Flannery O'Connor

CRITICAL COMPANION TO

Flannery O'Connor

CONNIE ANN KIRK

Facts On File
An imprint of Infobase Publishing

Critical Companion to Flannery O'Connor

Facts On File, Inc.
An imprint of Infobase Publishing
132 West 31st Street
New York NY 10001

Library of Congress Cataloging-in-Publication Data

Kirk, Connie Ann.
Critical companion to Flannery O'Connor / by Connie Ann Kirk.
p. cm.
Includes bibliographical references and index.
ISBN 978-0-8160-6417-5 (hc : alk. paper) 1. O'Connor, Flannery—Criticism
and interpretation. 2. O'Connor, Flannery—Handbooks, manuals, etc. 3.
Women and literature—United States—History—20th century. I. Title.
PS3565.C57Z735 2008
813'.54—dc22   2007006512

Text design by Erika K. Arroyo

Printed in the United States of America

VB FOF 10 9 8 7 6 5 4 3 2 1

This book is printed on acid-free paper.

*To my Family
and
To the Sisters of Mercy at
Immaculate Conception School
Wellsville, New York,
September 1963–June 1971*

CONTENTS

ACKNOWLEDGMENTS

Thanks go to my editor at Facts On File, Jeff Soloway, for accepting my proposal for this new volume in the *Critical Companion* series and for his patience and helpful suggestions concerning the manuscript. Nancy Davis-Bray at the Flannery O'Connor Collection at Georgia State College and University in Milledgeville was both congenial and helpful over a period of several months in directing me toward useful source material and photographs. I am grateful to Craig R. Amason, executive director of the Andalusia Foundation in Milledgeville, Georgia, who answered questions and also helped locate photographs. Thanks go to professor of history Nancy A. White of Armstrong Atlantic State University in Savannah, Georgia, for allowing me access to the O'Connor childhood home and backyard on my first visit to the city. I also want to acknowledge my former fiction and creative writing professors at Binghamton University who first introduced me to the work of Flannery O'Connor. These include Joanna Higgins, Gayle Whittier, and Larry Woiwode.

Finally and always, I thank my family for their unwavering love and support. Without them, my long and intense "visit" with Flannery O'Connor would not have been nearly as warm.

—Connie Ann Kirk, Ph.D., New York

INTRODUCTION

Flannery O'Connor was one of the most gifted and important American fiction writers of the 20th century. During her 39 years of life, she published two novels, one collection of short stories (another was published shortly after her death), and several essays and reviews. She also gave numerous lectures at universities and elsewhere and wrote hundreds of letters to a variety of correspondents, from famous writers like herself to students and fans of her fiction. A Georgia native with deep Irish-Catholic roots, O'Connor was devoutly religious. She once stated in a letter, "I write the way I do because and only because I am a Catholic" (*Habit of Being* 114). Despite this assertion, O'Connor's writing has been appreciated by non-Christian and Christian readers alike for its acerbic wit, penetration of complex themes, commentary on the South, and other attributes.

While her faith underpins all of her work, O'Connor's stories do not preach. Rather, they frequently show troubled or imperfect characters experiencing moments of grace and responding in complex and unexpected ways. Her stories illuminate the human condition on universal levels. O'Connor used her surroundings in the Protestant South as her most frequent canvas. On that canvas, she worked in an unusual technique. She drew vivid depictions of grotesque and odd characters performing violent or strange acts against fellow human beings. Through these extreme characters and acts, O'Connor disturbs, even shocks, her readers. Alongside these uncomfortable scenes, the author reveals a window that opens at a moment of opportunity for true and genuine change. Like her unusual characters, however, readers are not forced to select a predesigned conclusion. They are free to interpret whatever they may see in that window for its value or lack of value.

O'Connor's major works include two novels, *Wise Blood* (1952) and *The Violent Bear It Away* (1960), as well as two short-story collections, *A Good Man Is Hard to Find and Other Stories* (1955) and *Everything That Rises Must Converge* (1965). These and other writings have been gathered into four key collections by editors who knew the author: *The Complete Short Stories* (1971), which contains more short fiction than appeared in the previous collections; *The Habit of Being* (1979), O'Connor's collected letters, a popular book that increases understanding of the author's aesthetic, social, and spiritual sensibilities as well as serving as a primer in college creative writing workshops for the study of fiction writing; *Mystery and Manners: Occasional Prose* (1969), which includes essays and other writings that contribute to, among other subjects, an ongoing dialogue about art and religion, both separately and together; and finally, the 1988 Library of America edition, *Collected Works*, which includes the novels and stories above along with representative letters and essays and adds a few previously unpublished stories. It provides range and depth in a single gathering of the author's work.

O'Connor's fiction began to appear in college literature anthologies less than a decade after her death. As literary critics of the 21st century continue to survey the 20th-century American literary landscape, Flannery O'Connor is among those writer's most frequently highlighted. She is widely recognized as a master of the art of short fiction.

ABOUT THIS BOOK

Critical Companion to Flannery O'Connor provides high school and college-level students, teachers, library users, and general readers with a current, dependable, and comprehensive introduction to O'Connor's life and work. A chief guiding principle in writing the book has been to present complete and reliable information in a readable and easy-to-use format, but also to present that information in such a way as to invite readers' own interpretations and explorations of the author's work rather than to prescribe any one reading or school of criticm.

Another emphasis is the importance placed on the interconnectedness of O'Connor's fiction to her other writing—in particular, her essays and correspondence. By covering this material and offering extensive cross-references to and from it, the book invites readers to engage in a more comprehensive "case study" approach to reading O'Connor. Each of the genres O'Connor wrote in informs the others. Related topics, also cross-referenced, along with a chronology, a full bibliography of primary and secondary sources, and a complete index, round out the book to make the Companion the first encyclopedic, introductory resource of its kind in O'Connor studies.

The book is divided into four principal sections. Part I provides a thorough biography, including detailed information about O'Connor's family life, education, and career, with suggestions for further reading. Part II offers extensive treatment of O'Connor's two published novels; all 27 short stories from the two collections—A Good Man Is Hard to Find and Other Stories and Everything That Rises Must Converge—key stories from her master's thesis at Iowa; and the eight essays selected by editor Sally Fitzgerald for reprinting in the Collected Works, Library of America edition. Short stories and essays are organized alphabetically. Story entries each contain a synopsis, critical commentary, and list of related letters from The Habit of Being, along with suggestions for further reading. Essay entries contain summaries and cross-references to spark connections between them and O'Connor's fiction. Listings of further reading are also included for essays, where appropriate.

A special feature of this book is the section dedicated to O'Connor's voluminous correspondence. O'Connor is one of the few fiction writers for whom it is possible through published records to accurately trace and identify story origins, writing influences, reading, and other information about the author's concerns, interests, and experiences. Through her correspondence, O'Connor also spoke in detail about her writing practices. Many of the letters give advice to other writers. This advice is important not only because it influenced her contemporaries but also because it continues to be studied by writers today. Exploration of O'Connor or her fiction is incomplete without a study of the relevant correspondence. Winner of the National Book Critics Circle Special Award for 1979, The Habit of Being (the volume collecting O'Connor's correspondence) stands on its own as one of O'Connor's most important and influential "works." For that reason, brief summaries of each of the letters from The Habit of

Being are included here to enhance readers' understanding. The letters section also provides cross-references that encourage a deeper study of the author, her thinking, and her art.

Unlike the original letters, which are organized chronologically in *The Habit of Being* from June 19, 1948, to the author's last known letter, dated July 28, 1964, letter summaries in this book are organized alphabetically by correspondent, beginning with Louise Abbot and ending with James Tate. Entries within correspondent sections contain a summary of each letter, listed chronologically. Included in each summary is the date on which the letter was written, the location where the letter was written (if known), the page number of number and paragraphs in the letter as it is printed in *The Habit of Being,* a summary of the letter's contents, and cross-references to the fiction, essays, and related topics.

Part III of the book provides entries on related topics that address subject of interest in O'Connor studies. These include journals; writers who influenced the author; places O'Connor studied, lived, or visited; and other topics. Cross-references from related topics direct readers to other subjects but also back to the fiction, essays, and letters, providing yet another route for concentrated study and inquiry.

In using this book, readers are encouraged to make use of cross-references. In reading a typical short-story entry, for example, readers should use cross-references to the letters to see comments the author herself may have made about the story's genesis, creation, influence, or reception. Cross-references from the letters may lead readers to related topics and works that may suggest another perspective. To indicate a cross-reference, any name or term that appears as an entry in Part III is printed on first appearance in an entry in SMALL CAPITAL LETTERS.

Abbreviations

For the purposes of this book, citations to texts that are frequently referenced have been abbreviated as follows:

CS   *The Complete Stories of Flannery O'Connor,* edited by Robert Giroux (Farrar, Straus and Giroux, 1971)

CW   *The Collected Works of Flannery O'Connor,* edited by Sally Fitzgerald (The Library of America, 1988)

HB   *The Habit of Being: Letters of Flannery O'Connor,* edited by Sally Fitzgerald (Farrar, Straus and Giroux, 1979)

MM   *Mystery and Manners: Occasional Prose,* selected and edited by Sally and Robert Fitzgerald

PART I

Biography

Mary Flannery O'Connor
(1925–1964)

O'Connor's life was marked by early religious training that would stay with her all of her life; a recognized achievement in writing; a quiet but stimulating adult life on ANDALUSIA, her farm in MILLEDGEVILLE, GEORGIA; travel to give occasional talks and lectures; and a brave battle with LUPUS, which would lead to her death at the age of 39. Through it all, O'Connor remained steadfast in her ROMAN CATHOLICISM and in her dedication to her work as an artist. She also maintained several friendships through letters and visits at the farm.

CHILDHOOD THROUGH HIGH SCHOOL, (1925–1942)

Mary Flannery O'Connor was born in SAVANNAH, GEORGIA, on March 25, 1925. She was christened on April 12 at the CATHEDRAL OF ST. JOHN THE BAPTIST. Her parents, Regina Cline O'Connor and Edward Francis O'Connor, both came from Irish-Catholic families long established in Georgia. Edward's grandfather, Patrick O'Connor, immigrated from Ireland in the mid-1800s and set up a livery and wagon business in Savannah. Regina's father, Peter James Cline, was elected the first Catholic mayor of Milledgeville in 1888. The cathedral where the author was baptized was established in the 1870s, largely funded by another ancestor, John Flannery, who was married to Mary Ellen (Norton) Flannery, for whom Mary Flannery was named. When O'Connor was a young child, her father worked in his own business that was initially financed by a substantial baby gift in her honor from her mother's second cousin, Mrs. Raphael (Cousin Katie) Semmes. The gift has led some biographers to assume that Flannery was named after Cousin Katie's mother. Edward O'Connor owned and operated the Dixie Realty Company as well as its extension, the Dixie Construction Company. Young O'Connor traveled from Savannah to Milledgeville to stay at her mother's ancestral home at 311 West Greene Street each summer.

In 1931, O'Connor enrolled in first grade at ST. VINCENT'S GRAMMAR SCHOOL FOR GIRLS, located

Future author Flannery O'Connor at age three *(Courtesy Flannery O'Connor Collection, Georgia College & State University)*

at the cathedral, where she was taught by Irish nuns of the Sisters of Mercy. Since the school was near her home, she walked home for lunch rather than staying at school to eat and play with her classmates. This habit, along with being an only child, increased her dependence on herself and her own means for entertainment and companionship. Along with drawing and reading, O'Connor found herself studying and watching her immediate surroundings carefully. These surroundings included the domestic fowl that pecked and strutted about the yard outside.

Over time, she became unusually interested in one chicken in particular. Called a frizzled chicken because its feathers grew backward, the bird walked in directions that O'Connor found she could summon at will if she worked with it a certain way. Soon she trained the chicken to walk backward. The feat caught the attention of several local people, and news of it spread to New York. From there, the newsreel company Pathé News sent a cinematographer to Georgia to film O'Connor and her chicken's performance. The short movie was shown before feature films across the country in the 1930s. This early moment of national notoriety foreshadowed the fame that would return to O'Connor years later.

It is no surprise that O'Connor was talented at reading and writing in school; she also worked steadily at developing her knack for cartooning and art. Perhaps more surprising, she was remembered by classmates as one who chewed snuff in class, gave her teachers tomatoes rather than apples, and shot rubber bands from her braces when the nuns were not looking. Conversely, Sister Consolata remem-

O'Connor at age three, most likely in Savannah, Georgia *(Courtesy Flannery O'Connor Collection, Georgia College & State University)*

bered Flannery as mature for her age and as comfortable talking with adults, which is a fairly common trait among only children. In sixth grade, O'Connor was transferred to the SACRED HEART SCHOOL FOR GIRLS, though the reasons for the move are unclear.

Subsequent moves were the result of her father's work status. In 1938, the family moved from Savannah to ATLANTA, where O'Connor's father began to work for the Federal Housing Administration (FHA) as a real estate appraiser. O'Connor enrolled in seventh grade at St. Joseph's Church School, but her transition to the urban lifestyle of Atlanta was less than a happy one for both her and her mother. At the end of that school year, both Flannery and Regina moved to the Cline ancestral home in Milledgeville, leaving Edward in Atlanta for a time.

There was no parochial school in Milledgeville, so O'Connor was enrolled at PEABODY HIGH SCHOOL in the fall of 1938. Peabody was an experimental school, one of 10 such schools in the state. It was affiliated with the GEORGIA STATE COLLEGE FOR WOMEN (GSCW), also located in Milledgeville. The school was predominantly female, since most of the boys in town attended the Georgia Military Academy. O'Connor later voiced disapproval of the experimental curriculum at Peabody High. Students were allowed to choose their own courses of interest rather than take state-mandated subjects, and teachers rotated among subjects every six weeks. The author regretted having no history or classics in her secondary education; these were subjects she believed valuable to a future writer. Nevertheless, she took up reading somewhat haphazardly on her own, drawn to collections of humorous stories and to EDGAR ALLAN POE in particular, especially *The Narrative of Arthur Gordon Pym*. She also participated in extracurricular activities such as cartooning and serving as art editor for the school paper, the *Peabody Palladium*.

By 1940, Edward O'Connor had been ill several times in Atlanta with what would later prove to be lupus. He was forced to leave the FHA and retire to Milledgeville with his family. Also by then, his daughter's growing interest in art had caused her to establish a studio in the attic. She continued to write reviews and verse and submit CARTOONS for the school paper. Her high school education was in

O'Connor, about age 12 *(Courtesy Flannery O'Connor Collection, Georgia College & State University)*

social activities with her college classmates by living in a dormitory, O'Connor lived with her mother, two unwed aunts, and a boarder from the faculty. Uncles frequently visited them on weekends. Perhaps one note of independence might be observed in that it was about this time that she began to sign her work with the name Flannery rather than Mary Flannery as she was called at home.

One school activity in which she did participate was in submitting stories and poems for *The* CORINTHIAN, the college literary magazine. She also worked as art editor for the yearbook, *The* SPECTRUM, and submitted artwork such as linoleum-cut cartoons. Many of the cartoons were satires of college life. One cartoon, for example, poked fun at the U.S. Navy WAVES (Women Accepted for Volunteer Emergency Service) who marched around campus in formation to classes.

full swing when her father died on February 1, 1941, from lupus. At not quite 16 years old, O'Connor felt the loss of her father so deeply that she rarely discussed him during all the years afterward. That summer, she visited her maternal aunt and cousins in Arlington, Massachusetts. The following summer, O'Connor graduated from Peabody High as a promising member of the class of 1942.

GEORGIA STATE COLLEGE AND IOWA, (1942–1948)

Also in the summer of 1942, O'Connor enrolled in the freshman class at Georgia State College for Women, located only one block from home on Greene Street. While World War II raged on, she took part in a new, accelerated three-year program at the college that started in the summer. She majored in sociology and English. She took her studies seriously, but again her social life was limited by living at home. Rather than join in the

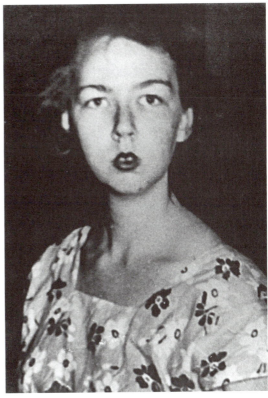

O'Connor, at about age 16 or 17 *(Courtesy Flannery O'Connor Collection, Georgia College & State University)*

The WAVES became a major part of the campus when the navy selected the college as a training center for military-store clerks.

Since there were other young women at the college who lived in town and not on campus, O'Connor had more in common with a few more of her classmates. One of O'Connor's best friends at GSCW was Betty Boyd (Love), who majored in mathematics. They met in the summer of their freshman year and stayed friends all through school. The accelerated program had only a few students, and both O'Connor and Boyd were among them. Betty came for dinner to the Cline house on Sundays, and she and Flannery laughed and worked on *The Corinthian* together. Boyd recalled later that at this time O'Connor still had her interest in domestic fowl; she often sketched a chicken out of her four initials, "MFOC."

At GSCW, O'Connor took classes in French literature, physics, sociology, American literature, the short story, English literature, economics, political science, U.S. history, and other subjects. Classmates later remembered her brilliance in school, yet also recalled that she was neither outspoken nor a show-off in class. She kept quiet in the back of the room, wrote outstanding papers, and offered comments or answered questions when asked, often lacing her responses with humor.

In 1943, O'Connor met Marine Sergeant John Sullivan, who was stationed at the campus naval base, when her Aunt Katie Cline invited him to Sunday dinner at Greene Street. Sally Fitzgerald, O'Connor's later friend and editor, pointed to Sullivan as O'Connor's first love. She said they attended one dance at GSCW, went to movies together, and shared stories about their Irish-Catholic families. Sullivan, it was said, encouraged O'Connor in her writing. When Sullivan was transferred to another naval base, O'Connor kept in contact with him through letters.

Among the many instructors O'Connor impressed at GSCW was George W. Beiswanger, her philosophy professor. Beiswanger had achieved both his M.A. and Ph.D. at the UNIVERSITY OF IOWA. He told O'Connor about the fellowships available there and urged her to apply to Iowa for graduate work. He wrote a letter of recommendation for her. O'Connor

A college photo of O'Connor *(Courtesy Flannery O'Connor Collection, Georgia College & State University)*

was attracted to Iowa. She recognized that her goal of becoming a published writer would be harder to achieve without more professional guidance and instruction in the field, and Iowa was developing a well-known and respected creative writing program then directed by writer Paul Engle.

In June 1945, O'Connor received her B.A. degree. Though she had applied to Duke as well as Iowa, she accepted a journalism scholarship to Iowa, made the journey west with her mother to find housing, and enrolled in classes that September. Her coursework included literature, advanced drawing, American political cartooning, magazine writing, and advertising. Now living away from home for the first time on E. Bloomington Street, Iowa City, she took part in student life, making friends with Louise Trovato, who was her roommate, and Ruth Sullivan, a classmate. O'Connor stayed in regular contact with home. She wrote to her mother every day and read the Milledgeville newspaper on a regular basis. She also still attended daily MASS.

Though she had accepted the journalism scholarship, once O'Connor arrived on campus, she applied for admission into the famed Iowa Writers' Workshop. In their first interview in his office, director Paul Engle could not understand O'Connor due to her strong Southern accent. He asked her to write down what she was trying to say to him. O'Connor introduced herself as a writer from Milledgeville, Georgia. Significant to Engle, as he noted later, she did not name herself as someone who wanted to become a writer but as someone who already saw herself as a writer. Engle looked over her application for the Writers' Workshop and saw immediately that she had outstanding natural talent. He admitted her into the program and accepted her proposal of a master's thesis comprising a collection of short stories. O'Connor later dedicated her thesis to Engle, even though he had less influence on her last two years in the program than he did earlier.

In 1946, she heard from John Sullivan that he was demobilized, had left the navy, and was entering the seminary to join the priesthood. Their correspondence trailed off soon afterward. Some observers think that O'Connor's relationship with Sullivan resulted in unrequited love. Sullivan eventually left the seminary, married another woman, and went into business. Though O'Connor met and spent some time with a few men in Iowa City, few if any romances stood out by comparison.

Meanwhile, O'Connor kept reading and writing with fervor at Iowa. She was exposed to the work of writers and critics such as JAMES JOYCE, FRANZ KAFKA, WILLIAM FAULKNER, Cleanth Brooks, and ROBERT PENN WARREN. She chose Joyce's collection of short stories, *Dubliners,* and Warren's *Understanding Fiction* as supplementary texts in a course on literary criticism. Her first publication occurred that summer. "The Geranium" was published in *ACCENT.* It was a short story that would become the title story of her master's thesis. In December 1946, she began work on her first novel.

In early 1947, O'Connor's Uncle Bernard Cline died, leaving Andalusia farm, including 1,000 acres of woods and 500 acres of fields, to O'Connor's mother and her Uncle Louis Cline. This bequest would prove important later on, but for the time being, O'Connor's life focus remained in Iowa. She submitted the first four chapters of her novel to the Rinehart-Iowa Fiction Award contest for a first novel and won the $750 prize in May. Rinehart held an option to publish the novel if it were completed to the publisher's satisfaction. In the spring, she submitted her thesis, *The Geranium: A Collection of Short Stories,* to the university. The thesis contained six stories: "The Geranium," "The Barber," "Wildcat," "The Crop," "The Turkey," and "The Train." "The Train" was also the opening chapter of her first novel. Her thesis was accepted, and she received her Master of Fine Arts degree in June 1947.

In September 1947, in order to keep working on her novel, she enrolled as a postgraduate at Iowa and took a class in European literature. Meanwhile, her story from her thesis "The Turkey" sold to *MADEMOISELLE* for $300. It appeared in the November 1948 issue under the title "The Capture." "The Train" was accepted by *SEWANEE REVIEW* for a payment of $105; it appeared in the April 1948 issue. While a postgraduate at Iowa, O'Connor met and enjoyed the company of fellow writers such as ROBERT LOWELL, Robie Macauley, Paul Griffith, Jean Williams (Wylder), and Clyde McLeod (Hoffman). By the time she completed the school year in early 1948, she had applied and been accepted to the well-known artist's colony YADDO in Saratoga Springs, New York, where she planned to continue work on her novel that summer.

YADDO AND EARLY CAREER, (1948–1952)

O'Connor arrived at Yaddo in June 1948. Her plan was to work on her novel in June and July. While there, she met writers Edward Maisel and Elizabeth Fenwick as well as painter Clifford Wright. Although she was a writer of the first order, O'Connor did not always believe she fit in with the lifestyle of the other artists at the colony. She still attended daily Mass, often going with the domestic staff. She was also seen frequently engaged in conversation with the staff around the mansion and grounds of the colony property.

Though Paul Engle offered her a fellowship at Iowa for the 1948–49 academic year, O'Connor was also invited to stay on at Yaddo past the summer, so she took advantage of that opportunity. She became part of a group of 15 artists at the colony, including poet Robert Lowell and writer Malcolm Cowley. In the fall, several artists left, but she remained with Lowell, Maisel, Wright, and another writer named James Ross. A few months later, Elizabeth Hardwick joined the few artists still living at the colony during the winter months when most artists were teaching or working at regular jobs. Earlier in 1948, O'Connor wrote to Elizabeth McKee and asked her to be her literary agent. By early 1949, she had nine chapters of her novel ready to send to her.

Aside from the people she met and the work she accomplished, O'Connor's experience at Yaddo was marked by an uncharacteristic involvement in political controversy. The director of Yaddo, Elizabeth Ames, came under Federal Bureau Investigation (FBI) scrutiny for allowing radical journalist Agnes Smedley to stay at the colony from 1943 until 1948. Smedley had been accused of being a Soviet spy, and Ames was being investigated for harboring her. Since a residency at Yaddo is competitive, the artists at the colony at the time, led by Robert Lowell, became suspicious of Ames's apparent favoritism toward Smedley. They met privately with the board of directors, asking for her dismissal on the basis that Ames had risked the welfare and status of the colony through her actions. In February 1949, O'Connor, with Lowell and Hardwick, left Yaddo and moved to New York City.

One effect of the controversy was that the press published a transcript of the Yaddo board meeting in a newspaper, which resulted in more than 50 writers coming to the aid and defense of Elizabeth Ames and denouncing Lowell and his supporters. In another meeting of the board, it was decided that Ames would stay on at Yaddo, but that a committee would look into establishing policies regarding the length of artist residencies.

In New York, O'Connor stayed for a short time with Hardwick and then moved to a Young Women's Christian Association (YWCA) residence at East 38th Street and Lexington Avenue. While in New York, she was introduced by Lowell to Robert Giroux, who was then an editor with Harcourt, Brace. She also met and began what would become an important lifelong friendship with Robert Fitzgerald, a poet and translator, and his wife, Sally. The Fitzgeralds had a large family. They invited her to live in their upstairs garage apartment as a paying guest at 70 Acre Road, Ridgefield, Connecticut, while completing her novel. In September, she took the couple up on their offer, working in the mornings, babysitting the Fitzgerald children in the afternoons, and eating dinner and engaging in conversations about literature and other topics with the Fitzgeralds in the evenings.

O'Connor worked at Ridgefield from March until Christmas 1950. She was released from her contract with Rinehart over editorial disagreements and contracted her novel instead through Robert Giroux with Harcourt, Brace. Her life as a writer working in the literary scene of New York and the Northeast region was just beginning. She decided on *Wise Blood* as the title for her first novel based on the influence of Robert Fitzgerald's translations of Sophocles' *Oedipus Rex* and *Oedipus at Colonus*. Just before her trip to Milledgeville to spend Christmas with her family, she began to feel pain and a weighty sensation in her arms and shoulders. The Fitzgerald family doctor gave her an initial quick diagnosis of arthritis but recommended that she see her physician as soon as she reached Georgia.

On the train south, O'Connor became so ill she had to be hospitalized as soon as she reached Milledgeville. There laboratory tests eventually revealed that she was suffering from lupus erythematosus, the same disease that killed her father. The young author was not told of the diagnosis, however. Instead, she and Regina moved out of the ancestral home on Greene Street in Milledgeville to the farm at Andalusia, presumably so that she could have a bedroom downstairs. There she learned to give herself cortisone-shot treatments. In and out of the hospital, the author continued to work on her novel while at Andalusia. In March 1951, she sent the manuscript to Robert Giroux and her agent, Elizabeth McKee, expecting a prompt reply. She did not hear from them until June, and then she was advised to send the manuscript to writer and critic Caroline Gordon for further comments and revision work. Despite this initial disappointment, O'Connor became friends with Gordon and responded well to her feedback, making heavy revisions on the novel. She submitted it again to Giroux in October and sent still more changes in December 1951. Early the next year, the book moved into production. *Wise Blood* was published in May 1952 to mixed reviews. Most local Milledgeville residents did not understand O'Connor's work. Some even became angry with the unpleasant characters and the violence in the story.

In June 1952, O'Connor felt well enough to return to the Fitzgeralds' home in Connecticut. As a surprise to the Fitzgerald children and as ever the friend of fowl, she sneaked three ducklings onto the plane to give to them. No doubt now that her first novel was in print, the author believed herself on her way to the literary career she had envisioned. Returning to the Northeast to live and work in the stimulating environment of other intellectuals and near the publishing capital of New York was part of that life. Unfortunately, after five short weeks, she fell ill again with a viral infection that triggered her lupus symptoms, and she had no choice but to return to Georgia.

There she underwent two blood transfusions, began an increased dose of ACTH cortisone, and went to bed for six weeks. At this point, the author was finally informed that she had lupus, for which there was, and still is, no cure. Her acceptance and understanding of the consequences of this diagnosis were signaled by her request that the Fitzgeralds send her remaining books and clothing still at their house. By then it was clear that her life in Milledgeville under the constant care of her mother had become a permanent condition.

LIFE AND CAREER IN MILLEDGEVILLE, (1952–1964)

One of the most inspiring aspects of O'Connor's life is that she did not let a possible death sentence keep her from pursuing her goals as a creative artist or living a full life with the dozen years she would have left. Her strong religious faith helped her deal with the crisis in which she found herself, an intellectual and writer living in a rural southern town. It was not just any small town but the very same town where she grew up, where she had to live under her mother's constant vigilance, where family roots ran deep and relatives still lived and dropped by for Sunday dinner, and yet a small town where very few people understood or appreciated the complexities of her work.

She and her mother set up a dairy farm at Andalusia. Her doctor allowed her to work mornings, but she was advised to rest for the rest of the day and avoid anything that might trigger her lupus symptoms. One of her first acts after finding out about her diagnosis in 1952 was to order a pair of peafowl and four peachicks. If she could not pursue beauty in the form of an artist's life away from Milledgeville, then she would enhance the natural beauty of Andalusia so she could enjoy being in its presence every day. She once wrote that she wanted to have so many PEACOCKS around her that she could never walk anywhere without seeing one. Her interest as a small child in the "frizzled" chicken that she taught to walk backward had apparently never left her; her fascination had, in fact, evolved. As she describes in her essay, "The King of the Birds": "My quest, whatever it was actually for, ended with peacocks. Instinct, not knowledge led me to them" (*Collected* 832).

Her mother complained that the peacocks would eat her flowers, but she apparently stepped aside as her determined daughter ordered them delivered anyway. As O'Connor's essay describes, the author regularly sat on her porch and studied the birds with intense scrutiny. She knew their wild cries in the night, their development from peachicks to full-grown birds, and their mating habits. She watched as they flew to the rooftops of the farmhouse and barn, as they pecked at their food and as they moved graciously about the yard, independently deciding when and where and why they would fan their magnificent plumage. She raised the birds until she had a flock as large as "40 beaks to feed" (*Collected* 834). True to form, the birds did eat flowers, and her mother was in constant battle

O'Connor in Milledgeville, Georgia, circa 1956
*(Courtesy Flannery O'Connor Collection, Georgia College
& State University)*

mode with the flock, putting up fences and endeav-
oring by other means to keep Flannery's birds from
devouring her garden.

O'Connor's adult relationship with her mother
at Andalusia has elicited scholarly interest. In
her chapter "Regina and Flannery" in *Flannery
O'Connor: A Life,* Jean W. Cash describes Regina as
a pioneer female farmer in the area who possessed
good leadership skills. She managed whites, blacks,
and internationally born workers on the farm and
kept close tabs on money. She was not without
her faults. For example, she held onto a 19th-cen-
tury view of African Americans as inferior to the
white race and believed the black workers on the
farm needed to be watched continually, even as she
developed fond feelings for them and treated them

well. There is evidence in her letters that Flannery
represented the first generation in her line to step
away from this view, but living at home with her
mother all her life except for five years perhaps
kept her from fully emerging out of its shadows.

Regina both protected and interfered with her
daughter's work habits. When callers came to visit,
Regina spoke most openly and freely with them
as one clearly more comfortable in social settings.
This often prevented Flannery and her guest from
talking alone about more sophisticated subjects.
When Flannery was invited to a function, Regina
was capable of refusing on her daughter's behalf,
even in her presence. Though she announced rules
for quiet during Flannery's work hours, she had
difficulty honoring them herself, often entertaining
guests of her own.

Though she liked to read mysteries and other
popular fiction, Regina had difficulty appreciat-
ing her daughter's complex work or even lasting
long enough to finish reading it without falling
asleep. After describing her mother getting up
and down to tend to small matters around the
house while reading one chapter of *The Violent
Bear It Away,* O'Connor wrote in a letter to Cecil
Dawkins, "I think the reason I am a short-story
writer is so my mother can read my work in one
sitting" (HB 340). Differences in reading prefer-
ences aside, it seems clear that without challenging her daughter's methods, Regina understood
that she provided some characteristics of the farm
women of her daughter's stories. Regina was a
constant supporter of her daughter's work, even
if she wished that Flannery would write popular
fiction, and Regina helped her with transportation
to lectures and other career-related events. Just
like her daughter, the capable, independent, even
dominant southern matriarch did not expect to be
living with an adult daughter any more than the
other way around. As Cash concludes, however,
both women managed fairly well to support each
other under difficult circumstances.

Besides the close and complex adult mother-
daughter relationship and the resident flock of peacocks, another feature of life at Andalusia was the
many visitors at the farm. Sunday dinner was a regular occasion, and they entertained visitors not only

from Milledgeville but also, as O'Connor's reputation grew, students, writers, and others who came to seek her out. Locals and people from the region included family in town and faculty or students from the universities in Milledgeville, Macon, or Atlanta, and friends from church. At one time, O'Connor hosted regular meetings at the farm to discuss literature with students from a friend's college class.

Among others who came to Andalusia and enjoyed Regina's hospitality and her daughter's conversation were writer Brainard Cheney and his wife, Frances, from Nashville, Tennessee; textbook representative Danish-born Erik Langkjaer (for whom Sally Fitzgerald claims O'Connor developed an infatuation); Jesuit priest James McCown, who had read and enjoyed O'Connor's stories; writer Louise Abbot; author KATHERINE ANNE PORTER; novelist John Hawkes; professor Theodore Spivey; Granville Hicks and his wife; and Thomas Stritch. Not least of all, her good friend Betty Hester first visited Andalusia in June 1956 and returned several times.

O'Connor also kept in touch with the outside world through her voluminous correspondence. As the collection of letters, *A Habit of Being,* shows, she maintained contact with approximately 50 correspondents and wrote nearly 800 letters from 1948 until her death. The vast majority of these letters were written from 1951 onward, and they were sent from Andalusia. Of these, the letters to Betty Hester, the mysterious "A" of *A Habit of Being,* were the most frequent and, many argue, the most telling about O'Connor's thoughts on writing, spirituality, and other subjects.

Hazel Elizabeth "Betty" Hester was a clerk living in Atlanta who wrote to O'Connor in the summer of 1955, telling her that she had read and enjoyed her work. Something in the way she discussed O'Connor's fiction struck a chord with the author, who wrote that Betty understood her writing close to her own image of it. A steady correspondence of nearly 90 letters from O'Connor to Hester have been printed in *A Habit of Being.* Approximately 250 letters from the author to Hester are reportedly housed at Emory University, a collection that was closed to scholars until May 12, 2007.

Hester was a wide reader who apparently suffered from mental illness much of her life. At the age of 13, she had witnessed her mother's suicide, and her father had abandoned the family before that. Hester had little higher education and an even smaller income, but her bright mind was active with curiosity about philosophy, theology, literature, and other subjects. O'Connor shared many of her thoughts on Catholicism and on her writing and was pleased when Hester became a Catholic but saddened when she left the church in 1961. When *A Habit of Being* was published in 1979, O'Connor's letters to Hester were labeled "A" for anonymous because Hester did not want her name revealed. She did not want scholars trying to contact her about her dear friend. Her identity was unknown to most O'Connor scholars for nearly 20 years, from 1979 until Hester's death by suicide in 1998.

O'Connor in 1961, sitting on the porch of Andalusia, her farm in Milledgeville, Georgia. *The Violent Bear It Away,* her second novel, had been published the previous year. *(Courtesy Flannery O'Connor Collection, Georgia College & State University)*

Hester visited Andalusia several times. The extent and intimacy of O'Connor's published letters to her suggest that O'Connor may have had lesbian feelings for her. Most scholars, however, disagree, pointing out that O'Connor was perhaps more asexual in nature. Sally Fitzgerald, her close friend and editor, and Jean Cash, her first biographer, suggest that O'Connor's romances with the opposite sex were limited to perhaps two or three men and that none of these were particularly passionate. Others point to her friendship with openly lesbian writer Maryat Lee to support the argument that O'Connor favored women. Whichever of the three natures is closest to O'Connor's dominant sensibility, for a seriously ill woman living permanently under the care of her mother, the opportunities to develop any relationships physically after

A studio portrait of O'Connor, taken sometime after 1955 *(Courtesy Flannery O'Connor Collection, Georgia College & State University)*

she returned to Andalusia must have been severely limited. Whatever the nature of their relationship when Hester visited the farm, the best result for readers remains the lively letters that O'Connor wrote to her friend when she was away.

Andalusia is important, not just because it served as O'Connor's home during the bulk of her writing career and because news of it appears in her correspondence but also because the farm serves as the setting or background for several of her stories. The most notable example, perhaps, is "The Displaced Person," which features a family of Polish immigrants and a peacock as a symbol of the transfiguration of Christ. Polish refugees came to work at Andalusia in August 1953, and in December, O'Connor was reading a draft of the short story to friends. Several O'Connor stories feature a mother and daughter living on a farm with no husband or father figure. Often, the daughter is very bright, imaginative, and disabled. Examples of these stories, among others, include "Good Country People" with Joy-Hulga Hopewell as the disabled daughter with a Ph.D.; "A Circle in the Fire," in which a farm woman is raising a daughter alone; and "The Life You Save May Be Your Own," with the mother, Mrs. Crater, and her mentally challenged daughter, Lucynell, both of whom get swindled by the shifty Mr. Shiftlet.

Despite the care she and her mother took with her health in adjusting her lifestyle around the farm, O'Connor's condition deteriorated fairly rapidly. By the end of 1954, she had to use a cane; by September 1955, she began to use crutches to avoid an operation, and by 1956 she was told after an X-ray that her hips were failing so quickly that she would need to use crutches all the time. She continued enduring injections of ACTH (adrenocorticotropic hormone). Starting in 1959, she suffered occasional necrosis in her jaw, which made eating difficult unless she took large doses of aspirin to help ease the pain. Her physician, Dr. Merrill, and other doctors discovered that the problem was caused by the cortisone used to control her lupus, and a lesser dosage was attempted. Her hip joints were injected with cortisone and Novocain, but the relief from pain lasted only two weeks. During the winter of 1962, she caught the flu, which raised troubles with her lupus; however, after another injection in her hips, she felt better for a time.

In August 1963, she suffered from anemia and was given iron supplements. Though her hips appeared to have improved by February 1964, another physical exam showed that her anemia was caused by a fibroid tumor. Despite the risk of reactivating the lupus, O'Connor underwent the operation to remove the tumor on February 25, 1964. She went home, suffering from a postoperative kidney infection. Though she continued to work diligently on her short stories, illness would never again release its grip. She lived only a few more months.

Fatigue was a continual problem in O'Connor's years at Andalusia. Her work schedule had to be kept to a few hours each day, and other modifications had to be made to her lifestyle to manage life on the farm. O'Connor was not against experimenting with technology to see if it might be of help in her daily work or to use it to keep entertained and stimulated while living quietly at the farm. The first phone was installed in July 1956. That same year, she used the $800 she earned from selling "The Life You Save May Be Your Own" to *General Electric Playhouse* to buy her mother a new refrigerator. In 1958, she learned to drive and passed her driving test on the second try, though she drove only when necessary. By late 1959, O'Connor had paid for new additions onto the farm house, including a sitting room, bedroom, and bathroom.

In 1962, she bought an electric typewriter, hoping it would take less effort to write her stories than it did on the manual typewriter. However, something about the quickness of the keys distracted her from being able to compose on it. In 1963, she and Regina purchased a new Chevrolet that was specially adapted to her legs, but driving became something she was increasingly reluctant to do. When she had written "Introduction" to *A Memoir of Mary Ann* in 1961 at the request of Sister Evangelist, the superior and the other sisters of Our Lady of Perpetual Help Cancer Home in Atlanta gave O'Connor the gift of a television set, which she surprisingly enjoyed. The sisters also sent her a secondhand record player in 1964, which she used to listen to records sent by her friend Thomas Stritch.

With all of her health problems, many readers perhaps assume that O'Connor retired to the farm when she was diagnosed with lupus in 1951 and rarely left, except for doctors' appointments and occasional stays in the hospital. The truth is that O'Connor was a brave and determined woman who traveled locally and around the country fairly frequently, visiting friends, giving talks and lectures, and taking one pilgrimage trip abroad. Locally, she appeared at club and literary meetings in Milledgeville, Macon, and Atlanta. In 1953, she made trips to Tennessee to visit Brainard Cheney and to Connecticut to see the Fitzgeralds. In 1955, she met authors Peter Taylor and Randall Jarrell at an arts forum at the Women's College of the University of North Carolina at Greensboro.

That same year, she traveled to New York City, where she appeared on the television show *Galley Proof* on May 31. Harvey Breit of the *New York Times* interviewed her, and she was shown the first scene of the televised version of "The Life You Save May Be Your Own," starring Gene Kelly in his television acting debut as the main character. On that trip, she attended her first and only Broadway show, TENNESSEE WILLIAMS's *Cat on a Hot Tin Roof*, which she did not like. She also ventured to Connecticut while she was in the Northeast, seeing Caroline Gordon, Sue Jenkins Brown, Malcolm Cowley, and Van Wyck Brooks. That July, she went back again to Tennessee to visit the Cheneys.

In April 1956, she gave a lecture at the Lansing, Michigan, chapter meeting of the American Association of University Women. A year later, she gave a lecture to an enthusiastic audience of 250 at the University of Notre Dame in South Bend, Indiana. In 1958, she agreed to travel with her mother at Mrs. Semmes's request and, with her funding, to take a pilgrimage to Europe. The trip entailed 17 days of travel to Ireland, London, Paris, LOURDES (where there is a grotto believed to have healing waters from an apparition of the Virgin Mary), Rome, and Lisbon. O'Connor waited in line to stand in the waters of Lourdes. She was more appalled by the souvenir shops and commercialization of the holy site as well as the unsanitary conditions of the waters with the steady immersion of sores and other ailments than she was enam-

ored of the site's potential for grace. She said later
that while she was in the water she "prayed for my
book, not my bones" (*Collected* 1251). Her books
did indeed survive her. Another highlight of the
European trip was the author's opportunity to have
both a general and private audience with Pope Pius
XII in Rome.

When fellow southern fiction writer EUDORA
WELTY needed a substitute to serve as guest
instructor at a University of Chicago writing program, O'Connor filled in for her for five days in
February 1959. For her part in the program, she
conducted two workshops with students and gave
public readings. The readings were, unfortunately,
not well attended, and O'Connor left not having
a very high opinion of the writing program in general. In 1960, she traveled to Minnesota, where she
spoke at St. Teresa's and St. Catherine's colleges
and to the Newman Club of the University of Minnesota in Minneapolis.

In 1962, she traveled to South Carolina and
Indiana, where she gave lectures at Converse College, and the University of Notre Dame, respec-
tively; and in October of that year she spent six
days speaking at four colleges in Texas and Louisiana. She also toured the city of New Orleans with
Richard Allen, who was curator of Tulane University's jazz museum. In early 1963, she traveled to
Northampton, Massachusetts, where she received
an honorary degree at Smith College and saw Robert Fitzgerald. Ill as she was, Flannery O'Connor
traveled outside of Georgia within months of her
death. In October 1963, she spoke at Hollins College in Virginia; Notre Dame of Maryland; and
Georgetown University in Washington, D.C. After
she returned from that trip late in the year, however, she never left Georgia again.

Lifestyle, visitors, correspondence, and travels
notwithstanding, it is O'Connor's writing and publishing career that makes readers most interested
in her life at Andalusia. At the farm, the author
maintained a steady work schedule of composing,
revising, and preparing manuscripts for publication.
The year 1952 marked not only the year that her
first novel, *Wise Blood,* was published, a happy time
for almost any author, but it was also the year when
her diagnosis of lupus was relayed to her. That same

Flannery O'Connor, at an autograph party in 1952,
sponsored by the Georgia College library staff on
publication of *Wise Blood (Courtesy Flannery O'Connor
Collection, Georgia College & State University)*

year, she wrote the stories "A Late Encounter with
the Enemy," which she sold to HARPER'S BAZAAR;
"The Life You Save May Be Your Own," (originally titled "The World Is Almost Rotten"); and
"The River." In that critical year, when it was clear
that Andalusia would be her permanent home, she
channeled any feelings she had about the situation
into work on a new novel.

In 1953, she continued working on her novel
and also wrote "The Displaced Person" and completed "A Circle in the Fire." That is the same year
she began to plan her story collection *A Good Man
Is Hard to Find and Other Stories* and continued
revising stories into 1954. In 1955, the author wrote

the short story "Good Country People" in what she described as four days. She wrote "A View of the Woods" in September 1956. In 1957, she wrote the essays "The Church and the Fiction Writer" and "The Fiction Writer and His Country." By January of 1959, she had completed a draft of her second novel, *The Violent Bear It Away*. Later that year, she wrote "The Comforts of Home."

In 1960, she wrote the essay "The King of the Birds" and the "Introduction" to *A Memoir of Mary Ann*. The latter was written at the request of Sister Evangelist, who was the Superior of Our Lady of Perpetual Help Cancer Home in Atlanta. Mary Ann had been an inspirational patient at the home. Sister Evangelist approached O'Connor, hoping she would write Mary Ann's story from notes taken by the sisters who knew her. When O'Connor declined, advising the nuns who knew her to put together their tribute on their own, Sister Evangelist convinced her to write the introduction to the memoir. O'Connor bet the nun two of her peafowl that the book would never be published, but when Robert Giroux told her that Farrar, Straus was going to print it, she lost the bet and paid the nun in full.

At the end of 1960 and the beginning of 1961, she wrote "Parker's Back" and "Everything That Rises Must Converge." Later in 1961, she wrote and revised from Caroline Gordon's feedback the story "The Lame Shall Enter First." In 1962, she began a novella called "Why Do the Heathen Rage?" but set it aside in 1963 to work on "Revelation." In the final year of her life, she worked on revising old and unfinished stories, fine-tuning them before she could no longer make any changes to the manuscripts. One of these stories was "Judgement Day" ("Judgment Day"), which is a companion story to "The Geranium," the first and title story of her master's thesis.

O'Connor proved that an author need not live in or near New York to see her work in print. In fact, her work was published with great regularity in both small literary journals and magazines with wide national circulations. "A Late Encounter With the Enemy" appeared in *Harper's Bazaar* in September 1952. "A Stroke of Good Fortune" was published in *Shenandoah* in 1953. Other publications that year included "The Life You Save May Be Your Own" in KENYON REVIEW and "The River" in *Sewanee Review*. "A Good Man Is Hard to Find" was published in *Modern Writing I*, edited by William Phillips and Philip Rahv.

The year 1954 brought the following publications: "A Temple of the Holy Ghost," *Harper's Bazaar*; "A Circle in the Fire," *Kenyon Review*; and "The Displaced Person," *Sewanee Review*. In 1955, the following stories were published: "The Artificial Nigger," *Kenyon Review*; the collection *A Good Man Is Hard to Find and Other Stories* by Harcourt Brace; "Good Country People," *Harper's Bazaar*; "You Can't Be Any Poorer Than Dead," NEW WORLD WRITING. The year 1956 brought "Greenleaf" to the *Kenyon Review*; "A View of the Woods" was published by the PARTISAN REVIEW in the fall of 1957. AMERICA published "The Church and the Fiction Writer" in 1957; "The Fiction Writer and His Country" appeared in *The Living Novel: A Symposium* edited by Granville Hicks. In 1958, *Harper's Bazaar* published "The Enduring Chill;" the *Kenyon Review* published "The Comforts of Home" in 1960.

Her second novel, *The Violent Bear It Away*, was published in 1960 by Farrar, Straus and Cudahy. The Catholic magazine *The* CRITIC published "The Azalea Festival" (previously titled "The Partridge Festival") in 1960; "The King of the Birds" appeared in HOLIDAY in 1961. Her "Introduction" to *A Memoir of Mary Ann* was published in the memoir in 1961; "Everything That Rises Must Converge" appeared in *New World Writing* in October of that year.

In 1962, the *Sewanee Review* published several articles about her fiction in the same issue with her short story, "The Lame Shall Enter First." In 1963, "Why Do the Heathen Rage?" appeared in the July issue of ESQUIRE. That same year, the New American Library issued both of her novels and *A Good Man Is Hard to Find and Other Stories* in a collection titled *Three by Flannery O'Connor*. "Revelation" was published in *Sewanee Review* in the spring of 1964, months before her death.

Although the most money she received for the first publication of her writing was for the essay "The King of the Birds," published in *Holiday* in 1960 for $750, and although O'Connor applied for and was rejected twice for a Guggenheim Fellowship, she did benefit from several fellowships, grants, and AWARDS throughout her career. In addition to the scholarship to Iowa for graduate work in journalism, the Rinehart-Iowa Fiction Award, and her residency at the Yaddo artists' colony, she was also awarded the *Kenyon Review* fellowship in 1952—a sum of $2,000, which she used to help pay for health-care costs, medicine, and books. She won second prize in the O. HENRY AWARD short-story competition in 1953 for "The Life You Save May Be Your Own." In 1954, three of her stories were nominated for O. Henry Awards, and "A Circle in the Fire" won second place. In 1956, her short story "Greenleaf" won the $300 first prize O. Henry Award. During her visit to the University of Notre Dame in 1957, she was awarded an honorary degree at St. Mary's College. In 1959, she received $8,000 from the Ford Foundation, a sum intended to assist her with living expenses for two years but which she planned to make last five times that long. In 1962, her story "Everything That Rises Must Converge" won another first prize O. Henry Award. In 1963, she received an honorary degree from Smith College in Northampton, Massachusetts. Not long before she died, she was told that her short story "Revelation" won her a third O. Henry Award first place.

FINAL DAYS AND LEGACY, 1964 ON

Following her operation for the fibroid tumor in February 1964, O'Connor was treated for the postoperative kidney infection in March and never fully recovered. She was hospitalized again that month and stayed in bed in early April after she was sent home. In May, she reported to her agent, Elizabeth McKee, that she was too ill to work further on revising her new collection of stories. She suggested that, instead of revising them further, they reprint the stories in their magazine-published versions instead. She signed the contract for *Everything That Rises Must Converge* on May 21, deciding on the title. Soon afterward, however, she was admitted to Piedmont Hospital in Atlanta. There, in her desire to continue working as much as she could, she hid stories under her pillow in case the health-care workers would tell her she could not work. On June

20, she returned to Andalusia and sent "Judgment Day" to Catharine Carver for feedback. She also asked Robert Giroux to postpone publication of the collection until the following spring.

On July 7, she received the Sacrament of the Sick (also known as Extreme Unction). In mid-July, she was still working, revising "Judgement Day" ("Judgment Day") from Carver's comments as well as "Parker's Back." By the end of the month, however, she admitted that she could no longer work, and she was admitted to Baldwin County Hospital in Milledgeville.

In the hospital on August 2, Flannery O'Connor slipped into a coma. Shortly after midnight, Monday, August 3, 1964, her kidneys failed, and she died. A low requiem Mass celebrated her life at the Sacred Heart Church on August 4. Afterward, she was buried beside her father at Memory Hill Cemetery. Her flat marble gravestone bears a cross with the Greek monogram for Christ, "I. H. S." underneath it, and reads: "Mary Flannery O'Connor / Daughter of / Regina Lucille Cline / and / Edward Francis O'Connor, Jr. / Born in Savannah, GA. / March 25, 1925 / Died in Milledgeville, GA. / August 3, 1964."

O'Connor's legacy is embodied in her works of fiction, essays, reviews, and letters that are available to all readers and writers. However, two other branches of her legacy are worth noting for students and scholars of her work. One is the physical location of her papers, books, and memorabilia; the other is a brief mention of artists other than authors who trace influences on their work to the Georgia writer. In 1946, with her first publication, "The Geranium," in *Accent,* the library staff at the Ina Dillard Russell Library of what is now known as Georgia College and State University established a Flannery O'Connor Collection. They began to keep reviews, newspaper clippings, and other materials about their hometown author as her career evolved. To these, they added yearbooks and other student publications from the local Peabody High School as well as Georgia State College for Women, the college as it was known in O'Connor's time at the school. In 1970, Regina O'Connor made a first donation of manuscripts to this collection, giving it credibility as an O'Connor resource and making the library a place of interest for scholars from around the world. At present, the Flannery O'Connor Collection holds more that 6,000 manuscripts and 700 books from the author's personal library, making it one of the premier collections for serious study of the author's work.

In addition to the collection, the author's home of Andalusia is maintained and kept open for public access by the nonprofit organization, The Flannery O'Connor–Andalusia Foundation, Inc. The foundation was established in 2001 to promote interest in and study of the author and to raise funds to maintain and improve the Andalusia property site and keep it open for visits by readers and scholars. The foundation also coordinates efforts with other O'Connor-affiliated institutions and organizations that have the same goal of promoting the author's work.

A second legacy beyond the obvious literary one shared by American, southern, and/or Catholic/Christian writers working since her time involves the range and reach of O'Connor's influence on other kinds of artists. Several musicians, for example, cite O'Connor in their work or have spoken about how her stories have come into play in their creative process. The best known of these include contemporary musical groups R.E.M. with their *Murmur* CD and U2 with their song "In God's Country." U2 thanked God, Desmond Tutu, and Flannery O'Connor in their 1988 Grammy acceptance speech. Bruce Springsteen, the popular singer and songwriter who is often praised for his narrative style, spoke in an interview in *Rolling Stone* and in his book, *Songs,* about reading O'Connor's fiction while writing the songs "Nebraska" and "The River" in his late twenties. He said that O'Connor wrote about particularly American characters in a way that mirrored his own thoughts. Both the late-night television comedian Conan O'Brien and actor Tommy Lee Jones wrote about O'Connor for their bachelor's degree projects at Harvard.

Scholarly work and reader interest in Flannery O'Connor is alive and well, as exemplified by more than 1,200 citations in the *Modern Library Association International Bibliography* under her name and more than 35,000 Web sites listed from a basic Internet search.

FURTHER READING

Cash, Jean. *Flannery O'Connor: A Life.* Knoxville, University of Tennessee Press, 2002.

Fitzgerald, Sally. "Chronology." In *Collected Works.* New York: Library of America, 1988.

Simpson, Melissa. *Flannery O'Connor: A Biography.* Westport, Conn.: Greenwood Press, 2005.

PART II

Works A–Z

"An Afternoon in the Woods"

This story was once going to be part of the collection, A Good Man Is Hard to Find and Other Stories but was deleted in favor of "Good Country People." As the final version of "The Turkey" and "The Capture," the story did not appear in any collection before Collected Works (Library of America, 1988). For that posthumous edition, editor Sally Fitzgerald worked from O'Connor's original typescript. The story gives further evidence of O'Connor's frequent urge to retool stories, even years after they were published in different forms and titles.

SYNOPSIS

One autumn afternoon, a 10-year-old boy, Manley, decides to have an adventure in the woods rather than go to a girl's birthday party. After he is dropped off at the girl's house with his present for her, Manley hides behind a truck, waiting for it to drive away, then heads off into the woods for the afternoon. He is wearing a white suit as well as a pair of silver toy guns in a holster. The first thing he does on his adventure is open the girl's birthday present, which had been wrapped in pink paper with a silver bow. It is a heart-shaped bottle of perfume with the words "Hearts and Flowers" printed on it; his mother and grandmother had picked it out. Manley crushes the bottle with a rock and buries it with the paper and bow in a ditch. This act of rebellion fuels him with energy, and he thinks he sees the woods and its colors more clearly than before. At the same time, the boy feels as though he is being watched.

Soon Manley spies a wild turkey a mere five feet away. At first he is afraid, but when he sees that it is wounded, thoughts run through his mind of catching it and bringing it home. He has visions of how bringing home a turkey would impress his family, just as Roy Jr., presumably his older brother, impressed them by killing a bobcat. Apparently bringing home game in his family is a means to receiving forgiveness—Roy Jr.'s transgression of backing the car into an ice truck the previous day was forgotten in the excitement of the bobcat. Manley speculates that his runaway from the party

and dirty and torn suit will be given the same absolution if he brings home a turkey.

The turkey, however, has some fight left in it and manages to zigzag its way along a ditch out of Manley's reach. When it falls, the boy catches up and grabs hold of its colorful tail feathers. When he sees its black eye looking at him through the leaves of a bush, however, he becomes startled and lets go, and the turkey gets away. Chasing after it, he fumbles and falls, breaking his glasses.

At this, Manley becomes discouraged and thinks about how natural it is that he should fail. The family is proud of Roy Jr. just for existing, whether he is "going bad," as his grandmother grandly proclaimed one day, or not. He begins to think maybe God is playing a trick on him by sending him the turkey. He begins a few cautious attempts at cursing, moving from a tentative "Oh hell," to "Goddammit" and more. He begins to fantasize about what his grandmother would do to him if she could hear him cursing, and this makes him laugh.

Soon the novelty of swearing wears off, and the reality of his torn clothes and broken glasses sets in. He thinks about having committed what he calls blasphemy with mixed emotions and is not sure whether to cry or laugh. Soon he sees the turkey once again, and this time it is motionless. He decides that God has given him the turkey to help him get out of his situation and considers it as a poor bribe on the part of God to bring him back from starting to "go bad." He hoists the dead bird over his shoulder and carries it to town.

There a man in hunting clothes sees him and curses under his breath, while others whistle or compliment him. All the while, he is thinking that it is a cheap trick on God's part if he thinks he will bring the boy back by letting him get off this easy. Three country boys begin to follow him, and the boy turns to God again. He thinks he will give his last dime to a beggar if he sees one before he leaves town. He prays for a beggar to appear, even though his conscience tells him that he is doing this to test the Lord.

Just as he is about to lose hope that he will see a beggar, Hetty Gilman walks toward him. She is an old woman in town who has been begging for money from everyone for more than 20 years. Manley cannot believe it; he holds out the dime, which she promptly swipes from his hand. Manley thinks that this must have been a miracle. Feeling good, he turns to offer the country boys a look at his turkey.

The tallest of the boys spits out real tobacco juice and asks Manley where he got the bird. Manley is honest and says that he found the turkey wounded in the woods. He begins to explain the whole story when the tall boy steps over and takes the turkey from him and walks casually away. Manley freezes until the country boys are in the next block.

He walks four blocks until he realizes suddenly that it is dark, and he breaks out in a run toward his house. All the while, he feels as though "Something Awful" is chasing him, reaching out at him with stiff arms and clutching fingers.

COMMENTARY

"An Afternoon in the Woods" is a full revision of its earlier incarnations, "The Turkey" and "The Capture." "The Turkey" was part of O'Connor's 1947 master's thesis, "The Geranium: A Collection of Short Stories," and "The Capture" (basically "The Turkey" with a new title) was published in MADE-MOISELLE in November 1948. When O'Connor wrote to Robert Giroux in November 1954 during their discussions about editing the collection *A Good Man Is Hard to Find and Other Stories,* she sent him this version of the story for possible inclusion and admitted that it is much rewritten from the *Mademoiselle* piece. However, by February 1955, she was suggesting that they drop this story as well as "A Stroke of Good Fortune" in order to include in the collection a story she had just completed, "Good Country People." Giroux agreed that the latter story was thematically more consistent with the collection.

O'Connor said that she was not "wildly fond" (HB 73) of "An Afternoon in the Woods" (HB 73). Even so, the story provides a glimpse at the author's powers of rethinking and retooling her fiction. She revised the latest version seven years after it was first written. The story is a strong example of several in O'Connor's canon that portray the development of a child's faith.

Readers may wonder whether Manley may be a child incarnation of an older character, Manley Pointer, who appears in "Good Country People."

It could be that this Manley does indeed "go bad," as his brother was feared to be doing by his family and grows up to become the diabolical salesman who steals artificial eyes and limbs from unsuspecting women. However, given Bible salesman Manley Pointer's statements to Hulga/Joy Hopewell that he never had religion or faith, this boy's level of faith in the story might be used to argue that he is a different individual altogether.

As his name suggests, Manley wants to prove himself to his family, especially in view of the exploits of his older brother, Roy Jr. This "manly" wish not only shows up in his quest to bring home the turkey but also in his avoidance of the girl's birthday party. A "manly" man prefers to wear his guns and a holster without regard to getting his nice white suit dirty. Manley has more universality as a name than Ruller, which the character bore in "The Turkey."

A boy's developing masculinity might also be expected to think as little of "Hearts and Flowers" perfume and pink packages as Manley does. Manley has been watching his brother develop, and he is also growing up himself. The events of this particular afternoon mark a change in his growing manhood but also, and perhaps more important, in his spiritual life.

The dichotomy of male and female and the exchange of gifts is an interesting motif in the story. Manley refuses to present either himself or the gift his mother and grandmother "wrapped up" in a white suit and pink paper to the birthday girl. He smashes not only the present but his own decorated appearance by dirtying and tearing his suit and breaking his glasses. His imaginary western gang bonds him with a group of males instead. His rebellion is at least partially an attempt to loosen the bonds held on him by the females in his life.

By the time he is in town, carrying the turkey and feeling bad for all of his transgressions, however, he wants to give a gift, the dime, to the beggar woman, Hetty Gilman. His feelings for females do not ease much as the story progresses even beyond this point, however. Hetty is portrayed as looking dissatisfied—the dime was not nearly enough. Women will want more from Manley than he has been willing to give them so far. Perhaps this Manley might be Manley Pointer as a child after all.

Setting plays an integral role in establishing a context for Manley's eventual spiritual discovery. In "'An Afternoon in the Woods': Flannery O'Connor's Discovery of Theme," Virginia F. Wray points out the increased role of the woods in this version of the story in contrast to the earlier version, "The Turkey" (and "The Capture"). She writes, "The woods . . . contain a knowledge and energy that are integral to Manley's afternoon experience" (50). Like the tree line in other stories such as "The Revelation" or the circle of trees in "Greenleaf," Manley's woods seem to harbor secrets and challenges that town settings cannot and do not in O'Connor's fiction. In O'Connor's fiction, the woods hold mystery, and the tree line marks the border between the reality of everyday life and its conflicts and a more metaphysical realm where mysterious events may take place. Manley encounters this firsthand. That afternoon, "[t]here was a peculiar life all through the woods, a kind of watching presence" (CW 763).

The colors in these woods are golden and fire-filled. Sunlight seems to direct Manley's path. The turkey leads him along, but the sunlight even strikes the bird, making him appear a bright bronze color. In this way, color fuses the turkey, the woods, and the boy under the influence of whatever presence is found inside the woods. Unlike the earlier version of the story where the boy wants to catch the turkey and bring it home to impress his family, the light in the woods foreshadows that something more complex and mysterious is happening.

Lightning does not strike when Manley begins to curse in the woods any more than it does to Ruller in "The Turkey." However, Manley's cursing goes beyond Ruller's game-playing and giggling. Manley does not just feel a bond with his older brother when he utters the curse words as Ruller does, but he is also fully aware that he has just engaged in the sin of blasphemy. His act bears more meaning and awareness and is therefore more serious in the later story.

Sin and redemption provide a motif, as they are in so much of O'Connor's fiction. Manley runs away from the birthday party and smashes the gift. He also tears and dirties his white suit and falls and breaks his glasses. All of these things will not sit well with the women, especially his mother and grandmother. Roy seems to have earned his way back into his parents' good graces by killing a bobcat. The heroic deed apparently assuaged some of the strain that had been building up from Roy's wrongdoings. When Manley first sees the turkey in the woods, he thinks maybe bringing home a turkey might work the same positive result for him and get him out of his predicament. He wonders whether God might have presented him with the turkey as a gift or a trick.

Maybe he is started down the wrong path just like Roy, and God has given him this chance at redemption. Manley thinks he wants to pay God back. He wants to do something good for God, so when the country boys start following him in town, he thinks he would like to stop and show them the turkey. Things are going so well, maybe he will even become a priest who reforms boys like these.

Then he starts to make bargains and to test God. He prays for a beggar to appear on the town's streets. When beggar Hetty Gilman appears, he gives her the dime. What he sees as a miracle performed for him makes him feel so invincible and powerful that he thinks he might be able to walk on water.

His "redemption" in the form of escape from trouble is, however, short-lived. His good deeds have been disingenuous. The country boys steal his turkey, and he is left as he was when he entered the woods—alone and needing to bear the responsibility and consequences of his torn clothes and broken glasses. Not only that, but as a result of his afternoon, he now also feels the cold hand of Something Else (possibility the devil, evil, sin) clutching out at him. He has learned that, just like his brother and just like every other human being, he has a capacity for wickedness.

CHARACTERS

Manley The main character of the story, Manley is an overweight 10-year-old boy with blue eyes that are always watering behind wire-rimmed glasses. For the girl's party, he is dressed in a white suit, but he is also wearing his toy pistols and holster. His escape from the girl's party, destroying her gift of the bottle of perfume, and his attire make his name particularly fitting. He expresses a moment of "manly" rebellion in the face of females who are older (his mother and grandmother) as well as his age (the girl). His thoughts turn frequently to his older brother and his family's fears that Roy Jr. is going "bad." Manley is manly in another way as well—in his struggle with God, he represents the human condition. O'Connor did not comment on whether this Manley may or may not represent a younger version of the character Manley Pointer in a later story, "Good Country People."

RELATED LETTERS

Robert Giroux, November 15, 1954 (HB 72); Robert Giroux, December 11, 1954 (HB 73); Robert Giroux, January 22, 1955 (HB 75); Robert Giroux, February 26, 1955 (CW 929). *Pages*: HB: 72, 73, 75; CW: 929.

FURTHER READING

Wray, Virginia F. "'An Afternoon in the Woods': Flannery O'Connor's Discovery of Theme." *The Flannery O'Connor Bulletin* 20 (1991): 45–53.

"Artificial Nigger, The"

The sixth story in *A Good Man Is Hard to Find and Other Stories* (Harcourt, 1955) was originally published in *The KENYON REVIEW*, Spring 1955 (vol. 17).

SYNOPSIS

Mr. Head wakes up to moonlight flooding the room. Today he is taking Nelson, now 10 years old, for his grandson's first real visit to the city. Nelson claims that it is his second visit, since he was born in the city. He likes to say this often as a source of pride because they live in the country. Mr. Head's intention is to show the boy all around the city to help deflate the boy's pride and convince him that the city is an unpleasant place that he would do well to avoid.

The boy is up first making breakfast, and this annoys Mr. Head. The boy is too eager. They discuss seeing blacks in the city. Mr. Head says that there have been no blacks (he uses the racial epithet for African Americans throughout the story)

in their country since before Nelson was born and that Nelson has never even seen one.

On the train, Mr. Head tells the boy to remove his hat, and they put their hats on their knees. Soon a large man with skin the color of coffee and two young women walk through the train. Mr. Head keeps asking the boy what he saw, and the boy says he saw a man, a fat man, an old man. Mr. Head announces to him that Nelson has just seen his first black man. The boy says that he told him "they" were black, not tan, and how is he supposed to know what to look for if he is not given correct information.

Finally they get off at the right stop for the city. Mr. Head decides to keep the dome of the terminal in view; that way they will not get lost. Mr. Head is determined to show him parts of the city that will make the boy disapprove of it. He shows him the sewer and has the boy stick his head down in it, but even that appears to have no effect.

Soon they are out of sight of the dome and enter into a neighborhood of black families. Mr. Head tries to tell Nelson that this is where he was born in hopes that this might cut his pride down a notch. Nelson says he is hungry, and they realize that they left their lunch bag on the train. Nelson fusses at his grandfather for losing track of it and accuses him of getting them lost. His grandfather continues with his story that this is where Nelson came from, and if he likes it so much, he can ask for directions from one of the black people who are staring at them from their doorsteps as they pass. Nelson is afraid of the men and does not want the children to laugh at him, so he approaches a woman. She tells him the way out in a cool voice that shakes him up. He takes his grandfather's hand in a rare sign of dependence.

They follow the direction of streetcar tracks and are soon in a white neighborhood. The boy is still shaken up, as his grandfather drills him about how foolish he looked speaking to the black woman. Nelson says that he wants to go home. He is becoming sleepy as well. Soon he lies down and falls asleep, exhausted. Mr. Head contemplates that finding his grandfather missing might heighten the boy's knowledge that he depends on him. He decides to step out of the boy's range of sight but close enough that he can keep an eye on him. He plays the sad trick for too long, and the boy resents him for the betrayal.

Mr. Head tries to pass things off, offering to get Coca-Colas, but Nelson stands with his back toward him. His grandfather begins to feel shame for his actions, and his misery only intensifies his guilt. When a dog barks, it startles him, and Mr. Head becomes desperate. He admits to a passerby that he is lost. The man gives him directions on how to catch the train at the suburb stop. Mr. Head is relieved and tells the boy that they are going to get home after all. The boy stares with cold eyes; home means nothing to him now that he has been betrayed by his grandfather. Mr. Head knows and feels the evil of his error, thinking that now he knows what people would be like if there were no such thing as salvation.

They continue to walk toward the suburb stop when the grandfather sees a statue of a black man sitting on a fence. Nelson stops a little distance away and studies the figure as well. Something about the figure and its broken stature moves both Mr. Head and Nelson to feel the divisions between them fade away. Mr. Head feels the need to say something wise to the boy. He tries, but what comes out is the statement, "They ain't got enough real ones here. They got to have an artificial one" (CW 230). As they both stare at the figure, the boy suggests they go home before they get lost again.

While on the train and when they disembark, Mr. Head realizes he has been a sinner all his life. He feels remorse for his sins, not just from that day but from his whole life. He also feels mercy has been given to him in a way that is inexplicable, a mercy borne out of agony and suffering. He feels that his sins have been forgiven by God from the day he was born, and this knowledge makes him ready to enter Paradise. Meanwhile, Nelson says that he is glad they went to the city once but that he will never go back again.

COMMENTARY

This story was reprinted in *The Best American Short Stories of 1956*, edited by Martha Foley, and in *Fiction in the Fifties: A Decade of American Writing—Stories*, edited by Herbert Gold, in 1959 (Doubleday). Subsequently, the story appeared in *The Complete Stories*, (Farrar, 1971) and *Collected Works* (Library of America, 1988). When the story

was going to appear in *The Kenyon Review* in April 1955, it was close to the time of the bus boycott in Montgomery, Alabama. Out of sensitivity to the times, editor John Crowe Ransom asked O'Connor if she might like to change the title. She responded that she did not. The statue was vital to the story, she noted, since it is through that object that Mr. Head receives his epiphany of mercy.

Readers may have seen a cement statue in the form of a black jockey holding a lantern on lawns. The statue depicted in this story, however, is not quite the same. In this version of these lawn "ornaments," a black man is holding a piece of brown watermelon. The general motif, however, is the same. The statue is about 12 to 36 inches tall and weighs 30 to 50 pounds. Frequently, the figures are brown or black and wear clothing that is painted red and white. In black figures, the whites of the eyes feature prominently against tar-black painted skin.

The genesis of the story comes from an anecdote O'Connor's mother related to her. One day she was asking for directions to a place where a cow was being sold. When she became lost trying to locate the house, she asked for directions. The man said that she could not miss the place because "it's the only house in town with a artificial nigger in front of it" (Magee, *Conversations*, 21). The phrase caught O'Connor's ear as well as her imagination. She wrote "there is nothing that screams out the tragedy of the South like what my uncle calls 'nigger statuary'" (HB 101).

The story has received increased attention as late 20th- and early 21st-century critics examine O'Connor's relationship as a southern writer to the sensitive issue of race in America. Because of the emotionally and historically charged word in the title, the story has been challenged or banned in some schools and other limited circles; however, most people read the story similar to the way O'Connor once described it in a letter, as suggesting ". . . the redemptive quality of the Negro's suffering for us all" (HB 78). O'Connor once wrote that this story was her favorite and probably her best written. Critics and scholars do not always agree with her assessment. Some argue that the ending seems forced or a bit contrived, uncharacteristic for O'Connor. The story is notable in that it is one of the few in which no death or physical violence occurs.

It is perhaps easy, with 21st-century hindsight, to have problems with this story, starting with its title and continuing with its use of the racial epithet throughout. Often readers find fiction that uses racial epithets in any form offensive and racist. Even though many readers credit *Adventures of Huckleberry Finn* by Mark Twain as a masterpiece that cracked open the problem of race in the United States, other readers find the more than 200 uses of the same racial epithet in that novel as reason enough to not read the book. This story provides a focal point for a discussion of O'Connor and race. However, read through the prism of her spirituality, the story also offers commentary on O'Connor's sense of the divine act of mercy.

By her own admission, it took O'Connor two to three months to write the story. It became the favorite of all her works, the one she never thought she could top. She said herself that it contains all the elements that she wanted to feature in her fiction—grace, mercy, mystery, and even an appearance by St. Peter metaphorically in Mr. Head's three denials that he is lost. Perhaps most important to O'Connor's feeling about the story is the sense that it contains elements she admitted she did not even quite understand herself. It was almost as though it were too big for her. "I have often had the experience of finding myself not as adequate to the situation as I thought I would be, but there turned out to be a great deal more to that story than just that" (HB 101).

Readers see in the story how racism is passed down through generations. Nelson, now age 10, has grown cocky. Mr. Head begins to think he is losing his authority and control over the preadolescent. He senses that he needs to earn back Nelson's respect before he enters into adolescence. When Nelson wants to go to the city, Mr. Head decides he will take him and show him a version of the city that will curb his appetite from ever wanting to go there again. He wants to cure his pride over being born in a city.

On the train, a coffee-colored man walks by, and Mr. Head asks Nelson who it is. The boy replies, with the innocence of youth yet uncorrupted, that it

was a man. When Head keeps questioning him, the boy replies that he was a fat man; then he says that he was an old man. It takes Mr. Head to notify him that the boy has seen his first black man. Head says this with some kind of triumph, as though proving to the boy that he is not as smart as he thinks he is. Nelson does not like being outsmarted, and he looks at the man now with hate, since he feels as though the man walked their way just so that he would be embarrassed. As a consequence, he thinks he understands why his grandfather dislikes blacks so much.

Mr. Head continues the lessons. He thinks this will keep Nelson believing that Head still knows more than the boy. He gives Nelson a tour of the different train cars, explaining things as though he came up with the ideas himself. He and Nelson cannot afford to eat in the dining car, but instead of admitting this to the boy, the grandfather points to the African-American man they saw earlier eating behind a curtain and says that they keep the blacks roped off there.

Mr. Head's attempts at showing Nelson how much he knows that the boy does not know has an effect on the boy even before they reach the city. When Nelson wants to get off at the first stop, his grandfather pushes him back and tells him that the second stop is the one they want, the main station in the city. These experiences make the boy understand that he depends on his grandfather more than ever, and he hopes that he never becomes lost. Being lost becomes another important story motif when they are in the city.

Mr. Head and Nelson become lost three times in the city, and the grandfather makes three denials. The first time occurs when Nelson notices they are going by the same storefronts they had seen before. Mr. Head denies being lost, saying the direction has just slipped his mind. The second time occurs when they walk through the neighborhood where many African Americans live. Nelson accuses him of making them lost, but his grandfather denies it for a second time. The third denial does not come with the grandfather making them lost again, but with the game he plays with Nelson and the passersby to try to teach Nelson a lesson.

Nelson wakes up from falling asleep on the street to find his grandfather gone. When the woman

[handwritten at top: Betray / grandpap → nelson]

fusses at him about tripping her up and making her groceries fall, Mr. Head denies any relation to the boy. The women cannot believe his treachery; it is obvious that the boy belongs to him since they look so much alike. Nelson does not get over his grandfather's denial of him, either. The three denials are like Peter's denial of knowing Jesus. As in the Bible, the denials culminate in Mr. Head saying that he does not even know the boy.

The final occasion of being lost occurs when a door opens for Mr. Head. He is frightened by the dog and finally is frustrated and exhausted enough himself not to keep up his superiority charade with Nelson anymore. They walk to the white suburbs, and there Mr. Head wails out loud that he is lost. "Oh Gawd I'm lost!" he cries. "Oh hep me Gawd I'm lost!" (CS 267). A man wearing golf knickers helps him find the right direction.

[handwritten left margin: religion / something to himself]

This admission allows Mr. Head to receive the grace and mercy he will feel when they encounter the statue of the black man eating watermelon. In the cement statue, Mr. Head suddenly sees the tragedy of the blacks' condition. Whites feel the need so strongly to be superior to blacks that they will stoop to putting cracked and broken statues of them in their yards if they cannot have them as slaves. The black man has been so objectified that he is not even human.

[handwritten left margin: sees the wrong of is nari]

Somehow, and in O'Connor's way, somehow mysteriously, seeing this object is like beholding the crucified Christ for Mr. Head. He realizes through the black people's suffering that Jesus' suffering brings mercy down over him for all of his sins. He knows that he has been forgiven, and this humbles him and Nelson, who feels it, strangely, too. One senses that neither Mr. Head nor Nelson will ever be the same again. For his part, Nelson says that he never wants to visit the city again.

CHARACTERS

Mr. Head Mr. Head is 60 years old and has a long tubelike face with a long nose and jaw. His eyes are alert and appear wise. He does not like to rely on mechanical devices such as alarm clocks. As a guide on the morning that he and Nelson go to the city, the narrator compares his look in the moonlight to Virgil summoned to Dante or Raphael called by

God to Tobias. The circles he moves in while they are in the city recall Dante's "Circles of Hell" in the *Divine Comedy*. Symbolically, like Virgil leading Dante through Hell, Purgatory, and Paradise, Mr. Head leads Nelson on a random tour of the city, "guiding" him and answering his questions.

Nelson Ten-year-old grandson of Mr. Head. He is always saying that he was born in the city and is proud of it until he finally visits the city with his grandfather. When his grandfather says that he will take him on his first visit, he protests, saying that it is really his second visit, since he was born there. At a certain point while they are there, Nelson appears to glow with excitement that he is from the city. It is as though he is developing part of his self-awareness and identity from what he sees around him. He even becomes intoxicated with excitement from his interaction with the cool, large black woman whom he meets.

Mr. Head works hard to quell the boy's pride in being born in the city, even to the point of having Nelson smell the sewer over a manhole. He explains the workings of the sewer underground, and this leaves Nelson appalled that such an underground world exists. Interestingly, at the end of the story, when he is back home in the woods and after he has somehow received the gift of mercy with his grandfather from seeing the black statue, he says he was in the city only once and does not plan to visit ever again.

RELATED LETTERS

Caroline Gordon Tate, November 14, 1954 (CW 926); Robert Giroux, November 15, 1954 (HB 72–73); Robert Giroux, November 30, 1954 (HB 73); Ben Griffith, May 4, 1955 (HB 78); Ben Griffith, May 4, 1955 (CW 931); Betty Hester ("A"), September 6, 1955 (HB 101); Betty Hester ("A"), June 1, 1956 (HB 160); Betty Hester ("A"), August 24, 1956 [Nelson] (CW 1,000); Betty Hester ("A"); January 23, 1957 (HB 200); Maryat Lee, March 10, 1957 (HB 209); Maryat Lee, June 28, 1957 (HB 227); Betty Hester ("A"), November 2, 1957 (HB 249); Sally and Robert Fitzgerald, November 4, 1957 (CW 1,048–1,049); Betty Hester ("A"), April 4, 1958 (HB 275); Cecil Dawkins, October

5, 1958 (HB 297); Betty Hester ("A"), December 20, 1958, (HB 309); Cecil Dawkins, "Geo. Washington Birthday" [1959], (HB 321); John Hawkes, September 13, 1959 [Mr. Head] (CW 1,108); Roslyn Barnes, June 10, 1962 (HB 479). *Pages*: HB: 72, 73, 78, 101, 160, 200, 209, 249, 275, 297, 309, 321, 479; CW: 926, 931, 1,000, 1,048–1,049, 1,108.

FURTHER READING

Allen, William Rodney, "Mr. Head and Hawthorne: Allusion and Conversion in Flannery O'Connor's 'The Artificial Nigger.'" *Studies in Short Fiction* 21, no. 1 (Winter 1984): 17–23.

Bart, Robert S. "The Miraculous Moonlight: Flannery O'Connor's 'The Artificial Nigger.'" *St. Johns Review* 37, nos. 2–3 (1986): 37–47.

Cheatham, George, "Jesus, O'Connor's Artificial Nigger." *Studies in Short Fiction* 22, no. 4 (Fall 1985): 475–479.

Desmond, John F., "Flannery O'Connor and the Idolatrous Mind." *Christianity and Literature* 46, no. 7 (Autumn 1996): 25–35.

Fiondella, Maris G., "Augustine, the 'Letter,' and the Failure of Love in 'The Artificial Nigger.'" *Studies in Short Fiction* 24, no. 2 (Spring 1987): 119–129.

Fowler, Doreen, "Deconstructing Racial Difference: O'Connor's 'The Artificial Nigger.'" *The Flannery O'Connor Bulletin* 24 (1995–96): 22–32.

Giannone, Richard, "'The Artificial Nigger' and the Redemptive Quality of Suffering." *The Flannery O'Connor Bulletin* 12 (1983): 5–16.

Monroe, W. F., "Flannery O'Connor's Sacramental Icon: 'The Artificial Nigger.'" *South Central Review: The Journal of the South Central Modern Language Association* 1, no. 4 (Winter 1984): 64–81.

Oates, Joyce Carol, "The Action of Mercy." *Kenyon Review* 20, no. 1 (Winter 1998): 157–160.

Okeke-Ezigbo, Emeka, "Three Artificial Blacks: A Reexamination of O'Connor's 'The Artificial Nigger.'" *College Language Association Journal* 4 (June 1984): 371–382.

Perreault, Jeanne, "The Body, the Critics, and 'The Artificial Nigger.'" *Mississippi Quarterly: The Journal of Southern Cultures* 56, no. 3 (Summer 2003): 389–410.

Robillard, Douglas, Jr., "Flannery O'Connor and the Tragedy of the South." *Flannery O'Connor Review* 1 (2001–2002): 94–98.

Saunders, James Robert. "The Fallacies of Guidance and Light in Flannery O'Connor's 'The Artificial Nigger.'" *Journal of the Short Story in English* 17 (Autumn 1941): 103–113.

Shaw, Mary Neff. "'The Artificial Nigger': A Dialogic Narrative." *The Flannery O'Connor Bulletin* 20 (1991): 104–116.

Strickland, Edward, "The Penitential Quest in 'The Artificial Nigger.'" *Studies in Short Fiction* 25 no. 4 (Fall 1998): 453–459.

Yumiko, Hashizume, "Urban Experience in Flannery O'Connor's 'The Artificial Nigger.'" *Sophia English Studies* 11 (1986): 41–58.

"Barber, The" (1947)

This is the second story from O'Connor's 1947 master of fine arts thesis, "The Geranium: A Collection of Short Stories," submitted at the UNIVERSITY OF IOWA.

SYNOPSIS

It is not easy being a liberal in Dilton. Three weeks before the "Democratic White Primary" for governor, Raber's barber, Joe, asks him for whom he is going to vote. When he answers Darmon, the barber asks him if he loves black people (whether he is a "n-lover"). Rayber replies that he loves neither whites nor blacks. When he had mentioned this same thing to his colleague Jacobs, a philosophy professor at the college, Jacobs replied that this was not a good way to be. When Rayber challenged him asking why, believing he could argue his point, Jacobs had said to never mind; he had a class.

The barber claims that the election comes down to all black and white. He is a Hawkson man; he believes that the blacks are trying to get too powerful. The barber calls those who sympathize with blacks "Mother Hubbards" and his opponent and those who support him, "Little Boy Blues." Apparently this Mother Goose language comes from Hawkson's speeches.

Rayber wants to argue the case for Darmon, but he cannot think fast enough. The barber calls to George, the black young man who cleans up at the shop. Rayber wants to make an argument that will be important for George to hear. He thinks about Jacobs and how he once taught at an all-black college. He wonders about George's political leanings.

The barber asks him if he is a Mother Hubbard, and Rayber admits that he will be voting for Darmon. The barber asks whether he has ever heard Hawkson speak, and Rayber replies that he has. Rayber suggests that the barber do some reading, and the barber says that all he needs to do is think. Big words do not replace thinking. Rayber asks him if he calls himself a thinker and wonders why he is bothering to take the man on. When Rayber visits the barber the next time, he does not lay out his political argument but thinks instead about what his wife will have for dinner.

Discouraged with himself, this time he goes home and begins to prepare his argument. He wants to read and discuss it with Jacobs, but Jacobs just shrugs and says he does not argue. He reads it to his wife, not sure which side she is on, and she says it is very nice. Neither Jacobs nor his wife give him the response for which he is looking. Finally he goes back to the barber shop.

At first the barber just comments on the hot weather. Then he talks about hunting quail with a black man and how Rayber ought to consider it; there is nothing like it. George is still working, sweeping, and the fat man is there reading a paper. No one brings up politics, so finally Rayber asks if the barber is still a Hawkson man. This reminds the barber that Rayber was going to give his arguments for voting for Darmon on this visit.

The barber calls over Roy and others to hear Rayber's speech. Rayber says that he is not there to make a speech; he just wants to discuss the election and the reasons for voting for Darmon. As the men gather around Rayber's chair, the tension in the room begins to tighten. Rayber asks Joe whether George might like to hear, since he has called everyone else over. The room goes quiet, and Rayber has the sense that he has gone too far. The barber says that George can hear from where he is.

Rayber tries to make the point that he was not trying to convert them to Darmon; he was simply trying to discuss why Darmon was getting his vote. The barber asks George if he has heard Rayber's speech. George answers that he did, and when the barber asks him whom he is going to vote for, George answers Hawkson. This is the breaking point for Rayber.

Rayber asks them whether they think he would mess with their ignorance. The barber says Rayber's speech was fine. Suddenly, Rayber hits the barber, who falls on the floor next to the chair. He looks up and tells Rayber that he thought his speech was just fine. Rayber runs past the other men in the shop and goes outside. His face is still half covered in lather, the barber's bib hanging down to his knees as he runs. After the election, Rayber changes his barber.

COMMENTARY (1947)

The story was first published in *New Signatures*, a 1947 anthology of student writing, and later appeared in the *Atlantic*, (vol. 226, no. 4); October 1970. It was collected in *The Complete Stories* published by Farrar, Straus and Giroux in 1971 and also appears in *Collected Works* published by Library of America in 1988.

Similar to the writer in the short story "The Crop," the college professor Rayber seems at times nearly paralyzed to act. In the barber shop, he hears talk about candidates for the Democratic White Primary race. Rayber favors Darmon, the progressive candidate, whereas Joe, the barber, and Roy and Joe's other friends in the shop plan to vote for Hawkson, the segregationist. Joe praises Hawkson's speeches to Rayber and in doing so implies that Hawkson's rousing speeches have had an effect on them as voters. Hawkson apparently has the power to argue his points in a way that makes men who may not engage in political discourse on a regular basis excited enough about his ideas to keep talking about them in the barber shop. Joe has even heard Hawkson give his speech several times in Mullin's Oak, Bedford, Chickerville, and Spartasville.

Rayber thinks all of the men in the shop are ignorant and at first does not want to give them the time of day in arguing the opposite viewpoint or to explain why he supports Darmon. What he thinks is their lack of ability to listen and to reason, however, turns out to be his own inability to act quickly and use language persuasively. Rayber is a slow and deliberate thinker. He is also timid. He overthinks the situation in the barber shop. Rather than engage in an argument then and there or dismiss the men in views as racist and ignorant altogether, Rayber allows himself to think about his own inability to engage in the argument. He allows himself to be baited into trying to set out the opposing viewpoint, even when he knows it will not change any of these men's minds.

The dynamic between Rayber and his colleague Jacobs reveals Rayber's personality. Rayber is timid and insecure and thinks Jacobs is better at their profession. He admires the way Jacobs appears to know more than Rayber thinks he actually does. Rayber thinks this is a good trait for a professor. He not only admires Jacobs, but he also imagines how Jacobs would handle the situation in the barber shop. He asks Jacobs to read over his argument in favor of Darmon. In seeking his advice, however, Rayber ignores perhaps the best advice that Jacobs offers him—not to argue, especially with the ignorant.

Rayber seems timid with his wife as well. On his second visit to the barber, he has forgotten about the political discussion but sits in the chair instead, thinking about how they always have the same dinner every Tuesday, canned meat layered with cheese. He imagines a conversation in which he challenges his wife with the monotonous menu, only to be told that if he does not like it, he need not eat it. Even in his imagination, he is the weaker character. At this point, the barber startles him by breaking into his reverie to ask about Darmon.

Interestingly, Joe and the others call those who support integration "Mother Hubbards," "babies," and "Little Boy Blue." These are images from nursery rhymes that are meant to deride whites who believe in associating with blacks and working for their equality. The terms denote weakness and childishness as though the liberal Democrats in town do not have a different but valid point of view, but they are instead too naïve or too weak to

stand up to black people's demands for equal rights under the law.

What the men in the barber shop and George, the young employee, need is an effective and inspiring speech that might make them think twice about their views or at the very least understand the more liberal viewpoint a bit better. They offer Rayber plenty of chances to make his case. However, Rayber actually proves their "Mother Hubbard" view of him correct. He is too timid in his argument and is not an assertive and forceful or dynamic speaker. In short, he is no match for Hawkson.

Though Rayber tries with deliberation to defend his reasons for supporting Darmon, the listeners take the speech as an attempt to change their minds and readily dismiss Rayber's efforts. This enrages Rayber, who did not expect to change their minds in the first place but only wanted to defend his own opinion against their attacks. Finally moved to act, Rayber unfortunately behaves in the barbaric way of which he believes his listeners were more capable of than he. He hits the barber and runs off.

The reader does not hear Rayber's speech, but it is not necessary to include it in the story since O'Connor dramatizes Jacob's reaction and Rayber's unnamed wife's critique of it. Both read the speech but are distracted the entire time. Jacobs is apparently busy marking in his grade book, and Rayber's wife is glancing at an open magazine. Assuming that both characters are liberals who share Rayber's politics, that neither of them is interested in or becomes engaged in Rayber's argument is telling about both Rayber's speech and their own "Mother Hubbardism." Neither Jacobs nor Rayber's wife would go as far as Rayber in attempting to debate the men in the barber shop. They do not engage with Rayber about reasons to support Darmon or offer any suggestions about how to do so more effectively. Jacob even admits to Rayber, "I never argue" (CS 21).

The story makes an interesting commentary on language versus action. Hawkson apparently uses language so effectively that he can enact change on the part of listeners who would not normally become so engaged in political discourse. Using language of their own, the men in the barber shop spread Hawkson's views and their own, cementing their vote as a bloc. Hawkson has succeeded through his use of language to spur more votes. His supporters in the barber shop are doing the same. For Hawkson, language has promoted action, and that action has promoted more language and more action.

Rayber's use of language lacks the power of Hawkson's. Rayber is not even effective in engaging the interests of those who agree with him. When he finally delivers his speech, his motives are misunderstood, and his listeners fail to get the message. Instead of his language spurring action, Rayber's language results in the direct opposite— except in one unexpected way. Rather than engaging his listeners to act, Rayber's speech leaves them unconvinced and even more assured of their own position. Rayber has failed not only to change their minds, which he did not expect to do anyway, but also to get them to see the merits in his own viewpoint. His listeners do not appreciate a well-argued position for its own sake. Jacobs was trying to tell him that, to the ignorant, the test of a good argument is only whether or not it succeeds in changing their minds.

The action Rayber's language precipitates is far removed from what he intended and is performed by an unexpected character. Rayber becomes so frustrated at his impotent speech skills that he becomes violent with the barber and runs out of the shop. Words have failed him. He has failed to combat his situation with language and reason and logic. When he is so misunderstood in the barber shop, he lashes out. It is almost as though O'Connor is saying that when language and logic fail, violence becomes an attractive option for the overly frustrated, another way of saying that war and violence result from the failure of diplomacy.

CHARACTERS

Rayber   A college professor in the town of Dilton. Rayber wishes to open the minds of the ignorant racists in the barber shop he visits as well as help the black man who works there, but he lacks skill with language. Ironically, the black man who works in the shop rarely speaks but keeps acting, doing his job. Rayber seems paralyzed in both speech and action until the climax of the story; when he does speak and act, both efforts turn out badly.

FURTHER READING

Larsen, Val. "A Tale of Tongue and Pen: Orality and Literacy in 'The Barber.'" *Flannery O'Connor Bulletin* 22 (1993–1994): 25–44.

"Capture, The"

See "Afternoon in the Woods, An."

"Catholic Novelist in the Protestant South, The" (1963)

This essay was originally presented as a lecture on October 18, 1963, at Georgetown University in Washington, D.C. O'Connor was invited to speak as part of the university's 175th anniversary celebration. The text was published in the school publication, *Viewpoint*, in spring 1966 and was first collected in *Mystery and Manners*, published by Farrar, Straus and Giroux in 1969. The essay also appears in *Collected Works*, published by Library of America in 1988.

SYNOPSIS

O'Connor writes that she has spoken at several Catholic colleges and is glad to find that Catholic students are embracing fiction more than they were 10 or 20 years ago. She says that Catholics have traditionally limited their imaginations to practical matters of survival, but now they are coming into their own in establishing themselves. She finds that Catholics are now realizing that they must cultivate their imaginations in order to have a fruitful religious life.

She desires a Catholic literature for the future that would also add to the nation's literature. She differentiates between Catholic and Christian, saying that the word *Christian* has come to be known as "anyone with a golden heart" (MM 192).

Fiction is what she writes, so she addresses herself to that form of literature. Catholics are embarrassed to read and write fiction, she says, because it mirrors their own experience. She describes a Catholic novel as one written by a devout Catholic and one in which readers may find Catholic themes. The novel need not be restricted to being categorized as a Catholic novel to be one and should work on many levels.

American Catholics theorize about what their fiction should be like, but they have few examples to show for it. Young Catholic writers are quickly discouraged by theories. The Catholic press quickly points out how Catholic novelists paint the church in a bad light or do not reflect the church. O'Connor contrasts this with Catholic scholarship, which had recently been debated in relation to the value of scholarship in general, with many scholars entering the discussion. Catholic writers, on the other hand, are rarely heard from, but instead the discussion is dominated by those not directly involved in writing fiction.

Novels by Catholics are frequently discussed based on the author's faith and nothing else, disregarding the role of the imagination. She collects Catholic press articles on the failures of the Catholic novelist. One of these made a suggestion that someone write a novel about life in a seminary; another suggested addressing factors that make Catholic life challenging. She states that the novelist does not work this way unless he or she is a "hack" (195). Instead, a novelist goes within and writes from there.

The two most important elements contributing to her own fiction are that she is a southerner and a Catholic. Living among mostly Protestants gives her a different perspective, one that she finds helpful. The Catholic novelist will not see human beings as inherently good or evil but will instead see them as "incomplete" (197), needing grace that comes through nature while at the same time transcending it. A possibility for grace remains open and unanticipated in the human heart. Christ and the devil are the centers of good and evil.

The sense of Catholic writers, like all writers and all people, are first impressed by one's environment, so southern Catholic writers first come to know the world through the region in which they live when very young. In this case, they find that imagination is not entirely free but is attached to place. Although writers may wish to write about a

place that suits their personalities better than their place of origin, this is not entirely possible. Part of the writer's experience, particularly the southern writer where the region is so strongly flavored, is coming to terms with that region and its role in his or her work. Writing a novel is a personal affair, an encounter with one's imagination and its particular elements, and those have been formed by the region in which one lives.

A failed Catholic novel disregards the author's culture and instead may try to make a culture out of the church itself. Because the church is not a culture, this is not possible, and the novel fails to engage properly.

The best connection between the southern writer and his or her region is through the ear. No matter who is speaking in the novel, if that character is from the South, readers interpret his or her speech to represent the region. This keeps fiction of the South communal and away from being personal. Though an author such as KATHERINE ANNE PORTER may break out of some of these bounds, most southern writers do not, and they do not need to do so to write effectively.

Though more current fiction relishes the outsider, the character who does not feel a sense of community or belonging to society, the South rejects outsiders, except on terms that it sets itself. It is not easy for the writer to reconcile the South's values of self-preservation that make it wary of strangers with its vulnerability to elements that are not necessarily good for it, such as those presented by Hollywood or Madison Avenue. However, O'Connor writes, fiction is better when it is social, not personal. Faulty manners are better than none at all.

A problem in this country for Catholic writers is that society is not predominantly Catholic but Protestant, and there is no region of the country that is notably Catholic and can help shape and anchor a work of fiction. This is why the southern Catholic, O'Connor believes, has an advantage. The South is known as the Bible Belt, so-called first in 1919 by H. L. Mencken. Generations have discussed Scripture on their front porches, and this has become a part of the fabric of the area.

Storytellers today lack stories against which to measure themselves. Stories are shaped against a backdrop of other stories with which the community is familiar. The South has the Scripture to serve this function. Many southerners have stories that help make their abstract beliefs more real. For example, it is one thing to be taught about faith with definitions, but it is quite another thing to hear and empathize with the story of Abraham shaking as he raised the knife over his son, Isaac. In the last 400 to 500 years, Catholicism has moved away from stories and embraced the abstract. This has limited the imagination and its power to provide valuable insights.

The best boon to the future of Catholic fiction is the renewed interest in reading the Bible. Although scripture is read at every MASS, many participants do not really think about the Bible that much unless they pursue higher education where they may study it in detail. This contrasts with the Protestant South where many more people, highly educated and illiterate alike, have heard Bible stories and made them part of their everyday thinking.

It is easy to consider the South's religious fervor as a kind of GROTESQUE. O'Connor finds it difficult to convince readers that she does not make fun of prophets from the backwoods when she writes about them, but she in fact shares their concerns. It is sometimes easier to show the power of grace by describing instances where it is lacking.

Though a Catholic writer may know the Bible well, she cannot assume that her readers do, and this makes the work difficult. The author, character, and reader need to share a common set of stories. Being a Catholic writer in the religious South helps the writer avoid some of the common pitfalls of the church. He or she is forced to avoid abstraction and write concretely.

Many readers are impatient with the southern Protestant stories and think that nothing else can come out of the South. However, O'Connor sees the possibility for a Catholic literature to emerge from the region since there are elements available nowhere else in the country to help this development along.

One of such element is that southern Catholics must live daily with the division between Catholicism and Protestantism, and this may help fuel fiction. The very scenes of intense belief and worship that characterize the southern fundamentalist and show a need for God that repel Catholics are also the scenes where Catholics may feel the most kinship with their community. In other words, these intense scenes reveal a need for God that Catholics recognize their church as fulfilling.

The Catholic novelist in the South has much to learn from it and then much to give it in return. The South can teach her to be less abstract and more concrete and to trust her imagination. The South, in return, can benefit from the older history and traditions of the Catholic Church as well as the strength of the individual Catholic's faith.

O'Connor finds many opportunities for the Catholic writer in the South. There is already a literary tradition there. The South is struggling with its identity, which is always fuel for good fiction. Belief can be more easily made believable in fiction in the South. Also, within short proximity, the writer can find life demonstrating ways from the Old Testament all the way to post-Christian nonbelief.

She believes that Catholic novelists will enhance southern literature. They appreciate and understand that the South's identity comprises a focus on Scripture, a shared history of loss and defeat, and a dependence on God. The South and the Catholic know that evil can never be conquered; it is an ongoing part of life.

Where the Catholic Church is not present in visual and actual terms, the Catholic novelist must pull from within to make up the lack. She must use her eyes in conjunction with her faith and what is needed for her writing to find materials for her fiction, no matter how "un-Catholic" they may seem. Especially living in a secular world, the Catholic novelist is particularly able to appreciate the Protestant South for its reminders of what Catholics have and what they should keep.

"The Church and the Fiction Writer" (1957)

This essay first appeared in AMERICA on March 30, 1957. The publication vexed O'Connor, however, because the editor, Father Harold C. Gardiner, changed one paragraph, distorting, in her view, her message. The essay was collected by Sally and Robert Fitzgerald in *Mystery and Manners: Occasional Prose,* published by Farrar, Straus and Giroux in 1969 as well as in *Collected Works,* selected and edited by Sally Fitzgerald and published by Library of America in 1988. In a note in that volume, Fitzgerald makes clear that she worked from O'Connor's original typescript, which restores the paragraph in question. She also addresses the issue of the paragraph in the notes.

SYNOPSIS

It is not helpful when considering effects of the church on the Catholic fiction writer to think only of the likes of GRAHAM GREENE. There are other aspects of the question, too, besides the successful fruition of art. There are also writing gifts that have not fully matured and those that have failed. O'Connor cites a 1955 edition of *Four Quarters,* a publication of LaSalle College in Philadelphia that ran an article about the lack of writers graduating from Catholic colleges. Later issues, she writes, printed letters from readers on the issue. In one of these responses, Philip Wylie claimed that a devout Catholic must be necessarily "brainwashed" (MM 144) and cannot, therefore, be a top-notch creative writer.

O'Connor argues that the lack of writers graduating from Catholic schools must be taken by those universities to be a problem of education, but that to the writer it is a personal issue. Each writer must decide what his or her obligations are to the church and gauge that in terms of what is necessary to write quality work. The fiction writer may have a bigger problem resolving this issue than other writers.

The eye is where matters are measured for the fiction writer. Msgr. Romano Guardini has said that the roots of the eye connect directly to the heart. For Catholics, these roots dive into mystery, that region that is so divided in today's world. Some try to eliminate mystery from the world, and others try to find it again, only in places other than religion. Wylie's comment that Catholics cannot "see straight" (MM 145) if they believe in mystery is matched by Catholics themselves who say that no matter what the Catholic does see, there are things that should not be seen, "straight or otherwise" (MM 145). It is ironic that the two share even a small point positioned on the same side.

There is an assumption that a Catholic writing fiction must be attempting to prove the faith true or that there is a spiritual dimension to life. However, any writer of fiction must "be humble in the face of what-is" (146). The fiction writer must stay within the limits of the concrete and not stray out to the abstract. Concrete details, not abstract ideas, are the tools of the fiction writer's trade; " . . . fiction can transcend its limitations only by staying within them" (146).

HENRY JAMES gauged the morality in a work of fiction by how much "felt life" (146) it contained. Catholic writers feel the presence of life from the mystery of God sending his Son to die for us. This ought to expand the writer's vision rather than narrow it. Mr. Wylie's view and those who are like-minded is that this premise is not based on reality as we know it. The Catholic writer who writes for an audience beyond the Catholic community will likely consider that it may be hostile to his or her ideas. There will be an even greater effort on the Catholic writer's part, in this case, to be sure that the work stands on its own merits. People told O'Connor that she cannot be an artist because she is a Catholic. She has answered that because she is a Catholic she "cannot afford to be less than an artist" (146).

A writer needs to set limits on any work he or she writes that come from within the composition itself, and these limits are overall more restrained than limits put on the writer by his or her religion. One such problem is the nature of grace. It is important to the Catholic fiction writer to keep faith connected to what he or she sees. Somehow, this attachment seems at risk of unraveling by those who want to control what the Catholic writer sees.

If the Catholic reader separates the nature of grace from reality, what is left is only sentiment and obscenity. The supernatural goes the way of cliché. Sentimentality is an excess of emotion that omits the process of fall and redemption. The innocence that is expressed is false. Obscenity is like sentimentality in that it distances sex from reality and meaning and relegates it simply to an experience.

Religious literature is often criticized for downplaying life on Earth in order to emphasize the importance of life in the hereafter. Fiction should make the supernatural more defined by really seeing and presenting accurately the concrete details of the natural world. Writing about the worst people and events on Earth, the writer places trust in God and gains an even more intensified sense of mystery. The reader may or may not be saved as the writer is through this experience.

FRANÇOIS MAURIAC advised working at cleansing the source, yet the writer must do this while writing at the same time. The writer must learn perspective—either stop writing because one erroneously views the demands of the church as too high for one's capabilities, or attempt to work within the limitations of what one is writing.

The church is correct in its efforts at protecting people from literature that poses danger to their souls. The Catholic writer should be grateful that the church provides this service, even if this means that one's own work is judged unsuitable to be read without permission. This leaves one concerned only with the limitations that are presented from within one's art. This is a summary of the paragraph as it was altered by Father Gardiner before the essay's publication in *America,* a change with which O'Connor adamantly disagreed: It is the author's function as well as the church's to save souls from literature that endangers them. While serving his art, he knows that not all readers will appreciate what he produces. If the church decides to keep readers from reading that author's work without permission, the Catholic author will be glad for the reminder from the church of his or her duty. The difference between the two versions is that O'Connor does not agree that it is the writer's duty to save souls from dangerous literature; she believes this is the church's role. She also does not agree with the implication that the writer leave the limitations and duties of creating her art (if her work is placed on a questioned list by the church) to take on the responsibility that is the church's and not the artist's.

Many writers would consider it easier to take on the responsibility of saving souls than it is to write a work of art. They may think it "better to save the world than to save the work" (150). Romanticism, as well as piety, fuels this kind of thinking. Failed education or the lack of a true calling as a writer makes this question more important to the would-be writer. Some among the pious of the church are guilty of spreading this idea. Wylie's claim about dogma and creativitiy has some valid points.

However, faith firmly placed in dogma does not change the reality of what is happening all around the writer. Faith adds to the story; it need not take away from the story. Stories are judged on their attention to the concrete, and that need not change when the writer is a person of faith. The Catholic writer who wishes to expose the mysteries of life must do so through a clear vision and portrayal of the natural side of life.

In order to bolster Catholic fiction writers, we need to persuade them that the church assures their freedom for creative expression; it does not limit it. This can perhaps be best accomplished by Catholic readers who can read fiction with more than an eye for what may be obscene. Many Catholic readers lack an objective critical sense about fiction, so they are continually offended because they do not know how to truly read it.

A truthful portrayal of life in fiction is more challenging to those of weak faith than strong. If a fiction writer is true to his or her art and pays attention to God's will within that framework, then blessings will come through in the work. The best of these, though perhaps least anticipated at the current time, would be a Catholic reader who is content with the story.

"Circle in the Fire, A" (1954)

The seventh story in the collection A *Good Man Is Hard to Find and Other Stories* (Harcourt, 1955), this tale was originally published in the spring 1954 issue of KENYON REVIEW (vol. 16). It was reprinted in *Prize Stories 1955: The O. Henry Awards,* edited by Paul Engle and Hansford Martin, and also in *The Best American Short Stories* of 1955, edited by Martha Foley. Subsequently, the story became part of *The Complete Stories* (FSG, 1971) and *Collected Works* (Library of America, 1988).

SYNOPSIS

Mrs. Cope is pulling weeds while Mrs. Pritchard tells her about a rumor of a woman who gave birth inside an iron lung. The air is dry and windy, and Mrs. Cope is more concerned about the potential for fire than she is about rumors. She asks Mrs. Pritchard if she ever prays for all they have to be thankful for. Mrs. Cope's child, Sally Virginia, sees a pick-up truck drop off three boys at the gate. One boy has silver-rimmed glasses and carries a pig-shaped suitcase. He is the middle-sized boy of the three, about 13 years old. He tells Mrs. Cope that his name is Powell Boyd, and that his father used to work at the farm. His companions are Garfield Smith, the larger boy, and W. T. Harper, the smaller one. When Mrs. Cope asks after Boyd, the boy tells him that his father died in Florida; his mother has remarried; and they all now live in a development in Atlanta. Mrs. Cope tells Boyd that it was nice of him to visit her. The boys wait expectantly. Finally, Harper tells Mrs. Cope that Boyd has been talking about how great the farm is, how he always rode horses when he lived there, how there is everything there, and how when he dies he would like to go there.

Mrs. Cope tells them that Gene, the horse Boyd remembers, died, and that the boys cannot ride any of the other horses now because it is too dangerous. She is always concerned that someone will get hurt on the farm and sue her. She asks the boys if they would like something to eat. Sally Virginia, the overweight 12-year-old child with braces on her teeth, kneels in her upstairs window, watching with excitement. It appears that the boys will stay, at least for a short time. Mrs. Cope brings the boys crackers and Coco-Colas and sees that Garfield is on the hammock, smoking. She asks him to pick up the butt he spits out on the ground; she is afraid of fire.

The boys tell Mrs. Cope about the development and how Powell does not like it. There are 10 identical buildings four stories high each, and the only way they can tell which is theirs, the boys say, is by the smell. Powell tells Mrs. Cope that the boys hoped to spend the night in the barn, that his uncle had dropped them off and would be back for them in the morning. Mrs. Cope does not trust the boys and remains concerned about fire, with their smok-

ing in the barn. When Powell offers to sleep in the woods, Mrs. Cope refuses that as well; her woods are very dry and would also be at risk for fire from their smoking. Powell notes that Mrs. Cope calls the woods hers. They say they will sleep in the field near the house, which she allows, and where, the child notes, her mother can keep an eye on them. Powell joins the boys; he wants to show the others around the place.

At sunset, the three boys come out of the woods, dirty and sweaty. They ask for some water. The smallest boy has a cut on his arm. It is obvious that they have been riding the horses. Mrs. Cope feeds them sandwiches and asks them questions about their families. Powell's mother works, and his friends say that Powell once was babysitting his younger siblings when he locked his little brother in a box and set it on fire. She asks the boys if they thank God each night for all he has given them. The boys go silent.

The sun sets, turning the white water tower a strange pink and the grass an unusual shade of green. Sally Virginia hangs her head out the window and makes a noise, gaping at the boys. The larger one stares up at her and complains that there is still another woman on the farm. Later, the child tells her mother that she would beat the big boy up, but Mrs. Cope tells her to stay away from all of them.

The boys are still there the next morning. Mrs. Pritchard verifies that they were riding the horses the day before because Hollis, the farmhand, saw them. They are also drinking milk out of the milk cans. They ask Hollis how he stands being at this place where there are so many women. Mrs. Cope seems to think she owns the sky, the woods, and everything in between, but only God owns these things and her, too. Hollis walks away. Mrs. Pritchard says that there is no way of stopping boys this age when they decide they are going to do bad things. Mrs. Cope decides she must get them off the property. The child tells her that she can handle them, but Mrs. Pritchard puts her in her place, and she retreats upstairs to watch from the window. Mrs. Cope and Mrs. Pritchard do not find the boys when they look, but it turns out they have let the bull out. At lunch, Mrs. Pritchard informs

Mrs. Cope that the boys are down the road, throwing rocks at her mailbox, about to knock it over.

Mrs. Cope confronts them and tells them that if they are not gone when she gets back from town, she will call the sheriff to take them away. Other than a piercing, mean laugh by the hog pen in the afternoon, the boys are nowhere to be found later in the day. Nothing happens all night either, despite Mrs. Pritchard's dour warnings. By the next day, Sally Virginia has had enough and puts on a hat and a loaded holster over her dress. She stalks the boys and finds them washing in the cow trough in the back pasture. The little boy says he wished he lived there; the big boy says he's glad he doesn't and would put a parking lot on it if it were his. Powell says that if it were not there anymore, they would not have to think of it again. He takes a small object out of his pocket and shows it to the others. They move back into the woods past the girl and begin to set the brush on fire.

At first the girl is numb with "some new unplaced misery," (*Collected* 250) then she runs. Mrs. Cope sees the smoke and tells all the workers to hurry and throw dirt on the fire. Sally Virginia sees the look of the new misery on her mother's face, a look that is older, as if it might belong to anyone. In the distance, the child hears shrieks of joy, as though from prophets dancing in a fiery furnace.

COMMENTARY

The story is reminiscent of several others in O'Connor's canon, in particular, "A Temple of the Holy Ghost" and "The Life You Save May Be Your Own." In the former, the reader follows the train of thought of a 12-year-old girl who is left upstairs in her room while her older cousins go to the local fair with boys. In the latter, a stranger arrives at a farm to manipulate the lives of a woman and her daughter. All three stories feature women farmers and their daughters. In fact, this scenario, which resembles O'Connor's own life situation living at ANDALUSIA under the care of her mother, appears in several of the author's works.

Mrs. Cope, whose name suggests that she finds a way to cope with most any situation, is an optimistic woman who works hard to keep up her farm. She employs blacks as well as Mr. and Mrs. Pritchard

to help her run the place. Apparently, years before, she employed Mr. and Mrs. Boyd and their family of children. Powell Boyd, the middle child, has such good memories of his life on the farm that years later he tells his buddies about riding horses there, finding anything one wishes, and that he would even like to go there when he dies. He has a child's idyllic memory of the place. With his father passing away in Florida and his mother remarrying and moving to the city, Powell finds that he longs for the way things were when he was younger and his father was still alive—the way they were when they all lived together in the country. In many ways, Powell appreciates the farm as much as Mrs. Cope does. She is always looking out at the woods and pastures and thanking God for them. Powell has remembered the same land fondly enough to tell his friends about it and to want to bring them there to share it with them. Unfortunately, Mrs. Cope does not stop to realize that she shares her love of the farm with Powell. Instead, she views his presence and apparent desire to stay there with his two friends as a threat.

The story opens with Mrs. Cope worrying about the dry conditions and about fire. Fire may represent trouble or evil or even hell in the story. When Powell Boyd arrives, we sense that trouble may not be far behind. The boys smoke, and apparently Powell has played with fire before, having supposedly set his younger brother on fire in a box. As Powell's background unfolds, it is clear that he is struggling with the changes in his life brought on since his father's death and his mother's remarriage. The development in Atlanta is too close and confining. The houses all look alike. City and suburban life do not agree with him, and he longs to return to the days in the country that he remembers so fondly when his father was alive and his family was all together.

Given the destroyer design on his sweatshirt that his hollow chest makes look as though broken, perhaps someone in his family was in the navy, or perhaps the shirt is a hand-me-down from a thrift shop. His mother is employed, and he is charged with caring for his younger siblings while she is at work, yet he is only 13 himself, still coping with his father's death. If he were truly a destroyer, the broken appearance of the ship on his shirt, as well as his wire spectacles (reminiscent of The Misfit's glasses in

"A Good Man Is Hard to Find") belie his power. He has held onto his memories of the farm as a means of coping with the rapid changes in his life.

If she were able to relate more to her employees as human beings, Mrs. Cope may have helped Powell had she realized all that the farm meant to the boy and that he was hurting. Instead, she becomes highly territorial about the property. Powell does not remember it as *her* farm where his father worked—he remembers it as a utopian existence before his troubles began. His comment to his friends that he would like to go there when he dies even suggests that he thinks of the farm as a kind of heaven.

Powell is not only affected when he discovers that things at the farm have changed or were never quite the way he remembered them, but he is also confronted with the even greater destruction of his dream that has helped him cope all along. Mrs. Cope keeps speaking about *her* woods and *her* horses and *her* land, and each time she does, she takes more and more of the ownership of Powell's dream, the last way of coping he had, away from him. The boys' comments against Mrs. Cope's ownership indicate a belief that no one owns heaven for him or herself. Heaven, and all that is below it, including human beings, belong to God. The boys are wiser than Mrs. Cope. For all she thanks God every night, she misses the bigger picture: that human beings own nothing of God's green earth for themselves; everything on the earth is interconnected and belongs to all. When the boys throw rocks at Mrs. Cope's mailbox, they are trying to destroy her name affixed to the property. Powell's despair grows. Soon there is nothing left for Powell to do in order to cope in his own convoluted way but to erase the memory of the farm as heaven from his own mind and from the boys' and Mrs. Cope's. He says, "If this place was not here any more, you would never have to think of it again" (*Collected* 249). The circle in the fire is reminiscent of ritual and the fires of hell, where angels fallen from the state of grace dominate the scene.

While all of this is happening with Mrs. Cope and Powell Boyd, Sally Virginia is trying to grow up and become a woman. She is insulted when the bigger boy curses at her and when he comments to Hollis that the place is owned by women, run by women,

and appears to be full of women. Garfield's misogyny feeds into Powell's disappointment at his mother's emotionally distancing herself from him by marrying another man and then going out to work, leaving him at home caring for the other children. With the strongest male figure in his life dead, Powell has built up rage against females. Hearing Mrs. Cope go on about owning the farm, taking even his memories away from him, builds this pressure even more.

Sally Virginia experiences her own buildup of rage at the boys and her mother's apparent lack of control over them. She asks her mother several times if she can deal with them, but her mother refuses to let her near them. At the same time, Mrs. Cope is cruel to her daughter. The child assumes a male role by putting overalls, a hat, and holster on over her dress and charging out toward the woods to bring justice back to the farm. Mrs. Cope sees her in the outfit before she leaves and asks her why she has to look like an idiot and when is she going to grow up, and she comments that sometimes she looks like she may belong to Mrs. Pritchard. She tells her that she looks at her and wants to cry. For a woman who is supposedly so grateful to God for all that she has, one has to wonder why she is not more grateful for her imaginative and loyal daughter.

When Sally Virginia misunderstands the boys' comments that they are burning the woods to clear it out for a parking lot, the reader is reminded that she is still a child. The red-and-white imprint of the bark on her cheek, however, suggests that something has happened to her in the woods. She has become aware of a "new unplaced misery" that she has never felt before. Some critics point to this passage and suggest that the child may be experiencing her first menstruation. The imprint of the bark on her face appears to be a sign that she has become united with nature in some way. O'Connor has used the motif before in "A Temple of the Holy Ghost" when the nun's crucifix presses into the child's face in an embrace and leaves an impression, uniting her with a deepened sense of spirituality. As she stops beside her mother staring at the fire, Sally Virginia notices her mother's face in a new light—she sees the same misery she feels. She is linked to her now in a new way, perhaps in the growing knowledge of womanhood.

The new misery, however, is also portrayed as anonymous and genderless. Mrs. Pritchard experiences it earlier in her toothache, but the narrator says that the misery as it appears on Mrs. Cope when her daughter sees it looks as though it could belong to a black person, a European, or even Powell Boyd. The misery may be interpreted in any number of ways. Perhaps the misery is the realization that the farm is not heaven and all that this knowledge implies. Perhaps the misery is that there is true evil in the world, around which deep faith in God, and not self-reliance alone, is the only way one may find to cope.

Readers may be surprised that for all the practical power the women have (the rumor of the distant Pritchard relative bearing a child from within an iron lung suggests this female power as well), they are ineffective against protecting their property from these young boys. Mrs. Pritchard states several times that there will be no stopping them. Perhaps she knows the devil when she sees him. Mrs. Cope is so used to Mrs. Pritchard always being the bearer of bad news that she does not believe her pessimism and passes off her warnings. She tries to feed the boys and thinks when she warns the boys of the sheriff in the incident at the mailbox that she has scared them off and they will be gone when she returns from town. Mrs. Pritchard, for all her unpleasant, negative outlook, seems more clear-eyed on the subject. She is enough of a realist to know better than Mrs. Cope that these unhappy boys will make it their business to cause trouble at the farm, no matter what.

O'Connor comments in her letters about one reader's surprise about a particular element of this story. The reader wrote to her that he was surprised that Sally Virginia is not sexually attacked by the boys when she enters the woods and sees them naked in the back pasture. He indicated that this lack of sexual attack when and where it might be expected puts an interesting tension in many of the author's stories. O'Connor says she had not thought of this before, but agrees that the boys were fully capable of harming the child, not out of passion for themselves, but out of revenge against Mrs. Cope: "They might well have done this if they had seen the child behind the tree. I didn't let them see the child behind the tree. I couldn't have gone through that myself," she writes (HB 120). Perhaps shielding Sally Virginia from the boys (she is also protected from the fire by standing outside the circle of flames) allows that O'Connor's young female character still retains some measure of empowerment over her "new misery."

CHARACTERS

Mrs. Cope Mrs. Cope is a small and trim woman, with a large round face and black eyes that seem to look larger behind her glasses. She is optimistic, thanking God every day for all that she has. She stands in contrast to Mrs. Pritchard, who is always looking at the negative side of things. When Mrs. Cope is confronted with young Powell Boyd and his cronies terrorizing the farm, her ability to "cope" is sorely tested.

Sally Virginia Cope Mrs. Cope's 12-year-old daughter is a reader and an observer. She is plump and wears braces. She watches much of the action of the story from her upstairs window. She wants to rescue the farm and her family from the intruding boys, but her mother tells her to stay away from them. When she makes a noise at them from her window, Garfield Smith curses that there is yet another woman on the premises. Finally, she puts overalls over her dress, a hat down over her eyes, and a holster with pistols on her hips and makes her way out to the woods to stop the boys. Instead, she senses a new kind of misery that she recognizes on her mother's face and thinks the boys are going to make a parking lot when the brush begins to burn.

RELATED LETTERS

Betty Hester ("A"), October 20, 1955 (HB 111); Betty Hester ("A"), November 25, 1955 (HB 119); Betty Hester ("A"), December 8, 1955 (HB 120); Elizabeth Bishop, January 13, 1957 (HB 198); Betty Hester ("A"), January 25, 1957 (HB 200). *Pages*: HB: 111, 119, 120, 198, 200.

FURTHER READING

Babinec, Lisa S. "Cyclical Patterns of Domination and Manipulation in Flannery O'Connor's Mother-Daughter Relationships." *Flannery O'Connor Bulletin* 19 (1990): 9–29.

Smith, Peter A., "Flannery O'Connor's Empowered Women." *Southern Literary Journal* 26, no. 2 (Spring 1994): 35–47.

"Comforts of Home, The" (1960)

This is the fifth story in the collection *Everything That Rises Must Converge* (FSG, 1965).

SYNOPSIS

Thomas's mother has disturbed the peace of their existence. His father is dead, and Thomas is a historian working at home. His mother sees a report in the newspaper about a 19-year-old girl who has passed a bad check and is now in jail. She feels compassionate toward the girl, realizing that she could be her own daughter. She decides to take her a box of candy, which is her token deed for any mission of goodwill, for the sick, newcomers in town, new babies. While she is there, the girl tells her story.

When she returns from the jail, the mother bursts into Thomas's study and tells him that they have no idea how the other half lives. The girl, who calls herself Star, has lived a horrible life. Thomas can see that his mother is moved by the girl's story, but he hopes that it will pass.

Two nights later, however, the girl is at the house for dinner. Thomas learns that her real name is Sarah Ham, though she calls herself Star Drake. His mother tells Star that her son writes history and is the current president of the local Historical Society. The girl is clearly disturbed. The lawyer had told his mother that the girl's stories were, for the most part, untrue. She was not insane enough to be hospitalized, not criminal enough to be put in prison, but not stable enough to remain in society. Thomas realizes he is looking at "the most unendurable form of innocence" (*Collected* 580). He hates that his mother has brought her to their home.

Star makes eyes at Thomas, calls him cute, and says that he reminds her of a cop she saw in a movie. Everyone was always putting something over on him, and the cop looked like he was going to explode any moment. When his mother asks him to take Star home after the meal, he is filled with rage but does as she asked. Star says that nobody likes her, and Thomas mutters that his mother does. Star says that she is an old lady who is behind the times. When Star would not get out of the car, Thomas pulls her out by her coat sleeve and leaves, the passenger door flung open as he pulls away.

At breakfast the next morning, Thomas tries to reason with his mother. He tells her that the girl is a slut and is only out to get what she can from her. His mother answers that she has nothing and they have everything. She and Thomas have the comforts of home, and the girl has nothing, not even a sense of morality. Thomas hears his father's voice in his head, telling him to put his foot down. His mother says that he is not like his father, implying that he has more compassion and a moral sense. However, she will not invite the girl to their home again. But instead of keeping her promise, the mother convinces Thomas to take the girl in for one more night when she gets into trouble again.

The girl has been at their house for eight nights, sleeping in the guest room. Her presence throughout the day and at meals bothers Thomas enormously. Sarah kids about killing herself, since not even God or the devil would want her, and Thomas tells her to go ahead and try. She slashes her wrists, but when they take her to the hospital, the doctor says she has hardly hurt herself. The mother, however, feels very low.

The mother tells Thomas to lock up his father's gun, but he says quite openly in front of the girl where it is and that she is welcome to it. The old woman puts away all the knives and sharp instruments and dumps out the rat poison. When Thomas discovers that the gun is missing and that the girl has been into his room at night, he decides, with his father's voice in his head, to finally go to the sheriff, a man named Farebrother. He makes arrangements with the sheriff to come to the house and search for the gun that is in the possession of a dangerous girl. In the meantime, he tells his mother that the girl can no longer stay with them and that if she is there that afternoon, he will move out.

When he returns, his mother is asleep and the girl is taking a shower. He does not want to move out and cannot make the motions necessary to locate his suitcase. In the meantime, he discovers that his father's gun has been returned to his desk drawer. The sheriff will have no need to come, and the girl will not be arrested for stealing the gun.

Thomas sees the girl's coat and red purse, and at the urging of his dead father's voice in his head, he plants the gun in the girl's purse. She sees him do it. When the mother comes out, the girl tells her what has happened, but the mother does not believe it. She says that Thomas is a gentleman and would not do such a thing. Thomas's father tells him to say that he found the gun in her purse, and he says this to his mother. She seems to hear his father in his voice.

There is a struggle between the girl and Thomas over the purse and the gun. Thomas's father shouts "Fire!" and the gun goes off. Thomas's mother lay on the floor between him and the girl. When the sheriff arrives, he surveys the scene and quickly divines a story that explains it. Thomas wanted his mother dead and came to the sheriff to set things up so that the girl would be blamed.

COMMENTARY

The story first appeared in *The* KENYON REVIEW, vol. 22; Fall 1960. It was also collected in *The Complete Stories* (FSG, 1971) and *Collected Works* (Library of America, 1988). It is the last story the author wrote about the complexities of an adult character living with a parent, a situation that echoed her own condition.

The title refers to one of the blessings that Thomas's mother thinks they have while Sarah Ham does not. Thomas, it appears, has an even greater share of comfort than his mother. As a 35-year-old historian still living at home, Thomas joins several of O'Connor's intellectual characters in living and working at home where the mother tends to his every need. Thomas does not have to provide the house, which his father's will no doubt provided, nor food that his mother not only prepares but serves to him either at the table or in his study on his request. Some might say it is not a bad life for an artist or an intellectual—the comfort of home and the care of a loved one to sustain one's work.

O'Connor writes that Thomas inherited the logic of his father without his ruthlessness and the goodness of his mother without her inclination to seek it out. This suggests that he has inherited the best of both parents. What he lacks, however, is a sense of his own identity separate from his work. His home is his home but also his place of work and his source of spiritual comfort. Though there is some suggestion of a meeting outside the house, to invade his home as Sarah Ham has done is to invade Thomas's very self. When Sarah is found to have stolen his father's gun in his desk drawer, Thomas feels that his privacy and core sense of self have been completely violated.

Though Thomas seems perfectly content with his lifestyle, he frequently deals with the shadowy figure of his dead father, who would expect more from him. His father was deceitful and willing to do what he thought he had to do to reach any given goal. He was assertive with people; no one walked over Thomas's father. This stereotypical view of manhood—not being pushed around, especially by a female—hounds Thomas in his relationship with his mother and in his dealings with Sarah's threat to their cozy arrangement.

Thomas loves his mother, and though he cannot speak with her about all of his interests, they get along well enough. She is proud of him and respects his work, which helps him tolerate her lack of understanding. No doubt he provides her with company and, presumably, some form of perceived protection. There are two threats to Thomas's "comforts of home," however. One is his father's presence in his imagination, and the other is his mother's constant effort to find people to help. When she sees Sarah's story in the paper, she acts, precipitating the ensuing events. Both Thomas's love and care from his mother and his sense of manhood from his father become challenged.

Sarah Ham is a confused and troubled young woman. Thomas and his mother are told that she is a psychopath who will lie about her past. It is clear that Thomas's mother did, as Sheriff Farebrother noted, bite off more than she could chew when she took in Sarah Ham. Thomas's failure is getting his mother to see this, putting his foot down, as his father might say, and getting Sarah out of the house and out of their lives. His love for his mother is strong, and he shares just enough of her good tendencies to allow Sarah back into the house after he once tried to get rid of her.

Thomas's manhood is challenged by Sarah. Some of these tests have sexual overtones. Thomas has apparently never married and turns away in disgust at Sarah's sensual glances, her moves toward him in the car, and other flirtations. A Freudian reading sees Thomas dropping the pistol in Sarah's purse as Thomas finally asserting his manhood. His mother tells Sarah that Thomas would never do such a thing, since he is a "gentleman." The word *gentleman* gives the gesture more sexual currency. Oedipal readings note Thomas's absent father and the fact that he lives with his mother.

Thomas's manhood is also questioned in the matter of action versus language, a familiar theme of O'Connor's. As he writes his history papers and articles, Thomas is in complete control and hard to match in terms of eloquence. When he tries to explain about Sarah Ham to the sheriff, however, he stumbles and repeats himself so that the sheriff has to struggle to understand what he is trying to say.

In the end, Thomas listens to the voice of his father in his head. Readers may believe it is not what he himself would do without this voice pressuring him. Perhaps Thomas's father is the devil. Perhaps the voice is some aspect of Thomas's personality inherited from his father that has been protected from society by Thomas's lifestyle. When society, in the form of Sarah Ham, enters into the protected cocoon and threatens it, the part of Thomas that is like his father wins out. In other words, Thomas may have been more like his father had he lived away from his mother's heavy influence in adulthood. Sarah not only disturbs Thomas's and his mother's comfort of home, but she also upsets the comfort of home in the social order of the community.

The sheriff, a representative of the law, is the polar opposite of Thomas's mother. He is corrupt, just like Thomas's father. He understands logic, prompting Thomas to go to him with the problem of what to do with Sarah Ham. It is unclear whether the sheriff intends to merely look for the gun at the house or make some kind of accident happen that kills off one of the two women plaguing Thomas. His name, Farebrother, suggests that the sheriff is

so much like Thomas's father that he could be Thomas's brother. He mentions to Thomas that Thomas's father, whom he knew well, would not have let these women run over him this way.

The end of the story is a tragic mismatch of justice. According to the sheriff's preordained fix on events, Thomas will likely be sentenced to jail for a senseless, accidental killing of his mother. His mother is dead. Sarah Ham will, in all likelihood, be hospitalized or jailed once again. The sheriff's and Thomas's father's kind of justice over those they see as the weak of the world wins out.

In an O'Connor reading, however, "doubting Thomas" may have had to live through or see with his own eyes the horrors of listening to his father and killing his mother in order to see how good his mother truly was.

CHARACTERS

Thomas   Thomas is an adult son who lives with his mother. He is a historian and president of the local Historical Society. He enjoys the comforts of home where he works in his study and lives with his mother cleaning and cooking for him. He has inherited his dead father's sense of reason without his ruthlessness and his mother's admiration of good but without her need to seek it out. Thomas's name suggests the doubting Thomas of the gospels. St. Thomas did not believe that the other apostles had seen the resurrected Christ when Christ visited them in Thomas's absence. He said he needed to see to believe, in particular, Christ's wounds from the crucifixion. Later, Christ appeared to Thomas, asking him to put his hand in his side and to touch his hands and see so that he would believe. In doubting himself, Thomas in the story allows himself to be taken over by the unattractive traits of both of his parents. He allows his mother to bring Sarah Ham into the house, and he allows his father's cruelty to inspire him to behave badly in what results in tragedy. Like St. Thomas believing on the eighth day when Christ shows him his wounds, this Thomas sees the sacrifice his mother made for goodness when she is shot on the eighth day after Sarah first enters the house.

Thomas means "twin," and there are several doublings in the story of the main character. Increasingly, his mother puts him and Sarah together in her conversation, telling him that he could be her. Thomas is the combination of the best traits of his parents, rather "twinning" them into the next generation. Sarah Ham mentions on meeting him for the first time that he reminds her of a cop she saw the night before in a movie. The cop looked like he was furious at having everyone always trying to put something over on him. Sheriff Farebrother, too, is a twin to Thomas's father, but as his name suggests, he is a brother-like figure to Thomas.

Sarah Ham Calling herself "Star Drake," Sarah Ham is a psychopath who is suicidal. She cannot keep a job and gets drunk and does not take care of herself. She is a liar. In short, she is someone an uneducated, friendly old lady with good intentions has no hope of redeeming. Sarah's name, *Ham*, as well as her chosen nickname, *"Star,"* suggests how much she likes to perform, how much she would like others to like her and look at her. Her eyes and expression "twinkle" and dazzle. Drake connotes a colorful male duck, perhaps one that makes noise for attention. Drake also has a more noble and aristocratic sound. *Ham* as a discordant word suggests that any attention Sarah does receive is undeserved and will not end productively. The name *Sarah* suggests Sarah from the Bible, Abraham's wife who gave birth to Isaac in old age. When she was told by the angel that she would conceive a son, she laughed.

RELATED LETTERS

Betty Hester ("A"), November 2, 1957 (HB 250); Maryat Lee, November 14, 1959 (HB 358); Cecil Dawkins, December 10, 1959 (HB 361); Betty Hester ("A"), "Wed." December, 1959 (HB 362); Betty Hester ("A"), December 19, 1959 (HB 363); Cecil Dawkins, January 28, 1960 (HB 371); Cecil Dawkins, "Geo Wash Birth" [February 22, 1960] (HB 375); Betty Hester ("A"), March 5, 1960 (HB 379); John Hawkes, November 6, 1960 (HB 416); John Hawkes, March 3, 1961 [Sarah Ham] (CW 1,146–1,147); Elizabeth McKee, May 7, 1964 (HB 575); Robert Giroux, May 21, 1964 (HB 579). *Pages:* HB: 250, 358, 361, 362, 363, 371, 375, 379, 416, 575, 579; CW: 1,146–1,147.

FURTHER READING

Angle, Kimberly Grace. "Flannery O'Connor's Literary Art: Spiritual Portraits in Negative Space." *Flannery O'Connor Bulletin* 23 (1994–95): 158–174.

Gentry, Marshall Bruce. "The Hand of the Writer in 'The Comforts of Home.'" *Flannery O'Connor Bulletin* 20 (1991): 61–72.

Millichap, Joseph R. "The Pauline 'Old Man' in Flannery O'Connor's 'The Comforts of Home.'" *Studies in Short Fiction* 11 (1974): 96–99.

"Crop, The" (1947)

"The Crop" is the fourth short story (pp. 52–66) from O'Connor's 1947 M.F.A. thesis at the UNIVERSITY OF IOWA, "The Geranium: A Collection of Short Stories."

SYNOPSIS

Miss Willerton lives with Lucia, Bertha, and Garner. After breakfast, Lucia and Bertha do the dishes while Garner goes into the parlor to work the *Morning Press* crossword puzzle, and Miss Willerton crumbs the table.

This day, she thinks she may write about a baker, perhaps a foreign one. She begins to compose a first sentence in her mind when Miss Lucia calls her out of her reverie and tells her to keep the catcher under the crumber brush or she will brush crumbs right onto the rug and Lucia will have to Bissel it again. Miss Willerton finally sits down in front of her typewriter, where she has freedom until lunch.

She decides there is not enough social tension with bakers to write a story about them. She considers people of other occupations—teachers, for example. In thinking about social problems, she begins to think about sharecroppers, about which she knows nothing.

Miss Willerton begins her story: "Lot Motun called his dog. The dog pricked up its ears and slunk over to Lot" (CS 35). She values first sentences as her strong suit. She reads the sentence over and over and changes words to avoid repetition and to achieve what she believed to be the strongest aural effect. She believes in what she calls "phonetic art," that literature appeals to the ear as much as the eye. She decides this is a good beginning and now knows she must plan the action of the story.

The story must include a woman. She thinks about how to provide a love interest while at the same time creating a story with sadistic violence. She enjoys planning passionate scenes but feels guilty because of what Lucia, Bertha, and Garner would think if they knew about them. Now she must plan her characters.

She envisions Lot as tall, disheveled, and gentlemanly, despite having a red neck and large clumsy hands. He would have straight teeth and red hair to show that he had spirit. The woman would be "more or less pretty—yellow hair, fat ankles, muddy-colored eyes" (*Collected*, 736). The woman would cook supper for Lot and whine about his not cutting enough wood for the stove. Her back would hurt. She would accuse him of begging for food, for not having enough nerve to steal it, and he would tell her to shut up. The tension would rise until the woman came at Lot with a knife.

Suddenly Miss Willerton cannot stand the tension and steps into the story to save Lot by hitting the woman over the head. An active scene ensues as Miss Willerton has entered the story and seemingly confuses fiction for reality.

Lucia tells Miss Willerton that she can go to the grocery store for her. While she is there, Miss Willerton is disgusted by the people she sees and does not make the connection between these real people and the characters she had envisioned earlier in her attempt to write a story.

Back home, Miss Willerton sets the groceries on the table and rereads the single sentence she typed earlier. She decides the sentence sounds terrible. She wants to write something more arty and vibrant. Suddenly she is struck with the idea to write about the Irish. They are a spirited people with their brogues and love of music and are full of rich history. The Irish people, she muses, have red hair, wide shoulders, and large, drooping mustaches.

COMMENTARY

This story was not published until after O'Connor's death when it appeared in MADEMOISELLE, April 1971, (vol. 72, no. 6) with an explanation by Robert Fitzgerald. Subsequently, it was printed in *The Complete Stories* (Farrar, Straus and Giroux, 1971) and *Collected Works,* (Library of America, 1988).

With the story's first publication in *Mademoiselle* in 1971, Robert Fitzgerald observed that though the story is not one of O'Connor's best, it could never be thought to be by anyone else. "We enjoy a small caricature of the shady type, the imaginative artist. . . . The exacting art, the stringent spirit, and the sheer kick of her mature work are promised here" (qtd. in *Complete,* 551). It is the only story in O'Connor's canon with a protagonist as a writer, so it is interesting to scholars primarily for that reason.

The author admitted in a 1948 letter to her agent, Elizabeth McKee, that the story was for sale to the "unparticular" (*Habit*, 6). She accepted the criticism of George Davis. Rereading as much of it as she could "stand" after receiving his comments, she admitted, "I should not write stories in the middle of a novel" (7). As one of her earlier works, the characters are not fully drawn, and the story overall is not considered among her most successful. However, the inverse mirror it presents to the reader looking over a writer's shoulder into a character-writer's thoughts and methods of fiction provides a rare viewpoint from which to consider O'Connor's own aesthetics early on in their development.

The story is about how not to write a story. Miss Willerton begins her work like many writers, with a first sentence she likes. However, she begins to analyze the sentence word by word before she moves on. Overanalyzing every sentence blocks her creativity. Note that the entire story with Lot, the woman, and then with Willie, is not written down at all. Miss Willerton's dreams get ahead of her writing, and the act of writing falters until it stops altogether as the author steps into her reverie. Also, the fantasy ends up having nothing to do with Lot rolling in the mud with his dog in the first sentence, the only sentence that is actually written down. The story shows the difference between fiction that develops from the imagination, carefully crafted by a writer, and fantasy, which is where many writer-wannabes leave off, allowing themselves to dream the story without carrying out the hard work required to share it with others.

Another aesthetic observation in the story is that writers need to have the proper balance of engagement with and detachment from their fiction as they create it. Not only does Miss Willerton enter her own story, but she also stands too far away from it at the same time. She has not allowed herself to be a creator of characters in a way that keeps her from stepping into the story herself, dissolving the necessary distance from writer and fiction and turning the story into a fantasy in her own mind. At the same time, she is oblivious to the similarities between her characters and the real people she encounters outside the grocery store. Her would-be story, then, has more to do with a momentary fantasy or entertainment than it does any semblance of art that speaks to the human condition.

Still another caution to writers is Miss Willerton's imposing themes on the story before it even begins, such as wanting to write a story with social impact that will impress a particular audience she is trying to cultivate. Her lack of understanding of her characters or the will to understand them better is exemplified by her disgust at the couple outside the store. The story suggests that, despite her lectures to local groups about "phonetic art," this author is more concerned with getting her mind off the realities of her daily life with Lucia, Bertha, and Garner than she is with writing. Her notion of language that appeals to the ear as well as the eye, while promising and intriguing, is undeveloped but telling—she talks of being a writer but has nothing to show for it. Miss Willerton might be compared with another would-be writer, Little Chandler of JAMES JOYCE's story "A Little Cloud" in *Dubliners*. O'Connor read Joyce and was likely familiar with the story.

The reader may also see glimpses of the young O'Connor herself working at this early period. The struggle for an idea to write about, the lack of character development (echoed in the limited development of Miss Willerton herself), Miss Willerton's comments about using violence in fiction as a kind of shorthand to certain character types, and the desire to appeal to certain critical audiences may reflect some of O'Connor's attributes at the time or those of Iowa classmates she observed and wanted to avoid. Ironically, in spite of Miss Willerton's failure to write the story within the story, the reader becomes engaged in Miss Willerton and what happens to her, precisely because O'Connor has avoided several of the traits Miss Willerton exhibits as a would-be author. O'Connor not only dreamed her up but wrote her down; Miss Willerton would have much to learn from her.

CHARACTERS

Miss Willerton Forty-four-year-old writer who thinks about writing more than she actually writes. She is forever planning out characters and stories but only seems to achieve a first sentence actually on paper. Perhaps her name suggests that she has the will but not the way to execute her desire.

RELATED LETTERS

Elizabeth McKee, June 19, 1948 (HB 4); Elizabeth McKee, July 21, 1948 (HB 6); Elizabeth McKee, December 15, 1948 (HB 7). *Pages:* HB: 4, 6, 7.

FURTHER READING

Fenwick, Ruth. "Final Harvest: Flannery O'Connor's 'The Crop.'" *English Journal* 74, no. 2 (February 1985): 45–50.

"Displaced Person, The" (1954)

This story is the last and longest of 10 stories in the collection *A Good Man Is Hard to Find and Other Stories*, published by Harcourt, Brace on June 6, 1955. It also appeared in *The Complete Stories of Flannery O'Connor* published by Farrar, Straus and Giroux in 1971 and in *Collected Works* published by The Library of America in 1988.

SYNOPSIS

Part I
Mrs. McIntyre owns and operates a dairy farm in rural Georgia. Workers on the farm, both black and white, include Mr. and Mrs. Shortley and Astor and Sulk. When the story opens, Mrs. McIntyre is welcoming a priest, Father Flynn, and a Polish

refugee family to the farm. Mrs. Shortley is observing everything, and through her point of view the reader glimpses the opening of the story.

The Polish refugees are a couple and two children. They are the "displaced people" of the story's title. Their arrival at the farm threatens Mrs. Shortley, who wonders whether they might take hers and her husband's jobs away from them. Mrs. McIntyre had made her help prepare a place for them to live before their arrival. They did not own anything from their old country, so furniture was pieced together, and they made curtains out of flowered chicken seed sacks. Mrs. McIntyre said they were lucky to get out of where they lived and come to a place like their farm.

Mrs. McIntyre introduces the Guizacs to the Shortleys. Mrs. Shortley considers the refugees' little girl pretty and has to admit that she is more attractive than either of her own two daughters, Annie Maude, 15, or Sarah Mae, 17. The foreign couple's son, however, does not compare to her own son, H. C. At 20, her son attends Bible school and is going to be a preacher.

As they all stand there, one of the PEACOCKS that still lives at the farm steps a few feet behind Mrs. Shortley. The priest looks agape over her shoulder, and when she turns, she sees the peacock had spread its tail in a magnificent display. The priest is clearly in awe of the natural splendor of fanned suns before him. Mrs. Shortley comments that it is just a peachicken.

When the priest's car leaves, Mrs. Shortley goes to the older black worker, Astor, and he asks her who is there. "Displaced Persons," Mrs. Shortley says from across the water. Then she goes to the barn to talk with Chancey about them while he works. She tells him that since Guizac does not know English, he will probably be of little use to Mrs. McIntyre, probably cannot even drive a tractor. Mr. Shortley comments that he would rather hire another black man. He adds that he will not have a pope of Rome tell him how to run a dairy farm. Mrs. Shortley tells her husband that they are not "Eye-talians"; they are Poles from Poland, where all the bodies were stacked up.

In three weeks, Mrs. McIntyre and Mrs. Shortley watch Mr. Guizac start up the silage cutter. So far, the refugee had demonstrated that he could drive a tractor and operate the rotary hay-baler, the silage cutter, combine, letz mill, and most any other machine on the property. He was also talented as a mechanic, a carpenter, and a mason. He had energy and saved his money and tried to save Mrs. McIntyre money as much as possible in his work. He had even sacked the other black worker, Sulk, when he caught him stealing a turkey and brought him before Mrs. McIntyre. She had had to tell him through his son, Rudolph, as interpreter, that all "Negroes" steal.

As Mrs. McIntyre and Mrs. Shortley watch Mr. Guizac work, Mrs. McIntyre comments about how pleased she is with him. She has only had poor white trash and blacks work for her before, but Mr. Guizac is her "salvation" after 30 years of running the farm. Mrs. Shortley allows the statement about poor white trash to pass without comment, but she mentions that the salvation Mrs. McIntyre feels she has from Guizac may be bought at the price of selling out to the devil. She tells her that Sledgwig told her daughter Annie Maude that their family of four would not be able to live long on the few dollars a month that they were paid.

Mrs. McIntyre asks whether Chancey Shortley is feeling better today. Mr. Guizac had taken over several of his responsibilities, and Shortley claimed to suffer from exhaustion. She suspects he is so tired because he has another job on the side, which Mrs. Shortley knows is true; he runs a whisky still, but she does not admit it to their employer. The blacks did not reveal it because the Shortleys did not tell her about theirs either; they had a mutual agreement. Mrs. Shortley tells Mrs. McIntyre that she heard that as soon as the Guizacs have enough money to buy a car, they plan to do so. Then, she adds, they will leave the farm.

Mrs. McIntyre says that Guizac cannot save enough money on the wages she gives him. She observes that if Mr. Shortley became unable to work, she could use Guizac in the dairy at all times, and that he does not smoke. She is always pointing that out to Mrs. Shortley. Mrs. McIntyre watches Mr. Guizac work and comments that the whole bottom field will be cut in two days at the fast rate he is working.

One night when Mrs. Shortley is in bed with her husband, she touches on the fear that Guizac or his family might discover the still. She speculates about the foreign ways of the Europeans, and she does not like the priest who brought the displaced persons to the farm either. Before she goes to sleep, she talks about how she does not want to see the displaced persons drive the blacks off the farm. She is too sympathetic, she says, to blacks and the poor.

Mrs. McIntyre looks and behaves differently since the Guizacs came to the farm. Mrs. Shortley thinks she acts like she is getting rich without anyone knowing about it, as though she has found a secret to success. The priest comes often to check on how the refugees are doing, and he walks around the place with Mrs. McIntyre, seeing all the improvements. Mrs. Shortley suspects he is trying to get her to allow another Polish family to come work at the farm. The priest likes picking up peacock feathers off the ground, but he does not fool Mrs. Shortley. She knows he is helping the foreigners bring in their devilish, fighting ways.

Mrs. Shortley overhears Mrs. McIntyre and the priest talking about money. She asks him if he thinks the Guizacs will leave because she does not pay them enough, and he says to pay them more because they have to be able to get by. Mrs. McIntyre says that in order to do that she will have to fire some of her other workers. The Priest asks if the Shortleys' work has suited her, and she complains that Mr. Shortley smokes in the barn. When the priest asks if the blacks have been any better, she says that they steal. When he asks her which worker she will let go, she admits that she plans to give Mr. Shortley a month's notice the next day.

Mrs. Shortley does not want to wait for her husband to be fired. She goes to their house and begins to pack. She tells Chancey to bring around the car; they are leaving. The daughters help pack, and soon the car is loaded. The family heads down the road away from the farm.

Part II

Mrs. McIntyre decides it is no loss that the Shortleys have left. She has seen many workers come and go since her husband, the Judge, died. She would miss Mrs. Shortley, though, since she was a good woman, and the couple was not quite white trash. She thinks back with Astor, the old black man, about the different people who have been there. He has stayed, he reminds her, and she remembers how he is the only worker who remembers the Judge, and he thinks this gives him seniority. When they speak about the Poles, he reminds her that the Judge always used to say the devil you know is better than the devil you don't. He does not tell her exactly what the Pole is doing that he finds peculiar since she does not seem to want to know. Still, Astor's suspicions make her start to watch him a little more closely.

She sees Guizac speaking to Sulk and showing him something that he pulls out of his pocket. When she confronts Sulk about it, he reluctantly shows her a photograph of a girl about 12 years old. She is wearing a First Communion dress with a wreath wrapped in her blond hair. Sulk tells Mrs. McIntyre that the girl is Mr. Guizac's cousin and that she is going to marry him. He is paying half of the cost of getting her to America. She is older now than she was in the picture, and she does not care whom she marries; she just wants to get away from Poland and come over here.

Mrs. McIntyre tells Sulk that he will get all of his money back; she will see to it. She goes into the house and cries. Her hopes that there would be no problems when the Guizacs are gone; he has become as much of a problem as all the other workers she has ever had. Soon she confronts Guizac with the photograph. She asks him why he would bring an innocent girl across the ocean to marry a Negro. He tells her that the girl is now 16. She tells him that her Negro cannot have a white European wife. She tells him to stop exciting her Negroes. He tells her that the girl's parents are both dead and that she is waiting in the third camp she has been in.

Mrs. McIntyre tells Guizac that this cannot and will not happen. She says that she can run the farm without him but not without her black help and she will not have him exciting and agitating them. She remembers Mrs. Shortley saying that she thought Guizac pretended sometimes to not understand English in order to get away with things. She suspects he might be doing that now. He nods and returns to work.

She thinks about how she has held back the world from taking over the farm for so many years. She thinks about how all her workers are the same, whether they are from Tennessee or Poland. She has managed the Herrins, the Ringfields, and the Shortleys, and she will stand her ground against the Guizacs as well: This is her place, and she will run it the way she wants it to be run. Guizac does good work. By the end of the day, there would be stubble around everything that needed mowing except for the graveyard where the Judge lay under his monument, the one on which the angel has been broken off.

Part III

When the priest comes again, Mrs. McIntyre tells him that Guizac is not working out after all. The priest urges her to give him time. She tells him that it is not his work that she questions; he is a very good worker. However, he does not know how to get along with her black workers. He also does not seem to be grateful to have his job.

When the priest begins to leave, a peacock again spreads its tail in front of him. The priest stands in amazement and says that Christ will come again in that kind of glory; the display reminds him of the Transfiguration. Mrs. McIntyre has no idea what he means and has only said that it is not her job to provide a home for the wandering people of the world. She says that Mr. Guizac did not have to come; she did not ask for him. The priest turns his mind instead to Christ now that the glory of the peacock's tail reminded him that he came to redeem us all.

Mr. Shortley returns to the farm before Mrs. McIntyre can hire a new white worker. He tells her he has nowhere to go, and that Mrs. Shortley had had a stroke and died in the car the day they left. She hires him back, though he is not nearly worth having around without his wife. It takes Mrs. McIntyre three days to get over the shock of her death. Shortley wants the dairy job back, but he is patient. He distrusts the foreigner because he reminds him of one who threw a hand grenade at him in World War I. Mrs. McIntyre explains that the Guizacs are Poles, not Germans, but they are all the same to Mr. Shortley. The blacks are glad Shortley is back.

During one of Father Flynn's visits, Mrs. McIntyre tells him that she is going to let Guizac go; she does not owe him a job. She tells him that as far as she's concerned, Jesus himself was another Displaced Person. She gives him an earful of how hard times have been since the Judge died and how she has tried to keep the farm going for 30 years. She is not made of money. The priest seems to retreat within himself while she goes on about her trials.

Mr. Shortley thinks that Mrs. McIntyre is withering somehow inside. He thinks the priest has a control over her and soon she will be going to MASS. He is waiting for the dairy job, so he is interested in when Guizac will be fired. She tells him she is waiting for the first of the month. The first comes and goes, however, and still Guizac is working on the farm.

Mrs. McIntyre approaches Guizac one morning with the intention of letting him go. Instead, she angrily tells him that this farm is her place and everyone working on it is extra. They are there at her pleasure. Mr. Guizac simply says "Ya," his typical response. She goes back to the house as though she has accomplished what she wanted.

Mr. Shortley decides he has had enough and will now press his case to whomever he sees. He tells Mrs. McIntyre about how he went to war, risking his life to prove that all men are made equally. He says he went to Europe to fight and shed his blood, and a grenade thrown at him by a man very like Mr. Guizac but with small eyeglasses nearly killed him. He asks the blacks why they do not go back to Africa. Sulk replies that he might get eaten if he were to go there. Mr. Shortley, now speaking more without his wife around to do the talking, says that it is not the blacks with whom he has a problem. Their grandfathers were brought here; they did not want to come. They did not run away from home, and it is those people with whom he has problems.

Sulk tells him that he does not like to travel. Shortley says that if he were to go anywhere now, he would go to China or Africa because it is easy to tell the difference between you and them. He complains that too many foreigners are learning English and that there would be less trouble if everyone stayed speaking his or her own language.

Mrs. McIntyre discovers that the town is buzzing about how she runs her farm because Shortley has been talking. She knows she must fire Guizac and so makes another attempt. He is working on the ground beside the small tractor. Mr. Shortley then backs out the large tractor from the shed and parks it on a slight incline. He gets off. Suddenly the brake releases on the large tractor, and it begins to roll down the incline in the direction of the small tractor and Mr. Guizac.

Mrs. McIntyre watches the large tractor slide down. One of the blacks sees the tractor and jumps out of the way but says nothing. Mr. Shortley glances slowly over his shoulder, and his eyes, the black's and Mrs. McIntyre's meet for a brief second, and no one says a word. Mrs. McIntyre is about to scream but does not. The tractor rolls over the Pole, breaking his backbone. Then the two men run to the man's aid, and Mrs. McIntyre faints.

Mr. Guizac is held by his wife and two children. The priest comes with the ambulance and administers last rites to Guizac, while the medical worker attempts to revive him. The body is taken away in the ambulance. Mr. Shortley leaves that evening to find another job, and Sulk also takes off, suddenly interested in seeing more of the state. Old Astor is not able to work without anyone to help him or keep him company. Mrs. McIntyre barely realizes that she has been left without any help at all to run the farm before she goes to the hospital with a nervous breakdown and then returns home. She sells off the cows at auction for a loss and retires to take care of her health.

The old priest still comes out to the farm to sit with the old woman. She goes blind and loses her voice. Father Flynn brings breadcrumbs to feed the peacock and then sits by her bedside, telling her about the church and its doctrines.

COMMENTARY

The story was originally published in SEWANEE REVIEW in October 1954 (vol. 62). Between publications, O'Connor heavily revised the story, as was her custom. After the revision process, the tale was more than twice as long; it included two new sections and underwent many changes to its first section. Inspiration for the story came from a family of Polish refugees, the Matisiacks, who came to live and work at ANDALUSIA in 1952 or 1953. O'Connor read an

early draft of the story at her friends', the Cheneys, residence in Smyrna, Georgia, in December 1953.

A film of the story was produced for television in 1977 with a screenplay adapted by Horton Foote and directed by Glenn Jordan. At more than 40 pages in the *Collected Works* edition, the story is O'Connor's longest short story. Its complex themes and closeness to the setting of Andalusia make it one of the stories frequently studied by scholars.

Structure

O'Connor divided this long story into three numbered parts. However, within two of these numbered parts are also section breaks. Considered together, this makes an actual total of six parts to the completed story. Part I contains three sections in all; Part II has one; and Part III has two sections.

As is her custom, O'Connor introduces her characters in the first section of the story. These include Mrs. McIntyre; Mrs. Shortley; the Guizacs from Poland; the 80-year-old priest, Father Flynn; and two black farmhands, Astor the older man, and the younger boy, Sulk. The reader is also introduced to the peacock that catches the attention of Father Flynn and will become a character in the story in its own way. A hint of the problems that will develop is also given in this section—Mrs. McIntyre believes her employees take advantage of her. Mrs. Shortley thinks her and her husband's job security is threatened by the arrival of the Guizacs, who are the wannabe immigrants or Displaced Persons.

Part two begins three weeks after the Guizacs arrive. The Displaced Person is doing well with his work. Mrs. McIntyre is pleased with his speed and efficiency and tells Mrs. Shortley that he is saving her money, something the Shortleys do not do. Mrs. Shortley manages to turn her fears about job security toward the Guizacs, telling the priest and the work men, Astor and Sulk. Her husband, Chauncey, is a more passive personality in the marriage, barely listening to his wife's rants and raves.

By the third part of the story, Mrs. Shortley has worked herself and her family into a frenzy that results in their packing up their belongings and leaving the farm very quickly. Mrs. Shortley leaves the story at this point as well by having a stroke on the way and dying. The attention in the story shifts to Mrs. McIntyre and her relationship with the Displaced Person.

In the fourth part of the story, the reader obtains more background about Mrs. McIntyre and her three husbands. Sulk tells of the Displaced Person's plan of having his cousin come to America and marry Sulk. The cousin is white, and Sulk is black. Mrs. McIntyre will not stand for such a plan. She is unhappy that Guizac has hatched this plan and sees it as disturbing the peace of mind of her black workers, whom she believes are essential to her farm's finances. She still complains about money and how everyone who comes to the farm seems to take advantage of her.

Mrs. McIntyre notifies the priest in the fifth part of the story that the Displaced Person does not know how to work with her blacks and so he is not working out. She must keep her black workers, no matter what. She cannot run the farm without them. While she is trying to explain this to Father Flynn, his attention is riveted on the peacocks. He mentions that God will come in a blaze of glory, as the peacock tail reminds him.

In the final part of the story, Mrs. McIntyre rehires Mr. Shortley when he returns. Now that she has her old worker back, she is in more of a position to let the Displaced Person go. Unfortunately, she has little experience firing someone and cannot come up with the courage or the words to do so. People have just left the farm on their own. With his wife out of the picture, Mr. Shortley agitates the black men into thinking about how Mrs. McIntyre has threatened all of their jobs by hiring a "foreigner." When the accident happens, no one on the farm except the Displaced Person's family has any sympathy or urge to rush out to help him. Mrs. McIntyre, Mr. Shortley, and Astor serve as passive accomplices in the accident. None of them truly wants the Displaced Person to survive.

Justice prevails in the story. The farm goes under financially. Mr. Shortley and the other workers leave. Mrs. McIntyre fails in health and finances and becomes bedridden. Only Father Flynn continues to come out to sit with her. On his visits, he continues to teach her about the church.

Displaced Persons

"Displaced Person," or D.P., was an official designation of post–World War II European, Russian Jewish, and other refugees. Many people who were liberated out of the concentration camps, Jews from Poland, Hungary, Romania, and Russia as well as others in different situations, were left homeless after the war. Some did not want to return to homes where they still feared for their safety. Others did not want to relive bad memories or rebuild from the rubble of raids and bombings. Still others sought a new life or reunited with relatives in other locations. For many, life was just too confusing to make sense of right away, and they needed a place to stay while they attempted to sort out their lives.

Camps for D.P.s were set up by the Allies after the war and were in existence from approximately 1945 until 1952. Some historical accounts claim that more than 250,000 Jewish refugees were housed in the D.P. camps or city centers during that period. Some of the D.P. camps were in the same locations as the concentration camps. Others were centers set in or around urban areas in Italy, Germany, and Austria. The camps and centers were administered by the allied authorities and the United Nations Relief and Rehabilitation Administration (UNRRA).

Though life in the camps or centers was crowded, poor in quality, and difficult, the people were free. Most spent their time trying to reconnect with relatives or plan their futures. The arts flourished, and journalism was free to tell people's stories and spread news of events and opportunities. Newspapers published pictures of children and others trying to reconnect with their families. Private organizations such as churches and other agencies occasionally stepped in and helped D.P.s locate relatives or move on with their lives.

There are several references and allusions to the war and the concentration camps in this story. Several of these involve piles of bodies, which are the ultimate Displaced Persons. At the arrival of the Guizacs, Mrs. Shortley remembers seeing a newsreel of piles of naked bodies with tangled limbs. She thinks of the image again when she tries to mentally process these foreigners by comparing their children to her own. In their room, Mrs. Shortley complains about the priest and the Guizacs. She is affected by the Polish language which she does not understand. She envisions a war of words between Polish and English, with words dead and dirty, piled up together naked like the bodies she saw in the newsreel.

In her vision of the Sun and the figure, she makes the prophecy that the children of wicked nations will be cut up and piled with legs and arms, feet and faces all mixed up. The Shortleys become piles of displaced bodies in the black automobile when they leave the farm early in the morning in the car crowded with their belongings. Finally, the Guizac family piles onto the body of their dead husband and father after the accident with the tractor. The last use of the piled-body image is particularly affecting since the family had survived the horror of the war only to end up in a posture similar to those who died in it or grieved over the bodies of dead loved ones.

Besides the displaced bodies reminiscent of the war, the Displaced Persons appear in many forms in the story. Father Flynn, himself an apparent immigrant with an Irish brogue, has come into contact with the Polish Guizacs, presumably through churches that help D.P.s relocate. Mrs. Shortley observes that there are 10 million more like them in Poland "where all them bodies were stacked up at" (CS 201) and that Father Flynn has told Mrs. McIntyre he can get her all the workers for the farm that she needs.

The Guizacs are the official Displaced Persons in the story. They were displaced from Poland and have come to America to have a better life. Mr. Guizac would like to bring his cousin over, suggesting there may be even more family to follow. Mrs. McIntyre notes that Guizac calls himself a Christian, and she cannot understand how someone who does would dream of marrying a white cousin to a black farmworker. The picture of the cousin in a white First Communion dress and wearing a flower wreath on her hair, plus the association with Father Flynn, suggest that the family is Polish Catholic. This is strengthened by the scene of Father Flynn putting something (likely Communion) into Mr. Guizac's mouth at the accident and saying words over him Mrs. McIntyre does not understand (likely Latin).

Mrs. McIntyre values the sustainability of her farm most of all. If Guizac is a good worker, then she favors having him and perhaps others in his family coming to make the farm more productive and her finances more stable. Mr. Guizac appears to be on this path with Mrs. McIntyre when he does his work so quickly and efficiently. He is a skilled worker, and he begins to save her money almost from the start, something no other previous employee, including the Shortleys, had done. Mr. Guizac's "displacement" to Georgia from Poland, however, shows itself in one inconvenient and fateful way—he does not understand the difficult and complex relationship between races in the southern United States.

It is perhaps natural that Guizac thinks that he could invite his cousin to America to marry the young man also working on the farm. It would not be the first time that immigrants brought family members to the United States by matchmaking them with friends of those already in the country. Perhaps his motives are somewhat devious; perhaps not. If Sulk indeed likes the picture of the girl and would like to meet her, that would not be so unusual, even today. Whether Guizac is knowingly taking advantage of young Sulk by having him help pay for the girl's trip, however, is an open question.

That Sulk agreed to marry the cousin and is helping pay her way over makes Guizac's methods for helping his family still in Europe questionable. He tells Mrs. McIntyre, however, that the girl had been in three different D.P. camps in three years. She is a 16-year-old girl from Poland whose mother and father have both died, her mother in the second camp. Presumably, the girl found an arranged marriage under unusual circumstances, with a chance to get out of the camp and come to America, a risk worth taking.

Mrs. McIntyre cannot understand why Guizac would set up such an arrangement for his white cousin to marry a black man, or as Mrs. McIntyre calls him "something like that" (CS 223). In her view, he is doing his cousin a disservice by making the innocent white girl marry a black man. It is beyond her understanding to see how Guizac can do such a thing and still call himself a Christian. Mrs. McIntyre shows ignorance not only in her feelings about race but also in her lack of understanding and compassion about the difficulties D.P.s had to live under in war's aftermath.

Whether his motives or methods are fully noble or not, Mr. Guizac makes a fatal mistake in the eyes of Mrs. McIntyre. He does not know, presumably, that blacks and whites did not freely marry in the mid-20th-century American South. In addition, because he is displaced out of his own culture and into a new one, he does not know how critical black workers are for a farm owner and widow like Mrs. McIntyre. Black workers had done so much of the work on farms in the South for so long that even in the 1940s, white farmers could barely envision a farm surviving without them. Mrs. McIntyre tells him that she can run the place without him, but not without her black workers, from whom she gets more work for less money.

Mr. Guizac becomes a displaced person in several ways beyond his official designation as a D.P. He is displaced because he has left a familiar culture and arrived in a new one that he does not fully comprehend. Probably he understood the jealousy of the other farmworkers when he clearly surpassed them in ambition and range of talents. The depth and complexity of the race issue, however, is new to him. Guizac also becomes physically displaced in another way that will kill him. His body ends up beneath a tractor that runs over him and breaks his back. His family rushing to lie over him is also displaced yet again. Now they find themselves in this new country with their husband and father dead and no other family members around for support.

Several other characters besides the official D.P.s might also be described as displaced persons. The Shortleys appear to have no goals of any kind beyond getting through what is required of them. Mrs. Shortley's jealousy of Mr. Guizac and her hearing that Mrs. McIntyre planned to fire her husband leads to her displacing Mr. Shortley and their two daughters, Annie Maude and Sarah Mae. She forces them to pack up all of their belongings and leave in a huff before four o'clock in the morning. She wants to make sure that they have left before Mrs. McIntyre has a chance to fire them. She wants to leave before the first milking of the day. In the meantime, the confused girls sit in the back of the car, displaced

on top of a stack of belongings with the family pets. Even the pets have been displaced from their homes.

When Mrs. McIntyre tells Father Flynn that she must let Mr. Guizac go, she remarks that even Christ was a Displaced Person. Father Flynn raises his hands a little, then lets them drop on his knees in exasperation and appears to think about it. Christ was displaced in the sense that he was an outsider all of his life. He left his home in heaven, one might argue, to come to earth in human form and preach and carry out his Father's will. He is displaced once again when he follows his mission to leave Nazareth where he grew up under the care of Mary and Joseph and begin his traveling and preaching.

Foreigners

The story points out the problem of ignorance and distrust among people from countries other than one's own. Mrs. Shortley is afraid of "foreigners." When she hears about the Guizacs and helps Mrs. McIntyre prepare for their arrival, she imagines them as not even human. What she imagines reveals how little she knows about the world. She envisions three bears walking in wooden shoes like Dutchmen with sailor hats and brightly colored coats with many buttons. The family she actually sees is instead dressed very much like herself and her children.

Mrs. Shortley quickly assesses the family, noting with revulsion that Mr. Guizac bends down and kisses Mrs. McIntyre's hand. Rudolph Guizac, the 12-year-old son, serves as interpreter. Mrs. Shortley does not like the daughter's name, Sledgwig, which she thinks sounds like the name of an insect. She has to admit that the daughter is prettier than either of hers, but she considers her 20-year-old son, W. C., superior to Rudolph.

Language seems to be of particular concern with the people on the farm and the Guizacs. Mrs. Shortley and Mrs. McIntyre call the family the Gobblehooks while they prepare for their arrival. Mrs. Shortley does not like the sound of Sledgwig Guizac's name. She distrusts Father Flynn partially because of his Irish accent. At one point, Mrs. Shortley even imagines the English language at war with Polish. She envisions the words tumbling on top of one another in some kind of struggle for domination.

Religion is another thing about the foreigners that Mrs. Shortley dislikes. She thinks that their religion, ROMAN CATHOLICISM, has not yet been "reformed," as though the Reformation were an advance from an ancient way of doing things, like technology. She thinks that Americans have a more progressive religion because Protestants are reformed Catholics. She shows no knowledge of any other religion than Christianity or that Protestants exist outside the United States. Mrs. Shortley also fears Catholics because they follow the pope. She is nervous about what influence "papists" may have on her family and her community. Her ignorance about Catholicism makes her turn Father Flynn into a kind of devil figure who wants to put Mrs. McIntyre under the influence of the pope and take control of the farm.

Distrust arises out of the farmworkers' insecurity. Mr. Shortley resents the Poles coming to America to take his and other Americans' jobs when men like himself went to Europe and helped liberate people during two world wars. Despite being told the contrary, Mr. Shortley compares Mr. Guizac to the Germans he saw in the war and thinks all Europeans are the same. Mrs. Shortley has the sudden feeling that the Europeans are always fighting and that if they start to come to the United States, they will bring their fighting ways with them and stir things up. The Shortleys envision that Guizac has had a pretty easy life; people do things for him and give him handouts, including a safe ocean crossing with the promise of a job and place to live. They are jealous of the Guizacs' brick house that they heard was raided in the night. They do not understand that the Guizacs were driven from their home, but instead feel resentment that the Guizacs' house was made of brick when theirs is made of wood.

The story shows how uneducated people sometimes think of others from different countries as well as how some American veterans felt after returning from the world wars. Some of the same sentiments about immigrants taking jobs away from locals were problems when immigration surged in the 19th century and continue on into the 21st century. O'Connor's status as a significant American writer flows from such insights about people.

Peacocks and Transfiguration

It is no accident that the peacock on Mrs. McIntyre's farm is the first "character" in the story. It appears in the opening sentence, following up the road behind Mrs. Shortley as she planned to wait for the car bringing the Displaced Persons to the farm. Together they look like a procession. The tail is not spread out, but it is glittering in the sun and raised up off the ground. Father Flynn sees it and remarks on its beauty. He mentions that the tail is full of suns. Mrs. McIntyre complains that the peacock is simply one more mouth she is responsible to feed. Mrs. Shortley, in a similar vein, remarks that the bird is just a peachicken, and the women exchange glances indicating they think Father Flynn's admiration of the bird is childish.

In another scene, the peacock sits in a tree, its tail hanging down like a map of the universe with its suns and planets. She makes no notice of it and simply stares beyond it. Astor, on the other hand, speaks with the peacock. He stands under Mrs. McIntyre's window and tells it things he may want her to overhear—how he disliked the two husbands she divorced, telling the peacock how the numbers of peacocks were going down husband by husband. She tells Astor to call her prior husbands "Mr." and that once the last peacock is gone, she would not be replacing him. Occasionally, the peacock walks around Astor and looks at him as though they were friends carrying on a conversation.

When Father Flynn sees the peacock's tail in full array, he drifts off in admiration and remarks that the sight reminds him of the Transfiguration and that Christ will come like that. Mrs. McIntyre has been trying to speak to Father Flynn about Mr. Guizac. Her comment about the Pole juxtaposed to Father Flynn's vision of the peacock presents a double meaning. She says, "He didn't have to come in the first place" (CS 226). She is referring to Guizac and how it is not her responsibility to give him a job, but the priest takes her comment to be about Christ. The priest responds, "He came to redeem us" (226).

Had he lived and been allowed to work and flourish, Mr. Guizac may have redeemed Mrs. McIntyre as well, by making the farm more successful. Guizac serves as a Christ figure in the story.

Mrs. McIntyre tells Mrs. Shortley, "That man is my salvation!" (CS 203). She also watches him work, but finds he does not seem "real" to her. "He was a kind of miracle that she had seen happen and that she talked about but that she still didn't believe" (CS 219). Guizac's death, like Christ's, provides Mrs. McIntyre with a means of potential redemption through her loss of the farm and the instructions she receives at the end of the story from Father Flynn.

Mrs. McIntyre is spiritually empty. The angel atop her husband's grave was stolen by former workers, the Herrins, when they quite and left the farm. The Judge had purchased the angel for the distinct purpose of putting it on his grave because its face reminded him of his wife's face. The Herrins take away Mrs. McIntyre's spirit, the will to live that had died with her first husband but remained somewhat alive in his memory and in the angel that guarded his grave. This was just one more way that Mrs. McIntyre felt betrayed and used by her employees.

The empty safe is another symbol of Mrs. McIntyre's lack of spirituality. She has kept the Judge's office as a memorial, just as it was when he died. The closet-sized space is described as dark and quiet like a chapel. In it, the rolltop desk serves as a kind of altar; the empty safe is described as a tabernacle. Mrs. McIntyre recalls that her husband always described himself as poor. She never feels as poor as when she sits before the empty safe/tabernacle.

The Transfiguration that Father Flynn refers to is described in the Bible, Mark 9:2–10, where Christ's divinity is made physically visible to some of his apostles:

After six days Jesus took Peter, James, and John and led them up a high mountain apart by themselves. And he was transfigured before them, and his clothes became dazzling white, such as no fuller on earth could bleach them. Then Elijah appeared to them along with Moses, and they were conversing with Jesus. Then Peter said to Jesus in reply, "Rabbi, it is good that we are here! Let us make three tents: one for you, one for Moses, and one for Elijah." He hardly knew what to say, they were so terrified. Then a cloud came, casting a shadow over them; then from the cloud came a voice, "This is my beloved Son. Listen to him." Suddenly, looking around, they no longer saw anyone but Jesus alone with them. As they were coming down from the mountain, he charged them not to relate what they had seen to anyone, except when the Son of Man had risen from the dead. So they kept the matter to themselves, questioning what rising from the dead meant.

Father Flynn sees in the radiance of the full peacock's tail the glory and beauty of the Transfiguration. His faith causes him to connect the beauty of nature with the revelation of Christ's divinity to the apostles as described in the Gospel of Mark. Mrs. McIntyre does not recognize what Father Flynn is referring to because either she did not know the Bible passage or is an unbeliever.

The Transfiguration showed the apostles that the human being, the prophet they had come to know and love, had a purpose and an identity that was beyond the normal and the earthly. There is a divine presence in Christ that the apostles rarely saw except through his good works and teachings. The effect of seeing Jesus transfigured in bright light and wearing dazzling white garments showed power and goodness. Christ conversing with Moses and Elijah raised him, for the apostles, to an equal plane with those holy men. Like the apostles at the Transfiguration, through his faith, Father Flynn recognizes the glory of God in the beauty of the peacock's tail.

Another aspect of this Bible passage is the voice of God the Father announcing to the apostles that Jesus is his son and they should listen to him. Father Flynn tries to convince Mrs. McIntyre to accept Mr. Guizac's presence on the farm and to listen to the word of God as he tries to give her instructions in the church.

The peacock and Mr. Guizac are figures of hope. Father Flynn is the only character to recognize the value and potential of both. He tries to help Mrs. McIntyre see that some of the answers to her problems—her loneliness, her flagging spirit, and her financial struggles in keeping the farm afloat—could be found in the beauty of the peacock and the hard work of Mr. Guizac, a man who wants to make a new life in America for his family. She fails to appreciate either form of goodness.

Whether Mrs. McIntyre will achieve her own transformation or transfiguration remains uncertain at the end of the story.

Andalusia

Critics and O'Connor scholars focus on the setting of this story, closely associated with ANDALUSIA. Biographers have noted that in *The Habit of Being* the author spoke about her mother hiring Polish immigrants to work on the farm. O'Connor read a draft of the story to her friends not long after the immigrants arrived.

Like the O'Connor farm, Andalusia, Mrs. McIntyre's farm has peacocks. Interestingly, however, instead of the large flock that O'Connor was known to have, the peacock flock has slowly diminished during Mrs. McIntyre's time on the farm. Her first husband, the Judge, had liked them and kept about 20 or 30 when he was alive. According to Astor, when she married Crooms, the flock dropped to 12, and when she married McIntyre, it dropped to five. Now on the farm there exists only one peacock and two peahens. Mrs. McIntyre kept them out of a superstitious fear about bothering the Judge in his grave if she had kept none of the birds. The Judge had enjoyed them because he said they made him feel wealthy.

The steady decrease in the peacock population parallels the level of Mrs. McIntyre's removal from life and from active engagement with and compassion for other people. With each husband, the flock numbers went down, as though the farther Mrs. McIntyre got from her memories of life with the Judge, the more unhappy she became. Remarrying did not cure her loneliness for the Judge. She kept a connection to him through the peacocks. O'Connor's mother did not approve of the birds' screams much more than did Mrs. McIntyre.

Both farms are dairy farms, and both employed white tenant farmers and black workers. O'Connor wrote in a letter that her mother, just like Mrs. McIntyre and Mrs. Shortley, made curtains for the immigrant workers out of chicken-feed sacks because she could not afford to buy curtains. Like Mrs. McIntyre, Regina O'Connor was a strong-minded businesswoman who ran the farm without the help of a husband, son, or even without much help from her daughter. Flannery was the bookish daughter who admitted in letters to not helping much around the farm. Instead, she wrote.

The connection of the story to Andalusia continued when the film company shot its adaptation of the story on location at the farm. O'Connor wrote about her mother having built a water tower that appears in the film.

CHARACTERS

Mrs. McIntyre A 60-year-old widow who owns the farm where the Displaced Person comes to work. She is small and has a round-shaped face with a small mouth with red bangs that almost meet her eyebrows. Her eyebrows are high and penciled in with orange. Her eyes are soft blue except when she inspects a milk can; then they turn a granite gray. She buried one husband and divorced two others. Her struggle to keep the farm afloat has skewed her thinking into a defensive posture against those who would like to help her as well as her own employees. She is hopeful that Mr. Guizac will be a valuable employee who presents no problems and increased profits, but when she finds out he is trying to get her young black worker, Sulk, to purchase his cousin as a bride, she loses hope.

Mrs. McIntyre had married her first husband, the Judge, principally for his money but also secretly because she liked him and enjoyed his company. She was 30; he was 75. When he died, she discovered that he did not have as much money tucked away as she had thought. She married and divorced her second husband, Croombs, who is now in the asylum 40 miles away. She also divorced her third husband, McIntyre, whom she suspects is most likely drunk and living in a hotel room in Florida.

Mrs. Shortley A large, married woman with an older son and two teenage daughters. She works with her husband on Mrs. McIntyre's farm. She seems to provide the owner with more companionship than labor. She is jealous of Mr. Guizac's hard work. When she finds out that her husband is going to be let go in order that Guizac may receive a raise, she gathers up her family and all of their belongings and goes away with them in their car. On their way, however, she has a stroke and dies.

Mrs. Shortley's character parallels Mrs. McIntyre's. She thinks she is better than both blacks and foreigners. She does not like the priest nor Mr. Guizac and thinks religion is only for those who cannot manage to stay good without it. She goes to church mainly for the social aspects and to sing. She is a foil to Mrs. McIntyre in that she is not considered by Mrs. McIntyre to be white trash, yet she sees herself above everyone else. She shares Mrs. McIntyre's pride and lack of compassion for others. She is ignorant of the world around her and its condition after the war and becomes suspicious of those who may be in a position to take advantage of her. Besides Father Flynn, she comes closest to being a friend to Mrs. McIntyre.

RELATED LETTERS

Robert Giroux, March 29, 1954 (HB 71); Caroline Gordon Tate, November 14, 1954 (CW 926); Robert Giroux, November 15, 1954 (HB 72); Robert Giroux, December 11, 1954 (HB 73); Betty Hester ("A"), November 25, 1955 [Mrs. McIntyre] (CW 970–971); Betty Hester ("A"), January 17, 1956 (HB 132); Betty Hester, May 19, 1956 (HB 159); Elizabeth McKee, January 3, 1961 (HB 425); Betty Hester ("A"), November 9, 1963 (HB 547). *Pages*: HB: 71, 72, 73, 132, 159, 425, 547; CW: 926, 970–971.

FURTHER READING

Asals, Frederick. "Differentiation, Violence, and The Displaced Person." *The Flannery O'Connor Bulletin* 13 (1984): 1–14.

Bolton, Betsy. "Placing Violence, Embodying Grace: Flannery O'Connor's 'Displaced Person.'" *Studies in Short Fiction* 34, no.1 (Winter 1997): 87–104.

Burke, William. "Displaced Communities and Literary Form in Flannery O'Connor's 'The Displaced Person.'" *MFS: Modern Fiction Studies* 32, no. 2 (Summer 1986): 219–227.

Donahoo, Robert. "O'Connor's Catholics: A Historical-Cultural Context." In *Flannery O'Connor and the Christian Mystery*, edited by John J. Murphy, et al., 101–113. Provo, Utah: Center for the Study of Christian Values in Literature, Brigham Young University, 1997.

Male, Roy R. "The Two Versions of 'The Displaced Person.'" *Studies in Short Fiction* 7 (1970): 450–457.

Martin, Karl. "The Prophetic Intent of O'Connor's 'The Displaced Person.'" *The Flannery O'Connor Bulletin* 23 (1994–95): 137–157.

Olschner, Leonard M. "Annotations on History and Society in Flannery O'Connor's 'The Displaced Person.'" *The Flannery O'Connor Bulletin* 16 (1987): 62–78.

Schellenberg, Susan. "A Response to 'The Displaced Person.'" *Flannery O'Connor Bulletin* 25 (1996–97): 30–33.

Smith, Peter A. "Flannery O'Connor's Empowered Women." *Southern Literary Journal* 26, no. 2 (Spring 1994): 35–47.

Stoneback, H. R. "'Sunk in the Cornfield with His Family': Sense of Place in O'Connor's 'The Displaced Person.'" *Mississippi Quarterly: The Journal of Southern Cultures* 36, no. 4 (Fall 1983): 545–555.

Young, Thomas Daniel. "Flannery O'Connor's View of the South: God's Earth and His Universe." *Studies in the Literary Imagination* 20, no. 2 (Fall 1987): 5–14.

"Enduring Chill, The" (1958)

The fourth story in the collection *Everything That Rises Must Converge* (FSG, 1965), it first appeared in HARPER'S BAZAAR in July 1958 (vol. 91).

SYNOPSIS

Asbury Porter Fox is a failing 25-year-old writer coming home from New York City to Timberboro, Georgia, presumably to die. His 60-year-old mother picks him up at the train station and notices right away that he does not look well. His sister, Mary George, is 33 and principal of a local elementary school. She is asleep in the car and is not sympathetic to Asbury's condition.

Asbury has had a chill for four months, and nothing has seemed to cure it. He has no energy and also suffers from headaches and other aches and pains. He has lost his part-time job at the bookstore because of so many sick days. He has lived on his savings until they ran out, and now he has had to come home. His mother says she will call for Doctor Block to examine him. Asbury is rude to his mother and everyone around him and thinks that what he has is beyond the country doctor's abilities to cure.

Mrs. Fox thinks he would benefit from hard physical work on the dairy and getting his head out of the arts for a while. To her, the more education she saw people get, the less they seemed able to do. After their father died, she had worked hard to see both of their children educated, but only Mary George seemed to have succeeded at finding work in her chosen field. Asbury's work had yet to be published. The year before, he had come home to write a play about blacks and wanted to work on the dairy for a short time to get to know the blacks firsthand who worked there. When he did so, he lit a cigarette in the barn with Randall and Morgan. He had also taken a drink of milk, but the two men would not do that, saying only that Mrs. Fox did not allow it.

Asbury has burned all of his writing except for a long letter to his mother, which has filled two notebooks. In the letter, he blamed her for all of his failings, including being unable to write. The letter would devastate his mother if she were ever to read it. In his room, he puts the notebooks into a drawer and places the key in his pajama pocket. He wants to give her the key before he dies so that she can read the letter afterward and know the part she played in his tragedy. The letter would leave her with an "enduring chill" that would let her see herself for what she really was.

Mary George thinks Asbury's illness is psychosomatic. He cannot write, so he gets sick; it is that simple. She says he is going to be an invalid instead of an artist. She says he needs two or three shock treatments to shake him out of the artist mentality.

Father Finn "from Purrgatory" arrives one day and visits Asbury. He does not seem aware that the family is not Roman Catholic, and he is deaf in one ear and blind in one eye. He says he does not know Joyce when Asbury questions him about JAMES JOYCE. Finn questions Asbury on the catechism and on his prayer life. He tells him that if he does not pray, he will not learn to be good or how to love Jesus. He must pray to receive the Holy Ghost. Asbury tells him that the Holy Ghost is the last thing he is looking for, and the priest says he may be the last thing he gets. Still, the Holy Ghost will not come until the young man sees that he is conceited, lazy, and ignorant. Mrs. Fox enters the room at Father Finn's raised voice and sends him away. He blesses Asbury anyway in Latin and says to call him anytime for another visit.

Asbury keeps looking for a significant moment after which he might give over and die. He cannot think of anything special but remembers how he had felt unified with the black workers in the barn when he had smoked with them. He asks his mother to send them in. Mrs. Fox again looks as though this is the last thing she wants to do, but she does send in Randall and Morgan. Clearly, she has told them to cheer him up and not to let on that he may be dying.

Instead of sharing a cigarette as Asbury had intended, when he offers the pack Randall takes the whole pack in a misunderstanding.

Discouraged once again, Asbury thinks now he will die with no significant last moment. He takes out the key to the dresser drawer where the letter to his mother lay, sets it on the nightstand, and dreams. A car pulls up with Dr. Block, and his mother comes rushing in. She tells him that he is not going to die, that they know what he has. He has undulant fever that he must have caught from drinking unpasteurized milk. He will have to endure the fever when it comes back over the course of his lifetime, but he will not die from it.

When the doctor and his mother leave, Asbury slips the key back into his pajama pocket. He looks around at the stains on the walls and ceiling of his room that he has known so well since childhood. Overhead he sees a familiar birdlike shape with the icicle in its beak. As he lies there, he sees a new life dawning and feels his old life give way. Suddenly, he sees the bird begin to move. He knows he will have to endure the fever all his life. The bird moves out of ice rather than fire, but it is on the move, the descent of the Holy Ghost.

COMMENTARY

Of all the stories O'Connor wrote about an intellectual adult living at home under the care of his or her mother ("The Comforts of Home" and others), this story's protagonist, Asbury Porter Fox, may be the most unpleasant of all. He is arrogant, dismissive of his mother, and of foul temperament. When the reader first encounters Fox, he is feeling satisfied over the look on his mother's face that shows him he looks as bad as he feels. Maybe his condition will teach his mother about death and make her grow up. He tells her he does not feel like talking, that he has had a bad trip. Before that, he had noticed that the sun was coming up over the woods, making them look oddly like temples to a god he did not know.

Fox does not know God or god in more ways than one. Neither is he the "god" that can educate his mother on the finer details of intellectual pursuits and sophistication, nor the humble person of faith who can count on God in times of trouble to get through difficult situations. The chill he developed in New York serves as a metaphor for his lack of faith and humility. The chill not only sinks down into his bones but keeps him from working until he loses all of his savings and must return home. There the chill endures because he will not give up his attitudes that he is better and smarter than everyone else around Timberboro.

What Fox calls the "enduring chill," is the long letter he has written to his mother to read after his death. The letter takes up two notebooks. In it, Fox blames her for everything that has gone wrong with his would-be writing career. In a fit of despair, he threw out all of his other projects—novels, plays, poems, and short stories. He did not like any of them. In the letter, he writes a sentence that he underscored two times—that he does not have talent and cannot create. All he has is the desire to be creative and to write. He thinks his mother did not raise him to develop his talent but left him with the desire to have it. He asks in the letter why she did not destroy his desire as well. The letter would devastate Mrs. Fox were she to read it, which is exactly Asbury's intent.

The enduring chill, then, is the chill of artistic despair and selfish discontent. The reader, however, understands the chill differently. It is equally caused by Fox's inability to take responsibility for his own failures. Ironically, Asbury's mother considers him an artist. Her first concern on seeing

him is that he may be about to have a nervous breakdown. Fox's sister, Mary George, thinks him no more an artist than a cow. Mary George serves as an informed observer of the relationship between Fox and his mother.

Fox's frequent comment that what is bothering him "is way beyond you" suggests that his ailment is not physical so that Dr. Block can cure it, nor emotional so that his mother's attention can assuage it. What is wrong with Fox is physical, but it is also beyond, just as he says. There is much wrong with Fox. It takes the priest he has visit him just to irritate his mother to identify the problem to both of them. He tells Fox's mother that the boy is "a lazy, ignorant conceited youth!" (CS 377).

The priest (who is old and has both vision and hearing problems) is not at all what Fox expects. Father Finn gives him a lecture about not knowing his catechism and tells him that he is ignorant. In many ways, the priest gives him the straight and plain talk that the young man has needed from an authority figure all his life. His mother has waited on him; Dr. Block, whose name suggests a blockhead of sorts, treats him as he did on house calls when Asbury was a child. When Fox's mother sees Asbury after the priest leaves, the young man looks shocked. The priest has come from "Purrgatory" and tells Asbury just exactly what he needs to hear most. The priest tells his mother that the boy is good at heart but ignorant.

Even after the visit by the priest, Fox is sure he is going to die. He doubts this only when his mother tells him that she will not sit by and allow it to happen. Her statement is so full of resolve and he obviously has had such a belief in the power of her control that for a moment he thinks she may be right. When he does not recover, however, he begins to look for meaning in what he believes to be his last days. In particular, he looks for one last meaningful experience before he dies. He thinks of the moment of what he calls "communion," when he was visiting the barn the previous summer, working in the dairy, and sharing cigarettes with the black workers. He did this because he knew it was against the will of his mother. He tells his mother that he wants to tell the black men who work for her goodbye.

He prepares for Morgan and Randall's visit to his room as though for "the last sacrament" (CS 379). When their visit is anything but meaningful, full of small talk and misunderstanding, Asbury gives up. In a hallucinogenic state, he gives his mother the key to the drawer and prepares to lose consciousness.

Instead, Dr. Block arrives and tells his mother that the young man has undulant fever, which he no doubt contracted drinking unpasteurized milk. The reader knows that Asbury drank this milk in the barn last summer. Asbury will live needing to deal with the fever from time to time, but he will not die.

All the while, the image of the water stain in Asbury's room dominates the story. Asbury remembers the stain from his childhood, lying in bed, looking up at it. It has always looked like a bird with an icicle in its beak. When the priest visits, he mentions the Holy Ghost (now called the Holy Spirit). A familiar symbol of the Holy Ghost is a dove. Asbury recalls his sister, Mary George, taking him to a revival when they were young. She pulled him up to the preacher and told the preacher that she was saved, but that Asbury needed saving because he was too big for his britches. She had told Asbury that she was going to give him a present. He ran away, and when he asked for his present, she told him that he was not going to get it after all. It was Salvation, and he would not get it because of the way he acted.

At the end of the story, the water stain bird hovers over Asbury. He realizes that he is not going to die but that he is going to live out his days looking up at that ceiling. The bird appears to him to begin to descend, emblazoned in ice rather than fire. The Holy Ghost is going to save Asbury in the way that art, the god he says he prays to by creating, has failed him.

CHARACTERS

Asbury Porter Fox Fox is a 25-year-old unsuccessful writer who has come home from New York City to Timberboro, Georgia, presumably to die. He is shaken by the light that he sees from the rising sun when he arrives home on the train. The story ends with another dawn, this time with Dr. Block

arriving to tell Asbury's mother that he had found the "bug" that was ailing her son. At the same time that the illness is diagnosed, the real illness that was "beyond" them all is also diagnosed and cured—Asbury's need to be saved. His old life wears away as he can see in the mirror at the end of the story. It has exhausted itself, and he must prepare for a new life that has shocked him with the power of its icy existence.

When Fox had gone to a lecture with his friend Goetz, he spotted a Jesuit priest listening to the lecture and paid attention to the priest's reaction. The expression on his face seemed to echo Asbury's own thoughts about what was being said—that there is neither death nor deity nor beings. When the priest finally spoke to their small group after the lecture, he mentioned that there is a real probability for people to change and become new with the help of the Third Person of the Trinity. He had handed Asbury a card with his name and address.

This Jesuit's act planted the seed that Asbury uses later to summon the priest who sets in motion his realization at the end of the story. Fox is shocked into belief by the violent realization of his own ignorance, both that unpasteurized milk will make one sick and that he has been a fool all along, one who has much to learn.

RELATED LETTERS

Betty Hester ("A"), November 2, 1957 (HB 250); Betty Hester ("A"), November 16, 1957 (CW 1,049); November 16, 1957 (HB 253); Betty Hester ("A"), November 30, 1957 (HB 256); Caroline Gordon Tate, December 10, 1957 (HB 256); Betty Hester ("A"), December 14, 1957 (HB 259); Betty Hester ("A"), December 28, 1957 (HB 261); Father James H. McCown, January 12, 1958 (CW 1,060); Elizabeth McKee, January 25, 1958 (HB 264); Alice Morris, February 28, 1958 (HB 271); Father James H. McCown, June 29, 1958 (CW 1,075); Maryat Lee, August 25, 1958 (HB 293); Dr. T. R. Spivey, October 19, 1958 (CW 1,076–1,077); Cecil Dawkins, January 28, 1960 (HB 372); Cecil Dawkins, November 8, 1963 (HB 546–547); Elizabeth McKee, May 7, 1964 (HB 575); Robert Giroux, May 21, 1964 (HB 579); Robert Giroux, June 28, 1964 (HB 589); Catherine Carver, July

15, 1964 (HB 593). *Pages:* HB: 250, 253, 256–257, 259, 261, 264, 271, 250, 253, 256–257, 259, 261, 264, 271, 293, 372, 546–547, 575, 579, 589, 593; CW: 1,060, 1,075, 1,076–1,077.

FURTHER READING

Aiken, David. "Flannery O'Connor's Portrait of the Artist as a Young Failure." *Arizona Quarterly* 32, no. 3 (1976): 245–259.

Angle, Kimberly Grace. "Flannery O'Connor's Literary Art: Spiritual Portraits in Negative Space." *Flannery O'Connor Bulletin* 23 (1994–95): 158–174.

Beringer, Cindy. "'I Have Not Wallowed': Flannery O'Connor's Working Mothers." In *Southern Mothers: Fact and Fictions in Southern Women's Writing,* edited by Nagueyalti, et al., 124–141. Baton Rouge: Louisiana State University Press, 1999. 233 pp.

Folks, Jeffrey J. "'The Enduring Chill': Physical Disability in Flannery O'Connor's Everything That Rises Must Converge." *University of Dayton Review* 22, no. 2 (Winter 1993–94): 81–88.

Walker, Sue. "The Being of Illness, The Language of Being Ill." *The Flannery O'Connor Bulletin* 25 (1996–97): 33–58.

"Everything That Rises Must Converge" (1961)

Title and first story of O'Connor's second collection of stories, *Everything That Rises Must Converge,* published by Farrar, Straus and Giroux in 1965.

SYNOPSIS

Julian Chestny's mother is under doctor's orders to lose 20 pounds to help lower her blood pressure. She goes to a "reducing" class downtown at the Y every Wednesday night. She is afraid, however, to ride the bus alone now that the buses are integrated, so she insists that Julian go with her. It is the least he can do for all she does for him. She is a widow who worked hard to put him through school and is still supporting him until he can get his career going. Julian knows that he will likely never get a job.

This particular week, Julian's mother has a new hat. It is purple and green and looks like a pin cushion. She is not sure whether she should wear it to her class, and she and Julian debate it. Julian thinks about how it would be easier to be in his situation if his mother were a drunkard who yelled at him. He has been out of school a year and is miserable taking care of her. When she says she wants to take the hat back home, he tugs on her arm to keep going.

His mother reminds him of the governor, the landowner, and other notable ancestors in the family. She begins to talk about his great-grandfather's plantation and 200 slaves. Julian tells her yet again that there is no more slavery, a recurring theme with his mother. She believes in separate but equal status for blacks and whites.

When the bus finally arrives, Julian hoists her up into it, but she smiles as though she is entering a drawing room where everyone has been waiting for her. The bus is half full with only white riders. She sits down on a seat facing the aisle beside a woman with blond hair and buck teeth. A woman with red-and-white sandals is sitting in the opposite aisle. Julian's mother begins to talk about the weather as though she expects everyone in the bus to listen to her and join in the conversation. Julian winces when she announces that she sees they have the bus to themselves.

The woman across the aisle comments on how unusual it is to have only whites on the bus nowadays. The other day she rode a bus that was full of blacks, "thick as fleas" (CW 490). Julian picks up a newspaper and uses it for privacy as he sinks into his thoughts. His mother has sacrificed too much of herself for him and has succeeded in spite of herself. He is educated and unprejudiced. He also thinks he is emotionally detached from her. He tells himself that she does not dominate him.

The bus stops suddenly. Someone from the back gets out, and a black businessman gets on. Julian watches his mother and the other passengers with bemusement as they make motions to one another.

The bus stops again, and a woman and her son get on. The little boy sits beside Julian's mother, and the large woman sits by Julian. He was hoping for the reverse. Since his mother thought all children were "cute," she would not suffer from the boy sitting by her. She immediately begins to talk with him. Sitting in this arrangement, Julian muses it was as though these two mothers had traded sons. It takes a moment for Julian to realize that this woman is wearing a hat identical to his mother's.

Julian hopes that his mother will be mortified when she sees the hat and so learn a lesson. His mother toys with the boy, telling the boy's mother that she thinks he likes her. The boy's mother fusses at him and brings him over to her. When the black businessman gets off at the next stop, the black mother plants her son between herself and Julian. The boy plays peekaboo with Julian's mother and gets a slap on his legs from his own mother.

The next stop is theirs, and when the woman pulls the cord at the same time, Julian has the premonition that his mother will try to give the boy a nickel as they all get off. He tries to take her purse from her, but she holds onto it. She cannot find a nickel, but she does have a shiny penny. On the sidewalk, she calls after the boy, offering him the penny. The boy's mother hauls off and hits Mrs. Chestny with her pocketbook and storms off with the boy.

Julian tells his mother she got what she deserved. She looks at him as though she does not recognize him. He gets her up off the sidewalk but instead of walking toward the Y, she turns in the opposite direction and tells him that she is going home. He follows, deciding to give her a lecture as they go. He tells her that the woman who hit her is not a bad woman; she represents the whole black race, which will no longer take being condescended to by whites. The old days are over, he says, and it is time she accepted that it need not be the end of the world.

After they walk a bit, he takes her by the arm and looks into her face. He does not recognize what he sees. She asks for Grandpa and Caroline, her black nurse when she was a child. After a few more steps, she falls to the pavement. Julian falls down beside her. Her face has become distorted and one eye roams around in its socket. He calls out "Mama!" and tells her he will go get help. He keeps running and going back to her, but it seems that he finds no one.

COMMENTARY

This story first appeared in New World Writing (vol. 19), edited by Theodore Solotaroff, in 1961. It was reprinted in The Best American Short Stories of 1962, edited by Martha Foley and David Burnett and was also the first-prize story in Prize Stories of 1963: The O. Henry Awards, edited by Richard Poirier. It was also published in First-Prize Stories, 1919–1963, edited by Harry Hansen.

O'Connor wrote in a letter that the title "is a physical proposition that I found in [Catholic theologian] Père Teilhard [De Chardin] and am applying to a certain situation in the Southern states & indeed in all the world" (HB 438). The concept from Teilhard is his theory of the Omega Point from his book The Phenomenon of Man. O'Connor reviewed the book for the Georgia Catholic diocesan journal, The Bulletin. Teilhard's theory is summarized by Max H. Begouen in the foreword to another of Teilhard's books, Building the Earth: "Remain true to yourselves, but move ever upward toward greater consciousness and greater love! At the summit you will find yourselves united with all those who, from every direction, have made the same ascent. For everything that rises must converge" (Begouen 11).

The story is arguably one of O'Connor's most mindful treatments of the Civil Rights movement and its immediate aftermath. Since African Americans are no longer forced to sit in the back of the bus, they now are integrated and may sit where they please. The process of true integration, however, went slowly, as O'Connor dramatizes with Mrs. Chestny and her conversation with the other white woman on the bus. Though both were now expected to be agreeable with a black person sitting next to them, the newness of the practice, the strangeness of it, in addition to their own prejudices causes them to make remarks and hope that no one of color will get on the bus at all.

Julian's rage at his mother grows throughout the story. The rage of an educated adult child against his or her less highly educated mother is a familiar motif in O'Connor's fiction. Julian's feelings begin with annoyance that he must accompany her to her reducing class simply because she is too afraid to ride the integrated bus at night alone. When he hears her old stories of their ancestors and slaves and the nurse Caroline, whom she loved, his spirits turn foul even more. Watching her speak to the other passenger and act on her prejudice makes him angry. When the woman's hat turns out to be just like his mother's, Julian feels a sense of bemusement and self-righteousness; his mother is getting what she deserves. When she refuses to ride the bus back home, he becomes frustrated. Finally, however, when she collapses, he becomes a child himself, crying "Mama" in his fear that something awful has happened.

O'Connor mentions Saint Sebastian in connection with Julian. When he is waiting for his mother to get going, he stands in the doorway like Saint Sebastian waiting for the arrows to strike him. Julian is a martyr to his mother, taking care of her because he knows he should. However, he is depressed and unhappy, "as if in the midst of martyrdom he had lost his faith" (CS 407). Saint Sebastian was a Roman saint who was tortured for his Christian faith. First he was attacked by arrows but was healed from his wounds by the widowed St. Irene. Eventually, however, he was beaten to death with a club for his beliefs. Perhaps the cold end to Julian's mother's life is the club that will awaken him to a better understanding of those outside of his generation.

The story features much mirroring, not least of which is the comical instance of the hat. At first Mrs. Chestny is looking at herself in the hallway mirror and analyzing what she thinks of her new hat and whether or not she should wear it that evening. As Mrs. Chestny prepares to go out, she comments that with a hat like that, "I at least won't meet myself coming and going" (CS 406) and mentions that the store clerk said the same thing in attempting to sell it. The phrase holds meaning. She has seen herself in the mirror before they left the house. Then she sees the black woman who gets on the bus wearing the exact same hideous hat. Whether she likes it or not or recognizes it or not, Mrs. Chestny is indeed seeing herself coming and going in the form of another woman who happened to like the same hat. Mrs. Chestny fails to recognize that such similarities bond her with her dark-skinned neighbors and show that they are not so different after all.

She is willing to allow that black people have the right to "rise." She is, however, a segregationist, wanting their rise to be on their side of town and hers on hers. The old ways are hard to break for a woman whose history, as recent as her own grandfather owning up to 200 slaves, plagues her experience. Julian cannot understand how his mother can adapt so easily to a change from an old mansion to all of the worn places they have lived since but who cannot change in her attitudes toward her black fellow citizens.

CHARACTERS

Julian Chestny   Though he is clearly frustrated with his mother's old ways of thinking about black people, a part of Julian longs for something of the days she describes from her childhood. When she talks about the plantation house, the decayed mansion, he tells her to stop, but he really thinks of the mansion with longing. He saw it once and appreciated more than she ever could—its elegance and beauty, the wide porch and high-ceilinged hall, the parlor, and the sound of the rustling oaks. He has never had the opportunity to live in such luxury, and somehow, though slavery made that lifestyle possible for his ancestors, Julian longs for the gracious life his mother and her relatives once had. Julian is not working, does not plan to work, and has apparently not accomplished much since leaving college. Like his mother, his situation in life and his attitudes are complex.

Julian tells his mother that only members of any present generation can say that they know who they are. When times change, people's situations change, and they no longer know who they are. The times when Julian's mother was close to her black nurse, Caroline, and both knew their places in relation to each other are long gone. Instead, his mother now rides in fear of black people sitting next to her on the bus. She does not know her place there since she refuses to change.

The reverse, however, is also true. Julian does not know who his mother is either since he is from another generation. The relationship between blacks and whites in the Old South was more complicated than the younger generation understood at first. Julian's mother cared for Caroline so deeply that it is she whom she calls out for as she lay dying on the sidewalk. While she has difficulty sitting beside a black woman she does not know, a black woman she did know from childhood was one of the people she most loved in life.

Julian's Mother (Mrs. Chestny) Julian's mother needs to lose weight, but she is not extremely overweight. She has gray hair in two wings that sprout from underneath her new hat and sky blue eyes that reveal a lack of experience in the world. In Julian's mind, she is nearly as innocent as a child. Even though she is a widow who, despite losing her husband, struggled hard to put food on the table and put him through school, Julian has the sense that her expression now, on the day he accompanies her to her reducing class, has probably not changed all that much from when she was just 10 years old.

She is the granddaughter of a plantation owner who once owned 200 slaves. Julian's great-grandfather was once governor of the state. She claims to know who she is and that this allows her to be gracious to blacks in the new environment. Both Julian and the reader understand that Mrs. Chestny does not see who she is in the context of the new world in which she has lived long enough to be part of. The new generation sees a racist and spoiled privileged member of the Old South who is blind to the struggles of her black neighbors. However, Mrs. Chestny is more complicated than that. The story illustrates the depth of the work ahead as the generations of Old South and New South attempt to "rise" together.

RELATED LETTERS

Maryat Lee, March 26, 1961 (HB 436); Roslyn Barnes, March 29, 1961 (HB 438); Thomas Stritch, September 14, 1961 (HB 449); Maryat Lee, November 3, 1961 (HB 453); Betty Hester ("A"), December 9, 1961 (HB 458); Father J. H. McCown, March 4, 1962 (HB 468); Maryat Lee, May 21, 1962 (HB 475); Betty Hester, March 2, 1963 (HB 510); Marion Montgomery, June 16, 1963 (HB 524); Betty Hester, September 1, 1963 (HB 537); Janet McKane, December 31, 1963 (HB 555); Elizabeth McKee, May 7, 1964 (HB 575); Robert Giroux, May 21, 1964 (HB 579). *Pages:* HB: 436, 438, 449, 453, 458, 468, 475, 510, 524, 537, 555, 575, 579.

FURTHER READING

Andreas, James. "'If It's a Symbol, to Hell With It': The Medieval Gothic Style of Flannery O'Connor in 'Everything That Rises Must Converge.'" *Christianity and Literature* 38, no. 2 (Winter 1989): 23–41.

Begouen, Max H. "Foreword." In Pierre Teilhard de Chardin, *Building the Earth.* New York: Avon, 1965.

Denham, Robert D. "The World of Guilt and Sorrow: Flannery's O'Connor's 'Everything That Rises Must Converge.'" *Flannery O'Connor Bulletin* 4 (1975): 42–51.

Desmond, John F. "The Lessons of History: Flannery O'Connor's Everything That Rises Must Converge." *Flannery O'Connor Bulletin* 1 (1972): 39–45.

Folks, Jeffrey J. "The Mechanical in Everything That Rises Must Converge." *Southern Literary Journal* 18, no. 2 (Spring 1986): 14–26.

Jauss, David. "Flannery O'Connor's Inverted Saint's Legend." *Studies in Short Fiction* 25, no. 1 (Winter 1988): 76–78.

Maida, Patricia D. "'Convergence' in Flannery O'Connor's 'Everything That Rises Must Converge.'" *Studies in Short Fiction* 7 (1970): 549–555.

Montgomery, Marion. "On Flannery O'Connor's 'Everything That Rises Must Converge.'" *Critique: Studies in Modern Fiction* 13, no. 3 (1971): 15–29.

Ower, John. "The Penny and the Nickel in 'Everything That Rises Must Converge.'" *Studies in Short Fiction* 23, no. 1 (Winter 1986): 107–110.

Petry, Alice Hall. "Julian and O'Connor's 'Everything That Rises Must Converge.'" *Studies in American Fiction* 15, no. 1 (Spring 1987): 101–108.

Russell, Shannon. "Space and the Movement Through Space in Everything That Rises Must Converge." *Southern Literary Journal* 22, no. 2 (Spring 1988): 81–98.

Teilhard, Pierre, de Chardin. *The Phenomenon of Man.* New York: Harper, 1959.

Wyatt, Bryan N. "The Domestic Dynamics of Flannery O'Connor: Everything That Rises Must Converge." *Twentieth Century Literature: A Scholarly and Critical Journal* 38, no. 1 (Spring 1992): 66–88.

"Fiction Is a Subject with a History—It Should Be Taught That Way" (1963)

This essay first appeared in *The Georgia Bulletin,* March 21, 1963. It was subsequently published in *Collected Works* (Modern Library, 1988).

SYNOPSIS

O'Connor mentions two recent incidents in Georgia where parents raised objections to modern fiction that their eighth and ninth graders were reading in school. She says that this happens with some regularity around the country. Usually the parent picks up a book the child is reading and flips through it quickly. Seeing a foul word or two in the book, the parent runs to the school board. At times, as in one of the two recent incidents in Georgia, the teacher who assigned the book loses his or her job, raising the ire of liberals.

The two Georgia incidents concerned John Steinbeck's *East of Eden* and John Hersey's *A Bell for Adano.* The cases received significant newspaper coverage. A columnist on the side of the teacher argued that students prefer reading contemporary novels to stuffy 19th-century works. The columnist also argued that the Bible itself contains several sections of provocative content.

In the case in which the teacher was dismissed, author John Hersey wrote to the school superintendent on the teacher's behalf. He argued that the book's theme is democracy and that it is not obscene. The "total effect" of the book would not be deemed obscene under the general guidelines of the law.

O'Connor does not wish to comment on either of the two Georgia cases in particular, but she does wish to point out that the incidents address a larger issue of what fiction is assigned to eight and ninth graders in high school. She presumes there is a list of appropriate titles composed by the state, but then the teachers are on their own as far as what they assign.

Some English teachers at the high school level, she says, are unqualified to teach literature. Rather than making thoughtful selections, they tend to assign books that they hope will keep their readers'

attention. We are in the first age when students dictate what they want to be taught. This does not happen in other subjects, such as algebra or French. Students are taught what they need to know. However, with literature, students are "too stupid now to enter the past imaginatively" (CW 850). While students before now learned to embrace Homer and Virgil, current students are offered the choice between HAWTHORNE and Hersey, and they choose the more contemporary work. This is a problem that has become so pervasive, says O'Connor, that it can only be driven out, like the devil, with prayer and fasting, and no one so far has come along who is strong enough to do it.

O'Connor proposes that fiction be taught as a subject with a history. In other words, students ought not to be studying contemporary fiction without first being exposed to works that came before it. Hersey and Steinbeck should be preceded by Cooper, Hawthorne, Melville, early HENRY JAMES, and Stephen Crane. These American novelists should be preceded in a course by reading good English novelists from the 18th and 19th centuries.

She argues that student readers are already surrounded by their own times and reading about times gone by gives a perspective from which to consider one's own era. One common example is the story of the student who wrote a paper about Abraham Lincoln being shot in a movie theater; this shows a severe lack of knowledge about the past.

Nineteenth-century English novels are pleasurable, and teachers should be able to find ways to make them accessible for eighth graders, both those who need simpler reading and those who are ready for more challenging discussion. Students should experience these works first, then move to 19th-century American novels to experience the "sea-change" (CW 851) difference between British and American novels of the same period and how a culture affects its literature. If students have this background in the novel behind them, they will be better prepared for the complexities of the 20th-century American novel.

Contemporary fiction is actually more complicated that that of earlier centuries. Modern authors leave readers a bit more on their own and merge readers and their emotions with the experience of the story more directly. Readers who have not obtained the background of earlier fiction are ill-equipped to contend with newer fiction and its intensity and will likely miss the novel's total effect.

Moral issues arise from this scenario. There is a difference in adultery as it is portrayed in *Anna Karenina* and the Bible and how it is portrayed in contemporary fiction. The difference goes beyond how adultery is treated as a sin in the first two instances and perhaps no more than a minor trouble in the latter one. Another difference is that modern fiction immerses the reader directly; virtually anything is possible.

Since morality is a source of disagreement in a diverse culture, high school students should certainly be prepared to read modern fiction with a good background in earlier literature. High school seniors could be assigned modern fiction based on parental consent and on their reading of earlier works.

High school teachers can help their students by giving them a taste of the best literature from periods leading up to the modern one. This is the way to teach literature. If students do not enjoy older literature, that is unfortunate, O'Connor asserts. Their taste in literature should not be solicited right now; instead, it should be cultivated.

"Fiction Writer and His Country, The" (1957)

This essay was originally a lecture given at the University of Notre Dame in South Bend, Indiana, in April 1957. It first appeared in print in *The Living Novel: A Symposium,* edited by Granville Hicks (Macmillan, 1957), then in *Mystery and Manners: Occasional Prose* (Farrar, Straus and Giroux, 1969), edited by Sally and Robert Fitzgerald. The piece was written as a response to a *Life* magazine editorial, "Wanted: An American Novel," from the September 12, 1955, issue.

SYNOPSIS

An editorial appeared in *Life* magazine asking who speaks in the name of America. The article deter-mined that the nation's first-rate novelists did not speak for their country.

The editorial spoke of the nation's prosperity during the previous decade and what it said was its success, compared with other countries, at creating a society without classes. It is also the world's most powerful nation. With all this positive energy in the country, its novelists were still writing about poverty. Novelists should be better representing what this country is really like and also infusing their writing with a spiritual sense of the joy of life.

Though literary critics responded to the editorial, previously no Christian novelist had taken on the article's particular desire for writing with a spiritual function.

O'Connor proposes that *country* should be differentiated from the more common term used in literary circles, *world. Country* works better because it is more particular. The fiction writer must be concerned with the elements that make up his own region and country and let that stand for the countries of the world. The Christian writer will add to this idea of country the abstract truths of his beliefs. It is important for the fiction writer to portray one country so vividly that it can represent the other countries of the world.

A Christian writer will think of his gift as coming from God. This will pertain even to what he thinks he can see imaginatively. He will prefer a flawed but alive character to one that is perfect but lifeless. Since he views his gift for writing as a vocation, he will be somewhat limited. He will not likely use his gift for that which he believes to be beyond its intended purpose.

A writer's country is the area immediately surrounding him. People think that southern writers have an advantage in this. It is possible that readers have become bored hearing about what is known as the "southern school." This title is ambiguous and seems to be a label given to writers in the South who presumably write about the GROTESQUE under the influences of EDGAR ALLAN POE and Erskine Caldwell.

One consensus about the southern writer seems to be that he is filled with "anguish." The thinking is that the southerner is upset by feeling so alienated from the rest of the country. The opposite is actually true—the anguish comes from the South's becoming too much like the rest of the country. We are losing not only our faults but also the positive aspects of our culture along with it.

Manners are becoming a thing of the past. Even poor manners are better than no manners at all. The South is full of amateur regional writers. Serious writers fear becoming one of them. One way in which some think they can avoid it is to examine what is happening to manners in society. Another way is to consider one's region not as the South but the whole United States. When one does this, there is an implication that one should write happy stories because of the prosperity and strength the country is supposedly enjoying.

A Christian writer may wonder about this call for happy stories in a society that is supposed to be feeling so well. He will feel that if he writes about what he sees, then this is more accurate than taking a poll. To write about an image manufactured about the country rather than the world as he sees it concretely is to "separate mystery from manners and judgment from vision . . ." (MM 30). A Catholic writer cannot do this because he knows that the writing will be sentimental or worse.

The best fiction is written by those whose sense of morality is tied to the way they see the world, not separated from it. Christianity does not limit the writer but instead frees him to see the world as it is and embrace mystery where he finds it.

Wyndam Lewis said that he writes about a rotting hill because he hates it, not because he loves it. Some people today think that writers write about rot because they actually like it. If they actually do like it, this comes out in their work. However, it is still possible that those who write about rot do so merely because it is what they see.

Some readers accuse today's writers of not writing about spiritual fulfillment and joy. O'Connor can only examine her own conscience about this. She does tend to write mainly about poverty, about those who are deformed in body or spirit, and her work does not tend to fill readers with a sense of the happiness that can be found in life. Since she believes that life should be focused around the Resurrection, she writes about the lack of this that she sees in the world around her. As a Christian, she

writes out of this belief, and she writes what she sees through that lens.

Some readers think that almost all of her characters are grotesque, yet she knows that many of them are not. One begins to think that because one is a Southern writer, this label will be affixed to all of one's work. The South did not invent Elvis Presley. The biggest problem with the Presley phenomenon is not the young man himself but his widespread popularity that extends way outside the South. What is and what is not grotesque may be more a question of who is doing the looking and through what lens.

Her opinion is that Christian writers will see the grotesque around them because they look at the world through their faith. Much of the focus on the perverse by readers is because of the gap between the writer's faith and the beliefs of readers. When a person believes in Christ's Redemption, that belief changes his day-to-day life in ways that secularism may not grasp.

The Christian writer must portray the distortions he sees in everyday life, which do not appear that way to readers, so that they do appear perverse. In order to draw attention, sometimes the writer needs to resort to violent means within the fiction. Ordinarily, what a writer sees in the world would be obvious to readers that agree with him. Some readers, however, need to be shocked into attention—"to the hard of hearing you shout, and for the almost-blind you draw large and startling figures" (34).

Artists do not speak for America—advertisers do that. Readers should not look to true artists for comfort. They should look to them to give them an accurate picture of the way things are, especially the way things are right now. It is a limited view, but it should be revealing.

An artist is always balancing the outer region of his country with his inner life, or region. Truth becomes the criterion against which all is measured, both in the artist's inner and outer life. Humility is key, and this is not a characteristic particularly prominent in the portrayal of a national profile.

In teaching catechumens, St. Cyril of Jerusalem told a story of being cautious of the dragon that sits by the side of the road. He said that we are all on our way to the Father, but first we must get by the dragon. Artful fiction tells the story of that journey past the dragon or the fall into its grip. In this way, only the courageous of any country are able to really listen to the true teller of stories.

FURTHER READING

Hicks, Granville (ed.), *The Living Novel: A Symposium.* New York: Macmillan, 1957.
"Wanted: An American Novel," *Life,* September 12, 1955, 48.

"Geranium, The" (1947)

O'Connor's first professional publication, "The Geranium" is the title and first story of her 1947 master's of fine arts thesis, "The Geranium: A Collection of Short Stories." It appears on pages 1–21 of the typescript.

SYNOPSIS

Old Dudley sits in a chair by the window of his daughter's New York City apartment. Every day he looks out the window and notices the geranium sitting on the windowsill of an apartment in the building across the alley.

On something like a whim, Old Dudley had once told his daughter that he would like to come to New York. Now it has become her duty to look after him, and both of them resent it. Now he lives in his daughter's apartment with her husband and son.

This particular day, the people across the alley are late putting out the geranium. Old Dudley listens to the sounds of the alley and the building. He hears the door to the apartment next door slam and realizes that it is the black man who has moved in next door. Maybe the man likes to fish.

His daughter tells him to mind his own business and not to go over there. Old Dudley bursts out and tells her that she was not raised to live with blacks next door like equals. He picks up another paper and sits down, looking out the window again. The geranium is still not there. It was never this late before. He thinks of the Grisby boy and Lutish back home. His daughter comes back in the room

and asks him to go down to apartment number 10 and ask for a shirt pattern.

Old Dudley becomes disoriented on his way back up the stairs and slips down three steps, landing in a sitting position on one of them. The black man from next door is there. He offers Old Dudley a hand up and tells him that he needs to be careful. Dudley does not look at him. The man tries to talk about hunting (he heard Dudley mumbling about it), but Dudley does not offer much in the way of conversation. The man tries to talk with him about where Dudley is from but gets nowhere. Finally, they reach Dudley's apartment, and Dudley goes inside.

Old Dudley is worked up from the encounter. He sees a man standing across the alley at the window where the geranium used to be. The man looks back at him and hollers over to ask why he's crying; he has never seen a man cry like that before. Old Dudley yells back asking him where is the geranium. The man says it is his plant, and he can put it out when he wants to do so. Anyway, he says, the plant fell off the windowsill. Old Dudley asks why the man has not picked it up.

The man tells Old Dudley to go pick it up himself. Old Dudley thinks he will. He will save the geranium and give it a better home. He starts out the door to the stairs when he thinks again of the black man patting him on the back and calling him "old timer." He will not have any of that again. He goes back inside and looks down at the plant. The man in the window is still there. He tells Dudley that he has not seen him pick it up. He tells him that he sees Dudley every day looking out the window at his place, and he does not like it. What he does is his business. He tells people that just once.

COMMENTARY

This story was published in ACCENT, summer 1946, (vol. VI). It also appeared in *Complete Stories* (FSG, 1971) and *Collected Works* (Library of America, 1988). Still a student, O'Connor submitted the story with "The Crop" to *Accent* in a single mailing on February 7, 1946, from Currier Graduate House at the State UNIVERSITY OF IOWA, Iowa City. The story bookends O'Connor's publishing career with its companion story, "Judgement Day." That story has the same characters and was written shortly before her death.

The geranium represents many things to Old Dudley and to the reader. As he looks for it to appear in the window across the tight alley, Dudley thinks of the Grisby boy back home. The geranium is like Grisby in that both of them are taken out in the sun for the day. Old Dudley tracks the geranium—it is set on the window sill from 10 each morning until 5:30 P.M. Grisby had polio, and he was taken outside in his wheelchair each day to get some sun. The implication from Old Dudley's thoughts is that a geranium that needs to be set out and taken in each day rather than have a more natural existence in the full sun has either something wrong with it or it is not being taken care of properly. It is living some kind of artificial existence, one which Old Dudley thinks everyone in the city is living.

Old Dudley thinks of the geraniums back home, as well. They grow better there in the southern soil and tended by green thumbs like his friends Lutish and Rabie. People in the city, who kept this geranium cooped up in a pot, do not deserve to have it. A geranium should be given a chance to root and grow. It should have much more vibrant colors than the pale pink of this variety that match old ladies' curtains. Pale pink seems a sickly color, lacking life and vitality.

All of these thoughts suggest how Old Dudley feels about being stuck in the city where his daughter has to take care of him. He is the one who is really cooped up; he is set out in his chair each day. What he needs, however, is to go back home and live under his own free will, however good or bad that may be for his health.

Old Dudley realizes that his daughter is doing what she sees as her duty. He also knows that she has siblings who are not doing this for him. He even acknowledges that it is really his own fault that he is in New York after all—for one minute, the city sounded like an exciting place to visit, and he said he would come. The problem now is that he feels trapped, like the pale pink geranium in the pot.

When Old Dudley learns that the geranium does not appear on the windowsill that day because it is lying on the ground down below, he is incredulous

that the man across the alley has not yet picked it up. When the man challenges Old Dudley to do so himself, he is willing to rescue the plant and take care of it. What holds him back, however, is facing another encounter with the new black neighbor. He remembers falling on the steps before. If he is too proud to have his daughter take care of him, his pride is even more wounded to have to be picked up and helped on the stairs by a black man.

Old Dudley's attitudes toward race are complex, and the story illustrates the ways an old southern white man can both refuse to be helped by a strange black man next door but at the same time go fishing with a black man in the South he feels comfortable with as a friend. Whites expected blacks to "know their place," but at the same time claimed them almost as family and certainly as friends. If the barriers of stereotyping and racial ignorance could be broken down, O'Connor appears to suggest, and relationships on a one-to-one basis encouraged, racism would have had a shorter life in this country.

CHARACTERS

Old Dudley   The old man is a widower who had found comfort in living with some old ladies in a boardinghouse in Georgia, seemingly taking care of them. There he had a sense of belonging and purpose with freedom to go out and hunt and fish and roam the countryside. In New York, Old Dudley is upset by how tight and confining life is in the apartment, in the building, and in the city itself. He notices that one can go nowhere and not find someone else there. Like the upturned geranium six floors down at the bottom of the alley, Old Dudley has been uprooted from the South and from his life.

Old Dudley's Daughter   The reader does not know what has happened to Old Dudley's daughter in the years between the time Old Dudley brought her up in Georgia and when she ended up living in New York City in a tight apartment with her husband and 16-year-old son. However, it is clear that she has given up many of the ways with which she was raised in favor of getting along in the city. She does not appear to long for the space of the South and the countryside. Instead, she seems intent on doing her duty, however, reluctantly, for her father. She tells him to let everyone in the city mind his or her own business and to leave people alone. She tries to get him to take walks and stay busy, even if it is simply going downstairs to get a pattern from her neighbor. Though she tries to talk with him, which is more than his son-in-law or his grandson ever do, soon she must revert to doing something else more important. Although she has enough respect for her father to know she should be taking care of him, she is too distant from him emotionally to know how much he is suffering.

RELATED LETTERS

Elizabeth McKee, September 30, 1948 (HB 7); Elizabeth McKee, January 13, 1955 (HB 74); John Lynch, November 6, 1955 (CW 967); Maryat Lee, February 24, 1957 (CW 1,023). *Pages:* HB: 7, 74; CW: 967, 1,023.

FURTHER READING

Darretta, John L. "From 'The Geranium' to 'Judgement Day': Retribution in the Fiction of Flannery O'Connor." pp. 21–31: Logsdon, Loren (ed.); Mayer, Charles W. (ed.) In *Since Flannery O'Connor: Essays on the Contemporary American Short Story*, edited by Loren Logsdon and Charles W. Mayer, 21–31. Macomb: Western Illinois University, 1987.

Fowler, Doreen. "Writing and Rewriting Race: Flannery O'Connor's 'The Geranium' and 'Judgment Day.'" *Flannery O'Connor Review* 2 (2003–04): 31–39.

Larsen, Val. "Manor House and Tenement: Failed Communities South and North in Flannery O'Connor's 'The Geranium.'" *The Flannery O'Connor Bulletin* 20 (1991): 88–103.

"Good Country People" (1955)

Ninth story of the collection, *A Good Man Is Hard to Find* (Harcourt, 1955), this tale appeared in HARPER'S BAZAAR the month the collection was published, June 1955. Along with "A Good Man Is Hard to Find," it is perhaps one of the most anthologized of O'Connor's short stories.

SYNOPSIS

Every day Mrs. Hopewell lights the heater in her room and her daughter Joy's, then fixes breakfast. Joy gets up and goes to the bathroom, and while she is there, Mrs. Freeman comes to the back door. She and Mrs. Hopewell talk in low voices while Joy is in the bathroom. Mrs. Freeman has two daughters, one of whom is 15 but is already married and pregnant. Mrs. Freeman gives Mrs. Hopewell a report on her daughter's state of nausea on an almost daily basis. Joy Hopewell is 32 years old. She has earned a Ph.D. that bewilders her mother. She is an atheist, and she also has an artificial leg. Her leg had been shot off in a hunting accident when she was 10 years old.

Mrs. Hopewell thinks highly of the Freemans and their daughters, Glynese and Carramae, whom Joy calls Glycerin and Caramel. She hired them to work on the farm because they were not white trash. They are good country people. They have worked for her for four years now. She allows Mrs. Freeman to take charge of a lot of the farm's business. Mrs. Hopewell could tell when she hired the Freemans as tenant farmers that Mrs. Freeman would need a lot to do and likes to be in charge.

Mrs. Hopewell thinks Joy has a poor attitude. She is often rude to people, perhaps because of her leg and how she has never lived a normal life, never experienced dancing or other kinds of fun. She seems to be full of bitterness. When she was 21 at college, she had changed her name legally to a name that Mrs. Hopewell assumed was the ugliest she could think of—Hulga. She was now legally Hulga Hopewell.

Hulga gradually learned to accept Mrs. Freeman's frequent visits since Mrs. Freeman took her place walking over the fields with her mother. One day Mrs. Freeman called her Hulga and continues to do so, though not in front of Mrs. Hopewell, who still refuses to do so. Hulga figured out that Mrs. Freeman's consideration of her must be because of her morbid curiosity about any hidden illness or infection. She noticed that Mrs. Freeman could listen to her mother's retelling of the hunting accident that took her leg over and over again.

This morning Mrs. Freeman is talking about her daughter again. Mrs. Hopewell, however, is thinking about what kind of conversation her daughter must have had with Manley Pointer, the Bible sales-man who had come by yesterday. He told her that he would not lie and tell her that he was posing as a college student. Instead, he had only a short time to live because of a heart condition. Mrs. Hopewell's eyes instantly filled with tears at the thought that he had the same condition as her daughter. She asked him to stay for dinner, though as soon as she did so, she regretted it. Joy took one look at him at dinner and then never looked at or spoke to him after that, even when he tried to begin a conversation with her directly. Oddly, when Pointer had begun to leave, he leaned over and said something to Joy, and she walked all the way with him to the gate.

Mrs. Freeman goes on with her talk, and Mrs. Hopewell responds with her repeated clichés, say-ing it takes all kinds of people to make the world. Hulga goes to her bedroom and locks the door. She is going to meet Manley Pointer at the gate at 10 o'clock. The salesman had flirted with her at the gate the previous day and enticed her to meet him.

During the night, she imagines that she had seduced him and then had to deal with his remorse. She would use the opportunity to allow her bril-liance to educate him to understand life more deeply. She meets him on the road, and he is as cheerful as ever, saying that he knew she would come. She wonders how he knew. He asks her age, and she says 17.

They walk through the pasture, where Manley asks about her leg and she asks him why he brought the Bibles. She tells him she does not believe in God, and he looks at her as though she is some strange animal in the zoo. He kisses her in the pas-ture, and though it is her first kiss, she thinks about it more than she feels it or is moved by it. Eventu-ally, they make their way to the barn.

After watching her climb to the hayloft without difficulty, the salesman climbs up. They kiss each other, though all the while Hulga is thinking. Pres-ently, the salesman tells her that he knew he loved her as soon as he saw her and asks her if she loves him. He says she must say so. Hulga talks to him philosophically at a level she knows he will not understand, saying that in one way she does love him. She tells him they need to be honest with each other. She tells him that she is 30 and that she

has a number of degrees. The salesman says that he does not care and asks her to prove her love.

Hulga expects the salesman's next move when, instead, he asks her to show him where her artificial leg goes on. She gives out a small cry. Even though she has learned to deal with her condition, the intimacy of working the leg remains hers alone. She barely looks at it herself when she puts it on each morning. Rather than expose her sensitivity about it, however, she simply asks him why he wants to see it. He gives her a long look and replies because it is what makes her different from every one else.

The remark hits home. Hulga decides that she is seeing true innocence in front of her, that he has discovered her essence. She surrenders herself to him completely. She shows him the leg, and when he asks to see her take it on and off, she does that as well. When he wants to do it, she allows him, think-ing that she will run off with him, and he will put her leg on and off each day. He takes it off again.

She tells him to put it back on, but he tries to kiss her again, looking back occasionally at the wooden leg. Then he tells her to wait, and he opens his valise and takes out a blue box with words on it, describing its contents as something to prevent disease. He takes out a deck of cards with obscene pictures on the backs and opens a Bible that is really a box with a flask in it. He says it is time they had a really good time.

Hulga is shocked. She asks him if he is not good country people. He says he is but that it never held him back and that he is as good as she is. She tells him to give her back her leg. He asks what is wrong with her; they have not gotten to know each other yet. He thought that she believed in nothing. He speaks in clichés like her mother. Hulga says that he is a Christian and says one thing and does another, just like all of them. The salesman tells her that he believes nothing of the sort.

When she screams for her leg, he quickly sweeps up the items back into the valise and puts the leg in with them. He makes his way to the hole in the loft and starts heading down. When just his head is above the hole, he tells her that she is not so smart. He has collected several things this way, including a woman's glass eye. He has believed in nothing ever since he was born. He says he uses a different name everywhere he goes, so she needn't think she will ever catch him.

Mrs. Hopewell and Mrs. Freeman are out in the field digging onions when they see the salesman come out of the woods. Mrs. Hopewell thinks he must have been selling Bibles to the blacks, and Mrs. Freeman comments about how simple a person he is and how she could never be quite that simple.

COMMENTARY

Mrs. Hopewell has kept the Freemans working on her farm for four years because she thinks they are "good country people." Good country people are not explicitly defined in the story. However, Mrs. Hopewell does say that she thinks Manley Pointer, the young Bible salesman, was boring when he stayed and had dinner with them. She says that he was not only boring but also sincere and genuine and that she thought he was good country people, whom she also calls the salt of the earth.

Mrs. Hopewell has a weakness for good country people like the Freemans. She allows Manley Pointer to stay and talk for two hours at her home because he gains her sympathy when he describes himself as a "just a country boy" (CS 279). Pointer implies that he may not be good enough for her to talk with, that she is more sophisticated. When she sees him look at the silver on her two sideboards, she decides that her house must be the most elegant he has ever seen. Unlike Hulga, she cannot be deliberately rude to anyone, and she impulsively invites him to dinner.

Mrs. Hopewell distinguishes between good country people and "white trash." White trash is never defined in the story either, but there is an implication that they do not like to work. Mrs. Hopewell's previous employees, whom she called white trash, did not stay longer than a year. Manley Pointer is clearly not good country people, and he does not seem to be white trash either. He turns out to be a force of evil that appears, like so many of O'Connor's devil figures, seemingly out of nowhere, then retreats intact and back into the nowhere from which he came.

Several dichotomies are found in the story—good country people and white trash; educated and uneducated people; those who believe in God and those who believe in nothing. Good country people, though perhaps unsophisticated, believe in God and hard work. They are responsible and try to be good to others. They are the salt of the earth, as Mrs. Hopewell says, because they keep businesses and farms going. There are many of them, and they do no lasting harm to society.

To Joy/Hulga Hopewell, good country people are simple and uneducated. They believe in God or say they do because they have not thought out the serious questions of faith for themselves. They speak in clichés because they do not take the time to think an original thought or form a unique means of expression. Joy/Hulga considers herself superior to good country people because she is highly educated and has come to the conclusion that God is a lie. Her philosophy degree has her thinking in existentialist terms that her mother does not understand and that what "science wishes to know [is] nothing of nothing" (CS 277).

Both Mrs. Hopewell and Joy/Hulga mistake Manley Pointer for good country people. When he tries to "seduce" Mrs. Hopewell into buying one of his Bibles, like her daughter, she at first is not taken in at all. When he appeals to her sympathy, she relents and impulsively invites him to stay for dinner. She does not, however, ever purchase a Bible. In this way, she is much less taken in than her daughter.

Interestingly, when Pointer mentions that she should have a Bible in the parlor, Mrs. Hopewell lies and tells him that hers is by her bedside when it is, in fact, in the attic. She does not tell Pointer that her daughter is an atheist who keeps her from having her Bible out, but she also does not tell him that it is stored away in an inconvenient place. Mrs. Hopewell may not have read the Bible any more recently than her daughter. Perhaps Joy/Hulga's views have had more of an effect on Mrs. Hopewell than one first realizes.

All Mrs. Hopewell loses out on in mistaking Manley Pointer for a good country boy when he is not, however, is some of her time and food and perhaps the cost of a new artificial leg. Joy/Hulga, who thinks she is so much more sophisticated and educated than her mother, has lost much more, but perhaps she has gained more as well.

Joy/Hulga thinks that she can seduce this good country boy, and then when he is feeling guilty over the seduction (as any good Christian country boy would feel), she will attack his mind and beliefs and try to confuse him about the existence of God for his own good. She will try to educate him. Joy/Hulga is miserable and seems determined to make everyone around her as miserable as she is. She lost her leg in a hunting accident when she was 10 and developed a sour disposition. She believes that she is more sophisticated than her mother and everyone else because of her education and her turning away from religion. Only the sophisticated and educated would have enough sense to turn away from God. Anyone who does not must be simple and ignorant.

Joy/Hulga learns a lesson in humility from the incident in the barn. She does not seduce Manley Pointer in the end, but he seduces her. When they first kiss, she is able to keep her mind clear. When he first makes his moves in the barn, she is able to do the same. However, when he figures out her secret, that she believes her artificial leg makes her different but that she is still special, he is able to break down her barriers against intimacy. He convinces her that he is a real innocent, and she begins to hope for the first time in many years that human contact is worth being vulnerable for after all.

At that moment, she surrenders her mind to him, which, to Joy/Hulga, is more important than her body. She begins to envision a future with this boy, losing her life to his, and allowing him to take her leg on and off in an act of real intimacy. When she sees the items hidden in his valise, however—instead of Bibles, he carries disease protection, liquor and playing cards with pictures of nudes on them—she is completely confused. Manley is not a good country boy at all. When he says that he has never believed in the Bibles he sells or in God or Christianity, she realizes that one need not be educated or sophisticated to be an unbeliever. He runs off, taking not only her leg to add to his GROTESQUE collection but also her glasses so that she cannot see. Pointer has taken advantage of her rather than the other way around.

Mrs. Freeman's comment at the end of the story is ironic. As the good country woman she is, she has common sense. Mrs. Hopewell approves of the common sense in her daughters and thinks Joy/Hulga lacks it, for all her education. When she sees Pointer leaving the woods, Mrs. Hopewell says that maybe the world would be better off if more people were as simple as he. Mrs. Freeman says that some people just cannot be that simple; she knows that she could not. She is likely speaking of Manley Pointer as anything but simple. He is one of those who could never be simple and innocent. She may also be speaking, ironically, of Joy/Hulga—that not every one would be as simple as she is to be taken in by him.

Names are an interesting motif in the story. Joy Hopewell changes her name to what her mother thinks is the ugliest sounding name in any language. Presumably, Joy/Hulga does this out of bitterness over her condition and as a means of acting out her frustrations against her mother. Joy/Hulga calls Mrs. Freeman's daughters, Glynese and Carramae, by the nicknames Glycerin and Caramel. She cannot identify with them and so trivializes them by substituting phony sweet names for their real names. Lastly, Manley Pointer tells Joy/Hulga that she will not be able to track him down once he leaves the farm with his trophy of her leg. He uses a different name every place he goes, he says, and he moves around often. Just as he uses false names to get away with his evil tricks, Joy/Hulga uses false names to avoid dealing with the two young women and a disability she cannot tolerate.

Joy/Hulga's glasses and the frequent mention of eyes are another motif at work in the story. She is described as having icy blue eyes that look away like someone who has blinded her own eyes out of sheer will power and intends to keep them that way. Joy/Hulga's turning away from God and her bitterness and withdrawal from other people has blinded her to the goodness in the world. Her mother tries to help her see that looking at the bright side of things makes life better and more tolerable. When she remarks that it would not hurt to smile once in a while, Joy/Hulga jumps up from the table and asks whether her mother has ever looked inside and seen what she is not.

Manley Pointer tells Joy/Hulga that he likes girls in glasses. When they are in the barn, he slips her glasses off and puts them in his pocket. Joy/Hulga cannot see the view outside the window without them. When he is ready to go, Pointer informs her that he once took a woman's glass eye by seducing her in the same way. Joy/Hulga has now been blinded, not through her own stubbornness but by a force even more determined than bitterness and self-pity, the devil himself.

Joy/Hulga Hopewell, it turns out, is anything but worldly and sophisticated. She acts like a child and is treated like a child by her mother. Mrs. Hopewell treats her as a child because she knows that her daughter has never enjoyed so many of the activities that adult life has to offer. It is as though both their lives and their relationship stopped on the day Mr. Hopewell accidentally shot off his daughter's leg. Joy/Hulga behaves like a child with no concern over her clothing. She wears a six-year-old skirt and a sweatshirt with a cowboy on it, mainly to spite her mother. Joy/Hulga's self-pity and sulking attitude is more childish than anything else. She cannot empathize with her mother, with Mrs. Freeman, or Mrs. Freeman's daughters. Her lack of empathy creates the situation in the barn. By not being able to put herself in the place of Manley Pointer, she is unable to figure out that he is an experienced charlatan who will take advantage of her.

O'Connor's fiction features several highly educated sons and daughters living with, or returning to, widowed or divorced farm mothers. "The Enduring Chill" is a good example. It is difficult not to associate these characters with O'Connor herself, who was forced to come home to live with her widowed mother after she was stricken with LUPUS, the same disease that killed her father. Most of the educated sons and daughters resent their mothers' strength and influence as well as the uneducated farm people and environment near whom they find themselves living. Perhaps writing fiction about exaggerated characters in this predicament was one way O'Connor found to cope with her own limitations and disappointment.

CHARACTERS

Hulga Hopewell (Joy)   She is a large, blond 32-year-old woman with a Ph.D. and an artificial leg. She is not ugly but has an unpleasant expression most of the time that makes her unattractive. Her mother still treats her like a child. Hulga legally changed her name from Joy to Hulga when she

turned 21. Her mother is convinced that her daughter thought until she could find the ugliest name possible. The name reminds her mother of the wide and blank hull of a battleship, and she refuses to use it. Hulga is a bitter character. She seems to bash and battle her way through life, stumping her artificial leg on the floor to exaggerate the sound, not allowing anyone to forget her infirmity.

Hull also refers to the leafy section of fruit, such as strawberries, or the dried outer covering of fruit or vegetables, such as pea pods; hulls are normally discarded. Like these kinds of hulls, Hulga feels discarded by life as a result of an accident. Her only goal in life seems to have been education. Now that she has gone as far as she can go, earning a Ph.D., she appears to have no other plans that make any practical sense to her hard-working mother.

A third word reminiscent of Hulga is *hulk*. A hulk is part of an old ship, perhaps jutting out of the sand on an abandoned island. *Hulk* also describes a large clumsy person or thing. Like a hull, the hulk of an ancient ship is one that has been discarded and long ago forgotten, unnecessary and useless. Since Hulga is described as a large woman who stumps around the house, the word *hulk* is apt. The name *Hulga* makes readers think of hulls and hulks. Either way, the connotation is completely opposite from her true name of Joy, which denotes happiness and blessing.

Mrs. Hopewell   She is a divorced woman who has raised her daughter and ensured that she be educated. She hires the Freemans as tenant farmers because they are a class above white trash. Mrs. Hopewell speaks in clichés, which puts her in sharp contrast to her highly educated daughter. Clichés suggest verbal and intellectual laziness; the reader sees that Hulga/Joy would have a difficult time around her mother and Mrs. Freeman. Mrs. Hopewell does not understand her daughter's books and thinks her daughter is brilliant but without common sense. Hopewell implies that she has an optimistic nature and is always hoping for the best, however clichéd and uncomplicated that viewpoint may be. She likely also hopes that her daughter will get well by coming to cheerfully accept her incurable deformity.

RELATED LETTERS

Robert Giroux, February 26, 1955 (HB 75); Thomas Mabry, March 1, 1955 (CW 930–931); Robert Giroux, March 7, 1955 (HB 75); Sally and Robert Fitzgerald, April 1, 1955 (HB 76); Ben Griffith, May 4, 1955 (HB 78); Alice Morris, June 10, 1955 (HB 86); Betty Hester ("A"), September 30, 1955 (HB 106); Betty Hester ("A"), October 20, 1955 (HB 111); Betty Hester ("A"), December 8, 1955 (HB 121); Betty Hester ("A"), May 19, 1956 (HB 158); Betty Hester ("A"), June 1, 1956 (HB 160); Betty Hester ("A"), August 24, 1956 (HB 170–171); Cecil Dawkins, November 5, 1963 (HB 546). *Pages*: HB: 75–6, 78, 86, 111, 121, 158, 160, 170–171, 546; CW: 930–931.

FURTHER READING

Atkins, Christine. "Educating Hulga: Re-Writing Seduction in 'Good Country People.'" In *"On the Subject of the Feminist Business": Re-Reading Flannery O'Connor,* edited by Teresa Caruso, 120–128. New York: Peter Lang, 2004.

Babinec, Lisa S. "Cyclical Patterns of Domination and Manipulation in Flannery O'Connor's Mother-Daughter Relationships." *Flannery O'Connor Bulletin* 19 (1990): 9–29.

Bauer, Margaret D. "The Betrayal of Ruby Hill and Hulga Hopewell: Recognizing Feminist Concerns in 'A Stroke of Good Fortune' and 'Good Country People.'" In *"On the Subject of the Feminist Business": Re-Reading Flannery O'Connor,* edited by Teresa Caruso, 40–63. New York: Peter Lang, 2004.

Chew, Martha. "Flannery O'Connor's Double-Edged Satire: The Idiot Daughter Versus the Lady Ph.D." *The Southern Quarterly: A Journal of the Arts in the South* 19, no. 2 (Winter 1981): 17–25.

Currie, Sheldon. "Freaks and Folks: Comic Imagery in the Fiction of Flannery O'Connor." *The Antigonish Review* 62–63 (Summer-Fall 1985): 133–142.

Edmondson, Henry T., III. "'Wingless Chickens': 'Good Country People' and the Seduction of Nihilism." *Flannery O'Connor Review* 2 (2003–04): 63–73.

Gatta, John. *"The Scarlet Letter* as Pre-Text for Flannery O'Connor's 'Good Country People.'" In *Hawthorne and Women: Engendering and Expanding the Hawthorne Tradition,* edited by John L. Idol, Jr. and Melinda M. Ponder, 271–277. Amherst: University of Massachusetts Press, 1999.

Havird, David. "The Saving Rape: Flannery O'Connor and Patriarchal Religion." *Mississippi Quarterly: The Journal of Southern Culture* 47, no. 1 (Winter 1993–94): 15–26.

Pierce, Constance. "The Mechanical World of 'Good Country People.'" *Flannery O'Connor Bulletin* 5 (1976): 30–38.

Steed, J. P. "'Through Our Laughter We Are Involved': Bergsonian Humor in Flannery O'Connor's Fiction." *Midwest Quarterly: A Journal of Contemporary Thought* 46, no. 3 (Spring 2005): 299–313.

Thiemann, Fred R. "Usurping the Logos: Clichés in Flannery O'Connor's 'Good Country People.'" *The Flannery O'Connor Bulletin* 24 (1995–96): 46–56.

Wood, Ralph C. "Flannery O'Connor, Martin Heidegger, and Modern Nihilism: A Reading of 'Good Country People.'" *The Flannery O'Connor Bulletin* 21 (1992): 100–118.

"Good Man Is Hard to Find, A" (1953)

Title and first story of the collection *A Good Man Is Hard to Find and Other Stories* (Harcourt, 1955).

SYNOPSIS

A southern family consisting of Bailey and his unnamed wife and three children, John Wesley, June Star, and an unnamed baby, decides to drive from their home in ATLANTA, GEORGIA, to Florida for a three-day vacation. At the beginning of the story, the grandmother (unnamed) uses a newspaper article about an escaped prisoner who calls himself The Misfit in her argument to her son that he should not take the family to Florida but to Tennessee instead. The Misfit was reportedly headed toward Florida himself, and she says that her conscience could not abide taking the children in the same direction knowing he was there. Her comment is an ironic foreshadowing of what happens later.

Even though she has lost the battle over where they are going, the grandmother is the first one in the car the next morning. She has hidden her cat, Pitty Sing, in a basket. She does not approve of Bailey's wife traveling in slacks and a green kerchief. At least if the grandmother were found dead on the highway, those who saw her would know that she was a lady, a statement that proves to be another foreshadowing.

The grandmother points out details along the highway. She comments on a black child wearing no pants, standing in a shack doorway, and a cotton field with a small graveyard in the middle. The children read comic books and then eat their lunch in the car. The grandmother promises a story if the children will be good, and she tells the story with drama and flair.

Before long, Bailey stops at a place called The Tower for a stretch and barbecue sandwiches. The proprietor, Red Sammy, is famous for his barbecue. Red Sammy's wife waits on the family, and they order sandwiches. Bailey's wife puts coins in the jukebox and plays "The Tennessee Waltz." Red Sam and the grandmother talk about the old days when one could leave one's door unlocked. He tells about foolishly allowing men to charge gas last week because they claimed that they worked at the local mill. "A good man is hard to find," Red Sammy says, and the grandmother agrees. Soon the family is on its way again.

The grandmother naps and wakes herself up with her own snoring until they are just outside of Toombsboro, Georgia. She tells the family she once visited a plantation there and urges Bailey to try to find the house. After traveling up and down hills on the rutted road with no plantation in sight, the grandmother has a sudden thought that makes her lose her grip on her valise, exposing Pitty Sing, who jumps out and onto Bailey's shoulder, causing a horrible accident. The car flips over.

Everyone but the children sit down in the ditch, 10 feet below the surface of the road. On a hill above, they spot a black, hearselike car driving slowly as though its occupants have seen them. The grandmother stands and waves to get their attention. The car stops, and a man with a black hat, blue jeans, and no shirt gets out with two younger men. As the man in the black hat walks carefully down the ravine toward them, the grandmother thinks she recognizes him.

When the grandmother says she recognizes the driver as The Misfit, he lets everyone know that it would have better for them all had she not recognized him. Immediately, the grandmother takes charge, trying to talk with The Misfit about his misplaced name and how he must have come from a good family since she can see that he is a good man. The two begin talking, though The Misfit appears not to reply to the grandmother's questions or comments all the time.

As they talk, The Misfit asks Bobby Lee to take Bailey and John Wesley out to the woods. Soon, the family back in the ravine hears two gunshots. Bobby Lee and Hiram return, and The Misfit asks them to take Bailey's wife, baby, and June Star to the woods. Now the grandmother is alone facing The Misfit. She loses her voice, until finally she is able to utter the words, "Jesus. Jesus."

"Jesus thrown everything off balance," The Misfit says, and compares Jesus' not committing a crime to the papers the authorities had on him that proved he must have committed one. A scream from the woods is followed by a pistol shot. The grandmother pleads with The Misfit not to shoot a lady; she will give him all the money she has. However, The Misfit is not after money now. Two more gunshots ring out from the woods. The grandmother calls out for her son.

The Misfit says that Jesus threw everything off balance when he raised from the dead. The grandmother suggests that maybe he did not raise from the dead. If he could have been there, The Misfit goes on, and seen it for himself to know for sure what happened, maybe he would not be the way he is now. The Misfit says that if Jesus did raise from the dead, then the only thing that people can do is throw away everything and follow him, but if he did not raise from the dead, then there is nothing left to do but enjoy life in any way one can, however harmful it may be to others.

At his questioning and emotion, the grandmother's mind clears for a moment, and she says, "Why you're one of my babies. You're one of my own children!" She touches The Misfit's shoulder. At the touch, The Misfit recoils as if bitten by a snake and shoots her three times in the chest. Then he drops the gun, takes off his glasses, and begins to clean them.

Bobby Lee and Hiram come back from the woods and see the grandmother sprawled in the ditch in a puddle of blood. The Misfit tells them to take her body out to the woods with the others. Bobby Lee says that she was a talker, and The Misfit says that she would have been a good woman had she had someone holding a gun to her head all of her life. Bobby Lee speaks about the fun they have all just had, and The Misfit tells him to shut up and that there is "no real pleasure in life."

COMMENTARY

This story was first published in 1953 in the anthology *Modern Writing I,* published by Avon and edited by William Phillips and Philip Rahv. The story was also reprinted in *The House of Fiction: An Anthology of the Short Story, with Commentary,* edited by Caroline Gordon and Allen Tate and published by Scribner in 1960. It remains the most anthologized and most well-known of all of O'Connor's work. Apparently, it was a favorite of the author's as well since it was the story she most often selected to read at public readings. She once indicated that its length was especially appropriate for this purpose.

The title of the story comes from a blues song written by Eddie Green, recorded in 1927–28, and popularized by the singer Bessie Smith. The speaker has the blues because she has discovered that her "man" is cheating on her. She tells any woman out there who has a faithful man to take her advice and give him plenty of affection because a good man is hard to find.

O'Connor heard the title when her mother showed her a news clipping with a picture of a girl in a ballerina tutu and a caption that stated she was dancing to Green's blues song. O'Connor wrote to the Fitzgeralds in January 1953 from ANDALUSIA that her mother asked her what she thought of the clipping, which she enclosed with the letter. She wrote the Fitzgeralds, "It kills me" (qtd. in *Collected* 907). She read the resulting story in public at least eight times partly because it was the right length for such an event and partly, as she once wrote to fellow writer KATHERINE ANNE PORTER, because it was so grim a tale that it was the only one of her stories she could read aloud without laughing.

Taken from O'Connor's Christian perspective, the title suggests that the story may be concerned with faith and resurrection, as well as how difficult it can be for people to believe that Jesus rose from the dead. "A Good Man," perhaps meaning Christ himself, is hard to find in the sense that faith in the resurrection can be a difficult gulf for nonbelievers or agnostics to cross over.

Those who seek the truth may find belief in Jesus Christ as a human being who walked the Earth, and they may be able to find faith in his wisdom and miracles. The act of the resurrection, however, is the stumbling block for many, as The Misfit suggests. Were it not for the resurrection, Christianity would not have been founded in the first place.

The believer himself may also be taken to be the "good man." Because The Misfit cannot make the leap of faith in Christ's resurrection and because he cannot know for sure if it happened, life has no meaning for him, and it degenerates into a downward spiral of violence and ambivalence. Because of his lack of faith, he is not only unable to find the good man, Christ, but he is also unable to be a good man himself as a believer. The truly devoted and ever faithful are just as hard to find as the belief in Christ's resurrection.

The grandmother, on the other hand, is a believer and has found Christ, at least on a superficial level. She has not been able, however, to find the "good man" in others. In other words, she has not been able to see Christ as Christian teaching requires, in her fellow human beings, especially those who may be very different from herself. She points out a black boy and tells June Star when the girl comments that he is not wearing any pants that he probably does not have any. Rather than try to understand the boy's situation, the grandmother simply says she would like to paint a picture of the boy. This comment is insensitive, as though the boy, her fellow human being in Christ, were nothing more than an interesting object on the landscape, not someone to whom she should feel connected.

The grandmother stands up for Edgar Atkins Teagarden when June Star criticizes him after hearing the watermelon story, but she measures his qualities not in personal characteristics but in the fact that he became successful by investing in

Coca-Cola. The grandmother uses the language of ministering to The Misfit when she tries to talk to him before she is shot, but she does not actually see him as a member of the human race, her own family, until the epiphany she has right before her death. Because she did eventually come to this realization at the moment of her death, however, the grandmother dies in a state of grace; her soul is saved by that single moment when her faith deepened and her concern extended beyond herself.

Before a public reading of the story at Hollins College in 1963, O'Connor called The Misfit not the devil, as some critics and teachers suggest, but "a prophet gone wrong" (*Mystery* 110). She suggested that he has a deeper and more mature capacity to believe and to counsel others than the grandmother has, though he does not believe in Christ. Perhaps this is why he recognizes the grandmother as a good woman at the end of the story and also why he sees that the gun to her head, the moment of death, was when goodness broke through for her. A truly good woman is just as hard to find in the world as a good man. O'Connor also indicates that the grandmother is not a witch, as some have called her, and that she is hypocritical but not totally bad.

At the same public reading, O'Connor explained her use of violence in the story and in her work as a whole. Violence creates the scenario that she desires to depict in her characters as a Christian. She says, "the man in the violent situation reveals those qualities least dispensable in his personality, those qualities which are all he will have to take into eternity with him" (114). This theme recurs throughout O'Connor's work, making this story a good sample of her chief fictional concerns.

CHARACTERS

Bailey When the reader first encounters Bailey, the grandmother's son, he is reading the sports section of the newspaper and listening to his mother tell him that he should not be taking his family to Florida. Starting out on what is supposed to be a three-day trip, he drives, wearing a yellow shirt with blue parrots on it. Bailey is balding and does not have a good temperament. When his mother expresses fear of his "wrath" later, we sense that Bailey can have a bad temper. He and his wife have

allowed their children to grow up rude and inconsiderate of others. He has not allowed his mother to change his family's plans to go to Florida, but he does relent when she and his children ask him to turn around on the highway to find the plantation. This act of going against his best judgment causes the family's destruction. The reader sees that Bailey is led around by his mother, who lives with him. He never assumes authority to earn respect. He does little but offer a couple of verbal protests to try to spare his family's life when confronted with The Misfit and his gang. Though he speaks up at least twice, he fails to take action, and when Hiram takes him up by the arm to haul him out to the woods, it is as if he is lifting an old man. Rather than protest or call to his wife, Bailey calls to his mother to wait for him, that he will be right back. His yellow shirt and yellow face after the accident suggest a lack of courage; his blue eyes match the blue parrots on the shirt, connecting him with parrots as one who simply repeats what he has already heard and does not think for himself. When the going gets tough, despite perhaps better intentions, Bailey lacks moral strength and physical backbone. Instead, he "bails" out, or gives up.

The grandmother Bailey's mother; O'Connor builds the grandmother as arrogant, hypocritical, manipulative, and interfering. Interestingly, as one of the major characters, she is also one of the three nameless characters along with Bailey's wife and the baby. She is small in stature and likes to dress neatly in coordinating Sunday clothes while traveling in case she should be found dead by the side of the road. She favors a ladylike appearance. The grandmother has mouthed the language of Christianity most likely most of her life. Just as The Misfit says, she could have been a good woman if she had had a gun pointed to her sooner in life. She realizes that all people are united as the children of God, but unfortunately, she realizes it just a moment too late. Even so, according to Catholic doctrine, she has died in a state of grace and is probably on her way to heaven because of it.

The Misfit An escaped Georgia convict who is on the run, reportedly headed toward Florida. He wears a black hat, jeans, no shirt, and silver spectacles that give him a scholarly look. He is the driver of the black, hearselike car that pulls up alongside Bailey's family after the accident. He has an earnest question to which he cannot seem to get an answer—whether or not Christ really came back from the dead. He says that if he were there at the time of Christ, he would have known for sure. If it is true, then people should drop everything and follow Jesus; if it is not true, then life is meaningless. Since he cannot prove the answer to himself one way or the other, he finds no meaning in life and no pleasantness.

One senses that The Misfit is more of a misfit because he cannot resolve the question to his satisfaction than for any other reason. He may have been a devout preacher had he convinced himself that the resurrection is true. In many ways, he is a more complex character than the grandmother he kills.

RELATED LETTERS

Sally and Robert Fitzgerald, May 7, 1953 (HB 59); Sally and Robert Fitzgerald, Friday [undated], 1953 (HB 60); Sally and Robert Fitzgerald, June 10, 1955 (HB 85); Betty Hester ("A"), October 20, 1955 (HB 111); Betty Hester ("A"), November 10, 1955 (CW 969); Cecil Dawkins, June 19, 1957 (CW 1,035); Betty Hester ("A"), January 31, 1959 (HB 317); Cecil Dawkins, May 21, 1959 (HB 333–334); Dr. T. R. Spivey, May 25, 1959 (HB 334); John Hawkes, September 13, 1959 (CW 1,108); John Hawkes, December 26, 1959 (CW 1,119); Andrew Lytle, February 4, 1960 (CW 1,121); Betty Hester ("A"), March 2, 1960 (CW 1,124); John Hawkes, April 14, 1960 (HB 389–390); John Hawkes, October 9, 1960 (HB 412); Louise Abbot, January 15, 1961 (HB 426); "Professor of English," March 28, 1961 (HB 437); John Hawkes, June 22, 1961 (CW 1,150–1,151); Ashley Brown, January 12, 1962 (HB 460); Cecil Dawkins, January 13, 1963 (HB 504); Betty Hester ("A"), March 30, 1963 (HB 511); John Hawkes, September 29, 1963 (HB 542); Betty Hester ("A"), November 9, 1963 (HB 548). *Pages*: HB: 59, 60, 85, 111, 317, 333–334, 389–390, 412, 426, 437, 460, 504, 511, 542, 548; CW: 969, 1,035, 1,119, 1,121, 1,124, 1,150–1,151.

FURTHER READING

Asals, Frederick, ed. *Flannery O'Connor: "A Good Man Is Hard to Find."* New Brunswick, N.J.: Rutgers University Press, 1993.

Bandy, Stephen C. "'One of My Babies': The Misfit and the Grandmother." *Studies in Short Fiction* 33, no. 1 (Winter 1996): 107–117.

Bellamy, Michael O. "Everything Off Balance: Protestant Election in Flannery O'Connor's 'A Good Man Is Hard to Find.'" *Flannery O'Connor Bulletin* 8 (1979): 116–124.

Blythe, Hal, and Charlie Sweet. "The Misfit: O'Connor's 'Family' Man as Serial Killer." *Notes on Contemporary Literature* 25, no. 1 (January 1995): 3–5.

———. "Darwin in Dixie: O'Connor's Jungle." *Notes on Contemporary Literature* 21, no. 2 (1991): 8–9.

Bonney, William. "The Moral Structure of Flannery O'Connor's 'A Good Man Is Hard to Find.'" *Studies in Short Fiction* 27, no. 3 (Summer 1990): 347–356.

Bryant, Hallman B. "Reading the Map in 'A Good Man Is Hard to Find.'" *Studies in Short Fiction* 18, no. 3 (Summer 1981): 301–307.

Church, Joseph. "An Abuse of the Imagination in Flannery O'Connor's 'A Good Man Is Hard to Find.'" *Notes on Contemporary Literature* 20, no. 3 (May 1990): 8–10.

Clark, Michael. "Flannery O'Connor's 'A Good Man Is Hard to Find': The Moment of Grace." *English Language Notes* 29, no. 2 (December 1991): 66–69.

Currie, Sheldon. "A Good Grandmother Is Hard to Find: Story as Exemplum." *The Antigonish Review* 81–82 (Spring-Summer 1990): 143–156.

Desmond, John. "Flannery O'Connor's Misfit and the Mystery of Evil." *Renascence: Essays on Values in Literature* 56, no. 2 (Winter 2004): 129–137.

———. "Sign of the Times: Lancelot and the Misfit." *The Flannery O'Connor Bulletin* 18 (1989): 91–98.

Donahoo, Robert. "O'Connor's Ancient Comedy: Form in 'A Good Man Is Hard to Find.'" *Journal of the Short Story in English* 16 (Spring 1991): 29–40.

Doxey, William S. "A Dissenting Opinion of Flannery O'Connor's 'A Good Man Is Hard to Find.'" *Studies in Short Fiction* 10 (1973): 199–204.

Dyson, J. Peter. "Cats, Crime, and Punishment: The Mikado's Pitti-Sing in 'A Good Man Is Hard to Find.'" *English Studies in Canada* 14, no. 4 (December 1988): 436–452.

Ellis, James. "Watermelons and Coca-Cola in 'A Good Man Is Hard to Find': Holy Communion in the South." *Notes on Contemporary Literature* 8, no. 3 (1978): 7–8.

Evans, Robert C. "Poe, O'Connor, and the Mystery of the Misfit." *Flannery O'Connor Bulletin* 25 (1996–97): 1–12.

Fike, Matthew. "The Timothy Allusion in 'A Good Man Is Hard to Find.'" *Renascence: Essays on Values in Literature* 52, no. 4 (Summer 2000): 311–319.

Fitzgerald, Sally. "Happy Endings." *Image: A Journal of the Arts and Religion* 16 (Summer 1997): 73–80.

Gordon, Caroline, and Allen Tate (ed.). *The House of Fiction: An Anthology of the Short Story, with Commentary.* New York: Scribner, 1960.

Hardy, Donald E. "Why Is She So Negative? Negation and Knowledge in Flannery O'Connor's 'A Good Man Is Hard to Find.'" *Southwest Journal of Linguistics* 17, no. 2 (December 1998): 61–81.

Jones, Madison. "A Good Man's Predicament." *The Southern Review* 20, no. 4 (Autumn 1984): 836–841.

Keetley, Dawn. "'I forgot what I done': Repressed Anger and Violent Fantasy in 'A Good Man Is Hard to Find.'" In *"On the subject of the feminist business": Re-Reading Flannery O'Connor,* edited by Teresa Caruso. New York: Peter Lang, 2004.

Kropf, C. R. "Theme and Setting in 'A Good Man Is Hard to Find.'" *Renascence: Essays in Values in Literature* 24 (1972): 177–180, 206.

Lasseter, Victor. "The Genesis of Flannery O'Connor's 'A Good Man Is Hard to Find." *Studies in American Fiction* 10, no. 2 (Autumn 1982): 227–232.

Liu, Dilin. "'A Good Man Is Hard to Find': The Difference between the Word and the World." *Short Story* 2, no. 2 (Winter-Spring 1992): 63–75.

Marks, W. S. "Advertisements for Grace: Flannery O'Connor's 'A Good Man Is Hard to Find.'" *Studies in Short Fiction* 4 (1966): 19–27.

Ochshorn, Kathleen G. "A Cloak of Grace: Contradictions in 'A Good Man Is Hard to Find.'" *Studies in American Fiction* 18, no. 1 (Spring 1990): 113–117.

O'Connor, Flannery. "A Reasonable Use of the Unreasonable." In *Mystery and Manners,* edited by Sally and Robert Fitzgerald. New York: Farrar, Straus and Giroux, 1970.

Owen, Mitchell. "The Function of Signature in 'A Good Man Is Hard to Find.'" *Studies in Short Fiction* 33, no. 1 (Winter 1996): 101–106.

Ragan, Brian Abel. *A Wreck on the Road to Damascus: Innocence, Guilt, & Conversion in Flannery O'Connor.* Chicago: Loyola University Press, 1989.

Renner, Stanley. "Secular Meaning in 'A Good Man Is Hard to Find.'" *College Literature* 9, no. 2 (Spring 1982): 123–132.

Sloan, Gary. "Mystery, Magic, and Malice: O'Connor and the Misfit." *Journal of the Short Story in English* 30 (Spring 1998): 73–83.

———. "O'Connor's 'A Good Man Is Hard to Find.'" *Explicator* 57, no. 2 (Winter 1999): 118–120.

Stewart, Michelle Pagni. "A Good Trickster Is Hard to Find: A Refiguring of Flannery O'Connor." *Short Story* 3, no. 1 (Spring 1995): 77–83.

Wray, Virginia. "Narration in 'A Good Man Is Hard to Find.'" *Publications of the Arkansas Philological Association* 14, no. 1 (Spring 1988): 25–38.

"Greenleaf" (1956)

"Greenleaf" is the second story in the collection *Everything That Rises Must Converge* (FSG, 1965).

SYNOPSIS

Mrs. May is awakened by a bull at her window. It has a wreath over its horns. She hollers to it to get away. She decides not to call Mr. Greenleaf at that moment, but the next day she tells him about the stray bull and that he needs to keep it penned up. Mr. Greenleaf tells her that the bull has been roaming before. He had put the bull in a pen, but he escaped. She tells him that he best get the bull taken care of and that if it ever gets loose again, he is to inform her at once.

Mrs. May sits at the dining room table with her two sons, Scofield and Wesley. Scofield is 36 and a businessman who sells insurance to blacks; Wesley is an intellectual. She thinks about her tenant farmers, the Greenleafs. They have been working on her farm for 15 years. She tolerates Mr. Greenleaf, but she cannot stand his wife. Mrs. Greenleaf liked to take the newspaper clippings to the woods, dig a hole and put them in it, and then cover them up. She would then fling herself on top of them and move her arms and legs around until finally she lay still. She called these rituals "prayer healings."

The Greenleafs have twin sons who are younger than the May sons. Their names are O. T. and E. T. Greenleaf. They had been in the army during World War II and had both married refined French women. When they returned from the war, they took advantage of the G.I. bill and went to college and purchased land and a house with a government loan. They each now had three children who were going to go to the convent school to be brought up with manners. By contrast, the May sons are rude and do not help their mother around the farm.

Scofield tells her that the bull belongs to O. T. and E. T. Greenleaf. Mrs. May goes to tell O. T. and E. T. that if they do not come after their bull at her place today, then she is going to have their father shoot it first thing in the morning. While she is at the Greenleaf farm, she goes to the milking barn and cannot help but notice how clean and well kept it is. It nearly takes her breath away. When she gets home, Wesley and Scofield tease her meanly and eventually get into a fight, tumbling over the furniture.

Mr. Greenleaf offers to drive the bull to his sons' farm the next day. Mrs. May talks to him about gratitude and his sons' lack of it from the days when they were boys and she let them wear her sons' old clothing. She tells him that they do not come for their bull because she is a woman, and that means they can get away with anything. Mr. Greenleaf tells her that his sons are aware that she has two men, sons of her own, on the property.

That night, Mrs. May hears the bull again at her window. She thinks Mr. Greenleaf has let him out on purpose. In the morning, she finds Mr. Greenleaf working with the milk cans and tells him to get his gun to shoot the bull. This upsets Greenleaf, who takes up his handkerchief. He says no one would ever ask him to shoot his own sons' bull.

She says she will drive him out to the middle of the field, and he can chase him to the empty pasture and shoot him.

Some time passes, and she decides to get out of the truck and sits down on the front bumper, with her head back on the hood. She thinks that she will honk in 10 minutes and see what is going on. She dozes for more than 10 minutes. When she rouses herself, she decides to honk to let him know she was still waiting. She then sits back down on the bumper.

The bull comes running out of the woods and straight toward the truck. Mr. Greenleaf is not behind it. Mrs. May yells that the bull is there but then sits still in disbelief at what is happening. Soon the bull charges into her, goring her with its horns. Mr. Greenleaf appears out of the woods and shoots the bull in the eye. The animal lifts up its head until Mrs. May slides forward, looking in death as though she is whispering some secret into its ear. *Startling*

COMMENTARY

Before appearing in *Everything That Rises Must Converge*, this story was published in *The Kenyon Review* in summer 1956 (vol. 18) and was reprinted as the first-prize story in *Prize Stories 1957: The O. Henry Awards*, edited by Paul Engle and Constance Urdang. It was O'Connor's first story to win first place in the O. Henry Awards. The story was also reprinted in *First-Prize Stories, 1919–1957*, edited by Harry Hansen; in *Best American Short Stories of 1957*, edited by Martha Foley; and in *First-Prize Stories, 1919–1963*, edited by Harry Hansen.

When O'Connor writes about this story in her letters, she describes having a delightful feeling in knowing that she is going to have a woman gored by a bull in a story. She does not know how or why yet, but that premise apparently began her journey in telling this tale.

The bull, odd as it may seem, may be seen as a Christ figure in the story. Early on, the bull wears a crown of thorns as it chews under Mrs. May's window. This could symbolize Christ's calling for Mrs. May to believe. More than one critic sees the story as a Christ figure courting Mrs. May toward belief. The "gentleman," as Mr. Greenleaf calls the bull,

religion

South values > intellectualism, & equality
military + & real religion
marriage

"Greenleaf"   81

does not like cars and trucks and has already gored the Greenleaf twins' truck. This foreshadows the ending where Mrs. May is lying against the bumper and trunk of the car and is herself gored. The horns penetrate her heart, and she falls over the bull's head, appearing to whisper some kind of last understanding or insight into its ear.

The Christ and religious imagery persists throughout the story. Mr. Greenleaf's face is described as looking like a chalice. Mrs. Greenleaf has her "prayer healings" during which she supplicates herself over clippings of tragedies in the lives of people she does not know and cries out the name of Jesus. The name *Wesley* is an allusion to John Wesley who founded Methodism and lived in SAVANNAH, GEORGIA, where O'Connor was born and spent her early years. Scofield may be an allusion to the Scofield study Bible. Other imagery includes the snake, references to the number seven, lilies, the devil, and judgment.

The final scene of the story parallels Mrs. Greenleaf's "prayer healings" during which she cries out to Jesus to stab her in the heart. What happens to Mrs. Greenleaf through her own method of prayer and devotion happens literally to Mrs. May. Mrs. May's belief has thus far been limited to respecting formal religion but not believing any of it is true. She thought that church was a place where her sons could go to meet some nice girls.

There are several parallels between the Mays and the Greenleafs. Mrs. May runs her farm by herself, but the Greenleaf twins run theirs together as a team. Their black worker says that they never argue. Mrs. May has Mr. and Mrs. Greenleaf as tenant farmers whom she thinks are inferior as employees and human beings. Mr. Greenleaf does not work quickly or efficiently and seems ignorant. Mrs. Greenleaf is a person whom Mrs. May can tolerate even less than her husband. Mrs. May considers Mrs. Greenleaf white trash who keeps her children dirty and does very little work around the house. She thinks that her prayer-healing ceremonies of putting the newspaper clippings in a hole in the ground and then wallowing and praying over them is the action of a crazy woman.

The sons of both families provide the most striking contrast between them. Mrs. May's sons,

Wesley and Scofield, do not help her around the farm. She thinks that they are ungrateful, and they appear to be. Wesley is a college professor and an intellectual. Scofield sells insurance to black families. Mrs. May thinks this work is beneath him. She is jealous of the success of the Greenfield twins, O. T. and E. T. Both of them went into the military in World War II, married French wives, and came back to the States and took advantage of the G.I. bill to get an education and build brick homes. When Mrs. May goes to their dairy farm to let them know about their bull and what she plans to do with it on her property, she looks inside their modern milk parlor. Unlike what she expects from observing Mrs. Greenleaf's dirty housekeeping, she finds the milk parlor spotless and radiantly white under bright light. It puts anything she has on her farm or could hope to have, to shame.

At one point Mrs. May admits to her own sons that she would rather have the ambitious Greenleaf sons than her own. Speaking this wish out loud makes her realize that it is so, and she breaks down crying. The Greenleaf boys grew up on her farm beside her own sons and have made so much more of themselves and their opportunities. Wesley had a bad heart that kept him from joining the army, but Scofield had served for two years. The Greenleafs became sergeants, but Scofield never made it beyond private first class. Mr. Greenleaf, now with something to boast about as he worked for Mrs. May, does not waste the opportunity to point out his sons' rank.

Finding religion to prepare for death

The ending of the story is ambiguous as to whether Mrs. May accepted the act of violence that took her life as a revelation. The narrator says that she had the expression of someone whose sight has been restored but finds the brightness of the light unbearable. Her whispering into the bull's ear could be words of acceptance, more complaints, or a dying wish or prayer.

CHARACTERS

Mrs. May   O'Connor once wrote to Elizabeth Hester that she did not know why a character like Mrs. May had to die; she just knew that she did. Like Mrs. Hopewell in "Good Country People," Mrs. May runs a farm by herself, with an "iron hand" as her friends say. Mrs. May has two sons living on the farm, however, who are no help to her at all. O'Connor likes the strong women who run farms, but she frequently writes of them as territorial, proud, opinionated, judgmental, and lacking in compassion.

Mrs. May is described as a small woman who is nearsighted and who wears her hair on top of her head like the crest of a disturbed bird. She has worked hard for 15 years and is becoming tired. Her sons are ungrateful, and her employees tolerate her condescension toward them. Perhaps one way to interpret her name is that Mrs. May is a person of possibility, even at the end of the story. She may or may not have been redeemed by the flash of light or inspiration that she sees as the bull charges her. Perhaps her claim to her sons that they will find out what Reality is when it is too late is another of the story's many foreshadowings. As a nearsighted person, perhaps Mrs. May's vision of Reality at being gored by the bull brings an awareness that it is she who has needed an awakening.

RELATED LETTERS

Betty Hester ("A"), January 13, 1956 (HB 129); Betty Hester ("A"), February 11, 1956 (CW 986); Betty Hester ("A"), March 10, 1956 (HB 146); Elizabeth McKee, March 15, 1956 (HB 146); Betty Hester ("A"), March 24, 1956 (CW 989–990); Elizabeth Fenwick Way, November 24, 1956 (HB 181); Betty Hester ("A"), November 29, 1956 (HB 182); Betty Hester ("A"), December 28, 1956 (HB 191); Sally and Robert Fitzgerald, January 1, 1957 (HB 192); Maryat Lee, March 10, 1957 (HB 209); Cecil Dawkins, November 5, 1963 (HB 546); Elizabeth McKee, May 7, 1954 (HB 575); Robert Giroux, June 28, 1964 (HB 589). *Pages*: HB: 129, 146, 181–182, 191–192, 209, 546, 575, 589; CW: 986, 989–990.

FURTHER READING

Asals, Frederick. "The Mythic Dimensions of Flannery O'Connor's 'Greenleaf.'" *Studies in Short Fiction* 5 (1968): 137–130.

Askin, Denise T. "Anagogical Vision and Comedic Form in Flannery O'Connor: The Reasonable Use of Unreasonable." *Renascence: Essays on Values in Literature* 57, no. 1 (Fall 2004): 47–62.

Coulthard, A. R. "Flannery O'Connor's Deadly Conversion." *The Flannery O'Connor Bulletin* 13 (1984): 87–98.

Giannone, Richard. "'Greenleaf': A Story of Lent," *Studies in Short Fiction* 22, no. 4 (Fall 1985): 421–429.

Gidden, Nancy Ann. "Classical Agents of Christian Grace in Flannery O'Connor's 'Greenleaf.'" *Studies in Short Fiction* 23, no. 2 (Spring 1986): 201–202.

Perry, Keith. "Straining the Soup Necessarily Thinner: Flannery O'Connor's 'Greenleaf' and Proverbs 11:28." *English Language Notes* 42, no. 2 (December 2004): 56–59.

Rout, Kathleen. "Dream a Little Dream of Me: Mrs. May and the Bull in Flannery O'Connor's 'Greenleaf.'" *Studies in Short Fiction* 16 (1979): 233–235.

Sexton, Mark S. "'Blessed Insurance': An Examination of Flannery O'Connor's 'Greenleaf.'" *The Flannery O'Connor Bulletin* 19 (1990): 38–43.

Shields, John C. "Flannery O'Connor's 'Greenleaf' and the Myth of Europa and the Bull." *Studies in Short Fiction* 18, no. 4 (Fall 1981): 421–431.

Smith, Peter A. "Flannery O'Connor's Empowered Women." *Southern Literary Journal* 26, no. 2 (Spring 1994): 35–47.

Walker, Sue. "Spelling Out Illness: Lupus as Metaphor in Flannery O'Connor's 'Greenleaf.'" *Chattahoochee Review* 12, no. 1 (Fall 1991): 54–63.

"Introduction" to A Memoir of Mary Ann (1961)

This essay was written in response to a request by Sister Evangelista, Superior of Our Lady of Perpetual Help Cancer Home in ATLANTA, GEORGIA, and was first published as part of *A Memoir of Mary Ann* by Farrar, Straus and Cudahy in 1961. Mary Ann was a young girl for whom the nuns had cared and who became an inspiration to many of them. She had suffered with a disfiguring facial tumor and had lost one eye. She lived with the nuns for nine of her 12 years. At first, Sister Evangelista asked O'Connor to write the memoir from the nuns' memories and notes. The author refused, but suggested that the nuns write it themselves since they knew Mary Ann, and she offered editorial help and an introduction to the memoir. O'Connor never expected to see the project in manuscript form, much less published. She even bet Sister Evangelista two PEACOCKS from her beloved flock that the book would never make it into print.

However, on January 23, 1961, Robert Giroux informed her that Farrar, Straus and Cudahy was going to publish the book. O'Connor honored her wager with the nuns and gave them two peacocks. In return for her help, the nuns gave O'Connor a used television set, which she enjoyed more than she or anyone else expected. The essay was later collected in an anthology of her nonfiction prose, *Mystery and Manners: Occasional Prose,* edited by Sally and Robert Fitzgerald (FSG, 1969).

SYNOPSIS

O'Connor writes that adults who write tales about pious children often get it wrong. The adults may misplace virtue for what only seems to be common sense to the child. She was never interested in reading about boys pretending to be priests or girls pretending to be nuns or even Protestant children who did not have the accoutrements of Catholic ritual but were thought to bring a ray of light in the world.

Against this backdrop arrived a letter in 1960 to O'Connor from Sister Evangelista, Sister Superior of Our Lady of Perpetual Help Free Cancer Home in Atlanta. The letter told about Mary Ann, a three-year-old who came to the home as a patient in 1949. She lived there until she was 12 years old and impressed all of the nuns with her courageous spirit. Her condition was GROTESQUE—she had been born with a tumor on the side of her face, and she was missing an eye. Sister Evangelista claimed that after meeting Mary Ann, one forgot her abnormalities and simply focused on her personality and the happiness that one felt in her presence. She requested that Flannery O'Connor help the nuns write the story of this little girl who had touched them so much.

O'Connor thought immediately, no.

The nun mentioned that others volunteered to write Mary Ann's story, but that the nuns wanted to be sure that they did not get a sentimental story.

They wanted Mary Ann to be portrayed truthfully. The writing, however, need not be nonfiction. It could be a novel with other characters in which Mary Ann played the central role.

O'Connor thought a novel was a horrible idea.

The author was invited to write the story of Mary Ann and to come to Atlanta to visit the home and soak up the atmosphere.

O'Connor writes that it is hard sometimes to explain that a professional writer cannot write just anything. She did not believe she could write Mary Ann's story. She looked again at a photo of Mary Ann in her First Communion dress, sitting on a bench. One side of her face looked completely happy; the other was disfigured. O'Connor looked at the photo longer than she thought she would.

She got up and took a book off her shelf. The photo had reminded her of NATHANIEL HAWTHORNE's story "The Birthmark." Coincidentally, Hawthorne's daughter Rose had founded the Dominican Congregation to which the nuns who had taken care of Mary Ann belonged. She read a passage from the story ending in "You cannot love what shocks you!" (qtd. in MM 216).

The passage and the photo convinced O'Connor that Mary Ann's story should be told factually, not as fiction. She wrote back that they should write the story themselves since they were the ones who knew and loved Mary Ann. She did offer to help them with editing and preparing the manuscript should they ever finish one. She sent off her response, never expecting to hear from the nuns about the matter again.

She writes of Hawthorne's *Our Old Home,* in which a gentleman is coaxed to pick up a horrible-looking child who was so ill that it was difficult to discern the child's gender. He writes of the man's struggle over his natural sense of reserve and repulsion at the child but of his final act of holding the child closely like a father.

O'Connor informs the reader that this gentleman was Hawthorne himself as was recorded in his notebooks, published by his wife after his death. She includes the notebook passage in the essay. Then she tells the reader that Rose Hawthorne, or Mother Alphonsa as she was known in her religious vocation, once said that these words of her father—telling of his being chosen by an ill child to be a father figure and of his eventual succumbing to the attentions of the child to hold him—were the most beautiful words her father had ever written.

Rose Hawthorne Lathrop, according to O'Connor, found much of what her father sought in life. She did not have his reserve but instead charged forward with warmth and compassion in the active help of those in need. Years after becoming a Catholic, she saw the plight of poor children with cancer in New York. They were not cared for at all, and they were essentially left to die. She moved to a tenement and started to take in these incurable child patients. An artist, Alice Huber, joined her efforts, and in time other women did as well. The group became the Dominican Order of the Servants of Relief for Incurable Cancer with seven free homes for children with cancer across the country at the time of O'Connor's writing.

She provides a passage of Mother Alphonsa's account of a troublesome boy who had lived for a time at the tenement while his grandmother was there temporarily as a patient. At the end of the passage, O'Connor writes that she congratulated herself on turning the task of writing about Mary Ann back to the nuns. They would probably have neither the writing ability nor the time to put the story together.

A manuscript, however, did arrive. The writing was flawed in many ways, but somehow O'Connor saw that the nuns had conveyed the power of Mary Ann's brief life. She saw that the story was incomplete and compared this to the unfinished nature of Mary Ann's own face. The little girl had been given six months to live when she came to the home, but there she was raised by 17 nuns and lived to be 12 years old. Death is a common theme in literature, but this was the story of the death of a little girl. She had been preparing for death rather than for life but in doing so had lived all the more vibrantly with parties and dogs and Coca-Cola and children who came to visit her.

O'Connor resisted the temptation to cut out some material about so many of Mary Ann's pious actions while living at the home, at least partly because she had nothing better to suggest be put in their place. She suggested that some of the nuns

come to MILLEDGEVILLE to discuss the manuscript. While they were there, she mentioned that Mary Ann probably had no other recourse during her life than to be a good child. At that, Sister Evangelista looked at her closely and informed her that they have had many "demons" in the form of poorly behaved children at the home. Mary Ann was special.

The nuns had read up on O'Connor since they last corresponded. They asked her why she wrote about so many grotesque characters, leaving O'Connor on the spot until another guest mentioned that this is exactly the kind of people with whom the nuns work as well. This incident made O'Connor think again about the nature of the grotesque in good and evil. It is not only evil but also good that is grotesque, an incomplete work in progress.

When Bishop Hyland gave the homily at Mary Ann's funeral, he said that many people might ask why Mary Ann had to die. O'Connor writes that he must have been thinking of her family and those who knew her personally. The larger question that others outside her world would think of was why she had been born.

It is commonplace to point to the suffering of children as a reason to deny the existence of God. Hawthorne's Alymers from "The Birthmark" have grown in number. Characters like Karamazov and writers like Camus cannot believe in God because of the suffering they witness. O'Connor says that this reaction is the result of an improvement in sensitivity at the cost of vision. Those who felt less in times past saw much more with their eyes of faith. Without faith, decisions are made by feeling alone. When the reason for these tender feelings is removed, it results in fear, and fear can cause terrible consequences such as gas chambers and forced-labor camps.

Though these thoughts seem far away from the story of Mary Ann, O'Connor writes, she cannot think of the little girl without also thinking of Nathaniel Hawthorne, who was so afraid of the ice in his blood, his natural sense of reserve. She sees a direct link from Hawthorne and his search and small act of charity with the child at the Liverpool workhouse through his daughter Rose who founded the order of nuns who treated poor cancer patients through the nuns who cared for Mary Ann and through Mary Ann herself. Hawthorne's small act of charity started something that resulted in Mary Ann's knowing what her death meant; his search resulted in her flowering.

O'Connor writes that this work of charity growing from person to person and invisibly over time and through generations is called by the church the Communion of Saints. It is a union of what human beings make of their individual states of grotesque or incompleteness. She says that the nuns told her they were concerned that they did not portray Mary Ann as full of life as she was. O'Connor writes that she thinks the sisters have done well and that through their memoir, the reader will clearly see the line that binds so many different kinds of people in Christ.

FURTHER READING

Desmond, John F. "Walker Percy, Flannery O'Connor and The Holocaust." *The Southern Quarterly: A Journal of the Arts in the South* 28, no. 2 (Winter 1990): 35–42.

Niland, Kurt R. "'A Memoir of Mary Ann' and 'Everything That Rises Must Converge.'" *The Flannery O'Connor Bulletin* 22 (1993–94): 53–73.

"Judgement Day" ("Judgment Day") (1965)

This is the ninth and final story that appears in the collection *Everything That Rises Must Converge* (FSG, 1965). [Note: Sally Fitzgerald, editor of the Library of America edition of O'Connor's collected works, believes the title should be spelled "Judgment Day," following one of O'Connor's typescripts, but the story was first printed (in CS) as "Judgement Day."]

SYNOPSIS

T. C. Tanner lives with his daughter in her apartment in New York City, but he means to go home to Corinth, Georgia, as soon as he can. He is saving up his strength for the journey. Yesterday he wrote a note to attach to his clothing, telling whoever may find him if he dies where to ship the body and where to write for the money to do so and to bury him. He has it all planned out. First he will walk, then ride in a taxi, and then a train. He would be home the next day.

His daughter married a Yankee who has a job that takes him away a lot, driving a van. She had come South to bring T. C. to New York to live with her. In Georgia, he lived in a shack with a black man named Coleman Parrum. A man named Doctor Foley bought the land on which the shack was, and when visiting one day, he asked the men to keep running the still on the place, but for him. If they refused, they would have to pack up and leave. Tanner says that he will not work for a black man.

Tanner's daughter tells him that part of his trouble is that he keeps sitting in a chair by the window, doing nothing but looking out the window. She does not want to hear his stories of damnation and judgment, either. She does not believe. At least at the shack where he would have to work for the black man, he could put his feet on the ground and breathe fresh air. His daughter lived high up in a pigeon hutch with lots of other people.

Tanner had watched people from the next apartment move out and other people move in. The new neighbor was black. Tanner called him Preacher and asked him if he might know somewhere nearby where the two of them could go fishing. The man became angry and said that he was no preacher from Alabama; he was an actor from New York. After enough of this talk on another occasion, the man slammed Tanner's head against the wall, and he had a stroke. The government check on which he had been depending to go home had to be used to pay his doctor bills.

Soon Tanner realized that he would not be going home. He at least wanted his daughter to send him home to be buried. He would go home in a coffin and jump out and shout "Judgment Day!" when Coleman came to get him.

His daughter goes to the store. He tells her that he is sorry that he became ill and that it is probably not so bad in this part of the country. She sits down for a moment and tells him that it is nice to have him speak pleasantly sometimes. She says she would not have her daddy be anywhere else than right with her. Tanner grows more impatient for her to leave.

When she leaves for the store, he plans his move. He makes his way out of the apartment and toward the top of the stairs. About halfway there, his legs give out. He falls forward and grabs the banister. Then he looks down the steep dark steps. Suddenly, he dives down them, landing about halfway. He begins to imagine the coffin box and Coleman finding him.

Instead of Coleman hanging over him, though, it is the black actor. He has a woman with him. Tanner calls for Coleman and says "Judgment Day!" just as he had planned, but the actor is sarcastic and says it just might be his judgment day. When the daughter finds her father, he has his hat over his face, and his head slammed between the railings of the banister, as though in the stocks. When the police arrive, they tell her that he has already been dead an hour.

She buries him in New York but finds that she cannot sleep. She has the body exhumed and sent to Corinth, and after that, she sleeps better and her general appearance improves.

COMMENTARY

This story is a revision of "The Geranium," which was the title story of O'Connor's 1947 thesis for the master of fine arts at the UNIVERSITY OF IOWA. The author worked off and on, composing different versions of the story until her death in 1963. A middle version was titled "An Exile in the East" and was published posthumously in *South Carolina Review* in November 1978.

The version discussed here is published in *Complete Works* (Library of America, 1988) and is considered the final revision. The text is taken from the carbon copies of her typescript which O'Connor was going over after obtaining comments from Catharine Carver weeks before her death. The final stages of her illness finally made her too weak to work any further. The latest revisions included changing the spelling of *Judgement* to *Judgment*. Readers looking for a consideration of O'Connor's attitudes about the subject of race may find study of this story's development over time informative.

T. C. Tanner has evolved from Old Dudley in "The Geranium" to be a similar old man but with more will to assert a change in his own destiny. Rather than sit idly by watching for the geranium to appear on the windowsill across the alley as Old Dudley does, T. C. Tanner is planning his escape from New York. He is terrified of dying in the city; he overheard his daughter telling his son-in-law that she has purchased a lot and will bury him in New York, even though she had promised her father she would take his body back South.

T. C. Tanner also acknowledges his relationship with black people more than Old Dudley does. He and Coleman built a shack together on land he knows is owned by a man who is at least part black, Foley. They ran a still, and when Foley tells them either to run the still for him or leave the premises, Tanner told him he had a daughter in the North and did not, as a white man, have to work for a black man. Later in the story, however, Tanner admits that he would rather have done that than to live with nothing to do in his daughter's apartment. Tanner keeps talking to his daughter about the coming Judgment. She is not a believer and finds his talk tiresome.

Unlike the black man in "The Geranium," the man who moves next door in "Judgment Day" is an actor who is very unkind. He resents Tanner's condescending attitudes and assumptions—that since he is a well-dressed black man, he must be a preacher from Alabama. Instead of helping the old man on the stairs, this neighbor grabs him by the shoulders and tells him that he does not take any flack from anyone, much less from a redneck. He throws him against the wall. This first gesture is the sign that this man is violent indeed, even perhaps capable of murder.

Readers may wonder who is judging whom in the story. Tanner has judged his situation of moving to the city with his daughter to be the wrong outcome for the last years of his life. Tanner misjudges the black man next door to be someone like Coleman who understands certain codes and relationships that existed between friendly blacks and whites in the South. Tanner warns his daughter of Judgment Day and jokes in his daydreams about shipping his body to Corinth and jumping up to his friends when they open the coffin and shouting, "Judgment Day!"

Tanner's appearance in death as though he were in the stocks is intriguing. One interpretation is that Tanner was imprisoned in his daughter's apartment. Another kind of imprisonment is that of his own making—his ignorance and pride in relation to people with dark skin. Still another interpretation is that he has been punished as the result of the judgment of the actor who represents a cold-hearted but real society at large.

Of course, there are two eventual judgment days in the story. One occurs when Tanner is killed by being shoved through the banister rails and left there after he has confused the actor for Coleman and annoyed the neighbor one too many times. Tanner's confused request to the "preacher" to help him up may be a sign that he has at last accepted the actor as an equal. However, Tanner may only be asking for help when he thinks he needs it, as he did with his daughter, and that he has not had a genuine change of heart.

The other judgment day might refer to Tanner's daughter's. When she finds that she cannot sleep after having her father buried in New York, she exhumes the body and ships it back to Corinth, thus avoiding the harsh judgment of the God in whom she claims she does not believe. Perhaps important to her belief system, the judgment of her conscience will now be clear that she has done her duty by her father and deserves a good night's sleep.

CHARACTERS

T. C. Tanner   A tanner is a trade worker who works skins into leather, so it is perhaps an appropriate name for the old white man who views individual blacks whom he has come to know, such as Coleman, differently than blacks as a whole. Tanner and Coleman are close friends, yet when Tanner tries to communicate with the black actor who moves in next to his daughter, he sees this man as a member of a group rather than as an individual. In a sense, Tanner "tans" all blacks—Coleman, Foley, and the New York actor—with the same broad brush. Rather than see them as individuals, he maintains certain expectations that match only his relationship with Coleman.

RELATED LETTERS

Robert Giroux, May 21, 1964 (HB 579–580); Catherine Carver, June 17, 1964 (HB 585); Catherine Carver, June 27, 1964 (HB 588); Robert Giroux, June 28, 1964 (HB 589); Catherine Carver, July 15, 1964 (HB 593); Betty Hester ("A"), July 17, 1964 (HB 594). HB *pages:* 579–580, 585, 588–589, 593–594.

FURTHER READING

Darretta, John L. "From 'The Geranium' to 'Judgement Day': Retribution in the Fiction of Flannery O'Connor." In *Since Flannery O'Connor: Essays on the Contemporary American Short Story,* edited by Loren Logsdon and Charles W. Meyer, 21–31. Macomb: Western Illinois University, 1987.

Fowler, Doreen. "Writing and Re-Writing Race: Flannery O'Connor's 'The Geranium' and 'Judgement Day.'" *Flannery O'Connor Review* 2 (2003–04): 31–39.

Napier, James J. "Flannery O'Connor's Last Three: 'The Sense of an Ending.'" *Southern Literary Journal* 14, no. 2 (Spring 1982): 19–27.

Nisly, Paul W. "Wart Hogs From Hell: The Demonic and the Holy in Flannery O'Connor's Fiction." *Ball State University Forum* 22, no. 3 (1981): 45–50.

Whitt, Margaret. "Letters to Corinth: Echoes From Greece to Georgia in O'Connor's Judgement Day." In *Flannery O'Connor and the Christian Mystery,* edited by John J. Murphy, et al., 61–74. Provo, Utah: Center for the Study of Christian Values in Literature, Brigham Young University, 1997.

"King of the Birds, The" (1961)

This essay was originally published under the title "Living with a Peacock," with one paragraph deleted, in the September 1961 issue of HOLIDAY. Along with the article appeared a picture of "Limpy," one member of the author's large flock of PEACOCKS, complete with a four-foot display of tail feathers in full array. O'Connor was unhappy both with the changed title to her piece, which she called "stupid" (qtd. in *Collected,* 1261) as well as with an omitted paragraph, which described the photographing process mentioned early in the essay in more detail.

The essay was reprinted under its original title in *Mystery and Manners: Occasional Prose* (Farrar, Straus and Giroux, 1970). Since the original typescript of the completed essay is missing, for *Collected Works*, the essay was reprinted under its original title but with the omitted paragraph taken from draft material and included in the notes.

SYNOPSIS

O'Connor first relates the story of teaching a chicken to walk backward at the age of five. Pathé News of New York sent a photographer to SAVANNAH, GEORGIA, to capture the feat of the Cochin Bantam walking forward and back, and the news of it spread across the country by newsreel. The writer says she mentions this at the beginning of her article about peacocks because from that moment on she began her fascination with fowl. She started collecting chickens with a passion. She made clothes for them and marveled at pictures of them in books. Whatever she was looking for in collecting chickens way back then, however, she found many years later when she started her flock of peacocks.

In the meantime, she had collected exotic fowl of various kinds from turkeys to quail to geese, pheasants, Japanese silk bantams, mallard ducks, and more. One day the Florida *Market Bulletin* advertised peafowl, and for some reason after seeing many similar ads, she told her mother she was going to order a peacock, a hen, and four young ones called peabiddies. When they first arrived by train from Eustis, Florida, that October, she could not stop looking at the birds but put them in a pen as she was instructed by the seller. The male did not have its enormous tail feathers at that time because these are shed during the summer and are not regrown in full until December.

The essay describes the growing pattern of peabiddies into mature birds. It takes two years for a young peacock to develop the pattern of suns in its magnificent tail. The best way to observe a peacock that is ready to fan its feathers is to wait. It will lift them but turn away from most watchers until it decides to face around. Observers who try to see the tail from the front by moving around the bird

will be met with disappointment as the bird turns in likewise motion away from them. When it is ready, or so it seems to O'Connor, the peacock will turn toward an observer so that its magnificent pattern of feathers will be visible.

The essay relates stories of various visitors to the farm, such as a telephone lineman who wanted the bird to show its display on command, and this it will not do. Some visitors were impressed with the plumage; others wanted to know what use the bird was in practical terms. The phone lineman, for instance, after stopping his truck to see the plumage finally arrayed before he left, seemed miffed at the arrogance of the bird and commented on its scrawny legs. Another visitor, an old man with five or six children who had driven up in a car to buy a calf, had a very different reaction. When he spied the bird, even with its tail folded, he removed his hat out of respect and commented that he had not seen one since his grandfather's time and that people used to keep them but did not so much anymore. When one of the children asked what it was, he announced, "Churren, that's the king of the birds" (*Collected* 837).

According to O'Connor's observations of her flock, the peahen need not be present for the peacock to display its feathers, and he will also attempt to raise his tail when surprised, brushed by a breeze, or for seemingly no reason at all. The peacock has a favorite place in the yard where it likes best to strut, which it will do in the spring and summer soon after breakfast until the day becomes too hot and then again in the late afternoon. The male often raises its voice in a shriek at the same time it raises its tail; the female's noise is more like a mule. The calls go back and forth during the night. O'Connor's birds roosted on the roof of the barn, the cedar trees, a fence post, and elsewhere, and much to her mother's chagrin, they ate flowers.

Regina O'Connor tolerated the birds, but that was about all. They ate her flowers and the fruit from her fig trees and made noises all day and night. She put a two-foot high wire fence around all of her flower beds, convinced they would not have sense enough to jump over it. A man selling fence posts visited them and stated he once had 80 peafowl on his farm. They made such a racket that his grandmother said either they had to go or she would. The woman was 85. O'Connor asked him which went, and he said that he still had 20 of the peafowl in his freezer. When she asked how they tasted, he said no better than chicken but that he would rather eat them than listen to them.

Despite her family and neighbors' annoyance and protests and the cost and bother of maintaining the birds, the author says she will hold onto her flock. The essay concludes with a recurring dream. She dreams she is a five-year-old peacock laid on a table for a celebratory feast, ready to be devoured by a photographer visiting from New York. She screams for help and wakes up, hearing the chorus of her flock in the night. She will keep her birds and let them multiply since she believes they will have the last word.

"Lame Shall Enter First, The" (1962)

The sixth story in the collection *Everything That Rises Must Converge* (FSG, 1965), it was first published in the SEWANEE REVIEW in summer 1962 (vol. 70).

SYNOPSIS

Sheppard tells his 10-year-old son, Norton, about a troubled boy named Rufus Johnson, age 14. Sheppard asks his son if he knows what it is like to share. Sheppard tells Norton that he gave Rufus a key to their house after he left the reformatory and told him he could have a place to stay there if he ever wanted it. Sheppard works as the city recreational director and spends Saturdays at the reformatory as a counselor. Johnson was both the smartest and most underprivileged boy with whom he had ever worked.

Sheppard is not getting too far with trying to create pity in Norton for Rufus. When Sheppard tells him that Johnson's mother is in the penitentiary, Norton cries and speaks about his own mother, how at least if she were in a penitentiary, he could go visit her. She has been dead for more than a year.

Rufus arrives at the house on a day when Norton is home sick alone. The boy tells Rufus that his father will be glad to see him, that he will get a new shoe for his club foot because he has been eating out of garbage cans. Johnson talks to Norton about Norton's father and how he talks too much.

Sheppard is glad to see Rufus when he gets home; he invites him to stay for a few days. Norton keeps speaking up about the things Rufus said about him, but Sheppard keeps trying to win over the boy. Finally, he leaves to bring home dinner, and Rufus asks Norton how he puts up with him; he thinks he is Jesus, Rufus says.

Sheppard debates the existence of hell with Rufus, and Rufus tells him that those who deny hell deny Jesus. The dead go there and burn forever, Rufus says. Suddenly, Norton asks his father if that is where his dead mother is, burning in hell. Sheppard tells him that she is not unhappy because she is not anywhere. It is hard for him to understand that Norton seems to want his mother to be in hell rather than nowhere. Johnson asks Norton if his mother believed in Jesus, and he says yes. Sheppard says no. Johnson says that if she believed in Jesus, then she is saved.

One day Johnson is picked up by the police for allegedly committing a crime. The incident makes Sheppard feel terribly guilty, and he tries to win back the boy's confidence. He gets him the new shoe, buys a microscope, and watches him as he reads through the encyclopedia. When he needs to go to a meeting one night, he takes the boys to a movie to pass the time. When he comes out of the meeting, a police car pulls up. They accuse Rufus again of more vandalism. Sheppard sticks up for him this time, telling them they were wrong before.

In another incident, the police blame Rufus because of his club foot. Sheppard vouches for him again, saying that he was there with him all along this time. Rufus tells him that he slipped out but that there were no witnesses. He tells him that Sheppard pretends to have a lot of confidence in him, but when things heat up, he folds like everyone else. Sheppard insists that he is going to save Johnson; he is still resolved. Rufus admits to the other crimes. He tells Sheppard to save himself; no one can save him but Jesus.

grotesque → Rufus

Soon Sheppard sees Rufus reading with Norton and asks what it is. Rufus tells him that it is a Bible they stole from a 10-cent store. He says that he alone stole it; Norton only watched because he cannot dirty his soul. Johnson is going to hell anyway, he says, unless he repents. He says that if he does repent, he may as well go all the way and become a preacher. Norton calls for him to repent, and Sheppard grows angry.

Sheppard tells Rufus to put the Bible away. He says that Rufus does not believe in it. Rufus says that Sheppard does not know what he believes. Rufus tears out a page and begins to eat it. Even if he does not believe it, he says, it is still true.

Rufus leaves, and Sheppard is alone with Norton. Norton looks through the telescope upstairs and suddenly cries out that he found his mother. He says that she is there, waving at him. Sheppard says that he is just seeing stars; there is nothing there but stars. Norton is waving wildly up at the sky.

After the police bring Rufus home again, Sheppard finally realizes that he has done more for Rufus than he has for his own child. He knows now that he filled his own emptiness over losing his wife with good works at the expense of Norton. He runs upstairs, thinking that he has discovered something important, that he has years now to make it up to Norton, and this makes him happy.

When he reaches Norton's room, he climbs to the attic. Unfortunately, the boy is not where he expects him to be. The tripod to the telescope has fallen over. Hanging over it from a beam is the boy, on his way to join his mother in the stars.

COMMENTARY *Starling*

This story is another that is frequently anthologized in college texts and elsewhere. It is also another of O'Connor's stories that deals with O'Connor's preoccupation with good works done by misguided people. Without faith, even good works are useless and have no fertile soil from which to grow.

Sheppard and his son are having trouble adjusting after the death of Sheppard's wife and Norton's mother. Sheppard eats cereal out of the box in the kitchen while he allows Norton to eat stale chocolate cake with ketchup for breakfast. Sheppard works full-time and adds Saturdays to his work

schedule, plus coaching a Little League team rather than spending more time with his son now that his wife is gone. He avoids dealing with Norton's intense feelings of grief as well as his own by being busier than ever under the excuse of helping others. The situation is getting worse as the story opens.

Sheppard asks Norton what he is going to do that day rather than suggest they do something together. He watches him eat the cake and then harasses him about the boy's intentions to sell seeds to try to win a prize of $1,000. He asks the boy whether it would not be better to spend his time caring for others or to spend the money that he might win on something helpful, like getting Rufus Johnson, who has a clubbed foot, a new shoe. This harassment brings Norton to tears, and he suffers at his father's torments to the point of getting sick. Norton is only 10 years old and in need of much help and attention. Steeped in his own grief, Sheppard does not see that he needs to help not others but himself and own son. *don't avoid the prob*

In his grief, Sheppard thinks doing good works for those outside the family will fill up the emptiness left within the family. He misunderstands Norton's great pain and instead thinks Norton is selfish. He turns instead to Rufus Johnson, whom he sees as an intelligent teenager who needs help. This is true, but just like Star Drake in "The Comforts of Home," sometimes the help that is needed exceeds the skills of the person who is willing to give it.

Though Sheppard is a trained counselor, he becomes just as selfish as Norton in his work with Rufus Johnson. Sheppard is greedy for success in turning the boy's life around by focusing on the teen's high IQ. He thinks that if Johnson is smart, he will be able to reach the boy and change him. He thinks that change in life is possible by appealing to the boy's intellect and showing him care and concern. The story is full of irony as it reveals that Sheppard is dead wrong. Most ironic of all, Rufus Johnson himself shows this to Sheppard and guides Norton to search for spirituality.

Sheppard equates intelligence with faith in terms of what has the power to control and guide one's life. When Rufus tells him that he is under the power of the devil, Sheppard answers that they are in the space age and that Rufus is too intelligent to buy into that phoniness. Instead of thinking that with faith anything is possible, Sheppard thinks the same of intelligence. Oddly, Sheppard has the arrogance to tell Rufus that he can explain the boy to himself. Clearly, Sheppard is wrong in the way he deals with both boys.

The father's misguided actions become more obvious on rereadings of the story. Norton hides in the closet, for example, yet his father does not see and sympathize with his son's fear at Johnson's sudden appearance in their house. Norton is supposed to accept the delinquent stranger, not only as a visitor but as a houseguest. Sheppard welcomes Johnson with open arms and offers him a home, even after Norton tells him that this boy has run through his mother's things with great disrespect and called Sheppard names.

Sheppard whips Norton in anger, even though he normally does not believe in such behavior by parents. He does this when Norton objects to Johnson staying in, of all places, his mother's bedroom. Sheppard prefers Johnson's intelligence to Norton's apparent lack of curiosity. Overall, Sheppard seems to wish that he had Johnson for a son rather than Norton. When he thinks that Johnson is being grateful, he even calls Johnson son but does not cross the hall to Norton when Norton calls to him. The next day Sheppard takes Johnson to get his new shoe but leaves Norton at home so that he can focus entirely on Johnson's reactions. Perhaps his trouble with Norton is that the boy reminds him too much of his wife. Norton's apparent selfishness is really the consuming sense of grief that both of them feel and that neither of them has handled.

Unlike the lame Rufus, the one who is metaphorically lame and "enters first" is actually Norton. Norton looks at his father "lamely" and "blindly." He has other subtle signs of being lame as well—his drifting eye, his upset emotional state. Norton is more lame than Rufus because he came from a good life, which has degenerated to a spiritually poor one. Rufus teaches Norton what Sheppard cannot because he lacks faith—that there is a Jesus and there is a devil. Sheppard says several times that he will not allow Rufus's belligerence to stop him from saving him. Sheppard continually says that he will save the boy, and Rufus tells Norton that the man thinks that he is Jesus. Even Rufus knows that only belief in Jesus can save.

At one point, Sheppard says to Rufus, "The good will triumph" (CS 474), and Rufus replies, "Not when it ain't true . . . not when it ain't right" (CS 474). This exchange, perhaps, best sums up a major theme of the story.

CHARACTERS

Sheppard Sheppard has a sensitive pink face and white hair that stands up like a halo around his head. His eyes are intense blue. His name implies a Christian connection to Jesus as the shepherd of a flock, but Sheppard does not believe in God or Jesus. He is the city recreational director, and on Saturdays he works at the reformatory as a counselor. He is fascinated with technology. His wife died more than a year ago. When she was alive, they used to eat outdoors often, even having breakfast out on the grass.

Sheppard is a character similar to Rayber in *The Violent Bear It Away* in that he tries to reform the wayward adolescent, Rufus Johnson (Tarwater), while at the same time keeping hold over his son, Norton (Bishop).

Norton Norton is a stocky boy of 10. His father thinks that he will be a banker or the administrator of a small loan company because he sees those as selfish professions and he thinks Norton is selfish. Norton has very large round ears that seem to pull his eyes too far apart on his face. As the story opens, he wears a faded green shirt with a cowboy across the front of it. His eyes are a lighter shade of blue than his father's, as though they have faded like his shirt. One of his eyes seems to move to one side.

Norton misses his mother terribly, and his need for her has made him what his father calls selfish. His father thinks that he never noticed Norton being so selfish when his mother was alive. The boy is likely in need of either professional counseling to help him with his grief or at the very least a father who does not leave him alone so much during the week and even on Saturdays.

Rufus Johnson At 14 years old, Johnson has the look of a man when Sheppard first meets him at the reformatory. His eyes are steel gray, and his thin dark hair hangs over one side of his forehead like a man's. His face is bony. His clubbed foot is encased in a heavy black shoe that has a sole four or five inches thick. The shoe is falling apart so much that Johnson's gray sock was hanging out of it the first day Sheppard met him.

Johnson knows, in O'Connor's worldview, something that Sheppard does not, something that he learned from his grandfather—that he, Johnson, is under the power of the devil. In this way, Johnson is wiser than Sheppard and just as smart as Sheppard thinks he is with his high IQ. What is unique, however, is that Johnson not only outsmarts Sheppard in terms of himself and saving him but also in what is wrong with Sheppard's family. He teaches Norton what Norton lacks, though Norton is too young to understand it fully or integrate it with what has happened to his mother. The tragedy occurs because of Sheppard's lack of faith and understanding and because of his neglect of his son. Startling

RELATED LETTERS

Betty Hester ("A"), July 22, 1961 (HB 446); Caroline Gordon Tate, November 16, 1961 (HB 454); John Hawkes, November 28, 1961 (HB 456); Cecil Dawkins, January 10, 1962 (HB 460); John Hawkes, February 6, 1962 (HB 464); Elizabeth McKee, May 28, 1962 (HB 475); Cecil Dawkins, September 6, 1962 (HB 490–491); Betty Hester ("A"), November 3, 1962 (HB 498); Dr. T. R. Spivey, January 27, 1963 (HB 506); Elizabeth McKee, May 7, 1964 (HB 575); Robert Giroux, May 21, 1964 (HB 579). *HB pages:* 446, 454, 456, 460, 464, 475, 490–491, 498, 506, 575, 579.

FURTHER READING

Asals, Frederick. "Flannery O'Connor's 'The Lame Shall Enter First.'" *Mississippi Quarterly: The Journal of Southern Culture* 23 (1970): 103–120.
Asals, Frederick J., Jr. "Hawthorne, Mary Ann, and 'The Lame Shall Enter First.'" *The Flannery O'Connor Bulletin* 2 (1973): 3–18.
Gordon, Sarah. "The News From Afar: A Note on Structure in O'Connor's Narratives." *The Flannery O'Connor Bulletin* 14 (1985): 80–88.
Magistrale, Tony. "O'Connor's 'The Lame Shall Enter First.'" *Explicator* 47, no. 3 (Spring 1989): 58–61.

"Late Encounter with the Enemy, A" (1953)

Originally published in *HARPER'S BAZAAR* in September 1953 (vol. 87), this is the eighth story out of 10 in the collection *A Good Man Is Hard to Find and Other Stories.*

SYNOPSIS

General Tennessee Flintrock Sash is 104 and lives with his 62-year-old granddaughter, Sally Poker Sash. Sally prays each night that her grandfather will live long enough to attend her college graduation. It has taken her 20 years of summer school to finish her degree. She was a teacher who did not have a degree when she began to work so many years before. She is less certain that her grandfather will make it to her graduation than he is.

Her desire to have him there was to show all of the current generation what background and history she has behind her. For the 20 years that she has spent in summer school, she has always returned to her own class in the fall and taught exactly the same way she always has. She wants to show everyone that old traditions are not forgotten. For his part, General Sash agrees to go to the ceremony but only if he can sit on the stage in his wheelchair where he can be seen. He likes to be seen onstage. He once appeared as a bit of a "prop" at an ATLANTA premiere of a Hollywood movie. Since then he has been "lent" out for similar kinds of occasions.

Sally is to receive a B.S. in elementary education and needs to line up with her class, so she cannot tend to her grandfather at the ceremony. A 10-year-old blond boy named John Wesley agrees to take care of her grandfather and make sure he gets up on the stage properly.

Unfortunately, when Sally sees John Wesley from her place in the procession line, he is at the Coke machine at the side of the auditorium and not with her grandfather. He has left her grandfather out in the sun in his wheelchair. Sally breaks loose from the line and gets Wesley back to the General. Meanwhile, the General is not sure what the procession in black robes is all about. There is something vaguely familiar about it, but he is not sure what. He wishes they would stop going on about the past—the living are alive now.

When the General is introduced, the boy bows for him, and this makes him angry because he thinks he can get up and bow for himself. Soon, however, it is clear that he is mistaken about that. As the graduates cross the stage to receive their diplomas, his memory surfaces and blurs about places like Chickamauga, Shiloh, and Marthasville, as well as his mother and his wife. The black procession still seems fuzzy but familiar.

When Sally crosses the stage to receive her diploma, she takes a look at her grandfather staring into space and holds her head high. When the ceremony ends, she finds her way to her relatives, and they all wait for John Wesley to wheel her grandfather over to them. As it turns out, he had taken him out the back way. As he stood in line for the Coke machine, the corpse sat in the chair.

COMMENTARY

Even the old man in this story acknowledges that the living are alive now and that some old traditions are not always so important. History is not something of great interest to General Tennessee Flintrock Sash. He has lived quite a bit it himself, after all and presumably remembered much of it, at least until he got so old. He is more interested in the celebrations and parades that honor his place in whatever history happened—the trappings of history that give him a place of honor and attention.

The soldier's granddaughter, Sally Poker Sash, herself no young woman at age 62, also neglects to appreciate the real significance of the reason for her graduation ceremony. Like her grandfather, she too is interested in outward appearances. She is proud of her heritage and wants nothing more from her entire 20 years of formal college education than to use the occasion of the graduation ceremony to showcase her family's link to the past. The degree itself, a B.S. in elementary education, appears to mean little to her. She continues to teach the same way each school year, even after taking classes each summer.

Both Sashes—whose name brings to mind the ceremonial sash that crosses over the bodies of soldiers, scouts, and beauty queens in parades—have their own late encounter with an enemy. Sally opposes the progress of education by denying her own education's influence on her daily work, and she epitomizes that by putting her grandfather onstage at the ceremony. It is as though her enemy is change, and she thinks her grandfather demonstrates that one need not change to be important and valued. By his presence at the graduation, Sally protests any need for change, either in southern culture or in the classroom.

General (or more realistically, perhaps, Major) Sash, on the other hand, has his own late encounter. In his mind, while he is onstage he visualizes a man in a black robe attacking him with words. Somewhat like his granddaughter, General Sash is also fighting progress. At more than 100 years old, he fights days of confusion daily, and imagines on this day that he has a black hole in his head. He is likely having a stroke onstage, one that will kill him. His encounter with the enemy, an imagined one to be sure, is met when he is in full uniform and in an honorary position in front of the public. The old man loses this battle, and his position in the wheelchair dead on display mocks those who would hold up old, empty symbols long after they have outlived their real usefulness.

The story is both humorous and tragic; O'Connor presents the South as a region that denys losing the Civil War. What it lost in military defeat, it gained in pride and tradition. However, popular culture, exemplified by the focus on young John Wesley's drinking Coca-Cola, which was invented in ATLANTA and by the Hollywood movie *Gone With the Wind* which premiered in Atlanta, shows that the old traditions are giving way to the new fads. The South, like General Sash and even his granddaughter, is losing many of its real traditions by not evolving with the natural change of events. Those who hold onto the old ways risk being petrified like the old man in his uniform.

When the history behind a symbol loses its value, the symbol itself becomes comic, as it does in this story. O'Connor's strokes of humor include the name John Wesley. Wesley was the founder of Methodism and once lived and preached in SAVANNAH, GEORGIA. The young boy has not learned to value tradition any more than the old man has learned to value history. He is off trying to buy a

Coke when he should be watching over the General. The New South devalues the history and traditions of the Old South, even as it is still charged by its elders with protecting them.

CHARACTERS

General Tennessee Flintrock Sash   The General is a kind of a stage name for Civil War veteran Major George Poker Sash. The stage name is interesting since it names a southern state as well as a common term for toughness and stability in the face of battle. It is doubtful that Sash was a general, and it really does not matter since he does not remember much of what happened to him anyway. The old man's memory has not faded purely from his age but mostly from the little importance he places on what actually happened to him and to the South and his role in those events.

Sally Poker Sash   Sally teaches elementary school and has taught it the same way for many years, despite taking college courses each summer for 20 summers to earn her degree. The degree is simply for show, especially the graduation ceremony where she wants to show off her family's deep heritage in southern history. Like her grandfather, Sally has endured her "war" of struggling to achieve a formal education only to miss its value in her life.

RELATED LETTERS

Elizabeth McKee, August 30, 1952 (HB 42–43); Elizabeth McKee, November 26, 1952 (HB 48); Betty Hester ("A"), May 2, 1956 (mentioning General Tennessee Flintrock Sash), CW, 995. *HB Pages*: 42–43, 48. *CW pages*: 995.

FURTHER READING

Knauer, David J. "A 'Late Encounter' with Poststructuralism." *Mississippi Quarterly: The Journal of Southern Culture* 48, no. 2 (Spring 1995): 277–289.

O'Shea, José Roberto. "Flannery O'Connor and the Grotesque: A Study of 'Late Encounter with the Enemy' and 'Revelation.'" *Estudios Anglo-Americanos* 16 (1992): 81–90.

"Life You Save May Be Your Own, The" (1953)

This short story was originally published in the spring 1953 issue of KENYON REVIEW (vol. 15) and then again in *Prize Stories 1954: The O. HENRY AWARDs*, edited by Paul Engle and Hansford Martin.

SYNOPSIS

An old woman and her daughter sit on their porch as Mr. Tom T. Shiftlet walks down the road toward their house. Without ever seeing him before, the woman decides he is a tramp. He stands just inside their yard and turns to face the sun, lifting one arm and another stump of an arm toward the sky, forming a crooked cross. He says he'd give a fortune to live where he could see such a sunset every evening. He looks over the farm property and rests his attention on the automobile and asks if the ladies drive. They engage in conversation about how things are not as they used to be. He mentions that doctors in ATLANTA have cut into the human heart. In the midst of their talk, Shiftlet asks the woman, "What is a man?" The woman does not answer. A bit later, he remarks that he is a man, even if he is not a whole one.

Mr. Shiftlet announces that there are tools in the box he is carrying, that he is a carpenter by trade. After more questions from Lucynell Crater, the mother, the drifter arranges to work around the place for food, agreeing that he is willing to sleep in the car. He mentions that the monks slept in their coffins, and the woman says that the monks were not as advanced as people are now. The daughter, also named Lucynell, watches Shiftlet work. He fixes several things and even teaches Lucynell, who is deaf and has never said a word, to say the word *bird*.

The mother makes suggestions to entice Shiftlet to become interested in marrying her daughter. She asks him to teach her the word *sugarpie*. When he almost has the car running, he asks her for money to buy a fan belt. She gives him the money, and he gets the car going. Lucynell continues working on him to marry her daughter and have a permanent home with a wife who will not talk back to him. Mr. Shiftlet says that he cannot marry because he has no money to give a wife a proper honeymoon. Lucynell says that her daughter would not know the difference. Her final enticement is to offer him the money to paint the automobile, as he wants very much to do.

The three of them go to town on Saturday, and Shiftlet marries Lucynell. He is unsatisfied with the ceremony in that it was simply paperwork and blood tests. He is not satisfied with the law. He has painted the car dark green with a yellow stripe under the windows. They take the old woman home and pick up a packed lunch for a two-day trip. The mother has paid for the trip. She is sad to see her daughter go; they have never been apart for two days before. Shiftlet and his new wife drive off in the direction of Mobile. He drives fast; he has always wanted a car and never thought he would have one. Lucynell depresses him when he looks at her. She immediately eats the lunch her mother has packed.

They stop at The Hot Spot, an aluminum-painted diner, where Shiftlet orders Lucynell ham and grits. She falls asleep at the counter. Shiftlet tells the boy waiter to give her the food when she wakes up, that he will pay for it now. The boy comments that her sleeping eyes and that pink-gold hair makes her look like an angel of God. Shiftlet tells him that she is a hitchhiker but that he cannot wait to take her on with him; he has to get to Tuscaloosa.

Shiftlet heads back out on the road as a storm is brewing overhead. He keeps seeing signs that say, "Drive carefully. The life you save may be your own." He stops to pick up a hitchhiker, a boy standing by the side of the road. The boy did not have his thumb up for a ride, but he gets in anyway. Assuming that he is running away, Shiftlet speaks to the boy about mothers. Shiftlet says that his mother was an angel of God but that he left her. He becomes emotional thinking about it. The boy grows angry and tells him to go to the devil, that his mother is a flea bag, and that Shiftlet is a pole cat. He flings open the car door and jumps out into a ditch.

Shiftlet is so surprised that he drives on for another hundred feet with the passenger car door open. He is more depressed than ever about the rotten state of the world. He prays that the Lord may wash the slime from the earth. Behind him, a turnip-shaped cloud descends until thunder and large raindrops splash onto the back of Shiftlet's car. He steps

on the gas with the stump of his arm out the window and races the oncoming shower into Mobile.

COMMENTARY

This story was anthologized in *The Complete Stories* (FSG, 1971) and *Collected Works* (Library of America, 1988). In 1955, the opening scene of the story was dramatized by NBC-TV on *Galley-Proof*, with narration by Harvey Breit, who also interviewed O'Connor. The next year, O'Connor sold the television rights to General Electric for its *General Electric Playhouse,* and with the money they paid her, she bought herself and her mother a new refrigerator. In her letters during the production process, she writes about names she has heard suggested for playing the role of Mr. Shiftlet—she once heard it would be Ronald Reagan, then tap dancer Gene Kelly. In regard to the latter, she joked that perhaps the producers would turn the story into a musical.

The title of the story comes from a public service advertisement in the 1950s asking drivers to slow down in order to save a life, which just may be their own. O'Connor makes a pun with this title and Shiftlet's actions at the end of the story when he drives off toward Mobile. He slows down and nearly stops as he drives the hitchhiker, just as he tells the mother that he taught Lucynell to speak by slowing down long enough to care and pay attention.

In a 1959 letter to writer John Hawkes, O'Connor writes that Mr. Shiftlet is "of the Devil because nothing in him resists the Devil" (HB 367). Like many of O'Connor's complete villains such as The Misfit, Shiftlet (perhaps there is more than a passing similarity in the sound of their names) possesses a deeper devilishness than first meets the eye. When he tells the women his name, for example, he tells them that his name could be any number of things and he could be from any number of places. Perhaps the truest thing to say to them is that he is a man, but then what is a man and why was he made?

The questions give a clue to Shiftlet's association with the devil. A Christian man knows what a man is and what a man was made to do. That he gives shifty answers to the women's questions associates him with uncertainty, mistrust, and trouble. When he comments that the monks sleep in their coffins when the mother tells him he will have to sleep in

Shiftlet → the grotesque character w/ startling action [handwritten]

the car, Shiftlet stands in contrast to the religious monks. Monks prepare for their future with the Lord; Shiftlet plots how to get himself this automobile. When he finally gets the car to start, his expression is as serious as if he had just raised the dead.

Shiftlet says he is not satisfied with the civil wedding to Lucynell. Even the doctor who removes a man's heart and holds it in his hand knows nothing more about it than any one else. Shiftlet is not satisfied with the law when the mother tells him that the marriage is legal. His restlessness continues when he explains to the old woman that a body can stay still but a spirit is like an automobile—it has to keep moving. Symbolically, Shiftlet's interest in the car represents his spirit that is on the move.

When the boy at the counter of The Hot Spot mentions that the sleeping Lucynell looks like an angel of God, Shiftlet claims she is a hitchhiker, and he cannot wait for her to wake up. Not only repulsed by what he has done to get the car, Shiftlet has moved into the spirit realm now by driving it. He must keep moving. He pays for her meal and deserts her. A man associated with the devil cannot tolerate an angel in his car any more than a monk can tolerate the devil sleeping with him in his coffin. The counter boy, on the other hand, touches Lucynell's golden hair with something like reverence.

[handwritten margin note: *a real man deep uncertain*]

Shiftlet picks up a real hitchhiker, but this young man refuses to be conned by the shifty driver. Shiftlet goes on about how good his mother was and how he was never sadder than the day he ran off on her. Readers do not know whether to believe Shiftlet or not this time when he sheds tears, but what matters most is that the boy does not believe him. He gets out in time before something bad happens to him, which O'Connor's readers know can be a distinct possibility.

O'Connor's description—of Shiftlet not being the devil himself but associated with the devil because he does not do enough to resist him—allows the character to pray at the end of this comic story. Disgusted with what the world has become, he prays that the slime be washed from the earth. No sooner does he say this prayer then great claps of thunder resound overhead, and the rain pouring down the back of the car washes Shiftlet and his spirit-car right out of those parts.

[handwritten margin note: *he is the slime of the earth*]

CHARACTERS

Lucynell Crater, the daughter   Almost 30 years old, Lucynell is a large woman with blue eyes and pink-gold hair. She is both mentally challenged and deaf. When Mr. Shiftlet asks, her mother claims that she is 15 or 16; she is too innocent for anyone to guess her real age. Mr. Shiftlet teaches her to say the word *bird*, which is the first word she has ever spoken. She watches him work. In her letters, O'Connor called this character the "idiot daughter."

The daughter does, however, have an innocent, angelic quality. Not only does her mother say so, but the counter boy at The Hot Spot does as well. The only word she articulates in the story, her version of *bird* may represent how in her disability and innocence she is filled with the Holy Spirit. That she shares her mother's name is intriguing; perhaps O'Connor gave her the same name to show that she is a more innocent side of her mother's nature.

Lucynell Crater, the mother   Mrs. Crater is an old woman who has been a widow for 15 years. She is described as the size of a cedar post and wearing a man's gray hat pulled down over her eyes when Mr. Shiftlet first comes to her place. She has no teeth and does not take the gum Shiftlet offers her when he arrives. She hires Mr. Shiftlet to work on her property and then manipulates him into marrying her daughter. Mrs. Crater "convinces" Mr. Shiftlet to marry her by seemingly making him feel hopeless about future prospects of a man with his disability. Though she is shrewd about Shiftlet's motives when he wants money, she misses that she is the one being conned, not the other way around.

The name *Crater* suggests the moon with its indentations and valleys. In the evenings, Shiftlet sits with the two women on the porch where the old woman's land ("three mountains") is silhouetted against the sky and it is "visited" by the moon and the planets.

Tom T. Shiftlet   Shiftlet is the name by which this character introduces himself and says that he is from Tarwater, Tennessee. However, he then tells Lucynell Crater that his name could just as easily be Aaron Sparks from Singleberry, Georgia, or

George Speeds from Lucy, Alabama, or Thompson Bright from Toolafalls, Mississippi. Whatever his real name might be, the name Shiftlet seems to fit his shifty character. When he arrives at the farm, he is described as wearing a black town suit with one sleeve folded up and a brown felt hat turned up in front and down in the back. He carries a tin toolbox. His hair is black and long, slicked down flat to his ears from a part in the middle of his head. He has clay-colored eyes, a long forehead, and a jaw that juts out.

He appears young and says that he is 28, but at the same time he looks jaded and dissatisfied with the world, as though he were much older. He rolls his own cigarettes. Shiftlet says he has worked as a gospel singer, a foreman on the railroad, an under-taker's assistant, and a singer on the radio with Uncle Roy and the Red Creek Wranglers. He says he also fought in the "Arm Service" of his coun-try and had visited every foreign land. Through his smooth talking, hard work, and manipulative techniques, he manages to steal the old woman's car and abandon her daughter at a roadside diner. Through the countermanipulations of the old woman, however, he has had to marry Lucynell Crater, the daughter, to get what he wants.

RELATED LETTERS

Elizabeth McKee, October 15, 1952 (HB 44); Sally Fitzgerald, Tuesday [November, 1952] (HB 47); Sally Fitzgerald, Thursday, [Undated; Fall, 1952] (HB 47); Elizabeth McKee, November 26, 1952 (HB 48); Elizabeth McKee, December 20, 1952 (HB 48); Sally and Robert Fitzgerald, December 20, 1952 (HB 49–50); Robie Macauley, May 18, 1955 (HB 81); Sally and Robert Fitzgerald, June 10, 1955 (HB 85); Betty Hester ("A"), September 8, 1956 (HB 172–174); Elizabeth Fenwick Way, September 13, 1956 (HB 174–175); Sally and Rob-ert Fitzgerald, December 10, 1956 (HB 185–186); Betty Hester ("A"), December 18, 1956 (HB 189–191); John Hawkes, December 26, 1959 (HB 367); Elizabeth McKee, October 28, 1960 (HB 414–415); Betty Hester ("A"), September 14, 1963 (HB 539). *HB pages*: 44; 47–50; 81; 85; 174–175; 186; 191; 367; 414–415; 539.

FURTHER READING

Chew, Martha. "Flannery O'Connor's Double-Edged Satire: The Idiot Daughter Versus the Lady Ph.D." *The Southern Quarterly: A Journal of Arts in the South* 19, no. 2 (Winter 1981): 17–25.

Clasby, Nancy T. "'The Life You Save May Be Your Own': Flannery O'Connor as a Visionary Artist." *Studies in Short Fiction* 28, no. 4 (Fall 1991): 509–520.

Desmond, John F. "The Shifting of Mr. Shiftlet: Flan-nery O'Connor's 'The Life You Save May Be Your Own.'" *Mississippi Quarterly* 28 (1975): 55–59.

Elie, Paul. *"The Life You Save May Be Your Own": An American Pilgrimage: Flannery O'Connor, Thomas Merton, Walker Percy, Dorothy Day.* New York: Far-rar, Straus and Giroux, 2003.

Griffith, Albert J. "Flannery O'Connor's Salvation Road." *Studies in Short Fiction* 3 (1966): 329–333.

Hegarty, Charles M., S. J. "A Man Though Not Yet a Whole One: Mr. Shiftlet's Genesis." *Flannery O'Connor Bulletin* 1 (1972): 24–38.

"Parker's Back" (1965)

This eighth story from *Everything That Rises Must Converge* (FSG, 1965) was one of the last pieces on which the author worked. It was published posthu-mously in *Esquire* in April 1965 (vol. 63).

SYNOPSIS

Parker regrets marrying his wife. He knows that he married her to have her, but now she is pregnant, and he finds her unattractive. She sits on the porch, snapping beans and watching automobiles go by. She does not approve of them. Parker works for a nearly 70-year-old blond woman who looks at him with the same expression as she does her tractor. She tells him to keep his shirt on when he works for her.

Parker met his wife by the side of the road. He was working on his truck when he sensed that a girl was watching him. He pretended to hurt his hand and waved it about, cussing and swearing. Suddenly, he was whacked on the side of the head with a broom that sent him down on the hood. When he got up, he saw that a woman was telling him not to curse in her neighborhood. He told her he hurt his hand, and she looked at it. As she did, she spied all the tattoos on his arm: an eagle, a cannon, a serpent, hearts, and a hand of cards. He saw her looking at them and tells her that she ought to see the ones she cannot see. She blushes and tells him that she does not like tattoos, but he does not believe her. In his experience, all women have been fascinated by them.

He continues visiting this girl whom he finds challenging, and her mother seems pleased to receive the fruit which he brings with him as a gift. She manages to ask him successfully what the O. E. in his name stand for; he tells her Obadiah Elihue. When he was in the navy, he nearly killed the man who leaked it from his personnel files. Her full name is Sarah Ruth Cates.

He is able to convince Sarah one day to take a ride in his truck, and he gets her into the back. When he wants to have his way with her, she insists they cannot without being married. Eventually, though he keeps telling himself not to, he ends up married to Sarah. They wed in the County Ordinary's office because she thinks churches engage in idolatry. Now she is pregnant.

She remains unimpressed with the tattoos that cover every part of the front of his body. To add a new tattoo, which is something he does when he is suffering from growing stress, he would have to begin putting them on his back. He has resisted this, since then he would not be able to see the tattoo without a mirror. She wonders what Jesus will think of him when he meets his judgment with all of his tattoos. Parker is an unbeliever, so it does not matter to him.

Parker becomes dissatisfied with his job and with his life. This warrants another tattoo, but the idea of getting another one that Sarah would not like weighs on his mind. She does not take to his idea of putting a Christian symbol on his back where only she can see it. At work one day, he is distracted by these thoughts. He drives the old woman's baler into a tree, where it catches on fire. The tree and one of his shoes is burning, but he is thrown away to watch in horror. He hears a voice that says, "God above."

He takes off in his truck to the city. He decides that he simply must get another tattoo, this one on his back. He looks through religious emblems in the tattoo artist's book. He stops when he sees one

image of Christ's face with the words, "Go back." It is an intricate design in squares that will require the artist two days to apply. Parker pays for it and has the tattoo put on.

When he goes back to Sarah, she does not open the door. She wants to know who is there, but she does not let him in until he says his full name, not O. E. She begins to tell him right away about the woman for whom he worked not having insurance on her tractor and what trouble he is in. Parker wants her to look at the tattoo, but she refuses. His only hope is to make her see it and hope that it will please her when she sees Christ's image. When she finally does look, however, instead of reading the image and words as a sign, she accuses him of idolatry. She says she can take lies and vanity, but she cannot tolerate idolatry. She chases him out of the house with her broom. He stands by a tree, crying like a baby.

Don't pray to idol, be one w/ god - deep vdd

COMMENTARY

The title of the story has several meanings. One is that much of the story is about Parker's back. Parker likes tattoos and has had many painted on his body since he was about 15 years old. Each time he grows restless or troubled, he eases the pressure by getting a new tattoo. He wants to be sure to be able to see them all; this is why he does not have any put on his back. So Parker's back in this sense is the only part of his body that has remained clean or bare of markings.

Another meaning of the title is that Parker runs away to the city after his accident with the tractor. The moment traumatizes him, and he runs, which is his typical reaction when he does not understand what has happened to him. He runs away after five years in the navy, for instance, after a bout of dissatisfaction after one of his furloughs. When he looks through the tattoo artist's book, looking for a religious image that Sarah Ruth might enjoy seeing on his back, he sees the two eyes of a Byzantine Christ and hears a voice in his head saying "Go back." He decides that this is a sign he should have the image painted on his back.

Yet another reference to the title occurs when Parker has the accident with the tractor. The tractor runs upside down into the tree and bursts into flame. Parker lands on his back, and his shoes burn.

Parker's back is also mentioned when his cronies in the pool hall in the city slap him there after the recent tattooing, making his back raw and sore.

The last reference to the title is a play on words, "Parker's Back," as in Parker is back. He returns home and to Sarah Ruth, hoping to make her happy with the image of God on his back. He knows that he cannot see it without the careful use of two mirrors, but he hopes that she will like it and accept him, rather than insisting on his being in the dark when he removes his clothing because she does not want to look at his tattoos. Parker forgets, if he ever really understood it in the first place, that Sarah Ruth did not want to get married in a church because she objected to statues and pictures. She thought of these images as idolatrous. Now she thinks the same thing of Parker's back and strikes it several times with a broom until welts rise up on Christ's face painted there. When Sarah virtually turns her back on Parker by throwing him out of the house, "Parker's Back" in this instance is the back of his wife turning away from him.

Caroline Gordon said of "Parker's Back," "Miss O'Connor seems to have succeeded where the great Flaubert failed: in the dramatization of that particular heresy which denies Our Lord corporeal substance" (CS xv). That God could also be man and came to save the world in that fleshy form is a belief of all Christian faiths. When Parker physically acquires an image of Christ on his back, he has sacrificed a part of him for his wife, which he held back before. In a symbolic way, Christ has been made flesh, and Sarah Ruth, the heretic, does not recognize either the image itself as that of Jesus nor the symbolism of her husband's action. Instead, she retreats and beats him with the broom just as she did the first day when she heard him curse at his truck to draw her attention.

Something has happened to Parker that has not happened for Sarah Ruth. His accident and the resulting burning tree and Parker's calling out to God echo the biblical account of Moses and the burning bush. In Exodus 3:2–6, the Lord speaks to Moses from a burning bush and tells him to remove his sandals since he is on holy ground. From that moment on, Parker knows "there had been a great change in his life, a leap forward into a worse unknown, and that there was nothing he could do

about it. It was for all intents accomplished" (CS 521). By the end of the story, with Parker beaten and symbolically leaning against a tree similar to a crucifixion, it is clear that Parker has begun a journey toward another place in his spiritual existence, a place Sarah Ruth has yet to recognize.

CHARACTERS

O. E. (Obadiah Elihue) Parker A 28-year-old gloomy man whose main interest in life is having tattoos painted all over his body and escaping when he feels another bout of unease and dissatisfaction. Parker's name is ironic since Obadiah in the Bible comforted Job. Parker is no comforter; he is more of an instigator of trouble than one who would work to take away the cares and difficulties of the world from others. Ironically, when Parker does finally try to do something to comfort his wife, she turns on him. He is lazy and untalented. The nearly 70-year-old woman for whom he works says that he breaks everything he touches. He received a dishonorable discharge from the navy.

In the single-chapter book of Obadiah in the Bible (Obadiah 1:4), there is a warning about pride as represented in eagles, "Though you go as high as the eagle, and your nest be set among the stars, From there will I bring you down, says the Lord." The eagle on the cannon was the first tattoo Parker received and the one that, when pressed to find a favorite, Sarah points to, mistaking it for a chicken.

Sarah Ruth Cates Parker Sarah is described through Parker's eyes as being "plain, plain." Her face has skin as thin and tight as an onion, and her eyes are sharp and gray like ice picks. Her hands are dry and rough. She does not like automobiles. She does not dip, smoke, drink whiskey, use makeup, or swear. She thinks Parker's tattoos are a "vanity of vanities." She is poor and so hungry that she takes an apple a little too eagerly for his taste from Parker's basket when he comes to visit.

Sarah is the daughter of a preacher who is off in Florida spreading the news. Sarah in the Bible was the wife of Abraham, and she gave birth late in life to Isaac. As in the Bible, Sarah's pregnancy, especially considering her detached feelings toward Parker even though they are married, surprises the reader. Instead of having the commitment to her husband that the biblical Ruth shows, Sarah Ruth follows her own set of convictions and values with little or no sign of softening them for anyone.

RELATED LETTERS

Betty Hester ("A"), December 24, 1960 ["that story"] (HB 423–424); Betty Hester ("A"), January 21, 1961 (HB 427); Betty Hester ("A"), July 11, 1964 (HB 592); Catherine Carver, July 15, 1964 (HB 593); Betty Hester ("A"), July 17, 1964 (HB 593–594); Maryat Lee, July 21, 1964 (HB 594); Betty Hester ("A"), July 25, 1964 (HB 594). *HB* pages: 424, 427, 559, 583, 585, 592–594.

FURTHER READING

Asals, Frederick. "'Obediah,' Obadiah': Guys and Dolls in 'Parker's Back.'" *The Flannery O'Connor Bulletin* 21 (1992): 37–42.

Bleikasten, André. "Writing on the Flesh: Tattoos and Taboos in 'Parker's Back.'" *Southern Literary Journal* 14, no. 2 (Spring 1982): 8–18.

Browning, Preston, Jr. "'Parker's Back': Flannery O'Connor's Iconography of Salvation by Profanity." *Studies in Short Fiction* 6 (1969): 525–535.

Burns, Dan G. "Flannery O'Connor's 'Parker's Back': The Key to the End." *Notes on Contemporary Literature* 17, no. 2 (March 1987): 11–12.

Corn, Alfred. "An Encounter with O'Connor and 'Parker's Back.'" *The Flannery O'Connor Bulletin* 24 (1995–96): 104–118.

Davis, William V. "'Large and Startling Figures': The Place of 'Parker's Back' in Flannery O'Connor's Canon." *Antigonish Review* 28 (1977): 71–87.

Driskell, Leon. "'Parker's Back' vs. 'The Partridge Festival': Flannery O'Connor's Critical Choice." *Georgia Review* 21 (1967): 476–490.

Fahey, William A. "Flannery O'Connor's 'Parker's Back.'" *Renascence: Essays on Value in Literature* 20 (1968): 162–164, 166.

Farnham, James F. "Further Evidence for the Sources of 'Parker's Back.'" *The Flannery O'Connor Bulletin* 12 (1983): 114–116.

Feldman, Kathryn. "Back to Back: Flannery O'Connor: Art and Reality." *Nassau Review: The Journal of Nassau Community College Devoted to Arts, Letters, and Sciences* 7, no. 1 (1995): 85–88.

Fowler, James. "In the Flesh: The Grace of 'Parker's Back.'" *Publications of the Mississippi Philological Association* (2004): 60–66.

Haddox, Thomas F. "'Something Haphazard and Botched': Flannery O'Connor's Critique of the Visual in 'Parker's Back.'" *Mississippi Quarterly: The Journal of Southern Cultures* 57, no. 3 (Summer 2004): 407–421.

Jorgenson, Eric. "A Note on the Jonah Motif in 'Parker's Back.'" *Studies in Short Fiction* 21, no. 4 (Fall 1984): 400–402.

Kilcourse, George. "'Parker's Back': 'Not Totally Congenial' Icons of Christ." In *Flannery O'Connor and the Christian Mystery*, edited by John J. Murphy, et al., 35–46. Provo, Utah: Center for the Study of Christian Values in Literature, Brigham Young University, 1997.

Mayer, David R. "Outer Marks, Inner Grace: Flannery O'Connor's Tattooed Christ." *Asian Folklore Studies* 42, no. 1 (1983): 117–127.

Napier, James J. "In 'Parker's Back': A Technical Slip by Flannery O'Connor." *Notes on Contemporary Literature* 11, no. 4 (September 1981): 5–6.

Petry, Alice Hall. "O'Connor's 'Parker's Back.'" *Explicator* 46, no. 2 (Winter 1988): 38–43.

Sessions, W. A. "How to Read Flannery O'Connor: Passing By the Dragon." In *Flannery O'Connor and the Christian Mystery*, edited by John J. Murphy, et al., 191–215. Provo, Utah: Center for the Study of Christian Values in Literature, Brigham Young University, 1997.

Slattery, Dennis Patrick. "Faith in Search of an Image: The Iconic Dimension of Flannery O'Connor's 'Parker's Back.'" *South Central Bulletin* 41, no. 4 (Winter 1981): 120–123.

Streight, Irwin Howard. "Is There a Text in this Man? A Semiotic Reading of 'Parker's Back.'" *The Flannery O'Connor Bulletin* 22 (1993–94): 1–11.

"Partridge Festival, The" (1961)

This story first appeared in *The* CRITIC, March 1961 (vol. 19). It was originally part of the *Everything That Rises Must Converge* manuscript, but O'Connor omitted the story from the collection before publication.

SYNOPSIS

Calhoun wants to write, but he is drawn to selling. He usually sells enough things such as air conditioners, boats, and refrigerators during the summer months to pay for his small living expenses during the rest of the year. He visits his Aunt Bessie and Aunt Mattie in Partridge for the Azalea Festival.

Why he is really there is to find out more about the murder. Ten days before the festival started, a man named Singleton did not purchase a button for the festival as a fund-raiser. Part of the festivities involved "trying" those accused of such innocent "crimes" in a mock trial on the lawn of the courthouse. As part of the event, Singleton was put in stocks and then thrown in the outhouse "jail" upon his "conviction." Singleton did not take kindly to this display of community condemnation. Ten days after the "trial," he showed up at the courthouse and shot five dignitaries.

Calhoun decides to go to town to learn more on the street about what had happened. He talks with a boy who thinks that Singleton was crazy. Calhoun tries to tell him that Singleton was only the messenger for Partridge's own inherent guilt. The boy does not understand.

Calhoun walks along and sees the remnants of a funeral. He hears disdain for Singleton when he watches it go by with another citizen. He is shocked at the town's feelings for Singleton. Calhoun enters a barber shop and is so revolted by the hatred in the barber's voice as he talks about Singleton that he tears the bib from around his neck and runs out of the shop.

Calhoun is not interested in a date set up by his aunts, and neither is the date, Mary Elizabeth. She takes him to her father's law office where they can watch the event on the street from an upstairs window. Calhoun learns that she is a nonfiction writer, while he intends to write a novel about Singleton. When he asks her what her opinion of Singleton is, she says he is a Christ figure.

Through their conversation at the window watching an event both despise, they dare each other to go to the institution in Quincy to meet Singleton firsthand. Both are afraid to do it. The next day it is raining, and Calhoun thinks she may not come, so he does not have to go either. However, she does arrive, and they take off in the pouring rain.

It becomes clear that Mary Elizabeth is terrified, just as Calhoun is, but she says something about being related to Singleton. By the time they reach the hospital, Calhoun has long given up the idea of doing the novel.

Mary Elizabeth gets them into the hospital by telling the officials that they are kin of Singleton's. The staff seems to know differently but not care. Singleton is soon unruly and grabs for Mary Elizabeth's knee. He tells her they are two of a kind and lifts his hospital gown.

Mary Elizabeth and Calhoun run out of the room. They drive away, and later Calhoun pulls off the side of the road. They hold hands as they sense the kinship each felt toward Singleton building a kinship between them. Reflected in Mary Elizabeth's glasses, Calhoun sees a master salesman looking back at him.

COMMENTARY

Like "A Late Encounter with the Enemy," "The Partridge Festival" speaks to the social side of southern tradition and its possibilities for hypocrisy. Even though there has been a murder in Partridge as a direct result of festival activities that resulted in the shooting of several men, the Azalea Festival continues on, as usual.

This kind of communal behavior enrages Calhoun. He hopes to write a novel about the murder that will expose the actions of the citizens of Partridge for what they really were. He sympathizes with Singleton and sees a bit of himself in the criminal. Singleton could not stomach the town's foolish behavior any more than Calhoun could.

Calhoun, however, is more of a salesman than a thinker or a writer. When he "interviews" the people of the town, he allows his emotions to be involved with their answers rather than abstractly to record them or analyze them. When he meets Mary Elizabeth, who shares his feelings, he meets another double. Mary Elizabeth elevates Singleton to Christ-figure status. When she hesitates to go to the hospital to meet and interview Singleton, Calhoun employs his salesman skills in daring her to go.

Despite Calhoun's and Mary Elizabeth's desire to see Singleton as a champion for their philosophies, it turns out that Calhoun's great aunts and the people of Partridge are right about him. Far from a thinking man who acts rashly to make a point about his community, Singleton is severely mentally ill. He behaves badly at their visit in the hospital by exposing himself to Mary Elizabeth.

In the car, Calhoun sees himself reflected back in Mary Elizabeth's glasses as a salesman. He has discovered that he misread not only all of the townspeople but also Singleton and his motives. Mary Elizabeth has also learned that, far removed from a Christ figure who would enjoy reading the intellectual books she brought, her hero had no idea what he was doing.

A further irony is that the Partridge festival was started by Calhoun's great-grandfather, who was one of the leading merchants in the town years before. No matter how much he tries to shake himself of the town, Calhoun seems destined to maintain his inherited trait for the sale.

This story was predicated on actual murder sprees in 1949 and 1953 committed by Marion Stembridge, who was a grocer and loan shark. Stembridge was charged with killing a black girl in 1949. Although he was convicted and sentenced to one to three years, he never served any time in prison. He then killed two lawyers in 1953 before killing himself. After the 1953 rampage, a man named Singleton honked his horn up and down a street in MILLEDGEVILLE, trying to warn everyone.

CHARACTERS

Calhoun One possible source for the name *Calhoun* may have been the town of Calhoun, Georgia. It is one hour north of Atlanta and is part of Cherokee lands. The Cherokee were made to endure the famous "Trail of Tears." Although Calhoun fancies himself an artist, his talents do not match his ambitions. O'Connor does not allow Calhoun to fully rebel from his community in the way that he would like. By having the strong ties he is trying to escape, Calhoun is destined to fail at his attempt to be a writer and a thinker. The implication is that since he does not deal with the truth of his circumstances and the history of Partridge, he fails as an artist.

Mary Elizabeth As a nonfiction writer, Mary Elizabeth is tied more to abstractions and ideas than Calhoun is. She allows the specifics of the Singleton case to support larger ideas. Calhoun, who calls himself a fiction writer, instead looks to describe Singleton and his situation in more concrete terms. When Mary Elizabeth says she thinks of Singleton as a Christ figure, she is calling him a martyr. As the lone rebel in the town standing against the folly of the festival and its traditions, Singleton, she implies, tried to save the community from itself. As a nonbeliever, however, Mary Elizabeth fails to understand that Singleton cannot be a Christ figure and also have murdered six people. When she leaves the hospital after Singleton exposes himself, Calhoun sees the nakedness of the sky in her face. Like Calhoun, she is left in shock; Singleton is not only not who she thought he was, but he is also mentally disturbed. He is hardly the rebel that she and Calhoun envisioned, and to both the world seems a much more complicated place.

RELATED LETTERS

Maryat Lee, September 6, 1959 (HB 348); Betty Hester ("A"), October 31, 1959 (HB 356–358); Betty Hester ("A"), June 25, 1960 (HB 401); Cecil Dawkins, August 10, 1960 (HB 404–405); Ashley Brown, February 13, 1961 (HB 431); Maryat Lee, Friday [c. March, 1961], (HB 434–435); John Hawkes, April 20, 1961 (HB 438–439); Elizabeth McKee, May 7, 1964 (HB 574–575); Elizabeth McKee, May 21, 1964 (HB 580); Robert Giroux, June 28, 1964 (HB 589). *HB pages:* 348, 357–358, 401, 404–405, 431–432, 435, 439, 575, 580, 589.

FURTHER READING

Driskell, Leon. "'Parker's Back' vs. 'The Partridge Festival': Flannery O'Connor's Critical Choice." *Georgia Review* 21 (1967): 476–490.

Johnson, Rob. "'The Topical is Poison': Flannery O'Connor's Vision of Social Reality in 'The Partridge Festival,' and 'Everything That Rises Must Converge.'" *The Flannery O'Connor Bulletin* 21 (1992): 1–24.

Malin, Irving. "Singular Visions: 'The Partridge Festival.'" In *Critical Essays on Flannery O'Connor,*

edited by Melvin J. Friedman and Beverly Lyon
Clark, 180–186. Boston: Hall, 1985.

Scouten, Kenneth. "'The Partridge Festival': Manuscript Revisions." *The Flannery O'Connor Bulletin*
15 (1986): 35–41.

"Regional Writer, The" (1962)

Originally the essay was a talk given by O'Connor
in the fall of 1962 to the Georgia Writer's Association on receiving a Scroll award for her second
novel, *The Violent Bear It Away* (Farrar, Straus and
Cudahy, 1960). The talk was later published in the
Winter 1963 issue of *Esprit* and also in *Mystery and
Manners: Occasional Prose,* edited by Sally and Robert Fitzgerald (FSG, 1969) and then in *Collected
Works* (Library of America, 1988).

SYNOPSIS

O'Connor is glad to receive the Scroll and is in fact
just happy to have her novel remembered two years
after its publication and especially with the correct title. She jokes about variations for *The Violent
Bear It Away* that she has heard. These include
"The Valiant Bear It Always," "The Violets Bloom
Away," and "The Bear That Ran Away With It"
(MM 51). She says that awards are proportionately
valuable to the distance from home at which they
are awarded.

In a previous talk to the Georgia Writers' Association, she recalls comparing a Georgia author to a
pig and a Talmadge ham. In that talk, she was saying that a pig (or an author) is a pig (or an author),
no matter from where it originates. This time, however, she is expanding her talk to speak about the
larger area that Georgian authors represent, that is
the practitioners of Southern literature.

It is a myth to say that writers are lonely and suffering. She says that this may be a story held over
from the Romantics. Fiction writers, in her view,
work in the most concrete of arts. Writing is communication. Southern fiction does well because its
most talented writers know that they are working within a community. Unlike other areas of the
country, the southern writer does not need to leave

the South in order to write about it. Those who do,
risk losing authenticity in their work and having it
tainted by theory.

If one calls oneself a Georgia writer, this sets
up a boundary that really provides a doorway to
one's subject matter. Many southern writers look
to their immediate surroundings for material—WIL-
LIAM FAULKNER in Oxford; EUDORA WELTY in Jackson; and Mr. Montgomery, this group's poet. The
Georgian writer does not speak for all Georgians,
but he ranks his work against a Georgian audience's
reaction to it. O'Connor tells an anecdote about a
local lady asking William Faulkner if she would like
his book. He tells her that he thinks she will like it,
since it is garbage. O'Connor says the book was not
garbage, and the lady probably did not like it, but
that a few in Oxford no doubt did like it. The praise
of these few in his hometown would mean more to
a southern writer than the praise of New York City
critics because critics in New York know little about
how to read and interpret southern literature.

She says it is good that southern audiences are
growing for southern literature. When she went
to college, no southern writer since Joel Chandler
Harris was taught, and those before him other than
EDGAR ALLAN POE were not widely known. Br'er
Rabbit was asked to hold up the southern end of
things against the likes of northern writers such as
NATHANIEL HAWTHORNE, Herman Melville, HENRY
JAMES, and Stephen Crane.

In the time during which she writes, many southern colleges came to offer arts festivals where writers can read and be appreciated. Southern writers
now need not leave to be appreciated or stay and be
ignored. They are becoming a part of the community about which they write and are valued for their
contributions. Another problem has developed,
though, and this is that too many writers now write
of a phony South taught to them through television
rather than through their own observations. The
result is fiction that could be set almost anywhere.

O'Connor relates an anecdote of a friend from
Wisconsin who bought a place in the Atlanta suburbs. The person who sold the house was from
Massachusetts and told the woman that she would
like the neighborhood since there were no southerners around for a couple of miles. The identity of

the South is blurring. It would be an ironic turn of events if the southern writer were to discover that just as his work was being appreciated by southern audiences, the true southern literature had evaporated.

Identity goes deeper than surface details. It is not found in white columns and clay roads or in mockingbirds. Identity is made up of that which does not go away but instead stays after any trial of change. God is the only one who knows it all, and the artist is the only one who digs deep enough to search for it.

"The best American fiction has always been regional" (MM 58). It has moved from the Northeast to the Midwest to the South. When there is a common past, the literature has stayed the longest in favor. In this, the South has a small, if temporary, advantage. The South has in its region the capacity to create great literature.

After he won the National Book Award, WALKER PERCY was asked why there are so many good southern writers. He answered that it was because the South lost the war. O'Connor says this is not because the war makes good subject matter but because "we have had our Fall" (59). This gives experience to the South that the rest of the country does not have; other areas of the country still live in relative innocence as they face the modern world. In addition, the South has a shared culture in the stories of the Bible through which to interpret its experiences and try to make sense of human limitations.

This is the kind of knowledge that the southern writer finds when he turns to his community, and it is not available in Hollywood or New York. Each writer functions best at a specific intersection of time, place, and eternity. The goal for each writer is to locate that spot for him or herself.

"Revelation" (1964)

This story is the seventh in the collection *Everything That Rises Must Converge* (FSG, 1965) and was published in SEWANEE REVIEW in the spring issue, 1964 (vol. 72).

SYNOPSIS

Mrs. Turpin and her husband, Claud, go to the doctor's office and wait in the tiny waiting room. The Turpins are farmers who raise a few hogs, chickens, and white-faced cows, as well as a few acres of cotton. They are there because a cow kicked Claud in the leg. There are several other people in the room whom the reader sees through Mrs. Turpin's eyes. One is a "white-trash" woman with a son; she does not make him move over so that Mrs. Turpin can sit down. Another is a pleasant and stylish woman with her young adult daughter, Mary Grace. Mary Grace is "ugly" and has a severe case of acne and a sour disposition. She sits reading a book titled *Human Development* throughout most of the story and is visibly bothered when there is any talking in the room.

Mrs. Turpin and the pleasant woman have a conversation. Mrs. Turpin says that Claud has to pick up the blacks who work the cotton on their farm nowadays and give them a ride back home in order to get them to work for him. She says she gives the workers ice water, too. Blacks will not work cotton on farms anymore without these kinds of benefits. The white-trash woman says that she would neither hose down hogs nor be nice to blacks. Mrs. Turpin helps a black delivery worker find the bell in the waiting room. He leaves. The white-trash woman says that all blacks should go back to Africa where they came from.

While all of this is going on in the waiting room, Mrs. Turpin thinks about how she is so happy to be just who she is, just one level below the highest class. At the same time as she is having these thoughts, she notices that Mary Grace keeps staring at her over her book. She has a mean expression, and her eyes seem to bore into Mrs. Turpin's whenever she looks her way.

Mrs. Turpin finally decides to meet the girl's challenge head-on and asks Mary Grace if she is in college. Her mother tells Mrs. Turpin that Mary Grace goes to Wellesley in Massachusetts, but she studies all summer as well. She has done well and taken many different kinds of subjects, but the woman thinks that this much work is not good for her and that the girl ought to go out and enjoy herself sometimes. She explains that she knows a girl who is ungrateful for the good education she is receiving and who has a sour disposition.

Mrs. Turpin says aloud that she is grateful for who she is. The comment makes her think of Claud and how somebody else may have married him instead of her, and this makes her grateful anew. When she goes so far as to thank Jesus aloud in the waiting room, Mary Grace lets her have it with her book. It hits her over her left eye. Then the young woman is upon her, attempting to strangle her. Much confusion ensues. Mrs. Turpin sees the girl's eyes rolling in her head, Claud's face, magazines flying, and the doctor appearing with a syringe. Soon the attack is over.

When Mary Grace is calming down, she keeps her eyes on Mrs. Turpin. The woman asks what she has to tell her since it seems obvious that she has something to say. The girl tells her to go back to hell where she came from and calls her a wart hog. When the ambulance takes the girl and her mother away, the white-trash woman describes her as a lunatic. She thanks God that she is not a lunatic.

Mrs. Turpin cannot get the girl's words out of her mind. That night in bed she thinks about them and turns them over and over, trying to understand what they may mean as though they were a message from God.

The next day she cannot stop thinking about the white-trash woman's disdain for hosing down hogs and Mary Grace's message. While she does her work, she prays to God. She asks him how she could both be saved and be from hell at the same time. She wants to know how she could be herself and also be a hog. She gives of herself to help both white-trash and blacks.

She can see Claud's truck out on the road and can see when it begins to return. She watches the hogs in the evening light—the young ones crowd and lay down by the sow. There is something about the light and the life force of this image that gets her thinking in a new way.

The light of the evening turns orange and purple. Suddenly she sees the light behind the tree line as a bridge. On the bridge she sees white trash washed clean, blacks wearing white, lunatics clapping merrily, and those like herself who try to be responsible and caring walking up the bridge behind

them. They are all being saved and going to heaven together. When she turns off the faucet and makes her way to the house, the crickets chirp, but she does not hear them. Instead, she hears souls singing hallelujah.

COMMENTARY

This story won first prize and was reprinted in *Prize Stories 1965: The O. HENRY AWARDs*, edited by Richard Poirier and William Abraham. O'Connor learned that the story had won this honor shortly before her death. The story was later collected in *Complete Stories* (FSG 1971), edited by Robert Giroux, and *Collected Works* (Library of America, 1988), edited by Sally Fitzgerald. Giroux called this story, along with "Everything That Rises Must Converge," works that "are as nearly perfect as stories can be" (*Complete* xv). Indeed, many critics have called this story O'Connor's best because it brings many of her recurring motifs and themes together in one successful, transcendent tale.

For example, Mrs. Turpin is a reincarnation of several other self-righteous women of the Old South. Other versions of Mrs. Turpin include Julian's mother in "Everything That Rises Must Converge," Mrs. McIntyre of "The Displaced Person," and Mrs. Hopewell of "Good Country People." These women have not observed black people from afar. They have known black men, women, and children firsthand and have lived on the same property with them, unlike many people today who live in suburban homes where they may have little or no direct contact with people of another race.

However, even though these women had every chance to get to know their black associates, their knowledge and understanding of them does not equate with their proximity in their day-to-day lives. Mrs. Turpin has had black people working on the Turpin farm for many years, yet she does not understand why giving them a ride to work is anything other than a handout to them to get them to do the work in the first place. Her attitude has not been changed by living around African Americans any more than the other women in so many of the stories in O'Connor's fiction.

The doctor's office is a good setting for O'Connor, a writer who spent a good deal of time in offices just like these. The chance meeting of people and groups in settings like elevators and doctor's offices allows the writer to present characters as though they are a cross section of society. In the second part of the story, after Ruby Turpin has been called a hog by Mary Grace, Ruby stares at the hogs in the pen at her farm. They resemble in number and behavior the people in the waiting room at the doctor's office.

Another masterly feature of the story is that the reader stays inside the mind of Mrs. Turpin throughout. This is a closer and more sustained personal point of view than O'Connor usually presents. The reader becomes Mrs. Turpin and has the story "revealed" to him or her in much the same way as the vision will be revealed to the main character at the end.

Mrs. Turpin benefits from a vision that the other women in O'Connor's stories do not. In this way, the story completes a movement that has been working throughout O'Connor's fiction. Unlike many other stories, although there is violence in Mary Grace's outburst, no one dies, and there is no tragedy as in O'Connor's other work. Mrs. Turpin is open enough and questioning enough to seek answers. Although she is self-righteous, she does have faith, and her faith opens her up to change and improvement. O'Connor hints at this by titling the book that Mary Grace throws at her *Human Development*.

Mrs. Turpin has been challenged by Mary Grace, who has called her a wart hog and has told her to go back to hell where she came from. Ironically, Mrs. Turpin has her vision by the pig stall. By hearing that she is a hog in her attitudes, she communes with them through a rare moment of humility, an act that allows her to see the vision. She prays for answers, and God answers her with the vision that all people are working their way toward purgatory and heaven together. Many of those who possess less than she and Claud, African Americans and others to whom she feels superior, are ahead of her in line.

For all of the women in O'Connor's fiction who do not see this vision, the fact that Ruby Turpin sees it in one of O'Connor's very last stories is an important step forward in carrying O'Connor's message to the world.

CHARACTERS

Mrs. Turpin (Ruby) Mrs. Turpin is in her 40s and weighs 180 pounds. She tries to be good to all people and has a pleasant disposition. She goes to church and works hard. She prays and tries to understand what God has in store for her. Mrs. Turpin also has a high opinion of herself. She ranks herself above people she calls white trash and also black people. Because she owns a home with land, she considers herself superior to those who do not. The only people above her are those who own a bigger house and much more land.

Despite her flaws, Mrs. Turpin is open to prayer and to the sense of mystery that she may not always know everything that God would want her to know. She is grateful for what she has. When she accepts that the words Mary Grace utters during her seizure might just possibly be a personal message to her, she is blessed with a vision, or "revelation." The vision shows her that she and the others are all the same, that Jesus loves them all and saves them all. Her good deeds do not get her to heaven; God's grace does.

Mary Grace She is the intelligent 18- or 19-year-old disturbed daughter of the pleasant woman in the doctor's office waiting room. Through Mrs. Turpin's eyes, she appears ugly; she has bad skin and a horrid disposition. She is reading a textbook, *Human Development*, and is annoyed that people in the waiting room are talking and disturbing her concentration. Her mother tells Mrs. Turpin that she is an excellent student who studies too much and should have more fun in her life. She is also ungrateful for what she has and is mean to people.

The girl's name is no accident in O'Connor fiction—Mary is the Mother of God, and grace is what is bestowed on Ruby Turpin when she sees the "revelation" at the end of the story. Mary Grace ends up being a messenger from God to Ruby Turpin because Mrs. Turpin is open to receiving the girl's ugly words in that way.

RELATED LETTERS

Cecil Dawkins, November 5, 1963 (HB 546); Betty Hester ("A"), November 9, 1963 (HB 547–548); Maryat Lee, November 29, 1963 (HB 551);

Betty Hester ("A"), December 9, 1963 (HB 552); Betty Hester ("A"), December 25, 1963 (HB 554); Elizabeth McKee, January 3, 1964 (HB 560); Betty Hester ("A"), January 25, 1964 (HB 562); Robert Giroux, January 25, 1964 (HB 563); Elizabeth McKee, February 14, 1964 (HB 565); Betty Hester ("A"), March 14, 1964 (HB 569); Betty Hester ("A"), March 28, 1964 (HB 571); Janet McKane, April 6, 1964 (HB 572); Elizabeth McKee, May 7, 1964 (HB 575); Maryat Lee, May 15, 1964 (HB 577); Betty Hester ("A"), May 17, 1964 (HB 578); Catherine Carver, June 17, 1964 (HB 585); Maryat Lee, June 23, 1964 (HB 586); Betty Hester ("A"), July 25, 1964. *Pages HB*: 546, 548–549, 551–552, 554, 559–560, 562–563, 565, 569, 571–572, 575, 577–579, 585–586, 594.

FURTHER READING

Babinec, Lisa S. "Cyclical Patterns of Domination and Manipulation in Flannery O'Connor's Mother-Daughter Relationships." *Flannery O'Connor Bulletin* 19 (1990): 9–29.

Britt, Brian. "Divine Curses in O'Connor's 'Revelation' and 2 Samuel 16." *Flannery O'Connor Review* 1 (2001–02): 49–55.

Cash, Jean W. "O'Connor on 'Revelation': The Story of a Story." *English Language Notes* 24, no. 2 (March 1987): 61–67.

Egan, Kimberly. "Ruby Turpin in Flannery O'Connor's 'Revelation.'" *Notes on Contemporary Literature* 28, no. 2 (March 1998): 8–9.

Frieling, Kenneth. "Flannery O'Connor's Vision: The Violence of Revelation." In *The Fifties: Fiction, Poetry, Drama* by Warren French, 111–120. DeLand, Fla.: Everett/Edwards, 1970.

Hardy, Donald E. "Free Indirect Discourse, Irony, and Empathy in Flannery O'Connor's 'Revelation.'" *Language and Literature* 16 (1991): 37–53.

Heher, Michael. "Grotesque Grace in the Factious Commonwealth." *The Flannery O'Connor Bulletin* 15 (1986): 69–81.

Johnson, Gregory R. "Pagan Virtue and Christian Charity: Flannery O'Connor on the Moral Contradictions of Western Culture." In *The Moral of the Story: Literature and Public Ethics*, edited by Henry T. Edmondson, 237–253. Lanham, Md.: Lexington, 2000.

Martin, W. R. "A Note on Ruby and 'Revelation.'" *The Flannery O'Connor Bulletin* 16 (1987): 23–25.

McMillan, Norman. "Dostoevskian Vision in Flannery O'Connor's 'Revelation.'" *The Flannery O'Connor Bulletin* 16 (1987): 16–22.

McNiff, John; Likha. "Flannery O'Connor: The Art of Revelation." *The Flannery O'Connor Bulletin* 10, no. 2 (1988–89): 24–56.

Napier, James J. "The Cave-Waiting Room in O'Connor's 'Revelation.'" *NMAL: Notes on Modern American Literature* 5, no. 4 (Fall 1981): Item 23.

Pepin, Ronald E. "Latin Names and Images of Ugliness in Flannery O'Connor's 'Revelation.'" *ANQ: A Quarterly Journal of Short Articles, Notes, and Reviews* 6, no. 1 (January 1993): 25–27.

Perisho, Steve. "The Structure of Flannery O'Connor's 'Revelation.'" *Notes on Contemporary Literature* 20, no. 4 (September 1990): 5–7.

Rath, Sura P. "Ruby Turpin's Redemption: Thomist Resolution in Flannery O'Connor's 'Revelation.'" *The Flannery O'Connor Bulletin* 19 (1990): 1–8.

Rowley, Rebecca K. "Individuation and Religious Experience: A Jungian Approach to O'Connor's 'Revelation.'" *Southern Literary Journal* 25, no. 2 (Spring 1993): 92–102.

Schroeder, Michael L. "Ruby Turpin, Job, and Mystery: Flannery O'Connor on the Question of Knowing." *The Flannery O'Connor Bulletin* 21 (1992): 75–83.

Slattery, Dennis P. "In a Pig's Eye: Retrieving the Animal Imagination in Ruby Turpin's 'Revelation.'" *Flannery O'Connor Bulletin* 25 (1996–97): 138–150.

Sloan, LaRue Love. "The Rhetoric of the Seer: Eye Imagery in Flannery O'Connor's 'Revelation.'" *Studies in Short Fiction* 25, no. 2 (Spring 1988): 135–145.

Srigley, Susan. "O'Connor and the Mystics: St. Catherine of Genoa's Purgatorial Vision in 'Revelation.'" *Flannery O'Connor Review* 2 (2003–04): 40–52.

Stephenson, Will. "Ruby Turpin: O'Connor's Travesty of the Ideal Woman." *The Flannery O'Connor Bulletin* 24 (1995–96): 57–66.

Tedford, Barbara Wilkie. "Flannery O'Connor and The Social Classes." *Southern Literary Journal* 13, no. 2 (Spring 1981): 27–40.

Tolomeo, Diane. "Flannery O'Connor's 'Revelation' and the Book of Job." *Renascence: Essays on Value in Literature* 30 (1978): 79–90.

"River, The" (1953)

This short story first appeared in the summer 1953 issue of *Sewanee Review* (vol. 61). It was subsequently collected as the second story in *A Good Man Is Hard to Find,* published by Harcourt, Brace and Company in June 1955. Later publications include *The Complete Stories* (FSG, 1971) and *Collected Works* (Library of America, 1988). O'Connor was intrigued by a writer named Robert Jiras who had approached her with a desire to make a documentary film of the story. In a 1956 letter to Betty Hester she questions how the sacrament of Baptism, which she saw as central to the story, might be "documented." The film was produced and directed by Barbara Noble in 1976.

SYNOPSIS

At six in the morning, Mrs. Connin arrives from her overnight shift to a dark apartment in the city to pick up a boy whom she will babysit for the day at her house in the country. The boy is four or five years old. The boy's father puts on his coat haphazardly, while his mother calls from the bedroom for an ice pack. Mrs. Connin tells the man that they may be back late since she plans to take the boy with her to a healing at the river. She tells him that she will ask the Reverend Bevel Summers to pray for the boy's sick mother.

Outside, Mrs. Connin tells the boy to wipe his nose and lends him her red-and-blue flowered handkerchief when she sees him go to use his sleeve. When Mrs. Connin asks the boy his name, he knows that his name is Harry Ashfield, but instead he tells her that his first name is Bevel, and Mrs. Connin is delighted with what she thinks is the coincidence that the boy's name is the same as the preacher's. As the trolley car arrives, Mrs. Connin tells Bevel that the healer did not help her husband because he did not have the faith; he is in the government hospital.

At Mrs. Connin's house, Bevel meets her children—J. C., Spivey, Sinclair, and Sarah Mildred. He sees pictures on the walls of Mr. Connin and also of a carpenter wearing a sheet with a gold circle around his head and surrounded by children.

He is going to ask who that is, but Mrs. Connin's boys take him outside. They pull a prank on Bevel that causes him to be chased by a shoat, a young hog. Mrs. Connin rescues him from the runaway hog, but the boy cries for a good five minutes as she holds him.

Bevel considers himself lucky this day because he learns things when he goes away from home instead of when a sitter stays with him at his house. When he asks, Mrs. Connin tells him about the man in the picture. She tells him that he is Jesus who made him. Bevel is confused because he always thought that the doctor made him and that Jesus was a joke since his parents always laughed at the name. Mrs. Connin reads him her great-grandmother's 1832 book, "The Life of Jesus Christ for Readers Under Twelve" and lets him look at the pictures. One of the pictures depicts Jesus driving a pig, symbolizing the devil, out of a man. Bevel slips the book into his coat pocket.

They walk to the river for the healing. The preacher, Bevel Summers, is a young man of about 19 standing in water up to his knees. He sings and preaches to the group of people gathered on the bank. His main message is that there is only one river, the River of Life, which is made from Jesus' blood, and that we have to lay our pain in the River of Faith. The Kingdom of Christ is to be found in the river. An old woman rushes forward and flaps around in the river like a butterfly. A huge old man named Mr. Paradise sits along the bank looking like a boulder, heckling the preacher. A few people testify to Jesus and wade into the water or dip in a hand or foot. The preacher goes on speaking and looking up to the sky while this goes on, seemingly oblivious to them.

Mrs. Connin calls out about Bevel having the same name as the preacher. The preacher baptizes Bevel, who is too shocked at being plunged upside down beneath the water to cry. He tells the boy that now he counts and that he did not count before. As Mrs. Connin asks him to pray for the boy's mother, the boy says that his mother is sick with a hangover, and Mr. Paradise laughs loudly from the bank.

When Mrs. Connin returns Bevel to his parents that night, she tells them that he has had a long day. His mother is reclined on the couch and does not get up. Mrs. Connin learns that Bevel's real first name is Harry, and the boy's mother learns that he was baptized that day. Mrs. Connin leaves, not taking the money the boy's father reaches out to pay her.

Bevel's mother pulls off his coat and feels the book inside. George, one of their adult friends who is still there from the party that day, sees the 1832 date in the book and pronounces it valuable as a collector's item. That night when Bevel goes to bed, his mother comes in and asks him what the preacher said. Bevel feels as though he has been pulled up from the river and tells her that he said that now he counts. His mother kisses his forehead and leaves the room.

Bevel gets up the next morning and begins yet another day of trying to find food and drink and something to do to pass the time. He plays with ashes from the ashtray, stares at his feet, and thinks of his wet shoes. The shoes remind him of the river. He manages to make his way back to the river, where he decides he will baptize himself. He fights the water not keeping him by going under it again and again. Meanwhile, Mr. Paradise catches sight of the boy, grabs some peppermint candy, and runs toward the river. Seeing the large man charging toward him as a pig carrying a club, the boy plunges underneath the water again. This time, he feels the current take gentle hold of him, moving somewhere forward and down; perhaps he may be finally going to the Kingdom of Christ. All fear and anger leave him. Mr. Paradise swims down the river after him, but he never sees the boy and comes up empty-handed.

COMMENTARY

In 1953, O'Connor wrote from ANDALUSIA to her friends Sally and Robert Fitzgerald that she had sold the story "about the child that got baptized" to *Sewanee Review* (*Habit* 60). This comment as well as the central images of the river, and Mrs. Connin's request to Bevel Summers to baptize the boy and his subsequent immersions show that baptism is a central theme. In Catholic doctrine, Baptism is one of the seven sacraments (the others are: Confirmation, Reconciliation, the Eucharist, Matrimony, Holy Orders, and the Anointing of the

Sick, also known as Last Rites). Baptism is more than a rite of initiation into the church, however; it is also believed to be a spiritual cleansing of original sin and the beginning of a new life in Christ.

Harry Ashfield takes on a new name, Bevel, signifying this new life, just as babies are christened with their names at Christian baptism. Though his story ends tragically with a presumed suicide (no doubt regarded as an accident within the world of the story, since Bevel is so young), in the spiritual sense, Bevel's life has been renewed through his search for the Kingdom of God. Like the grandmother in "A Good Man Is Hard to Find," Bevel has died in a state of grace, this time from just having received the sacrament of Baptism. As Bevel Summers preached that all should do, young Bevel has laid down the pain of his unhappy childhood in the river and has been redeemed from his suffering. Though many readers first see the story as tragic and sad, O'Connor uses imagery of ashes, skeletons, color, and music to render an ending that may be read as uplifting—the boy's transformation from death into spiritual life.

At the beginning of the story, when Bevel's father has not put him fully into his plaid coat, Mrs. Connin remarks that he isn't "fixed" right. His father says for her to fix him then, and curses, "for Christ's sake." This interchange about the coat foreshadows what will happen later and sets the tone for the story's imagery. Bevel will indeed be "fixed for Christ's sake," but not in the way his father intends. As his name implies, Harry Ashfield lives an ashen, barren existence in his parents' dark apartment in the city. Mrs. Connin is described as a skeleton when she arrives, and she remarks to the boy as they wait for carfare from his father that she could not long abide the smell of the dead cigarette butts in the ashtray. The broken planes of violent color in the watercolor on the wall are crossed by black lines, and Bevel's mother calls for an ice pack for her hangover. Water, representing life, is frozen into ice packs or constricted into abstract forms rather than landscapes or portraits at the Ashfields' apartment. Though the boy's father appears a bit more sympathetic toward him than his mother does, there is very little love or life in the boy's home environment. The boy is startled when his father suddenly calls as an afterthought from the bedroom for him to have a good time. His pet name for him, "old man," rather than possibly suggesting that the boy may be wise beyond his years, instead supports the notion that he is nearer to death than life as long as he lives in that apartment.

By contrast, young Bevel is innocent and sheep-like in his willingness to be led out of the apart-ment, and the reference to the lamb alludes to youth and new life and also both to Christ as the Good Shepherd and the sacrificial Lamb of God in Jesus dying on the cross. Life begins to show itself in small signs almost as soon as they leave the apartment. Mrs. Connin's handkerchief is deco-rated with red and blue flowers. The designs are flowers, living vegetation, not abstractions, and the colors of red and blue are traditionally the Catholic colors of the Sacred Heart of Jesus and the Virgin Mary. When Mrs. Connin tells Bevel's father that she would have painted the watercolor rather than paid money for it, she admits to Bevel outside that she would not have painted it. She seems puzzled at why anyone would want such a painting. Her aversions to the abstract painting as well as her difficulty dealing with the ashtray suggest that Mrs. Connin comes from a more animated world. The two take the Vine Street trolley out of the city, bringing to mind the Bible reference to Jesus as the vine of life from which spring the fruit of his follow-ers. Though the buildings of the city appear gray and unlit, life imagery continues with the descrip-tion of Mrs. Connin in the car. She looks like a musical skeleton, making a whistle as she sleeps.

On the walls of her small home hang photo-graphs and calendars depicting real people and the passage of time. Another picture is of Jesus in a golden halo as the carpenter, surrounded by chil-dren. Even the light-colored dog with its tail poking up through the floorboards of the house foreshad-ows the unlikely surprise of life beneath the surface. Bevel is frightened by the dirty shoat that chases him and turns out to be very different from the pink pigs wearing bow ties that he has seen in books. He is learning the valuable difference between a pig that is alive and one that is not.

The family forms the shape of a boat's skeleton as it walks toward the river. Jesus is called the fisher of men, and the boat alludes to this image. Jesus is also called the Word made Flesh in that his coming to earth as a human being fulfills prophecy in the Scriptures. The frequent skeleton imagery may represent people waiting for their flesh to be replenished by the word of God. Just as Mrs. Con-nin predicted, the gray skies clear with the white sun seemingly racing them as they make their way toward the river. The red clay road, honeysuckle, and purple weeds of the countryside show the country as a more colorful and vibrant place than the warts of the city skyline in the distance. The river itself is a muddy yellow-red. The preacher and his followers sing hymns; the religious symbols of a table of food (like an altar), light, and water blend with the music and the preacher's words to move several of the people to enter the water. The preacher's face is described as bony. As the one preaching the Word of God, he does not look like a complete skeleton, but the sign of his human nature is there. Bevel agrees to be baptized when the preacher asks him, but the startling plunge into the water does not take him to the Kingdom of Christ in the way that he thought that it would.

Back home in the dark apartment, Bevel rises early again the next morning and must find food on his own as well as something to do. His parents are passed out cold and will be until sometime in the afternoon when they will not make him a meal but will instead all go out to lunch. Sustenance in the form of healthy food and drink are not available to him in this deathlike place. He has not had any new books or toys to play with in some time. To make them new, he has torn what he has into pieces. However, new life cannot be made by tearing apart old things, and the reader senses the boy's deepen-ing despair. When he dumps out the ashes of two ashtrays, but not all (signifying that there are a lot of ashes in the apartment), on the floor so that his par-ents will think they have fallen and not blame him, and when he rubs the ashes into the rug, the sense of the boy's utter desperation in his ashen, lifeless world is complete. The trip back to the promise of the life-giving river seems inevitable.

The sun is high and hot and pale yellow in the clear blue sky as the boy makes his way back through the colorful countryside to the river. In his first attempts, he fails to stay under the water, and he begins to think that maybe the river and its promise is also a joke, like everything else in his life. He senses that the river will not have him, suggesting that perhaps he is not worthy. When he sees "Paradise," ironically Mr. Paradise, the large unbeliever with the cancerous ear, running toward him with the peppermint stick that looks to him like a red-and-white club, it reminds him of the hog with the bad ear that had chased him the day before. He plunges back under the water. This time the current feels like a gentle hand pulling him toward something. Despite not knowing exactly where it will lead, it is the movement of the current, suggesting the progression of life and time and place, that convinces him to let go of his anger and fear and, presumably, his life.

The river itself is the central image in the story. The red clay of the road leading up to it provides the explanation for why the water appears both red and yellow in the sunlight. The red of the water echoes Bevel Summers's preaching that the river represents, for Christians, the river of Jesus' blood, given to save the sins of all who believe in him. Summers calls the river the River of Blood, the River of Pain, the River of Faith, and the River of Love. It is the source of all that is good. In his young mind, Bevel misunderstands Summers's statement that he will go to the Kingdom of Christ if he allows himself to be baptized as though he were going to an actual place. When this does not happen, he decides to try baptizing himself rather than live another lonely, hungry day in his parents' dark apartment.

Bevel Summers, the preacher, has the reputation for being a healer, though according to his preaching, he does not promise healings as part of his services. Certainly nothing in the preaching leads one to believe he expects this to occur, though he blushes when he reports no healing at other services and others accuse him of not healing. He claims that he does not promise it. The pairing of "Bevel" Ashfield with Bevel Summers in the story is also interesting. In carpentry, a bevel is a slanted cutaway angle from a horizontal edge. With Jesus depicted as the carpenter with children around him in the picture in Mrs. Connin's house, perhaps both Bevels have come to Christ in a rather slanted way—Sum-

mers through his occupation as preacher and healer, and Ashfield as a young child not quite understanding what faith means. The slope down to the river from the bank may be seen as a sort of bevel as well. Both Bevels have made it down that slanted bank and into the water. Unlike the ash-filled world from which Bevel Ashfield comes, Reverend Bevel Summers's surname suggests the season of the fullness of life. The younger Bevel taking his name symbolically begins a new life and a move toward becoming someone out of the ordinary. Mrs. Connin had said that the reverend was no ordinary preacher.

Many readers question O'Connor's inclusion of the story's last paragraph, since the boy's departure and apparent death has already occurred. What is the function of this paragraph, which sees the situation from Mr. Paradise's point of view? If one considers that Paradise is the unbeliever along the riverbank and as the skeptic who nevertheless goes to the healings anyway, this provides one solution. In shifting the point of view to Paradise, O'Connor aligns the reader with the skeptic and away from the boy. The paragraph serves as a coda to the story, ensuring that the reader will accept that what has occurred from the boy's perspective has also occurred from an observer's, Mr. Paradise. It serves to move the story more into reality. Also, the reader actually may not be so closely aligned with Mr. Paradise after all. The reader sees Mr. Paradise's head bobbing up and down out of the water and his eyes look dull, his hands empty. The reader becomes yet another observer on the bank of the river and retains something akin to free will to decide for him or herself what has occurred.

CHARACTERS

Harry Ashfield (aka Bevel)   Bevel is four or five years old, has a long face with a bulging chin, and wide-set eyes. His eyes and nose seem to be running all the time when Mrs. Connin picks him up to take care for him for the day. He wears a plaid, button-down coat. As his last name suggests, Bevel comes from a family life that is barren of joy and meaning. On a whim, he takes on the name of the Reverend Bevel Summer, whom Mrs. Connin has called no ordinary preacher. He allows himself to be baptized by him in the river. He returns to the river the next day and is presumed drowned when Mr. Paradise comes up empty-handed after swimming after him.

Mrs. Connin   The shift worker with four children who babysits Bevel for the day and has him baptized in the river. She is described as a speckled skeleton wearing a long peagreen coat and felt hat and as a musical skeleton when she whistles while sleeping in the trolley. When Bevel does not recognize the picture of Jesus on her wall and asks her about it, she tells the boy about Jesus and reads to him from her great-grandmother's 1832 book of the life of Christ for children. She asks the preacher, Bevel Summers, to pray for the boy's sick mother and returns the boy to the city apartment. She refuses her pay when she sees and fully realizes the conditions under which the boy lives.

RELATED LETTERS

Elizabeth McKee, November 26, 1952 (HB 48); Elizabeth McKee, December 20, 1952 (HB 48); Sally and Robert Fitzgerald, [undated; Summer, 1953] (HB 60); Betty Hester ("A") August 24, 1956 (HB 171); Betty Hester ("A") September 8, 1956 (HB 174). *Pages HB*: 48, 48 (again), 50, 60, 171, 174.

FURTHER READING

Behrendt, Stephen C. "Knowledge and Innocence in Flannery O'Connor's 'The River.'" *Studies in American Fiction* 17, no. 2 (Autumn 1989): 143–155.

Coulthardt, A. R. "Flannery O'Connor's Deadly Conversions." *The Flannery O'Connor Bulletin* 13 (1984): 87–98.

Sexton, Mark S. "Flannery O'Connor's Presentation of Vernacular Religion in 'The River.'" *The Flannery O'Connor Bulletin* 18 (1989): 1–12.

"Some Aspects of the Grotesque in Southern Fiction" (1960)

This essay comes from a talk given by O'Connor as part of the Dorothy Lamar Blount Lecture Series at Wesleyan College in Macon, Georgia, on October 28, 1960. It was published in *Mystery and Manners: Occasional Prose* (FSG, 1969) and was edited from its typescript by Sally Fitzgerald for publication in *Complete Works* (Library of America, 1988).

SYNOPSIS

The benefit of listening to a writer speak is to hear about her experience, not her theories. In this O'Connor says she is like Samuel Johnson's blind housekeeper; she measures tea by putting her finger in the cup.

In the 1920s and 1930s, writers could better speak for themselves as a group than they can now. Writers at Vanderbilt put together a pamphlet called *I'll Take My Stand*. In the 1930s, writers were bound by their mutual sense of social responsibility. It is not the same today; today writers speak for themselves and would not presume to speak for their generation or for other writers.

In speaking about their work, fiction writers hope to show that they are realists. This is not an easy task for some writers, especially those whose characters are not necessarily found in typical American society. Southern writers cannot escape the label, and they are ranked based on how closely their stories seem to relate to real life. O'Connor says she is frequently told that rural Georgia is not really the way she depicts it with criminals roaming the roads and Bible salesmen running off with girls' wooden legs.

Readers do not read simply for a moral in a story anymore. Due to the effects of social sciences on readers, now they read to look for deeper meaning from the daily life exhibited by the novelist. Nathaniel Hawthorne perhaps anticipated this by insisting that he wrote not novels but romances. Realism should not be held to such a standard that it limits the novelist and the novel. The supposed opening up of fiction to the everyday turns back on itself when the public begins to expect the same thing of every writer. Writers only know freedom from limitations within their own work. If writers choose to write outside of the realism of everyday events, but their work has life, then it should be considered on its own terms.

Much fiction has a quality about it that becomes labeled GROTESQUE. Northerners seem to put this label on almost any fiction from the South, but,

[O'Connor suggests] let us set that aside. When writers depict characters and situations that the reader does not see every day, if ever, this may safely be described as grotesque. Rather than be tied to realism in the way the reader may instantly recognize it, this kind of realism turns toward mystery and cannot be anticipated.

While all novelists seek the truth, they will see the depths of reality in their own way. Some will raise science above mystery. They will write of what they see and of what can be explained through some kind of order. They will write of immediate concerns. Other writers still believe in mystery and that life will always be filled with it. They will write of the details of the order of life only to the extent that it helps them reach the realm of mystery. The story's theme for this kind of writer only begins to be explored once the logic of psychology and other disciplines do not work. This writer is most intrigued by the aspects of existence that we have not been able to explain, rather than those for which humankind has found reasons and proofs.

The novelist interested in mystery will be more concerned with "possibility than probability" (MM 42). His or her characters will confront good and evil and must act but not always through understanding the forces at work through their actions. These characters are something like Don Quixotes, leaning toward something that is absent.

The novelist interested in mystery does not ignore concrete details such as those recorded through the senses. This is where story begins; it is a basic tool of the fiction writer to address these matters. However, this kind of novelist will be more open to distorting these details to achieve aims in working toward mystery and possibility.

HENRY JAMES once said that JOSEPH CONRAD used to write in a way that took the most work. Writers of grotesque fiction work just the opposite—they are trying to find an image that will connect two points at once—the concrete detail and the invisible element that the novelist believes is there just as much as the visible one. Because these two elements are so disparate, the result is going to be "wild," "violent" and "comic" (43).

The fiction writer of the grotesque may not see his or her characters as so unusual, but the audience definitely will. The audience will tell the novelist why he or she has chosen to present such odd characters. When they are looked on favorably, they are told that the characters show the writer's compassion for humanity. O'Connor believes that this is a sentimental rendering.

Compassion is a word that appears on many book jackets describing authors. Human beings need to be forgiven and understood because they are human beings. It is difficult for such an author, then, to be against anything. When grotesque is used properly, judgment overrules emotion.

In 19th-century American literature, grotesques appeared in works about the frontier and were often meant to be funny. Current grotesque characters may be amusing, but that is not their primary function. They carry a heavy load. Novelists who see meanings beyond the visible and the concrete in the visible are like prophets.

Southern writers write about the "freaks" of the world because, unlike writers from other regions, perhaps they can still see them. In order to recognize a grotesque, one must be familiar with the whole person. Because the South is still based in a theological culture, this provides the sense of the whole being against that which the unusual may be measured. "I think it is safe to say that while the South is hardly Christ-centered, it is most certainly Christ-haunted" (44). Whether the individual southerner may or may not believe it, he must contend with the notion that he or she is made in the likeness of God. When a freak is thought to take that place in literature, that novel reaches a deeper place.

Another reason southern writers tend to use more grotesques is because there are so many good southern writers. One needs to find another path than WILLIAM FAULKNER or others who are also working the same territory. The southern writer is forced to go beyond the scene in front of him or her to a universal truth in the world of the prophets. When Hawthorne suggested that he wrote romances rather than novels, he was making this same turn. He was pushing fiction more toward poetry. For the time being, southern literature has brought together this idea of Hawthorne's romance with the grotesque and has been able to evade the current trend of creating literature that is a mere mirror of society.

American audiences today want novelists to mirror their society and help heal their wounds. It is not the task of the novelist to be a nursemaid. "The novelist must be characterized not by his function but by his vision" (47). Sometimes the audience will have blind spots to this vision, so this is another explanation for an author's use of the grotesque to show what he or she sees.

Serious writers need to be concerned not just with the elite who know how to read carefully but also with the general reader who reads to be raised up after a long, tiring day. O'Connor says she heard from a woman in California who complained that none of her stories lifted her up. O'Connor thinks that if the woman's heart was in the right place, she would have had her spirits raised from her stories. What people forget, she says, is the amount of work that must go into the redemptive enterprise.

The neat balance of Dante with his heaven, purgatory, and hell is not the same balance with which writers need to concern themselves today. He wrote in the 13th century. Things were different then. Now, people question everything. Writers need not go to other writers to find balance; they need to create a balance from within themselves.

The great novels of the future will not be those that the reading public thinks it wants or that critics outline as desirable. They will be novels that novelists themselves want to read because they have never been done before. They will require much of the reader and will be more in the direction of poetry than what the novel has traditionally been.

The novelist who wishes to write this novel will need to go underground to the springs that enliven his other work. He or she will need "to know how far he can distort without destroying" (50). He or she must go within himself or herself to the place where vision begins, where he or she sees human beings like trees that move.

O'Connor expresses her belief that southern writers must continue to try to understand this vision to keep southern literature alive and growing. She does not want to think of a southern literature where novelists write about the same kinds of characters in suits who are really more grotesque than the freaks they write about now. Southern writers should continue to challenge readers. It should not be their function to meet the needs of tired readers who are not willing to put in the effort required for reading that will lift them up.

RELATED LETTERS

Betty Hester ("A"), December 16, 1955 (HB 127). *Page HB*: 127.

"Stroke of Good Fortune, A" (1949)

This is the fourth story in the collection *A Good Man Is Hard to Find and Other Stories* (Harcourt, 1955). Some critics see the piece as the point of departure from O'Connor's earlier stories into her later, more mature work.

SYNOPSIS

Ruby Hill comes home from buying groceries and places a sack of collard greens on the table at the foot of the stairs. She is frustrated because when she asked her younger brother, Rufus, home from the war, what he might like in the way of home cooking, she thought that he might suggest something civilized. Instead, he said that he wanted collard greens. She and her husband, Bill B. Hill, had not had collard greens in the five years that they have been married. Bill is a salesman from Florida who sells Miracle Products. Ruby left her hometown of Pitman and came to the city when she married Bill and never looked back. Now the small town of Pitman is entirely gone. That is why Rufus came to live with her and Bill when he got home from the European theater. Ruby thinks she is the only one of the family who had any ambition, any "get." She writes a note on the side of the sack for Bill to bring it upstairs and begins a long and arduous journey one step at a time.

Ruby is sick and in no condition to climb so many steep stairs. Her palmist, Madam Zoleeda on Highway 87, told her that she will have a long illness followed by a "stroke of good fortune." Ruby thinks this means that she and Bill are going to move soon into their own house in a subdivision, which is something she has been wanting. She contemplates her age, 34, and how that is not old, but that her mother, who had had eight children, looked old. Even if she did not touch up her hair, Ruby thinks, she does not look as old as her mother at the same age. Her sisters as well had had many children—four each in four years. She recalls that when her mother had Rufus, she was the only sibling who could not stand the screaming and commotion for him to be brought into the world.

Each flight of steps contains 28 steps, and she is breathless. She sits down, only to sit on a toy pistol owned by six-year-old Hartley Gilfeet. His mother calls him "Mister Good Fortune." Ruby is nauseous but rises again. She wonders if she may have heart trouble. Mr. Jerger's door opens, and he tells her whose birthday it is that day—Ponce de Leon, the seeker of the fountain of youth. She continues on up the stairs after their conversation and thinks maybe she has cancer. On the third floor, she encounters Laverne Watts, a friend. She brings in Hartley Gilfeet's toy pistol and takes a seat. She notices her swollen ankles and says that she will not go to the doctor. Laverne tells her she thinks Rufus is cute.

The women talk about shoes, and Laverne tells Ruby she should see a doctor. Ruby tells her that she has not seen a doctor since she was carried to one when she was 10 years old but escaped. Laverne asks her what it was for, and Ruby says that it was for a boil. Laverne starts to dance around and sing the word *Mother,* but Ruby insists that Bill takes care of that. She is not pregnant. Laverne says that Bill slipped up this time. She teases Ruby that her stomach has grown so much that she must have two babies inside it. She ought to go to the doctor just to find out how many babies there are.

Ruby feels insulted and gets up to leave. She announces that she thinks her heart will be better tomorrow. She slams the door and looks at her bulging stomach. Her loose skirt is feeling tight. She feels a pain and then as though something inside of her is rolling over. No, she could not be pregnant. There was no child waiting to make her old. Bill Hill said it was guaranteed, and it had worked all this time. She puts a hand over her mouth. Madam Zoleeda had told her that she was going to receive a stroke of good fortune that meant that she would soon be moving. She begins to feel calmer.

Suddenly there is a bang downstairs and a shaking rumble. Hartley Gilfeet gallops up the stairs slinging two pistols. Mr. Jergers opens his door quickly enough to grab a piece of the boy's shirt, but he works himself free. His mother calls from above for him to shut up, that he has set the whole place shaking. Ruby holds onto a banister spoke and looks down to the bottom of the stairway from where she had come. Suddenly she connects good fortune with a baby. Saying it echoes back to her through all three flights. She feels the rolling sensation inside again, but it feels as though it were not in her stomach but somewhere out there and nowhere as though lying in wait, with lots of time.

COMMENTARY

This short story originally appeared under the title "A Woman on the Stairs" in the August 1949 issue of *Tomorrow* (vol. 8). It was republished with the current title in *Shenandoah,* Spring 1953 issue (vol. 4) before appearing in the *Good Man* collection in 1955. In one of its incarnations, the story was going to be a chapter in the novel *Wise Blood,* but O'Connor wrote later in a letter that she had the good sense to take it out. The story under its last and final title was later collected in *Complete Stories* (Farrar, 1971) and in *Collected Works* (Library of America, 1988).

In December 1954, O'Connor was working with her editor, Robert Giroux, on the stories to include in *Good Man.* She wrote that this story was one of which she was not particularly fond, along with "An Afternoon in the Woods." If necessary, she favored omitting both of them from the collection in order to include a story she liked better, "Good Country People," which she had written very close to the deadline for the collection. In a letter to her agent, she agreed that she did not favor the story. She called it Catholic in its own way and told Elizabeth McKee that she had wanted to take it out of the collection, but Giroux thought it went along with other stories thematically. O'Connor said that the story was "about the rejection of life at its source" (HB 85). She said that the story, however, was "too much of a farce to bear the weight" (85). She also wrote about the German edition of *Good Man* in 1961 and that it would be all right for the Germans to omit this story but not "The Displaced Person."

When O'Connor writes of rejecting life at the source, she is writing about how Ruby Hill is rejecting her pregnancy and that the story in some ways is about the Catholic belief that human life begins at conception and must be protected and nurtured. The rights of the unborn are still prayed for and argued for politically by Catholics. The story shows Ruby Hill coming to the realization that she is pregnant. It is a feminist story in one sense because Ruby Hill does not see herself as a willing mother.

Ruby Hill is 34 and wanted to leave her home town of Pitman, Tennessee, to go to the city and make something of herself. She is the only one in her family with ambition, or what she calls "get." She is disappointed when her brother, Rufus, comes back to the States from the war in the European Theater. She thinks he should be worldly and more sophisticated now, but instead when she asks him what he would like special for dinner, he tells her that he would like some collard greens. This disappoints her.

The palmist, Madam Zoletta, tells Ruby that she will have a long illness that will result in a stroke of good fortune. Since Ruby has been wanting to move to a bungalow in a subdivision after five years of marriage, she thinks that this is the good fortune that will befall her. However, she wonders what illness she may have that will last until she and her husband move.

O'Connor uses numbers in some rather obvious ways. For example, there are several instances where Ruby thinks of her age, 34. The normal gestation for a baby is 38 weeks, but a premature baby may be born fairly healthy at 34 weeks. Ruby's mother was also 34 when Rufus was born, and Ruby thinks that she looked old from that time forward. She does not want a child at age 34 as her mother had. There are 28 stairs to Ruby's climb to her apartment; there are 28 days in a woman's average menstrual cycle.

Perhaps one of the weaknesses in the story, even as O'Connor saw it, is that the reader and everyone else is in on the nature of Ruby's condition before she is. The palmist seems to know when she labels the end of the sickness as resulting in a stroke of good fortune. Mr. Jerger implies that

he knows when he speaks to Ruby about today being the birthday of Ponce de Leon who landed in Florida on Easter Sunday, looking for the fountain of youth. He tells her that he is young at heart, which harkens back to Ruby's thinking that she has heart trouble when it is really a youth quite literally tugging at the heart inside her.

Laverne Watts makes the most blatant hints that she knows what Ruby's problem is. She leans back and sticks out her stomach and sways back and forth as Ruby talks about her illness. She notes her swollen ankles. Finally, she hints so strongly by spelling out the word *Mother* that Ruby begins to deny what she is suggesting. She denies it by saying that Bill Hill has been taking care of that for five years. Laverne tells her that he slipped up this time, about four or five months ago, and that she thinks Ruby is having twins.

Bill Hill has noticed that Ruby is becoming fatter, but he has been happy about it. Even Bill seems to know and recognize what is going on with Ruby. Yet, Ruby's denial persists. The biggest reason Ruby keeps denying her condition is one that feminists recognize. Ruby had ambition to be something more than her mother and sisters. Her mother died a little more, she felt, each time she gave birth, and she gave birth eight times. Ruby's two sisters have four children each. If Bill had not been careful, she thinks, she could have had five children herself by now.

One of Ruby's problems, at least from what has been presented in the story, is that she did not, do much with the "get" she thought she had. She left Pitman and married slightly up the social ladder. Other than that, she has been living in the same fifth-floor apartment for five years. A related problem is that she dislikes children (for example, the rambunctious boy on the stairwell with the toy pistols, Hartley Gilfeet, whom his mother calls Good Fortune). She has not thought of herself as a mother. She still sees her little brother, Rufus, as a baby and cannot picture him being romantically involved with the interested Laverne Watts. Ruby remembers the turmoil that Rufus caused her mother when he was born, and so she wants nothing to do with the birthing process.

Another weakness that O'Connor likely recognized is that the reader is not given much of a clue as to how the story resolves itself—what Ruby will do with her new information. She makes the link between the pain she feels and the rolling sensation inside with the memory of Rufus hurting their mother. She speaks the word *Baby,* which might be read as a sign of recognition or the beginning of acceptance.

CHARACTERS

Ruby Hill   Ruby is 34 years old and large around the stomach. Ruby's name is ironic in that her stomach is swelling and her married name is Hill. She also has the struggle of climbing the stairs, like a hill, and the "hilly" challenge of understanding and coming to terms with what has happened to her. The name *Ruby* suggests the gem of good fortune that she holds within her. She thinks she has heart trouble, cancer, or gas instead of pregnancy. The name *Ruby* ties with the heart trouble she thinks she may have in that her red-blooded heart may have problems, not in its physical functioning but rather figuratively in Ruby's accepting the new life that is growing within her and her future role as a mother.

RELATED LETTERS

Robert Giroux, December 11, 1954 (HB 73); Robert Giroux, February 26, 1955 (HB 75); Sally and Robert Fitzgerald, June 10, 1955 (HB 85); Betty Hester ("A"), September 6, 1955 (HB 99–100); Elizabeth McKee, January 3, 1961 (HB 425); Cecil Dawkins, February 15, 1961 (HB 433). *Pages HB:* 73, 75, 85, 99–100, 425, 433.

FURTHER READING

Bauer, Margaret D. "The Betrayal of Ruby Hill and Hulga Hopewell: Recognizing Feminist Concerns in 'A Stroke of Good Fortune' and 'Good Country People.'" Teresa Caruso (ed. and intro.) In *"On the Subject of the Feminist Business": Re-Reading Flannery O'Connor,* edited by Teresa Caruso, 40–63. New York: Peter Lang, 2004.

Fitzgerald, Sally. "The Owl and the Nightingale," *The Flannery O'Connor Bulletin* 13 (1984): 44–58.

Haddox, Thomas F. "The City Reconsidered: Problems and Possibilities of Urban Community in 'A Stroke of Good Fortune' and 'The Artificial Nigger.'" *Flannery O'Connor Review* 3 (2005): 4–18.

Kahane, Claire. "The Maternal Legacy: The Grotesque Tradition in Flannery O'Connor's Female Gothic." In *The Female Gothic,* edited by Julian E. Fleenor, 242–256. Montreal: Eden, 1983.

Mayer, Charles W. "The Comic Spirit in 'A Stroke of Good Fortune.'" *Studies in Short Fiction* 16, no. 1 (Winter 1979): 70–74.

McDermott, John. "O'Connor's 'A Stroke of Good Fortune.'" *Explicator* 38, no. 4 (Summer 1980): 13–14.

Zoller, Peter T. "The Irony of Preserving the Self: Flannery O'Connor's 'A Stroke of Good Fortune.'" *Kansas Quarterly* 9, no. 2 (1977): 61–66.

"Temple of the Holy Ghost, A" (1954)

This is the fifth short story in the collection *A Good Man Is Hard to Find and Other Stories* (Harcourt, 1955). It originally appeared in the May 1954 issue of HARPER'S BAZAAR (vol. 88) and was collected in *The Complete Stories* (FSG, 1971) and *Collected Works* (Library of America, 1988). The story is one of the few in O'Connor's canon to include characters who are identified as Catholic, in this case Catholic school students, as she once was herself.

SYNOPSIS

Two sisters, Susan and Joanne, attend Mount St. Scholastica convent school. They visit their 12-year-old second cousin (unnamed) for a week. The sisters are 14, but the unnamed "child" of 12 is smarter than them both and knows it. The sisters call themselves Temple One and Temple Two and are crazy about boys. Alonzo Myers, 18, has brought the girls from the convent and has already been hired to take them back the following weekend. The child suggests that Alonzo could take the cousins around and entertain them, but both cousins protest. Alonzo smokes cigars, and the odor from them makes his riders keep the windows open.

The sisters, between giggles at the table, tell the child's mother about Sister Perpetua, the oldest of the Sisters of Mercy in Mayville. She had given them a lecture about what to do if a young man should make inappropriate advances toward them in the back seat of an automobile. They were to tell him politely to stop and announce that they are Temples of the Holy Ghost. The child does not think this is funny, and neither does her mother. The mother tells them that they *are* Temples of the Holy Ghost. The child thinks over this title and feels as if someone has given her a gift.

After dinner, the girl's mother collapses on the bed and comments that the sisters are going to drive her crazy if she does not find a way to entertain them for the week. The girl thinks of Wendell and Cory Wilkins, who visit their grandmother, old lady Buchell, on a nearby farm. They are 16 and have a car. The girl thinks that they want to become Church of God preachers because one does not need to know anything to become one. The girl's mother agrees that she can trust them.

When the boys arrive, the sisters sit with them on the swing. The boys sing and play the guitar and the mouth organ. Their songs sound like a cross between a love song and a hymn. One starts out, "I've found a friend in Jesus" and another is called "The Old Rugged Cross." The girls try not to giggle and to listen politely. When they are finished, the girls sing "TANTUM ERGO" to the boys in their Catholic-school-trained voices. The boys are not sure what to think. They wonder if they are being made fun of, and finally Wendell says that that must have been "Jew singing." The girls laugh, but the child kicks her foot on a barrel and tells him he is a dumb Church of God ox. The girl's mother arranges a picnic in the backyard for the cousins and their guests under the light of Japanese lanterns. The child decides she is not going to eat with them and goes to the kitchen to eat with the cook. The cook asks her why she is so ugly in temperament sometimes and tells her that God could strike her deaf and dumb, and then she would see how she would not be so smart.

After supper, the sisters and the boys go to the fair. The child wants to go but not with them, so she thinks that she would not have gone even if they had asked her. She goes upstairs. She can hear the calliope in the distance and imagines the tents, merry-go-round, and the children. She remembers the closed medicine tents that were for adults only and how she used to want to be a doctor. Now she

wants to be an engineer. She thinks about what it takes to be a saint and decides that she would like to be one but that because she lies and sasses her mother and is lazy and ugly toward others on purpose, she will not become one. She might be a martyr if she were killed quickly enough. She thinks over the various methods that might be used for her death as a martyr and which ones she could stand better than others. She goes to bed and at first forgets to say her prayers; then she jumps out and gets on her knees. She says the Apostle's Creed, and then thanks God with fervor that she is not a member of the Church of God.

At 11:45, the sisters come in. They turn on a dim lamp so as not to disturb the child, but she sits up anyway and wants to hear about everything they saw. She asks about the dancing monkeys and the fat man and the midgets. Joanne replies that they saw all kinds of "freaks" and that she enjoyed them, all except one. She tells her that there are some things a child does not yet know, but the child entices her to trade information by telling her that she has seen a rabbit have rabbits.

The sisters tell the girl about the tent with the individual inside who told the audience not to laugh at what was about to be shown. One side was for women and the other for men. The person was made this way and did not ask for it but was making the best of what God had made. If the audience laughed, they could be struck the same way. The child wonders if the person has two heads, but Susan tells her that the individual has both male and female body parts and showed them to each audience separately. Joanne asks about the rabbit, but the child simply tells them the rabbit spit the baby rabbits out of its mouth. She lies back in bed with her new information, and her imagination envisions the tent with the hermaphrodite talking about being the Temple of the Holy Ghost and the audience whispering Amen and clapping softly as though they knew there was a child nearly asleep nearby.

The next day, the girls wear their brown uniforms and are returned to the convent by Alonzo, the child, and her mother. The mother talks to the girls about how nice it was to have them visit and how she and their mother used to get along at the convent when they were girls. Before they know it, a nun has brought them into the convent, where they participate in Benediction. The child prays to be better, not to sass and be so irritable toward others. She thinks about the person in the tent at the fair as she looks at the Host in the monstrance. On the way home, the mother asks Alonzo if he had gone to the fair.

Alonzo replies that he did and did not miss anything and that it was good that he went when he did. Some preachers from town had inspected the fair and convinced the police to drive it out of town. After he says this, the child looks out over the pastureland and studies the sun as it sets. It looks red to her, like a Host drenched in blood.

COMMENTARY

The title of the story refers to the Catholic belief that one's body ultimately belongs to God and not to the person, that it harbors the spirit of God, and that the body should be respected and taken care of, not abused or defiled. The story helps explain the doctrine by showing the child's realization that her body is an important gift, that even bodies that others might consider unusual or freakish are loved by God as temples of the spirit. The story is also an insightful dramatization of a bright child's internal life of faith and imagination. Some aspects of the story suggest a rare commentary by O'Connor about the subject of Protestantism versus Catholicism. Finally, O'Connor herself once described the story as an exploration of the virtue of purity.

The focus on bodies and physical development is clear from the beginning of the story when the teenage girls arrive and act so differently from the child. They are developing through adolescence and have, in the opinion of their families, become overly interested in the opposite sex. As a consequence, they have been sent to the convent school to try to keep focused on their educations. The implication is that their bodies need to be protected from their sex drives and that their less than sharp minds do not seem strong enough to do that. Sister Perpetua has instructed them how to ward off advances from the opposite sex by informing any potential perpetrators that their bodies are Temples of the Holy Ghost. In Catholic belief, refraining from premarital sex and avoiding other acts of fornication outside of marriage are honoring God's temple that is one's body.

In contrast to the sisters, who are portrayed as silly and boy-crazy, the younger girl is described as thoughtful and discerning. While she does show some interest in the Wilkins boys, it is more as a source for her imagined stories than for anything else. She is younger and smarter than both of her cousins and the boys. She lacks patience and understanding with people around her. She has a strong, developing faith, which keeps her praying for the improvement of her faults that she is smart enough to identify accurately. She is wise enough, also, to know that her elder cousins are curious about reproduction and uses this knowledge to manipulate them into telling her what they saw in the tent at the fair.

The reader sees the child's faith at work through her prayers. She prays that she may improve her faults. She makes a "running start" and gets through to the other end of the Apostle's Creed. This is a humorous line by O'Connor, since the prayer is one of the longer formal prayers Catholics traditionally memorize and therefore is one of the more difficult for young people to recite. She then moves to a more fervent, informal prayer of her own in thanksgiving. Later, the girl prays at Benediction in the convent chapel. In Catholic doctrine, Benediction is the honor and adoration of the physical presence of the body of Christ in the Eucharist. The Host is displayed, exposed on the altar in a monstrance, and incense is burned in homage. A monstrance is an elaborate, circular frame often resembling the sun and its rays, raised on a stand. The child has made the connection between her body as a temple of the spirit as she has just learned from her cousins and her mother and the person's body in the tent. The performer at the fair explains that God made the person that way and that s/he does not dispute God's way. The performer is simply trying to make the best of an unusual situation.

During Benediction, the girl ponders the relationship between the hermaphrodite and the Host in the monstrance. This unlikely pairing need not be read as sacrilegious. In Catholic belief, the Host *is* Christ's body because Jesus says in Scripture, "This is my body" and again, "This is my blood" when he blessed and shared the bread and wine at the Last Supper. Catholics read Scripture at this critical time in Christ's life, just before his suffering and death on the cross, in strictly literal terms. They point out that Christ did not say that the bread symbolizes his body and the wine his blood. Catholic teaching regards questions about how bread may become body and wine become blood as one of the great and central mysteries of faith.

The child contemplates the role of the body and acceptance. She makes a connection that all these physical manifestations—her own body, the body of the performer at the fair, and the Host at Benediction, all are temples of the spirit of God. The red sun raised like a Host in Christ's blood at the end of the story replicates in nature the raised Host at Benediction and completes the circle of the girl's enlightenment about this doctrine of her faith.

In addition to her faith, O'Connor dramatizes the creative child's imagination by allowing the reader into her thoughts as she envisions and makes up various stories—the world war scenario with the Wilkins boys, the fair, the occupations in which she is interested, sainthood and martyrdom (including the story of the lions), the individual at the fair with the audience watching and whispering, and other examples. Actions of others around her, her emotional responses to those actions, and listening to what people say all influence the girl's imagination. When she cannot go to the fair with her cousins and the boys, for example, she goes to her room and pours her frustration into visions and ponderings. As she listens to the calliope in the distance, she allows her mind to wander, and her visions turn to miniatures stories, where she is often the hero.

In the story of the lions, for example, the girl ponders whether she could stand to be torn apart by lions as a means of martyrdom. She envisions herself in tights in an arena like the Coliseum, awash in the golden light of Christians hanging around the arena in cages of fire. A series of lions charge toward her, but each falls at her feet, instantly converted. Her faith is so strong that no lion ever harms her, and she even sleeps with them (reminiscent of the lamb, or Lamb of God, lying down with the lions). The Romans revert to burning her to try to kill her, but her body will not burn.

Finally, they cut off her head with a sword, and this act sends her directly to heaven. The child practices this final scene in her bedroom several times. O'Connor comments in a letter about this vision, remarking that it is the girl's childish way of looking at martyrdom as a young person. By the end of the story, she says, the child is embraced by the nun and has had the crucifix hanging from the nun's side pressed into her cheek. The child must accept Christ's Crucifixion and our own, O'Connor writes. From the girl's various stories, readers see a child with a vivid imagination who is able to convert aspects of her life's questions and problems into fantastic tales.

The mystery of the Eucharist was very real for O'Connor herself, both as a person and a writer. She writes to her friend Betty Hester, "Understand . . . that, like the child, I believe the Host is actually the body and blood of Christ, not a symbol" (HB 124). She once encountered a fallen-away Catholic intellectual at a dinner party who remarked that she now understood the Host as a symbol, albeit a good one, of the Lord's body and sacrifice. O'Connor writes that she objected to this characterization at the dinner, rising to say in a shaky voice, "Well, if it's a symbol, to hell with it" (125). She continues in her letter to Hester, ". . . it is all I will ever be able to say about it, outside of a story, except that it is the center of existence for me; all the rest of life is expendable" (125). It cannot be emphasized enough that understanding O'Connor's core belief in the mystery of the Eucharist in Catholic doctrine is central to an educated reading of her work.

Not only does the story dramatize the doctrine of the body as a temple of God and the child's faith and imagination, but the story also offers an unusual commentary about Protestantism versus Catholicism. The contrasts between the two beliefs in the story are striking. The Wilkins boys do not need to know anything to become Church of God preachers, whereas Catholics have convents dedicated to educating their faithful from a young age about the teachings of the church. Before the picnic, the girls sing the centuries' old chant of "Tantum Ergo" with their Catholic-school-trained voices. The Latin hymn was composed by ST. THOMAS AQUINAS in homage to the Eucharist and has been incorporated as part of Roman Catholic liturgy since the 13th century. The words to the hymn translated into English are: "Lowly bending, deep adoring, / Lo! The Sacrament we hail: / Types and shadows have their ending, / Newer rites of grace prevail: / Faith for all defects supplying / Where the feeble senses fail. / To the everlasting Father, / And the Son who reigns on high / With the Holy Ghost proceeding / Forth from each eternally, / Be salvation, honor, blessing, / Might and endless majesty. / Amen."

The centuries' old hymn looms as a weighty power over the more contemporary popular hymns the boys sing with their guitars and harmonica, "I've found a friend in Jesus" and "The Old Rugged Cross." The two styles of hymn set side by side in this way provide a strong contrast between ROMAN CATHOLICISM and American Protestantism. The implied superiority of the Catholic Church, at least in the view of the main character, continues as the girl prays that night a fervent prayer of thanksgiving that she is not a member of the Church of God. Some of these differences may have been written in jest by the author, who, after all, claimed that many of her stories were read too seriously by literary critics. This argument may be undercut, however, when considering the last and most important contrast in the story. While Catholicism is teaching the young girl that the hermaphrodite's body is holy and should be honored just as God made it, the Protestant preachers of the community condemn the fair and run it out of town.

Biographer Jean Cash reports some theories on the origin of the story. One is that a childhood friend from SAVANNAH GEORGIA, Loretta Feuger Hoynes, often visited MILLEDGEVILLE to see Flannery. According to Hoynes, O'Connor was a bossy friend whom Hoynes only visited because her mother pressured her to do so. She claims the friendship ended when she was a teenager. A friend of O'Connor's had a brother who asked Hoynes to the movies. On their return, Hoynes and the boy sat on the porch and swung and smoked. Hoynes claims that O'Connor put her out of the house with her bag and all, accusing her of being a "wayward woman" (Smith 18). Another account claims that the convent sisters are reminiscent of O'Connor's Florencourt cousins from Boston.

The story has an interesting afterlife in O'Connor's biography. She observes in one letter that no one except a few nuns has written or commented much on the story compared to her other work. She received one letter from a correspondent who admired all of her writing except this story. The admirer complained that the "It" in the story was a lie. The German editors of *A Good Man Is Hard to Find and Other Stories* chose this story and "A Stroke of Good Fortune" to omit from the German translation. O'Connor fought to keep in "The Displaced Person," which they also wanted removed.

O'Connor wrote to Betty Hester in December 1955 that the story "all revolves around what is purity" (HB 117). She wrote that of all the virtues, she finds purity to be the most mysterious and then offers a definition that purity may mean an acceptance of God's will for us in our own individual situations. One senses from her comments that O'Connor struggled with how to define purity and wrote the story, much as the child imagines her stories, as a way of exploring its many facets and what she thought of them.

CHARACTERS

Child/Girl The protagonist of the story, the child is described as 12 years old and smarter than other children her own age as well as many people who are older. She has a vivid imagination and an active religious faith and prayer life. She encourages her mother to invite the Wilkins brothers to entertain her visiting 14-year-old cousins for the week. After the girls return from a fair, she manipulates them into telling her about a "freak" show they saw there, which involves a hermaphrodite. She prays to improve her faults and also about what she has learned. She makes a connection between bodies as temples of God and the presence of God she believes as a practicing Catholic exists in the form of the Eucharist.

RELATED LETTERS

Sally and Robert Fitzgerald, March 5, 1954 (HB 70); Robie Maccauley, May 18, 1955 (HB 82); Betty Hester ("A"), October 12, 1955 (HB 111); Betty Hester ("A"), November 10, 1955 (HB 117); Betty Hester ("A"), December 16, 1955 (HB 124); Betty Hester ("A"), February 21, 1957 (HB 202);

Elizabeth McKee, January 3, 1961 (HB 425); Betty Hester ("A"), August 4, 1962 (HB 487). *Pages HB: 70, 82, 111, 117, 124, 202, 425, 487.*

FURTHER READING

Allen, Suzanne. "Memoirs of a Southern Catholic Girlhood: Flannery O'Connor's 'A Temple of the Holy Ghost.'" *Renascence: Essays on Value in Literature* 31 (1979): 83–92.

Donahoo, Robert. "O'Connor's Catholics: A Historical-Cultural Context." In *Flannery O'Connor and the Christian Mystery,* edited by John J. Murphy, et al. 101–113. Provo, Utah: Center for the Study of Christian Values in Literature, Brigham Young University, 1997.

Horton, James W. "Flannery O'Connor's Hermaphrodite: Notes Toward a Theology of Sex." *The Flannery O'Connor Bulletin* 23 (1994–95): 30–41.

Kahane, Claire. "The Maternal Legacy: The Grotesque Tradition in Flannery O'Connor's Female Gothic." In *The Female Gothic,* edited by Julian E. Fleenor, 242–256. Montreal: Eden, 1983.

Mayer, David R. "Apologia for the Imagination: Flannery O'Connor's 'A Temple of the Holy Ghost.'" *Studies in Short Fiction* 11 (1974): 147–152.

Michaels, J. Ramsey. "'The Oldest Nun at the Sisters of Mercy': O'Connor's Saints and Martyrs." *The Flannery O'Connor Bulletin* 13 (1984): 80–86.

Walden, Daniel. "Flannery O'Connor's Dragon: Vision in 'A Temple of the Holy Ghost.'" *Studies in American Fiction* 4 (1976): 230–235.

"View of the Woods, A" (1957)

The third story in *Everything That Rises Must Converge* was first published in the Fall 1957 issue of *Partisan Review* (vol. 24).

SYNOPSIS

Mary Fortune and 79-year-old Mark Fortune watch the construction around the lake. The old man had sold the land to a company that was going to build a fishing club there. They drive up each day in the man's Cadillac and watch the men work. The old man tells Mary, who is his nine-year-old grand-daughter, that cow pastures should not get in the way of progress. Mary looks very much like the old man, and he has often said that if he left anyone anything, it would be to her.

Mary is the daughter of his third or fourth daughter; Fortune cannot remember which. He does not value his daughter, in any case; she married an imbecile named Pitts and went on to bear him seven children. The old man allowed Pitts to farm on his land ten years before. He could keep what he farmed, but the old man retained ownership of the land and never let Pitts forget it. Just when the Pittses seemed to act as if they owned the place, the old man put them in their place by selling off a given lot of land. This put Pitts off because he wanted to buy the land himself.

Though his daughter spoke of staying on the land and carrying out her duty of taking care of Papa, the old man knew better. The Pittses were biding time for him to be dead and gone when they could take over everything. He had headed them off. He had already put everything in trust in Mary Fortune's name and named his lawyer instead of his daughter as his executor.

When they wanted to name the baby Mark Fortune Pitts after him ten years before, if it were a boy, he told them that if they linked his name with Pitts's, he would put them off the land. When the baby was born a girl who looked remarkably like him just the same, he suggested that they name her after his mother, Mary. Fortune takes to the little girl; they are so much alike. It pains him when occasionally Pitts makes the girl leave the dinner table while he ominously unfastens his belt, and they drive off. Mary tells her grandfather that she has never been hit. He tells her that she should not take such treatment from her father. The girl is used by both Pitts and Fortune to exact revenge one each other.

Fortune wanted to see the road in front of the house paved. He wanted a drive-in movie theater, a supermarket, a gas station, and a motel to set up on his land. He was not an old man who did not like to see change. He was all for progress. The old man takes Mary to see Tilman, the man who owns a roadside business and with whom he has been discussing the land sale. He goes in to talk with him after Mary asks him why they are here, and he tells her it is none of her business. She says she will not be there when he gets back.

When he comes back out, Mary is gone. A black boy tells him that she took off in a green truck with a man she called Daddy. He is angry that she will not stand up to Pitts; however, when he reaches home, she seems resolved. Mary continues to say that he should not sell the lot. He tells her that she is more like a Pitts than a Fortune, a remark that hurts him more than her. However, not long afterward, she does not wake him up to go watch the construction.

He coaxes her to go with him, but she does not know that he is heading to the courthouse to seal the deal with Tilman. He offers to buy her an ice cream cone, but she does not want it. When she refuses and they talk about the lot again and how she does not want it sold for all the reasons previously stated, the old man becomes angry. He asks her why she is concerned about her father's calves grazing when he beats her repeatedly. She insists once again that no one has laid a hand on her, and if they ever do, she will kill them.

The old man asks her if she is a Fortune or a Pitts. She replies that she is Mary Fortune Pitts. He tells her that he is all Fortune, and she gets a defeated look on her face that looks to him like a Pitts look. He is just as upset as if the Pitts look were stained on his own face.

Paperwork in hand from the courthouse, Old Fortune goes to Tilman's to complete the deal. As he does so, Mary suddenly appears in the doorway, throwing bottles, one of which hits Tilman in the leg. The old man pounces on her and subdues her. He thinks about what to do. She seems to respect her father for beating her for nothing; he thinks the time must have come for him to whip her for her bad behavior now. He drives off with her down the clay road.

He tells her to get ready over by a tree and that he is going to whip her. She tells him again that nobody has ever done that, and if they do, she will kill them. He tells her to take off her glasses. She tells him to take off his glasses. This makes the old man angry, and he yells at her not to order him around. He strikes clumsily at her ankles with his belt. His heart begins to bother him in all the commotion.

At this, she is on top of him. She kicks and hits and knocks him down. When he reminds her that he is her grandfather, she asks if he has had enough. She tells him that he has been whipped and by her and that she is all Pitts. This remark angers old Fortune beyond fury, and he takes advantage of her loosening her grip to switch positions. He takes hold of her head and rams it against a rock three times. In his rage, he kills the girl, saying that he does not have one bit of Pitts in him.

Afterward, the old man has a heart attack and dies. Both grandfather and granddaughter, who looked and acted so much alike, lie together on the ground. ~~ends up beating her~~

COMMENTARY

This story was reprinted in *Prize Stories 1959: The O. HENRY AWARDs*, edited by Paul Engle and Constance Urdang, and also in *The Best American Short Stories of 1958*, edited by Martha Foley. Later, the story was collected in *Complete Stories* (FSG, 1971) and *Collected Works* (Library of America, 1988).

On one level, the story is about family tensions and revenge. Frank Fortune uses his granddaughter to get back at his son-in-law, Pitts, and his daughter who married him. The source of Fortune's resentment toward Pitts is not clear, other than that he does not like him and that his daughter married him. The distrust runs so deep that he has arranged for his lawyer not his daughter and her husband, to take care of matters after he dies.

He also disagrees with them about the land and the best uses for it. Fortune likes progress. He is willing to sell off plots of his land for development. Pitts prefers to keep the land as it is. The Pitts's value the view they can see from the front yard. Mary Fortune agrees with her grandfather most of the time about the land. She watches with him from atop the Cadillac as construction crews work on one parcel of it. The yellow dress she wears echoes the yellow bulldozer at work in the garden.

Mary disagrees with her grandfather when Mark Fortune wants to sell the front lawn in a particularly nasty move against Pitts. The lawn is where Mary plays, where Pitts's cows graze, and most important where everyone can see a view of the woods. Critic Margaret Whitt points out that

O'Connor gives the woods a Christ-figure role in the story. The woods are described at least twice as walking on water, and they hold a degree of mystery that Mary appreciates, though her grandfather does not.

O'Connor's essay "Catholic Novelists and Their Readers" lends support to the Christ-figure interpretation. She writes that the Christian writer "is like the blind man whom Christ touched, who looked then and saw men as if they were trees, but walking" (MM 184). Although Fortune looks at the woods before his death, he fails to recognize their mystery as something that should be meaningful in his life.

Mary figuratively and literally holds her ground on her grandfather's latest scheme. In working to destroy the view of the woods, he has gone too far. He does not understand why she should disapprove of this plan when she was more like him than all the others and enjoyed the prospect of development on the family land in every plan before this one. Shopping malls and gas stations had sounded as productive to Mary as they had to him.

Frank reads any disapproval in this matter as a sign of the Pitts side of the family emerging through his granddaughter. For two people so alike in other respects, even their names, the difference in point of view on this one transaction does not sit well with Fortune. Mary is not disagreeing with him on her own but is siding with her father against him.

Fortune seems to hope to enjoy his own progeny without the "stain" of another man or family entering the gene pool. If the Fortune name could live on without any mixing, he would be pleased. He is so close to Mary as to drive out any Pitts influence: She would be no more a Pitts than he is. That is one reason why he resents her going so passively with her father to her presumed whippings. Fortune would not take any whippings from Pitts, so he expects Mary, his double, to do the same. Instead of going after Pitts for it, he chastises Mary for going along, as if, as a child, she has any choice. Pitts seems to be whipping Mary as a way of whipping Fortune. He sees the Fortune in his daughter as well and wants to drive that side of the family out of her as much as Fortune wants to drive out the Pitts side. Both men use Mary to antagonize the other.

Mary Fortune Pitts was named for Frank's mother. Had she been a boy, she would have been named Frank Fortune Pitts, but Fortune threatened to have his daughter and son-in-law removed from his property if they were to link his name with Pitts's in that way. When Mary was born and looked so much like him even from the first day, however, he allowed them to name her after his mother.

Fortune clearly places more importance on family acting and looking like him than he does on family relationships. Perhaps his mother's death sets in motion this lack of familial connection. He is not close to his daughter and remains close to his granddaughter only as long as she keeps reminding him of himself.

The Pitts name has been suggested as more naturalistic and Fortune as materialistic. Mary goes along with her grandfather's materialistic side until it comes to the moment about where she plays and where she has a view of the woods. The view of the woods holds special meaning for Mary and the other Pittses. Frank Fortune cannot appreciate the value of the view, so it is likely that he would never understand or relent in his desire to sell off the land.

In a Christian reading of the story where the view of the woods represents Christ, the more naturalistic Pitts value it and family, but Fortune does not. Mary dies in a state of grace because she is killed, and Fortune dies in a state of sin because he has killed.

CHARACTERS

Mark Fortune Fortune is 79 years old and a grandfather. He owns land that he sells off in portions as development encroaches on the rural countryside. His name suggests money. Fortune's mother died in childbirth, giving birth to him. It is intriguing to note that in a sense, Fortune actually kills two Mary Fortunes—both his mother by his birth and his granddaughter at his enraged hands. Bloodline means so much to Fortune that ironically it is he who damages it by not allowing it to complete its cycle from his mother through him and through his daughter to his granddaughter. For all the progress of commercial development that he favors, the progress of his bloodline seems unimportant to him. He cannot even remember which number daughter (either the third or fourth) Mary's mother is among his own children.

Mary Fortune Pitts Mary is very much like her grandfather in physical appearance as well as personality. Like him, she is short and broad. She has pale blue eyes that peer out from behind spectacles. She has his wide and prominent forehead and his scowl that is constant and penetrating. She also has his ruddy complexion. She is like him, at least her grandfather thinks, in temperament as well. She is intelligent, willful, and ambitious.

These traits come back to haunt Frank Fortune, who will die as a result of killing her. Ironically, it is Mary's insistence on embracing her Pitts family lineage that enrages Fortune, who insists that his Fortune bloodline is superior. Mark and Mary may as well have looked at themselves in a mirror and known what would befall them.

RELATED LETTERS

Mrs. Rumsey Haynes, September 13, 1956 (HB 175); Betty Hester ("A"), September 22, 1956 (HB 177); Elizabeth Fenwick Way, November 24, 1956 (HB 181); Sally and Robert Fitzgerald, December 10, 1956 (HB 185–186); Betty Hester ("A"), December 11, 1956 (HB 186–187); Betty Hester ("A"), December 28, 1956 (HB 189–190); Sally and Robert Fitzgerald, January 1, 1957 (HB 192); Betty Hester ("A"), November 2, 1957 (HB 249–250); Elizabeth McKee, May 7, 1964 (HB 574–575); Catherine Carver, July 15, 1964 (HB 593). *Pages HB:* 175, 177, 181, 186–187, 189–190, 192, 250, 575, 593.

FURTHER READING

Coulthard, A. R. "Flannery O'Connor's 'A View of the Woods': A View of the Worst." *Notes on Contemporary Literature* 17, no. 1 (January 1987): 7–9.

Edmondson, Henry T., III. "Modernity versus Mystery in Flannery O'Connor's Short Story 'A View of the Woods.'" *Interpretation: A Journal of Political Philosophy* 29, no. 2 (Winter 2001–02): 187–204.

Gentry, Marshall Bruce. "How Sacred is the Violence in 'A View of the Woods'?" In *'On the Subject of the Feminist Business': Re-Reading Flannery O'Connor,* edited by Teresa Caruso, 64–73. New York: Peter Lang, 2004.

Hewitt, Avis. "'Ignoring Unmistakable Likeness': Mark Fortune's Miss-Fortune in 'A View of the Woods.'" In *'On the Subject of the Feminist Business': Re-Reading Flannery O'Connor,* edited by Teresa Caruso, 129–154. New York: Peter Lang, 2004.

Kahane, Claire. "The Maternal Legacy: The Grotesque Tradition in Flannery O'Connor's Female Gothic." In *The Female Gothic,* edited by Julian E. Fleenor, 242–256. Montreal: Eden, 1983.

Magistrale, Tony. "An Explication of Flannery O'Connor's Short Story 'A View of the Woods.'" *Notes on Contemporary Literature* 17, no. 1 (January 1987): 6–7.

———. "Flannery O'Connor's 'A View of the Woods': An Expectation." *Notes on Contemporary Literature* 34, no. 1 (January 2004): 9–11.

Riso, Don, S. J. "Blood and Land in 'A View of the Woods.'" *New Orleans Review* 1 (1979): 255–257.

Roos, John. "The Political in Flannery O'Connor: A Reading of 'A View of the Woods.'" *Studies in Short Fiction* 29, no. 2 (Spring 1992): 161–179.

Violent Bear It Away, The (1960)

O'Connor's second novel was published by Farrar, Straus and Cudahy on February 8, 1960. It contains 12 chapters and is dedicated to the author's father, "For Edward Francis O'Connor / 1896–1941." Its title and epigraph come from the Gospel of Matthew in the New Testament: "From the days of John the Baptist until now, the kingdom of heaven suffereth violence, and the violent bear it away" (Matthew 11:12). Of O'Connor's two novels, this second work is considered to be the better written as well as the more satisfying book to read. Literary critics have found in it a rich source from which to mine ideas for contemplation, discussion, and debate, resulting in several critical articles.

SYNOPSIS

Chapter 1

The novel opens in third person omniscient point of view and continues through a series of flashbacks. The opening scene describes Francis Marion Tarwater, 14, becoming too drunk to finish burying his great-uncle, 84. The old man, also named Tarwater, had taken young Tarwater away at age seven from his childless schoolteacher nephew, Rayber, and a welfare-woman, Bernice Bishop, when they wanted to raise Tarwater after Rayber's sister had died. Though Bishop was twice the nephew's age, Rayber and Bernice later married and had one child, whom Tarwater also tried to steal away to baptize in the woods, but he had failed. Old Tarwater thought their baby's challenged mental state was God's way of preserving him from being totally corrupted by the schoolteacher nephew and the welfare woman. The elder Tarwater had once lived with the nephew as a charity case until he discovered that the schoolteacher was using him as research for an article for a teachers' magazine.

The great-uncle taught young Tarwater math, reading, writing, and history as well as schooling him in "the facts of his Redemption" (*Collected* 333). Elder Tarwater called himself a prophet and taught Tarwater the younger to believe that he would also soon be called to God's service. The morning he died, he had come downstairs and made breakfast as usual and then died before he could eat the first mouthful. His corpse sat upright in his chair, his eyes fixed on young Tarwater as the boy finished his breakfast. A tremor transferred from the old man to the boy.

The boy tried to dig his great-uncle's grave to his specifications. Old Tarwater had told him he wanted it 10 feet deep. The boy started to dig under the fig tree because he thought the old man would be good for the figs. As he digs, he has a conversation with himself, the "stranger." He remembers going into the city with his great-uncle, who went on business to try to have his property cleared from his schoolteacher nephew. They went to the schoolteacher's house, where the boy caught sight of his "dim-witted" cousin in the doorway, and then saw his uncle. The elder Tarwater wanted to baptize the boy, but the schoolteacher told him to get off his property or he would have him put back in the asylum where he belonged. He spoke about young Tarwater in a way that made the boy hiding in the bushes dislike him.

While he continues digging, but not very fast, he wonders what he should do now that the old man is dead. He does not want any part of being a prophet, yet at the same time, this is what he has been taught, so he sees signs sometimes that he has been called to this purpose. He did not like the city and when he asked his great-uncle why he was not doing any prophet work there, the man had told him that if the boy felt called to a mission, he should act on it but that he himself was not called at that moment. As he digs, a black couple, Buford Munson and his wife, approaches to buy some liquor from the old man's still. The woman feels bad for the old man's passing; she had a dream of his unrested spirit for two nights. The boy goes out to the woods to fetch their liquor but continues his conversations with his inner stranger. Soon he is lying on the ground drunk.

Buford Munson finishes digging the old man's grave and brings his body from the breakfast table and places it in the hole and covers him up. He places a cross at the head of the grave. When the boy wakes up from his stupor in the woods, he makes his way back to the house and sets it on fire. He runs to the road at about midnight and catches a ride with a copper flue salesman who is heading to Mobile. The salesman tells him that you cannot sell a flue to someone you do not love—love works 95 percent of the time. Suddenly, the boy looks through the windshield and thinks they are heading toward the fire, that they have turned around. The salesman tells him he must be crazy, that the light he sees is the city lights, not a fire. Tarwater tells him that he was asleep and he is just now waking up. The salesman tells him that he should have been listening to him; he has been saying things he needs to know.

Chapter 2

The copper flue salesman's name is Meeks. Tarwater does not trust him, but he stays in the car riding toward Mobile. Meeks directs to him a phone book in the backseat to look up his uncle's phone number and address. Tarwater writes the information on the back of Meeks's card, as instructed. Meeks tells him that he can call him any time. Meeks says that he will take him right to Rayber's door, but the boy wants to wait until daylight. Meanwhile, Meeks tries to tell him about the value of work.

Tarwater muses during the car ride. He knows two histories—one is about the world beginning with Adam, and the other is about the schoolteacher, his uncle, beginning with the teacher's mother, old Tarwater's sister. The boy's grandmother, as described by old Tarwater, had been a whore who took up with an insurance salesman named Rayber and had two children. One child was the schoolteacher, and the other was a girl who also became a whore at 18. At the prompting of the schoolteacher, she took up with a man and had Tarwater. When his grandparents and sister died in an accident, Tarwater's father shot himself. His uncle, the schoolteacher, tried to raise Tarwater as his own. His later wife, Bernice Bishop, convinced the schoolteacher to give up on the boy by becoming pregnant with a child of their own, who turned out to be the dim-witted boy.

Prior to this history, old Tarwater had tried to redeem his sister, then her son, and failed with both. His sister had had him committed to an asylum, where he lived for four years. When he got out, he had given up on bringing his sister to Redemption and decided to go after the schoolteacher who was still a boy. He persuaded Buford and Luella Munson to work for his sister, and through them he got into the house. He kidnapped the schoolteacher as a boy and took him to Powderhead, where he taught him and baptized him. The boy was not missed for four days. His mother was too drunk to notice that he was missing for three days, and his father did not come home to help for another day. The boy went back home with his father when he came for him but later tried to run away to get back to old Tarwater in the woods. When his great-uncle asked Tarwater why he thought that was, the boy told him that the schoolteacher knew it was less bad in the woods than it was at home, but neither situation was a good one. Old Tarwater insisted that it was because the schoolteacher wanted to learn more about God and the truth. Tarwater reminded him that the teacher had also come back when he was 14 and gave old Tarwater lots of sass, which the old man said came from his parents. Old Tarwater took pride in the school

teacher coming to tell him about the accident in person right after it happened and telling him that he had inherited the house.

The old man ended up living with the schoolteacher for a time. He had not been there 10 minutes when he baptized Tarwater, his great-nephew, as a baby in his crib. The schoolteacher did not want this to happen, but the old man did it while the schoolteacher was at the door with the paper boy.

The true falling-out came when old Tarwater saw the magazine article written by his nephew. It cited him as an extinct breed, one who needed to believe in the call of God so badly that he created a call for himself. The next day, the schoolteacher found the magazine in the empty crib with this note written on the back: "The prophet I raise up out of this boy will burn your eyes clean" (*Collected* 379). The old man told Tarwater that the schoolteacher liked to keep everything inside his head, but the old man was willing to act. When the boy asked why his uncle the teacher had never fought harder to get him back, the old man said that it was because the boy was too much trouble.

Meeks stops at a gas station and calls his girlfriend. He urges Tarwater to call his uncle, but he does not know how to use a telephone. Meeks helps him dial the number. The only sound on the other end is heavy breathing, which Tarwater attributes to the dim-witted child. Meeks takes Tarwater to the schoolteacher's house, opens the car door, and tells the boy to get out. He tells him that he may call on him at the number on the card next week if he grows hungry.

Chapter 3

At first Tarwater does not want to knock on the door, but finally he lifts the knocker and makes a racket in the neighborhood. His uncle comes to the door and lets him in, but he cannot hear the first words the boy says until he gets his hearing aid. The boy tells him that his great-uncle is dead and that he burned him, just as the teacher would have done. The teacher first looks upset, but the expression goes away quickly. He does not believe him. The boy begins to think this is a trap set by the old man himself, but finally they both trust what has happened. The teacher tells Tarwater that the old man did him a disservice, and it is not too late for him to rectify the matter by giving him everything that he would have given his own son. The dimwitted boy, Bishop, comes out, and Tarwater sees that he recognizes him. He wants nothing to do with his challenged cousin. At the same time, he remembers the old man's threat to the teacher that Tarwater would one day baptize Bishop.

Chapter 4

Rayber tries to make up to Tarwater for four days. The first night he sits by his bed as he lay in it, exhausted. He tries to talk to him about why he did not try to rescue him again from the old man. Tarwater asks him about the scar on his ear and about his hearing aid. The boy knows that the old man shot his uncle there, and his uncle tells him that the shot also affected his hearing. He tells him that he did not have a gun with him that day. Tarwater says that he could have come back with a gun, and the teacher tells him that he can do more for him now than he could have if he had been killed by the old man or killed him back then. They go walking, and Rayber shows the boy about the city. They go to museums, movies, art galleries, and department stores. The boy shows no interest in anything his uncle tries to show him. Oddly, in front of a tall building, Tarwater stops and says that he lost his first hat there.

Rayber is already planning to write about Tarwater. He tries to administer tests on him, but the boy refuses to cooperate. Tarwater tells him that he is free and that he will not be able to trap him in his mind. They go out to dinner, but Tarwater does not eat much, and he keeps notes on the cost of all the meals Rayber has fed him, including those at his house. He plans to pay him back; he does not want to be beholden to him. At the restaurant, Tarwater calls Bishop a hog, since he is eating so messily. Rayer tells him in a firm voice to forget him, and Tarwater looks at him as though he has figured something out. That night, Rayber discovers the boy missing from his bed.

Chapter 5

Rayber follows Tarwater through the hedge and into town. He does not know if the boy is leaving for good or just going for a walk, so he did not get shoes or suitable clothes; he follows barefoot and in his pajamas. The boy cannot seem to stop walking. He stops once in front of a store window, and Rayber thinks that he finally sees something he wants. He will return the next day and buy it for him. When the boy moves on and Rayber reaches to the window, all he sees is one remaining loaf of bread in a bakery window. The boy goes to a church with a neon sign over it. While Rayber listens and looks from the window to the evangelists speaking there, he relives his own experience of leaving his uncle when his father came to get him in the woods. He had given his reason to his father for not wanting to leave—he had been born again when old Tarwater baptized him in the woods.

A married couple is exploiting their daughter at the church for money. The girl does her own preaching; her mother says that she is called to do so. She preaches about God and love. Rayber watches her and listens from the window. Occasionally, she looks over at him from the lit stage, and it seems she sees him watching her. As she preaches, this happens more frequently, until finally she speaks of him to the audience, that she sees a damned soul who is deaf to the Holy Word.

Rayber drops to the ground, searching for the hearing-aid box to turn it off so that he cannot hear. He decides he wants to get home as soon as possible, with or without the boy. When he goes around front, Tarwater meets him. He grabs him by the arm and tells him that he hopes he has enjoyed the show. The boy says that he had gone in to spit on it, and Rayber answers that he is not so sure. The boy is more submissive to Rayber, but he is so full of rage that he does not notice, even when they get back home.

Chapter 6

Rayber realizes the next day that he missed an opportunity to begin to reach Tarwater. He and Bishop and the boy go to the natural history museum, and on the way Rayber remembers the time he tried to drown Bishop. When Rayber allows himself to feel love, he shuts it away.

They walk through a park, and Rayber sees that the park reminds Tarwater of Powderhead, and he sits down with Bishop in his lap. He thinks about the love this makes him feel and remembers the drowning incident. Tarwater wants to get going.

Rayber gets up and talks with him about the tabernacle he visited the night before. Rayber tells him that there is no need to even spit on it, since it is not important. Soon Bishop has loosened himself from Rayber and finds his way to a fountain and steps over the side into the water. Tarwater looks at him and moves toward him. Rayber realizes finally that Tarwater feels compelled to baptize Bishop in spite of himself. He reaches the boy and takes him out before his nephew has the chance to do his great-uncle's bidding. Tarwater takes off.

Chapter 7
Rayber takes Tarwater and Bishop to Cherokee Lodge. Thirty miles from Powderhead, it has a lake and cabins. He thinks he will take the boys fishing the first day, but his main intention is to take Tarwater back to Powderhead to face what he has done. He thinks if he can get him to do this, the boy may break down, and he can help him bring himself back from the trauma he has experienced.

He registers both Bishop and Tarwater as his sons. The woman at the desk eyes them all suspiciously; none of them is dressed well. When Tarwater realizes that Rayber has made it sound as if he is his son, he begins to write on the registration card. Rayber moves toward their cabin, allowing the boys to stay where they are. The woman tells Tarwater not to do whatever devil's work he is up to there. He tells her that one cannot just say no, one must do no (abstain). He says he did not ask to come there, and he did not ask that there be a lake set down in front of him.

As Bishop proceeds up the steps, he turns and sits in Tarwater's way. He is signaling that he wants his shoes tied. The woman at the desk figures Tarwater is mean and will not tie them, but he does. When she looks at the card, she sees that he has written his full name, Francis Marion Tarwater, his home, Powderhead, Tennessee, and a comment that he is not Rayber's son.

Chapter 8
Tarwater tells of his impressions over the last few days—the nights spent at Rayber's, the tabernacle incident, the park. He is waiting for a sign to see whether or not he should follow the old man's mission for him, whether or not he is a prophet. He has

been in a constant conversation with the stranger in his mind from the time he dug the old man's grave. When they get to the lodge, the stranger points out the lake and tells Tarwater that it is time to make his decision.

The boy eats a large breakfast at the lodge; then Rayber takes him out in a boat on the lake. They leave Bishop behind, and the woman at the registration desk rescues the boy from jumping in the lake to follow the boat. Rayber admits to Tarwater that he once tried to drown Bishop. He failed only for lack of nerve. Tarwater tells him that the old man always said he could not act. Rayber tells him he will take him up in an airplane, but Tarwater says he has already been up in one at a fair with the old man.

Tarwater feels nauseated in the boat from eating too much breakfast after he has not been eating much of Rayber's food previously. The old man had better food. Rayber tries to tell the boy how badly the old man treated him. Tarwater asks him if Bishop has been baptized, and Rayber tells him that he may not have had the guts to drown him but he has had the guts to preserve his self-respect. When he tells Tarwater that he can read him like a book, the boy leans over the side and vomits in the lake.

Rayber explains that it is as much a relief to get something off one's mind as off one's stomach. The boy grows angry and tells him to pull the plug out of his ear and turn himself off. Rayber tells him that he reminds him of the old man; he is just like him. At this, Tarwater pulls off his shoes and overalls and jumps into the lake and swims back to the dock. Rayber thinks he has struck a chord this time and decides to stay out on the lake for a while. He drops the boy's clothes into the water.

When he returns to the cabin, he sees Bishop watching Tarwater, who has put on the new clothes Rayber bought him. He notices something excited about the boy's demeanor. Rayber asks who wants to go for a ride, and only Bishop jumps up to go with him. He says they will leave Frank (as he calls Tarwater) to his thoughts.

Chapter 9
As he drives with Bishop, Rayber thinks about his wife. She could not stand Bishop and would not divorce Rayber because she feared she would get

custody of him. She was the reason Rabyer had not taken Tarwater away from the old man. She had seen something in the boy's eyes the day they went for him and Rayber was shot. There had been no change in his expression when the gun had blasted, and this expression affected her.

Before long, Rayber realizes he has driven over to Powderhead. He had not intended to do this today, but since they are there, he decides to have a look; maybe it will help him with his plan for Tarwater the next day. Walking through the woods with Bishop, he realizes that the property is all his, and he thinks that if he sold it, he could afford to put Tarwater through college. At the house, which is just ashes between two chimneys, he thinks he sees a vision of the old man standing there, waving a surprised greeting. When Bishop presses to be lifted up to see, Rayber is suddenly filled with a desire to get away as fast as he can. He knows he cannot return the next day. He picks up a corkscrew at a gas station to take back to Tarwater.

Back at the lodge, he gives Tarwater the corkscrew; he says that he has no use for it but thanks him anyway. Rayber watches as Tarwater takes a new interest in Bishop. He tells him to get up as he told him to. They go to the lodge to have dinner. Rayber has decided to just lay out his thoughts for Tarwater to consider, then let him decide whether he wants to go back with him and Bishop and go to school and live under his rules, or stay and fend for himself. He does not get too far in his talk when Tarwater tells him they are not alike as he thinks they are. He tells him that he can go ahead and baptize Bishop right then and there with the glass of water on the table. He knows that this has been a stumbling block for Tarwater to get on with his life.

Tarwater tells him that he is not like him; he can act. Rayber thinks maybe he has in mind to make Bishop his slave, and this will not do. After dinner, Tarwater takes Bishop out on the lake. Rayber tells him to be careful, and the boy replies that he will tend to Bishop. Rayber, relieved to have both of the boys gone for a while, lies down in his room. He considers how a life of indifference is the only way to keep his sanity with the background he has had.

He looks out the window once and sees the boys in the boat, Tarwater leaning toward Bishop intently.

When he looks again some time later, he cannot see the boat at all. He puts his hearing aid back in and hears a bellow. It continues for a while and then goes silent. He thinks then that Tarwater has not only baptized Bishop in the lake but he has also drowned him, as Rayber had tried but failed to do. Looking out the window, he collapses when he realizes that he will feel no pain over what has happened.

Chapter 10

Tarwater crouches by the side of the road until he is picked up by a truck driver delivering new cars. The driver tells him that he must talk to him to keep him awake; he is not picking up hitchhikers to do them a favor. The boy tells him he just wants to ride until the road they are on intersects with Route 56. The driver tells him to start talking. Tarwater says that he does not waste his life talking; he acts. The driver asks him what he has done lately; why are his pants wet.

Tarwater tells him that he has drowned a boy. He has also baptized him, but that was mainly because the words poured out of him and into the water. He needed to prove he was not a prophet, and now he has done it. He tells the driver he is hungry, and the driver offers him a sandwich. When the boy says he is not hungry and does not eat it, the driver says he is crazy. He tells him if he is sick to get out of his truck. The boy tells him that he has never been sick except for when he overeats. Getting sleepy, the driver asks the boy to tell him a joke. Tarwater does not know any jokes. Finally, the driver pulls over and falls asleep, snoring.

The reader learns how it went in the lake. Tarwater meant to drown the boy, but he did not mean to baptize him. The stranger had talked him through it. When the driver wakes up, he tells the boy to get out. Tarwater begins to walk the highway with new determination to plan and execute his own fate.

Chapter 11

Tarwater walks down the road. He comes to a shack and trades the truck driver's sandwich for a drink of water from a black boy. He moves on and reaches a store where he and his great-uncle had sometimes gone. The woman working there recognizes him and tells him that the blacks have told her what he did dishonoring his great-uncle's corpse. He has shamed the dead. He is about to say something to her, but instead a profanity escapes his lips, something he had not intended. He asks her to sell him a purple drink, but she will not, and he goes away extremely thirsty. He decides he will signal the first car that comes along.

A man in a lavender shirt and a panama hat picks him up. At first, they say nothing. The driver offers the boy a cigarette, something he has never had before. He also offers him some liquor from the glove compartment. Tarwater thinks back to his great-uncle warning him about taking rides with strangers and about poisonous liquor but shuts away the thought. He cannot open the bottle because the cork is stuck. Finally, he reaches in his pocket and gets the corkscrew his uncle had given him and opens the bottle. He takes one drink, but he is so thirsty that he takes another long swig, despite the burning of the liquid as it goes down. Soon, he is knocked out.

When he wakes up, he finds himself in the woods naked except for his shoes. His hat is gone; the man has taken it. His hands are tied loosely together with a lavender handkerchief. The man has also made off with the corkscrew. Tarwater rips off the handkerchief and gets dressed. He finds his matches and lights a fire to the patch of ground where he lay. He wants to burn anything the driver may have touched. He lights a pine bough and uses it to torch bushes on his way out. As he goes, he realizes that he is very near Powderhead.

Chapter 12

As Tarwater nears Powderhead, he feels a range of emotions. The stranger in his head now tells him to go down to the house and take what is rightfully theirs. The boy lights up another pine bough as a torch and ignites the forked tree where he and his great-uncle used to stand in the woods on their way home to look at the house below.

He walks nearer the house when he sees that the old man's corn is a foot high and the field is freshly plowed. Then he sees Buford on a mule and waves at him. He begins to run; he will eat with him. When he gets there, he sees his great-uncle's fresh grave. Buford looks at him scornfully and says that

it is because of him that his great-uncle is buried with a sign of his Savior over his head. It is because of him that his corn is plowed. Tarwater stares at the wooden cross and where it penetrates the ground. He stares so intently it is as though he is envisioning all the dead that the roots of the cross envelop underneath the ground. Buford smells the burning woods; he turns the mule and goes away.

Tarwater looks down over the field and sees a vision of a multitude of people. They are sitting on the slope and eating from a single basket. He searches and finds the old man among them. The boy is finally aware of the source of his hunger; he is so hungry that he could eat all the loaves and fishes after they are multiplied. He looks back and sees a burning bush and comes to know that this fire is the same one that spoke to Daniel, Elijah, and Moses and it would soon speak to him.

The boy throws himself on the old man's grave and hears the command, "Go warn the children of God of the terrible speed of mercy" (*Collected* 478). He stands, then stoops down and takes a handful of dirt from the old man's grave and smears it onto his forehead. Then he walks off in the direction where Buford went across the field. Leaving the burning woods and the road behind, he makes his way to the highway once more by midnight. He appears ready to envision his fate. Steadily, he makes his way toward the city, where the children of God are asleep.

COMMENTARY

Publication and Reception

The Violent Bear It Away was published in 1960 by Farrar, Straus and Cudahy. The first chapter originally appeared in New World Writing in October 1955 under the title "You Can't Be Any Poorer Than Dead." The chapter was also submitted with other work as part of the author's application for the Kenyon Review Fellowship in the fall of 1952.

Like her first novel, *Wise Blood, Violent* met with mixed reviews when it was first published. In an article entitled "God-Intoxicated Hillbillies" in the February 29 issue of *Time*, the reviewer was particularly harsh, turning attention from the book to the author herself. O'Connor was described as "a retiring, bookish spinster who dabble[d] in the variants of sin and salvation like some self-tutored backwoods theologian" (qtd. in Whitt 87). The article also mentioned LUPUS explicitly, a shot that O'Connor found particularly offensive and unfair. Her disease, the article asserted, made O'Connor "visit remote and dreadful places of the human spirit" (87). The reviewer claimed that the novel was written by a "secure believer" who used the book "to poke bitter fun at the confused and bedeviled" (87).

The *New Yorker* also saw little merit in the book in 1960. It gave the novel two sentences in the March 19 issue, which included describing it as a "dark ingrown Gothic tale" (qtd. in Whitt 87). In October 1960, the *Times Literary Supplement* stated that O'Connor's "sophisticated pessimism creates a number of unrewarding moral culs-de-sac" (87). Early comments from *Library Journal* were mixed. They asserted that the novel's lack of "convincing action" carried the "macabre tale to a successful conclusion." However, even in 1960, the journal recognized O'Connor's potential for a lasting place in literature with their further comment, "Recommended only for those libraries that want a complete collection of all potentially important young American writers" (85).

In the *New Republic*, Frank Warnke attempted to delve into the novel further and was puzzled by the title, which he evidently did not relate to the Bible passage from which it comes. About the title, he asked, "Does it have something to do with a national conviction that only violent actions performed by ignorant and underprivileged people are 'real' enough to write about?" (87). He read the novel as an allegory about "a mad and murderous John the Baptist baptizing an idiot Christ" and found the book overall to be about "the misery of man without God." He praised what he called O'Connor's "stylistic felicity" (87).

Since O'Connor's death, literary criticism about this novel has been more active than for *Wise Blood*. Critics see connections between the two novels, including the reluctant prophet or religious hero. Francis Marion Tarwater is another version of Hazel Motes. Both the boy and the young man were apparently chosen to be preachers or prophets without their approval, and both fail in their efforts, including through the use of violence, to

run away successfully from their mandate. Readers may not be sympathetic to either character. Those who appreciate both novels recognize their uniqueness. Those who favor *Violent*, as most critics do, appreciate a maturity in O'Connor's technique.

The Title, Violence, and Religion

When O'Connor won the Georgia Writers' Association Scroll for this novel in 1962, she gave an acceptance speech that mentioned the problems she had experienced with the title after the book was published. She expressed gratitude that the group not only remembered the book two years after its initial publication but also that the organizers got the title of her book correct. "I've had a hard time all along with the title of that book," she said (MM 51). Some of the wrong titles she had heard since its publication included *The Valiant Bear It Always* and *The Violets Bloom Away*. She related a story from a friend who went into a bookstore one day looking for her collection of stories (only the collection *A Good Man Is Hard to Find and Other Stories* had thus far been published). The storekeeper said that they did not have the book for which her friend was looking, but they did have another book by the same author called *The Bear That Ran Away With It*.

Though O'Connor recalled the title problems with amusement, her use of the Bible passage as a title for the novel no doubt came from her interest in theology. She admitted in letters that the title comes from the Douay Bible verse Matthew 11:12: "From the days of John the Baptist until now, the kingdom of heaven suffereth violence, and the violent bear it away." The Douay Bible, also known as the Reims-Douai or the Reims-Douay, is a Catholic English translation of the Latin Vulgate Bible. Catholic scholars who were exiled from England translated the New Testament and published it in 1582 at Rheims, which was then the temporary home of English College. The Old Testament was published in Douai/Douay in 1609–10. At that time Douay was part of the Spanish Netherlands, but it is now located in France.

The translators of the Reims-Douay included men formerly from Oxford—William Cardinal Allen; the chief translator, Gregory Martin; and

Thomas Worthington. Their main purpose in translating the Latin Vulgate Bible was to provide Catholics with an authoritative version of the Bible in English. Before that time, individual Catholics did not frequently read the Bible since the Catholic version appeared only in Latin, which was mainly read by the clergy. Since, by this time, several Protestant versions of the Bible were already in existence, the publication of the Reims-Douay allowed individual Catholics the opportunity to read the Bible for themselves and argue against the tenets of the Reformation. Notes provided in the Bible by scholars, in fact, addressed some of the Protestant reforms and interpretations directly. From 1749 to 1772, Bishop Richard Challoner ordered several revisions to the Catholic Reims-Douay Bible with the intent of making it more understandable to the everyday parishioner. Revisions were subsequently issued at other times as well, including on into the 20th century.

The passage from Matthew is a difficult one for scholars. O'Connor must have been struck by the passage's apparent and surprising tying of violence to heaven. Does the passage mean that from the time of John the Baptist until now, the kingdom of heaven has been under siege by violence, and those who commit the violence take heaven away? Or, does it mean that from the time of John the Baptist until now, the kingdom of heaven endures violence from those who would also take the violence away? Many interpretations have been argued through various Greek and other translations by scholars from several Christian denominations. What matters here is what the passage may have meant to Flannery O'Connor and how that meaning may enlighten readers.

Virginia F. Wray presented previously unknown evidence about the title in a 1977 article, "An Authorial Clue to the Significance of the Title *The Violent Bear It Away*" in the *Flannery O'Connor Bulletin*. In her brief article, Wray presents a discovery from among O'Connor's books, which are now housed in the Flannery O'Connor room at the Georgia College and State University in MILLEDGEVILLE. In the author's copy of the 1952 book *Personalism* by Emmanuel Mounier, O'Connor wrote "the violent bear it away" next to a passage on page 49 that she

had marked with a vertical line along the right-hand margin. The passage comes in the chapter "Confrontation" and in the subsection called "Jacob's wrestling." Here is the section that O'Connor marked:

> The person attains self-consciousness, not through some ecstasy but by force of mortal combat; and force is one of its principal attributes. Not the brute force of mere power and aggression in which man forsakes his own action and imitates the behaviour of matter; but human force, which is at once internal and efficacious, spiritual and manifest. Christian moralists used to give this dimension to their conception of fortitude, and the great aim of this fortitude was to overcome the fear of bodily evil—and beyond that, of death, the supreme physical disaster. For the lack of moral courage is often, quite stupidly, a fear of being hit. Moreover, they related fortitude to liberality and magnanimity; i.e., to generosity of nature: many are made cowardly by avarice and by lack of imagination. It is always an internal victory over death that reunites these two fields of energy: a person only comes to full maturity at the moment when he is seized of loyalties he values more than life itself. But in modern conditions of comfort and of indulgent care for the feelings, we have long cultivated, under the cover of philosophies of love and of peace, the most monstrous misunderstandings of these elementary truths (qtd. in Wray 108).

Wray does not elaborate on what this finding may mean but simply comments that the discovery helps provide a focus for an analytical approach to the development of O'Connor's title that may not be exclusively theological.

Mournier's book is a work of personalism, a philosophy that is subjectively idealistic. It asserts that personality unlocks the interpretation of reality. There are three main elements to the theory: 1) only persons are real; 2) only persons have value; and 3) only persons have free will. The theory opposes materialism, another philosophy that dictates people are made up of specks of dust and atoms and have no inherent integrity or value. Subscribers to personalism include the theologian

Bordan Parker Bowne, Martin Luther King, Jr., Pope John Paul II, Vaclav Hável, William Stern, and JACQUES MARITAIN.

Immanuel Kant, while not a strict personalist, contributed to personalism by stating that a person should not be valued simply as a means to an end for other people but that a person is of value and worth in and of himself or herself. Though personalism is not specifically a Christian-based philosophy, many Christians have embraced it. For them, Jesus is the ultimate person. He is real; he has value; and he has free will.

The passage above from Mounier may provide clues to O'Connor's feelings about her second novel and about the Bible passage from which she drew her title. Mounier says that people come to know their true selves best through confrontation. Moral courage is sometimes equal to physical courage. If one is not afraid of being hit, one has physical courage, but this is also a sign of moral courage. It is only through one's loyalties to a cause that is greater than one's life that a person matures and is truly tested. Modern life, with its concern for one's own feelings and comfort over those of others, has caused people to misunderstand these basic truths.

This philosophy relates to *Violent* in that young Tarwater is not a means to an end for all of the people who exert influence over him—his great-uncle, his uncle, his dim-witted cousin Bishop, the devil in the form of the stranger's voice, or the man in the lavender and cream-colored car. Francis Tarwater has worth and value in and of himself, and he also has free will. This is why no matter what happens to him or what he himself does, he still has the capacity to change. As dark as things become in the novel and in young Tarwater's life, because he has inherent value as a person, he can change and his change is worthwhile. In addition, the passage relates that it is through violence, and when a person is really down, that he will realize what matters more than his own life. O'Connor's characters are people for whom what matters more than life itself is the grace of God and redemption. Her characters are people who many readers would not call good or valuable and who come into violent confrontations. As a result of violence, many characters choose to accept God's grace. This happens with the grandmother in

"A Good Man Is Hard to Find," with Haze Motes in *Wise Blood*, and with Francis Marion Tarwater in *The Violent Bear It Away*. For some people, it would seem, the only way to heaven is through violence, whether it is enacted on them or by them.

In remarks at Hollins College, Virginia, before reading "A Good Man Is Hard to Find" on October 14, 1963, O'Connor spoke in some detail about her view of violence in literature. She said, "I have found that violence is strangely capable of returning my characters to reality and preparing them to accept their moment of grace. Their heads are so hard that almost nothing else will do the work" (MM 112). She acknowledged that the increased amount of violence in modern literature should not be an end in itself:

> With the serious writer, violence is never an end in itself. It is the extreme situation that best reveals what we are essentially, and I believe these are times when writers are more interested in what we are essentially than in the tenor of our daily lives. Violence is a force which can be used for good or evil, and among other things taken by it is the kingdom of heaven. But regardless of what can be taken by it, the man in the violent situation reveals those qualities least dispensable in his personality, those qualities which are all he will have to take into eternity with him; and since the characters in this story ["Good Man"] are all on the verge of eternity, it is appropriate to think of what they take with them (MM 113–14).

One way of describing the role of violence in O'Connor's fiction is that violence boils down her characters to their essential elements. O'Connor believes that people will show the essence of who they are when they are faced with their own impending death. All that has been taught to them; all that they believe; all that they fear and wonder about; the behaviors they have accumulated—what is most important to people will be dramatized in that moment. They have been tortured, hurt, scared, terrified, questioned, prodded, and probed. Death and whatever, if anything, they believe to be on the other side of this life is staring them in the face. That crucial moment is what fascinated O'Connor so often. What will this character do in that moment, the last chance he or she has to make any changes before facing the eternal unknown? Will that character accept the grace that O'Connor believes will be offered?

Notice how O'Connor references her second novel in the passage above: "Violence is a force which can be used for good or evil, and among other things taken by it is the kingdom of heaven." This comment suggests that O'Connor's reading of the Bible passage is that indeed heaven can be taken through violence, as though won in some kind of war for the soul. This would be one of the good and proper uses of violence. The matter is confusing to most Christians who believe in Christ's dying in reparation for one's sins or who believe in people doing good works as a peaceful and caring way to make their way toward heaven.

The matter is complicated enough and central enough to O'Connor that it warrants consideration of another one of her stories. In "Why Do the Heathen Rage?" for example, Walter's mother finds a book that Walter was reading open and turned upside down on the bathroom floor. When she turns it over and reads, she sees this passage: "Listen! The battle trumpet blares from heaven and see how our General marches fully armed, coming amid the clouds to conquer the whole world. Out of the mouth of our King emerges a double-edged sword that cuts down everything in the way. Arising finally from your nap, do you come to the battlefield! Abandon the shade and seek the sun" (CW 800). The story culminates in Walter's mother facing a realization, "Then it came to her, with an unpleasant jolt, that the General with the sword in his mouth, marching to do violence, was Jesus" (CW 800).

For O'Connor, people frequently do not make their way into heaven without facing or enduring some kind of violence first. Young Tarwater strangely "needed" the violence done against him by the man in the lavender and cream-colored car to fully give himself over to his calling as a prophet. "Tarwater's final vision would not have been brought off if he hadn't met the man in the lavender and cream-colored car" (MM 117). This is because the devil, in this case, the man in the car, sets up

Tarwater so that he may receive grace when it is offered. For all the bad things Tarwater has done and has had done to him, there is still a chance for him to see the light and accept his calling. In such a dark land among such enduring evil, however, this chance may have to be won through drastic measures. Drastic times require drastic means.

The role of violence in redemption is a mystery that O'Connor admitted is not totally clear. However, among the worst evil among us, for which no one would expect redemption, strange things can happen. Whether the forceful action is Old Testament references in this novel or the force from within of penance and self-sacrifice on Haze Motes or the violence from someone else as with Francis Tarwater, the effect is similar. Violence produces the same result, as though a General Jesus held a sword high and fought for the redemption of souls.

The violence-and-grace motif is one of O'Connor's frequent themes. It is not an element she consciously placed in stories from the outset, she said, but rather one that she observed from reading and thinking about her work after it was finished. She said that she discovered in reading her own work "that my subject in fiction is the action of grace in territory held largely by the devil" (MM 118). In less dark territories, the measures perhaps need not be so drastic, but in the land held almost entirely by the devil, who O'Connor believed to be a real entity with real goals and missions, violent actions might be the only means possible to redemption.

The title of the novel is complicated and open to interpretation despite the few clues the author left behind. However, it is clear that to O'Connor *Violent* and others of her stories involve the dramatization of surrender to grace through some measure of force in particularly evil situations. The violent bear it away because it is the only way possible for some people to stop the lives they have been leading and see clearly what God has been trying to show them all along.

Structure

The novel is just longer than 200 pages and took O'Connor seven years to complete. The structure of 12 chapters is reminiscent of the 12 disciples of Jesus. The novel is also divided into three distinct parts. The first part, chapters 1–3, is like the end of the story—it depicts the death of Old Tarwater, some background, and the launch of Francis Tarwater on his journey and his arrival at the schoolteacher's house to notify him of old Tarwater's death. The third part, chapters 10–12, is somewhat like a beginning. Through the violence of the final chapters, Francis Tarwater comes to terms with his calling and is reborn into his new life as a practicing prophet. The middle section is the longest, chapters 4–9. This section dramatizes a week of Young Tarwater's journey and his interactions with Rayber and Bishop in the city and elsewhere.

Parts 1 and 3 have some similarities in their role of framing the novel. In part 1, old Tarwater has died, and young Tarwater denies his destiny of taking up the old man's mantle of becoming a prophet. After digging the old man's grave for a few hours in the hot sun, he abandons the project when influenced by the voice of the stranger inside his head. The stranger talks him into having a drink at the still and torching the house when he returns. Young Tarwater decides to go to the city, where he will inform Rayber of old Tarwater's death and see how the stories he has been told about Rayber compare to how he sizes up the man for himself.

Part 3 also ends with young Tarwater's heading back toward the city. After all the violence he has inflicted on Bishop and the neglect and misguided actions he has suffered from so many of the adults in his life, he has finally grown to see and accept his calling as a prophet. He turns toward the city in order to fulfill his mission.

Part 2 occurs in the week between parts 1 and 3. As Margaret Whitt notes, O'Connor traces young Tarwater's six-day experience with Rayber in six chapters. Though the section is not structured evenly in one day per chapter, the drawing out of days in an equal number of chapters more closely simulates events as though they were happening in real time. Importantly, real time reflects time as Rayber prefers it, and it also reflects city life. Rayber is tied to the real and secular world that marks time daily and hourly, so the pace of the novel in the section where Rayber is part of the action and where much of the setting is the city follows more along this pattern.

The entire middle section is written from Rayber's point of view as he attempts to get to know Tarwater and tries to help him in the way that he thinks is best. The reader is filled in on the first four days of the six-day visit in chapter 4. These are marked by Rayber walking around the city with Tarwater and Bishop and showing Tarwater such city sights as the movies, railroads, an art gallery, the water works, department stores, city hall, the post office, and so forth. Chapters 5–9 take up the remaining two event-filled days. In chapter 5, Rayber chases Tarwater through town to the Carmody religious meeting. As he listens to the preaching and witnessing, he remembers his own experience with old Tarwater, being born again in the stream, and his father coming to get him. In chapter 6, it is the next day, and Rayber follows Tarwater into the park where the boy almost baptizes Bishop in the fountain. Chapters 7, 8, and 9 take place at Cherokee Lodge, the lake, and just outside Powderhead over a single day.

Within each of the three parts, O'Connor uses flashbacks to fill in background. The flashbacks also serve to link the four male characters—Old Tarwater, Rayber, Francis Tarwater, and Bishop. They are linked through time and events and through another technique O'Connor uses elsewhere in her fiction, including *Wise Blood*. It is a device known as doubling.

Doubling

O'Connor uses doubling throughout the novel, including doubling names, relationships and events, and physical traits. Doubling can result in planned confusion and repetition. It can also allow readers the opportunity to consider important differences between characters that otherwise seem alike.

Good authors choose names carefully, so when names are similar and occasionally confusing, there is usually a good reason. Readers of this novel, for example, often confuse old Mason Tarwater with the 14-year-old protagonist, Francis Marion Tarwater. If the characters are referred to by their last names only, readers must discern whether the character is the great-uncle or the great-nephew; the older self-proclaimed prophet or the younger, more reluctant one. This blurring of identities can only be deliberate. After completing the novel, readers should consider the effect of this technique.

Since Old Tarwater is dead, the blurring of identities surely heightens the sense that Young Tarwater carries on Old Tarwater's traits and desires with his own. It also highlights Rayber's difficulty in seeing and trying to change Old Tarwater's influence on, and apparent presence in, the boy. The more of Old Tarwater that Rayber recognizes in the boy, the angrier and more determined he becomes to change young Tarwater and drive out his dreaded great-uncle's influence.

Interestingly, if one Tarwater stands in for the other in the reader's mind, the reader aligns with Rayber's viewpoint throughout part 2 of the novel. Seeing the action through Rayber's point of view, the reader looks from the outside at both Tarwaters. The result is that either Tarwater may not appear quite as sympathetic as in parts 1 and 3. Through part 2, the reader is given the opportunity to stand outside the religious prophecy of the old man regarding his great-nephew and consider the situation from Rayber's secular viewpoint. The point of view is also confused, however, by a doubling of the relationship and events between the old man and Rayber through flashbacks in part 2.

The confusion between the two Tarwaters also foreshadows Francis Tarwater's actions at the end of part 2 and in part 3. In the end, young Tarwater assumes, to a certain extent, his great-uncle's identity and mission, he becomes a prophet. He will carry on his uncle's mission by going to back to the city and preaching about mercy. After young Tarwater discovers that what his great-uncle taught him is the truth, he is willing to fulfill his mission.

Another blending of names occurs between Bernice Bishop, Rayber's wife, and Bishop, the mentally disabled child. Old Tarwater thinks Bernice Bishop's name is comical; he thinks of her as the welfare woman. Bernice comes from the name *Berenice*, meaning "to bring victory." In her role as the one who brings her slow son into the world to be eventually baptized by young Tarwater, she is the one who brings victory to the young prophet. A bishop in the Catholic Church runs a diocese, which is a regional organization made up of several parishes from cities and towns. A bishop is higher in the church hierar-

chy than a parish priest or pastor but lower than the cardinals and the pope. The Bishops, both Bernice and her son, serve in this middle capacity as well between the uncles and the nephews.

Disabled as he is, young Bishop, as his name suggests, has an inherent integrity at which he does not have to work to achieve. Not coincidentally in this novel of doubles upon doubles, when Francis Tarwater sees Bishop, he recognizes how much he looks like his great-uncle, Mason Tarwater. Bishop resembles old Tarwater in features, and his eyes are the same gray color. However, Bishop's eyes are clear and seemingly bottomless. The clarity of his eyes is another important detail since it foreshadows the boy's eventual end by being drowned in the lake.

In addition to the confusion in names, the doubling of the uncle-nephew relationship also gives some readers trouble. Are Uncle Tarwater and nephew Rayber or Great-Uncle Tarwater and great-nephew Francis being discussed? This relationship rises to greater importance in the book than the father-son relationship between Rayber and his dim-witted son, Bishop. This is partly due to Rayber making it so. As Sheppard does to Rufus Johnson at the expense of his son, Norton, in "The Lame Shall Enter First," Rayber gives more attention to Francis Tarwater than he does to his own son, Bishop. Norton suffers from the death of his mother, and Bishop suffers from a mental deficiency that Rayber cannot accept.

In an interview at the College of St. Teresa in Winona, Minnesota, in October 1960, O'Connor was asked why there were so many uncle-nephew relationships in *Violent*. She responded, "That's near-enough kin without having to be father-son. Then you get into the son searching for the father sort of thing. Cousins would have been too far apart" (Magee 59). Old Tarwater is Rayber's uncle and Francis Tarwater's great-uncle. Likewise, Rayber is Francis Tarwater's uncle. Rayber is central to the action in that he is both uncle and nephew, and he stands at the fulcrum of his uncle's prophecy and his nephew's skepticism and later acceptance of that prophecy.

The most important doublings are the ones that exist between Francis Marion Tarwater; his uncle,

George Rayber; and his great-uncle, the old man, Mason Tarwater. All three resemble each other physically. When Rayber sees young Tarwater, he sees old Tarwater, and vice versa. The old man is even apparently physically present in the boy, Bishop, whom he has charged Francis to baptize. Their eyes are the same gray color, though Bishop's are clearer.

Both Francis and Rayber were influenced heavily in their childhoods by old Mason Tarwater. Like Francis, Rayber was kidnapped from his home in the city by Mason. At seven years old, Rayber went willingly out of his yard with his uncle, thinking that a visit to the woods sounded appealing. Though Mason Tarwater succeeded in baptizing him, Mason failed in his attempt to bring up Rayber as a future prophet. Rayber left Powderhead only four days after Mason baptized him when his father reluctantly came to get him at the request of Rayber's drunken mother.

Despite returning to parents who did not fully want him and who were not fully capable of caring for him, Rayber was brought up in the "real" world of the city and became a teacher. He did not accept his uncle's calling as a prophet but instead embraced the material world. He married Bernice Bishop, a woman who was growing old for childbirth. When she gave birth to the mentally disabled Bishop, Old Tarwater thought of the child as one who was saved by God from Rayber's bad influence.

Another important effect of the novel's doubling through the blurring of names is the similarity of relationships and situations and of physical characteristics. The technique helps dramatize the Catholic teaching of the Trinity—the three persons of the Father, the Son, and the Holy Spirit—in one God. One character need not stand in for one of the three persons in a one-to-one match. The blurring of identities and relationships allows the reader to have a sense of how it might be possible for more than one person to exist within one entity or being and vice versa.

The Sacred and the Secular

One of the significant themes of the novel is dramatized in the larger central section in which young Tarwater lives in the city with the school-teacher, Rayber. Rayber represents the secular world. He is interested in psychological and environmental influences on character but has allowed no room for a spiritual dimension in his thinking. He rejected the teaching that his uncle, Old Tarwater, attempted to give him. Young Tarwater, on the other hand, has kept the old man's teachings, despite his efforts to be rid of them. Like Haze Motes, he is by no means a perfect or even a totally willing prophet. His path will show the dominance of God's will over one's individuality. Rayber's journey shows that self-actualization may be possible but at the expense of losing one's spirituality.

Old Tarwater represents the spiritual dimension of life. He was "called" early to the ministry and went to the city to proclaim the Redemption. While there, he waited for a large sign—the sun bursting into fire and blood. However, no large sign came, and he learned through fire, as he told young Tarwater, that his prophet work was on a different scale than he had thought and that he ought not test the Lord. Instead, God came to him in a vision and told him that he was to take young Tarwater and raise him in the backwoods. There he was to teach him that he would also receive the call and to watch for the correct vision to show him his path in life.

Even as he is faithful, old Tarwater is particularly familiar with the Old Testament and the more grandiose of the visions and movements of the spirit. While he tells young Tarwater that Jesus is the bread of life and that he should not try to do the Lord's thinking for him, he also says that he and the boy remind him of Elijah and Elisha. He speaks in Old Testament terms of great chariots carrying souls into heaven and of Moses and the prophets. This talk stirs young Tarwater to think that if he were a prophet, he would be a greater prophet than old Tarwater. He would do large deeds. He would not be baptizing a dim-witted child to complete old Tarwater's sorry business. Young Tarwater sees himself like Moses striking water from the rock or Joshua making the sun stand still or Daniel staring down lions in the pit. This was old Tarwater's problem in his youth as well, but he learned that this was not always the way God chooses to work through his prophets. Much of the plot concerns young Tarwater's growth in maturity by learning the same.

Once old Tarwater learns his calling and his mission, he is relentless in trying to achieve his goals. He fails in his efforts to raise Rayber in the Redemption; however, he does succeed in baptizing him during the four days he has him at Powderhead. Even more important, old Tarwater succeeds in planting the seed of belief in Rayber. As a child, Rayber embraced the idea that there may be a better life. Life with old Tarwater was not perfect, but it had a dimension that the worse life he had with his drunken mother and neglectful father did not have. Rayber later hates that old Tarwater put this seed into him because it made living in the "real" world where he was forced to grow up that much harder. When one knows that there might be something else, one is never quite satisfied with what one has.

Rayber has been touched with the spiritual dimension of life, and it has left a permanent mark. He does not want to leave when his father comes for him. Despite all his protestations in the city in his adulthood, he values the old man and something about his teachings. He winces when young Tarwater tells him that the old man has died but then quickly covers up his feelings. At the preaching of the Carmody family, he is moved by the testimony of the young girl whom he seems to see almost as an angel. He nearly accepts that young Tarwater will baptize his son, Bishop, but tries to tell himself that it really does not matter. That he has been touched with the good news when he was young enough to have it make an impression endures. No matter how hard he tries, Rayber cannot shake the kernel of faith the old man planted in him.

On the other hand, Rayber was forced to deal with the secular world and make his way in it. When his father came to get him at Powderhead, the father said that he was taking the boy back from this place to the real world. The real world is the secular world, where spirituality cannot be proven to human understanding; therefore, it must not exist. Rayber attempts to explain the world to himself through education and psychology and science. Rationality and the modern world's discoveries must surely trump any Old Testament visions of burning bushes or simple stories of Jesus curing the sick.

The secular world clashes with the spiritual one when Rayber takes in old Tarwater for charity and observes him as though he were a scientific specimen. Old Tarwater reads the article about himself in the teachers' professional journal and revolts. He says that he needs to be free and not trapped inside Rayber's head. The secular life is not free, according to old Tarwater's beliefs, because it must always be contained within the mind. That which cannot be explained or understood by human beings' limited mental capacities either does not exist or does not matter. When old Tarwater tells young Tarwater that he is free, he means it. He is free because he is not limited by human understanding and knows that the human condition cannot be tidily explained and wrapped up by psychological theories or other systems. He can accept mystery.

This is one reason why Bishop's existence frustrates Rayber so much—Bishop demonstrates every day the limitations of the human brain, and this is something that Rayber cannot accept. In Rayber's version of the secular world, Bishop is a mistake; he has no reason for being around. Rayber tells young Tarwater not to trouble himself with Bishop, that he should just pretend that Bishop does not even exist.

O'Connor provides several examples with Rayber to show that God's will is stronger and more powerful than any secular understanding; that is, God's will will not be contained. First, Rayber has been exposed to the good news at Powderhead as a child and has never been able to escape the slight hope that it just might be true. Second, Rayber spends much of his life trying to disprove what he learned at Powderhead through education and other means, but the birth of Bishop disproves rather than proves his theories.

Young Tarwater reenters Rayber's life and not only murders Bishop but also baptizes him at the same time. Rayber loses on both fronts from the murder—as a father trying the best he can in a secular world with a mentally challenged son and as someone who did not want his child to be baptized in the Christian tradition. In the Christian view of things, Bishop automatically goes to heaven as an innocent youth whose soul has been washed clean from his baptism. Even as the voice that said the words of baptism over him came from the same adolescent whose hands killed the boy, the baptism is the stronger force, since it is the spiritual force that overrides all else.

Rayber also fails to recruit young Tarwater to his way of thinking. Young Tarwater escapes from Rayber and his influence not only physically by running off from Cherokee Lodge but also by seeing the vision after the incident with the man in the lavender and cream-colored car that sets his destiny as a prophet. Last, and perhaps most important, Rayber appears to be losing the battle between the sacred and the secular within himself. The scene with the Carmody girl touches him and reminds him of the glimmer of hope that he felt at Powderhead the few days that he was there with old Tarwater. The seed of belief keeps propelling him, keeps cropping up in spite of his denials. Rayber collapses when he realizes that he has lost his son in the real world and when he realizes that the old man's prophecy has come true. The prophet the old man raised up did indeed come back to burn him.

Not only does the spiritual world win over the secular in this novel, but the spiritual aspect also develops between old Tarwater and young Tarwater. Old Tarwater may have been a pure prophet in the sense that he listened for his mission and was persistent in carrying it out once he thought he understood what it was, but he was also more of the fire and brimstone kind of prophet, whereas Francis Tarwater takes on more of New Testament aspects of peace and love. The difference may be represented in their names—Mason works in stone, and Francis is like St. Francis with his message of peace and connections with nature.

The reader is not told of all of old Tarwater's transgressions in life, but certainly kidnapping two children and raising one without a worldly education might be read in the secular world as wrong. However, the reader does see his influence on young Tarwater and how all of this history leads the boy to arson and eventually murder.

The main difference between the two is perhaps best illustrated by their respective callings or prophecies. Mason Tarwater gives his message to young Tarwater as he describes being trapped by the men who would take him away to the asylum and to

whom he said the same thing, "Go warn the children of God . . . of the terrible speed of justice" (Three 159). Justice might be described as a non-Christian means of obtaining peace. It follows more along the lines of "an eye for an eye." If one has wrong done to him, then the one who has done the wrong must pay back for that wrongdoing. The payment must be in equal measure to the wrong that was committed. This is how justice is achieved.

Notice the difference in Francis Tarwater's message as he hears it at the end of the novel, "GO WARN THE CHILDREN OF GOD OF THE TERRIBLE SPEED OF MERCY" (*Three* 267). Mercy is a different concept from justice, one that is much more aligned with the teachings of Jesus and Christianity. In the Old Testament, people sought justice against their oppressors by God; in the New Testament, Jesus came to redeem everyone of their sins, to pay the price required by justice. His selfless act to pay for the wrongs of all sinners, Christians believe, showed God's never-ending mercy.

Through the trials of the novel, Francis has come to learn an aspect of spirituality that Mason did not experience, perhaps because Mason did not commit the level of sin that Francis did. Francis has learned that God is merciful, that he has been called to prophesy despite his sins and his doubt and testing of God. He will take that message back to the city and into his preaching.

Country and City

Closely aligned with the novel's concept of the spiritual and secular aspects of life are O'Connor's use of the settings of the country and the city. Of the two different settings, the country, especially the woods, is more representative of the spiritual realm. Like the boy in "An Afternoon in the Woods," the characters in this novel are closer to God when they are in the woods or on the water. The city represents secular life—institutions, material goods, inventions, a faster and less reflective lifestyle.

Powderhead is set as a clearing in the woods. The name of Mason Tarwater's property, sounding so similar to powder keg, suggests a place where power resides and where that power may be released through an explosion or fire. The reverse may also be true in considering the name—it is a place where one's brains are merely powder and not considered worth using to their full capacity. Old Tarwater frequently plants corn and other crops right up close to the edge of the land that the house occupies. The implication is that he uses every bit of land he can for farming or other natural purposes and does not inflict human civilization on any more land than necessary to survive. The old man's still that Buford Munson comes to share is also set back in the woods, but as the devil in the form of the stranger's voice indicates, the woods may also be the realm of the devil.

The property changes hands during the course of the novel. Old Tarwater inherits it. When he dies, the land passes to Rayber. Rayber visits Powderhead and remembers the paths through the woods that he enjoyed exploring so much as a child. Instead of thinking that he could move out to the land that he has now inherited, he reverts to his self-taught secularism. He thinks about selling the land and using the money to fund young Tarwater's education, which would make young Tarwater more like Rayber than old Tarwater. When Rayber looks through the break in the trees at the ruins of the house with the two chimneys sticking up, however, he experiences strange emotions and realizes that he has not yet processed the old man's death enough to know quite what it is he wants to do with the land. Rayber has many chances to embrace a spiritual calling, including this one. O'Connor mentions in a letter that she has hope for Rayber.

When one cannot be out in the woods in this novel, plants in the city provide temporary shelter. Characters stand in, stand behind, or step over, hedges and shrubbery. Young Tarwater waits outside Rayber's house in and behind the hedge when he is first dropped off by the flue salesman, Meeks. Rayber trips over shrubbery outside the window when he is moved by the Carmody girl's clear and direct preaching. The city park provides young Tarwater with an opportunity to baptize Bishop in the fountain. In the midst of the city, small natural environments bring spiritual influence into the secular-based world.

The city by itself represents secularism. Both old Tarwater and young Tarwater see their work as prophets as being called to prophesy to the children of the city. Old Tarwater sees himself entrapped

there first by his nephew as a charity case and then in Rayber's head and in the article written by Rayber for the teachers' journal. Old Tarwater is trapped in the asylum for four years until he realizes that he will be released if he stops preaching to the other patients. When he returns to Tarwater, he is determined to remain free in the woods and to raise young Tarwater free. Young Tarwater will be free of institutions like school and free of becoming an idea in someone else's mind.

Young Tarwater has the power of his calling behind him. He remains free, as his great-uncle has taught him, even when he goes to the city to seek out Rayber. He runs away from Rayber while in the city. He can leave any time he likes, and Rayber will probably not seek him out. Francis looks at all the sights that Rayber shows him, but the boy remains uninterested in any of them until they see the sign telling of the preaching meeting that night. He goes back there to hear more.

Nature wields its power over Rayber and Young Tarwater when Rayber takes Frank and Bishop to Cherokee Lodge and the lake. Here young Tarwater becomes emboldened to act. On the lake, young Tarwater intends to drown Bishop in the boat, but a force beyond him also appears to force out the words of baptism at just the right moment. Old Tarwater, Rayber, young Tarwater, and Bishop are all ultimately helpless against the force of God's as found in nature.

Children and Adults

Francis Tarwater is only 14 throughout the story, and the abuse he has endured already is more than any person should have to take in a lifetime. Bishop suffers from neglect and is thought poorly of by his father. Bishop senses his father's feelings for him, which is why he takes to Francis's influence so easily.

Children are very often portrayed as more knowing and wise than adults in O'Connor's fiction. They are frequently, but not always, rescued in the end. June Star and John Wesley in "Good Man" meet their deaths at the hand of The Misfit's comrades. Harry "Bevel" Ashfield drowns himself in "The River" in a sort of self-baptism. Rufus Johnson and Norton Sheppard are key characters in "The Lame Shall Enter First," and both have suffered at the hands of adults who should have done better by them.

Rayber has been mistreated by being raised by an uncaring father and an alcoholic mother. Kidnapped for four days when he was seven, he was exposed to a strong value system at Powderhead that left him profoundly confused when he returned to the even worse scenario he had to endure in the city. Even so, though young Tarwater claims that Rayber had a worse life with his parents, he has grown up to live in what Meeks calls a respectable neighborhood in the city and have a profession as a teacher who has published at least one research article in a professional journal. Tragedy strikes again, however, when Rayber's wife dies and he is left to care for his mentally disabled son on his own. Perhaps Rayber's greatest loss of all as a young person was his lack of opportunity to explore the pros and cons of religion for himself in the same way he was allowed to become educated.

Bishop is another child who suffers from neglect. Perhaps Rayber treats the boy this way because of his own father's treatment of him. However, it is more likely that Bishop does not fit in with Rayber's secular worldview. It is difficult to attach meaning to a physical anomaly without any kind of spiritual guidance or value system. Since Bishop is mentally challenged, Rayber has difficulty loving him, caring for him, and most of all taking a genuine interest in him. Though the boy does not appear to be physically neglected or abused, Rayber is disengaged as his father.

Lucette Carmody's youth and her gift for preaching are clearly exploited for money by her family. The exploitation sickens Rayber as he witnesses it firsthand at the evening meeting that he and young Tarwater watch. Something about her words and the way she looks directly at Rayber connects with his childhood experience at Powderhead. He is confused and shaken and misses the one opportunity he has to discuss the common experience he had at Powderhead with young Tarwater on their way back to the house.

Young Francis Tarwater has obviously been taken advantage of by adults. His father committed suicide over guilt from impregnating his mother, Rayber's sister. Francis's mother dies in a car crash. These unfortunate events lead to Tarwater's status as an orphan up for grabs—old Tarwater kidnaps him and raises him with no formal education in the backwoods. Some readers find this abusive; others think that old Tarwater gave Francis meaning to his life; he likely would not have received such insight with formal education and life with Rayber in the city. Unlike his own parents, Rayber lets young Tarwater down by not going back to Powderhead after his first attempt to rescue the boy resulted in his being shot and made deaf in one ear. Francis confronts Rayber with this fact after old Tarwater's death when he visits him in the city. Francis is left unsatisfied with the answer, which is one more way he is pushed closer to a firmer commitment to old Tarwater's teachings.

Motifs in the Novel

Deafness.   O'Connor uses deafness as a clue to those who will not hear the word of God. Rayber is struck deaf when old Tarwater shoots at him at age 24, and he tries to get young Tarwater back from Powderhead. Rayber then needs to wear a hearing aid, which connects to another device in his ear. When he first sees it, Francis Tarwater wonders if Rayber's head is run by electricity. Later, Francis tells Rayber to take out the hearing aid and turn himself off. Francis's lack of knowledge about modern technology links him with old Tarwater and the backwoods. He does not know how to use a telephone on the road with Meeks. He also recalls old Tarwater's saying that Rayber would try to control him by getting him in his head, and the hearing aid makes him wonder if this is the method his uncle may use.

Lucette Carmody looking out the window at the night church meeting says she sees one who waits in the window but who "is deaf to the Holy Word" (*Violent* 134). Rayber is deaf in not listening carefully to young Tarwater when he stays with him in the city. If he had been open to a dialogue with the boy, perhaps the uncle and the nephew would have found the truth about themselves and their place in the world together. Instead, Rayber turns a deaf ear figuratively as well as literally on old Tarwater's message.

As a future prophet, Francis Tarwater hears very well and remembers what he hears. However, he is compared with a deaf person when he shows no interest in all the sights and sounds of the city that Rayber attempts to share with him. He also hears but has trouble understanding what he hears when he uses the telephone to call Rayber and Bishop answers it instead, breathing into the receiver. Francis distrusts technology to help with one's hearing. He does not understand his uncle's hearing aid and thinks that it must be connected in some way with his uncle's thoughts.

Devil. O'Connor admitted in her letters that the stranger's voice that young Tarwater hears in part 1 of the novel and the man in the lavender and cream-colored car are both manifestations of the devil. The devil enters young Tarwater's thoughts while he is digging old Tarwater's grave and getting nowhere fast in the hot sun. The stranger's voice suggests that it is not worth the effort anyway. When the boy takes a few drinks at the still where he goes to fetch liquor for Buford Munson, the devil takes more of a hold on him. The stranger's voice is more persistent, and he speaks more readily and often. By the time Francis returns to the house, he has become convinced to burn the entire place down, corpse and all. When Francis does burn down the house and flees, the stranger's voice goes away.

The devil in the form of the man in the lavender and cream-colored car gives Francis a ride and offers him liquor. When Francis wakes up, he finds his hands loosely tied with a lavender handkerchief, implying that he has been raped.

Fire. Fire is one of the forces that cleanses and brings clarity. Old Tarwater claims that his eyes were cleansed by fire and that was what led him to accept his mission as a prophet. Much of his preaching to the boy includes Old Testament images of fire. Francis sets fire to the cabin at Powderhead, thinking he is burning old Tarwater's corpse and refusing him his trip to heaven. When he falls asleep in Meeks's car, Francis wakes up to see the city lights ahead and mistakes them for the fire of the house they have left behind. He thinks they are returning to the scene of the fire. Meeks has to tell him that they are city lights, not fire. When Francis tells Rayber about the old man's passing, Rayber asks Francis if God came for him in a chariot of fire,

as he always preached. Francis says that the old man had no warning. Lucette Carmody preaches to the audience gathered about being saved by the Lord's fire or perishing in one's own.

The light reflecting on the lake before Bishop's baptism looks like fire. Francis lights another fire toward the end of the novel after he is raped by the man in the lavender and cream-colored car. He burns the area clean of the evil he suffered there.

Hats. Many characters wear hats in the novel. While that fact alone perhaps does not merit attention (one is reminded of O'Connor's answer to a questioner about why The Misfit's hat is black in "Good Man." She merely indicated that many men in that area wore black hats), Francis Tarwater's hat takes on added significance. The hats give some clues to character, time, and changes. For example, the welfare woman coming through the cornfield to get Tarwater with Rayber wore a pink-flowered hat. Old Tarwater wore a putty-colored hat with the brim turned up all the way around and never took it off. It was on him when he died.

Francis Tarwater wears a new gray hat when he and old Tarwater visit the lawyers in the city to try to get the old man his title to the Powderhead property. When Francis looks out an upstairs window from one of the offices, his new hat falls into the street. Years later, when Francis is in the city with Rayber, he remembers the exact location where he lost his hat so long before and mentions it to Rayber.

Like old Tarwater, young Tarwater wears a gray hat that he does not take off when sleeping. When he wakes up at Rayber's the first morning, he clutches at it as though it is a weapon. When he runs away from Rayber's to hear the Carmody family preaching at the church one evening, all Rayber can see is the knob of the boy's hat rising and falling ahead of him as he tries to follow him. Bishop has a black hat like a cowboy's with which he plays occasionally and dips in the water of the lake. The man in the lavender-and-cream-colored car has a panama hat, but before he leaves young Tarwater, he ties the boys hands loosely with his lavender handkerchief and takes the boy's hat in what he considers an even trade.

Hunger, Bread, and the Sacraments. When young Tarwater goes to the city, he finds that he is increasingly hungry. Rayber frequently mentions being hungry also. For example, Rayber says at the Cherokee Lodge that he is so hungry he could eat a horse. Hunger suggests hunger for God's word and grace, not a physical hunger. Young Tarwater's hunger and thirst increase after he leaves Cherokee Lodge and moves closer to Powderhead. He tries to alleviate his thirst by taking the swig of whiskey that the man in the lavender and cream-colored car offers him. Unfortunately, it is this drink that knocks him out and allows the man as the devil to do evil. When young Tarwater begins to burn the woods in an effort to cleanse them of what has been done, his hunger increases. By the time he sees the vision of the old man in the clearing with the multitude, he realizes that his hunger has turned from a pain to a powerful tide, something he realizes then that only those called to be prophets of the Lord will truly feel.

Old Tarwater has taught Francis that Jesus is the bread of life. As the Bible says, whoever eats of the bread of life shall live forever, or whoever believes in Jesus and follows his teachings will do likewise. Of frequent images of bread, perhaps the most prominent occurs when Rayber follows Francis Tarwater through the city the night he runs off and he sees him stop in front of a store window, looking inside. He stays there only for a moment. When Rayber catches up to the window, he discovers a single loaf of bread on a bakery shelf, as though left there accidentally. Francis Tarwater is still hungry for the bread of life, the word of God. He is searching for the truth. He has been told the truth by his great-uncle, but he is going through his time of testing what he believes.

Readers have been both puzzled and mystified by this novel, which O'Connor once called in a letter to Dr. Theodore Spivey her "minor hymn to the Eucharist" (HB 387). The bread of life is a direct reference to the Eucharist. Critics reading closely have seen connections to all seven of the Catholic sacraments. The seven Catholic sacraments are: Baptism, Penance or Confession, Eucharist or Communion, Confirmation, Matrimony, Holy Orders, and the Last Rites or Extreme Unction.

Both Tarwaters conduct baptisms and believe ultimately in Jesus as the bread of life. In addition to these, Rayber confesses to young Tarwater that he nearly drowned Bishop. Both Mason and Rayber talk about Rayber's marriage to Bernice Bishop. Francis's adventure in the city becomes a confirmation of what he has been taught by Mason. In addition, when he feels the breath, not of the Holy Spirit but of the devil on him in the woods, he turns and sets the trees that separate them ablaze, cutting the devil off from reaching him. Another suggestion of Confirmation comes with the vision of the burning bush. Young Tarwater performs a kind of Holy Orders on himself in taking up the priesthood of his mission as a prophet when he lays prostrate in the dirt over Mason's grave. Some critics read the boy's painful hunger turning to a tide as the alleviating of pain that suggests the Anointing of the Sick, also known as Last Rites or Extreme Unction.

CHARACTERS

Relationships Among Characters The similarities of names can sometimes be confusing. The following listing shows the familial relationships among the characters:

— Old Mason Tarwater does not marry or have children of his own.
— Mason's "whore" sister Tarwater has two children with George F. Rayber, Sr., who is a life-insurance salesman. Their children are George F. Rayber, Jr. and his "healthy/whore" sister.
— George F. Rayber, Jr. marries Bernice Bishop, and they have one "dim-witted" child named Bishop Rayber.
— Rayber's "healthy/whore" sister takes a lover at Rayber's prompting in order to give her "confidence." The lover is a divinity student who commits suicide out of guilt from the affair and the resulting pregnancy. Their son is Francis Marion Tarwater ("Frankie" retains his mother's Tarwater surname because his mother was unmarried).

These relationships make:

— George F. Rayber, Jr. the uncle of Francis Marion Tarwater (Rayber is Francis's unmarried mother's brother).

— Old Mason Tarwater the uncle of George F. Rayber, Jr. (Mason is Rayber's "whore" mother's brother). Mason is also the great-uncle of Francis Marion Tarwater by being Francis's uncle's uncle.

George F. Rayber, Jr. The schoolteacher is the son of old Mason Tarwater's sister and an insurance salesman, George F. Rayber, Sr. He is very similar to old Mason Tarwater except that he wears black-rimmed glasses and a hearing aid. He is an intellectual in that he prefers education to religion and tries to understand the world by reading, experimentation, and the use of reason. He has been successful enough financially that he lives in a respectable part of town, according to what Meeks tells young Tarwater. Rayber's early experience with old Tarwater and his difficult upbringing make him reject the religious teachings that old Tarwater tried to instill in him. Nevertheless, a part of him retains the seed of faith, and he cannot quite shake off the influence of the old man.

Scholars thus far have not found proven sources for O'Connor's name for Rayber. St. George is the patron saint of England; he fought a dragon that had not been conquered after many tries. In the process, he also saved a princess. Many people were baptized due to his courageous act, and he has been taken on as a patron saint of soldiers.

In the context of St. George, Rayber would be named ironically. Francis Tarwater accuses Rayber of being too cerebral, of having no courage or ability to act. Rayber admits to young Tarwater that he lost his nerve when he once tried to drown his own son, Bishop. Soon afterward, when he knows that Francis and Bishop are out on the lake and he hears Bishop's groans and knows what is happening, he refuses to act once again. He neither saves Bishop nor tries to do so, and he does not run out to the lake even after he knows the act is done. Through his passivity, he is complicit in the boy's murder. In essence, young Tarwater "tends" to Bishop in the way that both of them know Rayber wants.

Rayber may or may not be the same schoolteacher also named Rayber in the short story "The Barber." In that story, Rayber tries to engage in intellectual discourse about the upcoming election with the barber and the patrons of the barber shop. He ends up hitting Joe, the barber. Since the Rayber of *Violent* is more of a thinker than a doer, this gesture alone may be enough to make an effective argument that the characters are similar but not intended to be exactly the same person.

Old Tarwater thinks that there is enough Tarwater blood in Rayber that he has a chance to see the truth the old man tried to show him when he was young. As in her first novel, *Wise Blood*, O'Connor suggests throughout this novel that the blood relatives of believers have an inherent calling by God in their blood that will always be hard for them to ignore. Rayber is one of these blood relatives, and it is clear from what he does and does not do that he has been struggling with this fact for some time and will continue to do so. His collapse at the realization of that he has no feelings about either Bishop's death or his baptism may be where he reaches bottom and finds that following another path may make life more meaningful after all.

Francis Marion Tarwater Francis is a troubled 14-year-old boy who has lived in the woods with his great-uncle and has no formal education. Francis was O'Connor's father's name, and she dedicated the book to her father. Since she wrote so little about him, at least in what is yet available to scholars, most critics have avoided making too many connections between her father and the protagonist of her second novel. It is nearly impossible, however, to believe that the author would not associate her father, to whom she dedicated this book, with the main character. Whatever connections are there may always remain a mystery.

Margaret Whitt suggests that Francis Marion may be derived more directly from Brigadier General Francis "Swamp Fox" Marion, an officer in the Revolutionary War. Among Marion's three major military operations was one to SAVANNAH, GEORGIA, O'Connor's birthplace. Although less than well known nationally, Marion managed to have enough regional notoriety that he eventually had 29 towns, 17 counties, and a college named after him. Whitt writes that the story of his nickname would have been known to Savannah elementary students, such as young O'Connor.

The nickname legend involved Marion being chased by a Lt. Col. Banastre Tarleton through 26 miles of swamp for seven hours. Tarleton finally gave up saying that they had best go after General Thomas Sumter instead, "as for this damned old fox, the Devil himself could not catch him" (qtd. in Whitt 94). The quote is pertinent because Francis Marion Tarwater does not allow the devil, in either the form of the stranger's voice or the man in the lavender shirt, to maintain his grip on him. Tarwater and Marion are similar in that both figures were small, had little patience, were overly sensitive, and were susceptible to dark moods.

To Catholics and others, the name Francis brings to mind St. Francis of Assisi, who is, among other things, the patron saint of animals and, by extension, of nature and the environment. Francis was born in Assisi in about 1181 or 1182 and died there on October 3 or 4, 1226. He was born to a wealthy father and had originally planned to work in his father's business or perhaps become a knight or a troubadour. He carried out some military missions and was held prisoner. While imprisoned, Francis began to think about religion and spirituality. He returned, however, to Assisi and planned to go out again to fight.

He had a vision in a dream, however, about God calling him to help his church, so he returned to Assisi and began to work with the sick. In another dream, he understood that he was called to rebuild God's church, and he took the vision quite literally. He set out to live as a hermit and fix the church of San Damiano, near his town. This embarrassed his father, who had him imprisoned and brought before the bishop for disobedience. Francis gave up all of his inheritance as well as all his possessions, even down to his clothes, living very simply, and he began to preach and write hymns and prayers. Soon he had several followers who joined him in his lifestyle of poverty, preaching, and prayer.

The founder of the Franciscans, Francis believed that God was present in all the creatures and elements of nature. He loved animals—birds in particular—a trait shared by Flannery O'Connor and witnessed by her father, Francis, when they lived in Savannah. One day, St. Francis and his companions were walking down the road when Francis noticed that the trees overhead were full of birds. He ran off the road, leaving his friends, and began to preach to the birds, giving them a sermon. The sermon, now known as St. Francis's Sermon to the Birds, was written down by one of the friars. This is a translation from the Italian:

> My brothers, birds, you should praise your Creator very much and always love him; he gave you feathers to clothe you, wings so that you can fly, and whatever else was necessary for you. God made you noble among his creatures, and he gave you a home in the purity of the air; though you neither sow nor reap, he nevertheless protects and governs you without any solicitude on your part.

After the sermon, the birds stretched out their necks and wings, and Francis walked among them, blessing and touching them. Francis went out of his way afterward to include animals, birds, reptiles, and even the "unfeeling creatures" of nature in his work. Young Tarwater's connection with nature as opposed to life in the city suggests kinship with the saint.

The name *Marion* may remind Catholic readers of the Congregation of the Marian Fathers of the Immaculate Conception of the Blessed Virgin Mary. Founded in Poland in 1673, the Marian Fathers is a religious order of priests and brothers dedicated to expanding devotion to the Immaculate Conception of the Blessed Virgin Mary and to supplication for the souls suffering in Purgatory. About Purgatory in relation to "Revelation," O'Connor wrote that the vision that Mrs. Turpin sees at the end of the story is of people rising into Purgatory. Marian books concern the Blessed Virgin. When O'Connor prayed at the grotto in LOURDES for her book rather than her bones, she may have thought that she accumulated Marian blessings on her project.

Though Francis Marion is likely an allusion to the Revolutionary War hero, as Margaret Whitt suggests, the prominent Catholic connections in the names must have been clear to this devout author.

Mason Tarwater   Dead at 84, he is the great-uncle of Francis Marion Tarwater and the uncle to George F. Rayber, Jr. He believes he is a prophet. When he was 70 years old, he kidnapped and baptized young Tarwater, taking him to his camp Powderhead, in the backwoods. Old Tarwater has a short head with no neck and silver-colored eyes that stick out of his head. When he is found dead at the breakfast table, he is wearing a putty-colored hat with the brim turned up all the way around and a gray coat over his T-shirt. His eyes are like two fish trying to work their way out of red-colored nets.

The name *Mason* brings to mind the stonemason. A mason builds walls with stones and mortar. As a prophet, Mason's belief in himself is rock solid. He knows what he wants to do and what he has to do to achieve his goals. He teaches Francis figures, reading, writing, and history. Mason's history lessons include Adam and Eve as well as Herbert Hoover, the Second Coming, and the Day of Judgment.

In addition, a mason may be a member of the Freemason fraternal society. The Freemasons expand their membership when men ask existing members to sponsor them to join. The society has traditions said to be "secret" and that involve recitations and performing certain rituals that advance masons to further degrees of membership. Many of the founding fathers, such as George Washington, were Masons. The name of Mason gives old Tarwater a sense of being rock solid and traditional in stature. It places him with the ranks of the older and well-established generation. As a backwoods prophet, Mason is secure in who he is.

Mason's connection to unchanging stone contrasts with Francis's connection with poetic and changing aspects of nature such as the animals and the birds. Both Tarwaters are associated with nature but in different ways.

Tarwater is an intriguing name as well. Tar is a sticky liquid that is derived from the distillation of organic matter such as coal, petroleum, wood, or peat. When one learns that tar was once used to mummify bodies in ancient Egypt, one cannot help but recall O'Connor's use of the mummy "new Jesus" in *Wise Blood*. Tar has been used to seal roof shingles, ship hulls, and sails to keep out water.

Tarwater is a cold infusion of tar into water, which has been used in folk remedies and medicines. Tar, then, seals off water from getting in to

places where one does not want it. But both Mason and Francis Tarwater are the opposite—both are the means by which water reaches a person by having it poured over them in baptism. Mason baptizes both Rayber and young Tarwater; young Tarwater has baptized Bishop already by the age of 14.

Compared with folk remedies, the Tarwaters are similar in their backwoods and unorthodox preaching and baptizing. Both Mason and Francis Tarwater perform baptisms, which Christians see as the remedy for a troubled individual's spirit.

RELATED LETTERS

Elizabeth McKee, October 15, 1952 (HB 44); Sally Fitzgerald, Thursday [undated, Fall, 1952] (HB 47); Sally and Robert Fitzgerald, February 1, 1953 (HB 55); Robert Giroux, June 14, 1953 (HB 59); Elizabeth and ROBERT LOWELL, January 1, 1954 (HB 65); Ben Griffith, February 13, 1954 (HB 68); Catherine Carver, April 2, 1955 (HB 76–77); Robie Macauley, May 18, 1955 (HB 81); Catherine Carver, June 16, 1955 (HB 86); Elizabeth McKee, June 29, 1955 (HB 88); Andrew Lytle, September 15, 1955 (HB 104); Betty Hester ("A"), December 16, 1955 (HB 127); Elizabeth McKee, January 12, 1956 (HB 127–28); Shirley Abbott, March 7, 1956 (HB 142); John Lynch, September 2, 1956 (HB 172); Betty Hester ("A"), September 22, 1956 (HB 177); Elizabeth Fenwick Way, November 24, 1956 (HB 181); J. F. Powers, December 9, 1956 (HB 185); Betty Hester ("A"), December 28, 1956 (HB 191); Maryat Lee, January 31, 1957 (HB 201); Maryat Lee, March 10, 1957 (HB 209); Betty Hester ("A"), July 12, 1957 (HB 229); Cecil Dawkins, August 27, 1957 (HB 239); Betty Hester ("A"), October 5, 1957 (HB 245); Betty Hester ("A"), October 19, 1957 (HB 248); Betty Hester ("A"), November 2, 1957 (HB 250); Granville Hicks, November 7, 1957 (HB 251); Cecil Dawkins, January 17, 1958 (HB 264); Sally and Robert Fitzgerald, April 10, 1958 (HB 276); Betty Hester ("A"), May 17, 1958 (HB 282); Cecil Dawkins, May 22, 1958 (HB 284); Cecil Dawkins, June 8, 1958 (HB 287); Betty Hester ("A"), June 14, 1958 (HB 288); Betty Hester ("A"), July 5, 1958 (HB 290); Betty Hester ("A"), October 25, 1958 (HB 300); Cecil Dawkins, October 26, 1958

(HB 301); Betty Hester ("A"), November 8, 1958 (HB 301); Father J. H. McCown, December 23, 1958 (HB 310); Robert Lowell, December 25, 1958 (HB 311); Sally and Robert Fitzgerald, January 1, 1959 (HB 315); Betty Hester ("A"), January 3, 1959 (HB 316); Cecil Dawkins, January 14, 1958 (HB 316); Betty Hester ("A"), January 31, 1959 (HB 317); Father J. H. McCown, February 2, 1959 (HB 318); Sally and Robert Fitzgerald, February 15, 1959 (HB 318); Catherine Carver, February 18, 1959 (HB 319); Maryat Lee, February 18, 1959 (HB 319–320); Cecil Dawkins, Geo. Wash. Birthday [1959] (HB 320); Betty Hester ("A"), February 28, 1959 (HB 321); Catherine Carver, March 24, 1959 (HB 322); Sally and Robert Fitzgerald, March 24, 1959 (HB 323); Catherine Carver, March 27, 1959 (HB 324); Thomas Stritch, March 28, 1959 (HB 324–325); Catherine Carver, April 18, 1959 (HB 327–328); Sally and Robert Fitzgerald, April 20, 1959 (HB 329); Maryat Lee, May 6, 1959 (HB 331); Caroline Gordon Tate, May 10, 1959 (HB 331–332); Betty Hester ("A"), May 16, 1959 (HB 332–333); John Lynch, June 14, 1959 (HB 336); Catherine Carver, June 23, 1956 (HB 337–338); Betty Hester ("A"), June 27, 1959 (HB 338); Sally and Robert Fitzgerald, July 1, 1959 (HB 338); Maryat Lee, July 5, 1959 (HB 339); Elizabeth McKee, July 17, 1959 (HB 340); Cecil Dawkins, July 17, 1959 (HB 340); Dr. T. R. Spivey, July 18, 1959 (HB 341); Catherine Carver, July 19, 1959 (HB 342); Betty Hester ("A"), July 25, 1959 (HB 342); John Hawkes, July 26, 1959 (HB 343); ELIZABETH BISHOP, August 2, 1959 (HB 344); Robert Giroux, August 9, 1959 (HB 344); Robert Giroux, August 14, 1959 (HB 345); Maryat Lee, September 6, 1959 (HB 348); John Hawkes, September 13, 1959 (HB 349); Cecil Dawkins, September 22, 1959 (HB 351); Betty Hester ("A"), October 3, 1959 (HB 351); John Hawkes, October 6, 1959 (HB 352); Robert Giroux, October 10, 1959 (HB 353); Sally and Robert Fitzgerald, October 11, 1959 (HB 354–355); Betty Hester ("A"), October 17, 1959 (HB 355); Cecil Dawkins, October 31, 1959 (HB 356); Betty Hester ("A"), October 31, 1959 (HB 357); Betty Hester ("A"), November 14, 1959 (HB 358); John Hawkes, November 20, 1959 (HB 359); Robert Giroux, December 5, 1959 (HB 361);

Betty Hester ("A"), December 19, 1959 (HB 363); John Hawkes, December 26, 1959 (HB 367–368); Robert Lowell, January 10, 1960 (HB 369); Cecil Dawkins, January 11, 1960 (HB 369); Betty Hester ("A"), January 16, 1960 (HB 370); KATHERINE ANNE PORTER, January 22, 1960 (HB 371); Cecil Dawkins, January 28, 1960 (HB 371); Betty Hester ("A"), January 30, 1960 (HB 372); Robert Lowell, February 2, 1960 (HB 372–373); Andrew Lytle, February 4, 1960 (HB 373); Robert Giroux, February 10, 1960 (HB 373); Elizabeth Fenwick Way, February 14, 1960 (HB 375); Robert Giroux, February 14, 1960 (HB 375); Cecil Dawkins, February 22, 1960 (HB 375); Maryat Lee, February 25, 1960 (HB 376); Cecil Dawkins, February 28, 1960 (HB 376); Maryat Lee, March 1, 1960 (HB 377); Elizabeth Fenwick Way, March 3, 1960 (HB 378); Betty Hester ("A"), March 5, 1960 (HB 379); Maryat Lee, March 5, 1960 (HB 379); Robert Giroux, March 6, 1960 (HB 380); Betty Hester ("A"), March 8, 1960 (HB 381); Charlotte Gafford, March 16, 1960 (HB 381); Dr. T. R. Spivey, March 16, 1960 (HB 381); Betty Hester ("A"), April 2, 1960 (HB 385); Betty Hester ("A"), April 9, 1960 (HB 386); Dr. T. R. Spivey, April 9, 1960 (HB 387); Thomas Stritch, April, 1960 (HB 388); Elizabeth Fenwick Way, April 13, 1960 (HB 388); John Hawkes, April 14, 1960 (HB 389); Betty Hester ("A"), April 16, 1960 (HB 390); Elizabeth Bishop, April 23, 1960 (HB 391); Betty Hester ("A"), April 30, 1960 (HB 394); Betty Hester ("A"), May 14, 1960 (HB 396); Elizabeth Fenwick Way, May 22, 1960 (HB 396); John Hawkes, June 2, 1960 (HB 399); Betty Hester ("A"), June 11, 1960 (HB 400); Betty Hester ("A"), June 25, 1960 (HB 401); Elizabeth McKee, June 26, 1960 (HB 402); William Sessions, September 13, 1960 (HB 407); Betty Hester ("A"), September 17, 1960 (HB 408); Robert Giroux, September 29, 1960 (HB 409); William Sessions, September 29, 1960 (HB 410); Betty Hester ("A"), October 27, 1960 (HB 413); Robert Giroux, November 4, 1960 (HB 415); Robert Giroux, November 12, 1960 (HB 417); Robert Giroux, January 23, 1961 (HB 429); Betty Hester ("A"), November 11, 1961 (HB 453); John Hawkes, November 28, 1961 (HB 457); Cecil Dawkins, March 4, 1962 (HB 467); Betty Hester ("A"), May 19, 1962 (HB 474); Betty Hester ("A"),

June 23, 1962 (HB 481); Betty Hester ("A"), October 6, 1962 (HB 494); Robert Giroux, November 5, 1962 (HB 498); Dr. T. R. Spivey, January 27, 1963 (HB 506); Janet McKane, February 25, 1963 (HB 509); Janet McKane, July 9, 1963 (HB 529); Janet McKane, July 25, 1963 (HB 532); Janet McKane, August 27, 1963 (HB 536); Catherine Carver, June 27, 1964 (HB 588); Robert Giroux, June 28, 1964 (HB 589). *Pages HB*: 44, 47–48, 55, 59, 65, 68, 77, 81, 86, 88, 104, 127–128, 142, 172, 177, 181, 185, 191, 201, 209, 229, 239, 245, 248, 250–251, 264, 276, 282, 284, 287–288, 290, 300–301, 310, 311, 315–325, 327–329, 331–333, 336–351, 348–353, 355–359, 361, 363, 367–382, 384–392, 394, 396, 399–402, 407–411, 413, 415, 417, 429, 438, 453, 457–458, 467, 474, 481, 494, 498, 506–507, 509, 529, 532, 536, 588–589.

FURTHER READING

Arnold, Marilyn. "Sentimentalism in the Devil's Territory." In *Flannery O'Connor and the Christian Mystery*, edited by John J. Murphy, et al., 243–258. Provo, Utah: Center for the Study of Christian Values in Literature, Brigham Young University; 1997.

———. "*The Violent Bear It Away*: Flannery O'Connor's Reluctant Compromise with Mercy." *The McNeese Review* 28 (1981–82): 25–33.

Asals, Frederick. *Flannery O'Connor: The Imagination of Extremity*, Athens: University of Georgia Press, 1982.

Baker, J. Robert. "Flannery O'Connor's Four-Fold Method of Allegory." *The Flannery O'Connor Bulletin* 21 (1992): 84–96.

Bamberg, Marie Louise. "A Note on the Motif of Midday Crisis in Flannery O'Connor's *The Violent Bear It Away*." *American Notes & Queries* 23, nos. 1–2 (1984): 19–21.

Benoit, Raymond. "The Existential Intuition of Flannery O'Connor in *The Violent Bear It Away*." *Notes on Contemporary Literature* 23, no. 4 (September 1993): 2–3.

Beutel, Katherine Piller. "Flannery O'Connor's Echoing Voices in *The Violent Bear It Away*." *Journal of Contemporary Thought* 4 (1994): 23–36.

Bieber, Christina. "Called to the Beautiful: The Incarnational Art of Flannery O'Connor's *The Violent Bear It Away*." *Xavier Review* 18, no. 1 (1998): 44–62.

Brinkmeyer, Robert H., Jr. "A Closer Walk with Thee: Flannery O'Connor and Southern Fundamentalists." *Southern Literary Journal* 18, no. 2 (Spring 1986): 3–13.

Burns, Stuart L. "Flannery O'Connor's *The Violent Bear It Away*: Apotheosis in Failure." *Sewanee Review* 76 (1968): 319–336.

Buzan, Mary. "The Difficult Heroism of Francis Marion Tarwater." *The Flannery O'Connor Bulletin* 14 (1985): 33–43.

Cash, Jean W. "O'Connor on *The Violent Bear It Away*: An Unpublished Letter." *English Language Notes* 26, no. 4 (June 1989): 67–71.

Demory, Pamela H. "Violence and Transcendance in *Pulp Fiction* and Flannery O'Connor." In *The Image of Violence in Literature, the Media, and Society*, edited by Will Wright and Steven Kaplan, 187–194. Pueblo, Colo.: Society for the Interdisciplinary Study of Social Imagery, University of Southern Colorado, 1995.

Desmond, John F. "Flannery O'Connor and the History Behind the History." *Modern Age: A Quarterly Review* 27, nos. 3–4 (Summer-Fall 1983): 290–296.

———. "The Mystery of the Word and the Act: *The Violent Bear It Away*." *American Benedictine Review* 24 (1973): 342–347.

Detweiler, Jane A. "Flannery O'Connor's Conversation with Simone Weil: *The Violent Bear It Away* as a Study of Affliction." *Kentucky Philological Review* 6 (1991): 4–8.

Donahoo, Robert. "Tarwater's March Toward the Feminine: The Role of Gender in O'Connor's *The Violent Bear It Away*." *CEA Critic: An Official Journal of the College English Association* 56, no. 1 (Fall 1993): 96–106.

Giannone, Richard. "The Lion of Judah in the Thought and Design of *The Violent Bear It Away*." *The Flannery O'Connor Bulletin* 14 (1985): 25–32.

———. "Warfare and Solitude: O'Connor's Prophet and the Word in the Desert." In *Flannery O'Connor and the Christian Mystery*, edited by John J. Murphy, et al., 161–189. Provo, Utah: Center for the Study of Christian Values in Literature, Brigham Young University, 1997.

Grimes, Ronald L. "Anagogy and Ritualization: Baptism in Flannery O'Connor's *The Violent Bear It Away*." *Religion and Literature* 21, no. 1 (Spring 1989): 9–26.

Kehl, D. G. "Flannery O'Connor's Catholicon: The Source and Significance of the Name 'Tarwater.'" *Notes on Contemporary Literature* 15, no. 2 (March 1985): 2–3.

Kinnebrew, Mary Jane. "Language From the Heart of Reality: A Study of Flannery O'Connor's Attitudes Toward Non-Standard Dialect and Her Use of It in *Wise Blood, A Good Man Is Hard to Find,* and *The Violent Bear It Away." Linguistics in Literature* 1, no. 3 (1976): 39–53.

Magistrale, Tony. "Francis Tarwater's Friendly Friends: The Role of the Stranger in *The Violent Bear It Away." Notes on Contemporary Literature* 15, no. 3 (May 1985): 4–5.

May, John R., S. J. "*The Violent Bear It Away:* The Meaning of the Title." *Flannery O'Connor Bulletin* 2 (1973): 83–86.

Mayer, David R. "*The Violent Bear It Away:* Flannery O'Connor's Shaman." *Southern Literary Journal* 4, no. 2 (1972): 41–54.

Muller, Gilbert H. "*The Violent Bear It Away:* Moral and Dramatic Sense." *Renascence: Essays on Value in Literature* 22 (1969): 17–25.

Olson, Steven. "Tarwater's Hats." *Studies in the Literary Imagination* 20, no. 2 (Fall 1987): 37–49.

Paulson, Suzanne Morrow. "Apocalypse of Self, Resurrection of the Double: Flannery O'Connor's *The Violent Bear It Away." Literature and Psychology* 30, nos. 3–4 (1980): 100–111.

Scouten, Kenneth. "The Schoolteacher as a Devil in *The Violent Bear It Away." The Flannery O'Connor Bulletin* 12 (1983): 35–46.

Shaw, Patrick W. "*The Violent Bear It Away* and the Irony of False Seeing." *Texas Review* 3, no. 2 (Fall 1982): 49–59.

Shrine, Mary S. "Narrative Strategy and Communicative Design in Flannery O'Connor's *The Violent Bear It Away.*" In *Studies in Interpretation,* edited by Esther M. Doyle, et al., 45–59. Amsterdam: Rodopi, 1977.

Smith, Francis J., S. J. "O'Connor's Religious Viewpoint in *The Violent Bear It Away." Renascence: Essays on Value in Literature* 22 (1970): 108–112.

Swan, Jesse G. "Flannery O'Connor's Silence-Centered World." *Flannery O'Connor Bulletin* 17 (1988): 82–89.

Trowbridge, Clinton W. "The Symbolic Vision of Flannery O'Connor: Patterns of Imagery in *The Violent Bear It Away." Sewanee Review* 76 (1968): 298–318.

Wilson, Carol Y. "Family as Affliction, Family as Promise in *The Violent Bear It Away." Studies in the Literary Imagination* 20, no. 2 (Fall 1987): 77–86.

Zornado, Joseph. "A Becoming Habit: Flannery O'Connor's Fiction of Unknowing." *Religion and Literature* 29, no. 2 (Summer 1997): 27–59.

"Why Do the Heathen Rage?" (1963)

This story is believed to be a segment of a third novel or perhaps a novella that was left incomplete. It was published in the July 1963 issue of ESQUIRE (vol. 60); *Complete Stories* (FSG, 1971) edited by Robert Giroux; and *Collected Works* (Library of America), edited by Sally Fitzgerald. An editorial note with the story when it appeared in *Esquire* read, "Flannery O'Connor's . . . third novel is as yet untitled, and she says it may be years before it's finished. This excerpt is from the beginning sections" (qtd. in *Complete* 554–555). O'Connor died weeks after the story was first published, and the novel-in-progress, really more a collection of fragments than the term suggests, remains incomplete.

SYNOPSIS

Tilman is brought home in an ambulance after suffering a stroke while at the state capital on business and after being in the hospital for two weeks. He does not seem to recognize his wife, his daughter Mary Maud who is a teacher, or his son Walter who is reading a book on the porch when the ambulance arrives. Only Roosevelt, the yard man who will now become chief nurse, brings a sign of emotion out of Tilman.

Mrs. Tilman faces Walter Tilman, who is 28 and still living at home, with a proposition. It is now time for him to take over running the place. Walter tells his mother that she is fully capable of doing so herself; they would all have been better off if she had taken over 10 years before. She tells Walter that he either take responsibility, or he will have to move. Walter tells her he thought this was home, and this makes her feel guilty when she realizes that he is homeless if he does not stay with her.

She tells him she is "only" a woman, and he tells her that a woman from her generation would be better at the job than a man from his. When she says she would at least be embarrassed to admit that were she from his time, he says that the only virtue of his generation is that they are willing to speak the truth.

Unlike his mother's father and grandfather, who were both lawyers, Walter has no occupation. Mrs. Tilman had thought he might like to be an artist or philosopher, but he says he refuses to write under a label. He writes letters, mostly, some of them under assumed names, to people he does not know. He reads books that have no current relevance, in Mrs. Tilman's view.

She remembers a book she found that he had left open on the upstairs bathroom floor. She read the passage and thought about it for many days. It was a letter by St. Jerome from around A.D. 370 to Heliodorus. It began, "Love should be full of anger" (CW 800). She has that, all right, she thought. The passage speaks about a soldier and a general. It scolds the soldier for leaving the desert.

When she thinks of the passage now, it suddenly hits her. The general in the passage who has a sword in his mouth, ready to do battle and conquer the world, is Jesus.

COMMENTARY

Ironically, Mary Maud, the daughter with the take-charge personality, is the member of the family who should get the task of taking over the house and land when her father becomes ill with a stroke. Because of her mother's sexism, however, Mary Maud is not even considered for that responsibility. Instead, the mother rages against her son, Walter, who is clearly neither interested in the task nor qualified or suitable to handle the work. At 28, Walter reads books and writes letters like a monk but appears to have little interest in other occupations.

Walter suggests that his mother take over the property, but she refuses solely on the basis that she is a woman. Her expectations are not met in Walter, who has a very different outlook on life and has been apparently allowed to read books and write

letters without making any other contribution to his family's well-being.

The title of the story likely comes from the Bible, Psalm 2:1 and Acts 4:25: "Why do the heathen rage, and the people imagine a vain thing?" Other versions of the passage are: "Why do the nations protest and the peoples grumble in vain?" and "Why did the Gentiles rage and the peoples entertain folly?" In one interpretation of the story, Mrs. Tilman misses the point of her son's preoccupations entirely. He is engaged in deep thought and spiritual questioning, where she is simply trying to handle mundane day-to-day responsibilities. Why is she raging against her son's soul-searching when that is really more important in life, more at the heart of existence?

Another reading of the story in relation to the passage would be an ironic interpretation of the first reading. Though Walter may be engaged, in the end, in the more important endeavor, life still must go on with bills paid and food on the table, and so forth. Why do the "heathen" rage, indeed? Perhaps because they must in order to provide basic human needs.

Mrs. Tilman reads a passage out of one of Walter's books that she finds in the bathroom. She thinks about the passage for some time and still does not understand it. Her main objection to Walter's reading seems to be that what he reads is not relevant to this day and time. It takes more thought until she is struck at the end of the story with the epiphany that the general is Jesus.

Notice how the passage echoes much of Walter's situation. His mother loves him with a love that is full of anger. She admonishes him when he spurns her request to take over the property. St. Jerome asks Heliodorus what right he has to be in his father's house, much as Mrs. Tilman is asking Walter. She wonders, like St. Jerome, where his fighting spirit is. She hopes the incident with his father will wake him up, much as St. Jerome tells Heliodorus to arise from his nap and come to the battlefield. Both Mrs. Tilman and St. Jerome are saying wake up and engage in life, take up their crosses and do God's will. The story tells us that eventually Heliodorus branched off from St. Jerome and became a noted churchman as the bishop of Altinum. He served his own kind of purpose but in a quieter way.

CHARACTERS

Walter Tilman Walter does not mind the till as in cash box, nor does he till the soil, as in plowing. Instead, Walter joins several other intellectual characters in O'Connor's fiction who share the traits of conceitedness, laziness, and rudeness. Walter shares the physical appearance of his mother's father and grandfather. He shares their smile that is uncommitted; he has the same set jaw and Roman nose. Like them, he will soon be bald, and his eyes are the same color—not green or blue or gray. Physical characteristics, however, appear to be where the likenesses stop. Unlike his mother's ancestors or his father, he has not found it his responsibility to get a job or contribute to the household.

The story speaks about generations and how Walter perceives his generation as one that is willing to have its men be waited on. He also says the strongest trait of his age is the willingness to state the truth. Stating the truth but not acting on it goes only halfway to accomplishing anything of merit. It is one thing to be well read and to think; it is quite another to use that knowledge for something useful, especially if one is not of any help to anyone.

RELATED LETTERS

Robert Giroux, November 9, 1962 (HB 498); Cecil Dawkins, January 13, 1963 (HB 504); Sister Mariella Gable, May 4, 1963 (HB 516–517); Betty Hester ("A"), June 22, 1963 (HB 526); Janet McKane, July 9, 1963 (HB 529): Cecil Dawkins, November 8, 1963 (HB 546). *Pages HB*: 498, 504, 517, 526, 529, 546.

FURTHER READING

Wray, Virginia. "Flannery O'Connor's 'Why Do the Heathen Rage?' and the Quotidian 'Larger Things.'" *The Flannery O'Connor Bulletin* 23 (1994–95): 1–29.

"Wildcat" (1947)

This story is the third in O'Connor's 1947 masters' thesis, "The Geranium: A Collection of Short Stories," submitted to the UNIVERSITY OF IOWA (p. 40–51).

SYNOPSIS

The story is divided into three brief, numbered sections.

I. The reader meets Old Gabriel, a blind black man, who has a keen sense of smell. Gabriel tells a group of men that they have nothing with which to hunt the wildcat. The men gently mock Old Gabriel by asking him how many wildcats he has killed. The men tell him that the wildcat is after the cows. Gabe tells them that it has come out of the woods for more than cows; it wants human blood.

Gabe asks the men if they could sit with him awhile, and they ask him if he is afraid to be there by himself. Indignantly, Gabe pulls himself up by a post and tells them they had best get going since Mose and Luke had already left an hour ago.

II. The second section is a flashback to Gabe's youth. He wants to go hunting for the wildcat with the men, but he is made to wait in the cabin with his mother, Reba, and Thin Minnie. In another cabin, Nancy waits with old Hezuh. Gabe tells the women that he can smell the wildcat. Soon there is a weight against the house and a scream, and Nancy comes to tell them that the wildcat jumped in through the window and bit Hezuh in the throat and killed him.

III. The third section returns to the present. Gabe goes to bed, still smelling the wildcat and letting his imagination roam. He is convinced the cat will get him tonight. He does not want to sit with the women. He is not afraid. He is convinced, however, that the wildcat will come to him as he sits in the cabin and not be caught being chased out in the woods. He waits, which is the only thing old people like himself know and ol' Hezuh back then, could do. The cat was going to come in and get him as it did Hezuh.

He hears scratching by the chimney, but it is only bats. He imagines himself moving toward the cat hole, smelling. There he sees across the riverbank the Lord waiting with angels and gold vestments for him to wear when he dies. He begins to climb up on a chair and then a shelf to get up higher. The shelf breaks and he falls, and as he does he hears an animal cry in the distance of two hills away. The wildcat has gotten a cow before it came for him. He thinks that tomorrow night it will come back.

The next morning, Mose and Luke are making breakfast, and Gabe asks them what they caught the night before. They say that they caught nothing, but they have set a trap at Ford's Woods and expect to catch the cat that night. Gabriel knows better. He does not eat the side-meat they offer him. In the darkness, animal cries join the wild beats of his heart.

COMMENTARY

Like "The Crop," this story was noted by the author herself as "unpublishable" and was published after her death with the permission of her literary executor, Robert Fitzgerald. It appeared first in the spring 1970 edition of *The North American Review,* (vol. 255, no. 1) and was then anthologized in *Complete Stories* (FSG, 1971). Robert Giroux, who edited *Complete Stories,* notes that this story was written prior to June 1947. Editor Sally Fitzgerald used O'Connor's original typescript when she included the story in *Collected Works* (Library of America, 1988). Usually considered by critics to be the weakest story in the master's thesis, it is one of the rare instances when O'Connor attempts to write from inside the mind of a black character and in dialect.

Many readers see the story as being about Gabriel as an old man waiting for death, much as Nancy in WILLIAM FAULKNER's "That Evening Sun" waits for her estranged husband, Jesus, to come back and kill her. The second section of the story is a flashback to Gabriel's youth when he was kept with the women one night when men went out "hunting" for a wildcat. The wildcat was not out where the hunters were looking but came to another cabin and killed Hezuh. Gabriel had smelled the cat that night, and he smells it this night, years later, when the hunters are out looking for another wildcat.

The wildcat does indeed represent death. Gabriel not only senses death both in the flashback in the story when he is a young boy but also when he is an old man. No one dies in the third section of the story except a cow, but one senses that Gabriel's death is still imminent because his intuition about the wildcat's behavior is validated through the flashback of his prior experience.

In a way, Gabriel himself is the wildcat. He has struggled with his place in life all these years. As a youth, he did not want to be left with the women in the cabin; he wanted to fight the cat and prove his manhood. The wildcat spared him that night; he was too young; it was not his time. The memories rise up again in old age. Gabriel knows the wildcat because he knows that his end is near. Though he is blind, he visualizes the angels greeting him with the Lord on the other side of the river where they will put gold vestments on him.

Even so, Gabriel speaks to the wildcat in his imagination and tells it that the Lord does not want to see him with scratches on his face. He knows he cannot fight against the wildcat as he may have done as a young boy. He no longer has the strength. He falls against a shelf out of worry when he hears and smells the wildcat come close to the cabin. Instead, the cat attacks a cow, just as the younger men said it would.

O'Connor rarely uses dialect, and this story suggests what may be some of the reasons why. Like a character's thoughts, sound must come from within. If the author is not comfortable thinking as a member of another race or social class or gender, the author will know that the thoughts and speech do not ring true. O'Connor was experimenting with this story, but she rarely if ever took this point of view in her fiction again. It was a position that, years later, author Alice Walker appreciated about her.

CHARACTERS

Old Gabriel Gabriel is elderly, black, and blind. He is one of the early examples of O'Connor's characters with a disability. A lack of physical description of him in the story echoes for the reader the character's own lack of knowledge about what he looks like. The angel Gabriel is considered in Catholic tradition to be the angel of mercy. In Luke 1:26–33, Gabriel tells Mary that she is going to bear the son of God:

> In the sixth month, the angel Gabriel was sent from God to a town of Galilee called Nazareth, to a virgin betrothed to a man named Joseph, of the house of David, and the virgin's name was Mary. And coming to her, he said, "Hail, favored one! The Lord is with you." But she

was greatly troubled at what was said and pondered what sort of greeting this might be. Then the angel said to her, "Do not be afraid, Mary, for you have found favor with God. Behold, you will conceive in your womb and bear a son, and you shall name him Jesus. He will be great and will be called Son of the Most High, and the Lord God will give him the throne of David his father, and he will rule over the house of Jacob forever, and of his kingdom there will be no end."

Old Gabriel announces to the young men that the wildcat will seek them out; they do not need to hunt it. As much as he can smell the wildcat when he is a young boy, he can smell it again in the third section of the story. This Gabriel does not announce an impending birth but a death. The other angels in the story are there to welcome Gabriel back into the fold of the seraphim.

Gabriel's name is also relevant in the way it relates to the Bible passage of Daniel 8 where the angel Gabriel interprets Daniel's vision of the he-goat attacking the two-horned ram. Gabriel tells Daniel, "Understand, son of man, that the vision refers to the end time" (Daniel 8:17). Old Gabriel knows that his "vision" refers to an end time of his own.

Wise Blood (1952)

O'Connor's first novel was published by Harcourt Brace on May 15, 1952. It contains 14 chapters and is dedicated "For Regina," the author's mother. A few chapters were reworked from stories that were previously published. For example, "The Peeler" originally appeared in PARTISAN REVIEW, December 1949 (vol. 16). "Enoch and the Gorilla" was published in NEW WORLD WRITING edited by Arabel Porter in April 1952 (vol. 2). "The Train" was revised to be the first chapter of the novel, but it originally appeared in a different form in SEWANEE REVIEW in April 1948 (vol. 56) and was the last story in O'Connor's master's thesis, occupying pages 87–102 in that manuscript.

SYNOPSIS

Chapter 1

Hazel Motes is riding on a train opposite Mrs. Wally Bee Hitchcock who asks him if he is going home. Motes appears to her to be in his early twenties. In his lap, he holds a black wide-brimmed hat like a preacher's, and he wears a bright blue suit with the price tag still attached. She spots the army duffel bag at his feet and decides that he is heading home from the service. His brown eyes appear the color of pecan shells, and the outline of his skull shows through the skin of his face. She finally makes out the price of his suit, $11.98. She finds his eyes most intriguing; she tries to look into them. They seem so deep and distant, but Motes is not looking at her; his gaze is fixed on the porter.

Motes gets up and has an exchange with the porter about a berth. He tells the porter that he is from Eastrod. The porter tells him that Eastrod is not on this line and that he must be on the wrong train. Motes and the porter talk about where they are from; the porter says he is from Chicago and that his father was a railroad man, but Motes thinks he recognizes him as a Parrum from Eastrod. He sits back down across from Mrs. Hitchcock.

Mrs. Hitchcock asks him if he is going home, and he tells her no; he is going to Taulkinham to "do some things I never have done before" (*Collected* 5). Mrs. Hitchcock talks about people whom she knows in that town and in Chicago and keeps talking, not catching what Motes has said to her. Suddenly, he tells her that she probably thinks she has been redeemed. This stops her chatter. She blushes and suggests that they go to the dining car since he must be hungry. There they have to wait a half hour. Mrs. Hitchcock begins a conversation with another woman, and they are allowed into the dining car, but Motes is not. Finally, he is seated in the dining car with three young women.

After he orders, he comments that he would not want to be redeemed if they were, and he asks them if they think he believes in Jesus. One of the women with an Eastern accent asks who ever said he had to believe in Jesus. While he eats, the women watch him. He waits for his bill, but the waiter makes several passes, winking at the women, before he finally brings Motes his check. Motes pays and goes out to find the porter.

Motes tries to squeeze past Mrs. Hitchcock, who is ready for bed, but they end up going the same direction. She cannot see who he is without her glasses. The porter provides the ladder for Motes to climb up into his berth. Motes insists that the porter is Parrum from his hometown, and the porter becomes more annoyed, telling him that he is from Chicago. Motes finally climbs into his berth, and while he is there he remembers all of the family members whom he has seen closed inside their coffins as the lid went down. He had expected them all to jump up at the last minute and not let the lid close, but none of them did so. He imagines the berth is like a coffin.

He thinks about Eastrod in the days when he grew up. There were 25 people there then, and three of them were Motes, but now no one is left. He had grown up going around with his preacher grandfather helping him preach, and he knew since the time he was 12 that he would be a preacher, too. However, the army called him up when he was 18. He thought he would shoot himself in the foot to avoid going since a preacher could make do without a foot, but then he decided he would go for four months. Instead, he stayed in for four years and never made it home in the meantime. He was also wounded in battle.

All the while he was in the army, he managed to stay away from the corruption in which the other soldiers took part. On his release from the army, he rode a train to Melsy, the nearest station to Eastrod. He bought his suit and hat in a store while waiting for the train. When he got to Eastrod, the house was empty and boarded up. The only thing inside was his mother's old chifforobe. He tied the chifforobe and put a sign on it saying that it belonged to him and that if anyone stole it, he would track him down and kill him.

Thinking of the chifforobe as he lies in the berth makes Motes think of his mother. She did not pop up and keep the lid from moving its shadow across her face any more than any of his other relatives did. Having this memory makes him squeamish about being in the dark berth, and he yells to the porter to get him out of there. The porter does not move. When Motes cries "Jesus," the porter says that Jesus has been gone a long time.

Chapter 2

When Motes gets to Taulkinham, he sees many blinking bright lights. He walks around the station a bit with nowhere to go. He could sit on the bench, but he wants to settle somewhere private. Finally, he wanders into the restroom and into a stall marked "Welcome." He sits there reading the graffiti on the walls and sees the address for a prostitute, Mrs. Watts. He writes down the address, walks out, and takes a taxi to her house. The taxi driver keeps asking him if he is a preacher since he looks like one and Mrs. Watts does not normally have preachers at her house. Motes insists that he is not. The taxi driver tells him that he has a look about him that says he is a preacher; it is not just his preacher's hat that makes him look like one. He tells him that nobody is perfect and that preachers understand sin better when they have committed it themselves. When he gets out of the car, Motes tells him that he does not believe in anything.

Mrs. Watts's house is a shack, but it has a glowing light in the window that makes it inviting. Motes steps up to the porch and looks through a crack in the shade. He sees a white knee. He makes out a large woman trimming her toenails. He goes into the house and sees a hallway with a door on either side. He stands in the doorway that is open a crack. Mrs. Watts sees him but looks away, continuing to sit on the bed and work on her nails. Motes enters the room and sits on a far corner of the bed. Then he picks up her foot, moves it, and keeps his hand on it.

Mrs. Watts asks if he is hunting for something, and she moves him closer on the bed. He tells her has come for her usual business, and she tells him to make himself at home. He tells her he wants her to know that he is no preacher. Mrs. Watts says that it is "okay, son, Mamma don't mind."

Chapter 3

On Motes's second night in Taulkinham, he spends time downtown in the marketplace. There he sees a man in front of a department store demonstrating a potato peeler on a card table. An 18-year-old boy named Enoch Emery and a blind man, tall with a black suit and hat, stand in the small group around the salesman. A young girl is with him, and she is handing out religious tracts. The blind man is begging, holding out a cup as he taps with his cane. The begging makes most of the people who had been watching uncomfortable, and they leave. The potato-peeler salesman becomes annoyed with the blind man for chasing off his business. Motes takes the tract that the girl hands out to him. It says, "Jesus Calls You" (*Collected* 21). Motes tears up the leaflet into tiny pieces and lets them rain down to the ground. He notices the look in the girl's eyes as she watches him do it.

Meanwhile, Enoch Emery wants a potato peeler, but all he has is $1.16, and the device costs $1.50. The girl wants one also, but she has only $1.00. The blind man and the girl walk off, but something in the way that the girl looks at Motes makes him drop $2.00 onto the card table, snatch a peeler, and walk off behind them. Enoch Emery sees him do this and follows him.

Emery tells him that he has been in town for two months and that he is employed by the city. He draws the information out of Motes that he has been there two days. Emery asks Motes if he is following the blind preacher, if he goes in for Jesus types. He tells him his sorry story of a woman who took him from his father and sent him to Rodemill Boys' Bible Academy for four weeks. Motes crosses the street at a red light and is stopped by a policeman. Emery vouches for him and clears him. Motes tells him that he is obliged.

Emery is lonely and wants Motes's company. He talks to him some more about how unfriendly the people of this city are. He tells him more about the woman to whom his father gave him and how he had prayed for a way to get away from her without killing her, and Jesus obliged. Now he is with his father in this city, or at least he was until his father took up with some woman. They catch up to the blind preacher and his daughter at a building with a dome and columns. The blind preacher says that the people are due out soon; they are his congregation. The girl tells him a story about a woman and a man who killed a baby and how Jesus made it so that the woman was haunted by the baby everywhere she went. Motes gives the girl the peeler.

The blind preacher tells Emery to go with the girl up the steps and hand out leaflets. He tells Motes to join him in doing the same. He thinks Motes has followed him, that he has a look a preacher has put on him, but Motes followed the girl to give her the peeler. Motes tries to preach his own sermon to the crowd as it emerges and moves down the steps. He claims that he is a preacher of a new church, the church without Jesus Christ Crucified. Who needs Jesus, he says, when he has Leora Watts.

He comes down the steps and crosses the street before the blind preacher calls out that his name is Asa Hawks, just in case he wants to follow him again. Emery catches up with Motes and tells him more about his life. He works at the zoo as a guard. Emery wants Motes to spend time with him, but Motes has made his way back to Leora Watts's house and wants nothing to do with Emery. Emery accuses him, "You act like you think you got wiser blood than anybody else . . . but you ain't!" (*Collected* 33). He shows him that the girl has given him the peeler and tells him that she invited him to her house sometime. He planned to go and take his mouth organ. Finally, Motes escapes Emery inside Watts's house.

When he finds her in the bedroom, Mrs. Watts takes off her clothes and puts on Motes's hat. He laughs and turns off the light. He remembers sneaking in as a child to see a naked woman at the carnival and how his stern mother seemed to know about it when he got home. She told him that Jesus died to redeem him. Young Motes had put stones in his shoes after that and walked in them for miles to try to pay back the Lord for his sin.

Chapter 4

The next morning, Motes feels like buying a car. The idea comes to him out of nowhere; he has never considered such a purchase before. He has $50, and he looks at cars in several lots before he goes to Slade's. There he sees a boy who is guarding the lot. Motes asks for Slade, and the boy says that he is Slade. Motes looks at a gray car with large wheels, bulging headlights, and a board where the backseat used to be. Finally, a man appears, and they bargain over the price of the car. The boy curses, using the name Jesus, which seems to bother Motes. When he asks the father why the boy curses so much, the older Slade has no idea.

They try the car, and Motes talks Slade down to $40 plus gas. The boy puts gas in the car, still cussing. Motes has not driven a car in several years, so he does not want the Slades watching him pull away. He tells them that he mostly wants it for a house in which to live. He forgets to remove the parking brake. Finally, he drives out and onto the highway and starts to go very fast.

On the highway, he comes up behind a truck full of chickens that is moving slowly. His horn does not work, so he ends up following the slow truck down the hill. A large boulder on an embankment at the side of the road is painted with a question: Would hell swallow up a blasphemer and whoremonger; in smaller print, "Jesus Saves." Motes is stopped in the middle of the road looking at the boulder when an oil truck pulls up behind him, and the driver gets out to tell him to get out of the road.

Motes tells the truck driver that sin came before the whoremongering and blasphemy. He does not have to run from anything because he does not believe in anything, he says. The truck driver loses his patience and looks as though he is about the lift the car out of the road himself. Motes asks him where the zoo is, and the driver asks him if he just escaped from there. Motes tells him no, that he has to see a boy who works there.

Chapter 5

On awakening, Enoch Emery realizes that the person to whom he could show his discovery is going to arrive today; he has wise blood like his father, so he can feel it. His shift reliever arrives late, as usual. After fussing at him about his always being late, Emery goes on his way. He likes to hide in the bushes and watch women swim at the pool. Today the woman with two children is back. He likes to watch from the bushes while she sunbathes; she lets the straps of her swimsuit fall down over her shoulders.

As he sits there, he sees a gray car drive by a couple of times and slow down, as though the driver is looking for someone. He sees Hazel Motes get out of the car and walk over to the pool. Motes asks him for the address for Asa Hawkes. Emery tells him that he will give him the address once he has shown

him something. Motes resists, but he finally follows Emery to the Frosty Bottle, where Emery always buys something to drink on his daily rounds.

The clerk at the Frosty Bottle is a drunk woman named Maude. She stares at Motes while she fills Emery's daily order. She tells Motes that he is a nice boy, a clean boy. Motes leans close to her over the counter and tells her that he is clean but that if Jesus existed, he would not be clean. Maude is startled and yells at both young men to get out of there. Emery thinks Motes has changed a great deal. He has either lost all his money or has the police after him; perhaps he has committed a murder. Still, he must show him his discovery.

He convinces Motes to follow him through the zoo to find the place. They pass all kinds of animals until finally there is a cage with nothing in it. Motes stands in front of it and sees an eye back in the corner. It is an owl. Emery tells him to keep moving. Finally, they reach a small museum building. In the dark, Emery shows Motes the shrunken man in the glass case. He tells him that Arabs had done this to the man. Motes's reflection looks back at them from the case. Soon the woman and her two children arrive and walk over to the case as well. Her reflection with that of her sons' faces joins them in the glass. The sight makes Hazel Motes jump back and run out of the room.

Emery chases him until Motes swings him around and asks him again for the address. Emery suddenly feels weak and falls and lands against a tree. When he looks up, he sees Motes standing over him, dropping a rock on his forehead. Motes is gone when he wakes up, and he feels the blood on his face. Somehow, he knows that what is expected of him is just beginning.

Chapter 6

That evening, Hazel Motes finds the blind preacher and the child's house by following them home in his Essex. Then he takes the car back to town and preaches about his "Church Without Christ" as people go into and out of the movies. The woman in the ticket booth tells him she will call the police if he does not leave. He does the same thing at three other theaters and then goes back to Mrs. Watts for the night.

The next day he goes to the blind preacher's building and rents a room. When the landlady asks what he does for a living, he announces that he is a preacher for the Church Without Christ. She asks him if it is a Protestant denomination or something foreign, and he tells her that it is Protestant. As soon as the landlady is gone, he goes to their room. The blind preacher is actually not really blind, but he hurries and puts on the black glasses. Motes tells him that he has started his own church and that he preaches on the street. This does not bring the response from Hawks that he expects. Hawks shuts the door in his face.

After Motes leaves, the child tells Hawks that if he helps her get Motes interested in her, she will leave, and he will be free to do as he wishes. She mentions that he can use the clipping, which is a 10-year-old newspaper article that describes preacher Hawks's intention to blind himself to show how much he believes in Jesus and redemption. The child says she likes Motes's eyes—he seems to not see what he looks at but keeps looking anyway.

That night, Motes does not go to Mrs. Watts. She had cut up his black hat. He decides that he will seduce the child to get back at Asa Hawks. The next day he buys a new hat, this time a white panama. In late afternoon, he returns to their room, and Hawks is ready for him. He talks to him about how God blinded Paul. He tells Motes he still has time to repent. He shows him the newspaper article, and Motes reads it three times. The child tells him that he did it with lime and that someone like him who blinded himself for justification ought to be able to help Motes be redeemed. Even someone with the blood of that person can do it.

Motes takes the article and tells them that no one with a good car needs redemption. He slips the girl a note that tells her he came there for her because she looks so good. When Hawks complains that Motes took the clipping, the girl reminds him that he has another clipping—this one telling of how he lost his nerve and spilled the lime down his face but not into his eyes. She goes out.

Motes wants his car repaired. He takes it to one garage that will not do the job and then finds another where the mechanic claims he can make everything run well because the car is good to start

with. He claims he is the best mechanic in town and that he has the best shop. Motes leaves his car with him, convinced that he is honest.

Chapter 7

Motes picks up his car at the garage the next afternoon to take it out for a spin. About a mile out of town, the child speaks up from the backseat, where she has been hiding. She slides over to the front seat beside him and asks about the note he wrote. First Motes is annoyed; then he remembers that he wants to seduce the child to get back at Hawks, so he plays along. The child tells him her name is Sabbath Lily Hawks, named so by her mother since she was born on the Sabbath. Her mother died in childbirth.

She explains that she is a bastard because her parents were not married when she was born. She has heard that bastards cannot enter heaven, and she asks him if this is the case in his church. Confused, Motes tells her that there is no such thing as bastards in his church, but at the same time he thinks that no bastard can be redeemed in his church either. He wonders how a man who blinded himself for Jesus could have a bastard for a child. He questions Sabbath about when her father believed. Sabbath tells him that she has a church in her heart where Christ is King. Motes tells him about his Church Without Christ, that it is a church where a new kind of jesus cannot waste his blood redeeming people because he is all man. She tells him a story of a child whom nobody loved and whose grandmother kept locked up in a chicken crate and drowned her in a well.

After parking the car and walking across a field, they sit underneath a tree, and Motes considers how it would be difficult to take the girl's innocence in the afternoon. The child plays with his hat and tries to get him to look at her, saying that she sees him. Finally, Motes decides he is going to leave and gets in the car but it will not start. They walk to the nearest garage, where a man takes them back to the Essex with some gas. He crawls underneath and then emerges. The car starts. The mechanic will not take any money for service or the gas. When they both go down the road, the truck and the car even up with each other, and Motes tells the mechanic that his car will take him anywhere. The man simply says that some things will get some people somewhere and drives away.

Chapter 8

Enoch Emery has a feeling that his life will never be the same. Something is going to happen to him, and the events all started to unfold the day he showed the shrunken man to Haze Motes. Emery goes about preparing. He cleans his small apartment. In it there is a bed, a chair, and a washstand with a cabinet portion that looks like a tabernacle. Two of the three pictures on his walls are his—one is of a small boy kneeling down beside his bed in his pajamas, praying that God bless his daddy; it is Emery's favorite picture. He is not sure why, but he steals a few items of food, eats less, and saves his money. With the money he saves, he thinks he will buy clothes, but instead he goes out and buys curtains, gilt paint, and a brush. He decides he will paint the inside of the cabinet gold.

After work, he goes to town, even though it is not where he wants to be. He buys popcorn at Walgreen's, where the salesman eyes his purse and comments that it may be made out of a hog's bladder. The purse belonged to Emery's father, and it is his prized possession because it is the only thing of his father's that he owns. He sits at the counter, and the clerk tries to fool him with a Lime-Cherry Surprise that is not fresh. He waits, and she gives him a fresh one. He goes to the movies and runs out of the theater at the third movie, which is about a baboon that rescued handsome children from an orphanage fire. Outside the theater, he spots Haze Motes preaching atop his Essex.

Motes is crying out for a new jesus for his Church Without Christ. He wants a man who is just a man to serve this purpose; everyone can look at him and know that they have been saved. This gives Emery an idea, and he knows what he must do. He decides to retrieve the shrunken man out of the park and surprise Haze Motes. He has just the place now to keep it in his room until Motes is ready for it.

Chapter 9

Things are not going as Haze Motes hoped they would. Hawks did not respond to him in a welcoming manner as a preacher should with a soul to save. His preaching on the street with his new church had thus far failed to gain any followers, so he was not able to spite Hawks with his preaching

skills. He no longer wanted to seduce Sabbath but wanted to protect himself instead. What he still wants is a disciple. Finally, one night he gets one.

While he preaches from the hood of his Essex outside four different movie theaters, another man is preaching outside them as well. This man has better skills and manages to attract people who will stand by and listen. Ironically, he preaches that his church is the same as Motes's, except that he calls it the Holy Church of Christ Without Christ. He refers to Motes as the Prophet he met two months before who changed his view of religion.

Motes tries to tell everyone that what the man is saying is a lie. The man's name is Onnie Jay Holy, and he asks the crowd for a dollar each and their names on a sheet of paper. Just as he is about to start collecting money, Motes tells people it does not cost money to know the truth. He tries to pull the Essex away, but it bucks forward and back until Holy manages to get into it, and they pull away. Motes tells him that he is not true, and Holy replies that he is a real preacher who used to be on the radio. Motes tells him to get out of the car, and Holy tells him that all he wanted was to learn more about the new jesus. Motes tells him that there is no such thing as a new jesus, and Holy says the trouble with intellectuals is that they never have anything to show for what they say. Holy tells him his real name is Hoover Shoats and that he knew from day one that Motes was nothing but a fraud.

Shoats gets his thumb slammed in the car door, and Motes slides down in his car to stay there. He hears Shoats come up to the car occasionally and shout at him that he will be out preaching on the streets, giving him competition. Motes blares his repaired car horn, scaring Shoats away. While Motes stays in his car, he dreams that he is both dead and buried. People keep stopping and looking in at him, some reverently and some making faces. Although he thinks that it is morning when he wakes from his nightmare, it is only midnight. He drives back to his room and decides to sneak in on Asa Hawks.

He picks Hawks's lock and lets himself in. Hawks is asleep. He steps over to his bed and looks down at him. Hawks's head is hanging over the side. Motes strikes a match near his face, and Hawks opens his eyes. They look at each other for a few moments.

Motes finally sees what was behind the glasses were eyes that could see all along. Hawks tells him to get out. Motes, in his white hat, disappears.

Chapter 10

When Motes parks outside the Odeon Theater the next night, his preaching is more impassioned. A couple of people stop to listen to him. He speaks about a conscience being nothing but a mirror; it does not exist. He says if someone thinks it does exist, he or she should track it down and kill it because it is nothing more than a shadow. As he preaches, he does not notice a car just like his pulling up with Hoover Shoats and a man in a blue suit and a white hat getting out. The man in the white hat sits on the nose of the car, and they begin to preach. Shoats has brought his guitar with him this time, and he calls the man in the hat with him the True Prophet.

A woman stops beside Motes and asks if the man in the hat is his twin. Motes replies that if you do not track it down and kill it, it will do the same to you. He gets into his car and goes home. When he arrives there, Sabbath Hawks is in his bed. She tells him that her father ran off after Motes found him out. If he wants to hit her, go ahead; she has nowhere to go, and she is staying right there.

Sabbath tells him that from the day she first saw him, she thought they were both dirty inside, even though he looked so innocent. She says the difference is that she likes it that way, and he does not. She asks if he wants her to teach him to like it, and he says he does. He takes off his pants and turns out the light. He gets into the bed, but he has forgotten to remove his hat. Sabbath grabs it and sends it whirling across the room in the dark.

Chapter 11

Wearing a long black raincoat, Enoch Emery steals the shrunken body from the city park museum. He places it in the tabernacle in his room and waits for something to happen. Nothing does. He waits some more. He sticks his head in the tabernacle and sneezes. At first he thinks it may have been the new jesus who sneezed, but then he realizes it was he. He kicks the door of the cabinet closed.

With an umbrella he borrows from his landlady and wearing a hat and a fake beard, Emery ventures out to take the small, babylike package of the new jesus to Haze Motes. He winds up standing under a movie marquee to keep dry, and a group of waiting children look him over. They are waiting for the star of a feature film, a gorilla, to arrive for an advertised appearance. He thinks about the time when he was four years old and was surprised when a tin of peanut brittle that he opened turned out to be a joke—a coiled spring popped out of it. Standing there, waiting with the children for the gorilla, he begins to think perhaps the new jesus is going to change his luck after all.

A truck with a poster on the sides pulls up, and a loudspeaker announces that Gonga the gorilla is inside. Free movie passes will be given out to the first 10 children who dare to shake his hand. When the gorilla emerges from the truck, most of the people are terrified, but one little girl lines up to shake his hand. After her, there is another and then two boys. Finally, Emery shakes the gorilla's hand. It is the first hand offered to him in the two months that he has been in that town. Emery starts to tell the gorilla that he has seen two of its movies and introduces himself and his experience there in the city. The gorilla leans forward until Emery can the human eyes behind the costume. A voice from inside tells him to go to hell.

Emery is mortified and runs off toward the address that he remembers for Sabbath Hawks. Sabbath tells him that Motes is sleeping, so Emery gives her the package. He is eager to be rid of it in case the police come looking for who stole it. He tells Sabbath that it is for Motes, not her, and to tell Motes that he is glad to get rid of it. After Emery leaves, Sabbath opens the package out of curiosity and cradles the shrunken body in her arms like a baby. Its condition is becoming more worn from all the handling.

Motes had heard the door when Emery left, and now he is awake. He decides that the best thing to do is to move to a new city and start all over again with his preaching of the Church Without Christ. He begins to pack his duffel bag, fingering the items in the bottom of the bag that he leaves there all the time. One of these is a Bible that, in fact, he does not allow himself to touch, and the other is an oblong case carrying his mother's glasses. He has forgotten that he has them, and he puts them on. He looks at himself in the mirror and sees his mother's face in his. This disorients him, and just as this happens, Sabbath walks into the room, carrying the new jesus like a baby and telling Motes to call her momma.

Motes reaches for the new jesus, misses because of the glasses, then reaches again and throws it against the wall. Then he takes the loose skin from where the stuffing has come out and throws it out the door. The rain splashes in on him. Sabbath tells him that she knew he was evil and that he would never let anyone else have any fun because he did not want anything but Jesus. Haze says that he has seen the truth. She asks where he is going, and he answers to another city to preach the truth. She then asks when he is going, and Motes says after he gets some more sleep, but Sabbath says that he will not be getting more sleep.

Chapter 12

Emery still thinks the new jesus will do something for him for his efforts. He still has hope, and he still has an ambition to be somebody. He wants to be someone for whom people will line up to shake his hand. He goes to the Paris Diner and orders a bowl of split-pea soup and a chocolate malted milkshake. The waitress cooks bacon and does not fill his order. He has been there many times before, and she has not grown to like him. There is only one other customer in the diner, a man who has finished eating and is reading the newspaper.

Emery tells the woman that he is in a hurry. Since the waitress appears in no mood to help him, he asks just for a piece of cake from the glass case. Then he slides over the stools and reads the back of the man's paper. When the man lowers the paper and looks at him, he asks if he might borrow a section that he is not reading. He lets the comics slip out of the paper, and Emery reads them; they are his favorite part of the paper. He also sees an advertisement for Gonga, the Jungle Monarch, and his appearance schedule in town. He sees that Gonga will make his last showing in 30 minutes at the Victory Theater. Emery has what he tells the waitress is an awakening. He tells her that he knows what he wants and he will not look the same if she sees him again.

Enoch makes his way to the Victory and climbs into the truck while the gorilla is shaking people's hands. When the movie is about to start, Gonga gets back into the truck, and it drives off. There are noises from the truck that are not those of a gorilla. Eventually, the truck stops off the highway, and Emery gets out. He has a long cut on his face and a lump under his eye. He digs a hole with his stick and buries his clothes and puts on the gorilla suit.

A couple sits on a rock off the highway, looking at the lights of the city in the valley. Emery walks down the road toward them with his hand extended. When he sees him, the man runs off. The woman then sees him and goes running down the highway. The gorilla looks surprised, drops its hand to its side, and sits down on the rock.

Chapter 13

Hoover Shoats is working the street preaching again with his Prophet made to look like Haze Motes, Solace Layfield. Layfield has consumption and a wife and six children. He makes $3.00 a night working with Shoats. On their second night together, Shoats made $15.35 after giving Layfield his cut. After Layfield takes Shoats home for the night, he sees another rat-colored car like his following him. Haze Motes is driving that car.

Soon Motes pulls up behind Shoats and rear-ends his car. Shoats stops, gets out, and asks Motes what he wants. Haze tells him to take off the hat and suit that look so much like his. Shoats tells him that he is not mocking him, that Shoats bought him the suit. Motes tells him that he preaches what he does not believe. He tells him that Shoats believes in Jesus.

Layfield takes off the hat and coat and begins running down the road. He runs out of the pants and looks like he is going to take his shoes off as well. It does not matter because now Haze Motes is driving toward him in the Essex. He runs him down and then runs over him. He stops and backs up and runs over him again. Then he stops the car and gets out. He leans over Layfield and hears the man making his last confession in the dirt, his face bloody. He is wheezing. Motes tells him to shut up. When Layfield wheezes for Jesus to help him, Motes slaps him in the back, and the man goes quiet. Motes does not hear any more breathing.

He goes back to the Essex and checks it for damage. He wipes the blood off the bumper, gets in, and drives off. He stays in the car all night. Early the next morning, he drives to a service garage to get his car serviced for his trip out of town. He follows the boy mechanic around the car while he works on it. The boy tells him that there is a leak in the gas tank and two leaks in the radiator. It will not hold water. The back tire might last 20 miles, driving slow. Motes has him put water in the car. All the while the boy works on the car, Motes curses, speaks about Jesus, and blasphemes. Finally, he takes off.

A police car pulls up behind Haze Motes within five miles of town. He has passed but not read a sign that says that Jesus died for you. Motes tells the officer that he was not speeding and that he was driving on the right side of the road. When he asks why the officer stopped him, the officer tells him it is because he does not like the look of him. Motes tells him that he does not have a license, and the officer says that he does not need one. He tells him to drive his car up to the top of a hill and park it facing the embankment. Motes thinks that perhaps the officer wants a fight, and he is willing to oblige. When he drives to the hill, the officer follows him; then they both get out. Motes is supposed to check out the view. While he does, the patrolman shoves his car down the embankment, where it rolls, bounces, falls apart, and lands on its top, 30 feet down. Motes stares out after it and sits down on the embankment, letting his feet dangle.

The patrolman says that someone without a car does not need a license. He offers to give Motes a ride, but Motes says that he is not going anywhere. He just stares off into space. The officer drives off. Motes walks three hours back to town. He goes to a store and buys quicklime and a bucket. When he gets to his room, the landlady sitting on the porch asks him what he is going to do with the lime, and he says that he is going to blind himself. The lady sits on the porch and considers blindness and death. She thinks that she would rather be dead than blind and then realizes that when she is dead, she will be blind. She wonders why a sane person would want to make his life less enjoyable. She cannot say.

Chapter 14

Haze Motes has blinded himself with lime, and his landlady lets him stay at the house because he can pay her rent regularly and on time with the money that he receives from the government for his war wounds. He rarely speaks and spends his days walking about half of the time, sitting with the landlady, Mrs. Flood, and eating meals she cooks for him. Sabbath had seen him blind himself and called all the boarders to come see him afterward. She ran off, saying that she never intended to live with a real blind preacher, and she missed her father. Sabbath has returned, and the landlady told Motes that she did not approve of certain living conditions and he would have to pay double if the girl lived with him. He gave her another $3.00.

The landlady feels justified taking Motes's money because she feels that it is her tax dollars come back to her. When she sees that Motes is willing to pay more for the girl to stay, she resents her taxes being spent this way and calls the welfare office on her. Since she is a minor, Sabbath Lily is taken away to a detention home. Mrs. Flood ponders Motes's condition and his mysterious habits. She knows that he is really blind. He refuses to wear dark glasses. At first this disturbs her, but then she finds herself looking in his eyes for something, she does not know what.

She finds money in the trash basket, and Motes tells her that it is there because he did not need it. She tells him about the poor and how much they need it, and he tells her she can have it, but her pride makes her say that she is not a charity case. On the other hand, Mrs. Flood frequently considers ways she might get Haze Motes to marry her so that when he dies, as his widow, she might take over his government checks. She suggests he buy a guitar to have something to do with his hands and to reconnect him with the world, but he does not do so.

Mrs. Flood takes care of Haze Motes by feeding him and taking care of him when he is ill. He gets the flu, and she gives him food and brings him back to health. He walks with difficulty around the four or five blocks around the house each day and develops a limp. In his room, she discovers that he has rocks and glass chips in his shoes. She empties them out and later sees that he has replaced them.

When she sees him in bed on another visit, she sees that he has wrapped barbed wire around his chest. She tells him that people have quit doing these kinds of self-punishment like monks or the old saints, and he says that as long as he is doing it, people have not quit doing it. She asks why he does it, and he says it is because he is not clean.

Mrs. Flood tells him that she cannot keep going upstairs and that an easier way for them to take care of each other would be if they got married. At this, he gets dressed, gets his cane, and walks straight out of the house. It is a very cold day, and she thinks he will be back. She reports his disappearance to the police under the guise of wanting him to pay back rent. Two days later, two police officers find Haze Motes lying in a ditch. One asks the other if he is dead, but they see him moving a hand along the edge of the ditch, as though searching for something to hold onto. He asks them where he is and if it is nighttime or daylight.

The police officer tells him it is day and he must go back to the house to pay his rent. Motes says he wants to continue on his way. The other officer decides to try out his new billy club on Motes and knocks him over the head with it. They put him in the squad car, where he dies. The officers do not notice he is dead, and they take him to Mrs. Flood. She tells them to put him on her bed. The officers leave, and she draws up a chair and holds his hand to her heart. Then she looks in his face and explores a pinpoint of light she thinks she sees in the tunnel of his eyes where he has disappeared. He seems far away, and she feels as though she is at the beginning of something she cannot begin. As she closes her eyes, she thinks she sees him as a pinpoint of light.

COMMENTARY

Publication and Reception

O'Connor originated and worked on the chapter-stories and the manuscript for *Wise Blood* as a novel while in the MFA program in creative writing at the UNIVERSITY OF IOWA, Iowa City, from 1945 to 1947. While she was there, she submitted four chapters of *Wise Blood* to the Rinehart-Iowa Fiction Award competition for a first novel. She won the $750 prize and the fellowship in May 1947. According to

the rules of the award, the writer would complete a manuscript while remaining at Iowa, and Rinehart would have first option on publishing the novel if the publisher found it satisfactory. O'Connor returned to Iowa for the 1947–1948 school year to work on the manuscript for *Wise Blood* under these arrangements.

In early 1948, O'Connor received an invitation to come to the YADDO artists' community near Saratoga Springs, New York, for June and July that summer. Not sure of her future beyond May 1948, the author accepted the foundation's offer. She was invited to return to Yaddo in September and stay for the remainder of the year. The author turned down a modest offer to return to the University of Iowa that fall and settled in at Yaddo for a longer stay and continued uninterrupted work on the manuscript. In January, she learned that she could stay at Yaddo beyond March and seems to have intended to do so. When several authors suspected foul play on the part of director Elizabeth Ames and the selection process for artists for the community, however, O'Connor joined ROBERT LOWELL and other writers who moved out in a well-publicized protest.

About this time, O'Connor contacted literary agent Elizabeth McKee and asked her to submit nine chapters of *Wise Blood* to John Selby, an editor at Rinehart, and request an advance. When there was a delay in the Rinehart response, O'Connor became impatient. When she finally received Selby's comments on the novel, she became angry. In her view, Selby talked down to her in his letter and clearly did not understand what she was trying to do in the book. She was not writing a "conventional" novel. She would take Selby's comments seriously "only within the sphere of what I am trying to do" (CW 1243).

O'Connor continued working on *Wise Blood* while living for a few months near Elizabeth Hardwick in New York City in 1949 and also when she rented a space in the house of Robert and Sally Fitzgerald in Ridgefield, Connecticut. Robert Fitzgerald was translating the Theban plays at the time. In Connecticut, she read *Oedipus Rex* for the first time and discussed the Theban plays and other literature with the Fitzgeralds. Her exposure to *Oedipus* provided her with the ending she was looking for to *Wise Blood*; about this time as well, she also shortened the title to its current form from a working title, *Wise Blood and Simple*.

When illness drove O'Connor away from Connecticut in late 1950 and back to MILLEDGEVILLE, GEORGIA, under the care of her mother, she continued to revise and polish the manuscript. In the meantime, Robert Giroux, then at Harcourt, Brace had expressed interest in the book and offered her a $1,500 advance. After submitting more chapters to Rinehart and having more difficulties with that publisher that eventually led to their release of her contract, O'Connor was finally able to sign a new contract with Harcourt, Brace in October 1950.

In 1951, at Robert Giroux's suggestion, O'Connor sent the manuscript to Caroline Gordon Tate, who offered invaluable comments that O'Connor took seriously and acted on. She also sent the manuscript to the Fitzgeralds for their comments and suggestions. Writing while still battling her illness, accepting blood transfusions and shots of ACTH cortisone, and making trips in and out of the hospital, she finally sent the last corrections to Giroux in December 1951. The book was published by Harcourt, Brace on May 15, 1952.

When the novel came out, O'Connor's Uncle Louis Cline used to tell her about the reaction of the locals. Some of them wanted to know why she could not write about "nice" people for a change. In an October 20, 1955, letter to Betty Hester, O'Connor admitted that some of the criticism she received from George Clay about the book being boring because Motes was not human enough had merit. She indicated that she was working to improve that on her next novel.

O'Connor received important encouraging comments about the publication of her first novel in public and in private from notable and working writers, including Robert Lowell, Caroline Gordon, and J. F. Powers. Many reviewers, however, were puzzled or turned off by the book. William Goyen in the *New York Times Book Review* said that her characters did not seem human. Oliver LaFarge in the *Saturday Review* called Hazel Motes "repulsive," (qtd. in Whitt 15). Other reviewers pointed to the oddness of the characters, their predatory natures, and the

crazy world O'Connor created that was populated by monstrous creatures and subhuman people.

After O'Connor's note to the 1962 10th anniversary edition, the novel received more clarity and appreciation. All the while, the book remained in print, however, and was translated into several languages. After the author's death in 1964, more critical attention began to be paid to all of her work, including *Wise Blood*. In 1979, a quiet art film directed by John Huston and starring Brad Dourif was produced by members of the Fitzgerald family. More recent critical attention has shed light on nonreligious aspects of the book, themes such as the depravity of the modern world, or country life versus city life.

Still generally regarded as the less successful of O'Connor's two longer works, *Wise Blood* continues to puzzle and mystify readers. In her 1962 introduction, O'Connor wrote that the form of the novel's lingering sense of mystery could only deepen.

St. Paul

When O'Connor was asked by Robert Giroux to write the introduction for the 10th anniversary edition of *Wise Blood*, O'Connor did not want to do it. She wrote to Cecil Dawkins in the summer of 1961 that she could not read the novel she wrote 10 years earlier one more time. O'Connor had to write the introduction anyway because a new copyright had to be issued and the introduction would provide the new material required for that to happen. One can only speculate how she managed to do the introduction—whether she reread any part of the novel at all or just wrote the brief preface from memory. What was it about *Wise Blood* that made its author not want to look at it again?

Did she feel her work since her years in graduate school in Iowa had improved that much that this older work was more painful to look at than nostalgic? Was the story dated some way in her imagination? Was she just tired of looking at it after so many years of translations and reviews? Could it be that the novel brought back dark personal memories for her since months before *Wise Blood* was first published she found out that she had LUPUS, the disease that killed her father and required her to move back to Milledgeville, Georgia, for good?

Whatever the reason for her reluctance, O'Connor had to live with the novel that she had created and write a new introduction. She began this way: "*Wise Blood* has reached the age of ten and is still alive. My critical powers are just sufficient to determine this, and I am gratified to be able to say it" (*Three* 2). She goes on to describe the book as a comic novel that was written in "zest" and which should be read in the same way. It was written without theories but with certain thoughts that a belief in Christ is a matter of life and death. Readers who disagree with that idea find in Hazel Motes a character who tries to rid himself of a lingering sense of Jesus. O'Connor admits that Motes's integrity comes from his inability to do so. Free will is many wills, not just one, she writes. Freedom is not something that one can describe simply; it is a matter of mystery. The role of novels, even comic ones, she writes, can only be expected to deepen that mystery.

The book, 232 pages long in published form, took O'Connor five years to complete. Looking through her papers after her death, O'Connor's friend Sally Fitzgerald found about 2,000 pages of material unused in the final draft. Though O'Connor had not mentioned it in the available letters, the rejected pages showed an evolution in the making of the novel that began with an underpinning of T. S. Eliot's *The Waste Land.* There is evidence that she fashioned some aspects of her protagonist in the early days after the speaker of that poem. Fitzgerald writes that O'Connor was clearly influenced by the masterpiece and by her shared Christian sensibility with Eliot. Her library contained 12 books by the poet. One lingering influence from the poem in the final version of the novel is the notion of the "raggedy figure" that moves from one tree to another in the back of Motes's mind. The shadow in Eliot's poem always walks beside a person by day but rises up to greet him in the evening. The shadow around Haze Motes becomes fractured by the shadows of others, and when it is alone behind him, it seems to recede backward.

Eventually, says Fitzgerald, O'Connor came to realize that Eliot's mythical allusions were not the world that she knew from her impressionable early years but instead were images she dis-

covered later and thought about more abstractly. When she changed her outlook and Haze Motes to what she knew more intimately—as Sally Fitzgerald suggests may have happened while she was at Yaddo—aspects of the novel began to move into place. O'Connor reached back to what she knew from her earlier days. What she knew was the story of St. Paul and his blindness on the road to Damascus before he became a firm believer and apostle for Christ. Rather than keep with the more abstract, mythical allusions, she would relate her protagonist to the St. Paul whom she knew better.

The story of St. Paul is one of a journey of disbelief turning to a firm belief in Jesus Christ as Savior and Redeemer. Saul, Paul's Jewish birth name, was educated in Jerusalem. He was a tentmaker, the son of a Roman citizen of some means. According to the seventh book of Acts, he was present at the martyrdom of the first saint, Stephen, and approved of Stephen's execution. Acts 9–19 tells the story of his journey and conversion.

Saul was one of the more eager of the persecutors of Christians in the times of the early church. He went to the high priest in Jerusalem and asked for permission to travel to Damascus and bring back any Christian men and women to Jerusalem and put them in chains. He received his papers and set out on his journey. As he neared the city, a bright light shone around him, throwing him to the ground and blinding him. He heard a voice. The voice said, "Saul, Saul, why are you persecuting me?" (Acts 9:4). When Saul asked who this was, he heard, "I am Jesus, whom you are persecuting. Now get up and go into the city and you will be told what you must do." (Acts 9:4–5). Saul discovered when he got up from the ground that he could not see. His companions, who heard the voice but saw no one, led him down the road to Damascus.

In Damascus, a disciple of Christianity named Ananias had a vision from the Lord. The Lord told him to go to the Street of Straight in the city and ask for Saul, whom he would find praying. Ananias was to lay his hands on Saul so that he could cure his blindness. Ananias first objected, telling the Lord all of the bad things he had heard about Saul persecuting the Lord's people. The Lord told Ananias that Saul was a chosen one for his work who would convert many Gentiles, kings, and Israelites. Ananias found the house with Saul and laid his hands on him and told him that the Lord whom he met on the road to the city has sent Jesus and the Holy Spirit to regain his sight and be filled with the Holy Spirit. The account in Acts continues, "Immediately things like scales fell from his eyes and he regained his sight. He got up and was baptized, and when he had eaten, he recovered his strength" (Acts 9:18–19). Saul went on to preach in Damascus, surprising those who knew him as a man who treated Christians so cruelly before then. Later, he also preached in Jerusalem and around many countries.

In Cyprus, Saul met a magician and false prophet who had called him to come tell the prophet about the word of God and to trap him before the proconsul. "But Saul, also known as Paul, filled with the Holy Spirit, looked intently at him and said, 'You son of the devil, you enemy of all that is right, full of every sort of deceit and fraud. Will you not stop twisting the straight paths of [the] Lord? Even now the hand of the Lord is upon you. You will be blind, and unable to see the sun for a time.' Immediately a dark mist fell upon him, and he went about seeking people to lead him by the hand. When the proconsul saw what had happened, he came to believe, for he was astonished by the teaching about the Lord" (Acts 13:9–12). Many Gentiles, kings, and Israelites converted from Paul's teaching, and he was frequently imprisoned for his work. While in prison, he wrote many letters to Christian believers, continuing to preach through his epistles.

The similarities between St. Paul and Hazel Motes may at first be difficult to see. O'Connor did not, after all, follow St. Paul's story exactly but only found in it an inspiration for her own character. Both Haze Motes and Paul were preachers, and both were blinded. Both were also confronted and tested by false preachers.

Haze Motes loses his faith as a result of testing God and not being open to God's will. When he was a young boy, he went around the countryside helping his grandfather preach. By the time he was 12, he decided he would also become a preacher. A change in his plans developed, however, when he was drafted into the army and sent off to war.

Remember that O'Connor wrote the story in the years immediately following World War II. Motes tried to remain as close to the ways of a preacher as he could while in the military. He did not cavort with women; he did not drink; he did not participate in anything that would damage his future training or reputation as a preacher. What he thought would be a four-month stint turned into four years, however, and he never made it home. He was also wounded by a hit of shrapnel in the chest.

Staying as innocent as possible amid a world torn apart seems to have taken its toll on Motes. Whether he was altogether mentally healthy before he went into the service or not, what he saw when he returned home flipped some switch in his brain and set him off on a road that would change his life forever, like St. Paul. The few members of his family who had been left in Eastrod were gone. His house was empty and boarded up. The only thing left was his mother's old chifforobe, an empty cabinet. After four years of personal restraint with an expectation to assume his life as a preacher in Eastrod, the emptiness of the house and the cabinet hit him dramatically. Seeing no need for goodness and the power to preach, and rather than trying to discern God's next plan for him, Motes interpreted the emptiness as a sign that none of his efforts in the military had been worth it. There was no one to save or to preach to. It was time to run away from this Jesus who had let him down and the idea that he was destined to become a preacher.

Readers later learn of an incident in Motes's past that foreshadows what will happen in the novel. As a boy, Motes went to a carnival and tried to see what was going on in a tent that was set off from the others. He lied about his age to the ticket seller. He said he was 12 when he was just 10 years old. The man reluctantly sold the boy a ticket. What Motes saw on display was a naked woman lying in a coffin. He was shocked and embarrassed. When he got home, his strict religious mother sensed his guilt and tried to pry out of him what he had seen. She told him that Jesus had died to redeem him from his sin, and she hit him with a stick across the legs. Haze did not tell his mother what he saw, but his overriding sense of guilt made him put rocks in his shoes to inflict pain and punishment on himself.

This would not be the first time he sought forgiveness or penance by physically harming himself.

The image of the coffin and his mother becomes mingled with the berth on the train in the first chapter of the novel. Motes shivers lying in the berth, envisioning his mother. He sees her lying in a coffin with the lid coming down on her. She does not rise up and stop the lid from coming down. Instead of having life after death, in his dream, Motes's mother has become a cold corpse with no hope for redemption. Motes exclaims involuntarily, "Jesus," at the horrible sight of the lid going down on his mother's coffin. He mixes these confused feelings with the tight quarters in the berth on the train. Hearing him, the porter comments idly that Jesus has been gone a long time.

To Haze Motes, he sacrificed and preserved his innocence as best he could all through the war for a Jesus who had not waited for him and who had long ago left town. He had been taken in, cheated, made a fool of. In a reversal in this part of his journey compared to St. Paul's, Motes's "birth" in the train berth, his presumed loss of faith, sends him down a dark path of making up for lost time in the world of sin and experience. He tells people he is going to Taulkinham to do things he has never done before. Motes is angry and disappointed; it is payback time. He leaves a note on the chifforobe that it belongs to him and if any people bother it, he will hunt them down and kill them. If the chifforobe represents the faith he received from his family in his youth, this becomes a rather prophetic remark. Haze Motes becomes a man on a mission to track down his faith and kill it.

Motes's road to Damascus turns into a figurative road back to eventual acceptance of his lingering belief. He cannot escape Jesus' hold on him no matter how hard he tries. He seeks out the services of prostitute, Leona Watts, but this leaves him only looking for some way to occupy himself the following day. He meets up with lonely young Enoch Emery but is annoyed and confused by the boy's immediate attachment to him. He meets two false preachers, Asa Hawks, the man who pretends to be blind to get money and who has his daughter, Sabbath Lily, helping him, and Onnie Jay Holy (Hoover Shoats), the radio preacher who wants to go into business with Motes. Then he sets up a car-pulpit of his own with Solace Layfield when Motes refuses his offer.

Motes's road, like Paul's to Damascus and elsewhere, is long and full of adventures. Motes keeps moving. Each time he tries to escape, the presence of Jesus persists. Motes rides on a train, walks, and finally drives. He resists putting down roots or even stakes for the night as long as possible. When he buys the car, he tells Slade that he plans to live in it. A car makes an appropriate home for a man on the move of a spiritual journey. On his first jerky ride in the "rat-colored" Essex, he winds up stopped in the middle of the road staring at a sign that says "Jesus Saves." He is proud of the car, saying it is well made and claiming that it was not made by foreigners or blacks. He preaches standing on top of it, as though this rolling Church of Christ Without Christ can move right along to the next street corner full of people at any time. Each time something happens to the car, he stands up for its quality. Not until he runs over and kills Solace Layfield and hears Layfield's last confession, and not until the sheriff pushes the car off the road out of commission does Motes finally realize that he cannot run anymore. He needs to stop and come to terms.

Like Paul in several cities, the marketplace also plays a role in Motes's journey. Paul brings his spiritual message to crowded cities and synagogues and meets with the magician and false prophet. False preacher Asa Hawks takes advantage of the crowd drawn by the potato-peeler salesman to begin to preach across the street. He is not afraid of turning religion directly into commerce. The salesman is angry with Hawks for stealing his customers, but the draw of sympathy for a "blind" preacher with a daughter handing out tracts along the street is strong.

False preacher Onnie Jay Holy is even worse. He arrives on the street with a blowhorn that can outhawk Hawks and Motes both. He is slicker and even more polished as a preacher, having experience on the radio. If Hawks turns religion into commerce for the sake of supporting himself and his daughter, Holy is out to turn it into as big a business as possible. His deceit is greater than Hawks's since he is not even using his real name, which is Hoover Shoats. His debt to commerce extends beyond

Hawks's as well; when Motes does not go along with his plan to go into business together, he hires Solace Layfield to dress up like Motes and pretend to be a prophet for the "profit" of both of them.

Enoch Emery is most taken with the commerce and materialism of the city and the modern world. He is frequently buying things. He is interested in the potato peeler and other gadgets. He buys popcorn at Wal-Greens from a boy making it in a noisy popcorn machine. He also buys a daily drink at the Frosty Bottle at the close of his shift at the zoo. He is taken in by the Gonga movie promotion at which a man dressed up in a gorilla suit hands out tickets to a show. He goes to see not one film but three. They are *The Eye*, about a scientist who performs operations via remote control; another film that is not named but is about the Devil's Island Penitentiary; and *Lonnie Comes Home Again*, about a baboon rescuing children from an orphanage and receiving a medal for its efforts. The films heighten Enoch's excitement and set up his future actions with the gorilla suit.

When Enoch hears Haze's preaching, he finds Haze the "new jesus" in the form of the shrunken mummy in the museum and steals it. He paints the inside of his empty cabinet gold as though to make a tabernacle for the new jesus. Enoch is more concerned with the trappings and rituals of religion than with how it transforms a person. Moving around as often as he did while growing up, Enoch never had a chance to learn the real meaning behind the symbols he encountered and the flashing lights of the city. Intimately concerned with what is going on inside him spiritually, Haze Motes walks right through the traffic light in Taulkinham and is stopped by the policeman. His distance from mechanical objects is also shown when he cannot drive the Essex well when he first purchases it; he has not driven in four or five years. More keenly aware of his surroundings in the city, Enoch knows what the colors of the traffic light mean and tells the officer that Motes is new to the city and that he will take care of him. Unlike Motes, Enoch's sense of religion is materialistic, like the city's, and it runs away with him, quite literally, when he disappears from the city and the novel in his gorilla costume, to places unknown.

St. Paul frequently preached in cities, and it is city preacher Asa Hawks who mentions St. Paul to Haze Motes. When Motes finds where Hawks and his daughter live, he asks Hawks, if God is so great, why it is that God has not cured Hawks of his blindness. Hawks reminds him that God blinded Paul. Unknown to Motes, Hawks had been preaching about Paul for an hour in front of 200 people 10 years before at a tent revival. He was preparing to blind himself as proof of his faith when he lost his nerve and poured the wet lime down his face with his hands, taking care not to get any in his eyes. The clipping from the newspaper the next day read, "Evangelist's Nerve Fails" (*Three* 59). Not long after Haze Motes meets Asa Hawks and hears his supposed story from the first news clipping, "Evangelist Promises to Blind Himself" (58), Haze will reenact his own gesture reminiscent of the blinding of St. Paul that marked the beginning of his turn in faith. This young man who will discover the hard way that he cannot escape his faith and must return to it and accept that it will succeed in carrying out this act of blinding against himself.

Oedipus, Eyes, and Blindness

Perhaps it should be no surprise that O'Connor had a breakthrough in her novel when she lived and worked at the home of Robert and Sally Fitzgerald in Ridgefield, Connecticut, and that this breakthrough was having Hazel Motes blind himself. Robert Fitzgerald was working on translations of the three ancient Theban plays at the time O'Connor was living with his family. She and the Fitzgeralds had dinner together each evening and later talked about literature. Discussion of ancient Greek drama and Fitzgerald's work were likely topics. In a February 13, 1954, letter to Ben Griffiths, O'Connor admits that if Griffiths sees a connection between *Wise Blood* and *Oedipus*, it may be due to the influence of Fitzgerald's work. She wrote, "I did a lot of thinking about Oedipus" (HB 68).

In Sophocles' three Theban plays, there is a blind seer named Teiresias. That someone would be blind but also able to "see" is an irony not far removed from a central theme of *Wise Blood*. Asa Hawks pretends to be blind, thinking that his blindness increases sympathy and credibility among those who would listen to him and make a donation. Not until Haze Motes blinds himself does he "see" the error of his ways and that his future is tied up inextricably with his faith. Not until he dies do pinpoints of light finally appear in the dark pits that have been his eyes throughout the book.

Even more relevant to O'Connor's story is the main character in the Theban cycle, Oedipus. Oedipus leaves the stage and blinds himself in the play, *Antigone*. He blinds himself when he discovers the horror that the woman who is his wife and the mother of his children is in fact his own mother. When Haze Motes realizes that he believes after all and that he now has many sins to live with and to "pay" for, he does the same thing to himself with quicklime. When he blinds himself, he follows through on the act in the newspaper clipping that Asa Hawks dared not do. Unlike Asa Hawks who lost courage in his effort to prove his faith to his followers, then turns whatever faith he once had on its head to "hawk" for money, Haze Motes knows that his faith is a matter of life and death. Motes has stopped looking for the motes in others' eyes and has found the board in his own and looked at it directly. Haze Motes—a sinner who has broken the law through fraternizing with a prostitute, assaulting 18-year-old Enoch Emery with a rock, having sex with a minor, and committing murder—is, ironically, the only real preacher in the novel.

There is much about eyes and sight in the novel besides Motes's blindness. Mrs. Wally Bee Hitchcock notices Motes's eyes on the train. They are the color of pecan shells and set in very deep sockets. They look almost as though they were passages that would lead somewhere. Hitchcock's view of Motes's eyes foreshadows the view of Mrs. Flood's at the end of the novel. Flood will look into his deep dark eyes in death and envision that they are deep passages to somewhere he has gone. She will close her own eyes and look at his through hers, imagining tiny pinpoints of light until Motes, for her, becomes the points of light. By the end of the book, Motes has finally seen who he is and where he has to go. He set out on his final journey as the result of being out in the rain unconscious and then beaten by the police officer with the new billy club.

Another relevant image is Motes's mother's eyeglasses. He took only two items from home when he went into the army—a black Bible and eyeglasses that once belonged to his mother. He took them in case he ever needed to see more clearly. Figuratively, he needs to see more clearly to find truth and redemption. He never read the Bible without wearing the glasses. The glasses tire his eyes, so he stops sooner than he would without them.

Reading the Bible through his mother's eyes, as it were, works in two ways for Motes. He sees religion through her eyes. Yet he rebels against the strictness of her teaching (exemplified by the guilt he feels about seeing the woman at the carnival) by using the glasses to read the Bible when he knows that they will make his eyes tired more quickly, forcing him to stop. His mother represents, then, not only the one who brought him to the faith but also the one through whom his problems with religion originate. Looking at religion through her eyes tires him, and he knows this method will fall short in coming to grips with his faith. What Motes needs to do is to put away his mother's glasses and read the Bible through his own eyes. However, he will need to go through the journey and events in Taulkinham before he comes to realize this.

After spending the night with Sabbath Lily, Motes decides it is time to go to a new town. He gathers up his things and in his effort to make more room in his bag for his second pair of shoes, he comes across the case holding his mother's glasses. He had forgotten they were there. He puts them on. Looking in the mirror, he sees his mother's image superimposed over his face, revealing the similarity between his face and hers. At just that same moment, Sabbath Lily enters the room in a mock Madonna pose, carrying Enoch's new jesus mummy like a baby in her arms. The combination of the jesus figure, the Madonna image, and his mother's face transposed onto his in the mirror is too much. Motes flings the mummy against the wall knocking its head off and throws its body out the window. Still wearing the glasses now dripping with rain, he tells Sabbath that he only wants to see the truth and he has seen the only truth that there is.

Losing his car to the patrolman marks the turning point in Motes's journey. His vehicle for keeping himself moving on the road of life is gone. Just like the empty house that he came home to in Eastrod, this new empty "house," the car in which he once said he would live is no longer available to him. He returns to Mrs. Flood's boardinghouse and replies matter-of-factly that he is going to blind himself when she asks what he is going to do. After he goes upstairs, Mrs. Flood meditates on how blindness would be equal to death to her and how she would sooner see committing suicide to blinding oneself. It occurs to her that when people are dead, they are blind, and this notion upsets her. All this while, she does nothing, however, to stop Haze Motes. After he has done the deed, she is horrified and then fascinated with his eye sockets, which he refuses to cover. She is also intrigued by his expression, the way he seems to see something, even though she had convinced herself that he is totally blind.

Eyes as a motif appear throughout the novel. For example, when Motes follows Hawks and Sabbath and Hawks asks why he followed them, he says it is because of the fast eye that Sabbath cast on him. Sabbath denies doing any such thing, and Hawks says that Motes did not follow her; he followed Hawks; he can sense it. When they distribute tracts on the steps of the theater, Motes tells Hawks to watch and see what he can see when he throws the tracts off the steps. Hawks shouts that he can see more than Motes can; Motes has eyes yet cannot see—this is one of the many true statements that Hawks makes about Motes. At the zoo, when Enoch wants to show the shrunken mummy to Motes, they pass by a cage that appears to have nothing in it. Motes looks into the cage and sees only an eye. Looking closer, he and Enoch see that it is an owl with one eye open staring straight at Motes. It is as though the world is watching him to see where this young man's struggle against his faith is going to lead.

The eyes of the shrunken mummy look like "two clean bullet holes" (51), mimicking Motes's own sunken sockets. Sabbath Lily plays peek-a-boo with Motes, saying "I see you," as she comes out from hiding behind a tree in her efforts to seduce him on the side of the dirt road (63). Inside the shack where Motes finds help for his car after the dirt road incident, there are two animals, a hawk with most of its tail missing and a black bear with one

eye. The headlights of the rat-colored Essex that serve as Motes's house-pulpit-escape are huge, like two giant eyes.

Seeing and blindness are important motifs in the book. Like St. Paul, Haze Motes "sees" God's truth most clearly when he is blind.

Doubling

In fiction, the term *doppelgänger* refers to creating pairs of characters who have similar traits, activities, or names but who may be different in one important way. Another way to think of a doppelgänger in fiction is as an alter ego, a shadow figure, or a foil to a character.

Doubles in *Wise Blood* involve not only characters but also, interestingly, pairs of objects. Character doubles include Haze Motes and each of the preacher figures whom he encounters in Taulkinham—Asa Hawks, Onnie Jay Holy, and Solace Layfield—and Motes and Enoch Emery. Objects include Motes's mother's empty chifforobe in Eastrod and Enoch Emery's empty cabinet that he paints gold; Motes's mother's coffin and the train berth; and the shrunken mummy and the woman in the coffin in the carnival.

Some readers may wonder why Haze Motes and Asa Hawks did not get along better than they did. Hawks preached about St. Paul and intended to blind himself in front of 200 people but lost his nerve and ran away. When Motes follows him and his daughter, Sabbath claims it is because of her, but Hawks thinks that Motes followed him, and he is right. Motes is drawn to Asa Hawks because Hawks is a street preacher, and that is what Motes once thought his mission on earth would be. He is also blind, or so Motes thinks, and there is something about this lack of sight that suggests to Motes that Hawks may know more than he is telling or to see more than Motes sees. When Hawks faces him after being followed, the preacher places his hands on Motes's face. It takes some moments before Haze knocks them away.

"Some preacher has left his mark on you," Hawks tells him. "Did you follow for me to take it off or give you another?" (*Three* 26). Hawks intuits Motes's being touched by his grandfather and mother as chosen to be a preacher and that at least part of Motes took this mandate seriously. He knows something about Motes that the other false preachers will not know. Hawks seems to have been a believer at least in the past, and perhaps still is in some respects, despite the failure and cowardice that drove him to his present lifestyle. Hawks senses something spiritually at work in Motes that perhaps he recognizes as the same thing that was once part of him or remains buried beneath the surface. Motes is a believer but cannot bear to see that about himself yet; perhaps Hawks, the unreputable and unblind street preacher, senses this faith before Motes does. As either a present or past believer, Asa Hawks is a step away from the kind of preacher Motes could have been had he not let the problems at Eastrod lead him astray.

The preachers whom Motes meets gradually move further away from this image and yet closer at the same time. Onnie Jay Holy is a radio man who uses a blow horn outside movie theaters to attract followers after the movies let out. He has a slick manner and a charismatic presence that attracts several people to listen to him. Hoover Shoats (Onnie Jay Holy's real name) is an imposter preacher of a more corrupt order than even Asa Hawks. His name implies his connection to the material world and an instinct or spiritual life not much above an animal's. A Hoover is a vacuum cleaner, a brand once so popular people used to say they needed to "hoover" the floor. A shoat is a young pig.

Hoover Shoats not only has no interior life, but he is also an imposter who is even more shallow than Asa Hawks. Unlike the failed and lapsed bad preacher, Hawks, Shoats is a complete showman. Like a performer, he has changed his name to Onnie Jay Holy, presumably because it has a livelier ring that will help attract audiences to his radio show and street preaching. Motes sees him preaching outside movie theaters, which supports this showmanlike quality and desire. Shoats thinks he can draw his audience most directly from those who like to be entertained. To Hoover Shoats, religion is nothing more than a commercial product, a form of entertainment to be bought and sold.

Haze Motes's similarities to Hoover Shoats may be more difficult to see than those to Asa Hawks. Motes comes close to a performance in his preaching. He does not mean to entertain, but he hopes to bring his audience around to his way of think-

ing. He seeks a disciple, a follower, to help him get his new church going. Unlike Shoats, who simply wants to sell his audience a show for donations, Motes does not want money, and he does not want to give the crowd a show. He wants to change hearts to find the truth along with him, however dark and terrible they may find that truth.

Shoats himself first sees the value of Motes to his plan. He tells Motes that he is on to something with his message but that he needs to be sweeter in the way that he talks to people. Shoats is no amateur. He is an artist at this preaching business, and he can see that all Motes needs is a little help with promotion. Shoats can gather the people and build up a crowd, and Motes can deliver the important preaching message, like a prophet. However similar Motes appears to be to Shoats (even their names rhyme), Shoats does not immediately recognize the important difference between them until Motes refuses his offer to work together for money.

After Motes's refusal, Shoats enlists the help of Solace Layfield to play the part of his prophet and to mimic Haze Motes preaching across the street, even down to his appearance in the suit and tie and hat. The doubling has now become too close for Motes to bear. After the night preaching is done, he chases down and runs over Layfield with the Essex, telling him, "Two things I can't stand—a man that ain't true and one that mocks what is" (*Three* 105). Motes is nothing if not true to his beliefs. Unfortunately, for Solace Layfield, he failed Motes's test. Layfield is not true because he pretends to be a prophet, and he mocks what is true by dressing up and copying Hazel Motes.

The doubling between Haze and the false street preachers is important to better understand the journey that Haze Motes takes in Taulkinham. Since his grandfather was a preacher and young Haze went around the countryside helping him, he has inherited the desire and knowledge of a preacher but has temporarily lost his faith. He has never, however, lost his desire to seek the truth. His preaching in Taulkinham, then, centers on the idea of finding the truth, even if that means founding a Church of Christ Without Christ—and without followers. Asa Hawks is the preacher who lost his nerve. Hoover Shoats is the preacher who only pretends. Solace Layfield neither lost his nerve nor effectively pretends but only copies Haze Motes to make a few bucks. As his name implies, the only solace he will find is lying in a field somewhere after Motes has ended his life.

Through these comparisons to different kinds of preachers, O'Connor shows the reader what kind of preacher Motes is. O'Connor uses doubling in an even more direct and obvious way when she sets up the comparison between Haze Motes and Enoch Emery. She does this partly through structure, alternating several chapters from Motes and Emery's points of view. Chapters 5 and 11 both open, for example, with Emery, but with no Haze Motes, at first, in sight.

At age 18 and the victim of a severely dysfunctional family, Enoch Emery might be seen as the Haze Motes that might have been, had he not gone to war or come home to complete devastation. He is a more innocent version of Haze Motes and as such is a preacher of sorts, but one without a mission. Ironically, he is the bearer of wise blood. Emery holds more inherent intuition running through his veins than experience.

Emery seems young and impressionable, even for an 18-year-old. He is looking for friendship and companionship in the city and keeps running into unfriendly people. He sees something in Haze Motes—just four years older than himself but with worlds more experience from the war—that suggests he might be able to strike up a friendship with him. It is a logical assumption. Emery is taking care of himself after never meeting his mother and being deserted in the city by his father. He has been back to Taulkinham only two months, and he has a job at the zoo. He is proud of this accomplishment and tells Motes in an effort to show how grown up he is and how the city has placed its faith in him to do this job. On the surface, Enoch Emery seems like a responsible young man who is attempting to make the most of his unfortunate start in life.

Like other young people of his time, and ours for that matter, Emery is fascinated with the material world. Odd for someone with such strong instincts or wise blood, he is naïve and gullible and does not understand what it is that Haze Motes is preaching when he mentions the need for a new

jesus. Emery takes Motes literally as needing some kind of new idol to worship and finds the mummy in the museum and steals it for Motes to use. He even builds the mummy a tabernacle by painting the empty cabinet in his room gold. To him, it is a perfect new jesus for Motes's Church of Christ Without Christ. Emery seeks to replace Christ with a material idol but not quite a material idol at that. He finds instead a dead and shrunken human being. Ironically, Emery's idol is bloodless—what is left of a human being without blood or soul—quite simply, an idol made of dust. Though Emery has wise blood running through him, he has apparently never thought of Jesus as anything beyond a symbol.

Emery's search for friendship and acceptance in a material world mirrors Motes's search for the truth in a world of false preachers and prophets. Motes's journey is much more serious, a matter of life and death. Emery's search is important but not so deadly. Failing at relationships by often rubbing people the wrong way, Emery finds the companionship he seeks through his attachment to animals. Animals are not human beings, and they are not material objects either, but they are the link between the two that makes Emery comfortable negotiating the two worlds. Emery moves more and more in the direction of animals. He carries a purse that is made of a hog's bladder, a symbol that also links him to the animal and material world. The purse is made of an animal, yet it has become an inanimate object, and drawing the connection even tighter, that material object holds money. Emery works in the zoo and is able to sustain himself with a routine of working, getting a drink at the Frosty Bottle every day after his shift, and frequenting Wal-Greens, the movie houses, and stores.

He is attracted to the popularity of the Gonga gorilla that stops by the street corner and hands out tickets. Children line up to see the gorilla, and he appreciates their enthusiasm and joins the line himself. When he attempts to make friends with the gorilla, the man inside the costume speaks a profanity at him. Emery takes the tickets that he receives and goes to the movies. There the strange connections between Emery, animals, attempts at popularity, and the material world continue.

When Emery sees the movie about the baboon that rescues the orphans and wins a medal for doing so, he becomes very excited as though this has given him an idea. He goes out and finds the Gonga promotion van with the man in the gorilla suit. He puts on the suit and attempts to make friends with human beings that way since he remembers how popular Gonga was with the children. The suit, as another link between material object and animal and friends, does not bring him any closer to his goal. Instead of harming himself as Haze Motes will do when he discovers the truth about himself, Emery simply disappears—to a jungle, a zoo, or another city; we are not sure. He and his wise blood, which he does not understand, have served their purpose in Haze Motes's journey that makes up the bulk of the novel. Emery continues off the page and off the stage on his own.

The similarities between Haze and Enoch include their youth and several other comparisons. Both are looking for something. Haze is trying to escape his past and the influence that his religious family, in particular, his preacher grandfather and his strict mother, had on him. Enoch was brought to Taulkinham by his father and has been searching for a friendly face in the city ever since. Enoch recognizes the wise blood in both young men. When he accuses Haze of thinking and acting is if his blood was "wiser," Emery tells him about his wise blood, which he inherited from his father. Just as Haze attempts to escape his destiny as a preacher, Emery tries to make friends in a material world where his wise blood is not of any use.

Emery's antics with the woman at the pool at the zoo, the mummy, and the gorilla suit provide comic relief for Hazel Motes's more serious journey. The material world is as unforgiving and lonely as the Church Without Christ, but it is not, perhaps one might argue, as damning. One can belong to a Church of Christ *With* Christ and still be enamored with the baubles and trinkets of the material world. One can also be a believer and still have difficulty making friends or finding a place for oneself in a given community. Young Emery needs guidance and maturity, but he is not a lost cause. In a February 1954 letter to Ben Griffith, O'Connor comically admitted that she was more like Enoch than the

gorilla and answers letters at once and with lengthy responses, possibly because she does not receive very many of them. She also wrote once to Betty Hester that her crutches made her feel like an ape. Emery's loneliness and clumsy efforts at fitting in may have been very much like her own.

Like the doubling of characters, several material objects in the novel reverberate as symbols. These include Motes's mother's chifforobe and Enoch Emery's gold-painted cabinet, the berth in the train and the rat-colored Essex, and the shrunken mummy and the gorilla suit.

The empty chifforobe echoes the empty cabinet in Enoch Emery's room. Motes ties up the chifforobe and puts a note on it that it belongs to him and that people who bother it will be hunted down and killed. Enoch Emery buys gold paint and paints his cabinet to look like a tabernacle for the shrunken mummy, the new jesus. Neither one of these acts is particularly logical or useful. If both cabinets are taken to symbolize tabernacles or receptacles of faith, then Motes shows at least some evidence of wanting to protect and preserve it. Emery's actions illustrate his misunderstanding of religion as material trappings and ritual.

The berth on the train where Haze Motes gets so upset in his dreams and illusions brings to mind both the coffin that he saw at the carnival and the rat-colored Essex. They are symbols of death, but a kind of death while moving or, as O'Connor called the car, a symbol of "death-in-life." Something in Motes dies when he is "birthed" on the train in the berth. He is ready to leave his old life behind and go to the city and do things that he has never done before. The shame that his mother made him feel after seeing the woman in the coffin propels him to find a place where he will never find shame again, and that must be a place where people know no shame or the place where sinners dwell. The car becomes his home away from home, quite literally. It is his heaven on earth and also another coffin image. Rather than give him life, however, the car helps him take the life of Solace Layfield. As long as he feels that he can jump in it and ride away from his problems, it is holding him back from facing them. Motes's problems cannot be escaped by changing towns. The car, just like the berth in the train, does not offer solace with a convenient escape route when things get tough but instead kills solace (Solace) altogether. It is not until the patrolman destroys the car that Motes realizes that he must face that which will not go away.

Emery's stolen Gonga suit helps him escape town. He has found temporary relief by wearing the suit. Emery is a human being making himself out to be an animal. By donning the suit, he places flesh and blood into the lifeless costume of skin and fur and fills it with life and movement. The shrunken mummy, on the other hand, is without blood and without life, though it used to have both. It is a human being turned into a skin, a costume. While Emery becomes larger in the suit, the mummy has been shrunk down to doll size from its normal height. The animal costume expands the GROTESQUE-ness of Emery and his actions; the shrunken mummy expands the grotesqueness of humanity, showing how insignificant it is without blood and spirit.

Women in Wise Blood

Women do not fare too well in *Wise Blood*; however, their role is still important in Haze Motes's journey. The mothers are failures; the casual women whom Motes meets reach him; any romantic interests that he may have had do not satisfy him. Sabbath Lily implies that a woman friend is not what Hazel Motes is looking for on his journey when she sees him blind himself and says that she did not expect him to be a real Jesus man.

Motes's mother looks much like himself, but she is a strict religious woman and disciplinarian. At 10 years old, when he returns from the carnival after seeing the naked woman, his mother senses that he has seen something objectionable and asks him what he saw. She slaps his legs with a stick and reminds him that Jesus died to redeem him from sin. His own guilt, however, is stronger than the guilt that she infuses in him, and it drives him to put stones in his shoes and walk in them as a means of punishing himself. The other mother in *Wise Blood*, Enoch Emery's mother, is also a failure. Emery never met her at all. His mother-surrogate, the welfare woman who took him away from his father and then placed him in the Bible Academy

for several weeks is also a religious fanatic who talks Jesus all the time and does not do much for creating a sense of well-being in the boy.

Motes meets several women on his journey toward rediscovering his faith. One is Mrs. Wally Bee Hitchcock, who rides with him on the train and chats with him. She judges Motes to be about 20 years old and on his way home. Motes is older than that and is not going "home" just yet. Mrs. Hitchcock talks too much. She talks about how she is going to Florida to see her married daughter Sarah Lucille and how time goes so fast it is difficult to know whether one is young or old. She is not sure she has ever made a trip this long before. When she finds out where Motes is going, she continues to talk about how she once knew an Albert Sparks in Taulkinham. The talk annoys Motes enough that he finally sticks his face in hers and says the line that readers and critics ever since have said and signals the rise in tension in this novel at the same time that it alerts the reader that this is going to be a different kind of book than perhaps first thought, "I reckon you think you been redeemed" (*Three* 6). The line pulls the reader, just like Mrs. Hitchcock, out of a sense of realism and into something else. O'Connor once said that she did not write realistic fiction but something more along the line of NATHANIEL HAWTHORNE's "romances," and this line is the first signal in this novel that things may not be altogether normal or as one would normally find on a typical train trip in 1940s rural Georgia.

Mrs. Hitchcock is nicely framed by Mrs. Flood at the end of the novel. Mrs. Flood is the landlady and owner of the boardinghouse where Asa Hawks and Sabbath Lily Hawks live and where Haze Motes takes a room. She sees Motes come back to the house after his car was destroyed by the patrolman, and she sees the bucket of quicklime and water that he brings with him. She sees him go up the stairs and asks him what he is going to do. When he tells her quite frankly that he is going to blind himself, she does nothing to stop him. She does act, how-ever, when Sabbath Lily wreaks havoc all around the house when she sees what Haze has done. Hitchcock tells Motes that the girl is just after his money, and since she is underage, she has Sabbath taken away and put in a home for wayward children.

She takes care of Motes after his blindness by cleaning his room and supplying his meals. She realizes that his income from the government due to his wounds in the war is not spent all on his rent and is certainly not spent on many other expenses, so she begins to think about their marrying in an arrangement that would allow her to stop taking borders and would give him someone to take care of him for the rest of his days. However, just as Motes was not swayed from his mission by Leona Watts or Sabbath Lily, Mrs. Flood's proposal does not sit well with him. He would rather roam the streets in the rain than risk having this kind of arranged marriage inflicted upon him. Even so, for her efforts at caring for him, Flood is somewhat rewarded. She tells him he has come "home" when the police officers bring back his body, and she is the witness to the small points of light that Motes's soul appears to create as it recedes from this life. Mrs. Flood's eyes become the readers' as witnesses of Motes's final fate.

Leona Watts, the prostitute, is overweight and unattractive with gaping green teeth. She lists her name and address in the men's room at the train station to solicit business. The taxi driver knows the address and tells Motes that preachers do not normally go there. Motes denies that he is a preacher. When Motes goes into the house, Watts tells him to make himself at home. She calls Motes "son," and when he tells her that he is there for the "usual business" but that he wants her to know that he is not a preacher, Watts says that "Momma" don't care that he is not a preacher. This seems to absolve Motes temporarily from his real mother. Watts, whose name Margaret Whitt suggests a low-wattage intellect, is, in a perverted way, another mother figure in the novel.

Finally, Sabbath Lily, the underage young woman who is entranced by Haze Motes, comes off as a diabolical figure. Her mother died the day she was born, on the Sabbath, but not before she could name her baby girl. Lily denotes Easter lilies and the purity of whiteness and Redemption. Sabbath Lily, however, is just the opposite of a pure young woman. After three tries—in her and her father's room, at the roadside after hiding in Motes's car, and finally hiding in his bed—she finally succeeds in seducing Haze Motes. She tells him that she is a bastard with no hope for going to heaven. She has grown to enjoy and revel in her own damnation and being bad as a result. Motes wants to enjoy being bad, and she says she can teach him. This above all else seems to work. Sabbath Lily performs with the shrunken mummy after Enoch Emery delivers the new jesus to Motes's room. Rather than giving the wrapped package to Motes as Emery asked, she opens it and walks into the room holding it in her arms like a baby in a mock Madonnalike gesture. This angers Motes, who destroys the mummy and prepares once again to leave. Later, when she sees that he has blinded himself, Sabbath Lily tells him that she did not expect a real-Jesus kind of man and runs around Mrs. Flood's house telling everyone what happened until Mrs. Flood has her taken away to a home for orphaned and abandoned children.

Women do not save Hazel Motes, but no human being is capable of saving him from his dilemma. The woman with the most clarity and intelligence may be one who makes the briefest appearance, the woman on the train. Motes watches her smoke a cigarette. She has the face of a game hen and small eyes that point directly at him. He leans toward her and asks her if she thinks he believes in Jesus. He would not believe in Jesus, he says, even if Jesus existed and were right here on this train. The woman replies coolly in a deadly Eastern voice, "Who said you had to?" (7), causing Motes to pull back abruptly and fall silent.

Wise Blood

The naïve teenager Enoch Emery highlights the title of the novel. He talks to Motes about how Motes seems to act superior, as though he has wiser blood than everyone else. Emery says that instead he has wise blood. He inherited it from his father, and his wise blood helps him know things that he would not know otherwise. It is a kind of inherited intuition.

Emery's wise blood lets him know that someone special is going to arrive soon or that today will be a special day. His blood tells him that he needs to help Haze Motes or that he needs to do a specific action. At the same time that Emery seems so in touch with his blood, Haze Motes is preaching his Church of

Christ Without Christ message by saying that Jesus' blood cannot redeem people for their sins.

Aside from the larger metaphor of Emery's and Motes's wise blood, smaller drops of blood show up at certain moments. After Haze Motes hits Enoch Emery with the rock and he wakes up, Emery touches his forehead and sees blood on his fingers. When he gets up, he sees a drop of blood on the ground that seems to pool outward. Seeing the blood reminds him of his wise blood, and shedding it makes him think that there must be a special purpose he is to fulfill and that maybe he will finally find out what that is. Something he can only sense but that is definitely larger than he is has been set in motion.

Blood also appears in Haze Motes's next violent act, when he kills Solace Layfield by running over him with the Essex. After Motes hears Layfield's confession, despite yelling at him to stop, and after Layfield dies, Motes checks the front of his car for blood. He cleans the few spurts of Layfield's blood off the car with a rag before driving back to town.

Motes wraps barbed wire around himself at the end of the novel in another one of his acts of repentance, and he also puts shards of glass and stones in his shoes. The reader knows that these acts cause Motes to bleed on a daily and repetitive basis. The stones remind the reader of Motes's duplicate action after seeing the woman at the carnival when he was 10. The barbed wire may remind the reader of the barbed-wire fence he carefully avoids after Sabbath Lily tries to seduce him at the side of the road. It is also reminiscent of the crown of thorns around the head of the crucified Jesus.

To a Catholic, blood would almost always bring to mind the blood of Christ, which is part of the Eucharist at MASS. Christian belief says that Jesus died to save human beings from their sins, to wash away sin and death and to redeem sinners in the sight of the Father. The belief is that Jesus shed his blood so that one's soul may go to heaven. Roman Catholics such as Flannery O'Connor celebrate Mass, where the Last Supper is commemorated. According to the gospels, at the Last Supper, Jesus blessed the bread and wine and instructed his disciples to eat and drink. He said that the bread and wine have become his body and blood and that his blood will be shed for them and for all the world.

To a writer working from a Catholic sensibility, it is reasonable to make the connection between wise blood and this special blood, the blood of Christ. It may be that Enoch Emery has inherited wise blood from his father and that he may not understand it, but wise blood exists nonetheless and is true. Since her characters are southern Protestants, however, and not Roman Catholics, O'Connor explains the connection in a September 13, 1959 letter to John Hawkes: "Haze is saved by virtue of having wise blood; it's too wise for him ultimately to deny Christ. Wise blood has to be these people's means of grace—they have no sacraments" (HB 350). Without benefit of the grace in the sacrament of the Eucharist at Mass, wise blood is the closest thing that the characters populating O'Connor's novel have.

Wise blood, or intuition, may be Enoch Emery's way of describing what he knows he has but cannot understand. The faithful have this same feeling—they believe but they do not always have logical explanations for their beliefs. What is astounding is that O'Connor has created a work that operates in a similar way for both faith and intuition. Readers believe and intuit that something in the story has affected them without always quite understanding what that effect is and why and how it is produced. The novel has a meaning that readers cannot quite pinpoint or articulate.

In "The Nature and Aim of Fiction," O'Connor wrote that the rat-colored car was Motes's pulpit and coffin and what he thinks of as his means of escape. He does not, however, manage to escape his dilemma until the patrolman wrecks the car. "The car is a kind of death-in-life symbol, as his blindness is a life-in-death symbol. The fact that these meanings are there makes the book significant. The reader may not see them but they have their effect on him nonetheless. This is the way the modern novelists sinks, or hides, his theme" (MM 72).

O'Connor explains that many people want to know the themes of her stories. If they can state the theme of a story easily, this makes the story more understandable and worthwhile. O'Connor points out that a well-written story cannot be so easily summed up in one sentence or through any abstract explanations or platitudes: "Some people have the notion that you read the story and climb out of it into the meaning, but for the fiction writer himself the whole story is the meaning, because it is an experience, not an abstraction" (MM 73).

Like faith and like intuition, the experience of reading *Wise Blood* continues to attract many readers even without the ability to articulate exactly what that attraction is.

CHARACTERS

Hazel Motes Motes is a 22-year-old World War II veteran just returned home after four years in the service. He has been wounded by taking a hit of shrapnel in the chest, foreshadowing the metal that he will bind around his chest later on. His injuries do not seem to hamper his movements. He is described as very thin with a long, narrow face and eyes that seem like two dark deep holes. When he buys clothes to go to Taulkinham, he purchases a bright blue suit and a black hat. The outfit makes him look like the preacher he claims he does not want to be.

Hazel Motes's name, like others in the novel, has reverberations with the novel's themes. Hazael was a king of Syria who, like O'Connor's character, tried to get rid of God by using violence against God's people (2 Kings 8–13). Hazel's shortened name, Haze, is used more frequently throughout the novel. Haze Motes is definitely in a haze of sorts; he cannot clearly see his future or what is in front of him or what God has intended for him.

The name *Motes* brings to mind the Bible verse, Matthew 7:3, "Why do you notice the mote in your brother's eye, but do not perceive the wooden beam in your own?" If the people in Taulkinham notice Mote and the problems he brings to town, how is it that they do not see the board in their own eyes of their own sinful ways and turn toward God or at least search for a more meaningful life. The same goes for Motes himself, who spends much of the novel finding fault with everyone else but himself. A mote is a speck of dust. The name in this context suggests the Bible verse Genesis 3:19, "For you are dust, and to dust you shall return." Without blood, the shrunken mummy is dust inside, as the reader sees when Motes throws its body out the window. Motes, however, has recovered his soul through

his journey and the events in Taulkinham. When Motes dies, Mrs. Flood feels as though she is at the beginning of something she can no longer begin and sees tiny points of light when she looks through her own closed eyes into his. Lastly, *mot* means "word" in French. Hazel Motes is someone who might be said to have a hazy or confused understanding of the word of God.

Enoch Emery The reader first meets Enoch on the street in Taulkinham where the potato-peeler salesman has set up shop. Enoch is watching and eying the people in the crowd enthusiastically when Haze Motes walks up and joins the crowd. Emery is described as having a face like a fox and yellow hair. He has been in the city for two months, brought there by his father, but he was born and raised there long ago. He has a job working for the city at the zoo, and he is proud of it. He never knew his mother, and a welfare woman took him away from his father when he was 12, and he lived with her in Boonville. The welfare woman prayed all the time. Later that year, she placed him at the Rodemill Boys Bible Academy for four weeks. As with the welfare woman, it was all Jesus all the time at the school.

One Enoch in the Bible was the son of Jared, who was the son of Mahalalel. Enoch lived 365 years and went to heaven without dying, "Then Enoch walked with God, and he was no longer here, for God took him" (Genesis 5:24). The reader does not see what happened to Enoch Emery after he runs off in the Gonga gorilla suit; he simply disappears. Emery is a black or dark gray mineral that is also known as iron spinel or hercynite. In a crushed natural form, the mineral is known as black sand. It is used as an abrasive, for example on emery boards, for filing nails. Enoch Emery does not seem abrasive by nature; however, his persistence strikes several characters that way.

Asa Hawks Asa was the king of Judah who was criticized by the prophets for going to Syria instead of to the Lord for help in war (2 Chronicles 16). His lack of faith is criticized by the prophets. Asa Hawks once came close to blinding himself to prove his faith in God, but doubt made him lose his nerve, or so the newspaper clippings in his possession tell the reader. Hawks is reminiscent of someone on a street corner hawking wares, which this character does. Hawks preaches as a false preacher for money while his daughter distributes tracts. Like a hawk, Hawks sees clearly at night behind his dark glasses and hunts the prey of his believers and those who will put money into his cup. He is neither blind nor completely foolish. He has been at this trick a long time and presumably survives and escapes like a clever hawk taking flight.

RELATED LETTERS

Elizabeth McKee, June 19, 1948 (HB 4); Elizabeth McKee, July 4, 1948 (HB 5); Elizabeth McKee, July 21, 1948 (HB 4); Elizabeth McKee, July 21, 1948 (HB 6); Elizabeth McKee, September 3, 1948 (HB 6); Elizabeth McKee, September 30, 1948 (HB 7); Elizabeth McKee, December 15, 1948 (HB 7); Elizabeth McKee, January 20, 1949 (HB 8); Elizabeth McKee, February 3, 1949 (HB 9); Elizabeth McKee, February 17, 1949 (HB 9); John Selby, February 18, 1949 (HB 10); Elizabeth McKee, February 24, 1949 (HB 11); Paul Engle, April 7, 1949 (HB 13); Betty Boyd, August 17, 1949 (HB 14); Mavis McIntosh, October 6, 1949 (HB 15); Betty Boyd, October 17, 1949 (HB 16); Elizabeth McKee, October 26, 1949 (HB 16); Mavis McIntosh, October 31, 1949 (HB 17); Elizabeth McKee, February 13, 1950 (HB 20); Elizabeth McKee, September 22, 1960 (HB 21); Elizabeth McKee, [undated; probably January, 1951] (HB 23); Robert Giroux, March 10, 1951 (HB 23); Elizabeth McKee, March 10, 1951 (HB 24); Betty Boyd Love, April 24, 1951 (HB 24); Elizabeth McKee, April 24, 1951 (HB 24–25); Mavis McIntosh, June 8, 1951 (HB 25); Mavis McIntosh, September 1, 1951 (HB 25); Sally and Robert Fitzgerald, September 2, 1951 (HB 26); Sally and Robert Fitzgerald, Tuesday, mid-September, 1951 (HB 27); Sally and Robert Fitzgerald, [undated; mid-September, 1951] (HB 27–28); Robert Giroux, October 16, 1951 (HB 28); Betty Boyd Love, October 18, 1951 (HB 28–29); Robert Giroux, November 23, 1951 (HB 29); Robert Giroux, December 3, 1951 (HB 29); Robert Giroux, January 23, 1952 (HB 30); Sally and Robert Fitzgerald, Thursday [undated; early 1952] (HB 31); Robert Giroux, February 6, 1952 (HB 32); Robert Giroux, February 24, 1952 (HB 32); Elizabeth McKee, March 14, 1952 (HB 32); Sally and Robert Fitzgerald, [undated; April, 1952] (HB 33); Robert Giroux, April 16, 1952 (HB 34); Robert Giroux, April 30, 1952 (HB 34); Robie Macauley, May 2, 1952 (HB 35); ROBERT LOWELL, May 2, 1952 (HB 35); Betty Boyd Love [postmarked Maya 23, 1952] (HB 36); Robert Giroux, May 24, 1952 (HB 36); Robert Giroux, July 19, 1952 (HB 37); Robert Fitzgerald, Tuesday [July, 1952] (HB 39); Sally Fitzgerald, [undated; Summer, 1952], (HB 40); Elizabeth McKee, July 16, 1952 (HB 42); Robie Macauley, October 28, 1952 (HB 45); Sally Fitzgerald, Thursday [undated; Fall, 1952] HB 47); Sally and Robert Fitzgerald, February 1, 1953 (HB 55); Robert Giroux, June 14, 1953 (HB 59); Sally Fitzgerald, Friday [undated; Summer 1953] (HB 61); Sally and Robert Fitzgerald, January 4, 1954 (HB 66); Ben Griffith, February 13, 1954 (HB 68); Ben Griffith, March 3, 1954 (HB 69); Sally and Robert Fitzgerald, March 5, 1954 (HB 70); Robert Giroux, September 3, 1954 (HB 72); Catherine Carver, April 2, 1955 (HB 77); Ben Griffith, May 4, 1955 (HB 79); Robie Macauley, May 18, 1955 (HB 81); Sally and Robert Fitzgerald, June 10, 1955 (HB 85); Catherine Carver, June 27, 1955 (HB 88); Elizabeth McKee, June 29, 1955 (HB 88); Ben Griffith, July 9, 1955 (HB 89); Betty Hester ("A"), September 6, 1955 (HB 101); Sally and Robert Fitzgerald, September 30, 1955 (HB 109); Betty Hester ("A"), October 20, 1955 (HB 111); Robert Giroux, October 21, 1955 (HB 113); Betty Hester ("A"), November 10, 1955 (HB 115–116); Betty Hester ("A"), November 25, 1955 (HB 117–118); Catherine Carver, December 2, 1955 (HB 119); Sally and Robert Fitzgerald, December 12, 1955 (HB 123); Father J. H. McCown, January 16, 1956 (HB 130); Betty Hester ("A"), January 17, 1956 (HB 132); Betty Hester ("A"), February 11, 1956 (HB 137); Betty Hester ("A"), February 25, 1956 (HB 140); Betty Hester ("A"), March 24, 1956 (HB 149); Denver Lindley, April 19, 1956 (HB 151); Maryat Lee, March 10, 1957 (HB 209); Betty Hester ("A"), November 2, 1957 (HB 249); Betty Hester ("A"), April 19, 1958 (HB 280); Betty Hester ("A"), July 5 1958 (HB 291); Caroline Gordon Tate, November 16, 1958 (HB 305); Betty Hester ("A"), January 31, 1959 (HB 317); Maryat Lee, March 29, 1959 (HB 325); ELIZABETH BISHOP, April

9, 1959 (HB 326); Betty Hester ("A"), July 25, 1959 (HB 343); John Hawkes, September 13, 1959 (HB 349–350); John Hawkes, October 6, 1959 (HB 353); Robert Giroux, December 5, 1959 (HB 361); Cecil Dawkins, January 11, 1960 (HB 370); Cecil Dawkins, January 28, 1960 (HB 371); Elizabeth Bishop, April 23, 1960 (HB 391); Cecil Dawkins, June 22, 1960 (HB 401); Betty Hester ("A"), September 17, 1960 (HB 408); Robert Giroux, November 12, 1960 (HB 417); Robert Giroux, January 23, 1961 (HB 429); Betty Hester ("A"), May 13, 1961 (HB 439); Betty Hester ("A"), June 10, 1961 (HB 442); John Hawkes, June 22, 1961 (HB 444); Cecil Dawkins, July 17, 1961 (HB 445); Betty Hester ("A"), October 14, 1961 (HB 451); John Hawkes, November 28, 1961 (HB 457); Cecil Dawkins, March 4, 1962 (HB 467); Cecil Dawkins, April 25, 1962 (HB 471); Sally and Robert Fitzgerald, May 7, 1962 (HB 473); Cecil Dawkins, September 6, 1962 (HB 491); Charlotte Gafford, October 29, 1962 (HB 496); Betty Hester ("A"), May 25, 1963 (HB 522); Cecil Dawkins, November 5, 1963 (HB 546). *Pages HB*: 4–10, 13, 15–17, 20, 22–36, 39–40, 42, 45–46, 54, 56, 59, 61, 65–66, 68–72, 77, 79, 81–82, 85, 88, 101, 109, 111, 113, 116–119, 123, 130, 132–133, 137, 140, 149, 151, 209, 249, 280, 291, 305, 317, 325–327, 343, 349–350, 353, 361, 370–371, 391, 401, 408, 417, 429, 439, 442, 444–445, 451, 457, 467, 471, 473, 491, 496, 522, 546.

FURTHER READING

Allen, William Rodney. "The Cage of Matter: The World as Zoo in Flannery O'Connor's *Wise Blood*." *American Literature: A Journal of Literary History, Criticism, and Bibliography* 58, no. 2 (May 1986): 256–270.

Arnold, Marilyn. "Sentimentalism in the Devil's Territory," In *Flannery O'Connor and the Christian Mystery*, edited by John J. Murphy, et al., 243–258. Provo, Utah: Center for the Study of Christian Values in Literature, Brigham Young University; 1997.

———. "*Wise Blood*: Flannery O'Connor's Lonely Gospel of Hope." *Drew Gateway* 46, nos. 1–3 (1975–76): 78–84.

Asals, Frederick. *Flannery O'Connor The Imagination of Extremity,* Athens: University of Georgia Press, 1982.

———. "The Road to *Wise Blood*." *Renascence: Essays on Value in Literature* 21 (1969): 181–194.

Bacon, Jon Lance. "A Fondness for Supermarkets: *Wise Blood* and Consumer Culture." In *New Essays on* Wise Blood, edited by Michael Kreyling, 25–49. New York: Cambridge University Press, 1995.

Beiswanger, George. "From the 'Office of Fiction.'" *Flannery O'Connor Bulletin* 25 (1996–97): 175–182.

Borgman, Paul. "Three Wise Men: The Comedy of O'Connor's *Wise Blood*." *Christianity and Literature* 24, no. 3 (1975): 36–48.

Brinkmeyer, Robert H., Jr. "'Jesus, Stab Me in the Heart!': Wise Blood, Wounding, and Sacramental Aesthetics." In *New Essays on* Wise Blood, edited by Michael Kreyling, 71–89. New York: Cambridge University Press, 1995.

Brown, Thomas H. "O'Connor's Use of Eye Imagery in *Wise Blood*." *South Central Bulletin* 37 (1977): 138–140.

Burns, Stuart L. "The Evolution of *Wise Blood*." *Modern Fiction Studies* 16 (1970): 147–162.

———. "Structural Patterns in *Wise Blood*." *Xavier University Studies* 8, no. 2 (1969): 32–43.

Byars, John. "Mimicry and Parody in *Wise Blood*." *College Literature* 11, no. 3 (Fall 1984): 276–279.

Carson, Ricks. "O'Connor's *Wise Blood*." *Explicator* 49, no. 3 (Spring 1991): 186–187.

Ciuba, Gary M. "From Face Value to the Value of Faces: *Wise Blood* and the Limits of Literalism." *Modern Language Studies* 19, no. 3 (1989): 72–80.

Cook, Martha E. "Flannery O'Connor's *Wise Blood*: Forms of Entrapment." In *Modern American Fiction: Form and Function,* edited by Thomas Daniel Young, 198–212. Baton Rouge: Louisiana State University Press, 1989.

Currie, Sheldon. "Freaks and Folks: Comic Imagery in the Fiction of Flannery O'Connor." *The Antigonish Review* 62–62 (Summer-Fall 1985): 133–142.

Donahoo, Robert. "The Problem with Peelers: *Wise Blood* as Social Criticism." *Flannery O'Connor Bulletin* 21 (1992): 43–57.

Duckworth, Victoria. "The Redemptive Impulse: *Wise Blood* and *The Color Purple*." *Flannery O'Connor Bulletin* 15 (1986): 51–5———.6.

Dyer, Joyce C. "'Something' in Flannery O'Connor's *Wise Blood*." *Notes on Contemporary Literature* 15, no. 5 (November 1985): 5–6.

Edmunds, Susan. "Through a Glass Darkly: Visions of Integrated Community in Flannery O'Connor's *Wise Blood.*" *Contemporary Literature* 37, no. 4 (Winter 1996): 559–585.

Ellis, Juniper. "O'Connor and Her World: The Visual Art of *Wise Blood.*" *Studies in the Humanities* 21, no. 2 (December 1994): 79–95.

Emerick, Ronald. "*Wise Blood*: O'Connor's Romance of Alienation." *Literature and Belief* 12 (1992): 27–38.

Feeley, Margaret Peller. "Flannery O'Connor's *Wise Blood*: The Negative Way." *Southern Quarterly: A Journal of the Arts in the South* 17, no. 2 (1979): 104–122.

Fitzgerald, Sally. "Happy Endings." *Image: A Journal of the Arts and Religion* 16 (Summer 1997): 73–80.

———. "The Owl and the Nightingale." *Flannery O'Connor Bulletin* 13 (1984): 44–58.

Fodor, Sarah. "Proust 'Home of the Brave' and Understanding Fiction: O'Connor's Development as a Writer." *Flannery O'Connor Bulletin* 25 (1996–97): 62–80.

Gentry, Marshall Bruce. "The Eye vs. the Body: Individual and Communal Grotesquerie in *Wise Blood.*" MFS: *Modern Fiction Studies* 28, no. 3 (Autumn 1982): 487–493.

Giannone, Richard. "Paul, Francis, and Hazel Motes: Conversion at Taulkinham." *Thought: A Review of Culture and Idea* 59, no. 235 (December 1984): 483–503.

Gray, Jeffrey. "'It's Not Natural': Freud's 'Uncanny' and O'Connor's *Wise Blood.*" *Southern Literary Journal* 29, no. 1 (Fall 1996 Fall): 56–68.

Green, James L. "Enoch Emery and His Biblical Namesakes in *Wise Blood.*" *Studies in Short Fiction* 10 (1973): 417–419.

Gregory, Donald. "Enoch Emery: Ironic Doubling in *Wise Blood.*" *Flannery O'Connor Bulletin* 4 (1975): 52–64.

Han, Jae-nam. "O'Connor's Thomism and the 'Death of God' in *Wise Blood.*" In *Flannery O'Connor and the Christian Mystery*, edited by John J. Murphy, et al., 115–127. Provo, Utah: Center for the Study of Christian Values in Literature, Brigham Young University. 1997.

Harrison, Margaret. "Hazel Motes in Transit: A Comparison of Two Versions of Flannery O'Connor's 'The Train' with Chapter 1 of *Wise Blood.*" *Studies in Short Fiction* 8 (1971): 287–293.

Haykin, Marti. "A Note on the Prints." *Flannery O'Connor Bulletin* 25 (1996–97): 103–104.

Kowalewski, Michael. "On Flannery O'Connor." *Raritan: A Quarterly Review* 10, no. 3 (Winter 1991): 85–104.

Kreyling, Michael (ed.), *New Essays on* Wise Blood. New York: Cambridge University Press, 1995.

Kwon, Jong Joon, "The Elements of Mystery in *Wise Blood.*" *The Journal of English Language and Literature* 37, no. 2 (Summer 1991): 465–490.

Lawson, Lewis A. "Flannery O'Connor and the Grotesque: *Wise Blood.*" *Renascence: Essays on Value in Literature* 18 (1965): 143–147, 156.

LeClair, Thomas. "Flannery O'Connor's *Wise Blood*: The Oedipal Theme." *Mississippi Quarterly: The Journal of Southern Culture* 29 (1976): 197–205.

Lee, C. Jason. "Criticism and the Terror of Nothingness." *Philosophy and Literature* 27, no. 1 (April 2003): 211–222.

Littlefield, Daniel F., Jr. "Flannery O'Connor's *Wise Blood*: 'Unparalleled Prosperity' and Spiritual Chaos." *Mississippi Quarterly: The Journal of Southern Culture* 23 (1970): 121–133.

McCullagh, James C. "Symbolism and the Religious Aesthetic: Flannery O'Connor's *Wise Blood.*" *Flannery O'Connor Bulletin* 2 (1973): 43–58.

McDermott, John V. "Dissociation of Words with the Word in *Wise Blood.*" *Renascence: Essays on Value in Literature* 30 (1978): 163–166.

Middleton, David L. "Meaning Through Form: A Study of Metaphorical Structure in Flannery O'Connor's *Wise Blood.*" *The Texas Review* 5, nos. 1–2 (Spring-Summer 1984): 47–57.

Nielsen, Erik. "The Hidden Structure of *Wise Blood.*" *New Orleans Review* 19, nos. 3–4 (Fall-Winter 1992): 91–97.

Peters, Jason. "O'Connor's *Wise Blood.*" *Explicator* 63, no. 3 (Spring 2005): 179–181.

Rath, Sura Prasad. "Comic Polarities in Flannery O'Connor's *Wise Blood.*" *Studies in Short Fiction* 21, no. 3 (Summer 1984): 251–258.

Rechnitz, Robert M. "Passionate Pilgrim: Flannery O'Connor's *Wise Blood.*" *Georgia Review* 19 (1965): 310–316.

Smith, Marcus A. J. "Another Desert: Haze Mote's Missing Years." *Flannery O'Connor Bulletin* 18 (1989): 55–58.

Sweeney, Gerard M. "O'Connor's *Wise Blood*." *Explicator* 56, no. 2 (Winter 1998): 108–109.

Tate, J. O. "The Essential Essex." *Flannery O'Connor Bulletin* 12 (1983): 47–59.

Weisenburger, Steven. "The Devil and John Hawkes." *Review of Contemporary Fiction* 3, no. 3 (Fall 1983): 155–163.

Whitt, Margaret. "Creative Responses to O'Connor's *Wise Blood*: Those Shoes Aren't Like Mine, the Eyes That Matter, and Maude with the Cow Dressed like a Housewife!" *Flannery O'Connor Review* 2 (2003–04): 84–86.

Witt, Jonathan. "*Wise Blood* and the Irony of Redemption." *Flannery O'Connor Bulletin* 22 (1993–94): 12–24.

Yaeger, Patricia Smith. "The Woman without Any Bones: Anti-Angel Aggression in *Wise Blood*." In *New Essays on* Wise Blood, edited by Michael Kreyling, 91–116. New York: Cambridge University Press, 1995.

THE HABIT OF BEING:

Letters

The Habit of Being: Letters of Flannery O'Connor (1979)

O'Connor's letters were collected and edited by her friend Sally Fitzgerald and published by Farrar, Straus and Giroux in 1979. The title of the collection comes from Fitzgerald's sense that O'Connor deliberately cultivated a "habit of art" to craft her stories and novels but that she also developed a certain way of living in the world or what Fitzgerald termed "a habit of being." Fitzgerald describes this as "an excellence not only of action but of interior disposition and activity that increasingly reflected the object, the being, which specified it, and was itself reflected in what she did and said. It is to this second habit that her letters attest, even as they shed a great deal of new light on the novels and stories she gave us in the practice of the first" (xvii–xviii).

The volume won the National Book Critics Circle Special Award in 1979 and has, since that time, been regarded as among O'Connor's most important writing, even though she did not collect the letters herself and they were published posthumously. In addition to providing a window into her personality, her relationships, and several views about her own work, the letters also give readers food for thought on topics such as literature and literary analysis, aesthetics, politics, illness, spirituality, the Catholic Church, and many other subjects. Fitzgerald published 260 letters in *Collected Works* (Library of America, 1988). Though some of the letters were previously unpublished, the vast majority of them were reprinted from *The Habit of Being*.

SYNOPSIS

Just less than 800 letters span 16 years of O'Connor's life in the collection. The range is far-reaching, from her first approach to Elizabeth McKee in June 1948 while working at YADDO where her opening sentence shows her directness, "I am looking for an agent," (4) to her last letter to friend Maryat Lee, written just six days before her death in July 1964, where she closes with characteristic frankness, "Dont know when I'll send those stories. I've felt too bad to type them" (596). As a book, the let-

ters have been embraced as autobiography, spiritual counsel, writing advice, literary criticism, humorous sketches, opinion pieces, and several other modes of writing. Many readers find HB one of the most readable, enjoyable, and accessible collections of letters. The letters work well alone, even out of context from O'Connor's other work; in fact, some people have read and enjoyed the letters without reading anything else the author has written.

The following is a complete listing of O'Connor's 49 correspondents from *The Habit of Being*: Louise Abbot; Shirley Abbott; Roslyn Barnes; ELIZABETH BISHOP; Ashley Brown; Catherine Carver; Alfred Corn; Cecil Dawkins; Paul Engle; Elizabeth Fenwick (Way); Robert Fitzgerald; Sally Fitzgerald; Sister Mariella Gable; Charlotte Gafford; Robert Giroux; Louise Gossett; Thomas Gossett; Ben Griffith; Eileen Hall; John Hawkes; Mrs. Rumsey Haynes; Betty Hester (aka "A" for anonymous); Granville Hicks; Sister Julie; Maryat Lee; Denver Lindley; Betty Boyd Love; Elizabeth Lowell; ROBERT LOWELL; John Lynch; Andrew Lytle; Robie Macauley; Father J. H. McCown; Mavis McIntosh; Janet McKane; Elizabeth McKee; Marion Montgomery; Alice Morris; WALKER PERCY; KATHERINE ANNE PORTER; J. F. Powers; "A Professor of English;" John Selby; William Sessions; Dr. T. R. Spivey; Richard Stern; Thomas Stritch; Caroline Gordon Tate; James Tate.

Correspondents from the list above selected by Sally Fitzgerald for *Collected Works* are: Louise Abbot; Elizabeth Bishop; Ashley Brown; Catherine Carver; Alfred Corn; Cecil Dawkins; Paul Engle; Robert Fitzgerald; Sally Fitzgerald; Sister Mariella Gable; Robert Giroux; Louise Gossett; Tom Gossett; Ben Griffith; Eileen Hall; Sister Julie; Maryat Lee; Betty Boyd Love; Robert Lowell; John Lynch; Andrew Lytle; Robie Macauley; Father James H. McCown; Janet McKane; Elizabeth McKee; Walker Percy; Katherine Anne Porter; J. F. Powers; John Selby; William Sessions; Dr. T. R. Spivey; Richard Stern; Thomas Stritch; and Caroline Gordon Tate.

In addition, in *Collected Works*, Fitzgerald included previously unpublished letters to these different correspondents than appeared in HB: Beverly Brunson; Helen Greene; Elizabeth Hardwick; Carl

Hartman; George Haslam; Erik Langkjaer; Thomas Mabry; Mavis McIntosh; and Marcus Smith.

Because O'Connor so frequently discussed her work in her correspondence, any thorough study of her fiction or essays is incomplete without consulting her references to those works in her letters. The letters receive emphasis in this *Companion* because of their inherent epistolary value and also because of the enlightenment they offer students of the author's other works.

CORRESPONDENT SUMMARIES

Each of the nearly 800 letters in *The Habit of Being* is summarized below alphabetically by addressee and then chronologically by letter. In the original collection, the letters appear in a straightforward chronological format. Reading the letters through by correspondent, as reflected in these summaries, provides interesting insights into the relationships O'Connor formed with many different kinds of people. It also dispels the myth that she was a recluse. Several of the correspondent groupings parallel a significant portion of the author's life, and some illustrate the poignant, interrupted closing of her many relationships near the time of her death.

Summaries chronicle developments in the author's thinking, work, methodology, relationships, and experiences from a different perspective than one sees in reading *The Habit of Being* cover to cover. These summaries neither replace the richness of O'Connor's language and tone nor provide all of the details that exist in the original letters. They are intended to help readers locate and review letters quickly. The summaries may also be helpful in a consideration of O'Connor's life and writing from a slightly different perspective.

Note: For the most part, "she" as the subject of a sentence in the summaries always refers to O'Connor. The subhead "Works" refers to those works by O'Connor mentioned in the letter. Works given in brackets signify works alluded to but not mentioned by name in the letter.

LOUISE ABBOT (nine letters) Abbot initially wrote to O'Connor under the ruse that she was a "lady-journalist," but she was actually a shy reader who wanted to meet her. O'Connor was glad Abbot

dropped the false pretenses. *Pages:* HB: 205, 223, 325, 353, 426, 535, 567, 570, 581.

Letters:

February 27, 1957 (p. 205; 2 par.): From ANDALUSIA. FOC makes arrangements with Abbot to meet at Andalusia. She tells her she looks forward to meeting her and that she is glad she has decided not to be a "lady-journalist."
Works: None.

June 2, 1957 (p. 223; 3 par.): From ANDALUSIA. The *Carolina Quarterly* has arrived, containing Abbot's story. FOC thinks Abbot's story is better than the one that won first prize. She offers comments on Abbot's story, why she likes it. She offers some suggestions about the woman's realizations in the story and how Abbot might make them more believable to the reader. She also says that the cactus is too obviously used as a symbol. She encourages Abbot to write more stories.
Works: None.

March 30, 1959 (p. 325; 3 par.): From ANDALUSIA. She is glad that Abbot will not be her "neighbor" at the local institution. She mentions that she need not travel to use the Ford grant and that she may purchase an electric typewriter. She tells Abbot that (Prof.) Spivey recently visited and that he reported cheerfully about school.
Works: "my novel" [*The Violent Bear It Away*].

[undated] Sat. 1959 (p. 353; 7 par.): From ANDALUSIA. FOC speaks about faith, doubt, and penance. She also discusses a priest's article about hell. Mystery is a good thing because it means that God is above our understanding and, therefore, above us. "[Faith] is trust, not certainty" (354). She closes by mentioning that they are building two rooms and a bath onto the house.
Works: None.

January 13, 1961 (p. 426; 1 par.): From ANDALUSIA. FOC discusses how she never thought ahead about point of view when she wrote "A Good Man Is Hard to Find." She will look up something about the short story for Abbot's visit and discusses arrangements. She is going to the doctor and an event related to the Civil War. She concludes, "I sure am sick of the Civil War" (426).

Works: ["A Good Man Is Hard to Find"].

August 18, 1963 (p. 535; 1 par.): From ANDALUSIA. FOC writes about getting together after Abbot's operation. She recommends that Simron for iron may help her feel better. She takes six a day for her hemoglobin.

Works: None.

February 21, 1964 (p. 567; 3 par.): From ANDALUSIA. FOC will have surgery to remove a large tumor before Abbot has her surgery. She asks Abbot to pray for her and tells her that they will get together when she is feeling better. She mentions liking Spivey's paper on her work.

Works: None.

March 20, 1964 (p. 570; 2 par.): From ANDALUSIA. She enjoyed the visit from Father Ellis the previous day. She tells Abbot that her operation was a success but unpleasant and hopes that Abbot will not need one of the same kind. She has developed a kidney infection as an aftereffect.

Works: None.

May 28, 1964 (p. 581; 3 par.): From ANDALUSIA. Her lupus has reignited following her surgery, but she still wants to meet with Abbot when she gets back home from the hospital. She tells Abbot not to worry about indifference in her faith and that it is not always good or very instructive to keep measuring it. She was allowed a visit in the hospital by Abbot, who was supposed to stay three minutes but stayed 30. She asks for Abbot's prayers, saying that she is "sick of being sick."

Works: None.

SHIRLEY ABBOTT (two letters) Abbott was a student who sent O'Connor questions and then a sample of her writing about O'Connor's work. O'Connor answered her questions and commented on the student's article. *Pages:* HB 142, 147.

Letters

March 7, 1956 (p. 142; 2 par.): From ANDALUSIA. FOC attempts to answer Abbott's questions. She is working on a novel now [*The Violent Bear It Away*]. The first chapter, "You Can't Be Any Poorer Than Dead" was published in *NEW WORLD WRITING #8*. She is not good at speaking about her work before it is finished. She found out how to write fiction in graduate school by reading and writing it.

Works: "You Can't Be Any Poorer Than Dead."

March 17, 1956 (p. 147; 6 par.): From ANDALUSIA. O'Connor gives Abbott writing advice, complimenting her on her writing maturity at her age. She responds to Abbott's analysis of her work. She explains matters concerning her faith in Christian dogma and how she does not feel restricted by it. It is not possible to be good without grace. Each of her stories is a new experience. Most of her readers would not guess that she writes from a Christian and Catholic perspective, which she believes distinguishes it. She enjoys Abbott's interpretation of agrarian aspects of her work.

Works: None.

ROSLYN BARNES (13 letters) Roslyn Barnes was a student at GEORGIA STATE COLLEGE FOR WOMEN who sought out O'Connor. Like the author, she also went to school in Iowa City. O'Connor gave her advice about her education and sought information from her as a scientist on whether Père TEILHARD [DE CHARDIN's] phrase, "everything that rises must converge" had any relationship to physics. *Pages:* HB: 410, 420, 422, 428, 432, 437, 443, 446, 479, 482, 486, 492, 493.

Letters

September 29, 1960 (p. 410; 5 par.): From ANDALUSIA. She recognizes where Barnes is living in Iowa City. She asks after Mrs. Guzeman, who was nearly 100 years old when she was there; she assumes she has since died. She thanks her for looking up a Mr. Santos; hers is Bienvenido, not James Santos. She mentions that Paul Engle will know. She wishes she could visit but will be doing well, given her health, to get to Minnesota and back. She tells her that if writing does not work out, she can switch to radiation work since that is also available at Iowa. She sends her regards to Paul.

Works: None.

November 28, 1960 (p. 420; 2 par.): From ANDALUSIA. She sends a clipping from the *Atlanta Journal*. There are two official societies in the South—Black and White that "are about to be loosed upon one another" (420). She mentions Dr. Helen Green of GSCW visiting Andalusia. Green likes to give Flannery dresses and only buys new dresses that are navy blue and on sale.

Works: None.

December 12, 1960 (p. 422; 3 par.): From ANDALUSIA. O'Connor says that Barnes may go into detective work if science and writing both fail her since she has located both Bienvenido Santos and Mrs. Guzeman. She is pleased that she is going to MASS to help discern whether or not she wants to become a Catholic. She went to St. Mary's in Iowa City and does not know whether Msgr. Conway was at the church to which Barnes goes when she was there.

Works: None.

January 23, 1961 (p. 428; 4 par.): From ANDALUSIA. She has sent her *The Divine Milieu*. MILLEDGEVILLE is celebrating the 100th anniversary of secession with a three-day event including a parade with floats bearing women in fancy dresses. She is sorry that Barnes's parents disapprove of her looking into Catholicism but tells her that Barnes should pray for them. Her health is moderate.

Works: None.

February 13, 1961 (p. 432; 3 par.): From ANDA-LUSIA. She likes fudge but rarely gets any. Barnes must be busy already rather than go into the candy business. She hopes that she gets the job that she seeks. She thinks that she was better off going to Iowa than taking the money at Emory. She forgot her missal and needed to use the paper one in the pew at MASS and was disgusted with the idiot English translations of the Latin. She thinks that some of the trials at bringing the Mass closer to the local congregations are misguided. The PEACOCKS have their tails up. Since the weather has been good, they misjudge it for spring.

Works: None.

March 29, 1961 (p. 437; 1 par.): From ANDALUSIA. Given how behind she seems to be these days, she is hoping to be on time to wish Barnes a Happy Easter. She speaks about floods in Iowa and having six geese. She is applying a theory of TEILHARD's to both the South and the world in a new story that was just sold to NEW WORLD WRITING.

Works: "Everything That Rises Must Converge."

June 17, 1961 (p. 443; 1 par.): From ANDALUSIA. Since Barnes is the only scientist whom she knows personally, she asks about the physical accuracy of "everything that rises must converge."

Works: ["Everything That Rises Must Converge"].

July 26, 1961 (p. 446; 2 par.): From ANDALUSIA. She thanks Barnes for the information on the rising/converging question. She is sorry to have taken so long to get back to her, but she appreciates the thoughts and says that they go along with her own limited understanding of the concept. She says Barnes is wise to consider the Papal Auxiliary Volunteers for Latin America (PAVLA) before making a fuller commitment to becoming a nun. She will recommend her, as she wishes. Barnes should also pay back her debts first.

Works: ["Everything That Rises Must Converge"].

June 10, 1962 (p. 479; 3 par.): From ANDALUSIA. She has read Barnes's thesis and is impressed with it. She wants to know more about Msgr. Ivan Illych, who knows her friend Caroline Gordon. If she had to use a story for a thesis now, it would be "The Artificial Nigger."

Works: "The Artificial Nigger."

June 29, 1962 (p. 482; 2 par.): From ANDALUSIA. She is glad Barnes is in her present location and has heard of Msgr. Illych from Caroline Gordon and Eric Langkjaer. She wants to know more about her situation. She had cub scouts at the farm one day and a nursery school the next. While the nursery-school students were there, she shot a five-foot water rattler, but the children were not affected. If there is anything she can send to Barnes, she would be pleased to do so.

Works: None.

August 4, 1962 (p. 486; 2 par.): From ANDALUSIA. She is pleased to hear about Msgr. Illych's efforts. She does not think Barnes will be among the half of the students whom he sends home. This must be what it means to "bear away the kingdom of heaven with violence; the violence is directed inward" (486). The church's warning about TEILHARD is appropriate because his work on grace is unclear. The move toward warnings and away from an Index is a good one.

Works: None.

September 17, 1962 (p. 492; 4 par.): From ANDALUSIA. Dr. Helen Green has not yet come to Andalusia, and her mother is now too busy with haying to ask her for a while yet. She thanks Barnes for sending her the information about teaching, but she does not know enough about English to teach. Caroline Tate at the University of California at Davis may know someone or may have done it herself were she not already under contract at Davis. She values instruction in languages as a pleasure and says that the more languages one knows, the more one appreciates one's own. It does not dilute one's mother culture but is rather a training of one's mind. They have built a new pond.

Works: None.

September 24, 1962 (p. 493; 3 par.): From ANDALUSIA. She sends a graduation gift that Barnes may use to go out to dinner. Helen Green has now been to the farm and gave a humorous description of her visit to Chula Vista. Green is relieved that Barnes is among nice people and

that she is not being fooled by the church. Green described attending services that FOC imagines must have been MASS, benediction, and/or compline. O'Connor enjoys the "rooster" or dove that Green gave her.

Works: None.

ELIZABETH BISHOP (three letters)   The poet wrote to O'Connor to tell her she admired her stories. Bishop is one of the most important 20th-century American poets. The hoped-for meeting between O'Connor and the poet never happened, despite both writers' desires. *Pages:* HB: 197, 265, 285.

See also: BISHOP, ELIZABETH.

Letters

January 13, 1957 (197; 4 par.): From ANDALUSIA. She thanks her for her letter and tells her how much it means to her that Bishop has read and enjoyed her work. She does not travel as much as Bishop; her work has traveled further than she. She speaks of the critical attention her stories have received in other countries such as Italy.

Cal (ROBERT) LOWELL once showed her a picture of Bishop in Florida that left her with the impression that Bishop moved North and South along the East coast with the seasons. She and her mother would be happy to have Bishop come visit them at Andalusia. The violence in her stories is not frequent there, and the good country people who are not so good do not stay around long.

She respects Bishop's work, though she cannot explain why she likes it. She used to live with the Fitzgeralds in Connecticut and recalls Robert admiring Bishop and her work.

Works: "A Circle in the Fire."

February 6, 1958 (265; 3 par.): From ANDALUSIA. FOC thanks Bishop for sending her *The Diary of Helena Morley.* She and her mother both enjoyed it. The story makes her think that blacks and whites might get along better in a Catholic country. She says it was nice of Bishop to call her on her way to South America. She gave her the wrong date for May Sarton's reading in SAVANNAH and hopes that it did not inconvenience her. She gives a brief account that was given to her by two local college professors. She and her mother hope that Bishop will be able to visit them on her way north.

Works: None.

June 1, 1958 (285; 5 par.): From ANDALUSIA. She tells Bishop that she went to Europe and the trip cemented her desire now to stay at home. Her crutches drew attention. They let her get on a plane first, and the Italians eyed their aluminum composition. She describes her trip to LOURDES in some detail. It was not as bad as she envisioned it would be. That which is supernatural about the place does in fact exist, but it does not push away the natural deficiencies, such as germs.

She finds the ceremonies of the convent somehow depressing. She wonders whether an old woman about whom she read who entered a convent in South America may be the same one Bishop tells about.

A rich college nearby wants to have T. S. Eliot come give a reading next year, and she would like a visit from Bishop if the school ever made it worth her while to come to the area.

Works: None.

ASHLEY BROWN (seven letters) Brown was a professor of English at the University of South Carolina. He admired O'Connor's work and visited her often at Andalusia. They shared an interest in contemporary literature. *Pages:* HB: 277, 285, 431, 460, 469, 533, 584.

Letters

April 14, 1958 (p. 277; 5 par.): From ANDALUSIA. She discusses her upcoming trip and its relation to her doctor's most recent findings. She tells about a change in plans about going to Milan instead of going to Ireland and England. They plan to also visit Paris, LOURDES, Barcelona, Rome, and Lisbon.

She has yet to read Peter Taylor's play but did not think his story in *The* KENYON REVIEW was as good as his others. She comments about KENYON's new editor.

KATHERINE ANNE PORTER came to Macon, Georgia, and did a reading; she came to Andalusia for lunch the following day. O'Connor found her pleasant company. O'Connor may be changing publishers soon, now that Denver Lindley is leaving Harcourt, Brace. She will go with Bob Giroux of Farrar, Straus. She asks when Brown is leaving for Yugoslavia.

Works: None.

May 26, 1958 (p. 285; 4 par.): From ANDALUSIA. She gives a brief account of the trip to Europe, including that she caught a cold that stayed with her for 17 days. She saw Gabrielle Rolin instead of Paris. The trinket stores at LOURDES were the devil's work in the face of the Virgin Mary. She has read Nabokov's *Pnin*, which she liked. She read Uncle Remus at the Fitzgerald's because she took it for the children, but they were only speaking Italian. She wants him to visit when he gets back from Yugoslavia.

Works: None.

February 13, 1961 (p. 431; 4 par.): From ANDALUSIA. She keeps a collection of newspaper clippings, and "The Partridge Festival" was inspired by the clipping that she sends him with this letter. She is now writing a story about a man who has Christ tattooed on his back. She has read *I Choose to Die* by B. Cheney. MILLEDGEVILLE is in the midst of celebrating the secession with parades and pageants.

Works: ["The Partridge Festival"], ["Parker's Back"].

January 12, 1962 (p. 460; 3 par.): From ANDALUSIA. She thanks him for the copy of WALKER PERCY's *The Moviegoer* and plans to take her time reading it. She also appreciates the passage from the *Purgatorio*. She is working on an introduction to "A Good Man" that she can do at an upcoming reading at the University of Georgia. After this reading, she plans to stop doing talks. She asks whether he has ever read anything by Albert Guérard.

Works: ["A Good Man Is Hard to Find"].

March 18, 1962 (p. 469; 3 par.): From ANDALUSIA. She likes the last volume of Waugh's *Sword of*

Honor trilogy and thanks Brown for lending it to her. She likes Waugh better than Ford, except she does like *The Good Soldier*. She failed to locate an interview with Waugh in *Sign* magazine to send to him and describes it briefly. Father Charles at the monastery gave her mother the Alice B. Toklas cookbook. Her mother is reading it and commenting.

Works: None.

August 13, 1963 (p. 533; 5 par.):   From ANDA-LUSIA. She thanks Brown for sending the EUDORA WELTY story. She would like to reread it. No one else, she thinks, could make the story work but Welty. She tells him about the car. It has a 327 engine and is not as dark green as they had hoped for, but she can drive it. Some people are helping her find out about the "boils" on her swans. She received Caroline's article about Ford Maddox Ford and wants to write her a letter. She hopes he enjoys San Francisco.

Works: None.

June 15, 1964 (p. 584; 4 par.):   From *Baldwin County Hospital.* She is happy to hear that he is going to Brazil. She sends ELIZABETH BISHOP her best wishes. She is in the hospital or she would have sent some peafowl feathers for him to take to her. Bishop once sent her an altar in a bottle. She has been in the hospital three weeks. Caroline and Father Charles came to see her. She wants him to give her an account of Brazil and for him to tell Bishop that she hopes that Bishop will visit.

Works: None.

CATHERINE CARVER (15 letters)   When Robert Giroux left Harcourt Brace to go to Farrar, Straus and Company, Catherine Carver became O'Connor's new editor at Harcourt. Giroux assured O'Connor of Carver's ability.
   Pages: HB: 76, 79, 83, 86, 91(a), 91(b), 95, 119, 319, 322, 327, 337, 342, 585, 588, 593.

Letters

April 2, 1955 (p. 76; 3 par.):   From ANDALUSIA. She is glad that Carver will be her editor since

Giroux left. She does not expect to come to New York, but perhaps Carver might make it to MILLED-GEVILLE. In the meantime, she will see Denver Lindley. She is eager to see reviews of *Wise Blood*, particularly the British ones. She is nowhere near finishing the novel that Neville Spearman announced would be published that fall.

Works: Wise Blood.

May 5, 1955 (p. 79; 2 par.):   From ANDALUSIA. The books have arrived, and she likes what she sees. She is glad that all of the Waugh quote was used. She mentions a review in the Virginia Kirkus Bulletin sent to her by her agent that says that she may write better novels than short stories. She has sold "Whom the Plague Beckons" [which will be retitled "You Can't Be Any Poorer Than Dead"] to NEW WORLD WRITING. She hopes that she did not make MILLEDGEVILLE sound too remote to Mr. Lindley and hopes that he will visit.

May 24, 1955 (p. 83; 3 par.):   From ANDALUSIA. She thanks her for information and copies of letters. She gave a talk in Macon recently, and one of the ladies of the club asked whether TENNES-SEE WILLIAMS was from Tennessee. She did not know. She asks that Carver change her hotel to accommodate her limited walking ability. She thinks that the only people watching television at 1:30 P.M. will be children who cannot afford a copy of *A Good Man Is Hard to Find and Other Stories.*

Works: A Good Man Is Hard to Find and Other Stories.

June 16, 1955 (p. 86; 5 par.):   From ANDALUSIA. She thanks Carver for the new novel contract and for her work about the pictures. She says that perhaps the reviews are of some benefit. Carver would find some of her mail amusing. Many of those who write her fan mail have various ailments or want to write. Lon and Brainard Cheney are the same person, and she uses the names interchangeably. He writes speeches for the governor of Tennessee.

Works: Wise Blood.

July 22, 1955 (p. 91; 3 par.): From ANDALUSIA. She is glad that the book is selling. She is just returning from a weekend in Nashville where the people at the local bookstore told her that it was selling well. She keeps receiving mail, but now it is starting to become depressing; the latest is from a mental institution. Her peafowls have hatched 13 peachicks. She hopes she will soon be stepping on peafowl everywhere. She says it is hot in Georgia but that she knows from experience that it can be equally hot in New York City.

Works: Wise Blood.

July 28, 1955 (p. 91; 4 par.): From ANDALUSIA. She thanks Carver's mother for pictures. She has been asked to speak about the importance of the short story at an AAUW gathering in Lansing, Michigan, the following April. It will take her that long to figure out what the importance is. Does Carver know? She may just say that this is not important to a fiction writer. Did Harcourt publish Karl Stern's *The Third Revolution*? If so, she hopes that the publisher will send her a copy. There are now 16 peachickens.

Works: None.

August 10, 1955 (p. 95; 2 par.): From ANDALUSIA. Today she received a letter from a man who claimed to have spent his childhood among people like her characters. Her mother would like five more copies of *A Good Man* to give to sick friends.

Works: A Good Man Is Hard to Find and Other Stories.

December 2, 1955 (p. 119; 3 par.): From ANDALUSIA. She thanks Carver for sending a forgotten manuscript as well as a book to the hospital. Her agent has sold *Wise Blood*'s French rights to Gallimard. Local readers continue to misunderstand her work, thanking her for the "dispensation." Another asked her about her leg and called her "sugar." She will be glad when she is too old to be addressed that way.

Works: Wise Blood.

February 18, 1959 (p. 319; 3 par.): From ANDALUSIA. She was glad to hear from Carver since she was just then also writing to her. She would like her to read her new novel manuscript. Caroline likes it, but she would like someone to read it who might not necessarily share her viewpoint. It is only 45,000 words. She would be glad to send Carver new PEACOCK feathers. Several ladies in town wear the feathers that she has given them in their hats.

Works: The Violent Bear It Away.

March 24, 1959 (p. 322; 1 par.): From ANDALUSIA. She sends the novel today. She is uncertain about whether it should be published and values and appreciates Carver's willingness to give it her opinion. She is not sure whether it should be published as a novel or with a collection of stories.

Works: [The Violent Bear It Away].

April 18, 1959 (p. 327; 4 par.): From ANDALUSIA. Carver's comments make so much sense that she began to revise the novel right after reading them. Robert Fitzgerald made the same comments from Italy. O'Connor spent a lot of time with her characters in the city. Since she has the ending, she thinks that she can go back and improve the middle section of the novel. She will send it to Carver again and also wants Denver to see it when she has revised the middle.

Works: The Violent Bear It Away.

June 23, 1959 (p. 337; 3 par.): From ANDALUSIA. She thanks Carver for the wire and agrees that the manuscript is improved. She has done more work on it after sending it to Carver. She will send it to Carver again but does not expect her to read it. She is much more satisfied with it now and will send it to Giroux by August. She remarks about Dick Stern's work with Carver and says that he mentions that Cary Grant could play his characters. She has Spencer Tracy chosen to play Tarwater. She is very grateful.

Works: [The Violent Bear It Away].

July 19, 1959 (p. 342; 4 par.): From ANDALUSIA. She writes about putting back a sentence that she took out. She has sent the manuscript to McKee to submit to Giroux. Robert Fitzgerald also thinks it much improved and especially likes the "missionary child." She discusses some changes that she has made to the manuscript from the version that Carver has. She invites Carver to show the manuscript to Denver. She feels like she has been fired from a job now that the work on the novel is completed. Writing is always better than the alternative.

Works: [*The Violent Bear It Away*].

June 17, 1964 (p. 585; 3 par.):   From *Baldwin County Hospital*. She has been in the hospital for a month. She has asked Giroux to wait until spring to publish the short-story collection. She discusses various stories that she may like to include in it. She is working on one story in long-hand in the hospital. She will be able to work if she is ever let out of the hospital.

Works: ["Judgment Day"], "Revelation," ["Parker's Back"].

June 27, 1964 (p. 588; 4 par.):   From ANDALUSIA. She asks Carver if she will look at "Judgment Day" for the collection. It is a rewrite of a 1946 story. She has been home from the hospital a week and is growing stronger. She believes that she can write two more stories by the end of the summer. Cecil Dawkins tells her that she should include the first chapter of her novel in the collection, but she is uncertain that it may pad the book.

Works: ["Judgment Day"], "You Can't Be Any Poorer Than Dead," *The Violent Bear It Away*.

July 15, 1964 (p. 593; 5 par.):   From ANDALUSIA. She discusses the revision of "Judgment Day." She sends "Parker's Back." She thinks that she will leave out the novel chapter from the collection. Has Carver read "The Enduring Chill"? She is not fond of it but may make it worse if she works more on it. The old man in "A View of the Woods" was named Mr. Fortune; Tanner is all right to use. She appreciates Carver's reading. She is still bedridden but gets up to write about two hours a day.

Works: ["Judgment Day"], ["Parker's Back"], "The Enduring Chill," "A View of the Woods."

ALFRED CORN (three letters)   Alfred Corn was a student and poet at Emory University in ATLANTA who was impressed when O'Connor gave a reading there. He was too shy to approach her at the reading but wrote a letter to her later. *Pages*: HB: 476, 484, 488.

Letters

May 30, 1962 (p. 476; 8 par.):   From ANDALUSIA. She writes to Corn about his concern over his apparent loss of faith at college. His faith is challenged, she says, by intellectualism at the university. There are many ways to experience God. Faith is something that must be worked at continually all through one's life. She has had to do this herself. She recommends Etienne Gilson's *The Unity of the Philosophical Experience* and Newman's *The Grammar of Assent* and invites him to write to her again if she might be of more help.

Works: None.

July 25, 1962 (p. 484; 3 par.):   From ANDALUSIA. O'Connor addresses Corn's questions about Rayber in her novel and ELIZABETH BISHOP. Rayber and Tarwater are fighting the same fight in themselves. Rayber wins; Tarwater loses. Rayber discovers the power and acceptance of his own free will; Tarwater submits to another authority. She hopes Corn will find Christianity is the best way for him. She hopes he will visit her someday. She would like to be able to place his face.

Works: [*The Violent Bear It Away*].

August 12, 1962 (p. 488; 4 par.):   From ANDALUSIA. She writes about free will in her characters Rayber and Tarwater. Both have it. Then she discusses free will in the Catholic Church and the role of bishops and priests and the Vatican Council in the church's authority. Catholics believe that the church was endowed by Christ with the ability to teach and advise followers throughout time and changing situations and that this authority is guided by the

Holy Spirit. This is why she trusts the church and does not think she must figure out all of the proper interpretations of Scripture for everyday life. She does not think literature would be possible in a predetermined world. Mystery grows with knowledge.

Works: The Violent Bear It Away.

CECIL DAWKINS (61 letters) Cecil Dawkins was from Alabama but was living and teaching at Stephens College in Columbia, Missouri, when she first wrote to O'Connor. Dawkins wrote to ask advice from O'Connor on teaching literature and about teaching her work especially. Dawkins was also a writer who eventually published a collection of short fiction called *The Quiet Enemy* in 1964 and a novel, *The Live Goat*, in 1971. She also wrote a piece that dramatized several of O'Connor's short stories together. The two writers shared a common southern Catholic heritage and were only two years apart in age. Their shared experience and interests helped their correspondence flower.

Pages: HB: 221, 226, 230, 233, 239, 242, 248, 253, 260, 264, 267, 276, 284, 286, 295, 300, 306, 316, 320, 326, 333, 340, 351, 356, 361, 369, 375, 383, 393, 397, 401, 403, 416, 424, 433, 435, 444, 461, 463, 467, 471, 483, 485, 490, 493, 501, 504, 539, 546(a,) 546(b), 551, 578, 586.

Letters

May 19, 1957 (p. 221; 4 par.): From ANDALUSIA. She thanks Dawkins for writing. She is pleased to know that college freshmen are now, unlike in her experience at undergraduate school, taught contemporary literature. She did not read KATHERINE ANNE PORTER, WILLIAM FAULKNER, or EUDORA WELTY until she was in graduate school. Literature used to be defined by students as the classics written before 1900. Contemporary literature had to be best sellers.

The freshman who sensed something religious in her stories is right. It is a central subject. She writes about unpleasant characters because that is what she can write. She recommends JACQUES MARITAIN's *Art and Scholasticism* to Dawkins's students. MILLEDGEVILLE has a population of 12,000 and is also a bird sanctuary. She invites her to visit if she is ever nearby.

Works: None.

June 19, 1957 (p. 226; 2 par.): From ANDALUSIA. A friend who was interviewed at Sarah Lawrence was told that HENRY JAMES's *The Portrait of a Lady* would be too difficult for the students. Stephens College has a bad reputation for academics, but Dawkins's comments make this not all true. The "missing link" in her stories comes from Catholic Christianity, not other religions. She writes about orthodox Protestantism in and out of context and grotesques.

Works: ["A Good Man Is Hard to Find"].

July 16, 1957 (p. 230; 5 par.): From ANDALUSIA. Dawkins is kind to offer a dog for her, but she will have to pass because PEACOCKS and dogs do not mix. She is irritated by writers who think they know so much about the South that they can tell southern writers to stop working with the myth. While getting away does give one perspective and she would likely have stayed away had she not become ill, she has written her best work while living in the South.

Being Catholic has shaped her view of the South. She agrees with Dawkins that Catholics can be unpleasant, but most of these are not people of true faith but are rather those who have some kind of false certainty. They do not think.

She refers to the French Catholic novelists—Bloy, Bernanos, FRANÇOIS MAURIAC—and philosophers—Gilson, JACQUES MARITAIN, and Marcel—as among the reading that has helped her on her intellectual faith journey. She has also read Germans such as Picard, Romano Guardini, and Karl Adam. She is disappointed in the American Catholic writers who seem to write only pamphlets to leave in the back of church. She was impressed with some intelligent people whom she met at Notre Dame. She sends Dawkins a journal dedicated to Caroline Gordon, that she may become acquainted with her work.

Works: None.

August 4, 1957 (p. 233; 4 par.): From ANDA-
LUSIA. Dawkins need not rush sending
O'Connor the journal *Critique*. She does not listen much to reviews anyway, except by people
whom she trusts. She gave a talk on the short
story at a regional writers' meeting of senior citizens, all wanting to publish and make money.
She selected the least bad story out of seven, and
it was critiqued by the others. The agent who
sold *Gone With the Wind* to the film studio was
there. She never referred to O'Connor by name.
The entire experience was like a circus.

She is not much help on the farm with her
crutches, other than gathering eggs. She has not
read Hermann Hesse or many Germans.

Works: None.

August 27, 1957 (p. 239; 6 par.):   From ANDA-
LUSIA. She is not sure what Dawkins does with
all the tomato juice on her farm with dogs. She
would like to see for herself, but her crutches
make her not want to leave home. She did not
read everything in the *Critique* and rarely recalls
reviews minutes after she has read them. She discusses the technique of choosing point of view in
fiction and says that it is easier to ignore it and
get on with the story in short fiction, but in novels, one must give it more thought.

She tries to avoid talking about religion with
the atheists she knows. Agents who attempt to
give literary advice are usually off the mark. Her
own agent does not do this. Her agent sends her
work to publishers of O'Connor's choice, and
she sends them herself to small journals, giving
her agent the commission. She will read Hesse's
Magister Ludi, which Dawkins sent.

Works: None.

September 22, 1957 (p. 242; 3 par.): From
ANDALUSIA. She believes in forming and keeping
habits for writing productivity. If one is a genius,
one may write without habits, but most people
have talent only and need them. The habits help
show you what you can do. She writes two hours
a day at the same time each day and at the same
place without interference. She has energy for that

long and no more. Each writer has to find his or
her own habits. One should, however, start with
a rested mind. Teaching can be exhausting and
draining of one's creative energy. She encloses an
article by Guardini on FYODOR DOSTOYEVSKY as
well as a piece by Caroline about the Greeks.

Works: None.

October 27, 1957 (p. 248; 4 par.):   From ANDA-
LUSIA. She appreciates the picture. Someday she
will send Dawkins one of her and her friends. She
has heard that KATHERINE ANNE PORTER writes
her stories all in her head before committing pen
to paper but that she has a hard time believing
it, perhaps because she cannot work that way. At
the moment, she is writing two pages a day on her
current story. She is never sure if it will work out
until she does it. Reading Shakespeare before one
begins may make one too focused on language too
early in the process. The story should come first.
Dawkins's job sounds taxing on her time. Students from Wesleyan College visit her for ideas
about writing, but they do most of the talking
when they come over and leave her exhausted.

She went to a progressive school where each
summer the teachers went to teachers' college
for new ideas and came back in the fall only
to ask the students what they wanted to learn.
Consequently, they learned very little, no history and certainly no Greek.

Works: None.

November 17, 1957 (p. 253; 6 par.):   From
ANDALUSIA. She has read none of the writers in *The Living Novel* either except for one
book by Wright Morris. She has read Dinesan's
Gothic Tales, which she liked. She is amazed that
Dawkins had to teach Jessamyn West's *Cress
Delahanty*. A young college man from Harvard
visited her and talked to her about his novel.
When he got into discussing the "love section,"
she carefully tried to let him know that fiction
was about people, but he did not seem to listen.
She has noticed that the girls at the local college have many ceremonies involving candles, no
matter how insignificant the occasion. She thinks

that this is because they have not been around religious services where candlelight has meaning.

She encourages Dawkins in her writing, saying that Elizabeth Hardwick mentioned once that all of her drafts could be written by a chicken. Growth comes in fits and spurts. Her first published story shocks her now. She sends her best wishes to the dogs and mentions that she has purchased three Chinese geese.

Works: None.

December 22, 1957 (p. 260; 4 par.): From ANDALUSIA. Caroline Gordon has taught her more than anyone, and she wonders whether Dawkins has read her *How to Read a Novel*. It is more for writers than for readers. She has never met KATHERINE ANNE PORTER; however, she knows some men who have met her and liked her. Elizabeth Hardwick is from Kentucky and is married to ROBERT LOWELL. Her most recent book is *The Simple Truth*. O'Connor thinks she is a good writer. She tells Dawkins about various fans who have written to her about her work and their own, including an accountant who says he has written stories like hers and a man in Florida with a broken leg who wants to collaborate with her words and his ideas.

Works: None.

January 17, 1958 (p. 264; 4 par.): From ANDALUSIA. She is writing her novel again after some time away working on a story. It is always difficult to get back into it again. She finds some good work among James Purdy's *Color of Darkness*, but most of it is bad. She has also read Wright Morris's *Field of Vision*, but the characters were not engaging. In the spring, she and her mother went to LOURDES and Rome. She has sent a book by FRANÇOIS MAURIAC for Dawkins to consider in relation to questions that she has about the church.

Works: [*The Violent Bear It Away*].

February 12, 1958 (p. 267; 4 par.): From ANDALUSIA. She appreciates Dawkins offering to lend her camera, but her trip is off on doctor's orders. She is going to the University of Missouri instead to work with student manuscripts

at the invitation of William Peden. She expects she will see Dawkins while she is there. She has not seen Jean Stafford's story. She is glad she was not there to listen to Dawkins's students analyze O'Connor's work. She had a story published in the fall issue of *Partisan Review*.

Works: Unknown.

April 14, 1958 (p. 276; 3 par.): From ANDALUSIA. She appreciates the picture book about Rome. She is almost ready to head out to Missouri. She describes KATHERINE ANNE PORTER in some detail. O'Connor does not intend to judge any story contest.

Works: None.

May 22, 1958 (p. 284; 4 par.): From ANDALUSIA. She is sorry to hear that Dawkins's father passed away and is having a Mass said for him. She is recuperating from her trip to Europe better than the one to Missouri. Mr. Peden seems to have good taste in story collections. Taking time off from the novel has helped. Harcourt has sent her three novels by Kingsley Amis. Their failures inspire her to keep writing. She will send directions for Dawkins's visit that summer. A snake attacked the Chinese goose eggs; the peafowl eggs will hatch around July first.

Works: [*The Violent Bear It Away*].

June 8, 1958 (p. 286; 4 par.): From ANDALUSIA. She likes Dawkins's story, "Pop the Blue Balloon." She will be pleased to get a copy of *In Defence of Reason* by Ivor Winters; she has not read it. She thanks her for the Midlands book, but it perpetuates the error that she is a convert. The mistake began with Dale Francis who wrote that she was a convert in *Commonweal*. *Critique* will dedicate its Fall 1958 issue to her and J. F. Powers. Powers's best stories are those about the clergy. Her novel is going well.

Works: [*The Violent Bear It Away*].

September 20, 1958 (p. 295; 11 par.): From ANDALUSIA. Dawkins's story, "Hummers in the Larkspur," is better than some in the Martha

Foley collection she has been reading. She makes suggestions for improvements on pages 11, 14, 15, and 19. They are small matters, but small issues add up. She suggests that Dawkins send the story to ACCENT. She thinks Dawkins is "a fine writer" (296).

Works: None.

October 26, 1958 (p. 300; 5 par.):   From ANDA-LUSIA. She comments on another of Dawkins's stories. She recommends a light use of dialect, a suggestion. Readers seldom read historical short stories as they do novels. She has an idiot in her new novel, so it will probably be called Southern Gothic.

Works: [*The Violent Bear It Away*].

December 9, 1958 (p. 306; 8 par.):   From ANDALUSIA. She does not like interviews; she mentioned HENRY JAMES and JOSEPH CONRAD as favorite authors, and the interviewer thought that she said James Conrad. She tells Dawkins to not be concerned with rejection slips. She has broken a rib. She speaks in depth about religion and Dawkins's questions about the church. She says it is the responsibility of the faithful to help. She suggests both prayer and study, but prayer will accomplish more.

Works: None.

January 14, 1959 (p. 316; 2 par.):   From ANDA-LUSIA. She is filling in for EUDORA WELTY at the University of Chicago since Miss Welty's brother is ill. She tells Dawkins that maybe she can visit her in Chicago while she is there. She has completed her novel.

Works: [*The Violent Bear It Away*].

Geo. Wash. Birthday, 1959 (p. 320; 4 par.):   From ANDALUSIA. She was glad to see her and Betty Littleton in Chicago. She mentions the *Chicago Review* and its editor, Richard G. Stern. She told him about Dawkins's work, and he asked her to send some stories there if she is interested. She tells her about Rockefeller money that she has

heard students at Iowa use for funding. She gives advice on ways to fund schooling at Iowa.

She writes about the verse Matthew 11:12, which is the source for the title of her new novel. She is not sure what she thinks of the novel yet. She may read "The Artificial Nigger" at the Vanderbilt reading coming up since it would not hurt, she says, anyone's feelings being read in her home region.

Works: [*The Violent Bear It Away*], "The Artificial Nigger."

April 3, 1959 (p. 326; 2 par.):   From ANDALUSIA. She congratulates Dawkins on receiving $1,000 for a story sold to the *Post*. She only received $425 for her highest sale. The sale ought to please her mother; O'Connor's mother was always asking if she really thought she was using her God-given talent to its utmost if her works were not selling and pleasing a great number of people. The question always leaves O'Connor trembling.

Works: None.

May 21, 1959 (p. 333; 3 par.):   From ANDALUSIA. She thinks Dawkins's "Benny Ricco's Search for the Truth" is one of her best stories. She makes a couple of small suggestions to improve it. She is also not crazy about the title. Jesse Stuart told a friend of hers after she read "A Good Man Is Hard to Find" at Vanderbilt that the audience identified with the grandmother character, so the story should have had the police come and rescue her at the end.

Works: "A Good Man Is Hard to Find."

July 17, 1959 (p. 340; 5 par.):   From ANDALUSIA. Her novel is done and in the mail to the publisher. Her mother is reading a copy. She stops reading frequently to take care of farm business and only seems to read a couple of pages at a time. One reason she may be a short-story writer is so that her mother can read her work without getting up. She does not envy Dawkins needing to talk for three hours every day. Knopf sent her John Updike's short stories that will be published in August. She likes his novel and some of the stories, but many of the stories are too slight. She does not see any benefit to the game of golf.

Works: [*The Violent Bear It Away*].

September 22, 1959 (p. 351; 5 par.): From ANDALUSIA. She and her mother are enjoying the cheese that Dawkins sent. She will try to read *Henderson the Rain King*. She is working on another story that will not be set in Milledgeville. Her novel's galley proofs are due October 1. Advance copies of the book should be out in December; she will try to get her one. They recently bought six cows at the Registered Guernsey Auction.

Works: [*The Violent Bear It Away*].

October 31, 1959 (p. 356; 5 par.): From ANDALUSIA. The Saxton fellowship may have had publishing commitments attached to it, so it is just as well that Dawkins did not get it. She hopes her agent is helping Dawkins decide on fellowships. Caroline Gordon has talked with her about her prose, and she has gone over page proofs. She has read William Styron's *Lie Down in Darkness*. He has talent, but the book was too long.

Works: [*The Violent Bear It Away*].

December 10, 1959 (p. 361; 3 par.): *From ANDALUSIA*. She does not have three stories; she has possibly two. She is working on one and finished the other, "The Comforts of Home." She sent it to Catherine Carver and to Caroline. Caroline liked it, but Catherine did not. She is revising it. She will send it to Dawkins after she revises it if she likes it better then. She recommends that Dawkins find out more about YADDO. The living conditions are good. The servants are friendly, and the scenery is spectacular. She urges her to think about writing a short novel.

Works: ["The Comforts of Home"].

January 11, 1959 (p. 369; 5 par.): From ANDALUSIA. Her copy of *The Violent Bear It Away* has arrived with a messed-up title page. She has not dared to read it yet to find typos in the printing, but she hopes that Dawkins will let her know where they are if she finds any. She gives

Dawkins more advice on her writing and her use of Judas and Christ motifs. She sent her the book by Karl Adam and explains why. She talks about the Pious Style and the church. She has received the French translation of *Wise Blood*. All French books are paperbacks. This one is attractive.

Works: The Violent Bear It Away, Wise Blood.

February 22, 1960 (p. 375; 2 par.): From ANDALUSIA. She thinks that Dawkins may be hearing too many Freudian discussions since she did not think of Oedipus. She wonders whether any character must have an Oedipal complex who does not like his father. She is content with the structure of the story and the novel. She hopes Dawkins is not throwing away work that does not meet some outside critical standard rather than go along with her instincts.

Works: ["The Comforts of Home"], *The Violent Bear It Away.*

March 23, 1960 (p. 384; 3 par.): From ANDALUSIA. She has the flu and just received Dawkins's letter. If she were offered the Harper deal, she would refuse it. She recommends that if the editor is a female to choose someone whom she already knows and likes. A friend of hers read Dawkins's story in the library and liked it. If Dawkins and Betty Littleton come to Andalusia that summer, she will have them meet.

Works: None.

April 30, 1960 (p. 393; 2 par.): From ANDALUSIA. She has been in the hospital for help with her swelling feet. He ruled out all the factors that were not causing it, but that is the only progress that was made. She tells her more information about Betty Hester and where she is from. Hester liked Dawkins's "The Buffalo Ranch." She is a good writer who does well with novels. She hopes that Elizabeth can place Hester's novel someday.

Works: None.

May 23, 1960 (p. 397; 5 par.): From ANDALUSIA. Atheneum is good news. She gives advice about possible publishers for Dawkins's work. She advises her to try for YADDO earlier next year and write somewhere more low key this year. Vitamins only make her eat more, so she is on Gevral, which is a food supplement. Dawkins's mother's response to "The Buffalo Ranch" does not surprise her. O'Connor's aunts think her stories are bad also. It is best to leave it alone and move on.

Works: None.

June 22, 1960 (p. 401; 5 par.):   From ANDALUSIA. She sends Caroline's comments on the "The Patridge Festival." To Enoch, the mummy is an idol, but it is the new jesus in the book overall. Paul Levine wrote a positive review of her book in *JUBILEE*. Levine had sent smart questions to her through M. Coindreau for an interview for a book featuring McCullers, TRUMAN CAPOTE, Bechner, Bellow, Salinger, and her. She sends a pamphlet about the Fulbright from Carol.

Works: "The Partridge Festival," [*Wise Blood*].

July 11, 1960 (p. 403; 2 par.):   From ANDALUSIA. Dawkins need not apologize for telling her friends to stop and see O'Connor at Andalusia. It is about the only way that she sees people now. She writes about one story a year. She recommends writing every day, whether anything comes of it or not. The writer must stay sitting at the typewriter for the words to come and an entry into the story to emerge.

Works: None.

November 8, 1960 (p. 416; 3 par.):   From ANDALUSIA. She is recovering from her trip to Minnesota and also an Arts Festival at Wesleyan where she was accompanied by Caroline Gordon and KATHERINE ANNE PORTER. She is amazed that Porter remembered one of O'Connor's chickens that she met two years before. She speaks with Dawkins about money and how it is feast or famine for writers. She took Catherine Carver to the cyclorama in ATLANTA from where Enoch's mummy came. Carver and her mother went upstairs to try to find it. Carver wanted to see it for herself. Carver asked the clerk if there used to be a mummy like that

there, and she said that there had. This satisfied her that Enoch must have taken it.

Works: [*Wise Blood*].

December 29, 1960 (p. 424; 5 par.):   From ANDALUSIA. She loves the PEACOCK in stained glass that was made by Russell Green at Stephens. They have put it in a windowpane in a new part of the house. Her mother thought that it was a partridge, but a guest said that it was peacock when asked. She was in the hospital again, this time for help in seeing why her bones are crumbling. They are working to reduce her steroids. In the meantime, all she can do is stay home and write, which she is doing.

She would be so happy if Betty Hester could publish something. Hester is at work on a new novel. O'Connor's room has just been repainted, and the experience was so disruptive that she says that she will never allow it to happen again. She has already spent the $750 for the peacock story but does not know when it will be published.

Works: ["The King of the Birds"].

February 15, 1961 (p. 433; 4 par.):   From ANDALUSIA. To help her with comments on the stories, she would have to read them again. She advises Dawkins, however, that if she has any doubt, then she should wait. O'Connor has regretted having "A Stroke of Good Fortune" in her collection. She asks what has happened to "Benny Ricco," a story of Dawkins's that she has liked.

A photographer is due at Andalusia tomorrow to take pictures of the peafowl. Another visitor was an 87-year-old man who wanted to talk with O'Connor about his book. He came with his wife of 40 and spent most of the afternoon talking about how publication was contingent on writing a sexy book. He left his recipe for stuffed duck. At Auburn, Madison Jones writes and wants to stop teaching, but so far none of his plans have worked. She gave him some geese to help him start a business that he hoped to build, but they all died. His books are good, but they receive little attention.

Works: "A Stroke of Good Fortune."

March 22, 1961 (p. 435; 4 par.): From ANDALUSIA. She has a cold, and so does her mother. She talks about the writing of plays. Her friend has committed to writing and producing plays, but although she is very bright, O'Connor does not think that she will break through. It is a tough business. She has been given a used portable television by the nuns in gratitude for helping to get their book published. Now she can tell Dawkins about all the commercial products like Geritol, Anacin, Bufferin, and so on. She and her mother do watch programs occasionally on the educational channel. She is watching four geese sit on their nests this spring.

Works: None.

July 17, 1961 (p. 444; 5 par.): From ANDALUSIA. She empathizes with Dawkins's writer's block. Caroline has told O'Connor that she has been writing too many essays and that this is affecting her fiction. *A Memoir of Mary Ann* is doing well. It will be a feature in *Good Housekeeping* and will receive $4,500. O'Connor's share is $1,125. She has decided not to write an introduction for *Wise Blood*. Has Dawkins read Forster's *Where Angels Fear to Tread*? Her favorite is *Passage to India*. They have sold their dairy cows and are moving into the beef business.

Works: ["Introduction" to *A Memoir of Mary Ann*].

January 10, 1962 (p. 459; 5 par.): From ANDALUSIA. She is concerned that Dawkins has been ill, and she had not heard from her for a while. Dawkins must have writer's stomach. Betty Hester has left the church, which leaves O'Connor sick. She is working on "The Lame Shall Enter First." Andrew Lytle of *SEWANEE REVIEW* has said that he will take it. She is supposed to give some lectures coming up as well. She is cheered up by hearing that Dawkins is writing again. There is always the temptation to write essays when one writes fiction. She wishes Dawkins would come to Andalusia. They have a goose that runs after cars and swans that go to the pond and return.

Works: ["The Lame Shall Enter First"].

January 26, 1962 (p. 463; 4 par.): From ANDALUSIA. She wrote to Granville Hicks about Dawkins's desire to go to YADDO. She recommends Haydn and Stegner to be Dawkins's sponsors. She met a man who says that Dawkins's father delivered him. Hester was a Catholic only five years. She talks about essays that are to be written about O'Connor for the *SEWANEE REVIEW* issue and mentions that maybe Dawkins might write one. Robert Fitzgerald may also do one as is Jack Hawkes. Hawkes has a theory that O'Connor's voice is that of the Devil in her fiction. He may like her latest story in that regard, which she has just sent him.

Works: ["The Lame Shall Enter First"].

March 4, 1962 (p. 467; 3 par.): From ANDALUSIA. She thinks Dawkins will enjoy YADDO. She discusses Granville Hicks, Iris Murdoch, her French translator, Maurice Coindreau, who did both *Wise Blood* and *The Violent Bear It Away*. The German translation of her stories is doing well, but a German friend of hers found it an odd experience to read about General Tennessee Flintrock in German. She has a strange feeling that she is a different person in a language other than English.

Works: *Wise Blood*, *The Violent Bear It Away*, ["A Late Encounter With the Enemy"].

April 25, 1962 (p. 471; 6 par.): From ANDALUSIA. She asks Dawkins's opinion on the introduction to *Wise Blood*. Her editor says that she has to do it so that they can put a new copyright date on it. The Hickses were asking about Dawkins when they visited, and she hopes that Dawkins and they will get to spend some time together at YADDO. She met EUDORA WELTY at the Southern Literary Festival and found her to have no airs; she was a pleasant woman. She tells a story of Welty contacting WILLIAM FAULKNER. She also went to North Carolina State and will go to Rosary College in Chicago, Notre Dame, and then Emory. She makes these appearances for the money, not because she enjoys them, and when she is done, she will stay home and write a lot of fiction. Many eggs are hatching, and she is hoping for baby swans.

Works: *Wise Blood*.

July 19, 1962 (p. 483; 6 par.):   From ANDALUSIA. Dawkins's account of YADDO brings back familiar memories, even the studio squirrel. She does not know why writers cannot write in their rooms and must have studios. Mrs. Ames apparently lost the dispute over getting a swimming pool, though she rarely loses. She sends her regards to staff members Jim and Nellie Shannon. Her one-eyed swan died. She is enjoying writing what may turn out to be a short novel. In the fall, she will be speaking at East Texas State College. She has not been to Texas before. She hopes that Dawkins is writing and tells her not to let all the time she has at YADDO frighten her.

Works: None.

August 1, 1962 (p. 485; 5 par.):   From ANDALUSIA. She is glad that Dawkins has been to Schenectady. She talks about when she was at YADDO and describes where she worked; one location may be the same room that Dawkins is in now. She asks if Dawkins went to see Elizabeth McKee. She comments about Betty Hester's finding Dawkins's work conservative.

Works: None.

September 6, 1962 (p. 490; 5 par.):   From ANDALUSIA. She is glad that Dawkins is going to stay at YADDO. The scenery is beautiful in the autumn and the winter, and most of the strange characters from the summer have gone back to school. She agrees that "The Lame Shall Enter First" is not working, but she does not see where Dawkins gets the notion that Sheppard is a symbol of Freud. Freud did not occur to her while writing the story, and it is hard to place him in a reading of it now. She thinks the story does not work because she does not feel for Sheppard as she does for most of her characters. She tells Dawkins that her theorizing might get in the way of her writing—she ought not to mix thoughts and feelings.

Elizabeth McKee was pleased with her meeting with Dawkins. She is glad the book is going to be published. A review of *Wise Blood* in the Chicago *Sun* also mentions it in relation to Nabokov's *Lolita*, so Freud follows her there, too. Dawkins likely

hears about Freud at Yaddo; she has an article that she will send about him and St. Thomas. Jung is more dangerous, she thinks, to religion. Worms are eating her mother's flowers.

Works: ["The Lame Shall Enter First"], *Wise Blood.*

September 20, 1962 (p. 493; 4 par.):   From ANDALUSIA. She is willing to be a reference for Dawkins for any purpose at any time. Dawkins need not ask each time. She recommends that Dawkins live in a small southern town rather than New York City, not to write a certain way but more to be in touch with people outside of her head. The weather has been pleasant.

Works: None.

November 24, 1962 (p. 501; 4 par.):   From ANDALUSIA. She sends a copy of her recommendation letter for the Guggenheim. Betty Hester wants to send something to Dawkins about Iris Murdoch. Hester is filled with ideas lately, mostly about the differences between men and women. She does not follow her.

Obolensky has never been her publisher. She discusses various publishers and editors. She is back from Texas and Louisiana. New Orleans is a city she can stand; it is Catholic and southern, and the people have an awareness of the devil. She met WALKER PERCY. She likes his book *The Moviegoer* and has corresponded with him for a couple of years. Has Dawkins read it? She is fooling around with something that she does not yet know whether it will be a story or a novel or nothing at all.

Works: None.

January 13, 1963 (p. 504; 2 par.):   From ANDALUSIA. She is pleased that Dawkins was able to earn $,1000 for her story in *Redbook*. The magazine must be becoming more literary like ESQUIRE. She is letting ["Why Do the Heathen Rage?"] cool down for a bit while she works on an introduction to her reading of "A Good Man" for the University of Georgia. She may also read at Troy State. One of the students there wrote to her saying that she could not understand her work that she was too stupid and was seeking enlightenment of what she was expected to get out of it. O'Connor had written back that she does not expect anything enlightening to come of the stories for readers. She just hopes that she might enjoy them and not overanalyze them as if they were algebra.

Works: ["Why Do the Heathen Rage?"], "A Good Man Is Hard to Find."

September 16, 1963 (p. 539; 3 par.): From ANDALUSIA. She is pleased with the paper that the letter is on; she purchased 500 sheets of it for 99¢. She is glad to hear that Dawkins will have a story in *Best Stories*. She has been writing fiction all summer but has now stopped in order to revise a talk that she will give at Notre Dame in Maryland and at Georgetown University. She will also spend three days at Hollins College on this trip. She is having ups and downs with finances and the IRS.

She likes Updike's *The Poorhouse Fair* but dislikes the sensitivity in *Rabbit Run* and his other work. She will read *Catch-22* when she finds it in paperback. She is currently reading *Eichmann in Jerusalem* and admires its author [Hannah Arendt] very much.

Works: None.

November 5, 1963 (p. 546; 4 par.): From ANDALUSIA. She is willing to allow Dawkins to try working with her stories. She writes about reservations in her using "The Enduring Chill" because she is not yet sure if it may work into a novel. She is now working on another story ["Revelation"] that she likes. Her mother has her stories stored somewhere where neither of them knows where they are, but Dawkins can find "Greenleaf" in *Southern Stories*. She asks about her using the girl in "Good Country People."

She likes how Dawkins's book looks. She wonders whether she might want to dramatize *Wise Blood*.

Works: "The Enduring Chill," ["Revelation"], "Good Country People," "Greenleaf," *Wise Blood*.

November 8, 1963 (p. 546; 4 par.): From ANDALUSIA. She discusses where she thinks she may be going with "Why Do the Heathen Rage?" and "The Enduring Chill." The main objective she would have in allowing Dawkins to adapt her stories for the stage would be in what money she might receive for it. She has no qualms about Dawkins working with her material and would only object to a Yankee director deciding to make a hero out of one of the "colored" idiots in her story.

Works: "Why Do the Heathen Rage?", "Enduring Chill."

December 1, 1963 (p. 551; 1 par.): From ANDALUSIA. She asks how Dawkins is doing and tells her that she recently purchased *Idiots First* by Bernard Malamud but was dissatisfied with it. She plans to go back to just reading books that are sent to her for free.

Works: None.

December 10, 1963 (p. 552; 4 par.): From ANDALUSIA. She sends Dawkins some nuts. McKee has not told her about film options for her stories, and they have been in print a long time. She thinks Dawkins will be safe using them. Reviews are the worst aspect of the writing business. KATHERINE ANNE PORTER sent her a review from France where *A Good Man* was reviewed alongside MARY MCCARTHY's *The Group*. She wishes her a good Christmas and offers to look at the play with Dawkins if she might come by when it is finished.

Works: A Good Man Is Hard to Find.

May 19, 1964 (p. 578; 4 par.): From ANDALUSIA. She will be glad to get *Catch-22* from Dawkins and will give it a try. She has been in the hospital but is home now. She found Mrs. Turpin from "Revelation" in her doctor's office; she found Mary Grace in her own mind. She has relatives at the house helping her mother. She asks whether Dawkins is working on the play. She will use "Enduring Chill" in her collection. She has suggested to Elizabeth McKee that they use the already published versions of other stories for the new collection since her energy level is so low. *Works*: "Revelation," "The Enduring Chill."

June 24, 1964 (p. 586; 3 par.): From MILLEDGE-VILLE. She has just returned home from being in Piedmont Hospital for a month. She has no insurance and favors Medicare. She has not yet finished *Catch-22*, though she has liked it thus far. She will finish work on her collection before she begins the Grace Paley book. She is thinking about whether or not to include "You Can't Be Poorer Than Dead." She has had four blood transfusions in the last four weeks. If she can get to her typewriter, she has enough blood. She is told that she will improve, but she expects the unexpected. *Works*: "You Can't Be Any Poorer Than Dead."

PAUL ENGLE (one letter) As important as the director of creative writing at the UNIVERSITY OF IOWA was to O'Connor's early work, there is only one letter to him as part of the collection. *Page:* HB: 13.

Letter

April 7, 1949 (p. 13; 11 par.): From MILLEDGE-VILLE. FOC writes that she left YADDO on March 1 and is moving to New York City, where she will live in a room and work until her money runs out. She writes of her discomfort over the 108-page sample from her novel that Rinehart has gone over. She believes that they want a "conventional" novel, not what she is writing. She has told Selby that she is willing to hear criticism on the novel, but she is not willing to write it to Rinehart's specifications. If their advice does not fit, she will ignore it. She cannot send a plot summary to them as they requested because she does not work that way, and Rinehart will not send more money without the plot summary because they have not been able to see what her plans are. They are at an impasse.

If Rinehart will not send her money based on what she has already sent them, then she would prefer to find another publisher. Others are already interested, based on the first two chapters that have been published. She hopes that one day she will not need to rewrite so much, but for now she must have all the time the work requires. She works all the time, but she works slowly. She did not receive a Guggenheim, and she asks Engle to tell Robie Macauley to write to her if he sees him. *Works*: [*Wise Blood*].

ELIZABETH FENWICK (WAY) (12 letters) Fenwick (Way) was a writer that O'Connor met at YADDO. They became friends, and Fenwick-Way helped O'Connor after Yaddo by helping her locate somewhere to live near her in New York City right after leaving there in 1949. O'Connor became aware that Fenwick-Way had been diagnosed with lupus and told this to Sally Fitzgerald in Europe in 1958. The two women met again at the Fitzgeralds in Ridgefield, Connecticut, that same year. Fenwick-Way's case of lupus, if it was indeed that disease, was of a less severe type than O'Connor's. However, O'Connor was always concerned about her friend's health and treatments. She feared that Fenwick-Way may not realize how serious a condition lupus is. *Pages:* HB: 67, 153, 162, 174, 181, 217, 233, 375, 378, 388, 396, 440.

Letters

February 12, 1954 (p. 67; 3 par.): From ANDA-LUSIA. She is not sure where to send her letter, and she forgets that people live in the North in winter. Giroux told her that they are not publishing Fenwick-Way's book, which upset him. She enjoys revising her work more than drafting it. She gives some advice about revision, including a tip she picked up in art class about rearranging it in reverse.

She has a limp that she has been notified comes from rheumatism, not LUPUS. It bothers her that she has been able to withstand lupus for four years and now has this new problem of rheumatism that is affecting her hips. She uses a cane, and her gait makes her appear drunk much of the time. She has not developed the characteristic rash of lupus in the butterfly shape. Her peachicken is a cock, which means if he survives that he will have a large tail span of four feet. He has eaten two smoking cigarettes out of people's hands.

Works: [*A Good Man Is Hard to Find and Other Stories*].

April, 1956 (p. 153; 3 par.): From ANDALUSIA. She thinks that the letter from Dr. Merrill sounds good. After her appointment with him in ATLANTA, Fenwick-Way could come visit her in MILLEDGEVILLE. Emotional times will aggravate her symptoms, but time is the only way out of them; having the right medicine helps, too. Let her know if she can do anything.

Works: None.

June 8, 1956 (p. 162; 5 par.): From ANDALUSIA. She likes each of Fenwick-Way's books better than the one before it. She has received her latest and liked it. Books are either dead or alive to her, and this one lives. She sees why Catherine Carver liked it so well. She likes the book jacket design as well.

She urges Fenwick-Way to see Dr. Merrill as soon as possible. She saw him the previous week and heard about a new treatment for LUPUS. She is doing fine right now, but they may try it on her later. Her mother is now reading Fenwick-Way's new book since she appreciated its jacket.

Works: None.

September 13, 1956 (p. 174; 4 par.): From ANDALUSIA. She has been wondering how Fenwick-Way is doing with her LUPUS. Her cousin has bad arthritis, and after visiting her, she feels better about her own situation. Margaret Marshall and Denver Lindley both wrote that they liked Fenwick-Way's book. Her money situation has improved because she just sold the television rights for "The Life You Save" to Revue Productions. Even with the 10 percent cuts for Harcourt and her agent, she has still made a good amount. She has purchased a new refrigerator with some of the money. The appliance does all kinds of tricks. If Fenwick-Way ever does visit Dr. Merrill, she should come to MILLEDGEVILLE for a visit.

Works: "The Life You Save May Be Your Own."

November 24, 1956 (p. 181; 3 par.): From ANDALUSIA. If Fenwick-Way can write a book in six weeks with LUPUS, she wonders why lupus has not been that good to her. The nervous breakdown changes her mind. She asks Fenwick Way

to have Harcourt send her a copy. She wants to be working on her novel, but she seems to keep writing shorter things such as lectures, essays, and stories. She has upcoming publications of stories. She needs to do the lectures since they help support her flock of 25 peachickens. She is going to write the president about the increasing cost of feed. She hopes that Fenwick-Way will visit her, as it is not so easy for her to travel.

Works: ["Greenleaf"], ["A View of the Woods"].

May 2, 1957 (p. 217; 3 par.): From ANDALUSIA. She and her mother felt bad when they received the telegram saying that Fenwick-Way was not coming after all. They had made preparations for her visit. She wants to know when the lupus rash goes away. She does not go outdoors herself without her hat. She had a good trip to Notre Dame and saw Robert Fitzgerald, who was helpful with the arrangements. Trips make her come back home and get back to work with renewed energy. There was a mix-up of turkey and goose eggs that has taken care of itself since "nature is red in tooth & claw" (217).

Works: None.

August 4, 1957 (p. 233; 4 par.): From ANDALUSIA. Congratulations on *Poor Harriet*! Both she and her mother enjoyed Fenwick-Way's new novel, and Way is fortunate to keep having such attractive book jackets. Her character of the woman with the ax was memorable for her; hers are the only mysteries that she reads. She sympathizes about renters since her father worked in real estate and her mother owns apartment houses. This house is the first that she has owned.

She hopes that Fenwick-Way feels better. The sun is not good for LUPUS patients. She is currently taking Hydeltra. It is hot right now, but it is probably worse in New York. Her mother wonders how Fenwick-Way calculated out her plot.

Works: None.

February 14, 1960 (p. 375; 3 par.): From ANDALUSIA. She would like the review period to be over and to be fully engrossed in her next novel.

The voice that Fenwick-Way senses in the novel is that of the Devil. "His idiom appleas to me . . ." (375). She completed the novel coolly, not with high emotion, and quickly thereafter wrote a short story that will be in THE KENYON REVIEW that summer or so.

Works: [*The Violent Bear It Away*].

March 3, 1960 (p. 378; 4 par.):   From ANDALUSIA. She discusses reviews from *Time, The Saturday Review, The Atlantic Monthly,* and *The New Yorker.* She has learned to drive and has her license, though she drives very little, afraid that she will kill someone. Fenwick-Way needs to hire someone to drive her down to visit. She thinks that Fenwick-Way would like William Golding's *Lord of the Flies,* which she is now reading. She is pleased that Fenwick-Way enjoys the evangelical child in the novel; the reviewers have ignored her.

Works: [*The Violent Bear It Away*].

April 13, 1960 (p. 388; 3 par.):   From ANDALUSIA. She appreciates the review from *The New Yorker* and the Japanese book. The review is typical. She has a rash and is also having trouble with a finger. She asks Fenwick-Way if the sensation in her fingers when she had trouble there was the same. She hopes that Fenwick-Way will see Dr. Sofer at Mt. Sinai for her lupus as she has heard that he is the expert on the disease.

Works: [*The Violent Bear It Away*].

May 22, 1960 (p. 396; 3 par.):   From ANDALUSIA. She appreciates the clipping and is not afraid to see bad ones. She does not scare too quickly. Her doctors tell her that her LUPUS is affecting the blood vessels near the top of her thigh bones. She agrees with Fenwick-Way that aspirin helps many things. She took eight aspirin a day for a month when she had problems with her jaw, and the problem and the pain went away. She heard from a woman that Dr. Sofer claims that lupus sometimes goes into remission for as much as 10 years. She may try to go see him.

Works: None.

May 17, 1961 (p. 440; 4 par.):   From ANDALUSIA. She appreciates the invitation from Fenwick-Way, but she is now doing well. She may go up to Dr. Sprung in Providence, Rhode Island, for a consultation sometime. The last six months, she has felt the best yet. She is taking Aralen for her skin rashes. She continues to discuss her disease and its various treatments with drugs. She has had cortisone and Novocaine shots in each of her hips, which helped at the time but did not last. She hopes that Harper will accept Fenwick-Way's book.

Works: None.

SALLY & ROBERT FITZGERALD (65 letters)
The Fitzgeralds were friends of O'Connor after she left Yaddo and moved to New York City for a brief period. She was introduced to the couple by ROBERT LOWELL in February 1949. The threesome became close friends quickly, and O'Connor was eventually invited to move to the Fitzgerald home at Ridgefield, Connecticut, and take a small garage apartment. In return for a space in which to live and work, she helped watch the growing Fitzgerald family. When illness struck and she was forced to move back to MILLEDGEVILLE, she maintained an active correspondence with the Fitzgeralds for the rest of her life. *Pages:* HB: 4, 14, 16, 21, 23, 26–28, 30–31, 33–35, 37–43, 46–48, 49–50, 54–66, 68, 70–72, 74, 76, 79–80, 85–86, 96, 108, 111, 122–123, 127, 130, 132–133, 135, 159, 161, 169, 185–186, 192, 196, 198, 207, 210, 216–218, 232, 243–244, 250, 256–257, 266–269, 272–274, 276–277, 281–282, 285, 288, 311, 317–319, 323, 327–329, 336, 338, 342–343, 345, 354–355, 379, 459, 464, 473, 503–505, 510–511, 518–519, 526, 529–530, 536, 550, 560–561, 568.

Letters

September 20, 1951 (p. 26; 6 par.):   From MILLEDGEVILLE. She assumes that the school year has begun and makes comments about the next baby probably being a girl. She and her mother are at the farm and will likely be there all winter. She continues working on the ending of her novel. She has not read far in ROBERT LOWELL's book.

She has 21 brown ducks with blue stripes on their wings that walk single file.

Works: [*Wise Blood*].

Mid-September, 1951 (p. 27; 6 par.): From MILLEDGEVILLE. She sends the novel that has been returned by the typist. She wonders whether Giroux or Caroline Gordon Tate would go over it again. Her mother sends a pickle recipe and invites the Fitzgeralds, including all their children, to the farm. The dairyman calls all cows *he*.

Works: *Wise Blood*.

[Mid-September, 1951] (p. 27; 6 par.): From MILLEDGEVILLE. She read *The Catcher in the Rye* in one day and liked it. She appreciates their sending the manuscript to Caroline. There is much discussion in Georgia about the separation of church and state. She asks where JACQUES MARITAIN may be teaching. Her mother is glad that they enjoyed the cake. O'Connor now has five geese and turkeys.

Works: None.

[Christmas, 1951] (p. 30; 3 par.): From MILL-EDGEVILLE. She wishes them all a noisy Christmas. Regina is preparing for a refugee family, including making curtains for their house out of sacks of chicken feed. She says that if she is able to return, she will eat the two weeks' rent that they would send her for the time that she was not there, so not to send back any rent money.

Works: None.

Thursday [Early 1952] (p. 31; 5 par.): From MILLEDGEVILLE. She enjoys the Reformation in England. The refugees have not yet arrived. She has been asked by the Macauleys to the Arts Forum in Greensboro where KATHERINE ANNE PORTER will be. Harcourt wanted O'Connor's picture taken, and none of them turned out well. They enjoyed the Fitzgeralds' Christmas card.

Works: [*Wise Blood*].

[April, 1952] (p. 33; 6 par.): From ANDALUSIA. She appreciates the Ford book information. She wonders whether they have seen her novel; she has only seen a copy owned by a woman who sells books. She does not like her picture on the back. Regina asks about FRANZ KAFKA and Waugh, mispronouncing the latter's name. She now has 11 baby geese.

Works: [*Wise Blood*].

Tuesday [July, 1952] (p. 38; 4 par.): From ANDALUSIA. To Sally. She hopes that she is doing better. Loretta has been handed over to the welfare woman. Dr. Merrill thinks that she caught a viral infection in the North. Her mother thought that she had gained weight.

Works: None.

Tuesday (July, 1952] (p. 38; 5 par.): From ANDALUSIA. To Robert. She did not want to leave Sally while she was ill, but she does think that she helped by taking away Loretta. E. H. came over to help when O'Connor told her about Sally's condition. She tells him that Sally was thinking of calling her mother. O'Connor went to her doctor in Atlanta who told her that she probably caught a viral infection that aggravated her LUPUS. She is glad that she knows that she has lupus. Keep her informed about Sally. Rosenfeld's review of *Wise Blood* in the *New Republic* was unfavorable.

Works: *Wise Blood*.

Sunday [Summer, 1952] (p. 39; 5 par.): From ANDALUSIA. She sends greetings from her bed to Sally's. She asks Sally and Robert to read and comment on an enclosed document. She will send the $2.85 that she owes when she is up and around. She has not read Simone Weil but has heard about her.

Works: None.

[Summer, 1952] (p. 40; 2 par.): From ANDA-LUSIA. To Sally. She likes the suggestion of J. F. Powers reviewing her novel. Dr. Merrill diagnosed her illness as lupus over the phone before he examined her.

Works: None.

Thursday [Summer, 1952] (p. 41; 5 par.): From ANDALUSIA. She is upset to learn that they have had highs and lows. She tells them to ignore her suitcases for now and send them when it is a better time for them. They would enjoy their new employees; she plans to write about them one day.

Works: None.

Tuesday (Summer, 1952) (p. 41; 5 par.): From ANDALUSIA. She is hoping that the vacation has helped things. She has had two blood transfusions. She would be grateful now for them to send her two suitcases with her belongings. She asks that they also send her a copy of *Art and Scholasticism.*

Works: None.

Thursday [Summer, 1952] (p. 42; 4 par.): From ANDALUSIA. The suitcases and book all arrived safely. She hopes that Sally is better since she is feeling better now. She hopes that they will send Powers's review of her book when and if it comes out. The locals are talking about Eisenhower and Stevenson. She is working on a new story ["A Late Encounter With the Enemy"].

Works: ["A Late Encounter With the Enemy"].

Tuesday [Late summer, 1952] (p. 43; 2 par.): From ANDALUSIA. She appreciates the Bible which arrived just in time for Bible Week at the local churches. She is feeling better and is working. She has ordered two peafowl and four peachicks from Florida.

Works: None.

The Sabbath [1952] (p. 46; 4 par.): From ANDALUSIA. To Sally. She has just completed reading Sally's review of Conrad Aiken's *Ushant* and thinks that she got it right. She does not know how Sally finished the book. She appreciates the camera and the coat and sends her the postage. Regina is making Sally a fruitcake. John Crowe Ransom asked her whether she might apply for the KENYON REVIEW fiction fellowship. She told her that Robert and Peter Taylor recommended her to him. She has heard that the ROBERT LOWELLS are in Rome.

Works: None.

Tuesday [November, 1952] (p. 47; 3 par.): From ANDALUSIA. She sends "The Life You Save May Be Your Own" for comments. She needs another transfusion, but she works every day. She sends Robie Macauley's novel since she had two copies. She and her mother are about to go vote and cancel each other's votes out.

Works: ["The Life You Save May Be Your Own"].

Thursday [Fall, 1952] (p. 47; 6 par.): From ANDALUSIA. She appreciates both letters and has used the comments to revise the story ["The Life You Save . . ."]. She sent that story for the fellowship along with the first chapter of her new novel [*The Violent Bear It Away*]. She hopes that the cake arrived before Thanksgiving. The second one was for Maria to eat in her room with her beer. They are pleased to hear of a fifth child on the way. She agrees with her about Macauley's book. Regina is chasing mules. The new farmwife was telling them about their preacher who invites biblical figures onto the platform to sit in a chair and testify. Then he sings as though he is them. The congregation is spellbound.

Works: ["The Life You Save May Be Your Own"], [*The Violent Bear It Away*].

December 20, 1952 (p. 49; 5 par.): From ANDALUSIA. She wishes them Merry Christmas and tells the Fitzgeralds that she received the Kenyon Fellowship. She intends to use the money for books, blood, and ACTH. The new and former farmwives met each other in town and did not seem to get along too well. Mr. Ransom tells her that he will take either "The River" or "The Life You Save May Be Your Own" for THE KENYON REVIEW.

Works: "The River," "The Life You Save May Be Your Own."

Monday [December 30, 1952] (p. 50; 4 par.): From ANDALUSIA. She received a card notifying her that the Fitzgeralds have given her a one-year subscription to KENYON REVIEW. Now she can see her Mr. Shiftlet in it. She has heard from Caroline and people in Iowa City that the ROBERT LOWELLS will take Paul Engle's place for a year. She, her mother, and the farmwife have had various ailments. She sends an article about a Florida pastor evangelizing on horseback.

Works: None.

January 25, 1953 (p. 54; 3 par.): From MILL-EDGEVILLE. Her first issue of KENYON REVIEW arrived. The journal also sent her a check for $1,000 with no note attached. Her uncle tells her about people's reactions to *Wise Blood*. The most recent one asked why she could not write about "nice people." Regina is working out a new farm family to come work for them. FOC is willing to visit Notre Dame again next year. With ACTH, she seems all right if she stays out of the sun and does not exercise.

Works: Wise Blood.

February 1, 1953 (p. 55; 5 par.): From ANDA-LUSIA. She likes Maple Oats and the O'Faoláin book; in fact, she likes everything O'Faoláin writes. She sends a poem, "The PEACOCK Roosts." She does not think poetry is a good thing for fiction writers to do. She and her mother discuss *Moby-Dick* in an elemental way. She mentions HEMING-WAY's *The Old Man and the Sea* and how she likes how the fish's eye looked like a saint. Her character is a 14-year-old named Rufus Florida Johnson.

Works: [*The Violent Bear It Away*].

May 7, 1953 (p. 57; 5 par.): From ANDALUSIA. She likes Robert's poem. A Harcourt, Brace textbook salesman came by. She wonders what they will name baby #5. She has heard of an essay by Malcom Cowley in HARPER's that discusses the state of the novel. She hopes she will see them soon.

Works: None.

June 7, 1953 (p. 58; 5 par.): From ANDALUSIA. She asks whether baby #5 is yet around. She and her mother pray for them. The Cheneys have visited. She has sold "A Good Man Is Hard to Find" to PARTISAN REVIEW Reader and is reading M. Gabriel Marcel. She enjoyed Sally's review in *Commonweal*.

Works: "A Good Man Is Hard to Find."

[Summer, 1953] (p. 59; 5 par.): From ANDA-LUSIA. She appreciates and enjoyed the Shakespeare poem that they sent. Her mother asked her if Shakespeare were Irish. Regina is getting ready to build a pond. She received an article from the Tates from the *New Republic* about literature and orthodoxy. She received a letter from Cal (ROBERT LOWELL) that he is now 36 and feeling statesmanlike at Iowa. She sold "The River" to SEWANEE REVIEW. She is painting again; she paints with a palette knife to avoid washing brushes.

Works: ["The River"].

Friday [1953] (p. 60; 5 par.): From ANDALUSIA. She sends a PEACOCK feather and a story, "A Good Man Is Hard to Find." She seeks comments on the story. Brainard Cheney sent a letter. She asks when the Fitzgeralds will go to Siena. She has painted a self-portrait with a pheasant cock. Regina's pond is completed. She enjoyed the Powers story, "The Devil Was the Joker" in *The New Yorker*, which she appreciates their sending since she does not subscribe.

Works: ["A Good Man Is Hard to Find"].

Friday [Summer, 1953] (p. 61; 5 par.): From ANDALUSIA. To Sally. She sends greetings to her and Barnaby, the new baby, and makes comments about the name. She sends an edition of *Wise Blood*, the cover of which she finds amusing. The doctor in ATLANTA is pleased with her progress. The farmwife is expecting ladies from church tomorrow for a meeting where she will do the lesson. She says that Doubleday must find publishing Homer profitable since Robert will do another translation, the *Odyssey*.

Works: Wise Blood.

[August, 1953] (p. 62; 3 par.): From ANDA-LUSIA. It may be problematic for them, but the only plane that she can get comes in to Newark. She flew to Nashville the weekend before and saw the Cheneys and Ashley Brown. Regina anticipates a new family who will work on the farm.

Works: None.

Tues. [September, 1953] (p. 62; 2 par.): From ANDALUSIA. She sends a blouse to Sally since they will not be in a house for her to send something for that. If Sally could use any hardware for the place in Italy, she should let her know. It seems her friends are all leaving the country— she got a letter from Ashley Brown in Dublin and Caroline in Paris.

Works: None.

November 11, 1953 (p. 64; 5 par.): From ANDALUSIA. Her mother is going to send them a fruitcake, but it takes a while to prepare and make it. She received their address in Italy from Caroline. She has sent Caroline several stories. She has seven stories and two less than good ones collected so far. The only American events that have happened since they left are that Regina has a new silage cutter and that the farmwife has new teeth. Her mother has tried to keep their employee, Shot, from borrowing money from Louis Cline.

Works: None.

January 4, 1954 (p. 65; 5 par.): From ANDALUSIA. They are upset that the fruitcake is not yet there. They sent it before Thanksgiving. She has received another year on her Kenyon Fellowship. A reader has written and asked what happened to the character in the ape costume in *Wise Blood*; he also wants an autographed photograph of her. She might think about coming for a visit in the spring. She is pleased that the *Odyssey* translation is going well.

Works: Wise Blood.

March 5, 1954 (p. 70; 4 par.): From ANDALUSIA. She will send some cake mixes for Sally. She will also mail a copy of "A Temple of the Holy Ghost," which is coming out in HARPER'S BAZAAR. Her ninth-grade cousin wrote a book review on *Wise Blood* because she knew Sister would not read it. She wonders if Cal, ROBERT LOWELL, is in Iowa or Cincinnati.

Works: ["A Temple of the Holy Ghost"], *Wise Blood*.

April 26, 1954 (p. 71; 3 par): From ANDALUSIA. The farmwife's daughter will be married on the fourth of July; she is 17. ROBERT LOWELL will not come back to the Catholic religion, which hurts her. She sends a picture of her self-portrait.

Works: None.

December 26, 1954 (p. 74; 7 par.): From ANDALUSIA. They feel bad that they did not see them, but the Fitzgeralds did well to get home. She and Regina are praying for Sally's father and had a MASS said. She has sent in the manuscript for her story collection. She is going to Greensboro in March to speak on a panel. Randall Jarrell will be there. Giroux explained ROBERT LOWELL's adventure in Cincinnati to her at lunch in ATLANTA. She won second prize for the O. HENRY AWARD this year; Jean Stafford won first, and Paul Engle was the judge. She is now walking with a cane. She is reading Romano Guardini and especially liked his *The Lord*.

Works: [A Good Man Is Hard to Find].

April 1, 1955 (p. 76; 5 par.): From ANDALUSIA. O'Connor and Regina ask if child #6 has yet arrived and what the name may be. She is ready to help with names if they would like. She met Randall Jarrell and Peter Taylor in Greensboro and was surprised by Jarrell's kindness. Her mother is receiving a three-ton truck as an Easter gift. She expects that Giroux will send them her book; it now contains a 10th story, "Good Country People." She recalls the ending of a poem that she heard in North Carolina about stacking stiffs like a cord of wood. She uses the cane less and walks fine.

Works: "Good Country People."

May 8, 1955 (p. 79; 4 par.): From ANDALUSIA. They are delighted to hear of Caterina Fitzgerald's birth; this makes three boys and three girls. She was honored by the Macon Writers Club at a breakfast where she spoke for 25 minutes. She will also speak soon to the Book Review Group of the Macon Women's Club. Harcourt should send them her book soon. Giroux is now with Farrar, Straus.

Works: None.

June 10, 1955 (p. 85; 6 par.): From ANDALUSIA. She agrees that "A Stroke of Good Fortune" is not one of the best stories in the collection; she is glad they got the book. She has returned from a week in New York where she gave an interview about the television version of "The Life You Save." The collection is receiving more notice than *Wise Blood*. Harcourt, Brace has an eager atmosphere. She stayed the weekend with Caroline Gordon Tate and Sue Jenkins. She also saw Malcolm Cowley and Van Wyke Brooks. She read "A Good Man," and Brooks told Jenkins that it was too bad that O'Connor saw life as a horror story. Cowley asked her if she had a wooden leg. She will apply for a Guggenheim.

Works: "A Stroke of Good Fortune," "The Life You Save May Be Your Own," *Wise Blood*, "A Good Man Is Hard to Find."

August 25, [1955] (p. 96; 3 par.): From ANDALUSIA. She is grateful that the summer is nearly over. Some of their farm help left at midseason. She is now taking Meticorten. The book is in a third printing.

Works: None.

September 30, 1955 (p. 108; 4 par.): From ANDALUSIA. She would come to Italy now except that she has just started using crutches. Apparently, this problem is new, not related to the LUPUS. The British edition of *Wise Blood* has come out and is earning reviews that are favorable but not insightful.

Works: *Wise Blood*.

December 12, 1955 (p. 122; 4 par.): From ANDALUSIA. She is pleased to read Robert's translation of the *Odyssey* and glad to own it. She wonders if they have seen the Cheneys lately. She must stay in the States due to her crutches. The French publisher, Gallimard, has purchased

Wise Blood. She now has 16 peachickens. Regina sends Christmas greetings.

Works: *Wise Blood*.

January 22, 1956 (p. 132; 6 par.): From ANDALUSIA. She sends Robert's article on Ezra Pound. She is reading "Theology and the Imagination" by Fr. William Lynch. She has been labeled a Catholic writer by Catholics and invited to a book fair in Rhode Island. She cannot go because of her crutches. A Jesuit drove up the other day and in a white Packard to tell her he liked *A Good Man*. Caroline's friend Maurice Coindreau is going to translate *Wise Blood* into French for Gallimard. She likes Caroline's novel.

Works: *A Good Man Is Hard to Find and Other Stories*; *Wise Blood*.

February 6, 1956 (p. 135; 3 par.): From ANDALUSIA. Ten days after the visit from the Macon Jesuit, she has been asked by Harold C. Gardiner, S. J. to contribute to *America*. Caroline had dedicated her book to Dorothy Day, but when Day did not like the book, the dedication was withdrawn. Now it turns out Day likes the book better.

Works: None.

December 10, 1956 (p. 185; 4 par.): From ANDALUSIA. They are pleased to hear from them and see the picture of the Fitzgerald family. She sends "A View of the Woods," which will appear in *PARTISAN REVIEW*; however, she welcomes their comments. Gene Kelly is rumored to be playing Mr. Shiftlet in the televised version of her story; it will be his TV debut. She is still on crutches.

Works: ["A View of the Woods"].

January 1, 195[7] (p. 192; 5 par.): From ANDALUSIA. She likes the long sweater and expects that she will wear it in their house, which is not insulated, all winter. She does not approve of the way Cardinal Spellman condemned TENNESSEE WILLIAMS's *Baby Doll* movie. She agrees that it is no good but disagrees with Spellman's methods. She was given $300 for winning the O. HENRY

AWARD this year. It was for a story in KENYON REVIEW. She has revised the ending of the story that she sent them over Christmas. Regina gave eyeglasses and a new shirt to a workman on the farm, but he did not seem to appreciate either.

Works: ["Greenleaf"], ["A View of the Woods"].

August 1, 1957 (p. 232; 5 par.): From ANDALUSIA. She got their address from Tom Stritch, who is not sure this one is correct. She asks about their health. Fr. Gardiner, S. J. called her and asked if she were angry with him. He asked her to do a piece on Catholic literature for a radio show. He apologized for changing the paragraph in the article in *America*. The doctor ("Scientist") tells her that her need for the crutches is not related to lupus and she may be rid of them in two to three years. Lynch is interviewing in New York; she preferred Notre Dame. She now has 27 peachickens, some of which her mother wants gone.

Works: None.

December 1, 1957 (p. 256; 4 par.): From ANDALUSIA. She and Regina sent them a fruitcake on Friday. The postman said it would take almost three weeks to get there. The European trip for the following spring is on. Her mother came home with a story the other day that ashes from cremated people are being sent to cannibals to make Instant People. Their black worker, Jack, has had his teeth removed and is waiting for a new set. He wants "pearly white" teeth like a gun handle with gold ones scattered in between.

Works: None.

February 11, 1958 (p. 266; 6 par.): From ANDALUSIA. The doctor tells her she cannot go on the trip. He says now that the condition of her hips is related to the LUPUS. She received the *Odyssey*. The bit in her story about using newspapers to stay warm is no reflection on her stay with them in Connecticut. She received an invitation from YADDO to apply again, but she does not intend to do so. Caroline writes that

ROBERT LOWELL has had another spell. He sent one of his students from Georgia to see her, and O'Connor sent back a five-feet long PEACOCK feather to him.

Works: None.

February 26, 1958 (p. 268; 4 par.): From ANDALUSIA. The trip may be on again. Cousin Katy tells them to go and go off the tour schedule. A priest has asked her to write about her experience visiting LOURDES, but she is not sure that he has thought through his request carefully. Both she and Regina have just left the hospital, where they shared a room. There was a black orderly there named Ulysses. She appreciates their invitation to visit in May and stay, but she will be doing well to make the trip at all.

Works: None.

March 11, 1958 (p. 272; 5 par.): From ANDALUSIA. She is glad to hear that they can meet them on the trip. Cousin Katie is determined that Flannery get to LOURDES. She was going to ask Louis to get pocket knives for her to give the Fitzgerald children but wanted to check that they are not too young. Poet James Dickey visited her; he is fond of Robert. It is good to learn that it is not cold where they are. She looks forward to seeing the Matisse chapel and will do well to make it to Lourdes.

Works: None.

March 21, 1958 (p. 273; 3 par.): From ANDALUSIA. They will not bring the knives. They worked out more details about the trip. The Fitzgeralds can probably lodge in their room at LOURDES if they want to go. Allen Tate has been given a medal by the Catholics.

Works: None.

April 10, 1958 (p. 276; 3 par.): From ANDALUSIA. Billy is going to Greece and hoped to see the Fitzgeralds. She is looking for a publisher now that Denver Lindley has left Harcourt, Brace. She expects to see them in Milan on April 24.

Works: None.

May 11, 1958 (p. 281; 6 par.):   From ANDALUSIA. During her trip, she most enjoyed seeing them and the pope. She appreciates the time they spent together. They did not make it to Fatima since Regina had a cold, but it was all right because she does not experience an increase in devotion to Mary from her shrines. Father B. hopes that O'Connor will be kind when she writes about the sites they saw. All on the trip found the Fitzgeralds to be good companions on the pilgrimage. She sends more books by Gustave Weigel.

Works: None.

January 1, 1959 (p. 315; 3 par.):   From ANDA-LUSIA. She received the dress the day before and thanks them; there is nothing like it near where they live. Regina claims to be leaving the dairy business each day. She will be done with the first draft of the Tarwater novel in about 10 pages more. It feels good to be almost done with the draft, though she does not know if what she has written is good or bad.

Works: [*The Violent Bear It Away*].

February 15, 1959 (p. 318; 4 par.):   From ANDA-LUSIA. She hopes they received a lot of money from the Ford Foundation; she received $8,000. She has returned from Chicago where she led two workshops for $700. She has finished her novel. Cousin Katie bequeathed her her childhood home in SAVANNAH. She hopes to live on the Ford Foundation grant for 10 years.

Works: None.

March 24, 1959 (p. 323; 3 par.):   From ANDALUSIA. She sends a manuscript and appreciates their comments. She is treated differently now that news of the Ford grant has gotten about. She hopes they are dealing with the pressure of the grant as she feels it as well.

Works: *The Violent Bear It Away*.

April 20, 1959 (p. 329; 3 par.):   From ANDALUSIA. She appreciates the comments. The character of Rayber has been problematic in the writing. She sends mustard-seed necklaces to her god-child and Hugh Fitzgerald. They can destroy the manuscript they have; she has other copies and will be revising the entire thing.

Works: *The Violent Bear It Away*.

July 1, 1959 (p. 338; 2 par.):   From ANDALUSIA. She sends the middle of the novel again for their comments. Billy Sessions asked her whether they might read his play. She has read it and thought it had good qualities, but she knows little about plays.

Works: *The Violent Bear It Away*.

October 11, 1959 (p. 354; 4 par.):   From ANDA-LUSIA. She appreciates the picture of St. Paul. Regina hopes they have a refrigerator in their new home. The farm workers are back with them. Caroline and Ashley Brown are visiting next weekend. She has made corrections, including putting back "not his son," as they suggested. She looks forward to their comments.

Works: *The Violent Bear It Away*.

May 7, 1962 (p. 473; 3 par.):   From ANDALUSIA. They are glad to hear from them and that they own a home. She has just returned from Notre Dame; she will return north to receive a degree from St. Mary's College. She asks if they might comment on the preface for the second edition of *Wise Blood*. They are out of the dairy business, but separating the truth from the lies with the farm help continues.

Works: *Wise Blood*.

August 3, 1962 (p. 486; 3 par.):   From ANDALUSIA. To Robert. She appreciates his piece in the SEWANEE REVIEW. She would like to know what he thinks of Jack Hawkes's article; they have debated his Devil for many years. Regina is making another pond. Caroline is going to California to teach about Emily Dickinson, Stephen Crane, and Henry James for nine months and $15,000. She has been told that Caroline discovered a devilish strain in Dickinson.

Works: None.

January 1, 1963 (p. 503; 3 par.):   From ANDA-LUSIA. She appreciates the scarf and will wear it with the long sweater. They have had a few visitors lately who also know the Fitzgeralds, including Claudio Gorlier. She is planning to buy a car soon.

Works: None.

March 15, 1963 (p. 510; 4 par.):   From ANDALUSIA. She has just returned from the symposium on religion and art at Sweet Briar. James Johnson Sweeney asked about them. She congratulates Robert on the Bollingen Prize that she has heard he won. Powers won the National Book Award; WALKER PERCY won it the year before; she won the O. HENRY; and KATHERINE ANNE PORTER will likely win the Pulitzer. She is pleased that all of these authors are Catholics, especially since so many people say that Catholics do not contribute to the arts. She has read about a woman in Texas who is building a chapel shaped like John Glenn's space capsule.

Works: None.

May 16, 1963 (p. 519; 3 par.):   From ANDALUSIA. To Robert. She has written to Smith College to send him an invitation to the Harvard Club. She and Regina will be in Boston with relatives. Tom Stritch agrees with her about the boredom of these events. She has read *Zen-Catholicism* by Dom Aelred Graham.

Works: None.

November 23, 1963 (p. 550; 5 par.):   From ANDALUSIA. She hopes that their children are all at school. She tells Ben to come south and visit. She hopes to see them when she reads at Brown and Boston College. Regina sends greetings. Their farm help, Louise, threw water on Shot and almost put out an eye, which she admitted later to hoping that she might do. She sends an interview with Conrad Aiken, who is now frequently in SAVANNAH. Kennedy's death has stopped commercial programming on television to show the funeral. It will take the air out of southern politics that is so often based on anti-Kennedy rants.

Works: None.

January 8, 1964 (p. 561; 4 par.):   From ANDALUSIA. She appreciates the leather figure of the ape. A visiting baby almost ruined it, but it was saved. She was ill in bed during the holidays. Lyndon Johnson's administration is flamboyant with Texas hats and so forth. She hopes Robert and Benny will visit.

Works: None.

March 8, 1964 (p. 568; 3 par.):   From ANDALUSIA. To Robert. She invites him and Benny to visit at Easter. She just got out of the hospital after surgery. The surgery was proclaimed a success, even though it is unwise to perform it on LUPUS patients. It is a pretty time of year for them to visit. Regina joins her in inviting them.

Note: This is the last letter to the Fitzgeralds in HB.

Works: None.

SISTER MARIELLA GABLE (two letters)   Sister Gable taught English at Mariac College for nuns. An independent thinker within the religious ranks, Gable got into trouble when she taught J. D. Salinger's *Cather in the Rye* in a Catholic high school. *Pages:* HB: 516, 591.

Letters

May 4, 1963 (p. 516; 11 par.):   From ANDALUSIA. She appreciates Sister's letter. She thinks that the questions about fiction from Christian and Catholic critics do not defeat the two of them; it is the people who do. She speaks about Christianity and fiction and how certain readers want the faith to always look positive in stories. This is not being true to what the writer sees. "The writer has to make the corruption believable before he can write more easily about Protestant believers than Catholics because they have outward expressions that are easier to dramatize" (HB 516).

In the gospel, the devils always recognize Christ first. She is working on stories and may have enough now for a new collection, but she is waiting and seeing. She needs Sister's prayers and thanks her for them. She has been writing for 18 years and is now concerned that anything new she might try will tax her abilities. She is pleased with the direction that Sister's paper about her work will be taking. The differences between Protestantism and Catholicism are more about the church than they are about God.

Works: ["Why Do the Heathen Rage?"].

July 5, 1964 (p. 591; 4 par.): From ANDALUSIA. She appreciates receiving the essay. Richard Stern has it wrong; she does not object to Sister's reading of her work. She does not have poor feelings toward Penecostals, though Stern seems to have something personal against them. She will refer people to Sister's essay and expects to learn things about her work from it herself. LUPUS, ("the wolf") is acting up. She has been in the hospital 50 days so far this year. She will write a letter to Richard and Sister together explaining the inspiration in her stories related to Catholics and Protestants.

Works: None.

CHARLOTTE GAFFORD (seven letters) Gafford wrote to O'Connor about her second novel. *Pages:* HB: 381, 465, 468, 481, 496, 514, 576.

Letters

March 16, 1960 (p. 381; 4 par.): From ANDALUSIA. She thanks Gafford for her letter about *Violent Bear*. Even good reviews, like the one in the *Boston Herald*, show her that most readers do not see what she is doing. She is glad to hear about a new baby who goes to church with them and prays for the others. She encourages her to keep writing and to send her work to the quarterly journals.

Works: [*The Violent Bear It Away*].

February 10, 1962 (p. 465; 3 par.): From ANDALUSIA. Gafford's thesis is good. The Misfit is a "spoiled prophet" who could do much. She speaks about a phone call made by some students from Vanderbilt. They wanted her to do their homework for them, answering such questions as why The Misfit's hat is black. She has marked a place in the thesis for her attention.

Works: ["A Good Man Is Hard to Find"].

March 13, 1962 (p. 468; 3 par.): From ANDALUSIA. Gafford's thesis director may never understand what Gafford is trying to do, especially if she continues to use religious language. O'Connor makes a quick explanation of her use of *grace* that she uses in talks with the words *allegorical, moral,* and *anagogical.* She sends her a review of her work from *Renanscence* that seems particularly mean-spirited and shows how even Catholics can mispresent one's work.

Works: None.

June 24, 1962 (p. 481; 3 par.): From ANDALUSIA. Her trip to Birmingham is not happening. She does not like to fly in February and thinks that it is a bad time for a festival. Panels of writers do not interest her.

Works: None.

October 29, 1962 (p. 496; 2 par.): From ANDALUSIA. She appreciates Gafford's efforts at recommending *Wise Blood* in THE BULLETIN. She does not think her work will persuade many people, but she appreciates the effort. Gerard Sherry will be the new editor under changes the archbishop is making to the paper. She hopes Sherry will keep Leo on the book page, but they will have to all wait and see.

Works: Wise Blood.

April 21, 1963 (p. 514; 3 par.): From ANDALUSIA. She feels bad about Madison Jones. She does not care for arts festivals. She is sorry she was in bed when Gafford's friend stopped by and asks that he stop by again sometime. She wishes Gafford and her children could go on a trip to Okefenokee Swamp and stop by Andalusia. One of their PEACOCKS likes to block cars by standing out in the middle of the road and fanning his tail. One must get out of the car to disengage him, and then he makes a loud fuss about it. She thinks Gafford would enjoy it there.

Works: None.

May 10, 1964 (p. 576; 2 par.): From ANDALUSIA. She thanks her for the violets that have been crystallized and the book of poems, *The Story Hour* by Sara Henderson Hay. She wonders if it might be appropriate for her to write and tell her that she enjoyed them; they are amusing. She is home but is supposed to stay in bed and do very little. She is trying to write a story in her mind so that when she gets to the typewriter, she may have it. However, she thinks better on the typewriter and a few other places.

Works: None.

ROBERT GIROUX (47 letters) Robert Giroux became O'Connor's editor and publisher. She first met him when she visited his office with Robert Lowell in February 1949.

Pages: HB: 8, 15, 20–21, 23–25, 27–37, 59, 62, 67, 71–77, 80, 85, 87, 113, 120, 122, 138, 270, 277–280, 286, 331–332, 334, 337, 340, 342, 344–345, 353, 361, 373–375, 380, 402, 409, 415, 417, 421–422, 428–431, 439, 451, 471, 473–474, 498, 549, 563–556, 567–568, 572, 575, 579–581, 583, 585–586, 588–599.

Letters

March 10, 1951 (p. 23; 4 par.): From ANDALUSIA. She appreciates his letter and encloses the manuscript. She hopes he will want to publish it. Her agents can talk more with him about it. She is better but will not be returning to Connecticut for a while. She appreciates his sending Karl Stern's *A Pillar of Fire*.

Works: [*Wise Blood*].

October 16, 1951 (p. 28; 1 par.): From ANDALUSIA. She sends the revised manuscript today in another package. She has made changes based on Mrs. Tate's comments. She is sending another copy to the Fitzgeralds.

Works: [*Wise Blood*].

November 23, 1951 (p. 29; 1 par.): From ANDALUSIA. She received a lengthy letter from Caroline with suggestions for the novel. If there is time, she would like to make some changes.

Works: [*Wise Blood*].

December 3, 1951 (p. 29; 5 par.): From ANDALUSIA. She sends the changes. She also sends her biographical statement. She will get a picture taken and send it and wants the proofs sent to her in MILLEDGEVILLE. She appreciates the effort to allow her to incorporate her changes.

Works: *Wise Blood*

January 23, 1952 (p. 30; 3 par.): From ANDALUSIA. She sends the revised manuscript and galleys and makes small corrective comments about shrubs and buzzards. She likes the way the sample page looks and wonders when the book will be published.

Works: [*Wise Blood*].

February 6, 1952 (p. 32; 2 par.): From ANDALUSIA. She is not sure what she should do about the enclosed. She sends the address of her Cousin Katie in SAVANNAH, where she wants work sent to the place that she will be visiting for a few days later in the month.

Works: None.

February 24, 1952 (p. 32; 2 par.): From ANDALUSIA. She has made changes to pages 20, 26, and 185 on the proofs. She is pleased to learn of the paperback edition.

Works: *Wise Blood*

April 16, 1952 (p. 34; 5 par.): From ANDALUSIA. She appreciates the copy of the novel, which she finds attractive. She does not like her picture on the back. She sends a list of people who may be willing to review it favorably: John Palmer, Philip Rahv, Kerker Quinn, Frederick Morgan, Paul Engle, Andrew Lytle, Robie Macauley, John Wade, R. P. Blackmur, Francis Fergusson, and ROBERT PENN WARREN. She asks that author discount copies be sent to Mr. and Mrs. Allen Tate (Caroline Gordon Tate), Mr. and Mrs. Robert Fitzgerald, Mr. and Mrs. John Thompson, Miss Margaret Sutton, Mr. and Mrs. J. D. Way (Elizabeth Fenwick-Way), and Miss Lydia Bancroft. Her remaining nine copies will go to relatives.

April 30, 1952 (p. 34; 3 par.): From ANDALUSIA. She appreciates the comments. She was surprised to see Evelyn Waugh's. She asks that Giroux also send a copy of the novel to Cal [ROBERT] and Elizabeth LOWELL.

Works: Wise Blood.

May 24, 1952 (p. 36; 3 par.): From ANDALUSIA. She has had a request from Captain W. of the Salvation Army for their reading room. Please send them a copy at her 40 percent author discount. She appreciates the clippings and MARY MCCARTHY's *The Graves of Academe.* She prepares herself for more bad reviews.

Works: Wise Blood.

July 19, 1952 (p. 37; 3 par.): From ANDALUSIA. She would like six more copies of the novel charged to her account and a review copy also sent. Caroline suggests sending a copy to Herbert Read in England. She enjoyed Connecticut but had to come home because she became ill.

Works: Wise Blood.

June 14, 1953 (p. 59; 2 par.): From ANDALUSIA. The paperback came out sooner than she expected. She appreciates the review he sent. She has 50–60 pages completed of a new novel, which requires prayer and fasting.

Works: [Wise Blood], The Violent Bear It Away.

March 29, 1954 (p. 71; 2 par.): From ANDALUSIA. "The Displaced Person" has been sold to *SEWANEE REVIEW.* She forgot about the collection but has 11 stories for it already. She asks that he send her Peter Taylor's *The Widows of Thornton* when it is published.

Works: ["The Displaced Person"].

September 3, 1954 (p. 72; 4 par.): From ANDALUSIA. *SEWANEE REVIEW* will publish her story in the next issue. She asks whether the collection might be published in spring if she sends him the manuscript in October. She likes Taylor's collection and appreciates his sending it. Nev-

ille Spearman, Ltd. in England will publish *Wise Blood* there.

Works: [A Good Man Is Hard to Find], Wise Blood.

November 15, 1954 (p. 72; 6 par.): From ANDALUSIA. She asked her agent to send her story collection manuscript to him by the first of December. She has put in the longer version of "The Displaced Person," but they can use the shorter one if he prefers. She rewrote "The Capture" from the way it appeared in MADEMOISELLE and retitled it "An Afternoon in the Woods." "The Artificial Nigger" has been sold to John Crowe Ransom. Caroline wants the proofs of the collection when they are ready; she plans to ask the *Times* to allow her to write a review. Sally Fitzgerald's father is dying in Houston, and she will be coming back to the country to be with him. O'Connor hopes she will come to MILLEDGEVILLE. She hopes Giroux will stop by as well.

Works: "The Displaced Person," ["The Capture"], "An Afternoon in the Woods," "The Artificial Nigger."

November 30, 1954 (p. 73; 1 par.): From ANDALUSIA. She is rewriting "The Artificial Nigger" from Caroline's comments. Which copy should she send him?

Works: "The Artificial Nigger."

December 6, 1954 (p. 73; 1 par.): From ANDALUSIA. She will send the revision by December 20 along with a revised first page for "The Displaced Person."

Works: "The Displaced Person."

December 11, 1954 (p. 73; 3 par.): From ANDALUSIA. She makes comments about various stories in the collection. They might take out "An Afternoon in the Woods" and "A Stroke of Good Fortune" and add "The Displaced Person." She prefers "A Stroke of Good Fortune" to the other because its theme relates more to the others. She will have the revision of "The Displaced Person" in the mail by Monday.

Works: "An Afternoon in the Woods," "A Stroke of Good Fortune," "The Displaced Person."

January 22, 1955 (p. 75; 1 par.): From ANDALUSIA. If they need a picture for the story collection cover, she asks that they use the painted self-portrait of her with a pheasant cock, enclosed.

Works: [*A Good Man Is Hard to Find*].

February 26, 1955 (p. 75; 1 par.): From ANDALUSIA. She has just completed a new story called "Good Country People." Caroline and Allen think it is her best story to date and that it ought to go in the collection. It would fit if they drop "A Stroke of Good Fortune" and "An Afternoon in the Woods."

Works: "Good Country People," "A Stroke of Good Fortune," "An Afternoon in the Woods."

March 7, 1955 (p. 75; 1 par.): From ANDALUSIA. She agrees that ending with "Good Country People" is a good idea. She sends a few sentences to add to the ending before the text goes to proofs.

Works: "Good Country People."

June 16, 1955 (p. 87; 5 par.): From ANDALUSIA. She sends a clause from her Harcourt contract about Catharine Carver serving as editor. Harcourt also sent her the Orville Prescott review of *A Good Man*, which is going into another printing. She appreciates his advice.

Works: [*A Good Man Is Hard to Find and Other Stories*].

October 21, 1955 (p. 113; 2 par.): From ANDALUSIA. She did apply for the Guggenheim and used him as a reference, as he suggested. *Wise Blood* has appeared in England and received good reviews.

Works: Wise Blood.

December 9, 1955 (p. 122; 3 par.): From ANDALUSIA. She appreciates his recommendation for the Guggenheim. Catharine Carver will leave Harcourt, Brace December 15. She is not sure what she should do. She knows of Denver Lindley.

Works: None.

April 17, 1958 (p. 278; 4 par.): From ANDALUSIA. The arrangements please her. She will go to New York on her return. Since she has never been to the city before on crutches, she appreciates the limousine. She hopes that he and the Eliots will have a pleasant time in Texas.

Works: None.

August 9, 1959 (p. 344; 4 par.): From ANDALUSIA. She sends page 104, revised. She also makes other small changes that she notes. She appreciates his wiring her to let her know that he liked the novel. She is eager to have it published next February.

Works: [*The Violent Bear It Away*].

August 14, 1959 (p. 345; 2 par.): From ANDALUSIA. She approves the change to 146 and sends a new page 141. She would like a copy of FRANÇOIS MAURIAC's *Questions of Precedence* if it has been reissued. She appreciates his work on her book.

Works: None.

October 10, 1959 (p. 353; 4 par.): From ANDALUSIA. She sends galleys with changes. She makes a reference to page 82 and a sentence about hunger. She appreciates his sending Caroline galleys as well. She would like to send corrected copies to ELIZABETH BISHOP, Granville Hicks, Alfred Kazin, Andrew Lytle, the Lowells, and ROBERT PENN WARREN. She appreciates the book by James Purdy.

Works: [*The Violent Bear It Away*].

December 5, 1959 (p. 361; 2 par.): From ANDALUSIA. She approves of the dust jacket for the novel, which makes her think of the British cover of *Wise Blood*. She received a letter from George Hardinge asking about the violent scene in the woods against Tarwater by the man in the car. She is afraid that present-day Christians do not know the Devil when they see him and wonders how the book will fare.

Works: [*The Violent Bear It Away*].

February 10, 1960 (p. 373; 4 par.): From ANDALUSIA. She appreciates the telegram concerning the positive review. She has heard that Granville Hicks is writing a good review for the *Saturday Review*. She requests another 10 copies of the book charged to her account. Catharine Carver is coming to visit for a few days in March.

Works: [*The Violent Bear It Away*].

February 16, 1960 (p. 375; 2 par.): From ANDA-LUSIA. She appreciates the Duhamel review and more books. The book has been around shops there for two weeks.

Works: [*The Violent Bear It Away*].

March 6, 1960 (p. 380; 2 par.): From ANDA-LUSIA. She appreciates the reviews. Many do not sound like they have read the book. A positive review in the SAVANNAH *Morning News* kept calling Tarwater Tarbutton and claimed that he was nine. She asks that, once Lent is over, he send a copy to Father Paul in Conyers.

Works: [*The Violent Bear It Away*].

September 29, 1960 (p. 409; 5 par.): From ANDALUSIA. She appreciates the advertisement. She writes about the Sister Superior's request to publish the *Memoir of Mary Ann* with an explanation of their project. The Dominican nuns were founded by the daughter of NATHANIEL HAWTHORNE. She asks if he would be willing to look at the manuscript when she is done editing it as best she can.

Works: [*A Memoir of Mary Ann*].

November 4, 1960 (p. 415; 2 par.): From ANDALUSIA. She appreciates the reviews and his willingness to take a look at the nuns' book. Caroline found the manuscript touching and thought it might be suitable for a secular publisher.

Works: [*The Violent Bear It Away*], [*A Memoir of Mary Ann*].

November 12, 1960 (p. 417; 3 par.): From ANDALUSIA. She appreciates the TLS clipping. There was another bad review in the *Observer* by Kinglsey Amis. She asks that he send JACQUES

MARITAIN a copy. She is happy with the outcome of the election.

Works: *The Violent Bear It Away*, *Wise Blood*.

December 8, 1960 (p. 421; 4 par.): From ANDA-LUSIA. She sends the nuns' manuscript after she has retyped it from their last-minute changes. Caroline and the nuns have suggested various titles, but O'Connor's is straightforward. Sister Evangelist is considering that a movie should be made about Mary Ann. She wishes him a good Christmas.

Works: [*A Memoir of Mary Ann*].

January 23, 1961 (p. 428; 9 par.): From ANDA-LUSIA. The nuns are dancing. She has lost one pair of peafowl in a bet with them that no one would buy their book. Sister Evangelist notified the bishop, and he was pleased. He did say that the comment overheard in the confessional must be removed since one ought not to overhear penitent's speaking. Sister Evangelist is content with Giroux having editorial control. She is the person whom he should contact. O'Connor's part of the money needs to go through her agent. The nuns want their money to go to the home in ATLANTA. Would he like a picture of Mary Ann? If so, there are several from which to choose. She approves a brochure made up for her book. If they do it, she would like it to have comments from Richard Gilman in *Commonweal* in it. She needs to speak with him about Wise Blood and putting it back in print. The galleys for *Mary Ann* should go to her.

Works: [*A Memoir of Mary Ann*], *Wise Blood*.

January 28, 1961 (p. 429; 8 par.): From ANDA-LUSIA. The bishop made changes in the manuscript, and Sister Evangelist gave them to her; she sends them along. She also sends a poem written by Mary Ann's sister—the nuns wonder if it might be included. The nuns request a quote from *The Merchant of Venice* for the front of the book. She likes her plain title to this last that they have come up with, *Brief Candle*. Mary Ann's parents told Sister Evangelist that they would prepare a statement saying that they approved of the book. She encloses the bishop's funeral sermon in full in case he might want to use more of it than she included in the text. Sister Evangelist seemed to think that the bishop thought that more of it would be in the book.

Works: [*A Memoir of Mary Ann*].

May 9, 1962 (p. 473; 3 par.):   From ANDALUSIA. She encloses a note for his comments on the second edition of the book. The nuns would like more copies of the British edition. She thanks him for the book by I. B. Singer and looks forward to reading it.

Works: [*A Memoir of Mary Ann*].

May 21, 1962 (p. 474; 1 par.):   From ANDALUSIA. She asks about deleting the last sentence of the author's note. She does not think that it adds anything.

Works: [*A Memoir of Mary Ann*].

November 5, 1962 (p. 498; 4 par.):   From ANDALUSIA. She may not have a collection together with just seven stories. She wants to title it *Everything That Rises Must Converge*. She has heard from Mr. Coindreau that Julian Green may translate *Mary Ann* and that the Spanish may be interested. The nuns tell her that they have heard from a translator in Brazil who is interested in a Portuguese version. She appreciates the book by Gogol and looks forward to reading it. She has seen *The Violent Bear* in Swedish paperback.

Works: Everything That Rises Must Converge, A Memoir of Mary Ann, The Violent Bear It Away.

November 10, 1963 (p. 549; 2 par.):   From ANDALUSIA. Sister Evangelist has written a Bible study and meditation book and has been having it typed by a woman in ATLANTA who then gives it chapter by chapter to O'Connor. She is supposed to ask him if he might be interested and encloses Sister's letters about the project. She is a conduit for the Lord's work through the nun and does as she is asked.

Works: None.

January 25, 1964 (p. 563; 2 par.):   From ANDALUSIA. She appreciates his letter about the complications of a book of Sister's type and will give it to her. She hopes it will explain it for her. She is getting ready to put together a new collection of stories. She has just finished a story, "Revelation," which may give a collection shape. She has eight completed stories now with another on the way. On average, these stories are longer than the ones in her first collection. She asks when he might like to publish the collection.

Works: ["Revelation"].

March 7, 1964 (p. 567; 4 par.):   From ANDALUSIA. She is just out of the hospital and cannot believe that Mary Ann's parents have been approached by an ambitious lawyer and are suing Farrar, Straus and Giroux and the Cancer Home over the book. She thinks they have been snowed by the lawyer. She has cancelled all lectures and will not have the book ready by this fall. She is very troubled over the Mary Ann Long affair.

Works: [*Everything That Rises Must Converge*].

May 21, 1964 (p. 579; 3 par.):   From ANDALUSIA. She appreciates his letter and is pleased to be able to reprint previously published stories without significant revision for the collection. She mentions various stories and the typescripts that she has of them around the house. She does not want to include "The Partridge Festival." She has been working on a new story, "Judgment Day," that seems more suitable. Regina and Sister Josephine have not heard from Mary Ann's parents, and everyone assumes they are ashamed of what happened in the dropped suit.

Works: "The Comforts of Home," "The Enduring Chill," "The Lame Shall Enter First," "Everything That Rises Must Converge," "The Partridge Festival," ["Judgment Day"].

May 28, 1964 (p. 581; 2 par.):   From Piedmont Hospital, ATLANTA. She has been in the hospital but will send manuscripts next week. She still has hopes for the last story.

Works: [*Everything That Rises Must Converge*].

June 9, 1964 (p. 583; 2 par.): From Piedmont Hospital, ATLANTA. She is still in the hospital and has not been able to send the manuscripts. Perhaps a spring release for the book would be better than Christmas. She will keep working on "Parker's Back" after she is released from the hospital. She appreciates the Xavier Rynne books.

Works: ["Parker's Back"].

June 28, 1964 (p. 589; 5 par.): From ANDALUSIA. She is finally out of the hospital and works a couple of hours a day now. She speaks about various stories and what to include and not include in the collection. She thinks that there may be nine or 10 long stories for the book.

Works: ["Judgment Day"], "The Enduring Chill," "You Can't Be Any Poorer Than Dead," *The Violent Bear It Away*, ["Parker's Back"].

LOUISE AND THOMAS GOSSETT (five letters)
The Gossetts were friends of the O'Connors from Macon, Georgia. Tom taught at Wesleyan, and Louise taught at Mercer from 1954 to 1959. *Pages:* HB: 255, 438, 566, 573, 576.

Letters

November 24, 1957 (p. 255; 2 par.): From ANDALUSIA. She invites Gossett over and to bring Miss Maire MacEntee as well. She has been thinking of asking Gossett and Louise. She wants to know what the southern literature is that Gossett is teaching. She sends good wishes to the dogs and tells him she has three Chinese geese.

Works: None.

April 10, 1961 (p. 438; 3 par.): From ANDALUSIA. They are up early with the chickens, as are all farmers, so the Gossetts should let them know if they cannot make it for breakfast. She offers congratulations on attaining education. She has just read a review that puts her novel down for not being hopeful. People want novels to do what religion does. Her mother is converting from the dairy business to the beef business.

Works: The Violent Bear It Away.

February 18, 1964 (p. 566; 2 par.): From ANDALUSIA. She wishes she could come, but she needs to go to the hospital unexpectedly and must cancel trips to Boston College, Brown, and the University of Texas as well. She asks him to have Father McCown, who is in Houston, to send her Gossett's book.

Works: None.

April 8, 1964 (p. 573; 3 par.): From ANDALUSIA. She likes Gossett's book, which she has not yet finished. Father McCown visited her in the hospital; he was going to give a talk in Macon on "Literary Horizons of Catholic Thought" at the St. Joseph's Guild, even though he does not know much about it. Her Aunt Mary is so ill that the family has been called to town. She is also reading Isak Dinesen's *Out of Africa*.

Works: None.

May 12, 1964 (p. 576; 2 par.): From ANDALUSIA. She spends all of her time in bed now; her condition has worsened. The operation aggravated her LUPUS. She is strong enough to write to the Gossetts because she just had a blood transfusion. Her Aunt Mary is also staying at the farm after her heart attack, being cared for by Flannery's mother. She expects to spend the summer in bed. She has not had active lupus since 1951. She is not allowed visitors and can only go to the doctor. Perhaps the Gossetts might visit in the fall. "I sure hope for better things then" (576).

Works: None.

BEN GRIFFITH (six letters) Ben Griffith was a writer who at the time of O'Connor's letters was teaching at Bessie Tift Women's College (Tift College) in Forsyth, Georgia. He later became dean of the Graduate School at West Georgia College. *Pages:* HB: 68, 78, 83, 89, 156, 222.

Letters

February 13, 1954 (p. 68; 6 par.): From ANDALUSIA. She appreciates Griffith's letter. She is more like Enoch than the gorilla. She discusses possible, subconscious sources for aspects of the novel. She did read Wordsworth's "Intimation" ode but does not see any direct connection; *Oedipus Rex* may be an influence from Robert Fitzgerald's translation. Some critics see connections with FRANZ KAFKA, though she has never completed *The Castle* or *The Trial*. She has read HENRY JAMES.

She is now working on a volume of stories and another novel. It took her five years to write *Wise Blood;* this novel may take at least that long. She thinks Griffith must not be from the South since most southerners do not know southern literature unless they have attended college in the North or somewhere like Vanderbilt. She has heard of Bessie Tift but does not know any alumni. The atmosphere at the girls' college in MILLEDGEVILLE is spoiled by the neighboring mental hospital, military academy, and reformatory.

Works: Wise Blood, The Violent Bear It Away.

May 5, 1955 (p. 78; 5 par.): From ANDALUSIA. She has received one letter about "The Artificial Nigger." It wondered whether Mr. Head symbolized St. Peter and Nelson, Christ. She could see the loose tie to Peter but not the Christ figure. "What I had in mind to suggest with the artificial nigger was the redemptive quality of the Negro's suffering for us all" (78). She further discusses the story.

She will write to Harcourt, Brace and have them send Griffith an advance copy of *A Good Man Is Hard to Find and Other Stories.* She would like him to read a long story in that collection, as well as "Good Country People." She is home all afternoons but Monday and would enjoy a visit from him. She would welcome Griffith writing about her work for the *Georgia Review.* When she spoke recently in Macon, the newspaper reported that she was of the realistic school; probably the reporter got that idea from the cover of *Wise Blood.* She will correct the characterization in her next talk in Macon. She is interested in distortion because it may be the one way that people will see.

Works: "The Artificial Nigger," "Good Country People," *Wise Blood.*

June 8, 1955 (p. 83; 8 par.): From ANDALUSIA. She appreciates the review as well as the Plunkett material as well as Griffith's story. She has read the story, and it reminded her of Chekhov's "The Lament" and Luigi Pirandello's "War." They appear in *Understanding Fiction* by Cleanth Brooks and ROBERT PENN WARREN. The book has been of great value to her, and she recommends it to him.

She gives writing advice at some length, particularly about showing and not telling; it cannot be forced. She recommends JAMES JOYCE's "The Dead." Chekhov made even the air and dirt work for him in the story. It is not easy work. Her ducks named Merrill, Lynch, Pierce, Fenner, and Bean will be frozen in August, but "Clair Booth Loose Goose" will be spared. She hopes he has a good time in North Carolina.

Works: None.

July 9, 1955 (p. 89; 5 par.): From ANDALUSIA She appreciates Griffith passing her books around to scholars. Some of her fan mail indicates that some of the men do not read further than the title and send her specifics about their being the good man she could not find. She sees the similarities between the main character and Haze Motes. Her editor has told her that the book is second only to Thomas Merton on their book list. Reviews in *Time* and the *Atlantic Monthly* are negative and miss the mark. She has not read *Memoirs of Hecate County* or Krafft-Ebing. She gave Plunkett to a friend.

Works: [*Wise Blood*], ["A Good Man Is Hard to Find"].

May 7, 1956 (p. 156; 2 par.): From ANDALUSIA. She would enjoy having Griffith, Thomas Gossett, and Alfred Kazin over on Friday. The bird in the self-portrait is not a PEACOCK but a pheasant. Some people think it is a turkey. She cannot make the lecture because she works mornings.

Works: None.

May 21, 1957 (p. 222; 3 par.): From ANDALUSIA. Griffith is welcome to fish at the farm any time. She can no longer make it to the pond since the bugs attack her. She has not yet read WILLIAM FAULKNER's *The Town* but did read *The Hamlet*. She needs to avoid the Snopes for reasons that are evident.

Works: None.

EILEEN HALL (one letter)   When O'Connor wrote book reviews for *The BULLETIN*, the diocesan newspaper, Eileen Hall was the book review editor. *Page*: HB: 142.

Letter

March 10, 1956 (p. 142; 9 par.):   She sends Hall a copy of an essay that has answered some of her questions and may answer some of Hall's. She talked to a priest about her work perhaps bothering young people or people with younger or more simple sensibilities, and he counseled her that she need not write for a certain age or audience. She writes about FRANÇOIS MAURIAC and his ideas in *God and Mammon*. She says if one writes an honest novel, the rest is up to God.

Some of the experience and mystery of life is sin. The Crucifixion means little if sin is not considered. In matters of bad taste or good taste, it is relative to the beholder. The worst cases of bad taste in fictional works are pornography and sentimentality. One has too much sex in it, and the other has too much emotion. A point can use both to be proven. What bothers her most is fiction that says something is right or wrong when it is just the opposite. "Fiction is the concrete expression of mystery—mystery that is lived" (144). She has asked many of these questions of herself.

Finally, she discusses the reviewing or lack of it of Gordon's *The Malefactors*, *Art and Scholasticism* by JACQUES MARITAIN, and *This God and Mammon*.

Works: None.

JOHN HAWKES (22 letters)   John Hawkes was a novelist of O'Connor's acquaintance. They frequently discussed how each treated the presence of the devil in their fiction. *Pages*: HB: 291, 343, 349, 359, 367, 389, 399, 412, 413, 415, 424, 434, 438, 443, 455, 464, 470, 500, 537, 541, 548, 553.

Letters

July 27, 1958 (p. 291; 4 par.):   From ANDALUSIA. She delayed in thanking Hawkes for the Faulkner books because she has been reading. She finds his style intimidating, leaving her wanting to raise chickens fulltime. She is impressed with Hawkes's books. A poet friend of hers, James Dickey, reads each of Hawkes's books when they are released. His student's story about Georgia does not have enough Georgia in it. She is happy that he stopped by and hope that he will come again. She is glad to know of his writing.

Works: None.

July 29, 1959 (p. 343; 3 par.):   From ANDALUSIA. She is glad to have his address because she has been thinking about him and will want to send him a copy of her novel. She is uncomfortable being between projects; she does not know where the next 60,000 words will come from, much less the next single word. She tells him the name of her novel and that she does not expect many to like it, though it will be meaningful to her if he does. She has been reading *The Real Life of Sebastian Knight*. She likes Nabokov's *Bend Sinister*. She hopes the Hawkes's will stop on their next trip to Florida.

Works: *The Violent Bear It Away*.

September 13, 1959 (p. 349; 6 par.):   From ANDALUSIA. His letter made her want to show him the manuscript copy of her novel, but she will wait. She writes about the new novel and what it has in common with *Wise Blood*. She believes one should write novels about what one most cares about, and for her this is the intersection of the Holy with doubt and lack of faith. Today's world makes it tough to believe. Non-Catholics do not have the sacraments, a fact that causes her pain. Haze's wise blood saves him. The old man in *The Violent Bear It Away* speaks for her. It is possible for The Misfit to be redeemed; Mr. Shiftlet is probably beyond redemption. The story tells about Mr. Head's redemption.

She enjoyed Andrew Lytle's *The Velvet Horn*. She is waiting for *The Lime Twig* with anticipation. She appreciates his interest in her books.

Works: [*The Violent Bear It Away*], *Wise Blood.*

November 20, 1959 (p. 359; 4 par.): From ANDALUSIA. She appreciates Hawkes reading and commenting on the manuscript. Her characters must go to the city because southerners are doing that these days. She writes that she has been reading about the Devil and finds that he cannot read people's thoughts but must read what they are thinking by their actions. She thinks about Rayber and other characters and their relationship to the Devil. She sends her best to his wife, Sophie.

Works: [*Wise Blood*], [*The Violent Bear It Away*].

December 26, 1959 (p. 367; 4 par.): From ANDALUSIA. She does intend that Tarwater's friend is the Devil. She remembers workshopping the first chapter at Iowa and hearing comments about the voice of the novel. Meeks does not resist the Devil in any way. When evil is strong in a scene, grace can enter and be noticed. The violent scene in the woods illuminates for Tarwater the depth of his failure. He should be receiving a copy of her new book soon, and she hopes that he will like the middle section better, which she revised on his counsel. She looks forward to the chapters of his book that he will send.

Works: "The Life You Save May Be Your Own," *The Violent Bear It Away.*

April 14, 1960 (p. 389; 4 par.): From ANDALUSIA. She appreciates his letter and has been occupied fending off a heart attack from reading reviews of her new book. Though Andrew Lytle thinks the Grandmother is a witch, complete with cat, Hawkes's students know that she is not pure evil and can allow grace to pass through her. They see this because they likely have grandmothers just like her. She explains how a Catholic writer can see the Grandmother as a vehicle for Grace, but Protestants may not. She hopes *The Lime Twig* will come soon and that he and Sophie will stop by on their way to Florida if they go this year.

Works: "A Good Man Is Hard to Find."

June 2, 1960 (p. 399; 2 par.): From ANDALUSIA. She asks him to have New Directions send her galleys of his book. She thought of Hawkes when she read a comment from Cal ROBERT LOWELL on her novel. It involves repetition. She thinks Shakespeare exhibited an aspect of the problem that Lowell describes when he wrote *King Lear* after *Troilus* and *Cressida*. Her old ladies are more comic than GRAHAM GREENE's characters.

Works: None.

October 9, 1960 (p. 412; 5 par.): From ANDALUSIA. She read *The Lime Twig* in one sitting. She admires the work. She is not good at logical analysis, but she can say that it is as though one nearly dreams it before that time of waking. She wants to read it again in about a month so that she may look with a more critical eye than being swept away by it. She is on her way to Minnesota where she will read and also meet up with KATHERINE ANNE PORTER, Caroline Gordon, and Madison Jones on a panel about southern culture at an arts festival. She thinks that no one else writes quite like Hawkes.

Works: "A Good Man Is Hard to Find."

October 14, 1960 (p. 413; 4 par.): From ANDALUSIA. He is welcome to use a quotation that she sent to New Directions or from her letter, whichever he chooses. Leslie Fiedler does not bother her, even if he makes too much of Freud. She sends a postcard about the Free Thinking Christian Mission that relates to both her and his work.

Works: None.

November 6, 1960 (p. 415; 3 par.): From ANDALUSIA. She sent the proofs to the third Georgia Hawkes reader since she knows that the reader could not afford the book. She sends her comments. She writes about a couple; the wife has LUPUS and saw mention of it with O'Connor in *Time* magazine. The couple has now visited three times. Hawkes might want to take a look at her story in *The* KENYON REVIEW that has a devil in it. She is dissatisfied with the story, though.

Works: ["The Comforts of Home"].

December 30, 1960 (p. 424; 3 par.): From ANDALUSIA. She jokes about the mythology of Thor and his goats that was explained to her by Caroline Gordon. The story gives the goat in the postcard picture of the Free Thinking Christian Mission a touch of the classics. Her friend would find a letter from Hawkes of value. She would like to see her work in print, but so far O'Connor's agent has not been able to place it. She might purchase an electric typewriter because she has been in the hospital and may need it to write. Such a tool might make her stories "electrify the general reader; or electrocute him" (425).

Works: None.

March 3, 1961 (p. 434; 4 par.): From ANDALUSIA. She sends some southern air to melt the snow. She appreciates his article on Edwin Honig's poetry. She heard from Elizabeth Way that David and Edwin Honig are starting a poetry magazine. Caroline has had an effect on Andrew, who wrote an article on her for the *Critique* issue about her work. It is disadvantageous to be thought of as a Catholic writer in that readers keep looking for the character who will undergo redemption. She is intrigued by innocent characters like Sarah Ham and Enoch and Bishop who get things moving. The sheriff's view is the Devil's.

Works: None.

June 22, 1961 (p. 443; 2 par.): From ANDALUSIA. She does not associate mental illness with divine inspiration. She describes what she thinks are differences in their uses of the Divine. "There is a hierarchy of devils" (443). She is attempting to write an introduction to a new publication of *Wise Blood* to be done by Farrar, Straus but is coming up short.

Works: None.

November 28, 1961 (p. 455; 8 par.): From ANDALUSIA. She tells a story of seeing a goat man on the side of the road about whom she has been meaning to write to him. The new baby is good news that she cannot top, but she does have a pair of new Polish swans. Andrew Lytle says that Hawkes may write an article on her, and if he does, she should send him a story, "The Lame Shall Enter First." She describes her Devil and his Devil in their work. Hers is a fallen angel named Lucifer. He has a history, and he wants to corrupt God's plan. Hawkes's devil, as she sees it, is more subjective and is on an equal plain with God rather than being one of God's creatures. He says if one separates from the herd, he becomes evil. However, the herd can be wrong, in which case the one leaving it is not doing evil but good.

She does feel a kinship with NATHANIEL HAWTHORNE—more than with any other American writer. It may be that she does write in the school of Hawthorne's "romances."

She did not end up writing the note to *Wise Blood* and let it go. She has heard about a professor's review of *The Violent Bear* interpreting it as involving homosexual incest. She can only hope that the next generation will not be educated in this way.

She keeps recommending *The Lime Twig* to readers and has lent her copy to someone. She hopes he is busy writing another book.

Works: ["The Lame Shall Enter First"], *Wise Blood*, *The Violent Bear It Away*.

February 6, 1962 (p. 464; 2 par.): From ANDALUSIA. She has had the flu but now sends the story "The Lame Shall Enter First." She admits the Devil's voice is hers in this story. She is pleased to be termed one of the "wild talents," even though she feels less so at the moment.

Works: ["The Lame Shall Enter First"].

April 5, 1962 (p. 470; 4 par.): From ANDALUSIA. She likes his article a lot and hopes that Andrew Lytle will print it. If he does not, then he should get it published elsewhere. Hawkes has been careful to separate what he thinks of her work from what she has said about it in their discussions.

He seems preoccupied with the notion of perversity. She thinks that she writes as she sees it without making characters and so on. perverse. He does not seem to use the word as most of the world does. Her letter is written in haste.

She is going to Raleigh to speak at North Carolina State College and then to Spartanburg to the Southern Literary Festival, where she joins EUDORA WELTY and Cleanth Brooks on the program. After that she is going to Chicago and Notre Dame. She hopes that he and Sophie are all right. She is moved and honored that Hawkes wrote the article about her with such thought and care.

Works: None.

November 24, 1962 (p. 500; 3 par.): From ANDALUSIA. She has just returned from Texas and Louisiana. She likes New Orleans best of all cities and would live there if she had to live in a city. The young woman from Macon he told her about came and asked her questions about her work. She has not read the critical article by Irving Malin. She prefers the word GROTESQUE to gothic in considering about her work.

Works: None.

September 10, 1963 (p. 537; 3 par.): From ANDALUSIA. She is glad to hear from him and has been wondering where he now lives. She is pleased to hear he is working on a novel. She recalls Hollis Summers and his wife. A nun once wrote to her and said that a friend of theirs went to "Loaf of Bread." She has been to YADDO but is not sure she could stand "Loaf of Bread." Her swan is doing all right considering it has a tumor. Experts who have come to look at it say it is fairly common in large birds. On the farm they are also anticipating a baby burro, and the Muscovy duck has set on the nest three times, most recently on Labor Day.

Works: None.

September 29, 1963 (p. 541; 2 par.): From ANDALUSIA. It is kind of him to arrange for her to visit Brown. She would prefer to read "A Good Man" with comments to giving a lecture. She finds it works better if she brings one story to life for them rather than speak to them about miscellaneous details they will soon forget.

Works: "A Good Man Is Hard to Find."

November 1, 1963 (p. 548; 4 par.): From ANDALUSIA. She has returned from giving a lecture that affirms her preference for giving a reading instead. For him at Brown, she would also be pleased to answer questions from students in a class. It is nice of him to offer for her to stay with them, but she does pretty well with guest rooms. What kind of work did he read recently at Boston College? Her trip has garnered her money for another pair of swans that are on their way from Miami. Her resident swan, Mr. Hood, does not know they are coming.

Works: None.

December 12, 1963 (p. 553; 1 par.): From ANDALUSIA. She has mailed James Laughlin a comment on Hawkes's *Second Skin*. She likes the book and considers Hawkes a magician in the way he can keep the reader's attention. Betty Hester will be visiting over the weekend, and she will show her the proofs. Hester will likely give a long analysis that will enlighten both of them. Hawkes is the only writer who makes O'Connor "see in a literal visual way" (553).

Works: None.

MRS. RUMSEY HAYNES (four letters) Mrs. Rumsey Haynes was president of the Lansing, Michigan, local chapter of the American Association of University Women (AAUW). She had invited O'Connor to speak at a meeting. *Pages*: HB: 135, 154, 175, 205.

Letters

February 9, 1956 (p. 135; 4 par.): From ANDALUSIA. She appreciates both of Haynes's letters. It is kind of her to invite her to stay all week, but she will probably be ready to fly home a day or two after the talk. A talk is easier to prepare if she knew the interests of the audience. Life on crutches makes her dependent on someone else to travel. If picking her up and taking her back to the airport is too much of an imposition, she hopes that she will let her know.

Works: None.

April 29, 1956 (p. 154; 3 par.): From ANDALUSIA. She enjoyed her visit and stay with Haynes. Her mother liked the box of candy and homemade cookies. Regina cleaned her room while she was away, and now it will take some time to get it back to the messiness to which she is accustomed. The peachickens ate her mother's strawberry plants while she was gone, and now she has to make peace between them, especially since she wants to have twice as many birds by this time next year. She sends her regards to the people whom she met in Lansing and to Rumsey.

Works: None.

September 13, 1956 (p. 175; 5 par.): From ANDALUSIA. She appreciates the tulip bulbs for her mother. The yardman is preparing a spot for them to be planted. She finds Haynes's comment about Scofield and Wesley being her first young male characters from the upper class interesting. She has just completed writing "A View of the Woods." In fiction, a writer puts an idea on reality, so that may be why Haynes feels a sense of unreality when she reads O'Connor's stories. Her mother is building a 22,000-gallon water tank and will write to them directly.

Works: Other, "A View of the Woods."

March 3, 1957 (p. 205; 3 par.): From ANDALUSIA. She appreciates the article about Gene Kelly. She was not impressed by his performance in the dramatization of her short story and rarely watches television. Their farm family is leaving for another job, so her mother is hiring another. This will probably result in another story. They are watching daily for the tulips to emerge. Flowers usually bloom there in February.

Works: None.

BETTY HESTER, AKA "A" (182 letters) Known as "A" in *The Habit of Being* in order to protect her identity while she was alive, Hester wrote to O'Connor an insightful letter about her work in 1955. The letter touched a chord from the level of understanding that Hester seemed to exhibit about O'Connor's fiction, and the author wrote back,

asking Hester to write again. So began the most extensive correspondence of *The Habit of Being*. Other than letters presumably to her mother which have not yet been published, O'Connor wrote more letters to Hester over the course of her lifetime than to any other single correspondent.

Pages: HB 90–121, 123–134, 136–138, 140–141, 144–146, 148–174, 176–180, 182–192, 196–200, 202–203, 206–208, 210–220, 222–226, 228–229, 234–238, 240–242, 244–5, 247–50, 252–253, 255–256, 258–259, 261–263, 270–275, 279–283, 287–294, 298–302, 305–306, 308–310, 316–317, 321, 323–324, 328, 332–336, 338–340, 342–343, 348, 351–352, 355–358, 362–364, 367–368, 370–372, 374, 379, 381, 383–386, 390, 393–396, 400–408, 411–414, 416–417, 419–420, 423–425, 427–428, 430–431, 439–442, 446–455, 457–459, 461–467, 474, 478–481, 483–484, 486–487, 491–492, 494–498, 501–503, 505–506, 508–513, 515, 518–519, 521–522, 526, 528–530, 533–535, 537, 539, 541, 543, 546–549, 552–554, 562–563, 565–566, 569, 571, 573, 578, 581–583, 587, 592–594

Letters

July 20, 1955 (p. 90; 5 par.): From ANDALUSIA. She is very appreciative to receive her letter. She is maybe more surprised to hear from someone who understands the intentions in her work as it is for Hester to find a writer who connects with her spirituality. They live 87 miles apart, but O'Connor thinks that they are much closer spiritually.

"I write the way I do because (not though) I am a Catholic" (90). The factual statement makes it the clearest. She is, though, a Catholic with modern sensibilities, and this can be a weight to carry within the church. The church itself causes suffering, yet it is the only thing that helps one tolerate life. At the same time, a believer suffers for the church willingly from a love of the food that is the body of Christ. One loves the very world one must endure.

The *New Yorker* article was not signed and is ridiculous. When Nietzsche talked about God being dead, he may have meant that the world is full of chickens whose wings are bred away only to increase their white meat.

She says it is tiresome to keep reading that *A Good Man Is Hard to Find and other Stories* is full of sarcasm and cruelty. Christian realism is difficult, and she has portrayed a few people on their journey toward Bethlehem. Reviewers who call these horror stories miss the real horror.

She would like Hester to write to her again. She would like to get to know the person better who comprehends her work.

Works: A Good Man is Hard to Find and other Stories.

August 2, 1955 (p. 91; 8 par.):   From ANDALUSIA. She appreciates her writing again. She fears that her fast response might burden Hester with a correspondence she neither wants nor for which she has time. O'Connor has time because she does not have a job outside the home due to her illness and she lives on a farm. She can only write creative work for a few hours each day. She raises PEACOCKS for a hobby, but they do not take much time either, so she has time.

She writes for an audience of people who think that God is dead; at least, those are the people of whom she is most aware when she writes. As a Christian, the only reality for her is the Incarnation, in which her audience does not believe. Jesus was God; if not, then he lied, and the Crucifixion brought him to justice.

Hester is correct in saying that O'Connor will most likely never fully comprehend her own work or her own reasons for writing it. She knows that she has a gift and that its movement comes from her exposure to the church, not from within herself. She has an awareness of the devil. She is no mystic or saint. Since she is a member of the church, no matter how insignificant she may be, she is part of the Redemption.

Has Hester read Simone Weil? She has not but has heard good things. Edith Stein and Weil strike her as the most interesting women of the 20th century.

Whether Hester is or is not a Christian, she and O'Connor both praise the God who lives.

Works: None.

August 9, 1955 (p. 93; 6 par.):   From ANDALUSIA. She continues to be reminded of Simone Weil from Hester's letters and encloses a piece for her to read. She does not know what it is like to be a convert or to have that kind of experience. Fr. Jean de Menasce once said that a person should not move into the church until is strikes him or her that joining will enlarge one's freedom, not restrict it. She supposes it is similar to marriage. A married couple discovers what the institution is in the beginning.

Probably many people come to the church through unconventional means. The workings of the church on the inside are also set up for the sinner, which confuses the self-righteous.

She must have read Aristotle and Plato in college but it did not register. She does read the *Summa* every night before bed for about 20 minutes. She loves St. Thomas and knows that he loved God. There is a story that St. Thomas was locked in a tower by his brothers who did not want him to be a Dominican. They sent a prostitute there to tempt him. Thomas drove her out. She feels for St. Thomas.

B. R. came to visit at the farm, but she does not know him very well. She once sent him a book of St. Bernard's letters when he was ill and in his note of thanks back he told her he is an agnostic.

She is glad Hester recognized the shirts. She once had one with a bulldog and Georgia on it, but she avoids such spectacles now, since her mother says it is tasteless to wear such announcements over 30.

She does have ideas about God and nature, but she will not write them now. She is preparing a lecture to give in Lansing, Michigan, at AAUW. She would like it to be something like an argument for distorting fiction. She has not read Nelson Algren.

Works: None.

August 21, 1955 (p. 95; 4 par.):   From ANDALUSIA. She appreciates Algren's book. He is not a good writer in the 200 pages she has read thus far. She has read Céline's *Journey to the End of the Night* and finds Céline to be the superior writer to Algren. When one writes about the poor, one has to write about the real poor last and put oneself first. She is reading an article by Wyndham Lewis on George Orwell. Her chief objection to Algren is messy writing.

Works: None.

August 28, 1955 (p. 97; 8 par.): From ANDA-LUSIA. It would be nice to have St. Thomas nearby to ask about the issue of fascism. Though St. Thomas and St. John of the Cross were unlike one another, they had the same belief which unified them. St. John would have ministered to the prostitute and tried to help her. St. Thomas knew that he had to drive her out with a poker or else lose the battle of temptation. O'Connor relates to Thomas in that she knows that she needs the poker, too.

She also writes against the wave of nihilism that surrounds us. The church has been the only thing standing between her and that way of thinking.

Being born a Catholic makes one experience what one has accepted far down the line. Some things she is only now experiencing from what she accepted long ago.

The Simone Weil piece is from *The Third Hour.* It is written by a Russian named Helene Iswolsky who teaches at Fordham. O'Connor used to date her nephew. She encloses the Edith Stein that she has not read. She thinks highly of Weil and Stein for what they have done but not for what they have written.

She explains a few names, Caroline Gordon Tate, Allen Tate, John Crowe Ransom, and ROB-ERT PENN WARREN. At Vanderbilt, the group named themselves the Fugitives. She has learned a great deal about writing from Mrs. Tate.

As a child, she read Greek and Roman myths and The Book of Knowledge. Later she read EDGAR ALLAN POE, especially *The Humerous Tales of E. A. Poe.* Many of the stories were quite funny. One was about a good-looking man who took out his teeth, wood arms and legs, voicebox, hair piece, and so forth. Another is about patients in a mental hospital who take over the establishment. She would rather not think about the influence that the story may have had on her.

In graduate school, she was exposed to WIL-LIAM FAULKNER, FRANZ KAFKA, and JAMES JOYCE. She also began to read Catholic novelists such as

FRANÇOIS MAURIAC, Bernanos, Bloy, GRAHAM GREENE, and Waugh. She read Djuna Barnes, Dorothy Richardson, and Virginia Woolf, and southerners Faulkner, the Tates, KATHERINE ANNE PORTER, EUDORA WELTY, and Peter Taylor. She also read the Russians such as FYODOR DOS-TOYEVSKY (but not Tolstoy), Turgenev, Chekhov, and Gogol. She has read almost all of JOSEPH CONRAD, omitted Dreiser and Thomas Wolfe, but read a few stories of Sherwood Anderson's. She has drawn inspiration or technique from NATHANIEL HAWTHORNE, Flaubert, Balzac, and Kafka. She has read almost everything of HENRY JAMES. She also read Dr. Johnson's *Lives of the Poets.* If she had to choose one work, however, what always comes to mind is Poe's *Humerous Tales.* He probably wrote them all while drunk.

Has Hester read *The Lord* by Roman Guardini? She can lend it to her, if she likes.

Works: None.

September 6, 1955 (p. 99; 7 par.): From ANDA-LUSIA. Her Webster's dictionary is dated 1948, so her use of words may be five years behind. However, she does not agree that she is a fascist. She sees that as an offense against the body of Christ. She does not believe in the use of force, and neither does the church. She sees the changes that they both envision occurring within the church through Christ.

They do not agree on the Incarnation, and she does not agree that emotional satisfaction is necessary for something to be true. It does not change the idea that God exists just because many people do not find that emotionally satisfying anymore. Faith is not this way, either. Hester may be a Romantic; she hopes that she will change her mind about O'Connor being a fascist.

It has always been hard and complicated to see Christ's divinity and humanity at once in the same person. The church emphasizes the body, and she has struggled with the idea of purity.

"A Stroke of Good Fortune" should not have been in the collection; Hester is correct about it. It was once going to be part of *Wise Blood,* but she moved it.

"The Artificial Nigger" is her favorite story. One often wonders if one is up to the task, but things seem to have come together there. There is the tragedy of blacks represented by the statuary as well as Peter's denials. It worked.

Hester is also right about O'Connor's disposition. It is a combination of Nelson's and Hulga's, and even that may be being falsely positive.

Works: "A Stroke of Good Fortune," *Wise Blood,* "The Artificial Nigger."

September 15, 1955 (p. 102; 7 par.): From ANDALUSIA. One of the large differences between her faith and Hester's is that she believes it is not possible to know God through science and its limitations. God is love and is perfect and powerful.

Redemption and its mysteries are seen on Earth through good and loving works such as prayer, giving alms, keeping the sick company, and respecting death through proper burial and other forms.

LaCroix does not judge atheists as lost and leaves their fate up to God. She once heard about a priest who was being considered for canonization into sainthood. In his background, it was found that at one time he claimed that a man who was blasphemous up to the moment of his death would surely go to hell. From that single statement alone, he was not deemed worthy to be a saint.

Psychologists shed some light on temporary matters of the brain and emotions. She has been reading Jung, Neumann, and the Dominican, Victor White's *God and the Unconscious.* She read Karl Stern's *The Third Revolution.* She appreciates Stern's comments about guilt, particularly the way that he compares the Greek concept of it to the Christian.

If Hester thought of her as a fascist, it is better to have that out in the open and allow O'Connor to defend herself. Hester's letters make her think about matters that help clarify them for herself, which she both appreciates and enjoys.

She calls everyone the poor, not just those living in poverty. According to St. Thomas, one need not be a good person to write well, a trait for which she is grateful. HENRY JAMES says that the morality of a piece is in proportion to the "felt life" perceived within it.

She applies Jung's *Modern Man in Search of a Soul* in her own way to the world. She is not a modern Catholic but a Catholic with modern sensibilities.

Works: None.

September 24, 1955 (p. 104; 4 par.): From ANDALUSIA. She is adapting to her crutches. They make her feel like an ape who has no business thinking about Aristotle or St. Thomas, yet Hester's letters have her becoming more of a Thomist as well as an Aristotelian. She believes that human beings were created in the image and likeness of God. Creation is good and more perfect where it involves free will. Msgr. Guardini speaks about humility in a way that she would do. The crutches make crossing the room necessary to be a deliberate and planned-out act.

She is no great fan of Céline's; she simply meant that Céline's *Journey to the End of the Night* shows him to be a better writer than Nelson Algren. It is true that part of the author must go into each character, but to say that each character reflects the author entirely is exaggerated. JACQUES MARITAIN's comment that art demands the full attention of a pure mind is correct. A pure mind in this case must be able to see exactly what needs to be omitted. If she were to put herself into a story whole, it would fail as a story.

She is currently reading the Weil books. She finished *Letters to a Priest.* She speaks about the similiarities in the titles *Waiting for God* and *Waiting for Godot.* She finds Weil's life comical as well as tragic. If she lived long and developed her talent to the point necessary, she would like to write a funny novel about a woman.

Works: None.

September 30, 1955 (p. 106; 6 par.): From ANDALUSIA. She discusses Guardini and Dr. Crane. Crane's columns appear in the *Atlanta Constitution.* Her comments about Simone Weil's life being both comic and tragic are a compliment. The heroine of her novel about a woman would not be Weil; her heroine is Hulga. One of the skills in writing fiction is to be able to control one's characters and not be dominated by them, including by putting too much of oneself in them. This is why she writes about simple people. She writes what she is able to write.

She discusses Guardini and Romanticism. She is reading Etienne Gilson's *History of Christian Philosophy in the Middle Ages.* She finds it surprising that it answers many of Weil's questions put to Father Perrin and thought about before by St. Justin Martyr in the second century. She has read Gilson's *The Unity of Philosophical Experience,* which she likes.

Crutches for her are not as bad as they might be for someone else since she is not athletic and she did not engage in sports. It is kind of Hester to get her books from the Atlanta library. She encloses an article about Elizabeth Sewell, whose books she has been trying to find. She is writing to Forham in an attempt to get hold of the GRAHAM GREENE articles in back issues of *Thought* as well as *The Death of the Imagination.* Reviewers see her spirituality as Lutheran rather than Catholic; some say she has no spirituality at all.

She has a friend in ATLANTA who is going to send her a novel by B. R. for comments. She hopes she likes it, for her friend's sake. However, she does not see many poets writing good novels. She will send an article that she has on St. Thomas and Freud if Hester is interested.

Works: ["Good Country People"].

October 12, 1955 (p. 109; 7 par.): From ANDALUSIA. Hester should keep the Weil books until she is done with them; she is still working her way through *Waiting for God.* She would like the articles back, but her filing system leaves much to be desired. She discusses more about books going back and forth between them. She is nearly done with *The Structure of Poetry.* She gets a 20 percent discount from Cross Currents Bookstore. She enjoys reading booklists. She did not know that the University of Georgia was using a textbook by Dr. Crane.

She will read the St. Thomas and Freud article again to make sure it is appropriate to send to her. She is not a fan of Freud, but she has found uses for parts of his theories. She is

a fan when she must write or speak about him; always "crafty: never deny, seldom confirm, always distinguish" (110).

She and her crutches are going to Nashville to Vanderbilt to hear Russell Kirk. She liked his book *The Conservative Mind,* and he has another out, *Academic Freedom,* which she has not yet read.

It would be better for her if they could drop the "Miss" title for one another. It is too formal and gives her airs to be called "Miss O'Connor."

Works: None.

October 20, 1955 (p. 110; 12 par.): From ANDALUSIA. If she is not a facist in Hester's imaginings, then she is Cupid. She sends a self-portrait to give Hester a better idea of what she looks like. She is five feet three inches tall and weights 130 pounds.

Hester's packages get delivered more quickly than hers because they are better wrapped. Perhaps they can keep reversing the wrapping paper and applying new stamps and keep using that for the next several years. Would Hester please check to see if the ATLANTA library has the novel *Tarr* by Percy Wyndham Lewis. He is an author whom she would like to explore further. She will keep the Nelsen Algren on her gift book shelf and appreciates it.

Which translation is she reading of the Theban plays? She recommends Robert Fitzgerald's. She is pleased to hear that Hester reads her stories out loud. She does the same. Unfortunately, she is prone to laughing at her own jokes, which is unbecoming when she reads her stories in public.

George Clay, who wrote "We're All Guests," wrote to her about her work. He liked "Good Country People," but thought *Wise Blood* was boring because Haze Motes was not human enough. He did not like the religious aspects of "A Good Man," "A Temple of the Holy Ghost," or "A Circle of Fire." She accepts some of his criticism about *Wise Blood* and is working on that in her current novel project. The stories he obviously knows nothing about.

She did not get to hear Russell Kirk speak because the day was different than she expected; however, she met him and was able to talk with him at length during the weekend. She relays a short conversation, their both being nonconversationalists. Kirk is founding *The Conservative Review,* the first issue of which is due out in two weeks.

Sleep is an interesting subject. She went without sleep for several weeks once. She compares sleeps now to a gift from the mother of God. She contains our lives in sleep as she contained the Lord, and we hope to wake up in peace.

Dr. Crane's column in the *Atlanta Constitution,* page 18, Tuesday, October 18, advises preachers to ask their congregations for donations of goods such as chairs, stoves, typewriters since Jesus said that your heart is where your treasure is.

Works: A Good Man Is Hard to Find and other Stories, "Good Country People," "A Good Man Is Hard to Find," "A Temple of the Holy Ghost," "A Circle in the Fire."

October 30, 1955 (p. 113; 5 par.):   From ANDALUSIA. She agrees that Weil is quite a ways away from the church, but she came in its direction so far that she finds that interesting. She believes in Purgatory and sees herself there. She read St. Catherine of Genoa's *Treatese* on Purgatory.

She sends more articles. Some are on artificial mysticism. She finds the solution in St. Teresa, St. John of the Cross, and St. Catherine of Siena. She is reading *Born Catholics* by Frank Sheed. She was given the book by a nun who made her take piano lessons, which she hated. She thinks more should be written within the church about the subject of conversion.

She sent her self-portrait to *HARPER'S BAZAAR* and to Harcourt, Brace, but neither used it. Hester must have more energy than she, staying up until 1:00 A.M. reading. She is done by 9:00.

Dr. Crane says that C students who give truthful compliments will earn more income within 10 years than will A students who do not smile.

Works: None.

November 10, 1955 (p. 115; 6 par.):   From ANDALUSIA. She has read Meissonier. She thinks Clay has talent but little else. H. Motes is like Abraham in sacrificing himself. He is a mys-

tic who sacrifices his sight. A flaw in the novel is apparently that he was not characterized as human enough for his reasons to be believeable. What does she think of the review of the stories in the KENYON REVIEW?

She discusses Dante and Pseudo-Dionysius. Hester would like Evelyn Underhill's *Mysticism.* She wonders if the Atlanta Public Library might have Hügel's *The Mystical Element in Religion.* She would like to read it.

In a store the other day, a woman teared up in the elevator out of sympathy over her crutches. It made her feel just like The Misfit. The woman told her to remember what John said at the gate. O'Connor got off quickly at the next floor, even though it was not hers. She asked someone later what John said and was told "The lame shall enter first." She thinks that it will likely happen because the lame will hit everyone else with their crutches and move ahead of them.

Works: [*Wise Blood*], ["A Good Man Is Hard to Find"], ["The Lame Shall Enter First"].

November 25, 1955 (p. 117; 7 par.):   From ANDALUSIA. She writes about purity and its relation to "A Temple of the Holy Ghost." She supposes one works the most on what one is least sure of, but she worked very hard with Haze and found very little struggle with Enoch. She was ill by the end of writing the book. Possibly some of her illness entered the book and some of the book entered her illness.

The man in "The Displaced Person" facilitated redemption in that he wrecked the evil farm. Mrs. McIntyre was put on a course of beginning suffering, a Purgatory in a sense. The story did not show this clearly enough, though she thinks that redemption need not always be clear and obvious and probably is not always. The PEACOCKS provide a design of the universe. The priest recognizes the Transfiguration in the peacock's raised tail.

Ben C. Griffith wrote to her about *Wise Blood* and was going to write a critical piece about her work for *Georgia Review,* except, it appears they did not want it and preferred another article which he wrote about James Jones. She needs to read her competition. Griffith sees a sexual tension in the stories. In "A Circle in the Fire," for example, the girl is not attacked sexually in the woods but is attacked nonetheless. She had not thought of these things but sees where his comments have validity.

She sends the *Thought* issue with the article on GRAHAM GREENE by Sewell. She likes the one by Fr. Lynch. She read Sigrid Undset's *Kristin Lavransdatter* some years ago. She does not need to read the Hügel biographies. She will read *Letters to a Niece* and wants also to read Frances Newman's *The Hard Boiled Virgin.*

Works: "A Temple of the Holy Ghost," [*Wise Blood*], ["The Displaced Person"], "A Circle in the Fire."

December 8, 1955 (p. 120; 6 par.):   From ANDALUSIA. She appreciates Hester's charity more than her observations, even though she does make acute observations. She disagrees with her on the reason behind any sexual attack on the child by the boys in "A Circle in the Fire." They would not do it because they were attracted to her but because it would be the surest way to hurt Mrs. Cope. She cannot force a character to undergo anything that she could not stand herself, so she did not have the boys attack the child in that way.

She enjoys the two Shirley Grau stories she has read. Among her contemporaries she likes Peter Taylor's *A Long Fourth*, parts of J. F. Powers' *Prince of Darkness* and *The Presence of Grace*, the early works of EUDORA WELTY. She finds TRUMAN CAPOTE's and TENNESSEE WILLIAMS' work both sickening. She likes Frank O'Connor among contemporary non-American writers. If one of the club women ever asks her if she is related to Frank O'Connor, she plans to respond that she is his mother.

Hester's friend was kind to say that she enjoyed her talk, but most club meetings do not expect a serious speaker to talk about serious topics. As far as realism goes, poets need to be realists because poetry requires it. St. Catherine of Genoa may be a poet and a realist; Mrs. Hopewell is the realist without being a poet, and Hulga is the reverse. She comments that she thought she

understood that Undset wrote a couple of novels set in the current century that did not work too well, but she has not read them.

Works: "A Circle in the Fire."

December 16, 1955 (p. 123; 8 par.):   From ANDALUSIA. She attempts to explain her aesthetics, though she has no set theory and probably contradicts herself in every which way. She does not believe that fiction is moral or immoral. She does think that the author's morality and dramatic sensibility must match. The devil is a better writer than Mlle. Sagan because he has both of these senses aligned.

As far as she knows, the church teaching is that the body and personality of the person will be fully integrated except that the person will be without sin. Heaven will be seeing and only wanting to see God.

She got the closest she can to an illustration of purity as she thinks of it through her story ["A Temple of the Holy Ghost"]. Purity is accepting God's individual plan for us.

At a dinner that MARY MCCARTHY and she attended some years ago, she was there with Mr. Broadwater, ROBERT LOWELL, and Elizabeth Hardwick. McCarthy had left the church and was talking about the Eucharist and really what a good symbol it is. In a trembling voice, O'Connor said, "Well, if it's a symbol, to hell with it" (125). The Eucharist is the center of her existence, and this is all she will be able to say on the matter outside of her fiction.

She spoke about St. Thomas and St. Catherine of Siena at the talk. She did not quote St. Augustine. She is to go to another literary event on Tuesday.

If her "celebrity" makes Hester feel odd, she should think about how it makes O'Connor feel. She may as well be identified with Roy Rogers's horse or Miss Watermelon of 1955. Celebrities only have friends who are old and knew her before, or new ones like Hester for whom she is grateful and who are willing and able to not think about it or let it bother them.

Works: ["A Temple of the Holy Ghost"].

January 1, 1956 (p. 126; 8 par.): From ANDA-
LUSIA. She encloses material that explains her
thoughts on the idea of things heading toward
womanhood. She tries to name accurately the
things of God in her fiction. She does not believe
that Nature is God but that God created and
sustains it.

She does not believe that one must submit in
order to renunciate. She also does not believe
that purity can be naïve. It must come from
either experience or grace.

She has mailed her another article by Sewell
and one on St. Thomas and Freud. Sewell has
a new article in *Thought* on Chesteron, but she
has not read it. Would Hester like to read Guardini's article on the Grand Inquisitor section of
The Brothers Karamazov? She would like to read
The Bridge edited by John M. Oesterreicher.

Her novel has stalled for the moment. She
started a short story when the novel bothered
her. She writes "because I write well" (127).

She is now used to the crutches, and it seems
she needs to be because the doctor said that she
may need them for a year to three years. She was
not active, so the hardship is not that much.

For Christmas, from Robert Fitzgerald she
received a copy of his translation in manuscript
of the *Odyssey*'s first seven books. She also
received a poinsettia from an anonymous giver.
She had never gotten an anonymous gift before.

She needs to write a talk for the AAUW in
Michigan on "Some Aspects of Modern Fiction"
and wonders about the intelligence of northern
ladies versus southern ladies.

Works: [*The Violent Bear It Away*], "Some Aspects
of Modern Fiction."

January 13, 1956 (p. 128; 6 par.): From ANDA-
LUSIA. She appreciates the copy of *The Hard Boiled
Virgin* and the two Weil books. She is not enjoying the first 50 plus pages of HBV—it is all told
and not dramatized; she is not a fiction writer. It
reminds her of *Marius the Epicurean* in this regard.

She sends the Guardini and a part of a report
from Iowa. It will make Hester even more
pleased that she does not have a college degree.

She discusses the moral basis of poetry in
terms of naming the things of God accurately.
JOSEPH CONRAD said his goal was to give justice to that which is visible in the universe. St.
Augustine said that the world's things came into
the world physically as objects and intellectually
into the thoughts of the angels.

The Catholic Church and Protestants both
read the Gospel and interpret it. She is currently
content writing a story ["Greenleaf"] in which
a 63-year-old woman will be charged by a bull.
She is not sure whether she identifies with the
woman or the bull. The risk of it may be what is
pleasing her.

Works: ["Greenleaf"].

January 17, 1956 (p. 130; 6 par.): From ANDA-
LUSIA. She is never prepared. The three kinds
of baptism are water, blood, and desire. She
thought that Hester was baptized with the latter
if none other, so she does not know what to say
about her news. Miracles like voluntary baptisms
always leave her speechless.

She does not mean to be pompous in saying
that she writes to try to accurately name the things
of God or that she has even achieved it. She only
means that she tries to "see straight" (131). She
asks God to help her see and write with clarity.

It is not her goal to be an angel. She is getting
along with them better, however. When she was a
child, she used to lock herself in a room and turn in
circles striking out at her guardian angel. The Sisters told the children in Catholic school that their
guardian angels never leave them, and she wanted
to, if not hurt him since that was impossible, at
least dust up his feathers. She had not thought of
angels for a long time until about two years ago
when she was sent the PRAYER OF ST. RAPHAEL on
a card by the *Catholic Worker*. She had forgotten
that Raphael was the archangel who helped guide
Tobias. She used the prayer in "The Displaced
Person" when Mrs. Shortley thinks about her true
country. The prayer solicits guidance toward joy in
order that we not miss our true country.

She has sold *Wise Blood* to Gallimard, a French
publisher.

Works: "The Displaced Person," *Wise Blood*, ["Greenleaf"].

January 30, 1956 (p. 133; 4 par.): From ANDA-LUSIA. She has sent the Dialogues of St. Catherine of Siena. If she would like it, she can send *The Church and Modern Man* by Guardini. As Hester gets more into the church, it is not likely that her intellect will dull but that it will not rule so tyrannically. Her packages have grown neater since she has been turning Hester's paper inside out.

Works: None.

February 11, 1956 (p. 136; 4 par.): From ANDA-LUSIA. She has thought more in terms of father and child than in the bride and bridegroom analogy. It is funny how she did imagine herself stopping aging when she was 12. She did not want to be a teenager. She felt more burdened as a child than she does now.

She has set the bull story aside to see what she thinks of it now that she has a draft. In the meantime, she is working on a talk for the Council of Teachers of English in March, the event in Michigan, and a BOOK REVIEW for *The BULLETIN,* a Catholic publication. The book review will be her first publication in a Catholic journal.

A Jesuit drove up to the farm in a white Cadillac a few weeks ago. He jumped out of the car and told her that he liked her stories. They had a good talk, and 10 days later, she heard from the editor of AMERICA wanting her to contribute.

Works: ["Greenleaf"], *Wise Blood*.

February 25, 1956 (p. 140; 6 par.): From ANDA-LUSIA. She reviewed *All Manner of Men* for the *Bulletin*. It is a collection of short stories taken from the Catholic press. S. wrote several pages about *Wise Blood* in a letter to her telling her that he did not like it.

Hester may be right that it is the parents who tend to burden children, but the fact remains that she never envisioned herself as an adult. The adults around her never left the 19th century, so they tended to get along fine.

Tarwater goes to his uncle in the city, and the uncle is an atheist out of the Protestant tradition. She needs to make him more human. In her bull story, she uses the sun; she tends to signal prominent features, unlike EUDORA WELTY who is much more subtle. She is frustrated with her talk in April and commits herself to keeping it to a half hour.

Works: *Wise Blood*, ["Greenleaf"].

March 10, 1956 (p. 144; 7 par.): From ANDA-LUSIA. She is delighted to have *The Bridge* edited by Fr. John Oesterreicher and notices that it is not a library book. The cancer home has a former dancer as a patient, showing how much grace is there. Does Hester know that it was founded by NATHANIEL HAWTHORNE's daughter? She thinks it may be God's retribution to Hawthorne for disliking the Transcendentalists.

Novenas are useful only in that they go for nine days and help people keep attention. The review of Caroline Gordon's book in *Time* disgusts her. Gordon may not succeed in all that she attempts in the novel because she is trying to do the impossible, but her effort is better than so many other works that they will recommend. Gordon has taught her a lot about writing.

Antagonists must contain a bit of the author, or they will not be fully drawn nor adversaries. She disliked dancing as a child and was repulsed by the company of other children. In the end she somewhat got what she wanted in having her leg ailments. She sends "Greeleaf" for her comments and will not be offended if Hester does not like it.

Works: ["Greenleaf"].

March 24, 1956 (p. 148; 6 par.): From ANDA-LUSIA. She asks for clarification on Hester's comment about the fender of the car in "Greenleaf." She thought a fender went across the front of a car and the bumper across the back. However, she has made car mistakes before, once having Mr. Shiflet step on the clutch to start the car in the version in KENYON REVIEW. She fixed the mistake before the story went into the collection.

A fiction writer must be a little bit stupid. She needed to get the bull's horns into the woman's ribs, but she did not care to explore why she wanted this. She thinks of the bull, the sun, and Mrs. May as all sympathetic. If personal matters are worked on through fiction, it must be unconsciously.

She has received an article on her written by a woman from the Texas State College for Woman and sent to MADEMOISELLE. It is called "Flannery O'Connor: The Pattern in the Fire." The woman who wrote it does not understand O'Connor's work.

The Tates knew Hart Crane. Caroline says that she is going to teach a course at the University of Kansas, where she forces her students to see the difference between TRUMAN CAPOTE's work and *Wise Blood*.

In order to celebrate Hester's joining the church, she intends to go to Communion on Easter Sunday with her in mind. Since they will then have eaten of the same food, they will know how this act increases both of them.

Works: ["Greenleaf"], *Wise Blood*.

April 7, 1956 (p. 150; 7 par.): From ANDALUSIA. She loves Mrs. May, Mrs. Cope, Mrs. Hopewell, and Bailey's mother. Mrs. Greenleaf; well, she was virtuous; you have to give her that. She sends the book page from *The Bulletin*. She received a letter recently about a young man in college who is paying his way going door to door selling both Bibles and contraceptives.

She has only read *Swann's Way* by Proust. She also received a letter from Michigan in relation to her visit that she is being asked to a tea given by the Newman Club of Michigan State. Before they invited her, they wanted to be sure that she was a practicing Catholic, which tells her that they either cannot tell that from her work or they have not read her work.

She has been on crutches for six months and went to ATLANTA for an X-ray. She was told that she will remain on crutches from now on.

Works: ["Good Country People"], ["Greenleaf"].

April 21, 1956 (p. 151; 6 par.): From ANDALUSIA. She has the St. Catherine. She sent *The Malefactors*, which Hester can keep or give away since she has another copy. She agrees with Hester that J. F. Powers's collection is not up to his first. For reviews, she thinks that it is possible to be honest and wrong, so she favors being careful and courteous.

Cal, ROBERT LOWELL, makes her sad. At YADDO, she watched him return to the church after having left it and his first wife. He became very emotional to the point of having a breakdown, leaving the church again. He married Elizabeth Hardwick and has been undergoing treatments of drugs and institutionalizations since. She prays that he will find it easy to return to the church. She loves him and will not be at peace until he has returned. He has written *The Mills of the Kavanaughs* and is writing his life story as a sort of therapy.

Their correspondence means something to her. Her interest in the correspondence may be too much concerned with her and her work, but her work does interest her. She does not feel that it is a duty to write to Hester and hopes that Hester will only write when she likes it as well and not out of a sense of obligation.

She leaves Monday for Lansing and will return on Friday.

Works: None.

May 5, 1956 (p. 154; 9 par.): From ANDALUSIA. She will be glad to be Hester's Confirmation sponsor. She was a godmother to a child in California by proxy once, and they needed a letter stating that she was willing to do so. If they need something like that for this, let her know. She has never been a Confirmation sponsor before.

Their book swaps have become a bit out of sync. She has already sent *The Malefactors* to Mrs. Rumsey Haynes. She enjoyed the couple. She did not end up going to the Newman tea; they had her instead speak to a very large luncheon of the National Association of Catholic Women. She was last in a long line of other speakers in front of about 500 people (like the old soldier in her story).

She may meet Billy Sessions in person after all, since he is due to visit Dr. Rosa Lee Walston at the English Department of GSCW. She hopes she will not hear from S. again. The letters are full of hate, and she advised him to stop writing to her.

Would Hester like to read Baron von Hügel's letters to his niece? She reviewed it for the *Bulletin* and thinks it is better than anything she has read in quite a while. The woman from Texas won an award for her article on O'Connor. She tried to explain to O'Connor what she meant about Gide, but O'Connor is still not sure about it. Still, she likes that the girl won the award.

Works: ["A Late Encounter With the Enemy"].

May 19, 1956 (p. 157; 8 par.): From ANDALUSIA. She discusses *The Malefactors* and HENRY JAMES. Gordon writes in the school of James, using a central intelligence as he does in *The Ambassadors* with the character Strether. Tate and her husband, Allen, have written about this in their book *The House of Fiction.*

While good fiction does not lie, neither can it tell a whole and complete truth. The story is about life as that is interpreted by the writer; it is not about a writer and how he or she has been influenced by life.

The two black people in her story "The Displaced Person" are on the the farm. She sees blacks from the outside; she would never dare try an internal view such as Shirley Ann Grau attempts.

She does not think Catherine in *The Malefactors* was a successful character. She needed more of a body presence. She sends Hester *A Short Breviary.* She says Prime in the mornings and Compline some nights but most not. She likes her prayers to repeat sometimes and sometimes to change and thinks that staying with the liturgy is a good way to pray.

Works: "Good Country People," "The Displaced Person."

June 1, 1956 (p. 160; 8 par.): From ANDALUSIA. It took her four days to write "Good Country People" and two to three months to complete

"The Artificial Nigger," and she thinks both stories are arguably equal in quality. The creative energy in each was different. It is not possible to know the energy entailed in writing a novel unless one writes one.

Sally Fitzgerald is five feet two inches tall, weighing no more than 92 pounds unless she is pregnant, and she is pregnant a lot of the time. She is due with their seventh baby next week; they have been married nine years. Robert married a non-Catholic and left the church; then the marriage was annulled, and he married Sally, who converted, and Robert came back to the church. They are both devout practicing Catholics.

She is reviewing Russell Kirk's *Beyond the Dreams of Avarice* for The BULLETIN. She could send *The Conversative Mind* if Hester would like it. She is pleased that Hester likes the breviary, on which the Fitzgeralds started her some years ago.

Her friend in Nashville lent her Wyndham Lewis's *Demon of Progress,* but it was lost in shipping when she sent it back to him. She is grateful that it was his copy, at least, but now she is uncomfortable sending library books.

Would Hester be interested in coming for a weekend to Andalusia this summer? She would like to show her her PEACOCK.

Works: ["Good Country People"], "The Artificial Nigger."

June 28, 1956 (p. 163; 6 par.): From ANDALUSIA. Hester tends to think too highly of her, and she would be in trouble with the devil if she believed what she said. It seemed like Hester was ready to leave almost the whole time that she was there. Regina likes guests to eat, so she should try to stay long enough to do that next time. "I have never been anywhere but sick" (163). Illness is like a place where nobody can go with you. Her family does not show their emotions, except perhaps annoyance. For help with her crutches, the only help that really is of assistance is if someone holds the door open for her. Does she smell the *National Geographic?*

Works: None.

July 13, 1956 (p. 165; 4 par.):   From ANDALUSIA. She is very grateful to receive a biography of Baron von Hügel and his *Essays and Addresses*. She has a chess set that she never plays. She assumes one needs more of a mathematical mind to enjoy it. She would like to learn but only play with someone who does not take it any more seriously than she does.

Has she read St. Theresa of Avila's *Interior Castle*? She has that. She is thankful for Hester's aunt's comments about her father and his connection to the Legion. She once read over some of the speeches he made there and was touched by their old-fashioned partriotism.

Works: None.

July 28, 1956 (p. 167; 6 par.):   From ANDALUSIA. She will get back the article from the Jesuit about Elizabeth Sewell. They now have a telephone. The lineman looked at her PEACOCKS a long time and then mentioned their long legs rather than being enamored as she thought he was. She has completed the biography about the baron.

Her father may have carried some of her artwork around. She drew chickens a lot when she was younger. She is not at high risk of idealizing him because she bears some of his faults along with his attributes and also bears the same health condition, LUPUS. He used to want to write as well but did not the have opportunities that she has had. Her success makes her happy when she thinks that this may help fulfill one of his dreams.

The church has done a lot to free women, perhaps more than any other element in history.

Works: None.

August 11, 1956 (p. 168; 6 par.):   From ANDALUSIA. She is writing a talk on the Catholic fiction writer for a women's group in Macon. Her father did write a lot, but he would have written good creative pieces if he could have. She enjoys the telephone and thinks that it is a good invention. Her mother is taken up with it, which relieves her, too.

Works: None.

August 24, 1956 (p. 170; 6 par.):   From ANDALUSIA. It does not seem that Hester is reading the story ["Good Country People"]. Hulga hates the Bible salesman until she realizes that he hates her. She is not as smart as she thought she was. Her faith was trodden down by her fine education, and her intellectual pride has driven out her purity. She never kissed anyone before, but she may or may not have loved before. Hulga is like O'Connor, but so are so many of her other characters. One should not try to analyze the author through her fiction. In talking about the technique in writing the story, she may have also led Hester astray. The story came easily; she was fairly unconscious of technique as she wrote it.

She has been reading Jean Guitton's *The Virgin Mary*, which she recommends. She will be meeting a man on Sunday who wants to make a movie out of "The River." It is a story about baptism; how does one do a documentary on such a subject as that?

Works: ["Good Country People"], "The River."

September 8, 1956 (p. 172; 5 par.):   From ANDALUSIA. She believes the artist has a right to choose to write about the negative just as much as the positive. She quotes from Msgr. Guardini. Does Hester read the *Catholic Worker*? She sends a piece by John Lynch. She discusses Herbert Marshall McLuhan and *The Mechanical Bride*.

The man came to discuss dramatizing "The River." He has never made a movie before, so she is not sure if anything will come of it, but she liked the man, who stuttered. She sold the television rights to "The Life You Save May Be Your Own" to *General Electric Playhouse*. Ronald Reagan is involved, and she would be stunned to see him play Mr. Shiftlet. She is taking the money from the sale of the rights and buying her mother a refrigerator.

Works: "The River;" "The Life You Save May Be Your Own."

September 22, 1956 (p. 176; 6 par.):   From ANDALUSIA. She does not think about attributes of people in terms of feminine or masculine. She tends to divide people by bothersome or not bothersome. She is having trouble with her novel, but at least she is not writing a film.

Works: None.

October 6, 1956 (p. 177; 5 par.): From ANDALUSIA. She has revised ["A View of the Woods"] using Hester's three suggestions. She and Regina and N. went to a cattle auction, which she describes. Purgatory must have some element of learning about how close vices and virtues are. In the Communion of Saints, we can bear the burdens of those who burden us. She does not write from abstraction, so she cannot answer questions about why characters like the bull, Mrs. May, Mr. Fortune, or Mary Fortune have to die. She just knows that they do.

Works: ["A View of the Woods"].

November 12, 1956 (p. 179; 3 par.): From ANDALUSIA. Her recording will be aired Friday, November 23 at 7:30 P.M. on WGKA-FM. She does not like the sound of her voice on the recording. H. C. Gardiner, S. J. did not know that Hester was in the audience of his recent talk. He misquoted O'Connor.

If Hester visits, she can show her the scroll she received from the Georgia Writers' Association.

Works: None.

November 17, 1956 (p. 179; 4 par.): From ANDALUSIA. She thinks Hester's comments about Self-Condemned are true. Has she seen *Rotting Hill?* O'Connor liked it.

Her mother tells the story better of what happened yesterday involving a cow jumping into the water trough. They had to get a wrecking truck to pull her out.

A writer need not understand emotions in his or her story, just create them. She sends her talk for Wesleyan in December. She is to give another speech at Emory, though the folks there have been quite nice to her.

Works: None.

November 29, 1956 (p. 182; 11 par.): From ANDALUSIA. She has heard unofficially that she

is going to win the O. HENRY AWARD. She sends a piece by Powers on "Greenleaf." She discusses B. and his fiction. She addresses meaning in fiction in that she does not engage herself with it that much. A writing teacher is more or less a midwife.

When she asked a writer at Emory if he had any good students, he told her that teaching writing is a fraud. She thought in return that he could probably have used more of it. She is pleased Hester sent the picture. She talks about a goose they cooked for Thanksgiving.

She speaks about her lecture and Hester's comments. She would like Hester to come but comprehends her reasons. She refers Hester to a poem in *Commonweal* by Carol Johnson, who is the only writer to whom she wrote first. She thinks her poetry is worth keeping an eye on.

Works: "Greenleaf," *A Good Man Is Hard to Find and other Stories*.

December 11, 1956 (p. 186; 11 par.): From ANDALUSIA. She sends the magazine from Chicago that she gets from Ben Griffith. She also sends four letters from C. J. She does have *The Tower of Babel*, if she is interested. Harold C. wants to shorten her article for AMERICA rather than have her do it. She is not pleased with that notion since it will be under her name. She has not read Gordon's *The Forest of the South*. She discusses "Old Red" and "Summer Dust." Lon Brainard Cheney thinks that her best novel is *None Shall Look Back*, but she has not read it. *Critique* published an issue on Caroline the previous spring.

She does not recommend writing exercises, though she agrees with experimentation. Hester would not be engaged enough in anything written simply as an exercise. She would be better off thinking of a character and make that character come alive. The character will suggest its problem and the solution will come about on its own. It is better to find meaning through the story than to have meaning imposed on it from the beginning. She should write a draft, then see what she has, and then work to bring this out more clearly. The man living with the bears reminds her of Cal [ROBERT] LOWELL's imaginary policeman friend who is half man and half bear. She thinks she will ask her agent to sell all of her stories to be made into musical comedies.

Works: "A View of the Woods."

December 28, 1956 (p. 189; 7 par.): From ANDALUSIA. She never thought that she would own a copy of Simone Weil's *Notebooks of Simone Weil*. It was kind of Hester to read ["A View of the Woods"] another time through. She discusses this story. She discusses Powers and his comments about Mrs. May.

Msgr. Guardini has an article in the fall issue of *Cross Currents* about *The Idiot* as a Christ symbol. She is sending Hester a subscription that will go back to that issue. She has a Christ or a figure of redemption in her novel. She has not heard from Harold C. Gardiner S. J. nor from the O. HENRY people.

She writes about a letter from her agent detailing the airing of "The Life You Save" on February 1 on the *Schlitz Playhouse* at 9:30 P.M.

Works: ["A View of the Woods"], "The Life You Save May Be Your Own."

December 29, 1956 (p. 191; 5 par.): From ANDALUSIA. The O. HENRY AWARDS just sent her a check. It is better to write a piece out and see how long it will be than to decide its length ahead of time. She recommends Percy Lubbock's *The Craft of Fiction* and Brooks's and ROBERT PENN WARREN's *Understanding Fiction*. She sends good wishes for the new year and appreciation for her letters.

Works: "Greenleaf"

January 12, 1957 (p. 196; 8 par.): From ANDALUSIA. She sends a piece by Harold C. Pitts should be the Christ symbol if there is one. Sally Fitzgerald once reviewed Simone Weil in *Commonweal*. She likes Elizabeth Hardwick Lowell's *The Simple Truth*. She has not heard about a baby. N. has a job selling magazines like *Ladies' Home Journal*. Her mother is guarding the azalea that she received anonymously at Christmas in order to keep it alive to plant in the spring. From

SAVANNAH, she loves azaleas and has wanted one for some time. The Brooks and the [ROBERT PENN] WARREN have many of her youthful notes in them, but she has sent the two books.

Works: None.

January 25, 1957 (p. 198; 14 par.): From ANDALUSIA. She has just completed Hester's story and likes it very much. She questions whether it may be too long and wonders about the humanness of the hero. Her use of the MASS is, in general, fine, with a couple of questions. She questions the character Janelle. The tramp is good; Jennie Mae might speak less. It would be helpful to have a suggestion of why the boy is so terrible. After revision, she recommends that Hester send the story to ACCENT, *Epoch*, or *NEW WORLD WRITING*. Avoid calling streets Oak or Main. Let her see the revision. She discusses Martha Foley and Paul Engle and "The Artificial Nigger" and "A Circle in the Fire."

She has read Frank O'Connor's *The Mirror in the Roadway*. The Lowells had a baby girl. She discusses Caroline's *Aleck Maury* and "Old Red." She will return the story with any further comments.

Works: "The Artificial Nigger," "A Circle in the Fire."

February 21, 1957 (p. 202; 7 par.): From ANDALUSIA. She thinks the scene with the window-washing is very funny but does not follow the ending. She discusses B. and what she had read. B. does not like "A Temple of the Holy Ghost." She did not approve of the review of the O. HENRY stories in *Commonweal*, not only of her own story but the others as well. The male reviewers criticize Jean Stafford and MARY MCCARTHY, the latter because she is more intelligent than they are.

There is an article in the *Constitution* by Celestine Sibley about her talk at Emory. It quotes her citing a novelist that completing a novel is like giving birth to a piano sideways. She wishes that she could be better understood. It also sounds like she loathed the audience. The event is over, and she is glad. The G. farm help has taken a job down the road, and they must hire someone new.

Works: "A Temple of the Holy Ghost."

March 9, 1957 (p. 206; 8 par.): From ANDALUSIA. She likes the revised ending. She suggests Hester send the story to Arabel J. Porter at NEW WORLD WRITING and also to try *Epoch*, ACCENT, and the University of Kansas City *Review*. How did Hester like O'Connor's picture in *The* BULLETIN? She will be giving a talk at Notre Dame on April 15. She did see the television play. She sent her the Edith Stein book and the one about Fénelon. New farm help, Mr. F. and family, have arrived. Her agent's secretary sent her comment on the television play and that they planned to investigate a possible musical with Rodgers and Hammerstein. O'Connor is not sure whether or not this was a joke.

Works: None.

March 23, 1957 (p. 210; 8 par.): From ANDALUSIA. This title is better than the other one but still not quite right for the story. She will not interfere by writing to Mrs. Porter if Hester does not want her to, but the help would be that Mrs. Porter and not some assistant would review the story herself. Madison Jones's novel, *The Innocent*, is a very good novel but got a bad review in *Commonweal*. Regina took Shot in to take his written driver's test. She had to read him the questions. Harold C. edited her article for AMERICA and wrote to tell her. She is reading a book about HENRY JAMES by Elizabeth Stevenson.

Works: None.

March 26, 1957 (p. 211; 3 par.): From ANDALUSIA. Her article will be in the AMERICA issue for the 30th, not the 23rd. Her mother has taken the rug out from under her and replaced it, cleaning underneath with turpentine.

Works: None.

April 6, 1957 (p. 213; 6 par.): From ANDALUSIA. She explains the paragraph that was changed in AMERICA and her feelings about it. The priest is not necessarily wrong but observes these matters

of the artist from a distance. She is stopping doing things for service clubs but does still do work for the church, such as *America* and *The* BULLETIN. It is about the only charity or volunteer work she is able to do. Has she read *Art and Scholasticism*?

She waits for her $50, but the college where she recently read was fairly unpleasant. She read in the basement. She discusses Hester's story. Confirmation should not go long with 40 other people. She is pleased she had her sacraments when younger. She writes about Mr. F.'s family.

Works: None.

April 20, 1957 (p. 216; 6 par.): From ANDALUSIA. She sends the speech she gave at Notre Dame and an article by Sally Fitzgerald on Gardiner. At the talk, she was approached by a Lutheran who sympathizes with Catholics. She said she hoped that O'Connor would be a Catholic writer who would do something. She meant what she said, and O'Connor asked her to pray for her, and she said she would. Instances like this make the trips and speeches worthwhile. She speaks about dreams and the artist.

She sent her *Art and Scholasticism*. B. mailed her his story, and she liked it. She is getting a copy of *The Red Priest* and has turned down an opportunity to speak to the Georgia Library Association. She needs to prepare a two-page talk for the GSCW for an AWARD that they are giving her, which should not be too bad, except that she must endure a tea and social.

Works: None.

May 4, 1957 (p. 218; 7 par.): From ANDALUSIA. She discusses Joyce Cary novels. B. met up with Dorothy Day, and they talked about *The Malefactors*. Hester is wrong about Sally Fitzgerald; she has a sharp mind and high principles. Her Uncle Louis told her that he saw Hester. She is receiving a $1000 grant from the National Institute of Arts & Letters, along with Robert Fitzgerald and MARY MCCARTHY. Does she like JACQUES MARITAIN? Dreams are inappropriate for fiction. Form is made by the truth.

Works: None.

May 18, 1957 (p. 219; 5 par.):   From ANDALUSIA. She should not be sorry that she sends an unsuccessful story. The writer learns from these. She offers comments on the story. One writes stories not from an *idea* but from character or from plot. Father Tavard will be sending her some of his articles since O'Connor gave him her address. She has a peachicken that lost a foot, probably from a sling blade. She sends Dorothy Day's article from *Catholic Worker*.

Works: None.

June 1, 1957 (p. 222; 7 par.):   From ANDALUSIA. She writes about Mr. F. and his family who left the farm. She will write their story. Regina is working on getting Shot his driver's license and has enlisted professional help. She did not go to Koinonia with Fr. McCown and the Gossetts. She writes about her peafowl. The one with one leg must be kept away from the others, or they will kill it. She has not managed to find a wooden leg for it, and it may not be possible. She has purchased a four-room yellow house with her savings and will rent it out. She is mailing her a painting for her Confirmation.

Works: None.

Saturday [June, 1957] (p. 224; 1 par.):   From ANDALUSIA. She announces that Willie Shot Manson received his driver's license granted by the State of Georgia.

Works: None.

June 15, 1957 (p. 225; 6 par.):   From ANDALUSIA. She was sorry that her mother insured the package because she thought that would mean that Hester needed to go after it. She discusses *The Spoils of Poynton, The Portrait of a Lady*, and *The Sacred Fount*. Judge HENRY JAMES comments on *Lady* not the others. From the X-ray, the doctor says that her bone has not gotten worse. She does not like her name listed as Mary F. O'Connor for the Confirmation sponsors. Hester should wear old shoes to the farm since it is muddy and because of the manure.

Works: None.

June 29, 1957 (p. 228; 4 par.):   From ANDALUSIA. Mailer's *The Deer Park* has made it, but she is at present reading about St. Bonaventure. Harold C. S. J. wants her to write out her talk for the *Catholic Hour* since NBC will not be able to tape it. The peafowl without the leg does not need Hester's sympathy for being alone. All it thinks about is where its next food is coming from and how it cannot be killed. At the moment, it is resting in the shade. It is all right if Hester gets there before 11:30.

Works: None.

July 12, 1957 (p. 228; 6 par.):   From ANDALUSIA. If an editor keeps a manuscript, that is a compliment. She has completed reading *The Deer Park*. Has she read *The Romantic Agony* by Mario Praz? They have purchased a Santa Gertrudis bull. She read Powers's *Prince of Darkness* back when it first came out. She would like Hester to see Robie Macauley's *The End of Pity*. She is not positive she will use the title *The Violent Bear It Away*, but it works for her for now.

Works: [*The Violent Bear It Away*].

August 9, 1957 (p. 234; 10 par.):   From ANDALUSIA. When she gets *Modern Age*, she will send it to her. She writes about the jamboree. Phinizy Spaulding wrote to her about a paper he wrote as an undergraduate called "Children in the Stories of Flannery O'Connor." She discusses Hester's writing. She sent a review of Baron von Hügel's *Essays and Addressses* for *The* BULLETIN, which had run out of book material. The bull has arrived, and Regina named it Banjo.

To Waugh, a Catholic novel is one that concerns itself with conflicts about the faith; to her it is any novel written by a Catholic, which includes herself. She goes to bed at 9 o'clock but stayed healthy during Ashley's visit when he stayed up until one. She was told that her piece was read by Paul Horgan on the *Catholic Hour*. He was a teacher of hers at Iowa. At the time, he did not even know that she was in the room but was a good teacher who once noted about 40 problems with a story.

Works: A Good Man Is Hard to Find.

August 24, 1957 (p. 237; 7 par.): From ANDA-LUSIA. She has sent her *God's Heralds, The Two-Edged Sword,* and *The Path Through Genesis.* She is reading a FRANÇOIS MAURIAC novel, *Lines of Life,* which first appeared as *Destinies.* She gives advice on Hester's writing. Phinizy Spaulding visited to talk with her about William Alexander Percy, about whom he is writing his thesis. Her Uncle's house, Bell House, is going to be demolished. They are receiving the furniture from it at Andalusia. She sent her Robie's *Time.*

Works: None.

August 26, 1957 (p. 238; 2 par.): From ANDA-LUSIA. Her uncle has taken a room in Hester's area. He misses his house, so if she sees him, please offer him a smile. William Sessions is a good writer.

Works: None.

September 7, 1957 (p. 240; 3 par.): From ANDALUSIA. The one-legged peacock has been accepted back into the flock. Cozzens revealed himself in saying that Ernest Hemingway's *The Old Man and the Sea* should be in *Little Folks Magazine.* Hester's comments may be true about Madison Jones's *The Innocent,* though O'Connor tends to remember a work not in detail but very generally either favorably or not.

Works: None.

September 21, 1957 (p. 241; 6 par.): From ANDALUSIA. Hester need not read quickly nor return the Robie or *Thought.* She is reading a biography of St. John of the Cross and Rabelais. She writes about *The Lines of Life* and *The Lamb.* She has never heard of the Female Orphan Benevolent Society. When she said that Hester should write what was easy, she meant what was possible. All while she has been writing, the only easy writing for her has been Enoch and Hulga; "the rest has been pushing a stone uphill with my nose" (241).

If Hester does not write fiction, what will she focus on? She contemplates other forms, reviews, poetry, autobiography, poetry, and drama. She does not like the *Denver Register,* and the dancing nuns appear as though they are doing the Charleston.

Works: [*The Violent Bear It Away*].

October 5, 1957 (p. 244; 5 par.): From ANDA-LUSIA. She discusses the Female Orphan Benevolent Association and Mr. Q. She had not considered Robie and his attitudes toward women. The sun has been missing for nine days. Though it depresses her, an old woman's fan mail about her work depressing her does not keep her up at night, so she is one up on the woman.

Works: None.

October 19, 1957 (p. 247; 5 par.): From ANDA-LUSIA. She is not sure how she should answer the letters about which she speaks. She writes about Father H. She talked her mother out of seeing the movie *The Ten Commandments* without reading the book first. Then, she felt guilty, so she went with her to see *The Three Faces of Eve.* It was the first time she had been to a movie theater in a few years and she does not plan to go for a few more, though the *Eve* movie was not too bad.

She received a phone call from ELIZABETH BISHOP. She enjoyed the call very much and thinks Bishop sounds like a pleasant person.

She is writing a story as a break from the novel. It feels like taking a mountain vacation.

Works: [*The Violent Bear It Away*].

November 2, 1957 (p. 249; 6 par.): From ANDALUSIA. She neither sent nor has read *War and Christianity Today.* She has received copies of the British edition of her story collection from her agent. They changed the title of "The Artificial Nigger" and have a horrible cover on the book of a large African man in much pain. The agent will try to pursue what seems like a breach of contract with the change in title to get the book out of their hands.

Her SAVANNAH cousin wants her and her mother to go on a pilgrimage to Europe, all expenses paid. She discusses this. She also discusses ["The Comforts of Home"]. Cal ROBERT

LOWELL wrote to her about "A View of the Woods" in PARTISAN. Her new story now has the title "The Enduring Chill." She has ordered three Chinese geese.

Works: [*Wise Blood*], "The Artificial Nigger," ["The Comforts of Home"], "A View of the Woods," "The Enduring Chill."

November 16, 1957 (p. 252; 7 par.):   From AN-DALUSIA. They enjoyed her visit. She may look tired because she is in fact tired all afternoons. It is part of the disease. Regina is reading about LOURDES. She has been asked to give a talk in April at Marquette in Milwaukee. She should ride the bus more often, but she is an integrationist and does not like the kinds of things that the drivers say. She has completed work on ["The Enduring Chill"]. "Nobody appreciates my work the way I do" (253). Jack told them that the wind they had on Thursday was a tornado. Her mother was recorded commenting on it on the radio and said that the voice they heard did not sound like hers.

Works: ["The Enduring Chill"].

November 30, 1957 (p. 255; 5 par.):   From AN-DALUSIA. She sends the Plunketts. She should have better reasons for rejecting A. T. as a poet. Her doctor has her taking shots, and her mother has completed the LOURDES book. She received Caroline's *How to Read a Novel*, which she will review. She can send *The Living Novel, a Symposium* edited by Granville Hicks if Hester is interested. She is still revising "The Enduring Chill" but will send it soon.

Works: ["The Enduring Chill"].

December 14, 1957 (p. 258; 4 par.):   From ANDALUSIA. She has not read *The Golden Bowl*. She explains her purpose in going to LOURDES. She will not be going to Chicago or to the Arts Festival in Colorado. She is doing a major revision of "The Enduring Chill."

Works: ["The Enduring Chill"].

December 28, 1957 (p. 261; 2 par.):   From ANDALUSIA. She has everyone who visits go

through that book page by page. She likes the picture of the saint sawed down the middle. Allen Tate suggested that she put the Holy Ghost in the story earlier, which is good advice. She may use Asbury in more stories.

Works: ["The Enduring Chill"].

January 11, 1958 (p. 261; 4 par.):   From AN-DALUSIA. One of the older field workers, Henry, died last night, so they will have a big funeral there. She discusses matters around Henry's death and family. She has revised the beginning and the ending that she sent to Hester. She thinks more of the Irish after meeting an Irish delegate to the UN brought out to the farm by the Gossetts. They must air out the room from all the cigarette smoke on Monday night.

Works: None.

February 26, 1958 (p. 270; 5 par.):   From ANDA-LUSIA. Her aunt Mary gave her the fancy paper. They just left the hospital after being there a week. Caroline looks better than the picture of her. The review of *The Living Novel* left out anything about Catholicism. She is not strong enough yet to think about Robie or J. F. Powers. Her group will talk about Rev. Kirkland, Ring Lardner, and Stephen Potter. Her goose eggs froze and the Muscovy duck ate them. They will start over. She is not sure why her mother made the comment about Shot getting lighter.

Works: None.

March 7, 1958 (p. 271; 4 par.):   From ANDALUSIA. She sends letters from Caroline Gordon. She appreciates Hester sending the picture of William to his mother. She recalls not enjoying Powers's story about baseball, though it has been a decade since she read the collection. Her favorite of Robie's are "The Legend of Two Swimmers" and "The Chevigny Man." She received a bad review in *Commonweal*.

Works: None.

March 20, 1958 (p. 273; 3 par.):   From ANDA-LUSIA. Has Hester read *Fear and Trembling*? Did

O'Connor send her the issue of *Thought* with the article about Kierkegaard and St. Thomas? Ashley wrote on "Caroline Gordon and the Impressionistic Novel." He may send Sewanee Review the chapter on *The Malefactors* on Allen's advice. He titles that chapter, "The Novel as Christian Comedy." Rutgers Unviersity Press is considering the book.

Joe Christmas is a character in William Faulkner's *Light in August.* Hester should read it. "I keep clear of Faulkner so my own little boat don't get swamped" (273).

Works: None.

April 4, 1958 (p. 274; 4 par.): From Andalusia. She has been alone at the farm since her mother went to the hospital with back pain. The doctor thinks she will be still able to make the trip.

She has not read Caroline Gordon's *None Shall Look Back.* She discusses religious conversion and novels. In "The Artificial Nigger," Mr. Head is changed though he also remains stable. She describes a lunch at the farm with Katherine Anne Porter, who had given a reading in Macon on the 27th and was brought over by the Gossetts. She told her that if she went to Lourdes, she would pray to complete her [*Ship of Fools*] novel that she has been working on for 27 years.

Works: ["The Artificial Nigger"].

April 19, 1958 (p. 279; 5 par.): From Andalusia. She discusses Father C. They are ready to make the trip with their tickets, baggage, and traveler's checks. They will be in New York when she gets this letter. E. sent good wishes for Lourdes. She is pleased that Hester is working on a short novel. Let the length be dictated by the story. She has been plagued with nightmares about Katherine Anne Porter's 27-year novel. It must be dreadful to work on a thing that long and have it still not running. She hopes this never happens to her.

O'Connor has a new publisher after her editor at Harcourt, Brace resigned. She is now with Robert Giroux at Farrar, Straus & Cudahy. Giroux edited *Wise Blood* and *A Good Man,* and she is very pleased to be back with him. She will be ready to complete her novel with this new contract when she returns.

Works: Wise Blood, A Good Man Is Hard to Find and other Stories.

May 5, 1958 (p. 280; 5 par.): From Rome, Italy. She thanks her for her letter that was there when they got there. She describes her experience in Lourdes. They saw St. Peter's and had a general audience with the pope and writes about this as well as who else was at the audience.

Works: None.

May 17, 1958 (p. 282; 7 par.): From Andalusia. She is not going to Missouri because she has a high blood count and a cough. She went to Lourdes primarily because Sally Fitzgerald made sure she went into the water. Hester should choose a Saturday to visit and pick up a plaque and a medal that B. has given her. She must get her novel done through sheer will since she is no longer enjoying it. She wishes she could work on something she found pleasure in doing. She saw Caroline in New York. George Eliot was likely to be writing by her conscience but not Christianity.

Works: [*The Violent Bear It Away*].

June 14, 1958 (p. 287; 8 par.): From Andalusia. The man who committed suicide likely did not know where to put his suffering. She sent her the Missouri article. There will be an article about her work in the *Georgia Review* that summer by Jane Hart. It is called "Strange Earth: the Stories of Flannery O'Connor." The title cracks her up.

She has found a superb short story writer and recommends Hester find this book, *The Magic Barrel* by Bernard Malamud. She hopes Hester can lose her gallstone. The local high school driving instructor who taught Shot is now teaching her. She hopes to learn in the 11 or fewer lessons that it took Shot.

She never liked *Alice in Wonderland* or *Pinocchio.* She was a *Peter Rabbit* person. Child experts give them too much credit for having good taste. Banjo has had its first calf.

Works: None.

July 5, 1958 (p. 289; 5 par.): From ANDALUSIA. She appreciates the Malamud. City life would be good only for the paperbacks. She is still thinking about "The Hypothesis for Catholic Fiction." Writers like her do not put the institution of the church into their work. Hester could write a good critical paper with enough time to work on it.

It would be better for her to like O'Connor's book and then review it. There will be no biographies of her since her life is so boring. Hester may write one day about her novel or stories.

Works: Wise Blood.

July 19, 1958 (p. 291; 4 par.): From ANDALUSIA. She appreciates Saul Bellow's *The Victim*. She is currently reading Bernard Malamud's *The Assistant*. She passed her driver's test with a 77 and is now a licensed driver. She is trying to convince Regina to buy a car with automatic transmission and power steering in order to help her mother live longer and make it easier for O'Connor to drive.

Critical articles need to be specific. The last issue of KENYON REVIEW has a good article on Powers. Hester's point is not wrong, but she has not got all of her argument on paper as yet. If she would like to read a real surrealist novel, she can send her a novel of John Hawkes, whose work she admires. His "is the GROTESQUE with all stops out" (291).

Works: None.

August 2, 1958 (p. 292; 4 par.): From ANDALUSIA. She disagrees with Hester about Purdy's abilities. The farm family is returning. She will send the Hawkes book when she finds some wrapping paper. Hawkes stopped with his family a couple of months ago on his way to Florida. Hawkes is a professor at Harvard. They passed up buying Regina's cousin's car. It was red and white, and he said that the inside was as a pretty as a funeral parlor. He is going into the army.

Works: None.

August 30, 1958 (p. 294; 3 par.): From ANDALUSIA. She was hoping that Hester sent a story when she saw the brown envelope, but it was not. She is not interested in joining a third order per E. They have their new car. It is black like a hearse. She will pick her up in it the next Saturday that she comes to visit. Uncle Louis got it for them in Atlanta. Next time, send her a story.

Works: None.

October 11, 1958 (p. 298; 3 par.): From ANDALUSIA. She likes the Danielou character. Her mother enjoyed *The Nun's Story*, though the picture on the front made O'Connor feel ill. *Critique* is dedicating an issue to her and Powers. The pieces on her will likely be by Caroline and Louis Rubin. She sends one by Caroline that she likes more and more. The banana bread is gone between a friend who came to visit and her and her mother.

Works: None.

October 25, 1958 (p. 300; 2 par.): From ANDALUSIA. It will be helpful to her to be done with the business at Birmingham-Southern College and be able to devote all of her attention to the novel. She thinks now that she can complete it. She has been enjoying a history of Georgia written by a professor at GSCW. She did not know that they live on the border of the Creek Nation. She would like Regina to read it; then she will send it to Hester.

Works: [The Violent Bear It Away].

November 8, 1958 (p. 301; 5 par.): From ANDALUSIA. No true comparisons can be made between *The Malefactors* and *Lucky Jim*. Has Hester read Iris Murdoch? She is good.

Though she does not recall much beyond that she liked them when she read them some years ago, she read Cary's *Herself Surprised*, *The Horse's Mouth*, and *To Be a Pilgrim*. She has nearly reached the end of Tarwater. She talks about the article about the Japanese in *Commonweal*. She is reading Pasternak and a book by Henry Miller about Greece. She is also reading Martin Buber's *The Eclipse of God*. She had lunch yesterday with Clair Huchet Bishop, whose work has been published in *Commonweal*.

Works: None.

November 22, 1958 (p. 305; 3 par.): From ANDALUSIA. She writes about the crisis theologians, who are Protestants writing at a level beyond any Catholics today. The 20th century needs its St. Thomas to write about theology. Father Murchland has the notion of crisis, and he writes in *Commonweal*.

Her bitterness about C. is underserved. She tries very hard to overcome her obstacles and makes the best that she can with what she has been given. The cousin in SAVANNAH who sent them to Europe is dying. However, she had the blessing of learning that O'Connor's bones are getting better after visiting LOURDES and that O'Connor has not needed to use her crutches for more than a week.

Works: [*The Violent Bear It Away*].

December 20, 1958 (p. 308; 4 par.): From ANDALUSIA. It is about time that they reviewed Brainard Cheney (Lon)'s book. She asked why it had not been reviewed as yet and heard back that it was because it was about blacks. She followed up on this with Cheney, who took it up with Ralph McGill, so now it is reviewed. Why is Hester reading *A Stillness at Appomattox*? The Civil War has not been a great interest of hers. She will receive $350 for reading "The Artificial Nigger" in Nashville. She sends Christmas blessings.

Works: "The Artificial Nigger."

December 25, 1958 (p. 310; 2 par.): From ANDALUSIA. She thinks that *The Odyssey: A Modern Sequel* by Nikos Kazantzakis is a wonderful book. She tells a story about the farm-work couple. Jack and Louise were drunk, and Louise came to the house saying that she could not go back because Jack had loaded the gun and said that he would kill her. Regina went over and got the gun away from him. When they came over for their gifts Christmas Eve and the liquor had worn off, Regina returned the gun with a sermon about not killing during Christmas. They have stayed home to make sure that nothing else has happened.

Works: None.

January 3, 1959 (p. 316; 2 par.): From ANDALUSIA. She has read Malraux's *Man's Fate* but nothing else. She has just read Voegelin's second volume. She will have a first draft of her novel complete in about three or four more pages. She assigns this blessing to LOURDES more than the improvement in her bones. She is more grateful to complete the novel. She will now have to go back to the beginning to revise, but getting this far lets her know that the book is possible.

Works: [*The Violent Bear It Away*].

January 31, 1959 (p. 317; 4 par.): From ANDALUSIA. She is still calling the novel *The Violent Bear It Away*. She likes the title more and more but the book less and less. She plans to send it to Caroline, the Fitzgeralds, and to Hester. It is 43,000 words. She will work on it more when she returns from Chicago.

She plans to read "A Good Man Is Hard to Find" in Chicago. She will leave out the section about the black boy with the britches. She is pleased to hear that Hester is now writing a novel; she always thought she needed that much room. She recommends HENRY JAMES for structure though not for style. She reread *The Aspern Papers* and "The Beast in the Jungle."

The French translator of *Wise Blood*, M. Coindreau, is writing an article about southern life and American literature, including southern preachers. He wants to visit her. The title of his piece will be *La Sagesse dans le Sang*. He sees one outcome of the article as preparing the French public for Haze Motes.

Works: The Violent Bear It Away, "A Good Man Is Hard to Find," *Wise Blood*.

February 28, 1959 (p. 321; 5 par.): From ANDALUSIA. Caroline has returned *The Violent Bear It Away* full of marks and comments. Has she read *Lolita*? She sees it as a comic novel operating within its own rules. She does not like William Ready's writing about it or his book *The Poor Hater*.

She has not seen Cal ROBERT LOWELL's *Life Studies*. KATHERINE ANNE PORTER's book is due out in September. She is displeased with her own novel, even though Caroline liked it very much. She cannot find the word *rebarbative* in her dictionary; if Hester finds its meaning, she should let her know. Her Chinese goose laid a couple of eggs. This is always a positive thing. When Hester can come for a visit on a Saturday for some fresh air out in the country, she should let her know.

Works: The Violent Bear It Away.

March 27, 1959 (p. 323; 6 par.): From ANDALUSIA. Hester's stories "want" to be novels; it is her form. She makes comments on the draft, which she likes very much. She would like to send it to her agent when Hester gets it done. It is better to have an agent help one sell a novel. She thought Hester would like to hear the good news!

Works: None.

April 18, 1959 (p. 328; 3 par.): From ANDALUSIA. Regina has been in the hospital for three days. She needs to write back to a graduate student who has asked about why her work is so GROTESQUE. She finds it difficult to explain that it is because that is what she can do. She may earn a Ph.D. if she adds to many more student papers.

They have elected Miss Gum Spirits of Turpentine for the year, which is always worth waiting for. The other one worth watching for is Miss North Georgia Chick.

Works: None.

May 16, 1959 (p. 332; 2 par.): From ANDALUSIA. Henry James does not try to avoid vulgarity and is in fact a master of it. Has Hester read *What Maisie Knew?* She finds the book moving. She will work on Tarwater for the remainder of the summer.

Works: [*The Violent Bear It Away*].

May 30, 1959 (p. 334; 3 par.): From ANDALUSIA. Tom Gossett took them yesterday to the [Holy Ghost] monastery. If one enjoys HENRY JAMES's work, it does not matter if you like him or not. She writes about how much she still enjoys Baron von Hügel. She writes about charity and

St. Thomas and St. Catherine of Genoa. Hester has H. Motes's activities out of order. First came the lye in the eyes that left him unable to do charity, then the rocks and barbed wire.

Works: None.

June 13, 1959 (p. 335; 3 par.): From ANDALUSIA. They need to spend nights with Miss Mary Cline, since she is not doing well. A murder occurred in their neighborhood, and now there are 75 members of law enforcement and volunteers trying to track down the killer. Robert Fitzgerald reports that Sally wanted to cry when she saw the picture of Cal ROBERT LOWELL on the back of *Life Studies*. Lowell checked himself into a hospital before the book was released.

Works: None.

June 27, 1959 (p. 338; 4 par.): From ANDALUSIA. Occasionally, she wishes that she lived in the city where the culture is, but the feeling does not last very long, and she is more grateful that she lives in the country. Ashley likes Iris Murdoch's *The Bell*, but she has not read it. She read *Under the Net*, and earlier book. She finds the church's position on birth control as one of its most spiritual in a materialistic world. She expects to send her the novel in a month.

Works: None.

July 11, 1959 (p. 339; 3 par.): From ANDALUSIA. Hester's novel has returned from Macmillan. If it were her novel, she would either send it to Catharine Carver at Viking or to her agent. She recommends Jacopone da Todi and St. John of the Cross if she is interested in reading mystics. She can lend her Angus Wilson's *Such Darling Dodos*. The advance copy of John Updike's stories is a letdown. She also has a copy of a reissue of Nabokov's *The Real Life of Sebastian Knight*. Hester should know Nabokov if she does not already. She recommends *Pnin*. She likes Peter Taylor's current story in *Kenyon* better than the story that won the O. HENRY. Regina has been saying they have not seen Hester for quite a while. Won't she come visit?

Works: None.

July 25, 1959 (p. 342; 4 par.): From ANDALUSIA. She appreciates Hester's comments on the novel. She writes about Tarwater. If she has the strength, she may write about Tarwater in the city one day. She is interested in the violent because they are not natural. She is "much more interested in the nobility of unnaturalness than in the nobility of naturalness. As Robert [Fitzgerald] says, it is the business of the artist to uncover the strangeness of the truth" (343).

This novel is both less GROTESQUE and less humorous than *Wise Blood.* She does not go to book parties, so her activities after the book comes out will remain the same.

Works: [*The Violent Bear It Away*], *Wise Blood.*

August 22, 1959 (p. 348; 3 par.): From ANDALUSIA. She recommends George P. Elliott's stories. She did not care for the one that won the O. HENRY this year. Hester should read *Life* if she wants to know more about E.

Her friend in New York has just written to her that she is reading *Go Tell It on the Mountain* and finds so many similarities between James Baldwin and O'Connor. Hester has told O'Connor that she thinks Baldwin is a whiner. They had a visit from Madison Jones.

Works: None.

October 3, 1959 (p. 351; 4 par.): From ANDALUSIA. She is feeling down from seeing her novel in galley prints. The Sunday supplement will show up in about a month. They photographed her reading [*Familiar Reptiles*], feeding the animals, and gazing out at nothing. She looks like a witch. She was unprepared for the questions that they asked, and she does not look forward to seeing the article in print.

She writes about Cardinal John Henry Newman. Jack Hawkes will be at Brandeis University speaking and has invited her, West, and Djuna Barnes along. He asked to see her novel, so she sent it but now regrets it. If he does not like it, he is too much of a gentleman to say so.

Works: *The Violent Bear It Away.*

October 17, 1959 (p. 355; 4 par.): From ANDALUSIA. She likes the book better now that the corrected proofs have come in. She sends Jack Hawkes's letter about the novel. He is tactful, but she finds his opinion good and fair.

There is no Catholic literature in the sense of writers working around a central premise, but we do have several good Catholic poets. She names Raymond Roselipe, Ned O'Gorman, John Logan, John Frederick Nims, John Edward Hardy, two nuns, Leonie Adams, and Robert Fitzgerald. She has Martin Turnell's *The Novel in France* if Hester wants to see it. Alfred Kazin mentions O'Connor in *Harper's,* and Elizabeth Hardwick's article about book reviewers is in that issue. She can send it.

She can be counted among those who do not like the MASS being said in English. Besides being resistant to change, anxious, and lazy, she does not like the sound of human voices speaking together in unison unless they are singing.

Works: *The Violent Bear It Away.*

October 31, 1959 (p. 356; 7 par.): From ANDALUSIA. When Hester is in the library again, she should look up the interview with FRANÇOIS MAURIAC in the fall KENYON REVIEW. Mauriac said he sat next to Cardinal Spellman at an event and believed that he would have bonded more with the Dalai Lama spiritually. So tells Dr. Spivey.

She acknowledges that Hester is likely right about the MASS dialogue, but someone is always speaking more loudly, and this would be less possible with the discipline of song.

She writes of comparing herself to Hawkes. Rayber cannot be the devil since he fights against what is in him too much. She thinks it is an open question if he is saved or not, but she would liked him to be.

She tells of a letter from John Hawkes and his experience at Brandeis. It seems he thinks as she does in that he is writing to an audience that does not believe in the personhood of the devil. He likes *The Velvet Horn.* She has read Honor Tracy's *The Straight and Narrow Path,* which she found to be funny but too long. The better length for a book like that is Evelyn Waugh's *The Loved One.*

What does Hester think of her changing the Partridge story to one about peanuts? This might make things better for Calhoun.

Works: [*The Violent Bear It Away*].

November 14, 1959 (p. 358; 2 par.): From ANDALUSIA. "I am not afraid that the book will be controversial, I'm afraid that it will not be controversial" (358). She discusses Tarwater and admits that no one would have written this novel but her. She liked William Sessions's friend Minna.

Works: [*The Violent Bear It Away*].

Wednesday, [December, 1959] (p. 362; 2 par.): From ANDALUSIA. She has not made the moral theme clear, so yes, she does not get it. She is working on ["The Comforts of Home"] again. She gives most of her attention to Catharine Carver's gut reaction to her work.

Carver does not understand Thomas because she has just the story to go on; Hester understands him because she knows O'Connor well. The story, however, must show Thomas disclosing himself rather than O'Connor writing about him so much. "A story has to have muscle as well as meaning, and the meaning has to be in the muscle" (362).

Works: ["The Comforts of Home"].

December 19, 1959 (p. 363; 5 par.): From ANDALUSIA. She thanks her for the article on coffee. She is going to give a talk at the Jesuit college Spring Hill in Mobile in April, and maybe she will use something from it. She has now seen the cover of her novel. Francis Marion Tarwater appears in a black hat amid corn the color of clay. It looks like something out of the School of Southern Degeneracy. The cover, however, could be worse. On the back cover is a quote from Caroline's article in *Critique* which will likely get things fired up.

Once she puts "The Comforts of Home" back together, she plans to send it to Robie. She did not like the review of *The Devil's Advocate*. She has heard that TRUMAN CAPOTE reads well. He steps up on a stool and sounds like a young girl, but soon after he begins, according to Dick Stern, one forgets all that.

Works: [*The Violent Bear It Away*], "The Comforts of Home."

December 25, 1959 (p. 367; 1 par.): From ANDALUSIA. She thinks it is lucky that she has found St. Thomas's thinking in *Summa* and the *De Veritate* on prophecy. According to St. Thomas, a prophet's vision comes from his imagination, not his morality, and there is a difference between having a vision and announcing it. She finds great pleasure in these books and in Hester's presence in her life.

Works: None.

January 2, 1960 (p. 368; 4 par.): From ANDALUSIA. She appreciates the St. Thomas and is going to write to Regnery and ask for the volumes. She needs them to help work out the prophet. She needs to get through these talks and plans not to take any more invitations this year to do them. The *Davenport Messenger* makes the suggestion that readers should get hold of PÈRE TEILHARD DE CHARDIN's new book before the church puts it on the Index. She will send it to Hester if she would like.

She found *Breakfast at Tiffany's* unexpectedly boring so she does not plan to read TRUMAN CAPOTE's *The Muses Are Heard*.

Part of the task of writing is getting onself over the feeling of dread one has when setting oneself to the task. The middle of a book is the hardest. Once it is three-fourth done, you are past the worst. To avoid overeating, eat raw carrots, crunching loudly like Bugs Bunny.

Works: None.

January 16, 1960 (p. 370; 4 par.): From ANDALUSIA. The *Library Journal* review, the first for the novel, is very negative. They say she writes as a moralist and not as an artist and does not dramatize the work enough. The review is written by a woman in the Concord Public Library. The reviewer says that Tarwater is the most recent character of O'Connor's group of "poor God-driven Southern whites" (371). She sends Hester a couple issues of *Village Voice*.

She sends a section of the talk that Carol Johnson plans to read in North Carolina about philosophy in the novel. She thinks it is humorous and that she would like to hear the lecture. She will send "The Comforts of Home" after she types it up from revisions.

Works: [*The Violent Bear It Away*].

January 30, 1960 (p. 372; 2 par.): From ANDALUSIA. She does not expect any positive reviews from her novel except from the Catholic press. She has heard already from two Jesuits, Sister Bernetta Quinn, and Madison Jones all with positive comments.

Has Hester heard of Stanley Kramer? One of the Jesuits who wrote to her wants to show it to Kramer's agent since he thinks it would make a good film.

Works: [*The Violent Bear It Away*].

February 13, 1960 (p. 374; 3 par.): From ANDALUSIA. It is fitting that Hester's novel does not reflect her new beliefs as a Catholic. The imagination is formed in childhood, so her work will instead reflect need. *Time* magazine sent down a reporter and a photographer, so apparently they are planning to do an article on the novel. She has heard that a medieval studies professor at Boston University wrote a favorable review for *Catholic World* and that Granville Hicks will be writing one for the *Saturday Review*.

From the *Time* interviewer's questions, she realizes how difficult it is to avoid labels. He wanted her to characterize herself. He asked if she considered herself a Catholic writer, a southern writer, and if so what kind? She stammered for the whole hour and then stayed awake all night thinking of more developed and qualified answers.

Works: None.

March 5, 1960 (p. 379; 4 par.): From ANDALUSIA. She sends another review, this one the most humorous that she has seen thus far.

She asks for the return of "The Comforts of Home" so that she can send it to the Fitzgeralds. Hester should reread *Dubliners*. They have had

a cold snap with no water or lights and the PEACOCKS with frozen tails.

She does not know where Hester gets the idea that O'Connor was frequently ill as a child; she was not. Also, Hester's comments that her characters have a relationship of love with God but not with each other seems off base to her when one considers the grandmother reaching out to The Misfit. It is true what she says about many of characters not wanting to be devoured by the will of another. The most pure form of love about which she has written is Rayber's for Bishop. Rayber feels the need to destroy it because of its purity.

Works: "The Comforts of Home," *The Violent Bear It Away*.

Monday p.m. [March 8, 1960] (p. 381; 3 par.): From ANDALUSIA. It seems foolish to her that one must love a character in order to write about him or her; however, she does love Tarwater. The airplanes must improve if she were ever to fly to Brazil, but she will invite Hester over if ELIZABETH BISHOP ever visits Andalusia. She encloses the review by Harold Gardiner, S. J. Tarwater would be surprised by the priest's notion that Tarwater drowned Bishop to end Bishop's suffering.

Works: [*The Violent Bear It Away*].

March 19, 1960 (p. 383; 6 par.): From ANDALUSIA. She agrees with Hester's comments on Cecil's "The Quiet Enemy." It is difficult to send an author appreciation for a book if you do not approve of it. HENRY JAMES found a way. She sends another and asks for her prayers for this man.

Elizabeth Fenwick alternates between writing a novel for her own enjoyment and expression and a mystery that she writes for money. She also has LUPUS and is a very pleasant woman to know and have around. They met at YADDO, and she lived beside her when she stayed in New York. She has strange responses to O'Connor's books.

Did Hester see the article in *Commonweal* about Golding? Ashley brought her *Lord of the Flies* when he was there last, and he is the kind of reader who likes someone like Golding many years before that work catches on. She has not completed reading *Flies* but the novel makes her think of Hester thus far.

She saw one picture of ELIZABETH BISHOP that Cal ROBERT LOWELL showed her once. Bishop sent Cal one of her standing next to an unclothed female Indian.

Works: None.

April 2, 1960 (p. 385; 5 par.):   From ANDALUSIA. She appreciates Hester's birthday wishes. She still has all of her teeth at 35. R. M. likes Thomas Wolfe, which she thinks does not work favorably for his liking good fiction. When she replies to Dr. S., she will send it to her. It was yet another study of her character, saying that she is fearful of the Spirit. She asks who would not be?

She has been ill and wants to get through the speeches coming up and will avoid making more for at least three months. She would like Hester to let her know if she sees a very negative review in the *New Yorker.* She also heard that there was a fairly neutral one in the *New Republic,* which she has not seen either.

She would prefer not to think about what makes a book great. After she is done making speeches, she may think more about ritual. The Hollywood murder and Lana Turner might be best handled by Hester by letting it go where it will.

Works: None.

April 9, 1960 (p. 386; 4 par.):   From ANDALUSIA. She enjoyed going to Spring Hill. Father Watson wrote about Father Gardiner's review in AMERICA, but it was not published, so he has sent it to *Commonweal,* which may not publish it either. Hester would be happy to see what Fr. Watson wrote about Fr. Gardiner's review.

She writes about the Devil. She tells Hester to watch for another story by Cecil called "The Buffalo Ranch" in *Paris Review.*

Works: None.

April 16, 1960 (p. 390; 5 par.):   From ANDALUSIA. She sends more letters, including one from Gabrielle Rolin in Paris, one that Caroline wrote to the *New York Times* about Tarwater needing a

mother figure, and one speaking favorably about the novel from ROBERT PENN WARREN.

She got hives, and the doctor has told her that she must not go to the meeting in SAVANNAH. Once he said that, the hives went away, but she is still not going to talk to the National Council of Catholic Women.

Cecil wrote and thanked her for introducing her to Hester and appreciates Hester's letter. In the February issue of *Encounter,* KATHERINE ANNE PORTER writes about Lady Chatterley, and it is good to see. O'Connor may clean her desk, now that she does not have a talk to prepare or fret over.

Works: None.

April 30, 1960 (p. 393; 5 par.):   From ANDALUSIA. Because she is not talented with unfamiliar phones, she did not call Hester while she was in Emory Hospital, but she thought about doing so. They will have Fr. Paul and the Abbot for lunch tomorrow. She writes about the cancer home in ATLANTA, Mary Ann, and the Sisters' request of her.

KATHERINE ANNE PORTER does not write negatively about D. H. Lawrence but instead about the fuss over *Lady Chatterley.* She makes some refreshing comments. She writes about her friend who likes Jung and how she may have made him feel about the church.

The reviews in *Commonweal* and *The* CRITIC pleased her.

Works: [*The Violent Bear It Away*].

May 14, 1960 (p. 395; 3 par.):   From ANDALUSIA. She talks about Cal ROBERT LOWELL and an uncomfortable rumor that he called her a saint. Abbot called the young girl a strong character. According to Dr. Spivey she should have had more sympathy in her book toward Tarwater because there is a little of him in all of us.

Works: [*The Violent Bear It Away*].

June 11, 1960 (p. 400; 5 par.):   From ANDALUSIA. She received B.'s novel in the mail and is in the middle of reading it. She was instructed to send it

Hester when she is done. The woman concerned with the dog books did not arrive. R. W. Flint wrote a good review of *The Violent Bear It Away* in the PARTISAN REVIEW. She sends a portion of *Conversations with Catholics* to be published by Lippincott. She does not understand why the mummy was not clear to these readers. She sent Fr. Lynch, S. J.'s *Christ and Apollo.*

Works: The Violent Bear It Away.

June 25, 1960 (p. 401; 4 par.): From ANDALUSIA. She sends Caroline's comments on "The Partridge Festival." Enoch found the mummy to be an idol, and it represents the "new jesus—a shriveled man" (402) in the book overall. Paul Levine wrote a favorable review on the book in JUBILEE. He is also doing a book to be published by Harcourt, Brace on six writers, McCullers, TRUMAN CAPOTE, Buechner, Bellow, Salinger, and her. He interviewed her with smart questions. She sent a flyer from Carol.

Works: "The Partridge Festival."

July 9, 1960 (p. 403; 3 par.): From ANDALUSIA. She has not read Buechner, but she prefers Malamud to TRUMAN CAPOTE and Powers to McCullers. As the writer of fiction, she is more concerned with her characters than with what they may represent. Haze does not like the shriveled man because it is horrible. Haze has been tainted by the modern world and throws away the mummy because this act of rejecting it has meaning for him. She did not write about them in abstraction but in considering what the characters would do next.

According to Fr. Paul, B. thinks Jesuits are made differently from other people. He will soon discover the similarities if they exist.

Works: [Wise Blood], [The Violent Bear It Away].

July 23, 1960 (p. 404; 3 par.): From ANDALUSIA. A group of people visited Andalusia on Monday. It included six nuns from the cancer home, a Trappist abbot, and Msgr. Dodwell. The sister superior has to be one of the funniest women she has ever met. She is doing the principal writ-

ing on the book about Mary Ann. The founder of their order was NATHANIEL HAWTHORNE's daughter, and she just read her biography. She will send it if Hester is interested.

When Haze rejects the mummy, he is turning away from what he thought he was looking for but discovers he must reject. She hopes that John Kennedy gets elected. "I think King Kong would be better than Nixon" (404).

Works: [Wise Blood].

September 3, 1960 (p. 405; 5 par.): From ANDALUSIA. Her advice is to write stories and send them to Elizabeth McKee and get about the business of writing another story. If she should take a course in anything, it should be a course in typing.

She received a letter from T. last week. Hester likely saw the review of *The Leoopard* by Giuseppe de Lampedusa written by Richard Gilman. Gilman stayed overnight and talked with her about writing a critical article for *Commonweal* or *Commentary* on her work. He tried to name what she does, and she cannot think of a label for it, either. She suggested that *Commentary* would be the better periodical for the article if they accepted it. He agreed with her.

So far she has read 100 pages of Iris Murdoch's *The Bell* and likes it better than *Under the Net*. She has been working on the nun's project for several days. She got much good from Hester's visit.

Works: [A Memoir of Mary Ann].

September 17, 1960 (p. 407; 3 par.): From ANDALUSIA. She explains that what she likes about *The Bell* is particularly the woman character who destroys a community while keeping some of the good in it. She recommends *The American Novel and Its Tradition* by Richard Chase.

Has she received any comments on *Miss Nancy*? If Hester's new novel is one that feels like it has to be extracted from her, she should write it quickly. She has seen the British cover now of *The Violent Bear It Away*, which is still unsatisfactory, though better than the one for *Wise Blood*.

Works: The Violent Bear It Away, Wise Blood.

October 1, 1960 (p. 411; 5 par.): From ANDALUSIA. She does not approve of Chase's points about the Christian novel, though she likes the rest of the book. She has heard from Caroline Ivey about Harper Lee. She said that the members of Lee's hometown of Mayborough, Alabama, did not approve of her writing fiction about a similar episode that actually happened in the town. O'Connor thinks Lee's book is a children's book and would best be looked at on that basis. She would have liked it at age 15. Without the rape, it is similar to *Miss Minerva and William Green Hill*.

She has sold an article for $750 about her PEACOCKS to *HOLIDAY*. That is more money than she has ever received for any article that she has written. She writes about *The Secret of Dreams*, a Catholic Book Club selection written by a Spanish Jesuit. Is Hester watching the Kennedy-Nixon debates? They do not see them.

Works: None.

October 27, 1960 (p. 413; 3 par.): From ANDALUSIA. She sends some reviews and discusses one. MARY McCARTHY has apparently written an article called "The Fact in Fiction" in *PARTISAN REVIEW* in which she discusses miracles in fiction.

She returned from Missouri. She enjoyed meeting the nuns, especially Sister Bernetta Quinn. In a poem, "Three Poems for Three Nuns," by William Goodreau in *Critic*, the last nun is Sister Bernetta.

They are having a dinner party this weekend with Caroline, Ashley, KATHERINE ANNE PORTER, Madison, Louis Rubin, and Deen Hood.

Works: [*The Violent Bear It Away*].

November 12, 1960 (p. 416; 2 par.): From ANDALUSIA. She is writing an introduction to the nun's book about Mary Ann and will likely send it to Hester for her comments. She will send *The Nephew* by James Purdy if she is interested. She agrees with Hester's good opinion of *The Leopard*.

Works: ["Introduction to *A Memoir of Mary Ann*"].

November 25, 1960 (p. 419; 4 par.): From ANDALUSIA. She is upset that Hester did not come

and wonders what may be wrong. She asked B. about it, and he said that O'Connor may have agreed with critical comments that he made on Hester's writing and that Hester may now be depressed over it.

Hester needs to be able to let the outcome of her talent be God's will. If she makes herself vulnerable to criticism that keeps her from writing, she should avoid that like sin. The sisters, Regina, and Caroline all liked O'Connor's introduction to the Mary Ann book. She sends Caroline's comments.

Works: ["Introduction" to *A Memoir of Mary Ann*].

December 24, 1960 (p. 423; 4 par.): From ANDALUSIA. She was pleasantly surprised to discover how much she enjoyed Proust after reading 50 pages in the hospital. When she got home, the furniture and belongings were piled in the center of the room. The pipes had frozen, and they had a mess, so she has not read any more Proust. She looks forward to reading it all next year and appreciates the Greek plays Hester sent her.

They discovered that her bone deterioration is coming from the steroids that she has taken for a decade to control the LUPUS. Dr. Merrill is going to try to take them away from her.

Jubilee will publish the introduction to Mary Ann. The nuns are delighted and will have this publication if nothing else about Mary Ann. She has begun work on a new story and is having a grand time with it ["Parker's Back"].

Works: ["Introduction" to *A Memoir of Mary Ann*], "Parker's Back."

January 21, 1961 (p. 427; 6 par.): From ANDALUSIA. She speaks about conversion and a girl who visits the farm occasionally. She received a letter that interpreted her book from a Freudian sexual angle all the way through. She asked him to attempt to regain some simplicity. She is on page 513 in Proust.

"Parker's Back" is not progressing as well as she would like. There is too much humor in it for the seriousness of it to shine through. She likes Hester's title, *Odyssey of a Demon*.

Works: "Parker's Back."

February 4, 1961 (p. 430; 6 par.): From ANDA-LUSIA. She writes about TEILHARD DE CHARDIN and a notion of obedience among the dead. She does not think his books will be put on the Index.

She writes about conversion and how there is the first one and then a deepening of belief. Conversion is a process.

She has begun to think of Mary Ann's book as a miracle. She had told the nuns when they approached her about helping them with it that the sainted girl's first miracle would be in finding a publisher for her book. Giroux's response was that he had a few hesitations about the book but none of them were important.

She has been reading FRANÇOIS MAURIAC's *Mémoires Intérieurs*. She is sending it to Hester because they are almost identical in their views of Emily Brontë. She has not read *Wuthering Heights* in a long time, so she would have to read it again to follow Hester's interest.

Apostate priests write against the church or leave the priesthood and claim to be saved through the Bible.

The pageant was successful, and organizers may throw it every year now. It is a good way to make money.

Works: ["Introduction" to *A Memoir of Mary Ann*].

May 13, 1961 (p. 439; 3 par.): From ANDALUSIA. The only flaw she has found in Hester is the way she wraps a package. The one today was so tight that her fingers bled, and her mood turned sour for the remainder of the day when she finally got through the packaging to the books. She implores Hester to buy some string and use it to simply tie the package that way.

She has read Iris Murdoch's *The Severed Head* and is working her way through Murdoch's *The Flight from the Enchanter*. Cecil wants to write an introduction to *Wise Blood*; O'Connor told her to go ahead, though she cannot be certain that Giroux would use it. If not, perhaps Cecil can publish it somewhere else.

Works: Wise Blood.

May 27, 1961 (p. 440; 4 par.): From ANDALUSIA. B. wrote to them, but they also heard from Father Paul that B. had asked him to tell them the news. Regina was pleased for B. and the girl.

Ashley lent her *The Sand Castle* a while ago, and she has read it. Hester should write something about Iris Murdoch for *Commonweal*.

Dr. Karl Stern wrote to her about the introduction to *Mary Ann* in JUBILEE. A girl also wrote to her asking what she would charge to look at about a dozen of her stories.

She reread *A High Wind in Jamaica* based on Hester's view of it.

Works: "Introduction" to *A Memoir of Mary Ann*.

June 10, 1961 (p. 442; 4 par.): From ANDALUSIA. Shot had an accident on the farm with the hay baylor [bailer]. He was pulled in to his elbows while working on it with the machine running. Regina and Lon Cheney were there and got a mechanic to help him out and a doctor to examine him. He is now in the hospital where he will be for some time suffering from cuts and third-degree burns. Regina drove him there in the car. This is a major accident; they have had many small instances, but this is different. Shot is lucky to be alive.

She remains unconvinced that *Wise Blood* needs an introduction. She would like Hester to check out *The Moviegoer* by WALKER PERCY at the Atlanta Public Library. She thinks both of them should read this book.

She sends a review sent to her by Catharine Carver that appread in the *Paris Review*. CAL ROB-ERT LOWELL is apparently back in the hospital.

Works: Wise Blood.

July 22, 1961 (p. 445; 3 par.): From ANDALUSIA. Burns & Oates of London has purchased the *Mary Ann* book. They want to change the title to *The Death of a Child*, and she convinced the sisters to allow the change. It is nearly amusing to watch how quickly this work of the Lord's is moving along.

She has received comments back from Ash-ley and Caroline on her story "The Lame Shall

Enter First." As usual, Caroline said it was not yet dramatized enough.

She received a book from Houghton Mifflin last week called *Clock Without Hands* by Carson McCullers. She thinks it may be the worst book she has ever read. She will send it if Hester wants to read it. She thinks McCullers may have lost whatever talent she may have had. McCullers's other three novels at least had fairly good writing.

Works: ["Introduction" to *A Memoir of Mary Ann*], "The Lame Shall Enter First."

August 5, 1961 (p. 446; 6 par.): From ANDALUSIA. She has usually heard back just fine from the paperback people. They have received many postcards from B., who sounds very happy with his new marriage on August 3.

Ford Maddox Ford and Caroline know each other well, and he taught her much of what she knows. She likes Ford's *The Good Soldier,* though not the Tietjens series or his biography of JOSEPH CONRAD.

Carol Johnson has written cards telling them that she is seeing Greece from the back of a young man's motorbike. She has not read *Mirror in the Roadway* or Spengler. Since there is so much attention given to Iris Murdoch, Hester could probably place her article on her in *Commonweal* or *Thought.*

Works: None.

August 19, 1961 (p. 447; 3 par.): From ANDALUSIA. Regina noticed that B.'s wedding invitations are for August 26, though he was married already on the 3rd. They are not sure what is going on. It might be Billy's style to have two weddings.

Shot has not yet left the hospital. He is having skin grafts, and his left arm is not usable but it is said it may improve.

The *Mary Ann* book has been taken up by the Catholic Digest Book Club. O'Connor is listing possible reviewers who will receive copies on October 20 for the December 7 publication. She will put Hester on the list.

Works: A Memoir of Mary Ann.

September 16, 1961 (p. 449; 6 par.): From ANDALUSIA. Did the article by Beckett on Proust get to her? She sent it after the *Critique.* Her visit next weekend is good. They will meet her at the mailbox.

Shot is out of the hospital but is not doing any work as yet. He spends much of his time sitting and thinking about what he will do with the insurance money and wages that he has received from the accident.

She plans to leave the swans in the backyard until they have young; then she will move the parents to the pond and raise the young swans. The swans make noise but are really pretty content.

She asks Hester to bring the D. S Savage book when she visits. She is currently working on a story that will give Jack something to think about in their discussions about the Devil and that she is on the Devil's side. She may retitle the story to "The Lame Will Carry Off the Prey."

She wonders if they will see B. and Anna Magnani.

Works: ["The Lame Shall Enter First"].

September 30, 1961 (p. 450; 5 par.): From ANDALUSIA. They will enjoy the candy and the rum. Louise claims that Hester did not use the bed when she was there. When they asked her where she thought Miss Hester slept, she said maybe the floor. This is a matter Hester will need to straighten out with Louise when she visits the next time.

She is concerned about sending the library book since Hester did not receive the Proust. She will, however, send it without insurance and hope for the best. She mentions Mr. Coindreau's responses to the book in a small matter.

Though she does not think about the Communist world, she knows that Hester does, so she sends her the enclosed. Hester should write up some of her thoughts and send them out for publication.

Good Housekeeping is profiling the sisters' book. They took pictures of Sister Evangelist.

Works: A Memoir of Mary Ann.

October 14, 1961 (p. 450; 5 par.): From ANDA-LUSIA. Regina was not sure about when to give Louise the dollar that Hester left since Louise has been drunk the last two Mondays. She decided to give it to her there and then rather than wait for her to be sober. At first, it did not appear to sink in that the money was hers. After about an hour, Louise's senses cleared, and she was very happy.

Rather than define the novel and exclude what novelists have done with the form, including herself, she would rather leave the novel undefined and fairly open. ERNEST HEMINGWAY, for example, used the novel to examine his manhood; Virginia Woolf used it to experiment; A. Huxley presented lectures in it.

Dr. S. sent her two books; one she already has is *God and the Unconscious* by a Dominican, Victor White. The other is *Myth and Ritual in Christianity* by Alan Watts.

B. wrote to say that life is good and that his new wife is a good cook. He plans to begin work on his Ph.D. Maybe married life will settle him down to work.

Robert Giroux wrote to tell her that they are planning to reissue *Wise Blood*, and would she like to make any corrections. She cannot bring herself to read the book again, so she is going to say that there are no corrections and that she also cannot write an introduction.

Works: Wise Blood.

October 28, 1961 (p. 451; 4 par.): From ANDA-LUSIA. No news is so sad for her than to hear that Hester has left the church. She knows that she has to do what she believes and that she will not have a lower opinion of her for doing so. However, she thinks that she will have diminished her life and her appetite for it. She does not think Hester will do as some people and inflate their faith in themselves now with a lack of faith in Christ. In fact, Hester is likely to believe less in herself without a faith in Christ. In any case, she wants to tell her that faith comes and goes. If she feels drawn back in the slightest way to find faith once again, she should come back without any feelings of guilt.

She would like Hester to review the *Mary Ann* book, if she still thinks she can under the circumstances. However, she would not like her to review her introduction to the book because it will not ring true to her.

They have heard a rumor that Shot may sue them. Jack tells them that someone else is putting him up to it. On the other hand, Regina has been told by the insurance agent that since Shot took the compensation insurance payment, he will not be able to sue.

The sister at Marillac tells Cecil that she and O'Connor would not be able to meet there because it is for nuns only and is closed to the public. Cecil has writer's block, not helped by the fact that her roommate, who never cared much before about writing, sat down and wrote a good novel in about two months.

Works: A Memoir of Mary Ann.

November 11, 1961 (p. 453; 5 par.): From ANDALUSIA. She did not get Hester's letter on Monday, as usual, but did receive it Tuesday. She was afraid that Hester had thrown her friendship with O'Connor out with the church. She was prepared to write a letter on Wednesday to argue that this need not be so, and she is glad to see that such a letter is unnecessary.

She did not mean to imply that Hester felt guilty over leaving; she realizes that if she did, she would not have left. She is pleased that the church helped her find herself and thinks that the natural comes before the supernatural, so it may be that she needs to explore her renewed sense of self-esteem now first before she could return to the church. O'Connor knows that one finds Christ when the suffering of others means more than one's own.

Andrew Lytle has asked Jack Hawkes to write an article for *SEWANEE REVIEW* about O'Connor's work. This surprises her. Lytle says that Hawkes's work is too general about evil.

She had a good time in St. Louis, Missouri, and found several people there who thought that they could be Tarwater and so felt they understood *The Violent Bear It Away*. She met their writing teacher, Sister Mariella Gable, before in Minnesota. Gable taught *The Catcher in the Rye* in one school until parents complained. The bishop asked her to quit, but she argued her side of things and was reassigned to somewhere in the Dakotas. Gable likes Iris Murdoch.

Works: The Violent Bear It Away.

November 25, 1961 (p. 454; 4 par.):   From AN-DALUSIA. She certainly did not mean by her letter that Hester does not care for others. She thinks that Miss Nancy probably does not deserve the attention that Hester gives to her. She is thinking of a different kind of care for others, one that involves grace such as Sister Evangelist has. One need not be a religious to have this either, but it is also something that neither she nor Hester nor ELIZABETH BISHOP possesses.

She was wrong to guess that Hester would have less confidence now; she clearly has more. Since faith blinds, Hester is now able to see for herself, and since faith longs for the out of reach, now what Hester wants she can obtain. It is good for Hester to take time off for six months. When she returns to writing, she will probably be able to do anything she likes. O'Connor will look at her article on Murdoch. She knows little about Murdoch, but she can comment on the writing of the piece.

It has been a miserable week. Louise's niece, Shirley, arrived with a baby, and Louise's mother, Camilla, who is 100 years old, needed to come and stay on the farm while they were there. This meant for tight sleeping conditions and a Louise with strained nerves when she was sober.

She is not sure of what Andrew is speaking in relation to Jack Hawkes's work, but it is probably not what Hester suggests. He likes *The Turn of the Screw* and would probably be interested in Hester's article on Hawkes.

Works: None.

December 9, 1961 (p. 457; 5 par.):   From ANDA-LUSIA. It is probably a good idea to forget about her Murdoch essay for now while she is becoming herself. O'Connor thinks that Hester is trying to be like Iris Murdoch in the paper now. Hester's gift

is intellectualizing concrete details into ideas. She may be able to write novels, but perhaps not as easily as she can do other things. At the moment, Hester has truth mixed up with psychology.

She does accept that Murdoch's system of truth and morality is superior to the church's, but Hester would expect nothing else from her. She is curious, however, how Hester could be a member of the church for five years and not have a clearer understanding of the church's teachings. Self-abandonment is not the same thing as not being yourself or hurting oneself.

Neither does writing for oneself wash with her. There is always a desire to be heard when one writes, and Hester, of anyone, has that desire. O'Connor is never so far out of herself as when she writes and never so absolutely herself at the same time. She is able to abandon herself and be herself in the act, and this is what self-abandonment is like in the church.

On Sunday, Miss M. moved away from the farm. Louise was drunk and jumped in the truck with them and their two police dogs, which she was afraid of when sober, and was gone for two days. She did not explain what happened or where she was when she returned.

She heard from friends in Texas that they went looking for a paperback copy of her story collection and were told the store did not have it but that they did have another work by the same author called *The Bear That Ran Away With It.* She envisions her new collection title, *Everything That Rises Must Coverge*, being transformed into "Every Rabbit That Rises Is a Sage."

Works: A Good Man Is Hard to Find and other Stories, [The Violent Bear It Away], Everything That Rises Must Converge.

December 14, 1961 (p. 458; 4 par.):   From ANDALUSIA. She and Regina agree with Hester completely about Jenny Sessions. Regina does not favor anything foreign, but she likes Jenny and thinks that she makes a good match for Billy. They are pleased over the marriage.

Cecil's roommate sent her the novel to look over. She calls this kind of book a prairie novel—there is a sense of time and place, but not much happens. She is not sure what she will say about it because though it is sensitively written, it is very low key. She sees why Cecil and this woman are compatible.

When Bill and Jenny Sessions were there, Dr. Spivey also came, and they entertained each other so much that she did not have to do a thing. He was very funny and talked of *La Dolce Vita*. He still has his condition of psychosomatic blindness. The doctors say that there is nothing wrong with his eyes.

She sends holiday wishes.

Works: None.

January 13, 1962 (p. 461; 6 par.): From ANDALUSIA. Cecil and Betty came by the farm, but they just missed them. They will likely be back in the summer. In her view, Cecil needs to live in the South, where she can be closer to the things that she hates in order to write about them.

Louise's mother died last Sunday, and the funeral will not be until this Sunday at the People's Undertaking Parlor. Apparently, the body is kept out back until there is a casket choice, then the body is brought to the front. Louise's daughter, Lucy Mae, is going to call and let them know if she will make it from Florida for the funeral. Whenever Lucy Mae arrives, Louise speaks about going down to Florida with her, so they will be glad to know when and if that issue is settled once again.

Has she read *Set This House on Fire* by William Styron? She agrees with Milner that there are few Christian novelists working in the South.

She likes Trollope and is trying to get hold of *The Last Chronicle of Barset*. If Hester has not yet seen his mother's story about visiting America in 1830, she should read it.

She just heard from John Hawkes in one of his polite and elegant letters. He has a new job in Utah found for him by Bernard Malmud and Albert Guérard. He will teach the novel seminars and give a lecture open to the public called "Wild Talents in the American Novel."

She can send HENRY JAMES's *The American*

Scene if Hester would like it. It contains a part on SAVANNAH, where he expresses a dislike for the loss of mystery.

Works: None.

February 10, 1962 (p. 464; 4 par.): From ANDALUSIA. She has had the flu, and Regina, since she can have a flu shot, has had a bad cold. She appreciates the books. Being ill, she will read them quickly and get them back in time for their due date. She is concerned about Hester's account of her time and her mood swings up and down. She thinks an even routine of doing the same activities at the same time every day is very helpful to this kind of thing; in fact, it helps one survive.

The sisters have altered her existence—on the 14th she will be in orbit, then touring the White House that evening with Jackie. Regina wants to invite Mary Jo and Miss White out to see these things with them on their television, since they do not have one.

Works: None.

February 24, 1962 (p. 466; 2 par.): From ANDALUSIA. Louise got drunk and stayed in bed this week. Regina tried to get her up and go to the doctor, when the aspirin she gave her did not work. Jack said she was no better and should go to the doctor. Louise refused to go. She is 56 years old and has never been sick, nor gone to a doctor before. She would not budge. They went to town and bought some Absorbine Jr. for her and Regina rubbed her back. That did not help either, but still Louise would not go to the doctor.

They went to Eatonton and picked up Shot's mother, Ida. Ida thinks very highly of herself and her curative powers. She made a poultice of mud and salt and gave that to Louise, but that did not help. Finally, even Ida said Louise had to go to the doctor because she was not passing water. Louise still did not want to go, but Ida got her into the car and off they went.

When Louise and Ida came out of the examination room, Louise clearly felt better and admitted that she did. Ida joked with them afterward about Louise's ignorance. Louise had never heard of a specimen before. In any case, Louise had the flu and is now recovering after the doctor gave her a shot of penicillin. Regina says that she will make sure Louise gets a flu shot next year.

The next day, Father Mayhew arrived, and they were grateful that it was not earlier.

Works: None.

May 19, 1962 (p. 474; 5 par.):   From ANDALUSIA. They will be glad to see her, and Louis will enjoy bringing her back with the mail that day.

It is all right with her if Hester writes about her work in combination with the other two women; however, the piece should be about her work and not about her soul. She does not like seeing Hester falling down the drain of thinking that what one worships does not matter but only how one worships. She finds worship a duty.

She was shown *The English Journal* by the sisters at Rosary College. The author did not understand her work at all, saying that Haze, Tarwater, Mr. Head, and Nelson all had nothing happen to them. There was something dumb also about violence in PEACOCKS. The sisters agreed with her estimations of the piece.

Archbishop Hallinan, the new archbishop of ATLANTA, visited the farm yesterday. She was delighted to learn that he has read every one of her works and thinks highly of them. He even quoted from *The Violent Bear It Away* in one of his speeches. She would like him, though, even if he were not so favorable to her work. The church has found the right person for the job this time.

She recommends *The Lotus and the Robot* by Koestler, which she is now reading.

Works: [*Wise Blood*], *The Violent Bear It Away*.

June 9, 1962 (p. 478; 5 par.):   From ANDALUSIA. They are enjoying the candy, especially Louis and Mary Jo. The bourbon will last longer than the candy and will be enjoyed just as much, if only by her. She encourages Hester to visit without bringing anything but herself. She would like her to visit soon so that she can see the new bookcases. They have absorbed many of the books from her room,

but at the rate that publishers send her novels, that will not last long. She makes frequent gifts to the library of the books publishers send her. However, she advises the librarians to read them and decide what books to remove before they go out to the public. Private censorship is all right with her.

It was rather boring to get her honorary degree, but seeing Tom made the trip worthwhile. They presented her hood, which is now wrapped in newspaper and put away in a closet. That is about it for honorary degrees.

Jack Hawkes had much good news. He received a Guggenheim and a grant from the National Institute of Arts and Letters and will be going to Grenada, British West Indies, for a year. He rewrote the article for Andrew while keeping his thesis, and her understanding is that Andrew is going to accept it.

Dr. Spivey will be married on June 30 to a teacher from Sandy Springs. He and the teacher both share an interest in dreams. He dreamed that O'Connor was out searching for blacks and interpreted this to mean that she is progressing on a spiritual journey.

Regina had completed *The Fox in the Attic* mainly out of duty in finishing what she begins. Regina is now reading KATHERINE ANNE PORTER's book. She has read about half of the Hughes book and has not yet started *Ship of Fools*.

Works: None.

June 23, 1962 (p. 480; 5 par.):   From ANDALUSIA. She sends four books by Simone Weil. She was going to send the other two, but the package was already large. She will send *The Notebooks* and *The Fox in the Attic* next week.

She disagrees with Cecil who liked *A High Wind in Jamaica* better than *The Fox in the Attic*. Regina is reading *Ship of Fools* and complains regularly about reading a sickening scene right before eating. For example, she read a scene about a seasick bulldog right before going out to the Sanford House for a meal. She thinks KATHERINE ANNE PORTER has difficulty anticipating what is to come, but she is excellent at describing the particular and making it real.

Dr. Spivey did not explain the dream that much, other than to say that the blacks in it represent O'Connor's instincts. Unfortunately, she was host to an "air plant." Ashley Brown, the original such plant, is on his way to Africa.

The German translation of *The Violent Bear It Away* cannot accurately translate that title, so they are asking her for a new one. What does Hester suggest? They suggest *The Bursting Sun*, but neither they nor she likes it. She has thought of *Food for the Violent* or *The Prophet's Country* but does not like either of those either.

They had a visit from the Hoods in Florida. They made coffee and took it out with them to to pond early one morning to fish. Deen slurped while the jackass, Ernest, drank the coffee.

Works: *The Violent Bear It Away*.

July 21, 1962 (p. 483; 3 par.): From ANDALUSIA. Did Hester see the program on television with Ray Moore and five candidates for governor? She could not have written a better scenario exemplifying Georgia politics herself. She saw it on rerun and will watch it again if they run it again.

We all have a responsiveness that is left untapped. Maryat has developed hers from a real lack previously. Some of these are run out of us by the wrong kind of education.

She likes the bulldog in *Ship of Fools* and has made her way across the Atlantic minus about a third with KATHERINE ANNE PORTER. Though the book may not be a great one, she thinks it is well made, as though sculpted.

Works: None.

August 4, 1962 (p. 487; 5 par.): From ANDALUSIA. Even though they felt bad not to see Billy, both she and Regina thought that mononucleosis was nothing to mess around with. She consulted with her doctor, who told her that people can be a carrier as much as three months after infection, so she warned Billy that about exposure to Jenny.

She, too, liked the review of *Franny & Zooey*. She had read a couple of the stories in *The New Yorker*. She liked Dick Gilman's review of it in *JUBILEE* even better.

Cecil visited her friends in Schenectady, the Pollers; she was taken there for dinner by the Hickses. It was good for her to get away from the arty types at YADDO. After one is there awhile, one longs for people like the Pollers, who are an insurance salesman and a former librarian. At Yaddo, there is too much talk about form and various sleeping pills.

The sisters brought Mary Ann's family to the farm last Saturday. Meeting them made her feel closer to Mary Ann. Mary Ann's sister did not come since she has had tumors removed. The father is dying of cancer, and his face is full of warts. It was moving to meet them and come in contact with the real Poor of God, those who have been touched by God in that way and for whom it is their vocation.

It is strange that only Hester and a few nuns have ever mentioned "The Temple of the Holy Ghost," and it has never been anthologized.

Works: "Temple of the Holy Ghost," A *Memoir of Mary Ann*.

September 8, 1962 (p. 491; 3 par.): From ANDALUSIA. If she understands correctly that Hester is going to New York, then that is a good thing. Fourteen years ago, she stayed at the Y on 38th or 37th Street, perhaps, off Lexington Avenue. She could pay $2 a day and that included breakfast. Between Madison and Park there used to be a good co-op cafeteria where she could afford to eat without worrying about contracting some disease.

They called B. when they heard. Jenny is fine, but B. spent the bulk of their conversation explaining how he had been in bed since getting his wisdom teeth out, and the event was the first thing that got him out of bed.

A typewriter requires all 10 fingers to operate, whereas a pen only requires three, so the typewriter would seem in that case to be more personal.

Works: None.

October 6, 1962 (p. 494; 5 par.): From ANDALUSIA. She is glad to hear that Hester enjoyed New York and is on a bit of an art binge. Has she seen *Voices of Silence* by Malraux and the book on painting by Gilson? She ordered Hester an art book that she thought that she would save for her for Christmas, but when she got it, the dust-jacket was half torn off from careless packaging, and she saw at once anyway that it was a book that she would enjoy and Hester would not. It was a book of Daumier's drawings.

Mrs. M. has contacted her and invited her to accept a scroll this year. Since Mrs. M. was sick the year before, she can include *The Violent Bear It Away* in the AWARDS ceremony because they are giving awards for the past two years together. O'Connor refused to go to the dinner but accepted to appear at the box lunch at the Historical Society the day before. This still means that she needs to prepare a thank-you speech. She plans to say something about being honored at home meaning more than anywhere else, such as the Nobel Prize. N. is improving and may even come to miss the hospital and the joke-cracking nuns. Hester should visit them now that she has been to New York and Washington, D. C.

Works: The Violent Bear It Away.

October 19, 1962 (p. 495; 4 par.): From AN-DALUSIA. She appreciates the musicians. It would be good to be able to paint whatever one wanted to paint. She has more eye than ability. She used to paint musicians, but the Hoods liked them, so they are now hanging over their mantel. She just received a Professional Beer Can Opener from Mrs. Hood. It looks like some kind of medieval machine, but it actually works, and she will use it.

She likes *Morte D'Urban* by Powers more than she thought she would. She had seen a couple of chapters in *The New Yorker* and ESQUIRE and had based her first impression on that. Richard Gilman asked her to review it for *Commonweal*, and she turned it down because she did not think that she would like it; however, it turns out that she does. She has an extra copy if Hester would like to see it.

She appreciates Hester asking to send her papers, but she is trying to get rid of paper rather than attract it. She will also pass on the Sewell for now. She was sent an inscribed novel by Neville Braybrook, whom she thinks writes in the same foggy style.

Works: None.

November 3, 1962 (p. 497; 5 par.): From ANDA-LUSIA. She sent Hester an article titled "The Lady and the Issue" that reminds her of Hester's current thinking on the sexes. Hester is nearing the church's thinking on this matter in a way. If she continues along the track of raising her ideas to highest truth, however, she risks becoming a crank. She is unfamiliar with Iris Murdoch's examples, but her own story "The Lamb Shall Enter First" has an implied good mother in it for whom the boy is searching.

She does not have *Voices of Silence* and was lent it by the Phillips. They were visited by a mystical kind of person, R., who went outdoors to enjoy Nature. Regina saw her lying on the ground when it was only 50 degrees out. She demanded that she get up, that she will surely catch a cold. R. claimed it was "more sacramental" to lie down on the grass. Two days later she had a cold. Mother is always ahead of everyone.

She has heard from M. Coindreau that *Set This House on Fire* by William Styron is very popular in France and that he is being compared there to WILLIAM FAULKNER. Coindreau did the translation. John O'Hara will be awarded the Nobel Prize now that Steinbeck has received it.

Works: ["The Lame Shall Enter First"].

December 21, 1962 (p. 502; 5 par.): From ANDA-LUSIA. She waited until she received Hester's letter before opening the package. She had no idea that this would be in it; she was sure it was out of print. She wants to send it back, because surely Hester could not have had time to read it herself before she sent it. She is enjoying it in the meantime.

Regina did contribute to the choice of candy jar. She wanted her to send something attractive, perhaps in consideration of the vegetable dishes O'Connor sent last year.

She likes the electric typewriter for retyping material; it saves energy. It is always ahead of you, so she does not like composing on it.

Office parties sound like they could give Hester lots of fuel for fiction. They have had an artist at the farm sent by *JUBILEE* to take her picture. He stayed in a Volkswagen bus out in the woods while he was there. Finally, he could not take the picture because he kept sensing her resistance to allowing her true nature to be captured on film, so he took off in his bus to Florida to pick fruit.

Works: None.

January 19, 1963 "Gen. Robt. E. Lee's Birthday" **(p. 505; 3 par.):** From ANDALUSIA. She now has a calendar with important people's birthdays on it, so she will inform her. She has not heard about *The Bulletin*, but Hester needs to give the editor more than one issue before she judges him. Father Mayhew is going to do a regular column, which is to the editor's credit to discover and use this talent. They have found a device they can put on the car so she can drive it and they will not have to buy a new one.

Works: None.

February 2, 1963 (p. 508; 4 par.): From ANDALUSIA. She sends her greetings on Ground Hog's Day and thinks that her idea is a good one. She just completed reading the autobiography of Katharine Trevelyan. They will be meeting Mr. Sherry next Thursday. Louise has been giving Regina problems this week with pretending not to know what she is talking about. They met the woman who does not believe in tithing yesterday, saying that they will keep Miss O.'s cook if she does not pull through her current illness.

Works: None.

February 16, 1963 (p. 508; 2 par.): From ANDALUSIA. She hopes that Cecil will not get the job at the *New Yorker*; she is waiting to find out. She liked G. E. Sherry and finds him respectable. He is willing to listen to her thoughts about the racial articles in the paper. He is willing to learn more about the region. He wants to have good BOOK REVIEWS. She thinks that the newspaper business is like the housewife's life, "eat it and forget it; read it and forget it."

Works: None.

March 2, 1963 (p. 510; 4 par.): From ANDALUSIA. Dr. A. Brown tells her to let Hester know that Iris Murdoch will have her new novel out soon; it will be about a unicorn.

Mr. Sherry has asked her to write something for his supplement once a month. She has refused but has agreed to write occasionally and will give him something for the first issue. She wants to write about the teachers who are assigning Steinbeck and Hersey to eighth graders.

Miss O. continues in life and in keeping her cook. "Everything That Rises Must Converge" has won the O. HENRY AWARD. She nearly forgot about the prize now that it is run by someone at Harvard.

Works: "Everything That Rises Must Converge."

March 30, 1963 (p. 511; 4 par.): From ANDALUSIA. After 20 years of writing, she is most sure of her own failures at being articulate. She would go to battle for that which she cannot say. She read "A Good Man Is Hard to Find" at the University of Georgia the other evening. The audience was great because they were familiar with the story and caught all the jokes. When she read the part about Red Sammy Butts, though, there was an unusual amount of reaction. She found out later that Red Sammy is a little too much in character like their football coach, Wally Butts.

In reading the French translation, *Les braves gens ne courent pas les rues*, she came across Red Sam described as *"le joyeaux vetéran."* She is looking forward to reviewing the rest of it. The Muscovy duck has reappeared from the pampas grass with nine ducklings, a beautiful sight.

Works: "A Good Man Is Hard to Find."

April 13, 1963 (p. 512; 5 par.): From ANDALUSIA. She sends *The Unicorn* by Iris Murdoch, which was sent to her by Catharine Carver. She has lost the sense of what is published and what are review copies since the strike with the *New York Times Book Review*. She depends on it to see what is coming. Carver also sent her Ivan Gold's

Nickel Miseries. She likes the title. Gold once visited Andalusia unannounced. From his picture on the cover, she sees he has a beard now and has turned from a Brooklyn boy into an artist.

They are having a lot of company after Easter. This includes Mr. F. from Main, Dr. L. from Wheaton College, and a Franciscan missionary sister. They will host a class one afternoon from Shorter and the Newman Club for supper. The Literary Guild is coming for a picnic, and several Methodists from Emory will be over to have a conversation about FYODOR DOSTOYEVSKY films that they have been watching.

She delayed work for an hour the other day to watch W. C. Fields in *Never Give a Sucker an Even Break.* She likes Fields that much that she would put off her work to see his. However, she thinks she could have written a better movie for him than this one.

The Muscovy duck has taken up with two drakes, and her flock is being raised by a bantam hen. She will probably have nine more ducklings soon. Perhaps Hester's friends will put up with her musings about metaphysics, but it is not O'Connor's interest.

Works: None.

April 27, 1963 (p. 515; 5 par.):   From ANDALUSIA. Hester can keep the book, but if she would rather ask for it when she would like it, that is all right, too. O'Connor could keep her attention on it for only about two-thirds of the way. It stopped being a story and became more of a philosophical text, and that is what lost her.

Regina's black friend has asked for an article on "Woman's Day" for Mother's Day. She was asked to write on on "The Value of Sunday School" last year, which was much more her kind of topic.

The woman has still not secured Miss O.'s cook. She seems to resent the fact that Miss O. has not died and points out that she is losing her faculties, which can be a worse fate. She has been distracted from the cook/Miss O. issue, however, lately because someone recently ran into her car.

Regina slammed her hand in a car door, which has slowed her down some, though not much.

She does not know where Hester gets all the time she does to read. She has H. F. M. Prescott's *Man on a Donkey* but has not yet read it. She hopes to read FYODOR DOSTOYEVSKY over the summer.

Works: None.

May 11, 1963 (p. 518; 5 par.):   From ANDALUSIA. When she has the flu next time, she will try reading the H. F. M. Prescott. It has been in the house a long time, but she cannot remember how or from whom she got it. She has not read Bergson's or Meredith's essays about comedy. It is better not to be too self-conscious about one's work and better to keep it coming from the body, not the head.

Regina is back in business. She is now working on installing a creep-feeder. Such a machine feeds the calves but not the cows. As the calves feed, more feed creeps out for them.

She and her mother are going to Boston on May 31 to visit her aunt and cousins and for her to get another honorary degree, this time at Smith. She needs to find a way to take herself out of the running for these. She hopes to see Robert Fitzgerald, who may be in the area. He will be a professor at Mount Holyoke in the fall; they are enrolling Benny (Benedict) Fitzgerald at Portsmouth Priory.

ELIZABETH BISHOP wrote to her that she was sending her a gift by way of a friend and that she hoped O'Connor would not be offended. She likes items made by the natives where she is, and this is a crucifix in a bottle. The item recently arrived, and it is not a crucifix but an altar in a bottle, complete with Bible, chalice, two candles, tools for the crucifixion hanging from a cross, and a rooster atop the cross. It is all made of wood and paper, and she likes it very much. Hester will have to look at it when she visits the next time.

Works: None.

May 25, 1963 (p. 521; 4 par.):   From ANDALUSIA. Miss O. has died, and M. can now go to family graduations that are coming up. There is a question of the will and who gets the night nurse.

She has finally received the Philip Rahv anthology; not much money from it, but she is in good company. Waugh's early work does not measure up, in her opinion, to *Men at Arms*. Signet will publish her three books together in a single volume in October. They have asked for another introduction, but she told them to let the one for *Wise Blood* stand for all. She is working in fiction right now and does not want to stop to write nonfiction.

She does not intend to read Beauvoir. Simone Weil is strange enough, but it interests her. When she wrote about the blood and the head, what she meant was that the head can tame what is in the blood at times; at other times, the blood can be nourished by what is in the head. They work together.

She is reading C. Vann Woodward's *The Burden of Southern History*. The subject matter normally disinterests her; Woodward can write.

Works: *Wise Blood*.

June 22, 1963 (p. 526; 6 par.):   From ANDALUSIA. They thank her for the bottle and the candy. It was good of her to get there by bus and then take the ride with Louis Cline back. Louis eats the candy by the handful. Regina gets after him about it.

CAL ROBERT LOWELL defends Hannah Arendt. Talk of the Arendt issue fills the book section.

It is funny to hear the reaction of those around her to her inclusion in *ESQUIRE* with "Why Do the Heathen Rage?" It was as though now she were getting somewhere. It surprises her that so many rural Georgians around there read that magazine. Norman Mailer is in the same issue and spent some time bashing other writers. It seems like so many of the young male writers do that.

She thinks Hester's opinions of morality are unrealistic.

B. called all excited, and she cannot remember about what, though Regina showed her an announcement of the birth of Regina's godchild. They make terrible godmothers. She never remembers the birthday of her Fitzgerald godchild and cannot remember the first name of her other godchild. She sends a clipping that she finds amusing about high school English teachers.

Works: ["Why Do the Heathen Rage?"].

July 6, 1963 (p. 528; 5 par.):   From ANDALUSIA. This letter will probably not make sense since she is trying to write with a man putting up curtain rods in her room. Her mother has made new curtains. He is quiet now but will be back at it soon.

She was given the clipping about telephone teaching from a former Milledgevillian who now teaches at Columbus High. She was the one who taught the class. They learned by doing—they went throughout middle Georgia seeing sites, including the Indian mounds at Macon, the Mansion and ANDALUSIA in MILLEDGEVILLE, and Turnwold in Eatonton, which is Joel Chandler Harris's house. They returned to school and wrote about what they liked. The teacher told her that one girl wrote about O'Connor's swan hissing at her. They do, then they look, and then they telephone. The teacher claims that they ask good questions. They had read Ayn Rand or another bad writer, and one student asked one of the speakers on their field trip what he thought about Absolutes.

She was given the book of Elizabeth Sewell's poetry by the man at Smith. She does not understand the serious ones, but she quite enjoys the nonsense poems, including one about ST. THOMAS AQUINAS sailing off with the owl and the pussycat. She will send it to Hester if she would like to see it. She would like to read the novel if Hester still has it.

She is trying to complete Madison Jones's latest novel. It is so unfortunate that as soon as his books are published, they drop out of sight.

The man doing the curtain rods claims he gets a hemorrhage every three years. When she suggested that maybe it is an ulcer instead, he told her that he bleeds out of his nose. The doctor told him that if it did not bleed there, it would bleed in his brain, and he would die.

Works: None.

July 20, 1963 (p. 530; 3 par.):   From ANDALUSIA. Fitzgerald translated only the *Odyssey*, not the *Iliad*, but it is now in paperback. He has done the Theban cycle, *Oedipus at Colonus* alone and two with Dudley Fitts. Paul VI is a good pope, but any pope will do.

She thought that the package was of the Simone Weil books, but she is glad that she opened it and is now reading Elizabeth Sewell's *Now Bless Thyself*. She has heard from Maryat that she needs to read Hiram Haydn's *The Hands of Esau*. Haydn is Cecil's editor at Atheneum and also editor of *The* AMERICAN SCHOLAR. Maryat claims that the book describes what she is like on the inside, so with some hesitation, O'Connor will give it a look.

Works: None.

August 3, 1963 (p. 533; 6 par.):   From ANDALUSIA. She is glad to hear of the move. She would be all right living in a neighborhood that she did not like as much in order to have more room. Her space is her room, which is invaded fairly regularly. However, her desk is her domain. No one touches the desk but her.

They have a new car, one that she can drive because it has power brakes, and they do not need the driver to lift a foot to use them. She still hates to drive, however.

Ashley asked about her and wants her to know that Iris Murdoch has written a play or will have one produced in London. She does not recall this literary information that Ashley always seems to know. He told her that Caroline was friends with Elizabeth Sewell. She will send her the *New York Review* that has an article by Edmund Wilson about painting.

She has a friend in Athens who wrote an essay, "Getting James Baldwin Off My Back." She has likely read *The Ring & the Book*. She remembers taking Tennyson and Browning in college.

Works: None.

August 17, 1963 (p. 534; 2 par.):   From ANDALUSIA. Photographers are horrible. She thinks one's face is sacred to that person and should not be able to be broadcast without their permission

anywhere someone chooses. There are probably many images of her floating around in places that she has no control over.

It has been another active week around the farm. Louise got drunk again and threw boiling water at Shot. Regina had to take him to the emergency room. Louise was glad that she burned him, and when O'Connor asked Regina later if Louise still felt that way, she said that now she wishes that she had killed him.

Works: None.

September 1, 1963 (p. 537; 3 par.):   From ANDALUSIA. The new bookshelves sound like they will do the job, and she only hopes that Hester let the paint dry before putting her books on them. The birds in the picture are chukar quail.

She agrees with her about the EUDORA WELTY story and only wishes that it were not in the *New Yorker,* where the northern liberals get hold of something like that and think they know about southern living. It is not good to write topical fiction; she got away with it in "Everything Rises" because she put a plague on everyone's house about the race issue.

She is displeased over the publication of an interview of hers in an ATLANTA magazine, sent to her by B. F. She was asked about the race crisis bringing about a renaissance in southern literature, and she said she most certainly did not think it would. They changed the word *race* to *social* so that none of the article makes sense now. She is angry about it and newspaper people in general. Tom Stritch has been visiting most of the week.

Works: "Everything That Rises Must Converge."

September 14, 1963 (p. 539; 3 par.):   From ANDALUSIA. She has heard from Jack Hawkes that they are now in Providence, Rhode Island. His new novel, *Second Skin*, will be out in January. That is a very Hawkeslike title.

Another moviemaker has sent a script, this time for "The Life You Save." He did not change much from the original.

She is reading *Eichmann in Jerusalem*, sent to her by Tom Stritch. The haunting boxcars were the least of the events. Hannah Arendt is an intelligent writer.

Works: "The Life You Save Must Be Your Own."

September 28, 1963 (p. 541; 4 par.):   From ANDA-LUSIA. Though it might be dangerous to try to analyze too much, she is pleased to hear that she has thought through the matter of free will.

She reports that Ernest the burro has become a father. They have been on the watch since before she went to Smith, and one day she saw Marquita in the oat field, conversing with a smaller creature with a white mouth. He is about one-eighth her size. She called everyone, and they went out to greet the baby burro. Regina gave him the name Equinox, and she added O'Connor. Hester needs to make a visit to see him. She will send a picture soon.

Hester has asked about O'Connor's book dedications. She has published three books in 18 years. The next dedication will be to Louis I. Cline, who is older than 70. Thomas Stritch is older than 50, but he would apparently have more time.

They attended a luncheon yesterday with the governor at the college. She was shaking his hand while he smiled at someone else, and he smiled at her while he was shaking the hand of someone else, but all this did not concern her too much.

Works: None.

October 26, 1963 (p. 543; 3 par.):   From ANDA-LUSIA. It is not possible for human beings to both love and understand others. This is only possible for God. O'Connor loves many people but understands none.

She is back from Hollins, Notre Dame of Maryland, and Georgetown. The money from the trip should help pay bills for the next six to eight months. She read at Hollins, but gave talks at the other two, and she is now ready to get back to writing.

In Roanoke, a reporter tried to imitate her southern accent. In Maryland, a reporter tried to make a case for he and she wrote in a similar style. She did not buy it for a second. In Wash-ington, all they wanted to talk about was integration, and she moved around those questions the best she could.

Miss Mary Cline is in the hospital after falling after a concert that she attended with the Garners and Aunt Julia. They are seeking a gentlewoman of about 50 who might stay with her.

Works: None.

November 9, 1963 (p. 547; 5 par.):   From ANDA-LUSIA. [Cecil] wants to do a dramatization of "The Displaced Person." She wants to write a play using several characters from different O'Connor stories. Cecil is talented, and Elizabeth McKee and her firm are now handling plays, so perhaps something will come of it.

Miss M. fired the black woman whom they asked to spend nights with her. The woman used to work for a woman down the street, reading her the Bible. Miss M. said she did not need to pay 50 cents for someone to read her Scripture and claims she feels better. Hester's aunt and she are welcome for dinner any Saturday.

Someone wrote to her about an interpretation of "A Good Man Is Hard to Find," and she was very polite in her response, explaining that they were going to Florida and that it could not be anywhere else. Many students write to her such as the one saying that he may taking up writing as a hobby and wanting to know if experience or imagination were more engaged in the process.

She just finished a story ["Revelation"] but has no idea yet if it is good or not.

Works: "The Displaced Person," "A Good Man Is Hard to Find," ["Revelation"].

November 23, 1963 (p. 549; 3 par.):   From ANDALUSIA. She has been too sick to be near the typewriter. Before she got sick, however, she completed the draft of a story ["Revelation"]. She does not know what she thinks of it at present and cannot think of that right now, especially the last paragraph. Hester's comments will be helpful.

"I am sad about the President [Kennedy]. But I like the new one" (549).

Works: ["Revelation"].

December 6, 1963 (p. 552; 5 par.):   From ANDA-LUSIA She is glad to hear that Hester likes ["Revelation"]. She has sent it to only one other person, Catharine Carver. It is a test to see what Catharine thinks of it since she is a stoic New Englander.

The story took her just eight weeks to write. Many things fell into place at her pleasure. She saw Claud and Ruby in her own doctor's office.

She thought that Kennedy's funeral was a needed tonic for the nation. "Mrs. Kennedy has a sense of history and of what is owing to death" (552). O'Connor is feeling better with her anemia.

She will give Hester the galleys to John Hawkes's *Second Skin* when Hester visits. Hawkes has won a Ford Foundation grant, which pleases her.

Works: ["Revelation"].

December 25, 1963 (p. 554; 4 par.):   From ANDA-LUSIA She hopes Hester is not in bed as she is. She fainted and has been in bed since. She is going to try out some new medication.

C. Carver liked her story ["Revelation"] and thought it was one of her best, though darkest. She thinks Ruby is evil and that the vision proves it. Carver suggested she leave out the vision, but she is going to leave it in and make the scene stronger to highlight Ruby's character. She has fought this problem in all of her writing.

Works: ["Revelation"].

January 25, 1964 (p. 562; 5 par.):   From ANDA-LUSIA. Everyone and everyone's health seem to be improving, including Regina, her, Louise, and Aunt Julia. Caroline really likes ["Revelation"] and read it to her class, who laughed. Even though she likes it, she still wrote six pages on grammar. Ward Dorrance in Washington also likes the story. She plans to type it and send it to *SEWANEE REVIEW*. She could get $1500 for it from Esquire, but agrees with her character Mr. Shiftlet that some people ought to want more than money.

She is glad to hear that Hester is moving on from metaphysics. Jack Hawkes would like Hester's passionate views on the novel. It would be kind of Hester to read it in galleys and write to him.

She has a tin ear to music and cannot analyze it for herself. She needs others to recommend works to her.

Works: ["Revelation"].

February 15, 1964 (p. 565; 6 par.):   From ANDA-LUSIA. She might go to the hospital for an operation soon. What did Hester think of Hawkes's work? She has received her two new swans, but the weather has not allowed her to go out and enjoy them much yet. Andrew Carl Sessions sent his godmother a picture of him in a cowboy outfit. Thomas has sent them many records. The classical ones sound much the same to each other, and all the rest sound to her like the Beatles. She is now reading *I'll Take My Stand*.

Works: None.

March 14, 1964 (p. 569; 2 par.):   From ANDA-LUSIA. She dislikes galleys, and as far as she is concerned, Hester can tear them up for bird's nests. She has a nurse who strikes her as just like Mrs. Turpin. She does not have much energy, so she may not write letters very often for a while.

Works: "Revelation."

March 28, 1964 (p. 571; 2 par.):   From ANDA-LUSIA. The operation has reignited her LUPUS. They went to the doctor's office from "Revelation" yesterday. Did Hester see the interview on CBS with Cassius Clay and Eric Sevareid? It was worth watching.

Works: "Revelation."

April 10, 1964 (p. 573; 2 par.):   From ANDALUSIA. She writes about Mary Lou finding Sister on the floor with a temperature. She has been taken to the hospital and is not expected to make it. Regina has notified the family. She asks that Hester not call her Uncle Louis about it because it is hard for him to talk about.

Works: None.

May 17, 1964 (p. 578; 4 par.):   From ANDALU-SIA. It is true what Hester says about her uncle; he rarely mentions her father. She wonders how city dwellers get around. She has received positive feedback from "Revelation," which was published in the spring issue of SEWANEE REVIEW. Maryat told her niece when she asked why she made Mary Grace ugly that Flannery loves the character. Maryat knows what she is talking about. Both she and Miss Mary are there, and that at least makes it easier on her mother.

Works: "Revelation."

May 30, 1964 (p. 581; 1 par.): From Piedmont Hospital, Atlanta, Georgia. She should not be concerned with what O'Connor's uncle says about the health of relatives. She will have him bring Hester to visit her.

Works: None.

June 10, 1964 (p. 583; 3 par.): From Piedmont Hospital, Atlanta, Georgia. She cannot handle telephone calls right now. Letters are fine, and she is allowed visitors for about 10 minutes each. She invites Hester to visit that weekend. It looks more and more like she will always be in the hospital. She has become acquainted with all the nurses who would like to write.

Works: None.

June 27, 1964 (p. 587; 4 par.): From ANDALUSIA. She compliments Hester and her aunt for finding the good in people. It is a gift that she does not have. They have put the pottery in the parlor rather than in her room. Even though her mother indicates that it is a paperweight, she says that O'Connor's room must be cleaned up to use it there for that purpose. There was nothing done while they were away. Cardinal Spellman should not write good novels; it is proper that his novels are bad. If they were good, she would be concerned about the church.

Works: None.

July 11, 1964 (p. 592; 1 par.): From ANDALUSIA. She sends the manuscript of "Parker's Back" rather than a letter. She appreciates her comments. She needs to wait about a year to know how she really feels about her stories.

Works: ["Parker's Back"].

July 17, 1964 (p. 593; 4 par.): From ANDALUSIA. She agrees with Hester's comments on "Parker's Back" and discusses changes. She researched it in *Memoirs of a Tattooist*. She talks about "Judgment Day" as a much-changed version of an earlier published story. She is glad Hester got a raise. WALKER PERCY has written an interesting review of Richard Hughes's *Fox in the Attic* in SEWANEE REVIEW.

Works: ["Parker's Back"], ["Judgment Day"].

July 25, 1964 (p. 594; 2 par.): From ANDALUSIA. She writes about Caroline's views of the tattoos and appreciates Caroline's advice. She was fortunate to get the story written at all. The transfusion has not helped much.

They will be able to be concerned about the reading of "Revelation" rather than its royalties since she has just found out that it won first place in the O. HENRY AWARDS.

Works: ["Parker's Back"], "Revelation."

GRANVILLE HICKS (four letters) Hicks put together a book symposium called *The Living Novel, a Symposium* and asked O'Connor to contribute. *Pages:* HB: 201, 205, 251, 475.

Letters

February 21, 1957 (p. 201; 2 par.): From ANDALUSIA. She sends a copy of her talk but thinks that he will see that it is not what he is looking for. It is not about the novel genre in particular and is geared toward students. She does not consider herself an intellectual and is not good at speaking about theories and abstractions.

Works: None.

March 3, 1957 (p. 205; 2 par.): From ANDALUSIA. She is writing a talk now for Notre Dame on regionalism and religion in fiction and would be glad to send it to him for his purposes as well if his deadline is such that she might have it done by then. She is feeling displaced writing these papers rather than her stories.

Works: None.

November 7, 1957 (p. 251; 2 par.):   From ANDA-LUSIA. She likes both the book and that fact that she is in it. She does not concern herself with whether or not the novel as a genre is alive or dead, just whether the novel that she is working on is alive or not. She gives permission for him to have her portion of the volume published wherever he may seek.

Works: None.

May 21, 1962 (p. 475; 2 par.):   From ANDALUSIA. All in town are glad to read in the interview that MILLEDGEVILLE is a more fascinating place than Charleston. The *Union Recorder* reprinted the entire interview because of it. A letter came prompted by the interview from a woman in Oklahoma who writes with purple ink and sent poems with a common theme of the Bible.

Works: None.

SISTER JULIE (three letters)   Sister Julie was a Dominican nun from the ATLANTA group who worked on the book about Mary Ann. *Pages*: HB: 480, 492, 502.

Letters

June 17, 1962 (p. 480; 4 par.):   From ANDALUSIA. She sends a PEACOCK feather tip lost in fighting with the other cocks over the fewer number of hens. She is reading *Word of God* and the *Word of Man*. She writes each day but asks for prayers that something will come of it. She still has hope that her swans will nest.

Works: None.

September 19, 1962 (p. 492; 4 par.):   From ANDALUSIA. She was pleased to hear from sister. KATHERINE ANNE PORTER looks weak in the photograph she sent. She would rather speak at colleges than conferences since there are too many writers at conferences. She did not see Brother Antoninus's poem in *The Atlantic*. The swan is still alone. She sents best wishes to Sister Mary Brian.

Works: None.

December 12, 1962 (p. 502; 4 par.):   From ANDALUSIA. She appreciates receiving the poem by Brother Antoninus; it is the only one of his that she has read. If all of his work is like this, she would enjoy it. She urges not believing what the *Atlantic* says about the South. She has just returned from Texas and Louisiana where she saw both extreme conservatism and extreme liberalism. The swan is spending time with three Muscovy ducks. Their pipes froze in a recent freeze. She sends Christmas greetings.

Works: None.

MARYAT LEE (79 letters)   Lee was a playwright and writer who lived in New York. Along with Betty Hester, Lee consistently received lengthy letters from O'Connor, though those to Lee were usually more playful and contained much about O'Connor's views of race relations in the South, an interest of Lee's. Readers should be aware that many of these letters are full of sarcasm, running jokes, and jibes.
    Pages: HB: 193–197, 200–201, 203–204, 208–210, 212–213, 215, 220, 224–225, 227–228, 212–213, 215, 220, 224–225, 227–228, 245–247, 264–266, 269–270, 278, 283–284, 288,–289, 293–294, 319–320, 325, 329–331, 339, 348–349, 358–359, 370, 376–380, 392–339, 395–396, 398–399, 406, 418, 421–423, 425–427, 432, 434–436, 441, 444, 447–448, 452–453, 462–463, 475, 482–485, 489–490, 495–496, 499, 515–516, 530, 532, 534–535, 538–539, 544, 551, 560, 562, 574, 577–578, 580–586, 590–592, 594–596.

Letters

January 9, 1957 (p. 194; 5 par.):   From ANDALU-SIA. Not many days after Lee visited, O'Connor and Regina spotted the Lee gardener driving down the street, looking very happy. She speculated that Lee had the black gardener joking and laughing all the way to ATLANTA but realized they should not tell what they saw for fear it would get Lee in trouble. Lee's brother said that his sister went to the airport with friends, which was a nice way of getting out of any racial argument with those who would disapprove.

The humor in the situation often belies the horror of it. Dr. Wells had an education meeting about 10 years prior to which he invited two black educators. Separate but equal was the norm at the meeting, including two different Coke machines. That night, however, someone who had probably no more than a fourth-grade education burned a cross on Wells's lawn. Suddenly, education was important to the ignorant.

She has received four poems to critique from their mutual friend. Neither she nor her mother noticed any rudeness. However, her mother always being present does affect O'Connor's speaking abilities, and she wishes that she had a private office.

She is pleased that she liked her stories. One comes to know oneself as much as through what one throws away as what one keeps. She looks forward to reading Lee's play and to seeing her again at Andalusia when they can be more relaxed.

Works: None.

January 31, 1957 (p. 200; 5 par.): From Andalusia. Lee's brother visited and brought the book. While she thought it was nice of him to come, she realized that he got something for it; he has invited her to speak at the Georgia State College for Women chapel in about a week's time. She enjoyed the morality play. She hopes Lee's longer play will move more quickly for her; she has the same trouble with her novel. She has set it aside for a few weeks while she writes a lecture called "How the Writer Writes," for Emory's Adult education program. They need things kept simple.

It is too bad about Graham Greene's *The Potting Shed*. She liked an article on Greene that she read by Elizabeth Sewell in *Thought*. O'Connor's view is that Greene attempts to make religion agreeable to the modern-day reader by disguising it in seediness; however, he goes a bit too far—and then must rescue it through a miracle.

The most recent Klan activity in the area was the positioning of a "burning" cross, an electric one of red lights, on the lawn of the Court House.

Works: None.

February 24, 1957 (p. 203; 6 par.): From Andalusia. Lee's brother introduced her as a writer who had both been on and not on the best-seller list. She decided to ignore the dubious distinction. She has been thinking about Lee's agents against her own. Miss McIntosh is old and keeps her hat on while sitting at her desk. Miss McKee is younger and talks out of the side of her mouth. She appreciates the Atkinson review. What did Walter Kerr say about *The Potting Shed*?

Lee should follow the voices if she is hearing them in her work. O'Connor was asked if she writes from experience or imagination, and she has not thought about it much. She knows she does not do research. She thinks we have gained most of our experience in childhood. She knew homesickness and from that wrote her first published story about an old man who traveled to live in a New York slum. It would be nice to hear voices to help with the work, but she does not.

If Lee would like to see one of her stories dressed up for television as though for burial, she should be watching Friday, March 1. At Emory, someone said that he was working on "interpersonal relations," and someone else explained that as working with blacks and whites.

Works: None.

March 10, 1957 (p. 208; 5 par.): From Andalusia. She sends material for her to read on the Japanese ship. She recommends that Lee not marry a foreigner; this is Georgia advice. She appreciates the offer for her to use Lee's apartment while she is gone, but O'Connor does not see navigating the city by herself on crutches. She is writing a talk to give at Notre Dame. She is pleased that Lee likes the remainder of the stories. "The Artificial Nigger" is most likely the best story she will ever write, and it is her favorite. She wants to hear all about Lee's experience on the Japanese freighter.

Works: "The Artificial Nigger."

March 15, 1957 (p. 209; 4 par.): From Andalusia. She sends something for Lee to recline on while on the Japanese ship. She may yawn into it when she is reading *Wise Blood*. If she gets into any trouble in Tokyo, O'Connor has a pen pal who is an assistant professor of English at the Japanese Defense Academy. He called her style in "Greenleaf," "glamorous," the first person to ever use that term related to her work. He ought to be able to get anyone out of any jam.

She will not be able to make the trip after Notre Dame; she likes to be at different places but does not enjoy the process of getting there. Apparently it is Lee who is responsible for her brother miseducating 520 female students into thinking that the best-seller list is a worthy goal. She hopes her ship journey will give her adequate time to feel guilty.

Works: *Wise Blood*, "Greenleaf."

April 4, 1957 (p. 212; 6 par.):   From ANDALUSIA. Peafowl get their name from all the peas they eat—green, black-eyed, sweet. The PEACOCK sheds tail feathers in August, and that is where one's collection comes from. O'Connor sends Lee a feather from last August. The peacock was not hurt in giving it to her.

Lee's brother asked her if she was going to New York; he knew that his sister had asked her. She asked why should she go, and he said for the "atmosphere." She told him she would tolerate the atmosphere around MILLEDGEVILLE instead. She has only one other Japanese acquaintance, a Mr. Sanobu Fujikawa, who used to live in Kamakura City. He was here on a Fulbright scholarship and was interested in contemporary American literature. Some friends from Nashville brought him by.

For souvenirs, she would like a saber-toothed tiger complete with cub, a button from Mao's jacket, and some of the Asian chickens that she does not have. She does wonder about the people whom Lee will meet. The ATLANTA Chamber of Commerce sent the similar office in Tokyo a goodwill gesture of a sack of grits. They received a letter of thanks with the notification that the grit seeds were planted but that nothing had grown from them.

The football players at Notre Dame will have to come in off the fields to see a living novelist

speak before them. She might just make faces at them; she will not use the word *beauty*. Keep in touch about her trip.

Works: None.

April 17, 1957 (p. 215; 5 par.):   From ANDALUSIA. Has she arrived in Yokohama? It must rival her own experience getting through the Chicago airport. She hopes she has a gun with her; the only things she knows about the Orient she learned from *Terry and the Pirates*, which she no longer reads.

The talk at Notre Dame was not just for students, but it was also attended by the general public. She earned $100 for her trouble. She estimates that the audience was made up of 25 percent each of students, seminarians, clergy, faculty and spouses, and graduate students, though that would add up too high in percentages.

As usual, Regina cleaned and tidied up her room in her absence. This time she installed ruffled curtains. She cannot replace the dust, but she will have the curtains removed. She could do without getting honored at the GEORGIA STATE COLLEGE FOR WOMEN, which is to happen again soon on Honors Day, especially if the honor does not include any money, but Maryat is not to whisper a word of this to her brother, or else O'Connor will call her a liar. She asks that she not forget the saber-toothed tiger she has requested.

Works: None.

May 19, 1957 (p. 220; 4 par.):   From ANDALUSIA. She sends good wishes from MILLEDGEVILLE. She hopes that Lee has not gotten ill in Japan. She and Lee's brother and sister-in-law worked a receiving line for GEORGIA STATE COLLEGE FOR WOMEN parents. She lost interest, but Lee's sister-in-law was diligent in checking the names on name tags and saying them as she greeted each person. It seems Lee must decide whether she will live with a man or not. She will keep her in her prayers. She wants the saber-toothed tiger, not its tooth. She wants to begin a zoo.

Works: None.

June 9, 1957 (p. 224; 6 par.): From ANDALUSIA. Lee may come South, and that gets no sympathy from O'Connor. She speaks of David Faulkes-Taylor and Donald Ritchie. She quotes William Alfred's *Agamemnon*, "Pity the man who loves what death can touch." Faulkes seems crazy if he thinks they can move to a "progressive" southern state. E. Wynn visited them at the farm and wants to know if Maryat marries the man. The most interesting people one would like to have visit again are usually the most shy about coming. Her mother is considering moving into the beef business so they are looking at Santa Gertrudis bulls. When asked about his business, Lee's brother says that he thinks Faulkes is into sheep, though not personally. This seems to be an indication of how serious they take Maryat's relationship with the man. When she goes to Japan, she will bring her own washtub and soap.

Works: None.

June 28, 1957 (p. 227; 5 par.): From ANDALUSIA. Lee has her prayers, no matter how things go with her marriage question. She said in "The Artificial Nigger" what she said in the letter; it is her vocation to say it in fiction. Is she producing the play in New York? She goes to Athens at the end of the month to give a talk. She would like to know what Ritchie said to Lee that she found so interesting on the ship. Let her know if Lee marries, though making it legal is not really important to her; making a relationship sacramental is. Lee's aunt will probably not die from such a telegram— her own cousin was 83 when her first novel was published, and she thought it might kill her. It only seemed to strengthen her resolve.

Works: "The Artificial Nigger."

October 8, 1957 (p. 245; 6 par.): From ANDALUSIA. She is relieved to get her letter, though the other letter it refers to she did not receive. She apologizes if she did or said anything to cause hurt feelings. She is sure she must have said something to deserve a harsh letter if Lee did write one. There is no way that she would not want to keep Lee as a friend. She is immune

to "crusty" letters. E. Wynn told her she received a marriage announcement from Lee. She was glad to hear it. She hopes that she managed to write a new play in Japan. Carson McCullers will have a play produced soon called *The Square Root of Wonderful*; she does not like the title.

Lee should visit soon before Georgia secedes. The American Resettlement Association is making a move to keep blacks in separate neighborhoods. She is paying attention to peachickens. It used to be her goal to have so many peafowl that she would step on one every time she went outside. It seems now there are so many from the productive peahens that they are beginning to step on her.

Works: None.

February 2, 1958] "Ground Hog Day" (p. 264; 3 par.): From ANDALUSIA. She thinks the excerpts from Lee's play are very good and looks forward to seeing the entire play. She understands that it takes a lot of work and fortitude to get a play put on stage. She would find it difficult to give her work to actors. Yes; they will be going to Rome. When they return, she is supposed to read at the University of Missouri. At least, she would rather read than lecture and wants to be the stage's next Charles Dickens. The story she wants to read has a one-eyed Jesuit in it plus some other distinct characters. She keeps studying her geese.

Works: None.

February 11, 1958 (p. 266; 6 par.): From ANDALUSIA. She is not going to Rome or anywhere else for the time being, though she will make the trip to Missouri. She has LUPUS *Erythematosus*, also known as Red Wolf. Her father died of it at age 44. Her medicine may keep her alive until 96, or at least that is her doctor's hope. The medicine comes from pigs, so she is grateful to those butchered in Chicago. She would be delighted to read the play, but only if Lee has another clear copy. They have been having hurricanes and tornadoes lately, and she would hate to see it blow away. She has heard that Lee's friend Mr. Tillich as well as KATHERINE ANNE PORTER will both be at Wesleyan this year. She is going to eat her Chinese goose's eggs; there are five of them, but they all froze. Her letter is short, but she does not live in New York where she can see Shakespeare. She has no television either.

Works: None.

Thurs., 1958 [undated] (p. 269; 6 par.):   From ANDALUSIA. She thinks it is unwise to send a synopsis; the play should stand on its own, and the first impression of it should not be presented as a novel. She makes comments on Lee's prose in the synopsis. She is no playwright, but she wonders if it might work better to write another version of the play that is simpler. Then send both plays and see which ones the producers like better. They have had a freeze, and several things are iced over and not working, including their water, electricity, damaged trees, and PEACOCKS' tails. Bob Giroux sent a review of her novel that was positive but seemed to praise it for hillbilly readers.

Works: [*Wise Blood*].

April 15, 1958 (p. 278; 2 par.):   From ANDALUSIA. She read the Ford Foundation letter again before writing her nomination of Lee and discovered that they do not accept nominations of playwrights. She will keep the information and see if she can find out what some of the clauses mean that might make her still eligible. The people around town have been talking to her about Lee. One asked if she were any good as a writer; another asked if she were going back to her husband; others commented that Lee's friend had bangs, which indeed she did. Another mentioned that Lee did not wear much clothing and hoped that she did not catch a cold; O'Connor returned that she thought that it had been quite hot. On the question of whether or not Lee was a good writer, she evened up the matter with Lee's brother by saying that his sister was off and on the best-seller lists.

Works: None.

May 20, 1958 (p. 283; 5 par.):   From ANDALUSIA. She thinks it is impossible for people to be truly honest because we are no longer in the Gar-

den of Eden, and honesty is something only God can give. You can also expect it from those you pay to give you an honest opinion, but never expect it from family. It is too high an expectation. She wonders if a university theater that has asked her to give them a play to put on might be of any use to Lee, as in having her play produced at a university press. She did not get a lot of help from books on writing, but she did use *Understanding Fiction* by Cleanth Brooks and ROBERT PENN WARREN. It has some good stories in it for examples of the scope of what is possible to do.

Their cousin is sending them on a trip. "Experience is the greatest deterrent to fiction" (283). She hopes that she will see her either in Milledgeville or New York.

Works: None.

July 2, 1958 (p. 288; 3 par.):   From ANDALUSIA. She flunked her road test the previous Wednesday by driving in the wrong gear and landing in a person's lawn. The tester thinks she needs more practice. She got a 100 on the written test, but that did not help her much. If she sends her story to Arabel, be sure to tell her that she published *Dope*, the play. They killed a black-diamond pilot rattlesnake by the stairs the day before. She hopes she lives to see Lee if she ever comes back to visit.

Works: None.

August 25, 1958 (p. 293; 4 par.):   From ANDALUSIA. It seems they thought to write to each other at the same time. She returns the Ford Foundation materials; if they decide to allow playwright nominations in the future, let her know. She knew the story "The Enduring Chill" was too long as soon as she read the last published paragraph. The general premise is the slow descent and recognition of the Holy Spirit, which lands through ice rather than fire. She will revise the story before it goes into any collection. She received the book of *Paris Review* interviews. She thought the most humorous one was with Nelson Algren. They are close to electing a new governor from three segrationalists. Lee is living in the wrong place.

Works: ["The Enduring Chill"].

February 18, 1959 (p. 319; 3 par.): From ANDALUSIA. She got a call from the telegram office, which read her message to her. She has written a couple of unimportant letters but wonders if Lee is getting mail. She sends good wishes to Poppy. Has she heard of the theater program at the University of Illinois? Charles Shattuck administers the program that brings a playwright to campus in Urbana, Illinois, and puts on their play. She has heard good things about it lately. She has completed her novel; its title is *The Violent Bear It Away*.

Works: *The Violent Bear It Away*.

March 29, 1959 (p. 325; 3 par.): From ANDALUSIA. It is wise to take no advice but on money matters from an agent; that is all they know about. One of her friends is saying that the segregation issue in the Georgia schools will arrive at a climax when the governor closes the schools. The citizens will realize that this means no college football, and they will make him open the school again. The French translator of *Wise Blood* is to visit them next week. There is little to do to entertain such a guest in town other than the reformatory, monuments, and the insane asylum. Eatonton is the home of Uncle Remus, but that is about it.

Works: *Wise Blood*.

April 25, 1959 (p. 329; 4 par.): From ANDALUSIA. She cannot see James Baldwin in Georgia. She could meet him in New York, but not there. She thinks the story she read of his was good, but she abides by the customs of the community where she lives. She has just returned from a writers conference in Vanderbilt. She dislikes cocktail parties and thinks there were too many writers there. Once a year is enough of these things.

She thanks her for the broker advice, but she will not have money to invest. Her cousin bequeathed her a house in SAVANNAH that needs some repairs, including the roof. Her other rental house needs a hot water heater. That tenant is only two months behind on rent.

A friend from Tennessee, Brainard Cheney, would most likely enjoy meeting James Baldwin. He recently went to New York to research blacks and whites meeting socially that he wanted to observe for his novel, but he had no luck finding any.

Works: None.

May 6, 1959 (p. 331; 4 par.): From ANDALUSIA. She sends her congratulations on her new residence. She is sure it feels good to get out of the city, even if her arrangement sounds a little too much like Walden Pond. The *Village Voice* reminds her of her character Asbury. He and his mother seem to be suitable for another work of fiction, but she always feels pulled to another story when she finishes the last one.

Lee's mother sounds a lot like her. She wonders about the status of *Kairos*, Lee's play. Robert Giroux visited and put them at ease about being such a New Yorker at the farm when he changed his clothes and put on moccasins and began taking pictures of the peafowl. She does not know what she would do without them. She is enjoying reading a novel by Muriel Spark, *Memento Mori*.

Works: None.

July 5, 1959 (p. 339; 3 par.): From ANDALUSIA. It is hot, and they have the local reformatory boys visiting as they do most years about this time. The boys escape, and other boys follow them through the woods to their place. Since she enjoys typing on her novel at present, she is assuming that it is done. This is her favorite phase of the publication process—before it is printed and suffers from readers' misunderstanding.

Works: [*The Violent Bear It Away*].

September 6, 1959 (p. 348; 5 par.): From ANDALUSIA. She appreciates the offer to use Lee's apartment, but she does not have any plans to go to New York. She attended only one autograph party and hated it so much that she will never do another. It has taken her seven years to finish her novel. Along the way, she takes breaks by writing stories. She is now working on a somewhat less challenging story, ["The Partridge Festival"]. She will write an essay to present at Lee's brother's school in the fall and will be open to giving the lecture elsewhere that might pay. She read 80 pages of Dr. Pasternak but read so slowly that she needed to return it before she was done. She was not sure she liked the formlessness, but a friend told her it was like a shipwreck with floating treasures all around. You make your own form.

She mentions a Jules Feiffer cartoon about Eisenhower, an interview with Lorraine Hansberry, and Allen Ginsberg's claim that marijuana is the way to find God. The beats bother her with their sentimental attitudes toward their own bohemian ways.

The trick is to write a time-release kind of piece that works like medicine. They could see the play on Monday but not realize they are sick until Wednesday. This technique has worked well for her so far.

Works: "The Partridge Festival."

November 14, 1959 (p. 358; 4 par.): From ANDALUSIA. She thinks about Lee living in the cold and how it does not help anyone's prose to be freezing. Sometimes it can get so cold, even there, that she cannot work. She is reworking "The Partridge Festival," or she would send it to her. She is also working on a new story, "The Comforts of Home." An interview with her and a young girl came out in the paper recently. The article looked as though it tried to make them white trash. A photograph showed her and the Negro dwelling behind her and did not mention that she did not live there. The article brought all sorts of unwanted mail from people who do not understand what she is about.

She is wondering if Lee might be getting too self-conscious about her work. She and her work might benefit from getting away from Walden Pond. She is welcome at MILLEDGEVILLE for Christmas.

Works: ["The Partridge Festival"], ["The Comforts of Home"].

January 13, 1960 (p. 370; 3 par.): From ANDALUSIA. Lee's niece, Dean, came over with some things from Lee and told them about Lee's oper-

ation. Since O'Connor will likely die before her, she bequeaths her her painted rooster, her set of St. T. *De Veritate*, and her easel. She will read the Act II of the play sent over tomorrow.

Works: None.

February 25, 1960 (p. 376; 4 par.): From ANDALUSIA. She hopes she had a good sleep and trip home, though she misses her already and invites her back any time. She will paint that afternoon. *Time* and the *New York Times* book reviews were the only remarkable thing about publishing her book. She is not surprised that *Time* did not like it, but she wishes they had not portrayed her and the book as unhealthy. She needs to get working.

Works: [*The Violent Bear It Away*].

March 1, 1960 (p. 377; 4 par.): From ANDALUSIA. She is frustrated that Lee is wasting her talent while waiting and dealing with those she must work with in the theater. Lee seems to have forgotten to send her the day's work that is mentioned in her most recent letter. She thinks that Lee has enough discipline and works hard. She will attempt to think of what the matter might be, possibly too much of something. Would she like her to send the two copies of *Violent Bear*? She will be glad to inscribe them. She has heard about but not seen a good review of the novel in *Atlantic Monthly*.

Works: *The Violent Bear It Away*.

March 5, 1960 (p. 379; 5 par.): From ANDALUSIA. It does not satisfy her to know that B. has written to *Time*, but Lee should not mention it because B. has done this kind of thing before. She does not want any more attention drawn to her LUPUS. She has already received unwanted mail from the review.

She has purchased paint but is not sure if the colors make the picture better. She may not be done with it, but she probably is. They are back in business with water and electricity. She wonders what Madam Karlweis thinks of the play Lee completed in MILLEDGEVILLE. She would like to review it in the *Union Recorder* if it is produced.

Works: None.

April 28, 1960 (p. 392; 3 par.): From ANDA-LUSIA. She has not seen Lee's Parker pen, but she will sell it if she does and send her half the money. The paintbrush and book arrived, and with green stamps she has purchased a fishing tackle box in which to put her paints. Lee's experience with the black woman on the bus was unfortunate. O'Connor once sat beside a black woman in Chicago who was very talkative and was eating grapes. She offered some to O'Connor, but she refused. When she asked O'Connor where she was from and she told her Georgia, the woman made an exclamation and spit grape seeds all over the floor.

She is uncertain if the advice from the sculptor is relevant to writing. Wyndham Lewis said that George Orwell (she thinks) got his style simply by writing however and whatever words came naturally into his head.

Works: None.

May, 1960 (p. 395; 3 par.): From ANDALUSIA. She sends Lee a picture of her brother. Dean tells her that Lee's telegrams have been upbeat, so the recital must have gone well. Lee was the only person not there when they went to the event that lasted an hour. An elderly woman dropped her cane in the middle of a piece, but she was the only impolite person who made as if she had noticed.

Works: None.

[May 20,] Wednesday, 1960 (p. 396; 3 par.): From ANDALUSIA. She sees her at Walden Pond amid her tomatoes. She offers Lee another invitation to MILLEDGEVILLE. She is uncomfortable critiquing the writing of strangers, so she is pleased that her comments on Lee's friend's work sounded appropriate to her.

She thinks ROBERT PENN WARREN is a pleasant gentleman. Lee should read *All the King's Men; Band of Angels* is not his most successful. She could send her his long poem, *Brother to Dragons,* if she is interested.

Works: None.

May 24, 1960 (p. 398; 5 par.): From ANDALUSIA. It was nothing but a miracle that the man

brought her wallet back to her. Will her friend be coming by the farm or writing her a letter? Even though there are many differences between them, she thinks they have a kinship, and that is why she was able, if she was, to help her with her writing.

In the mornings, she writes by hand and finds that she is less critical. In the afternoons, she types, and that is much more exhausting for her. She edits and revises as she types. The typewriter seems to put her in that frame of mind.

Was she in Carmin Real? Is that what she means? She does not know any other way to tell someone his or her writing is mannered than to come out and say it. Allen Tate told her that a line about a field of dead cotton was mannered and should be a dead cotton field. It was not all his fault; he would be a better critic if he had better things to critique.

Works: None.

May 31, 1960 (p. 398; 5 par.): From ANDALUSIA. Ayn Rand's fiction is pretty low and deserves to go in the garbage. Lee's friend asked her to read her novel, but she does not plan to do so. It is better for the friend if she does not. Kabuki theater is something that is beyond her. She sends prose by Lee's brother. She recommends Gevral for feeling out of sorts. She takes it just like the old people.

Works: None.

September 6, 1960 (p. 406; 5 par.): From ANDALUSIA. It is not that she forgets to write, it is that Lee lives in too many places. She saw Lee's sister-in-law at the Piggly Wiggly. She seemed bored with *La Ronde* and said that Lee would be visiting down there soon. She is going to Minnesota to speak at two convent schools. One of the deans wrote *The Metamorphic Tradition in Modern Poetry,* about Auden, Jarrell, William Carlos Williams, and Stevens. She will be a bumpkin in that company.

She regrets that Lee is not putting on *Kairos.* She owes $9.95 this month for chickenfeed, so she must get on with more pressing work.

Works: None.

"Garfield's Birthday" [November 19, 1960] (p. 418; 4 par.): From ANDALUSIA. Lee's friend's story is good. She recommends Lee send it to *NEW WORLD WRITING* and other journals. She is pleased to hear that Lee considers her a good Protestant. She thought Elizabeth Wynn's minister and his wife were more, something more like Unitarians. When they came, she was glad to see that he was a godly man. He understood what she meant by the "Christ-haunted South" without any explanation from her.

Now that the election is over, the wealthy women of MILLEDGEVILLE are doing a postmortem. There will be Kennedys in all the offices, and Mrs. Kennedy will not bring any style to the White House; these are important matters. George Haslam told her that there are rumors now that they will name the baby Martin Luther Kennedy. Since he is now elected, it is time to begin to criticize.

The Secession Pageant is going to be written by Lance Phillips, and the proceeds will go to the Youth Center. Susan Hayward from Hollywood and Carrolton, Georgia, will be there.

Works: None.

December 8, 1960 (p. 421; 2 par.): From ANDALUSIA. She would be wise to learn to disregard criticism and keep on working. She has troubles of her own, now with her jaw. It is acting the way her hip bones did. She is going to Piedmont Hospital for an examination, and if they do not know quite what to do, she will go to Johns Hopkins.

Works: None.

December 22, 1960 (p. 422; 6 par.): From Piedmont Hospital. She was glad to hear Lee's voice and get her letter. She has received several gifts while she is in the hospital. The cancer-home sisters brought her crescents, her friend in Florida sent her a fake spider to scare the nurses with, and her aunt brought six egg custards. Her mother says that after all of the tests, Piedmont will have a lot of money and the doctors will have data, but she will be in the same state in which she came. She also received a two-volume

set of *A la recherché du temps perdu*, but she hopes she is out before she could have it read. The food is terrible; does she not agree?

When she checked in, the clerk asked her who was her employer, and she said she was self-employed. When she asked her the occupation, she said writer. The woman looked at her and asked her to repeat that and then asked how to spell it. She needs to end this letter because she has to eat before 12.

Works: None.

[January, 1961] (p. 425; 3 par.): From ANDALUSIA. It is unfortunate to hear about the gentleman's play. A book survives bad reviews, but a play closes. Lee should pick up fiction soon, as she keeps telling her. Lee has likely read about Georgia's integration of schools. She feels better, but there is little news.

Works: None.

February 14, 1961 (p. 432; 4 par.): From ANDALUSIA. She asks once again for Lee to have a vacation at MILLEDGEVILLE, the bird sanctuary. She is pleased that Lee has had her fill of Mlle. N. The pageant written by Lance was successful. There is some talk and hope of making the town into another Williamsburg. The Civil War will pay off yet. She recently purchased 100 shares of Keystone B and 100 shares of Thriftimart. She is a budding capitalist. She sends "The Partridge Festival."

Works: ["The Partridge Festival"].

Friday [c. March, 1961] (p. 434; 4 par.): From ANDALUSIA. She lies on her couch with a cold most of the week. She is glad Lee likes "The Partridge Festival" but needs it back to work on since that is really the only copy. If she needs to read someone, read Proust. It takes all seven books to follow where he is coming from. "I am falling out of my chair" (435).

Works: ["The Patridge Festival"].

March 26, 1961 (p. 435; 4 par.): From ANDALUSIA. She received a Waring blender on her birthday. She knows it must be from Lee. She is taken with it and has been looking through the book that came with it. She may make bourbon balls if Lee is around for Easter. Her jaw can take these blended foods just fine.

She has just completed a story called "Everything That Rises Must Converge," and has sold it to NEW WORLD WRITING. She likes it and will send her a copy. She did not get her story, so she must be typing it.

The nuns from the cancer home chose their two peafowl that they won on a bet about their book about Mary Ann ever getting published. The sister superior said that her brother gave them a television to give to O'Connor as a gift for her part of the work on the book. One of the first images she saw was Lee's brother on the college's station. Television does not do much for him. She is going to make the bourbon balls and send her a box of them.

Works: "Everything That Rises Must Converge."

May 31, 1961 (p. 441; 2 par.): From ANDALUSIA. The drug she takes is Subtiltryptasin and is manufactured by a Danish company, Dyk-Julden, in Konstanz, Germany. Her shot lasts about two weeks, and she is thinking about hip replacements.

Works: None.

June 24, 1961 (p. 444; 3 par.): From ANDALUSIA. It is likely better to wait to see what Dr. Sprung wants to do. Deen Hood says she heard that Dr. Sprung is strange. Probably those who try unconventional means get called that. She will not have more shots until July 26 since her doctor is on vacation. She recommends that Lee listen to any comments by Catharine Carver at NEW WORLD WRITING. She is probably the person in Philadelphia she heard about.

Works: None.

Thursday [August, 1961] (p. 447; 4 par.): From ANDALUSIA. They will not be going to Europe because too many people who would be at the conference were out of the country or otherwise occupied. It sits well with her because she had not looked forward to the trip. She needs the

doctor letter returned. Dr. Merrill will probably know about Subtiltryptasin if she ever needs it. It is unwise for Lee to take thyroid pills on her own. If it is thyroid, that will be good news. Did she spot the article about PEACOCKS and the picture in the September issue of HOLIDAY? She did not like the fact that they changed the title and omitted an important paragraph. She is pleased with the rest of it, especially the picture.

Works: None.

August 25, 1961 (p. 448; 2 par.): From ANDALUSIA. She is very concerned at Lee's self-prescribing pills when she has no idea what is wrong with her. She has not had the proper tests, and she must go see a good doctor and stop trying different pills on her own. O'Connor had sweats with her LUPUS, and they were an indication of chemical imbalance.

She has purchased two swans for $65. They were cheap because one is blind in one eye.

Works: None.

November 3, 1961 (p. 452; 3 par.): From ANDALUSIA. She understands that Lee must be exhausted. Is there any way that she might return to New York City from taking her mother across the mountains by way of Georgia? She recommends her story in NEW WORLD WRITING 19, ["Everything That Rises Must Converge"].

Works: ["Everything That Rises Must Converge"].

January 20, 1962 (p. 462; 2 par.): From ANDALUSIA. Did she receive the nuts she sent for Christmas? She is surprised that she did not see Lee in Georgia over the holiday, wearing her Russian hat. She is looking to have another operation. She may not be allowed to have it, but she is exploring it.

Works: None.

January 25, 1962 (p. 463; 3 par.): From ANDALUSIA. Lee does not sound too healthy. Tell her if she has hypoglycemia; she does not know anyone with that. She enjoys G. Marcel's plays. Has Lee read them? She will be pleased to send her various publications, including William James's *Meta-*

physical Journal. She will look forward with Olivia (the Lee family cook) to seeing her at Easter.

Works: None.

May 21, 1962 (p. 475; 4 par.): From ANDALUSIA. If she came south and pretended to be a light-skinned black, she could get sent back north for free, maybe even to Hyannisport. She would like to know how the reviews have gone for Ossie Davis's play *Purlie Victorious.* Lee could not have read "Everything That Rises Must Converge." For Mother's Day, she gave Regina what she wanted—a jackass named Ernest.

Works: "Everything That Rises Must Converge."

June 26, 1962 (p. 482; 4 par.): From ANDALUSIA. They will be pleased to have her stay with them while she is in town. She concerns herself with the wrong aspects of her story. She thinks that coming south will be good medicine for her and her work.

Works: None.

July 26, 1962 (p. 485; 3 par.): From ANDALUSIA. She enjoys her starched Japanese shirt. She likes KATHERINE ANNE PORTER's later work better than her earlier stories. She likes "Noon Wine." If she brings her tent, she can camp at ANDALUSIA.

Works: None.

August 17, 1962 (p. 489; 2 par.): From ANDALUSIA. The book is on its way. She inscribed it to Helen Nash and wrapped it before she remembered that she was Dr. Nash. The Ku Klux Klan met on the opposite side of the road from them Saturday night. They did not know about it until it was over, but when they heard, they burned a cross just for tradition. Georgian politics would curl her hair.

Works: None.

September 6, 1962 (p. 490; 2 par.): From ANDALUSIA. Her television reports that the stock market is not doing well. She read all of Proust and liked the first few books and the last one best. She does not want to read it again. The parts in society were the best.

Works: None.

October 9, 1962 (p. 495; 2 par.): From ANDALUSIA. Lee needs to come south and go see Dr. Burrell. She knows firsthand about the lack of honest doctors in New York. Lee should listen to her and take her advice.

Lee's friend would probably have to be connected with Harvard to have Frank O'Connor look at her work. She suggests Hiram Haydn, an editor at Atheneum.

Works: None.

October 27, 1962 (p. 496; 2 par.): From ANDALUSIA. Since Lee is seeing Dr. Saltzer, she will not be concerned now. Lee's diet sounds fine since she can eat eggs and cheese. She will be traveling to East Texas State College, University of Southwest Louisiana, Loyola in New Orleans, and Southeast Louisiana College between November 15 and 21. She is giving four talks in six days, and hopes that Lee will not be in MILLEDGEVILLE those dates.

Works: None.

November 9, 1962 (p. 499; 4 par.): From ANDALUSIA. She is glad Lee feels better. Dr. Saltzer deserves a chance. He wrote her that he suggested a specialist for LUPUS. She has a cold and hopes that she can get rid of it before she must go to Texas. She is pleased that Lee read and liked her "Converge" story. Her mother liked it, though most of her stories put her to sleep. Regina is taking the changes in the church well. They get Catholic papers that talk about the changes. O'Connor likes the job Kennedy is doing as president. She would like to read about Lee's condition somewhere.

Works: ["Everything That Rises Must Converge"].

November 17, 1962 (p. 499; 2 par.): From ANDALUSIA. Lee would love Texas. They are proud of their "white people," by whom they mean honest, not white-skinned. They hang both American and Texan flags on the lawn at General Walker's place in Dallas. She is in Louisiana at present and will stay alert for interesting sights.

Works: None.

April 29, 1963 (p. 515; 3 par.): From Andalusia. Lee should be careful about her diet. She met some people whom Lee knows at Sweet Briar. Meeting a million people was a difficult way to earn $500. She went to Troy State in Alabama and then the University of Georgia, where she felt at home. A Baptist minister from Billy Graham's college, Wheaton, visited the farm last week.

Works: None.

July 31, 1963 (p. 532; 3 par.): From Andalusia. Can Lee tell her more about the Hyperglycemia Foundation and the doctors and what they are doing to help her? She doubts such a thing can be legitimate or very helpful. Corn is an inexpensive remedy; almost all the animals at Andalusia eat it. She might buy her Hiram Haydn's *The Hands of Esau* and send it to her. Are there any other books she could send that she would like to read?

Works: None.

August 15, 1963 (p. 534; 2 par.): From Andalusia. She sends Lee her notes. Lee sounds better. O'Connor should begin to charge $1 per hour for medical advice and $5 for literary. Is she feeling better?

Works: None.

August 23, 1963 (p. 535; 4 par.): From Andalusia. It is best to tell and show doctors only the facts, not anything one imagines. Does she like the boardinghouse? They have a Chevrolet that she is to practice driving each day. Lee may have lupus with this new pain in her joints.

Works: None.

September 10, 1963 (p. 538; 4 par.): From Andalusia. She has been imagining her weak and not well, and she has been working with a Catholic family. Jim Bishop's work does not make it as far south as Georgia. She could send the book about Mary Ann for the family's children. She has heard that young people read it in Catholic school and like it. It is good he is making her write about her cousins. She saw the

Lee car the other day and thought it might be her, but it was her brother. She is pleased that she has no steel hips after all; her recent X-rays show that her own have gotten better than they were before.

Works: None.

October 31, 1963 (p. 544; 2 par.): From Andalusia. She has had a Mass said and has sent the book. How long will she be there? Integration is not happening there yet, and she wonders whether a deal is being made behind closed doors. They might get the new school. Lee needs to avoid coming there to start trouble.

Works: None.

November 29, 1963 (p. 551; 3 par.): From Andalusia. Since there is currently no one to hate, there is a standoff in some southern politics. Southerners are going to like Johnson. She would like to send her some pecans but is not sure where to send them. She is very pleased right now with a new story she has written ["Revelation"].

Works: ["Revelation"].

January 18, 1964 (p. 562; 3 par.): From Andalusia. She fainted prior to Christmas and was put in bed for 10 days. She has not been worth much since. Her mother has also been sick with the flu. She talks about some more politics, CORE and the Young Republicans. She is pleased to hear that Lee is feeling better.

Works: None.

April 16, 1964 (p. 574; 2 par.): From Andalusia. Her family has many members who have lived a long time, around 96. Miss Mary has pulled through. Dr. Merrill is treating her kidney infection, and she has been able to do some work the last couple of days. Her fingers swell, and it is good for her to type. Lee must be right about pulling back from entangling herself with that woman with whom she talked about it. It might put her in prison if she tried to deal with her.

Works: None.

May 15, 1964 (p. 577; 4 par.): From ANDALUSIA. Lee is correct; Ruby Turpin sees the vision. She likes both Mrs. Turpin and Mary Grace. She is like Jacob, but female and from the country. The vision is of Purgatory. Lee's Presbyterian niece probably does not see that. She has had a blood transfusion and was able to work; she loves working. Her hemoglobin was down to eight. Her body does not make its own blood at present, which is one of the effects of LUPUS, apparently. She wishes Lee would go see Dr. Sofer.

She had 10 transfusions in her spell in 1951, so this is not as bad as that. She could hear the celestial chorus when she went home on the first of the month. It was singing "Clementine" repeatedly, and she thinks that this light-headedness must be a result of the lack of blood to the head. She does not hear it now after the transfusion.

Works: "Revelation."

May 20, 1964 (p. 579; 1 par.): From ANDALUSIA. She is on her way to Piedmont Hospital, where Dr. Merrill will treat her. Her other doctors have run out of treatments for the time being.

Works: None.

May 21, 1964 (p. 580; 4 par.): From ANDALUSIA. John Howard Griffin in blackface was the man Billy Sessions was going to bring down, but they never made it. She would have got up from the seat if Griffin had sat by her and moved to sit by a real black person. She did not like his *The Devil Rides Outside* or *Nuni.*

She does not care for blacks who try to speak for everyone when they do not know what they are talking about, like James Baldwin. Baldwin can do a good job explaining being black in Harlem, but he does not know how it is to be everyone. Martin Luther King is not a saint, but he works with the skills he has and does what he needs to do. She normally uses the question if she would like the person if he or she were white to help determine how she feels. She dislikes Baldwin under this rule but likes Cassius Clay. The Muslims are not good enough to have Clay.

She plans to have a new collection of stories published that fall, but they will be republishing already printed stories rather than having her revise them. She has so little energy these days that she would like to use it for new work.

Works: None.

June 8, 1964 (p. 582; 3 par.): From Piedmont Hospital, ATLANTA. She received three letters from her in the same day. They were full of stories about political parties and fundraisers. She is still in the hospital; it is going on three weeks now. She is not sure she is progressing, or even if that is possible. Lee will likely be in a location where her letter does not go.

Works: None.

June 16, 1964 (p. 584; 4 par.): From Piedmont Hospital, ATLANTA. Her doctor says that they can begin to think about sending her home. She has her salt intake raised from two grams to around five per day. She has to stay low on proteins because they irritate the kidneys. She tells Lee a story about Davy Crockett and Edward Everett. A cattle drive came down Constitution Avenue in "Washing D. C." Everett joked in front of Crockett that the cattle were Davy Crockett's constituents. When Everett asked where the cattle were going, Crockett answered Massachusetts to teach school.

She has her phone number but probably will not call since it is expensive and would take too much energy right now for her to figure out how. This fact makes her feel down.

Works: None.

June 19, 1964 (p. 585; 1 par.): From Piedmont Hospital, ATLANTA. She is going home the next day. She will have transfusions today and tomorrow and looks forward to the food at home. She will have to limit visitors and work.

Works: None.

June 23, 1964 (p. 586; 2 par.): From ANDALUSIA. She does not know why Lee does not find her anecdote about Davy Crockett funny. Dr. Fulghum is back in charge of her care. He wants to see ["Revelation"] to see whether or not he should sue her. She tells him that it is his doctor's office in the story, but that much else has been changed.

Works: ["Revelation"].

July 1, 1964 (p. 590; 3 par.): From ANDALUSIA. She is not sure whether Lee is in Chester or not. Jackie Robinson is in Albany. She has not heard much from W. C. because she cannot have visitors. If she lives, she is sure she will hear a lot.

The little energy that she has she can spend on her collection, since she cannot have visitors. The medicine and the illness seem to be competing to see which one will kill her. Dr. Merrill has cut her medicine in half. She does not hear "Clementine" or "Sweet Low, Sweet Chariot" anymore.

Regina and her aunt are supposed to attend a luncheon given by Lee's sister-in-law for her cousin who is getting married. However, Regina has her hands full at the moment with Shot's legal problems. He was driving drunk, left the scene of an accident, and did not have his license on him. He may be going to jail, but currently he is out on bail.

Works: None.

July 10, 1964 (p. 591; 3 par.): From ANDALUSIA. She sends a letter full of stickers that someone gave her. She released the grasshopper in the cage that Lee gave her because it reminded her of blacks in jail. The duck ate him. She likes Gunter Grass's *The Tin Drum*. Regina helped Shot. He got a $100 fine and a year parole. He would be in jail were it not for her mother.

Works: None.

July 21, 1964 (p. 594; 3 par.): From ANDALUSIA. She goes to Baldwin County Hospital tomorrow for another blood transfusion. She thought she was doing better; then the kidney infection comes back. Her blood level is below eight again. She will read *The Tin Drum* while she is there. It seems like the attention on the racial issue has moved to Harlem. What is it like to live in the

city now? She still works on her story, ["Parker's Back"]. However, she's tired just moving to the other side of the room.

Works: ["Parker's Back"].

July 26, 1964 (p. 595; 3 par.): From ANDALUSIA. It is not hot there, and even in the rain, the weather is pleasant. She and Senator Russell are just as pleased that the riots are in Harlem, Brooklyn, and Rochester rather than there.

She does not feel well. She had the blood transfusion and now takes a double dose of medicine for the kidney but is scaling down the cortisone. She really does not know how she is anymore.

She was impressed by Lee's letterhead. So many people leave hardly any room for the letter.

Works: None.

July 28, 1964 (p. 596; 2 par.): From ANDALUSIA. Lee should let the police know about the phone call. She is not sure when she will send the stories, since she has not felt well enough to type them.

[Note: This is the last letter that Flannery O'Connor wrote. Her mother found it on her bedside table after the author died. Regina O'Connor mailed the letter.]

Works: None.

DENVER LINDLEY (seven letters) Lindley became O'Connor's editor at Harcourt, Brace when Catharine Carver left the company. *Pages:* HB: 123, 129, 148, 151, 206, 222, 247.

Letters

December 16, 1955 (p. 123; 4 par.): From ANDALUSIA. She will be pleased to have Denver be her editor now that Catharine Carver has left; however, since Harcourt, Brace seems to be losing editors fairly regularly, this has her concerned. Elizabeth McKee has asked her to wait until she is back from England to make any other decisions. She is pleased to hear that Georgia writer Lillian Smith liked her speech, though it was plain. Lindley did not miss much.

Works: None.

January 15, 1956 (p. 129; 2 par.): From ANDA-LUSIA. She read and admires Caroline's novel *The Malefactors*. She would like to have her work translated by Maurice Coindreau but imagines that Gallimard will determine that. She has read that the American novel in French suggests that the French translations are typically bad. For example, the French think Erskine Caldwell is a good writer.

Works: None.

March 18, 1956 (p. 148; 2 par.): From AN-DALUSIA. She and her mother enjoyed Lindley's visit and hopes he got back to New York safely. It is kind of him to ask to buy her pictures, but her mother will not allow them to be sold. If they were to leave the walls, then paintings of sweet-peas and dewdrops by her great aunts when they were young would undoubtedly replace them. It is worthwhile for that reason to keep her pictures on the walls instead and the others in the attic. She appreciates his liking her drawings, though, since she believes he knows a bit about art.

Works: None.

April 19, 1956 (p. 151; 1 par.): From ANDALUSIA. She appreciates the advice and has asked that *Wise Blood* not be published in any country occupied by Russia. They would likely use The Misfit as propaganda about the normal American man of business.

Works: *Wise Blood*, ["A Good Man Is Hard to Find"].

March 6, 1957 (p. 206; 3 par.): From ANDALUSIA. She saw the television play but did not like it. As bad as that was, having to endure the praise of the locals for having her work televised was worse. She is famous with children now, who point at her on the street. She wrote to Madison Jones about *The Innocent* receiving poor reviews, and he seems to be doing all right about it. She has recommended that John Lynch send his collection of stories to Lindley for a look.

Works: "A Good Man Is Hard to Find."

May 21, 1957 (p. 222; 2 par.): From ANDALUSIA. She appreciates Fr. Bruckberger's pièce de théâtre,

though she is enjoying it slowly due to her French. She has become inspired by the sketchbook to buy some paint and put something on Masonite. They enjoyed his visit, but he missed the rattlesnake that Mr. F. trapped under a crate. It is still around, so maybe he will see it when he comes again.

Works: None.

October 9, 1957 (p. 247; 2 par.): From ANDA-LUSIA. She likes Dillon Ripley's work over J. G. Cozzens and may be the only reader in the nation to do so. She got through 250 pages of Cozzens's *By Love Possessed*. Her mother says that she will wait for the *Reader's Digest* version, and she told her mother that that was a wise choice.

Works: None.

BETTY BOYD LOVE (seven letters) Betty Boyd was O'Connor's closest friend at Georgia State College for Women. Boyd married James Love. *Pages:* HB: 14, 18, 22, 28, 36, 43.

Letters

August 17, 1949 (p. 14; 4 par.): From New York City. She asks about how she is at Los Alamos. She is going to rural Connecticut with her novel to live with friends, the Fitzgeralds. She will save money. One of their former teachers is at Columbia and suggests that she will be full of champagne ideas to mix with the hogwash. She hopes Love will tell her about California.

Works: [*Wise Blood*].

October 17, 1949 (p. 15; 2 par.): From Ridgefield, Connecticut. She sends a clipping of a laundry ad. She has read Nathaniel West's *The Day of the Locust* and thinks that she would like it. She was also reminded of the character in *Sanctuary*. Boyd should read *A Sea Change* by Nigel Dennis. Her conflict with her publisher is still in play; they will not release her, and all she really wants to do is finish the book. She writes about four hours each morning. Robert Fitzgerald is a poet who is translating *Oedipus* and teaches at Sarah Lawrence College.

Works: [*Wise Blood*].

November 5, 1949 (p. 18; 5 par.): From Ridge-field, Connecticut. She sends her congratulations about Los Alamos and wonders if it were on the map before the bomb. Rinehart released her, and she now has a contract with Harcourt, Brace. Their former instructor, Helen Green, wrote her a lengthy letter. She thinks that she is the smartest woman at their old college. When she was home, she talked with her about YADDO and the social sciences. Is she missing anything important from not reading "Orphan Annie?" She is just back from New York City and finds that one benefit is seeing lots of people whom one can be glad one does not know.

Works: Wise Blood.

December 23, 1950 (p. 22; 3 par.): From Baldwin Memorial Hospital ("as usual"). She writes from her bed in the hospital where she is being treated for rheumatoid arthritis. She is taking cortisone. She will be at the bird sanctuary of MILLEDGEVILLE for a few months afterward. She is enjoying the play *Murder in the Cathedral* and asks for a letter.

Works: None.

October 18, 1951 (p. 28; 2 par.): From MILL-EDGEVILLE. She sends belated congratulations on the Love's daughter, Margaret Ellen. She has been in Emory Hospital much of the summer but hopes to avoid it from now on. She is beginning to raise ducks and now has 21. She asks her to write.

Works: None.

May 23, 1952 (p. 36; 4 par.): From ANDALUSIA. She survived the book signing and knows that she signed one for her. The book received good reviews in *Newsweek*, the *New York Tribune*, and the *New York Times*, but she has yet to see any money. She saw Miss B. who spent the night with her Aunt Mary Cline. She has also seen Lucynell Cunningham Smith. Though having a baby must be taxing, does she have any plans to visit Georgia?

Works: None.

September 20, 1952 (p. 43; 5 par.): From ANDA-LUSIA. She appreciates the picture. Both she and the baby look sturdy and strong. She gave her signed book to Lucynell to ship to her. She thinks Lucynell is very nice. B. has epilepsy, and she feels that she overreacted about her. She appreciates her writing about the book earlier. She would have written back sooner, but she went to Connecticut for five weeks, then fell ill, and spent the next six weeks in bed. The thinking behind her book is Catholic. She wonders if she likes *Dead Souls*. She enjoys Tolstoy but finds Gogol essential. The college is gearing up for another year with the usual fiascos.

Works: [Wise Blood].

ELIZABETH & ROBERT LOWELL (seven letters)

Robert "Cal" Lowell was a poet O'Connor met at Yaddo. Writer Elizabeth Hardwick [Lowell], whom O'Connor also met at Yaddo, invited O'Connor to stay at her apartment in New York City when they all first left the artists' colony in 1949. O'Connor loved "Cal" Lowell and grieved over his straying from Catholicism. *Pages:* HB: 20, 35, 57, 65, 311, 369, 372.

Letters

[Early 1950] (p. 20; 2 par.): From MILLEDGEVILLE. She will not be able to see them as planned because she has to go to the hospital for a month and then be at home another month. Please send her a card.

Works: None.

May 2, 1952 (p. 35; 4 par.): From ANDALUSIA. To Robert. She was very glad to hear from him and that he likes the gorilla. She has asked Robert Giroux to send him the whole manuscript. She has been in Georgia for a year and a half due to arthritis but will soon be back in Connecticut to see the Fitzgeralds. She now lives with her mother on a farm where her mother raises cows and she tends to ducks and pheasants. Her mother was insulted by a comment that Evelyn Waugh made on her work. She agrees with Elizabeth about siteseeing. She sends her regards to

Omar Pound if he ever sees him. One doctor she met knew Ezra Pound from St. Elizabeth's.

Works: [*Wise Blood*].

March 17, 1953 (p. 57; 4 par.):   From ANDALUSIA. She is pleased that they enjoyed the tale. She imagines that Iowa City must be relaxing after Europe. She has LUPUS and must take ACTH to help manage it. Her father had it also but did not have the treatments available now, and he died. She has the strength to write, which is what she should be doing anyway. "What you have to measure out, you come to observe closely, or so I tell myself" (57). She snuck three live ducks onto Eastern Airlines last year for the Fitzgerald children. She lives on a farm with her mother and raises peafowl that she enjoys studying with intensity.

Works: None.

January 1, 19[54] (p. 65; 4 par.):   From ANDALUSIA. She is pleased to hear that they have a good car. She does not drive. She is not fat but healthy and she should not gain any more weight. She met a man at the Cheneys who told her that she wrote a good book but that she does not look like a person who could have written it, and she agreed. She visited the Fitzgeralds this summer. She is working on stories at the moment to avoid working on her new novel. She had a story in HARPER'S BAZAAR about a Confederate general, but only ladies in hair salons ever see that publication. She is preparing a collection that she will title *A Good Man Is Hard to Find and Other Stories.*

Works: ["A Late Encounter With the Enemy"], *A Good Man Is Hard to Find and Other Stories.*

December 25, 1958 (p. 311; 4 par.):   From ANDALUSIA. To Robert. She is not terribly pleased that he remembers her breaking an unopened bottle of rum (not gin) on slippery steps. Liquor at ANDALUSIA is stored in the bathroom cabinet between the plunger and the Drano and you have to be near death to have any. In the spring, they visited the Fitzgeralds in Levanto. Sally joined them on trips to Paris, LOURDES, and

Rome. She looks forward to reading his book and hopes to finish her own. She sends her love to Elizabeth and Harriet. If they raised Harriet in the South, she would not have to be educated.

Works: None.

January 11, 1960 (p. 369; 3 par.):   From ANDALUSIA. To Robert. She appreciates the old animals. She feels like one since she has just completed one book and must start another. Georgia PEACOCK feathers hold up better than Massachusetts feathers—she gives hers to elderly ladies for their hats. She wishes Elizabeth and Harriet a happy new year and again urges them to bring Harriet south for her education.

Works: None.

February 2, 1960 (p. 372; 3 par.):   From ANDALUSIA. To Robert. She will keep his letter about the book close by to reread when the bad reviews start. She loses her confidence and clarity about her own wrangling at times. She may write again about prophets. Prophecy is more about seeing than having the ability to explain a vision clearly. He should bring Harriet to ANDALUSIA, where she could give her a Chinese goose and a PEACOCK. Today is Ground Hog day.

Works: [*The Violent Bear It Away*].

JOHN LYNCH (six letters)   Lynch reviewed O'Connor's collection *A Good Man Is Hard to Find and Other Stories.* He taught at Notre Dame and was also a writer. *Pages:* HB: 114, 138, 172, 210, 336, 459.

Letters

November 6, 1955 (p. 114; 4 par.):   From ANDALUSIA. She appreciates the copy of the review and is surprised that a Catholic publication would have it. She "writes the way [she does] because and only because [she is] a Catholic" (114). She is curious about in what ways, if any, the teaching at Notre Dame differs from that at Stanford or Iowa. She has not read his fiction but recognizes his name, she assumes, from *Commonweal*. She will read the 1947 O. HENRY

AWARDS. Her first story came out about then but it was not the best quality.

Works: None.

February 19, 1956 (p. 138; 6 par.): From AN-DALUSIA. She was pleased to hear about writing instruction at Notre Dame. She tells him about Robert Fitzgerald teaching there for a short time one summer. She has just reviewed *All Manner of Men* for the diocesan paper, The BULLE-TIN. She liked "The Burden" better than "The Knife." She hopes, though there is very little money from publication, that the Atlantic Press will take his stories. She has not seen *Ave Maria* but can imagine that it would turn off people to Catholicism. Her Catholicism operates at a deep level. Like him, she was once concerned that her work would upset her mother and relatives, too, but they are strong. She thinks that a big family is better than many books and that teaching is the worst drain of all on creative energy.

Works: None.

September 2, 1956 (p. 172; 3 par.): From ANDA-LUSIA. She appreciates the stories. His longer story has more power, which makes her wonder if he might write a novel one day. She has subscribed to *Four Quarters* after seeing his story and the symposium in it. She is now writing a lecture to give at Macon Parish Catholic Women's Council. The topic is supposed to be "What Is a Wholesome Novel?" They see obscenity in modern fiction because they do not recognize anything else.

Works: None.

March 16, 1957 (p. 210; 3 par.): From AN-DALUSIA. She appreciates his asking her to come to Notre Dame to speak. She needed reassurance from Robert Fitzgerald that it would be all right to talk the way she does, not like I. A. Richards. She will send Denver Lindley Lynch's story collection. She hopes the chicken pox is done.

Works: None.

June 14, 1959 (p. 336; 4 par.): From ANDALUSIA. She was in Chicago during very bad weather.

If she had known he was there teaching, she would have tried to see him. Both she and Robert Fitzgerald got Ford Foundation awards. The Fitzgeralds live less expensively in Italy; they send their oldest daughter to the best boarding school in Rome for $500; they will probably never return. She has nearly completed her novel and will soon start on the next one. The nuns at Winona College of St. Theresa have invited her to speak at some Catholic colleges in Minnesota. They have killed a rattlesnake, and she had three peachickens hatch but little else has been happening.

Works: None.

December 31, 1961 (p. 459; 4 par.): From ANDA-LUSIA. She was glad to hear from him that he still likes New England. The baby will bring happiness. She purchased two swans this fall and has now set out to be an expert on them as she is PEACOCKS. She hopes that he will visit if he ever comes south. Happy New Year to him and Gunny. Since the Fitzgeralds have purchased a farm in Perugia, it is looking less and less like they will return to the States.

Works: None.

ANDREW LYTLE (two letters) Lytle was one of O'Connor's professors at Iowa. A writer himself, Lytle edited *The* SEWANEE REVIEW and published O'Connor's work in several issues. *Pages*: HB: 104, 373.

Letters

September 15, 1955 (p. 104; 3 par.): From ANDA-LUSIA. She asks Lytle if she may use his name as a reference for a Guggenheim. She has not made much money from her collection of stories and is at work on a novel, so she is applying for the fellowship. She thanks him for the letter he sent to Harcourt, Brace the previous spring. What keeps her from being a regional writer is being Catholic and vice versa. The first chapter of her novel is to be published in NEW WORLD WRITING.

Works: [*Wise Blood*].

February 4, 1960 (p. 373; 4 par.):   From ANDA-
LUSIA. She is glad he liked her book and that
knowledge makes her feel better. She thinks a
lot about grace. There are times of grace in most
of her stories, and her characters choose either
to accept it or reject it. The Grandmother in "A
Good Man" accepts it when it is offered, but this
does not stop The Misfit from killing her anyway. "This moment of grace excites the devil to
frenzy" (373).

Works: [*The Violent Bear It Away*], ["A Good Man
Is Hard to Find"].

ROBIE MACAULEY (five letters)   MacCauley
was a writer who met O'Connor at Iowa. *Pages:* HB:
20, 45, 63, 80, 101.

Letters

Undated, 1950 (p. 20; 5 par.):   From Ridgefield,
Connecticut. She had written to Dilly Thompson to learn where he and Anne were and discovered they were at Iowa. She heard from Paul
Engle that everything was doing well there. She
and Enoch are living in Connecticut with the
Fitzgeralds. She enjoyed his story in *Furioso*. She
has left Rinehart and gone with Harcourt, Brace.
She sends best wishes to him and Anne.

Works: [*Wise Blood*].

October 28, 1952 (p. 45; 4 par.):   From ANDA-
LUSIA. She is not an analyst who could explain
why, but she enjoyed his book. She appreciated
the free copy. She heard from Paul Engle that he
did not like the title of her novel or the ending
but was most concerned that there was no mention of Iowa on the cover. He claims that it was
formed there and that she should have thought
to mention it. She says that she had, indeed,
sent that information to Harcourt but that they
prepared the jacket copy, not she. She wonders
where the Lowells are. Perhaps Macauley will be
appointed a member of the Mark Twain Society.
She will write about how much she likes his book
to the woman who sent it to her.

Works: [*Wise Blood*].

October 13, 1953 (p. 63; 4 par.):   From AN-
DALUSIA. She just read his story in the *PARTISAN
REVIEW*. His stories make her think of JOSEPH
CONRAD's work, such as *Secret Agent* or *Under
Western Eyes*. She has read almost all of Conrad's
work. She visited the Fitzgeralds in Connecticut.
She had a visit from someone named Lane who
claimed to have been at a party where Macauley
and Anne were also in attendance. She has also
been to visit the Cheneys in Nashville.

Works: None.

May 18, 1955 (p. 80; 8 par.):   From ANDALUSIA.
She is pleased that he likes her stories. They
were a joy to write, not like her novels. She is
starting her second book. She will visit New
York on May 30 for the purpose of being interviewed by Harvey Breit about the dramatization
of "The Life You Save." She has never been to
Washington, just over it via Eastern Airlines.
The panel at Greensboro was not good, even
worse because he and Anne were not there.
Ashley visited and told her that Macauley
thinks highly of Dr. Frank Crane, as she does.
She enjoys his columns. She asks him to thank
W. P. Southard for enjoying her work. The people who write to her mostly do not understand
what she is doing. One man from California was
starting a magazine called *Hearse*; two students
called her their pin-up girl; a lady from Boston
could not believe that a Catholic could have the
thoughts it would take to write "A Temple of the
Holy Ghost." She seems "to attract the lunatic
fringe mainly" (82). She will be pleased to get
the television episode finished. He had better
write to her before her next book comes out in
what could be as late as 1984.

Works: *Wise Blood*.

September 11, 1955 (p. 101; 5 par.):   From ANDA-
LUSIA. She appreciates his sending *A Good Man*
to the people at *Encounter*. Harcourt reports
that it has sold 4,000 copies. She is pleased
he is putting together of his good stories set
in Germany and Japan. She will be in Lansing,
Michigan, giving a talk at AAUW on what is

supposed to be "The Signficance of the Short Story." She encloses some columns with the author's picture.

Works: A Good Man Is Hard to Find and Other Stories.

FATHER J. H. MCCOWN (26 letters) Father J. H. McCown, a Jesuit priest, drove up out of the blue to Andalusia one day in his white Packard and told Flannery he admired *A Good Man Is Hard to Find and Other Stories.* They became fast friends. *Pages:* HB: 130, 134, 139, 157, 160, 171, 259, 263, 288, 303, 309, 318, 362, 385, 399, 414, 420, 462, 468, 470, 488, 497, 500, 513, 570.

Letters

January 16, 1956 (p. 130; 4 par.): From ANDALUSIA. She appreciates the books and sends him a paperback of *Wise Blood* in case he has not seen it. She is pleased that she read the Michelfelder book. Like that book, she writes of loss of faith in *Wise Blood*, though it is not set among Catholics. She has read most of the works by Bloy, Barnanos, and FRANÇOIS MAURIAC. After a while a Catholic fiction writer must turn elsewhere than them and GRAHAM GREENE. She likes ERNEST HEMINGWAY, who seems to be searching for a Catholic sense of life and JAMES JOYCE who cannot seem to drop Catholicism no matter how hard he tries. It could be that as a reader she appreciates finding the Holy Ghost in fiction through the ways in which he has hidden himself. She likes the Eric Gill autobiography.

Works: Wise Blood.

February 6, 1956 (p. 134; 4 par.): From ANDALUSIA. She wrote to Father Gardiner about Michelfelder. She discusses pornography and sentimentality in fiction. They are quite similar. It is better to treat them as sins against the form of art rather than against morality. She has just read a funny book, *Two Portraits of St. Theresa*, by Father Robo. She and her mother invited him back and enjoyed his visit.

Works: None.

February 20, 1956 (p. 139; 5 par.): From ANDALUSIA. She should not send him a book that she does not want to keep. She has heard of the woman he mentioned but not read anything by her. She sends a letter from John Lynch, whom she thought taught writing at Notre Dame. She received a letter from Father Gardiner, looking for reviewers' names for Caroline Gordon's new book. Recently Regina went to buy cows and asked for directions. The man told her to turn this way and that and the place could not be missed because it was the only one with an artificial nigger. The idea took such hold of her that she decided she would write a story with that object in it. She thinks it is the best of all of her stories, not least because she thinks there is a lot in it that she does not yet understand.

Works: ["The Artificial Nigger"].

May 9, 1956 (p. 157; 2 par.): From ANDALUSIA. She has stopped reading the books he sent her, since it would be easier to tell him that she had not read them than to tell him that she did not like them. She has a good ear for speech but uses it without discipline. Novels are art, and it is wrong to treat it as anything else. JACQUES MARITAIN expresses St. Thomas's view as "that art is wholly concerned with the good of that which is made" (157).

Works: None.

May 20, 1956 (p. 160; 1 par.): From ANDALUSIA. She was glad to see him among the Macon group. Seeing him among them reminded her of Waugh's Father Rothschild, S. J., who showed up in disguise on a motorcycle among unlikely companions.

Works: None.

August 28, 1956 (p. 171; 2 par.): From ANDALUSIA. She appreciates his reading and comments. She will revise. A woman writing in *JUBILEE* wants to know why Catholic magazines do not review "wholesome" books. Perhaps her article should address what a wholesome book is—one that is whole. He should write the pamphlet since readers will listen to a priest more than a novelist.

Works: None.

December 20, 1957 (p. 259; 2 par.): From ANDA-LUSIA. She needs some spiritual counsel. The first is that she has accepted the invitation of a nearby Episcopal minister to host a group every Monday night at Andalusia that will discuss literature and theology. She is to be the Catholic representative among several Protestants. They want to talk about Gide, but Gide is on the Index of works not to be read by Catholics. He once told her he would look into finding out whether or not he could give permission to Catholics to read books on the Index. She wonders if he could do this. Second, she asks about a young woman who writes to her who said that she was told it was a mortal sin to eat meat on Friday. O'Connor wants to know what he thinks: If the woman did not know it was that bad an offense, would it be a mortal sin?

Works: None.

January 12, 1958 (p. 263; 4 par.): From ANDA-LUSIA. She sends him her most recently published work. She appreciates his finding out about permission to read certain authors and will use the *epeikia* dispensation. She will need to add Sartre to Gide, though the group is still reading 35-cent books and has not gone near these yet. The young woman whom she wrote about is convinced that she has lost her faith and does not want to find it again. She has recommended *The Stumbling Block* by FRANÇOIS MAURIAC to her.

Works: None.

June 29, 1958 (p. 288; 2 par.): From ANDALUSIA. His mother sounds like hers. He should visit with her sometime; the mothers would agree about many things. She recommends *The Magic Barrel* by Bernard Malamud. It is very good, spiritual. She agrees with the saying that the Jews are in front of the Catholics in intellectual matters because they have more brains.

Works: None.

November 15, 1958 (p. 303; 4 par.): From ANDA-LUSIA. She would visit his mother except that

they no longer have someone to drive them, and this makes it hard for her to travel. She has sent a magazine devoted to articles on her and J. F. Powers. She likes the article by Sister Bernetta Quinn, the best on her. They have been to ATLANTA to the doctor for two days. They are sorry they missed Father Ware and Father Galvin. She is reading Martin Buber's *The Eclipse of God*. She also recommends *Holy Pagans of the Old Testament*.

Works: None.

December 23, 1958 (p. 309; 6 par.): From ANDA-LUSIA. She thanks him for the published materials. She has been looking for a list of paperbacks so that she might see what she could afford. She recommends Dom Aelred Graham's *Christian Thought and Action*. She does not know why Powers was not at the reception in Minnesota. Her doctor has told her that recalicification is happening with the bone. She says it may be LOURDES or prayer, and she hopes she can keep walking around without her crutches as she is now a little bit at a time. She asks his prayers for her novel—the writing is at a key part, and she would rather complete the story correctly than be able to walk. She will send *The Magic Barrel* once Christmas is over.

Works: [*The Violent Bear It Away*].

February 2, 1959 (p. 318; 3 par.): From ANDA-LUSIA. She asks for his prayers for her trip to Chicago in the winter. She wrote and heard back from his brother. B. says there has been a renewal of contracts for one year; however, they may not be worth much. A bill has just passed in the legislature forbidding anyone older than 21 from going to college or older than 25 to start graduate school. She hopes that this level of desperation has not yet hit Mississippi.

Works: None.

December 18, 1959 (p. 362; 1 par.): From ANDA-LUSIA. She needs to find an explanation of St. Ignatius's statement about the end sanctifying the means. She corresponds with a Protestant teacher who spouts lots of Jung, and Jung hates St. Ignatius. He has given her Jung's *The Undiscovered Self* in paperback. It equates communism with the church.

Works: None.

April 6, 1960 (p. 385; 2 par.): From ANDALUSIA. The day before, she met and had dinner with several of his relatives, including his mother, sister, brother, cousin, sister-in-law, and cousin-in-law. She had a good time and would like to see them again. His brother from New Orleans was not there but may come to Georgia soon. If McCown makes it to Georgia, they hope he will visit.

Works: None.

June 2, 1960 (p. 399; 2 par.): From ANDALUSIA. She appreciates the account of Miss O'Connor, Spring Hill, and his role in the Azalea Trail. She will send him her story about the azalea festival if it ever is published. He should bring his friends to their house when they are in Macon. Surely one of the many people he knows there would drive him over. When she is there, many folks ask after him.

Works: None.

October 28, 1960 (p. 414; 2 par.): From ANDALUSIA. They were hopeful to see him visit last July, but he did not make it. She appreciates the book. She would be glad to meet John Howard Griffin, but they would not like to see him in blackface. That must have looked terrible.

Works: None.

December 4, 1960 (p. 420; 2 par.): From ANDALUSIA. She appreciates the material he sent. She advises his looking at John Updike's *Rabbit Run*. It is "the product of a real religious consciousness. It is the best book illustrating damnation that has come along in a great while" (420). She will soon be in Piedmont Hospital for a bone examination.

Works: None.

January 24, 1962 (p. 462; 5 par.): From ANDALUSIA. She will send him Seán O'Faoláin's collection of stories after it arrives and she has read it. He and the Gossetts should be receiving NEW WORLD WRITING with her story in it soon. McCown's mother liked the *Mary Ann* book; the nuns are having a great time now that they are authors. Tom attended Mass but missed the communication between the priest and the congregation that Father McCown had. She asks him to send the travelogue. She has a friend who will teach catechism to Peruvians as a member of the Papal Volunteers. He has relieved a lot of her suffering; thanks.

Works: [A *Memoir of Mary Ann*], "Everything That Rises Must Converge."

March 4, 1962 (p. 468; 3 par.): From ANDALUSIA. She and Regina enjoyed the travelogue. He might publish it in *JUBILEE* if it were shortened. She asks for more information about Our Lady of Guadalupe. She appreciates the issues of *Catholic Mind* and especially likes the article, "Theology and Population." She is glad he likes "Everything That Rises Must Converge." She has no more copies, but she will try to get his brother one. She wishes she wrote more stories like that, but her well has been feeling dry lately. She asks that he pray the Lord may send her some more ideas since she is feeling as though she may be out of them.

Works: "Everything That Rises Must Converge."

March 27, 1962 (p. 470; 2 par.): From ANDALUSIA. She turns 37 that week and is feeling a bit old. St. Mary's College at Notre Dame is going to give her an honorary doctorate degree. She is sorry to hear about his mother's hip problem.

Works: None.

August 5, 1962 (p. 488; 2 par.): From ANDALUSIA. She sends him a letter from Roslyn Barnes, who is a Papal Volunteer in Cuernavaca. She knows he will pray for her. Barnes's family has not supported her mission work. She hopes his mother has left the wheelchair.

Works: None.

November 2, 1962 (p. 497; 2 par.): From ANDA-LUSIA. Roslyn Barnes came by to visit instead of going home to her family because they are angry with her. She is going to teach chemistry in a Jesuit college in Valparaiso with limited Spanish skills.

Works: None.

November 23, 1962 (p. 500; 4 par.): From ANDA-LUSIA. She sends him a check to do something for children out of the money she made on her trip. Roslyn is happy in Chile; she sends her letter. She has not heard about a book from the Gossetts. She appreciates the books he sent.

Works: None.

April 19, 1963 (p. 513; 3 par.): From ANDALUSIA. She is pleased he has returned to his regular group. The Gossetts have been concerned about his ulcer, so perhaps he could send them a line. Roslyn would also like to hear from him. She told her about her friend who wanted to be sent to Mexico but was told he was too old at 50. She said that many workers there were much older. She does not mention his book because it is the opposite of bad.

Works: None.

March 21, 1964 (p. 570; 2 par.): From ANDA-LUSIA. She is out of the hospital but is still fighting various infections and spending time in bed and out. She is still too weak to help him too much, but she would advise anyone interested in reading Catholic fiction to begin with the French writers FRANÇOIS MAURIAC and Bernanos. For English, she recommends Waugh, GRAHAM GREENE, and Muriel Spark, and Americans Powers, WALKER PERCY, Wilfrid Sheed, and perhaps Edwin O'Connor, whom she hears recommended but she has not read. For nonfiction, the most essential is Père PIERRE TEILHARD DE CHARDIN, S. J. She apologizes for not giving more ideas, but she is full of viruses. She will be battling illness until they know whether or not the operation has reinvigorated the lupus.

Works: None.

MAVIS MCINTOSH (two letters) McIntosh was Elizabeth McKee's partner in the literary agency. *Pages:* HB 15, 17 (2).

Letters

October 6, 1949 (p. 15; 2 par.): From Ridgefield, Connecticut. She thank Mavis for the contract and doubts that her novel will reach 90,000 words. Her typewriter is being looked at.

Works: [*Wise Blood*].

October 31, 1949 (p. 17; 6 par.): From Ridgefield, Connecticut. She has been thinking about Selby's release statement for a while. She finds it offensive, and it proves that it would not be good for her to work with him. She does feel, however, that she should give them the manuscript once more since they still seem to think they have rights to it. She makes a proposal for possibly moving the book from Rinehart to Harcourt, Brace. She is pretty sure they are not going to want the book. She is giving all parties the opportunity to be fair. She will try to be in New York this week and see her. She sends these ideas before she visits so that she may be aware of what she is thinking. She appreciates her efforts with these difficult people.

Work: [*Wise Blood*].

JANET MCKANE (30 letters) McKane was a primary school teacher from New York who wrote to O'Connor about her work. O'Connor was touched by McKane's heartfelt and insightful letter, and they began a correspondence that lasted through O'Connor's final illness. *Pages:* HB: 507, 509, 512, 519, 522, 529–32, 561, 564, 569, 571, 577, 582, 585, 589–92, 595.

Letters

January 30, 1963 (p. 507; 3 par.): From ANDA-LUSIA. It moves her to know that McKane has had a MASS said for her. She is also glad to hear that she likes her work and gives them thought. She sends an inscribed copy of *A Memoir of Mary Ann* and thanks her again for her prayers.

Works: [*A Memoir of Mary Ann*].

February 25, 1963 (p. 509; 5 par.): From ANDA-LUSIA. She appreciates the two books. They do not have a bookstore there, and those she orders from Brentano's can take six months to receive. She had tried to find the C. S. Lewis book before with no luck. She speaks of "passive diminishments" in *The Divine Milieu* by Père PEIRRE TEILHARD DE CHARDIN. He says that one should bear the difficulties one cannot change but work hard to get rid of those one can. She went to LOURDES and prayed for her novel and not her bones, though she is on crutches. Her novel was completed, so in that sense her prayers were answered. She sends a feather from one of her PEACOCKS since her copy of *The Divine Milieu* has been lent out. She has about 30 of the birds that screech in five different tones. She sends her best and hopes to remain in her prayers.

Works: None.

March 31, 1963 (p. 512; 2 par.): From ANDA-LUSIA. She appreciates the books on LOURDES and Miss Tabor's poetry. She read both while sick in bed with her annual spring cold. She would like to show the poetry to the chaplain at the state mental hospital in town. She is a friend of ROBERT LOWELL, who once was in the Catholic Church and suffers mental illnesses. She tells the chaplain that the hospital could have a writer that would help the patients who are well enough to move on from weaving baskets to something stimulating. He might like Tabor. In TEILHARD DE CHARDIN, she means that the patient must be passive toward his or her disease after trying all means possible to get well.

Works: None.

May 17, 1963 (p. 519; 7 par.): From ANDALUSIA. It was funny to her to find out how much the man was charging for his PEACOCKS. She sees them advertised regularly in the *Georgia Market Bulletin* for $17.50 each. She appreciated the issue of *Commonweal*; even though she subscribes herself she sometimes misses things like the review of Alice B. Toklas's book and the one written by Alice Ellen Mayhew. The latter is a sister of a friend of hers, Father Mayhew.

Her Catholic education was all in SAVANNAH up through sixth grade and one-half. From the time when they moved to MILLEDGEVILLE on, she went to public schools and was just as pleased. Perhaps the schools have changed since then.

There are many Georgians named Kelly and so forth. The Irish who immigrated to Georgia and kept the faith had to sacrifice to foster it there. Her great-grandfather provided a place for MASS to be said in his hotel room and then later on the piano at his house. Presently, there are three Mass times now each Sunday, but they have no Catholic school. They had a school for three or four years, but the diocese transferred the nuns to the city, where they claimed they were more needed.

She is reading *On the Theology of Death* by Karl Rahner, though it is difficult and slow going. In regard to Ignatian meditation, she is not very good at meditating or contemplating. Her mind wanders when she tries to think about the mysteries of the rosary while saying it. She has taken to reading prayers from a book prime morning and compline at night. She admires TEILHARD DE CHARDIN's *Mass upon the World*.

Her LUPUS is currently contained.

Works: None.

June 5, 1963 (p. 522; 6 par.): From ANDALUSIA. She appreciates the Rumer Godden book and the other materials. She can see what she means about New York since she lived there in 1949 for four months. She stayed in a room on the 12th floor of a building at the corner of Broadway and 108th Street. She went to daily Mass at the church on 107th and enjoyed riding the subways and buses. It would be different now because she cannot get around, and most of the city would be lost to her. She visited the Cloisters Museum twice and was much taken by a four-foot-tall sculpture there of the Madonna and child laughing. She would like to see it again but probably never will.

The North does have a sense of place, but it does not have a history of defeat like the South. Defeat makes for strong emotions among those who share that historical experience. She received Karl Barth's *Evangelical Theology: an Introduction* to review for the diocesan paper.

On the farm, they have four new peachicks and five ducklings. The farm is full of life—she walked outside the other day and beheld 14 PEA-COCKS with their tails fanned. She knows what she means about light in people. She sees it rarely and can never describe it.

Works: None.

June 19, 1963 (p. 524; 6 par.):   From ANDALUSIA. She does not like her picture taken. The pictures in *JUBILEE* were taken by an arty photographer who made ANDALUSIA look like Oklahoma after the Dust Bowl and her like a burdened Okie. The photo in *The* CRITIC is a little more her likeness, but not by much. She also does not like the interview in *Critic*. It is best not to solicit her opinions because she either should not give them or does not have any to begin with.

The bird in her self-portrait is a pheasant cock, not a PEACOCK. She used to raise them, but they were more work because they needed to live in cages where peacocks can roam free and take care of themselves. She likes the pheasant because it looks like it has horns, which give it the appearance of the Devil. She painted it soon after a spell with LUPUS, which makes one's faces full and puffy. She painted both herself and the bird from memory.

She liked the interview with Hans Küng in the *Catholic World*. She was sent an issue of *Christian Century* where there is an article accusing Küng of being anti-Semitic in *The Council, Reform & Reunion*. She will send the Freedom speech from *Commonweal* to her friend who is a Presbyterian with Catholic sympathies.

She owns all of Muriel Spark's works but has not read G. Fielding. She looks forward to *An Episode of the Sparrows*.

When she lived in New York, she did not do too many cultural things or see many sites. She did not see a play or go to the Frick museum. She did see the Natural History Museum, and the public library was too overwhelming. She went out to buy something to eat once or

twice a day, usually at the Columbia University cafeteria.

The peacocks are beginning to shed again, so when they do she will gather some feathers to send to her that she can put in a vase.

Works: None.

June 30, 1963 (p. 526; 5 par.):   From ANDALUSIA. She is pleased that McKane has dropped using the salutation "Miss." She discusses suffering and joy as shared experiences with Christ. She will leave her Catholic library to the town library some day. She is reading another book about TEILHARD DE CHARDIN, this one written by an Episcopalian. She likes how it focuses on Teilhard's views of the Sacred Heart of Jesus. It is perfectly fine for her to not agree with what she says in interviews. She gives mostly half answers anyway. Her cousin who teaches first grade in Boston schools also speaks about how children want to throw things away. The book she spoke about before and finished was *The Theology of Death* by Karl Rahner. She could reread it many times and still not fully understand it.

Works: None.

July 9, 1963 (p. 529; 7 par.):   From ANDALUSIA. She liked reading the children's comments on the poetry. She does not know much about children but enjoys watching them. The Virgin and Child statue she spoke about is not the one on the card. It may have been sculpted out of wood or stone; it had no color. Another reason she remembers it is because the Child's face reminded her so much of her friend Robert Fitzgerald's. The character in *ESQUIRE* was Walter Tilman of "Why Do the Heathen Rage?" She works with him every morning, and they do not always get along. She will send an inscribed copy of *The Violent Bear It Away* to her; she has several copies that did not sell in England. She is not clever about inscriptions and always thinks of a quotation too late, but she will make it out to McKane from her.

She is pleased to get her picture; she reminds her of an aunt of hers. Regina says she reminds her of a friend of theirs who has gone to Hawthorne to try to become a Dominican nun.

McKane may remember what she learned in college because she took time with her classes. She went to college during the war and finished in three years. She did not like her high school but enjoyed college, though she remembers little subject matter from either.

She wonders what chapter and verse notation the quote from Jeremiah comes from. She appreciates the map of New York City. She thought the summer there was hotter than Georgia.

Works: ["Why Do the Heathen Rage?"], *The Violent Bear It Away.*

July 25, 1963 (p. 531; 5 par.): From ANDALUSIA. She was pleased to read the article on Chagall. She has not felt that tied to the Irish in America, though she has met true Irish from Ireland, whom she prefers. Thomas Kilroy came to visit once with his wife. He was from Ireland, and his wife was from New York. He taught at Notre Dame, but they were going back to Dublin, where he would write. He told her that the South reminded him more of Ireland. She does not like the "Over-Irish" who express so much of themselves on St. Patrick's Day with a parade and so forth as they have in SAVANNAH.

If she ever gets to New York again, she would like them to meet and have dinner. She once had an aunt who sent her the Sacred Heart pamphlets each month; if McKane could do that, she would appreciate it.

Works: The Violent Bear It Away.

January 5, 1964 (p. 561; 5 par.): From ANDALUSIA. She appreciates the letter and the card with Holy Land flowers. She is very tired, though she is feeling a bit better. She did not receive her package from Boston; she does enjoy the woodcarving with the animal. She appreciates all of her thoughts. The storm in MILLEDGEVILLE was bad, but it did not affect them much.

Their Sicilian burro is named Equinox, and its mother was Marquita. She has a cross on her back and is supposed to be the kind Jesus rode

into Jerusalem. The Mexican burro is named Ernest. She is too tired to write a longer letter.

Works: None.

January 27, 1964 (p. 564; 3 par.): From ANDALUSIA. She enjoyed the picture with the red scarf. She appreciates the year of Novena MASSES. She is pleased the church does not pay much attention to single people, like herself.

Works: None.

March 12, 1964 (p. 569; 2 par.): From ANDALUSIA. She will read the MASS in her missal if she cannot come. It was so nice of her to have the high Mass said for her in the Byzantine church. She looked at the hymns; their congregation does not sing. She has received a bizarre pamphlet sent to her by some nuns in Canada. It is called "A Check on the bank of Heaven" made out to "Flannery O'Connor, 300 Hail Marys." It has pictures of the Christ Child as "President" of the said bank and the Virgin Mary as "Vice-President."

Works: None.

April 2, 1964 (p. 571; 3 par.): From ANDALUSIA. She appreciates the pictures and will keep the one with McKane in it and return the others. She knows Ridgewood, New Jersey, somewhat. She read MASS prayers this morning. They have tried five different drugs on her kidney infection that have not worked other than to give her bad side effects.

Works: None.

April 6, 1964 (p. 572; 5 par.): From ANDALUSIA. The rose quartz pendant is striking, and she will be pleased to wear it when she can get out and look at it in the meantime. She liked hearing about the Byzantine MASS. She does not like pious books and does not pray well for others, though she does in her fashion. She enjoyed C. S. Lewis's book on prayer as well as his Miracles. Her 82-year-old aunt is failing, and the family has gathered. She has requested a copy of "Revelation" for her.

Works: ["Revelation"].

May 15, 1964 (p. 577; 7 par.):   From ANDALUSIA. She thanks her for the MASS said by the Paulist priests. She likes the memorial stamps; does McKane have a collection of them? She appreciates Muriel Spark's *The Girls of Slender Means*. She likes the mug with the stripes the best, but enjoys them all. She is feeling improved and was able to work for an hour today and the day before. She hopes McKane rests and takes care of herself. Her doctor always tells her to stop before she tires. She will send a children's book that she may like to use with her class. She was sent it to review but knows nothing about children's literature.

Works: None.

June 5, 1964 (p. 582; 4 par.):   From Piedmont Hospital. She is upset to learn that McKane is in the hospital. She has said a Rosary for her but can do little else at present. She will see if she can stay awake for another five decades on the Rosary tonight.

Works: None.

June 19, 1964 (p. 585; 3 par.):   From Piedmont Hospital. She gets to go home tomorrow. Though she will have to stay in bed, it will be good to be home. She just received three letters from her from the Pink Ladies at the hospital. It is always a pleasure to hear from her. In answer to one of the letters, she enjoys Hopkins, "Margaret, are you grieving / Over Goldengrove unleaving? . . ."

Works: None.

June 27, 1964 (p. 587; 2 par.):   From ANDALUSIA. She appreciates the Russell stamps. St. James will work. She will not get to go to church for some time. It is good to be home. She watches T. Traveller and Equinox chase the swans. She is working on revisions, she is sure, from the prayers of her friends. She hopes McKane feels better.

Works: None.

July 1, 1964 (p. 589; 1 par.):   From ANDALUSIA. She appreciates the FRANÇOIS MAURIAC book but may not read it for a while. She is feeling poorly from a cut in her medication dosage and wants to put the energy she has into her work. She will send her the PRAYER OF ST. RAPHAEL. The angel is supposed to help you meet those you were intended to meet in your life. The prayer was written by Ernest Hello.

Works: None.

See also: PRAYER OF ST. RAPHAEL.

July 8, 1964 (p. 591; 2 par.):   From ANDALUSIA. She has far less energy since her medication has been reduced to half. The priest brought her Communion the day before. She asked him also for the Sacrament of the Sick, or Extreme Unction. She is glad to see that most of the restaurants celebrating the fourth of July are either integrated or disinteresting to those who would like to see them all integrated.

Works: None.

July 14, 1964 (p. 592; 4 par.):   From ANDALUSIA. She sends the prayer to St. Raphael that she thinks was written by Ernest Hello. She appreciates seeing the child's letter and returns it. She thanks McKane for her prayers, saying that she does need them.

Works: None.

July 26, 1964 (p. 595; 1 par.):   From MILLEDGEVILLE. She appreciates the cards. That is a Muscovy duck in the picture, not a goose. The duck's name is Sister. She hatches more ducklings than any of their other ducks and sets about four times a year. The other birds in the picture are a guinea and peahens. She recommends reading Milton and Shakespeare over *The Art of Plain Talk*. She also recommends *The Ethics of Rhetoric* by R. M. Weaver, which she regrets giving away as a graduation gift.

Works: None.

July 27, 1964 (p. 595; 2 par.): From MILLEDGE-VILLE. She thanks her for the burro and the books. She hopes to be able to read the books later. She can enjoy the burro now; it looks like Equinox. She went to the doctor today, which always exhausts her. Patients must go to see him rather than the other way around since he has had three heart attacks.

[Note: This was the second to last letter O'Connor wrote before she died.]

Works: None.

ELIZABETH MCKEE (30 letters) McKee was an agent in New York who would become O'Connor's literary agent. *Pages*: HB: 4–11, 15–18, 20–1, 23, 32, 42, 48, 74, 77, 84, 88, 120, 127, 146, 264, 289, 340, 402, 408, 414, 425, 475, 504, 560, 565, 574, 580.

Letters

June 19, 1948 (p. 4; 3 par.): From YADDO. [Note: This is the first letter in the HB collection.] "I am looking for an agent" (4). She mentions that writer Paul Moor suggested McKee. She tells McKee about her current work-in-progress, *Wise Blood*, which won the Rinehart-Iowa Fiction Award. She also tells her about publications of chapters from the novel and about her slowness as a writer and when she expects to have the novel completed. She will be in New York if McKee might want to meet with her, and she will also send her some of her work for review.

Works: [*Wise Blood*], "The Train," ["The Peeler"], ["The Heart of the Park"], "The Turkey," ["The Crop"].

July 4, 1948 (p. 5; 4 par.): From YADDO. FOC is glad McKee is interested in her work. *PARTISAN REVIEW* still has her chapter that she has promised to send to McKee for review. She would like McKee to go over her contract with Rinehart. She regrets not meeting McKee, who she has learned from Paul Moor will be in Europe when she is in New York.

Works: ["The Heart of the Park"].

July 21, 1948 (p. 5; 4 par.): From YADDO. FOC sends McKee some of her work. She explains her work process in that she does not outline first and needs to write out her novel to see where it is going. "I don't know so well what I think until I see what I say; then I have to say it over again" (5). She does not number pages but guesses that she must have at least 50,000 words done on the novel. She thinks the novel will be about 100,000 words. She has sent McKee the best chapters so far. She talks about possible travel plans and mentions that she sends the story "The Crop" "for sale to the unparticular" (6).

Works: "The Crop."

September 3, 1948 (p. 6; 2 par.): From MILL-EDGEVILLE. She will be in New York on September 14 and 15 on her return to YADDO. McKee mentioned once that she could set up meetings for her with John Selby and George Davis; she would like her to do that now. She has mailed John Selby a copy of chapter 9 of the book, the one that *PARTISAN REVIEW* is going to publish. She will be staying at the Woodstock Hotel.

Works: None.

September 18, 1948 (p. 7; 4 par.): From YADDO. She was pleased to hear from her. She would like to know if the following people might support her applying for a Guggenheim Fellowship—Philip Rahv, ROBERT PENN WARREN, and Arabel Porter, who is editor of *NEW WORLD WRITING*. She will likely contact her to make hotel reservations in November. At Yaddo, there will only be her, Clifford Wright, and ROBERT LOWELL. She will send her a copy of "The Crop" once she types it. "I am altogether pleased that you are my agent" (7).

Works: "The Crop."

September 30, 1948 (p. 7; 2 par.): From YADDO. She sends two copies of "The Geranium" and one copy of "The Train" to use to show Mr. Rahv about her work. She has not yet sent "The Crop" because she has been working steadily on the novel.

Works: "The Geranium," "The Train," "The Crop."

November 14, 1948 (p. 7; 2 par.): From YADDO. ROBERT LOWELL will recommend her for the Guggenheim, so she would like his name added to the list if it is not too late.

Works: None.

December 15, 1948 (p. 7; 4 par.): From YADDO. She sends George Davis's letter. She agrees with his critical remarks after rereading "The Crop" and asks that it be returned to her. It is not a good idea for her to write short stories while she is in the midst of writing a novel. It was kind of Davis to write the letter for the Guggenheim. She has seen Paul Engle's and ROBERT LOWELL's and Mr. Moe's will make three. She may send chapters of the novel in January, but she works slowly and may not.

Works: ["The Crop"], *Wise Blood.*

January 20, 1949 (p. 8; 2 par.): From YADDO. She sends the first nine chapters of her novel. Please show them to John Selby and begin contract negotiations. If Rinehart does not want the book, Alfred Kazin told her that Harcourt, Brace was interested. She is sending chapter 6 to KEN-YON REVIEW. If they reject it, she will send it to SEWANEE REVIEW.

Works: [*Wise Blood*].

January 28, 1949 (p. 8; 3 par.): From YADDO. She will be at Yaddo for sure only through April. She has requested a stay through July coming back in October, but she is doubtful of both getting that and the Guggenheim, which makes earning an advance on the novel that much more important. She will come to New York only when she must. How long does Rinehart need to make their decision on her book? She recommends James Ross from Yaddo to her. He is looking for an agent. He wrote a book called *They Don't Dance Much* that did not sell many copies and wants to place some of his stories. He would like to hear from McKee if she decided to contact him.

Works: [*Wise Blood*].

February 3, 1949 (p. 9; 2 par.): From YADDO. She is very satisfied with the $1,500 advance offer from Harcourt, Brace and doubts that Rinehart would give her that. Her main requirement is that the publisher they choose not change the book and that they try to sell it. After she hears back from Selby, she will ask her to make hotel reservations so that she can come to New York and discuss with her and with Theodore Amussen the offers from Rinehart and Harcourt and then decide.

Works: [*Wise Blood*].

February 17, 1949 (p. 9; 3 par.): From YADDO. She does not appreciate Selby's comment about her being a "straight shooter." All she can gather from his letter is that they do not like the novel and want a conventional one instead of the unconventional one she is writing. If Harcourt is sure to take it, she would like to remove it from Rinehart. Is is possible for McKee to get the manuscript back, or must they break their relationship first? She is eager to have the publishing business out of the way so she can return to writing.

Works: [*Wise Blood*].

February 18, 1949 (p. 10; 2 par.): From YADDO. She will come to New York, though she is not sure much can be accomplished by seeing Selby in person. She is writing him a letter first, outlining her views and what she wants so that he will know what to expect. She would like McKee to make appointments with Selby or William Raney and also Amussen from Harcourt, if possible. She will be staying at Elizabeth Hartwick's apartment.

Works: None.

February 24, 1949 (p. 11; 3 par.): From YADDO. It is too bad that McKee has to cancel the meeting with Selby for Tuesday; she does not get to New York until Tuesday evening but will be available after that. There are problems at Yaddo, and all the writers are leaving there as a group on Tuesday. She will be staying in New York probably for about a month. She will first be at Tatum

House but not for very long. Does McKee know of any places to stay? She is certain now that she will not be going back to Yaddo unless some big changes take place. She hopes McKee is well.

Works: [*Wise Blood*].

October 26, 1949 (p. 16; 5 par.): From Ridgefield, Connecticut. She appreciates her letter and Selby's release document. As usual, the document is unclear. It appears to her that Rinehart wants the right to have the manuscript returned to them for consideration if Harcourt does not end up publishing it. This does not strike her as a release. She thinks that they should sign with Harcourt and hopes that they will publish, but she does not want Rinehart to have another chance at the manuscript. This letter has cemented her conviction that she does not want to work with John Selby of Rinehart.

She would like to meet with her or Mavis when she is in town and find out more about how the Harcourt deal was obtained and also more about Mavis's conversation with Selby. She should see the proofs from "The Heart of the Park" soon from PARTISAN REVIEW. She sends her regards to George Davis. The novel is going so well now that it is almost quick.

Works: [*Wise Blood*], ["The Heart of the Park"].

February 13, 1950 (p. 20; 2 par.): From MILLEDGEVILLE. She appreciates her letter. She is out of the hospital and plans to return to Connecticut by March 20. She is eager to return to the book once she gets her strength back.

Works: [*Wise Blood*].

April 27, 1950 (p. 20; 1 par.): From Ridgefield, Connecticut. She appreciates her letter. She plans to come to New York in May and would like to have lunch. Bob Giroux asked about her book and when it might be coming out.

Works: [*Wise Blood*].

September 22, 1950 (p. 21; 1 par.): From Ridgefield, Connecticut. She appreciates her note. She is still in Connecticut, still writing. Bob Giroux

mentioned that they could put the contract date at the beginning of the year. She intends to work until then and see what she has.

Works: [*Wise Blood*].

Likely January, 1951 [undated] (p. 23; 4 par.): From Emory University Hospital, ATLANTA. She appreciates her letter. She is now in Emory University Hospital in Atlanta and is much better. She expects to be home the following week. She has completed the first draft of *Wise Blood* and sent it to Robert Fitzgerald for comments. He likes it, and so does she. She is working on getting a copy to her and another to Harcourt. She will add a chapter and revise others once she gets home, all of which will take time.

Works: [*Wise Blood*].

March 10, 1951 (p. 24; 4 par.): From ANDALUSIA. She sends Giroux's letter. She sent him a corrected copy of the manuscript and will send her one on Monday. She believes this is now the last draft. She inquires about Scribner's if Harcourt decides they do not want it. She is taking ACTH, which makes her feel better.

Works: [*Wise Blood*].

April 24, 1951 (p. 24; 1 par.): From ANDALUSIA. She asks if McKee might make sure that Harcourt, Brace received the manuscript, which she sent on March 12. If they do not want the manuscript, she would like it back and for McKee to send it elsewhere.

Works: [*Wise Blood*].

March 14, 1952 (p. 32; 1 par.): From ANDALUSIA. She appreciates the letter and advance check. It is kind of the publisher to send her money, but she wants to be sure she has a signed contract so that she knows she will not have to pay the money back.

Works: [*Wise Blood*].

July 16, 1952 (p. 42; 4 par.): From ANDALUSIA. She has returned to Georgia. Martin Greenburg wrote to see if she had any stories they could consider for *American Mercury*, and she sent him to McKee. It is all right to give him two stories if he can pay for them. She had lunch in New York with Caroline Tate, who advised that *Wise Blood* be sent to her British publisher, Herbert Read.

Works: [*Wise Blood*].

August 30, 1952 (p. 43; 1 par.):   From ANDALUSIA. She is fine with Miss Morris's changes to the story; they make it better. When do they plan to publish it?

Works: ["A Late Encounter With the Enemy"].

October 15, 1952 (p. 44; 5 par.):   From ANDALUSIA. She sends a revised version of "The World Is Almost Rotten." She likes the new title. McKee could send it to *SEWANEE REVIEW* if Discovery does not buy it. She is very eager to see a royalty statement and has questions about it. When will she see it? Also, could she find out when *HARPER'S BAZAAR* will publish the story they purchased? She is currently working on something that may evolve into a novel.

Works: ["The Life You Save may Be Your Own"], ["You Can't Be Any Poorer Than Dead"/*The Violent Bear It Away*].

November 26, 1952 (p. 48; 3 par.):   From ANDALUSIA. She sends "The River" that McKee could send to *Hudson Review* unless she has another idea. Where is her royalty statement, and what is going on with Mr. Shiftlet? She might send a chapter of her new novel. What about the timing for publication of "A Late Encounter With the Enemy" in *HARPER'S BAZAAR*?

Works: ["The River"], ["The Life You Save"], ["A Late Encounter With the Enemy"].

December 20, 1952 (p. 48; 5 par.):   From ANDALUSIA. Although it is close to Christmas, she finds she must write on an important matter. In communications with Mr. Ransom about the Kenyon Fellowship, he wrote that he would like to publish either "The Life You Save" or "The River." She would like McKee to pull "The Life You Save" from consideration with *NEW WORLD WRITING*

(they have had it long enough anyway) and not send it to *SEWANEE REVIEW*. She would like *KENYON REVIEW* to have it. If this is not possible, she would like to send Ransom "The River." However, her first choice is to have *Kenyon* publish "The Life You Save," especially since McKee thinks she may be able to sell the other story. She would like to refrain from any talk of money with *Kenyon*. If she does get any, she will send McKee the 10 percent commission directly. She received the fellowship of $2,000 that she needs. She sends Christmas greetings and hopes to hear from her soon. She also thanks Mavis for the royalty statement.

Works: "The Life You Save," "The River."

January 13, 1955 (p. 74; 1 par.):   From ANDALUSIA. She sends a carbon copy of "An Exile in the East," which is a reworking of "The Geranium," published in ACCENT. She sends both stories for review since she does not want to go to prison for selling the story twice, even though ACCENT did not pay for it when they published it.

Works: "An Exile in the East," "The Geranium."

April 5, 1955 (p. 77; 3 par.):   From ANDALUSIA. *NEW WORLD WRITING* is probably fine, especially since they seem to print novels in progress. She prefers, however, that they get more compensation for the piece, so if *HARPER'S BAZAAR* wants it, it is all right to let them buy it. She wants it clear in the publication that it is a chapter from a novel and not a stand-alone short story. The title, "You Can't Be Any Poorer Than Dead" is the chapter title, not the book title.

She recently sat by John Selby at a literary breakfast in ATLANTA; both were polite. She is sorry to learn that Giroux is at another publisher but will work all right with Miss Carver. Mr. Lindley may drop by if he is in Georgia.

Works: ["You Can't Be Any Poorer Than Dead"].

June 9, 1955 (p. 84; 2 par.):   From ANDALUSIA. She was told a clause in her contract with Harcourt, Brace should read "void unless . . ." She has signed just one copy, and it may be too late, but she would like McKee to check on the matter. She sends a self-portrait so she can judge her painting ability.

Works: None.

June 29, 1955 (p. 88; 6 par.): From ANDA-LUSIA. She appreciates her response about the contract and will be all right with it since she is. She appreciates the copy of the Gollancz letter. She has heard from Neville Armstrong that *Wise Blood* will be out in the middle of July. Could she look at the contract and see whether she is committed to them for another novel or short stories? She is not sure. Please return the copy of "An Exile in the East" since she may like to revise it some more. She is pleased to hear that McKee likes her self-portrait. It is better in color.

She did not like TENNESSEE WILLIAMS's play *Cat on a Hot Tin Roof* and thought she could write something like that herself. After thinking about it, it may be best not to be certain of that.

Works: Wise Blood, "An Exile in the East."

December 5, 1955 (p. 120; 5 par.): From ANDA-LUSIA. What do they do now that Catharine Carver is leaving Harcourt, Brace? This may mean a turning point for her to leave or stay with them herself. She would like to redo the contract saying that she will stay only if Denver Lindley is her editor. Does she return their $500 if she leaves them? She will leave Harcourt, Brace if Giroux would take her, so please speak to him about it. She is distressed by these events and looks forward to hearing from her soon.

Works: None.

January 8, 1956 (p. 127; 2 par.): From ANDA-LUSIA. She has thought about it and prefers to stay where she is at Harcourt, Brace with Denver Lindley since a change is too distressing to her at present. She sends regards for the new year.

Works: None.

January 12, 1956 (p. 127; 2 par.): From ANDA-LUSIA. She sends the contract. It has been probably a lot of needless fuss since it is probable that she will have a collection of stories ready before

another novel. She will send her a story in the next few weeks. Should Neville Spearman pay her $60 before she signs a contract for stories? She is doing well and gets along on crutches now as though she had been born with them.

Works: None.

MARION MONTGOMERY (four letters) Montgomery was a contemporary writer of O'Connor's. *Pages:* HB: 444, 465, 524, 575.

Letters

July 9, 1961 (p. 444; 1 par.): From ANDALUSIA. She enjoyed his book, *The Wandering of Desire.* She will be glad to speak well of it to Elizabeth Laurence, from whom she received the galleys.

Works: None.

February 16, 1962 (p. 465; 5 par.): From ANDALUSIA. Though she has never introduced anyone before, she will be glad to do so for him at the Macon Writers Club. If he has any juicy pieces of information about himself other than where he was born and so on, that she could use, please send it along. She could mention something about him being in trouble with the law or being saved or being in poor health. Whatever he sends, she will work with. The club will enjoy history and has a breakfast for historians. They have had some from Athens and one from Deepstep.

Works: None.

June 16, 1963 (p. 524; 3 par.): From ANDALUSIA. He is correct about thinking about big problems over small ones. Her big problem is discovering the right word. She did not thank him for introducing her at Georgia and also for The Sermon of Introduction. The *Atlanta Journal-Constitution* published an unsigned mention of "Everything That Rises Must Converge." She sends her regards to the couple from Georgia who are now at Converse and to Andrew Lytle.

Works: "Everything That Rises Must Converge."

May 10, 1964 (p. 575; 2 par.): From ANDALUSIA. She enjoyed his novel, *Darrell*, both while in the Baldwin County Hospital and at home. She could write a comment for the book if she were feeling better. She was unhappy to miss the Irish poet, but she was under doctor's orders to stay in bed. She now has an electric typewriter that she hopes to be using regularly soon.

Works: None.

ALICE MORRIS (four letters) Morris was the fiction editor at HARPER'S BAZAAR. She first accepted "A Late Encounter With the Enemy" for publication. *Pages:* HB: 77, 86, 271, 273.

Letters

April 28, 1955 (p. 77; 2 par.): From ANDALUSIA. She will send the picture of her if the woman from Macon ever sends it to her. There is another photo that O'Connor likes better that also features some turkeys. She is pleased that Morris likes "Good Country People" and that HARPER'S BAZAAR will publish it. A woman in Macon told her about reading her under the dryer, which satisfied her.

Works: "Good Country People."

June 10, 1955 (p. 86; 3 par.): From ANDALUSIA. She appreciates the piece on the Dead Sea Scrolls and the article by Brother Hartford. She sends a letter from Mrs. N. of Boston. She will be glad to help with any questions or complaints the magazine might receive about the story. This time they may hear less from angry Catholics and more from purist atheists.

Works: "Good Country People."

February 28, 1958 (p. 271; 3 par.): From ANDALUSIA. She is pleased that "The Enduring Chill" will be published by Harper's. She wants to ensure that Morris purchased the version with the second opening and closing. She may revise the story slightly. She did write a sentence to introduce the story, but she is better at just writing the story, and Morris can change the sentence if she likes. Better yet, just put an arrow pointing to the story and let the women under the dryer find it that way.

Works: ["The Enduring Chill"].

March 15, 1958 (p. 273; 2 par.): From ANDALUSIA. This is the last version of the last page that she will send. Catherine Tate from Princeton likes the new page, and so does she. She appreciates Morris's patience.

Works: ["The Enduring Chill"].

WALKER PERCY (one letter) Percy was a contemporary southern writer. *Pages:* HB: 470.

See also: PERCY, WALKER.

Letters

March 29, 1962 (p. 470; 1 par.): From ANDALUSIA. She is glad that the South lost the Civil War and that he won the National Book Award. The judges surprised her with their good judgment.

Works: None.

KATHERINE ANNE PORTER (one letter) Porter was a contemporary writer to O'Connor. *Pages:* HB: 371.

See also: PORTER, KATHERINE ANNE.

Letters

January 22, 1960 (p. 371; 2 par.): From ANDALUSIA. She appreciates Porter's note and request for a signature. She is glad to have the book in print, though now she sees all its flaws. She wishes Porter could see her Chinese geese that have arrived since she visited. They are noisy and they fight. The peafowl also fight; however, the peafowl fight four feet above the ground and the geese on the ground, so they have not attacked each other.

Work: [*The Violent Bear It Away*].

J. F. POWERS (one letter) Powers was a Roman Catholic writer. *Pages:* HB: 185.

Letters

December 9, 1956 (p. 185; 2 par.): From ANDALUSIA. She may have to bring Mrs. May back as another character and begin again. She can be tempted by death. She is working hard on *The Violent Bear It Away*, which died when it became a novel instead of a short story after chapter one. She understands that he is teaching at the University of Michigan; she was in East Lansing last year. Emerging writers may earn a degree in Hotel Management. The English faculty were not a happy bunch; they said their new library specialized in the second installments of three-part series.

Works: [*The Violent Bear It Away*].

"A PROFESSOR OF ENGLISH" (one letter)

The identity of this academic is anonymous in *The Habit of Being. Pages:* HB: 582.

Letters

June 6, 1964 (p. 582; 2 par.): From Piedmont Hospital. She appreciates his letter but cannot answer literary questions since she is in the hospital. The name for Mrs. May must have come to her because she was aware that English teachers would ask why she named her that. She thinks those looking to analyze her work "sometimes strain the soup too thin" (HB 582).

Works: "Greenleaf."

JOHN SELBY (one letter)

Selby was the editor-in-chief at Rinehart that had the first contract on *Wise Blood*, which eventually went unfulfilled. The publisher asked things of O'Connor that she did not feel she could deliver. *Pages:* HB: 10.

Letters

February 18, 1949 (p. 10; 4 par.): From YADDO. She appreciates his letter of the 16th. She hopes to meet with him while she is in New York and has asked Elizabeth McKee to set up a meeting. She wants to write to him beforehand, however, about her views on her novel and on the criticism of it in his letter.

She is not writing a "conventional novel" (10). She believes her novel will benefit, and is strongest, in the very areas of concerns that Selby has so far with the manuscript. She is willing to accept criticism but only from those who understand her intent for the book. She asks plainly whether Rinehart is still interested in publishing the kind of book she is trying to write. They can discuss it further on Thursday.

Works: [*Wise Blood*].

WILLIAM SESSIONS (15 letters)

Sessions was a writer from Georgia who visited Andalusia and became friends with both O'Connor and her mother. He converted to Catholicism. *Pages:* HB: 164, 166, 178, 180, 189, 212, 240, 243, 250, 407, 410, 484, 502, 509, 521.

Letters

July 8, 1956 (p. 164; 3 par.): From ANDALUSIA. She has been praying for him and received Communion Friday for his intentions. Born Catholics sometimes envy converts. Has he read the Hopkins-Bridges letters? Bridges asked Hopkins how he could learn to believe, thinking perhaps he would get a metaphysical response. Hopkins said, "Give alms" (164). Philip Burnham appeared often in *Commonweal*; she asks that he write to her about Burnham and himself.

Works: None.

July 22, 1956 (p. 166; 3 par.): From ANDALUSIA. She is about halfway through Jean Guitton's book. She is also reading the biography of Baron von Hügel by Michael de la Bedoyere as well as von Hügel's *Essays and Addresses*. She agrees that Hopkins's response to Bridges did not help him at the time. She would send him JACQUES MARITAIN's letter to Caroline about *The Malefactors* to show the woman in the bookstore if she had not lent it to someone who has not yet returned it. He does not think she was false or mean with Dorothy Day or Peter Maurin. Caroline will write the introduction to the French edition of O'Connor's novel or short stories. In addition, Caroline is working on *How to Read a Novel* and a *Books on Trial* article titled "How I Write a Novel."

Works: None.

October 11, 1956 (p. 178; 3 par.): From ANDA-LUSIA. She has recently seen the paperback edition of her collection. The cover has a man clutching for a mussed woman in a haystack with a pitchfork and suitcase full of whisky bottles off to the side. They did not take her suggestion of putting wooden legs all over the cover since they know what they are doing. She has not heard of such an ailment as athlete's heart, but anyone who must exercise has her sympathy. The water tank is built, but it leaks, so Mr. Clavin is taking care of it. The project seems to be never-ending.

Works: *A Good Man Is Hard to Find and Other Stories.*

November 23, 1956 (p. 180; 5 par.): From ANDA-LUSIA. In her opinion, he should definitely submit his stories to publishers and keep writing. "A Summer at Madame's" is the best one technically speaking and is ready to send out as it is. The other one is more ambitious and more interesting to her. The scenes are all right, but the story could benefit from more unity. It is not easy for a writer to criticize other people's work because they will tend to want to make it like their own. He should not make any changes she suggests unless he also sees what she means by the suggestions. She would send the stories out as a pair rather than one at at time. This shows editors that he is beyond the many writers who can only write one story. She hopes the goose digested well.

Works: None.

December 27, 1956 (p. 189; 2 par.): From ANDA-LUSIA. She and her mother are both enjoying reading *Three Mystics* about St. Theresa, St. John, and El Greco. They have started using the pitcher and appreciate it very much. For Christmas, she asked for meatballs and turnip greens, and that is what she got. She has read Father George Tavard's book and has written to Arabel Porter, so she hopes his manuscript has been sent.

Works: None.

[Spring, 1957] (p. 212; 3 par.): From ANDALUSIA. Her mother sends the message that he is not to bring anything but himself. She enjoys his com-pany and that he eats what is put in front of him. She was not aware that Isaac Rosenfeld died; she thought he was young but did not really know anything about him. They look forward to seeing Sessions on the 27th.

Works: None.

September 1, 1957 (p. 240; 3 par.): From ANDA-LUSIA. She encloses characters from Carrollton that might keep him company. Her mother keeps saying that he cannot talk where he is and to write him a letter. Her uncle has given them some things from Bell House, such as rockers for the porch. The front of the house now looks like a rest home. She has not rocked for several years but will now get more practice. They would like to hear from him about what he is studying in Germany. There is less exciting news on the farm to share in return. Their news all tends to come from the barnyard. For example, they have a new Santa Gertrudis bull. He weighs 1,100 pounds, has brown eyes and is red in color. He is 17 months of age and has been tested for both Bangs and TB.

Works: None.

September 27, 1957 (p. 243; 5 par.): From ANDA-LUSIA. They were pleased to hear from him. Regina wants to save his letters and give them to him when he returns so that he will have an account of his trip. She tells her that he is most likely taking lots of notes over there himself. They ask if they can send him anything that he cannot get in Germany. She sends Sally Fitzgerald gingerbread mix and home permanents for her hair, but perhaps there is something more of interest to him that they could send. Perhaps something like Instant Tea or Coffee, Supersuds, corn plaster, or Hadacol?

God's Little Acre has just been announced to be obscene by the Georgia Literature Commission. They are still talking about *The Dice of God* and whether or not that book by an Alabama author meets their criteria. The book was taken to the commission by some men in Macon who had read only the obscene parts. They call the parts obscene that cannot be read in front of a lady.

Does he plan to visit Heidegger, Msgr. Guardini, Karl Adam, Max Picard (is he still alive?), Marcel, and Claude Edmond Magny? The Fitzgeralds look forward to seeing him. The Bell House has been taken down; all that is there now are two beech trees. They may call it the The Beechtree Parking Lot. Her uncle gave them the birdbath from the place that gives the western side of the house an antique look.

Works: None.

November 3, 1957 (p. 250; 4 par.): From ANDALUSIA. They appreciate the letter from Italy and the cards. Her mother especially likes the card with the woman with the hat. She presumes he is visiting the Fitzgeralds now. A mutual friend visited them two Sundays ago. She told them that she is writing the history of West Georgia College. She always makes O'Connor feel like she has finally made it out of third grade. Her wealthy cousin in SAVANNAH wants to give Flannery and her mother a trip to Europe. It is a 17-day pilgrimage that includes Ireland, London, Paris LOURDES, Rome, and Lisbon. It will not cost her anything. She hopes they will see the Fitzgeralds in Rome.

Works: None.

September 13, 1960 (p. 407; 4 par.): From ANDALUSIA. She is sorry that he did not enjoy *The Violent Bear It Away*. He sees too many sex symbols in his reading and has read too much literary criticism. It is not a realistic novel, so it does not suffer from a lack of realism, as he contends. The old man is a prophet, not a churchgoer. She is a descendant of NATHANIEL HAWTHORNE, who said he wrote romances, not novels.

She will not take up his comments specifically because his view of the book is too far removed from her own. She hopes he does not put so much Freudian reading into his classes with students. They deserve better than that.

They look forward to seeing him at Thanksgiving.

Works: *The Violent Bear It Away*.

September 29, 1960 (p. 410; 3 par.): From ANDALUSIA. She is pleased to learn that he does not usually read Freud into everything and not with his students. He needs to remember that Tarwater is a Protestant, not a Catholic. As such, he allows himself to hear a voice and follow it. Catholics would not follow a voice unless it abided by church teachings. A feature of Protestantism is that it contains within it that which could start it in the opposite direction. One end of it is open to Catholicism; the other to lack of faith entirely. The old man and the child can both receive inspiration and tell the truth.

Works: None.

July 21, 1962 (p. 484; 2 par.): From ANDALUSIA. Mononucleosis is not something Dr. Fulghum recommends their having around since it is infectious. They are sorry to say, in that case, that they should see him not now but perhaps three months from now. He should consult with a new doctor about his being around Jenny as well.

Works: None.

December 17, 1962 (p. 502; 2 par.): From ANDALUSIA. They hope they will get to see him and his family. She hopes Andrew will enjoy his first Christmas. A woman they both know fills herself with theories, which are worse than Furies.

Works: None.

February 23, 1963 (p. 509; 3 par.): From ANDALUSIA. Since they have not heard from them in such a long time, she is writing to see how they are. They made it through Georgia's winter. How is Regina's godchild? She hopes he is working hard on the Ph.D. and can then not worry about knowing anything for the rest of his days after that.

Works: None.

May 18, 1963 (p. 521; 2 par.): From ANDALUSIA. Regina thanks him for the card. At the moment, she is haying. She has been stung by a couple of wasps and slammed her hand in a car door, but she still runs the place. Recently they had Minna Berg and Father Paul over for lunch. They had a cake for Father's birthday. The talked about him and showed Minna pictures of Andrew and Jenny, which she admired.

Works: None.

DR. T. R. SPIVEY (13 letters)   Dr. Ted Spivey taught English at Georgia State University in ATLANTA. He visited O'Connor to tell her how much he admired her work, and so began a correspondence. *Pages*: HB: 294, 296, 299, 303, 330, 334, 336, 341, 345, 360, 381, 387, 506.

Letters

September 9, 1958 (p. 294; 2 par.):   From ANDALUSIA. She has read a book he might be interested in; it is called *Israel and Revelation* by Eric Voegelin. She hopes he will stop by again when he is in the area because she enjoyed his visit.

Works: None.

September 28, 1958 (p. 296; 5 par.):   From ANDALUSIA. *Diary of a Country Priest* is the Bernanos novel. The German theologians are Romano Guardini and Karl Adam. *The Lord* is Guardini's most well-known work. She has not seen another called *The End of the Modern World*. He writes often of FYODOR DOSTOYEVSKY. She encloses an article about Gabriel Marcel. *The Mystery of Being,* his Gifford lectures, are accessible. His notebooks are beyond her. She has not yet read the *Torchbook Eckhart*. She wants to read Baron von Hügel's *The Mysteical Element in Religion* about St. Catherine of Genoa. She has just completed *Literature and Belief* by M. Jarrett-Kerr. His view is that the best Catholic novel is *The Betrothed* by Manzoni. Voegelin is not Catholic.

Works: None.

October 19, 1958 (p. 299; 4 par.):   From ANDALUSIA. She would have to read Gabriel Marcel again to know whether or not she agrees with Spivey's assessment. The story is more about knowing oneself than it is conversion. The way of the world since the 18th century has broken people's sense of religion and the Holy Spirit. The power of God

to do things such as the Incarnation and Resurrection seems to be unbelieved. Everything must be reduced and understood on a human level.

Works: None.

November 16, 1958 (p. 303; 7 par.):   From ANDALUSIA. She is grateful for the Buber book, *The Eclipse of God.* She discusses Guardini and Spivey's impressions as well as her thoughts so far on Bernanos's *Diary of a Country Priest.* She also discusses Pascal, the Jansenist influence in the church and in Irish fiction. She is reading Pasternak and quotes from *Dr. Zhivago,* "Art has two constants, two unending concerns: it always meditates on death and thus creates life. All great, genuine art resembles and continues the Revelation of St. John" (qtd. on 305). She is pleased he has dropped both the prefix Miss and Dr.

Works: None.

April 26, 1959 (p. 330; 5 par.):   From ANDALUSIA. She advises him on a girl he has written to her about. She says she seems to be young and not well taught. She needs an adviser, and any confessor will do for that job; difficulties are not talked over in the confessional. A Catholic college probably would not be good for her since the nuns are not savvy about the ways of the world, especially for someone who has had problems that are of the world. There are bad Catholics, just like anyone else. The girl most likely sees more ignorance than sin. She can send her a copy of Baron von Hügel's letters to his niece if she might like to read them. He seems to reach many American Catholics. She had a pleasant time at Vanderbilt.

Works: None.

May 25, 1959 (p. 334; 4 par.):   From ANDALUSIA. He needs to ignore some of Baron von Hügel's endearments to his niece and not consider this his most serious work. However, it does give his impressions of women's education. A new book on TEILHARD DE CHARDIN's thought will be out next month. Her editor knew him for a month and thought highly of him. She is enjoying a book, *The Disinherited Mind* by Erich Heller, which contains essays on Goethe, Nietzsche, Rilke, Spengler, FRANZ KAFKA, and others. She knows very little about the literature of Germany.

She read "A Good Man Is Hard to Find" at Wesleyan the week before last. One of the teachers asked about the significance of the Misfit's hat and its color of black. He thought he represented Christ. She said no, he did not, and his hat is black because many men in rural Georgia were black hats.

Works: "A Good Man Is Hard to Find."

June 21, 1959 (p. 336; 4 par.): From ANDALUSIA. It seems dreadful that he has decided to read the beat writers. She has not read the article in PR. They know they should escape materialism but seem to lack a discipline about what to run toward. Finding oneself in the path of Grace requires giving of oneself, self-denial. The beat poets are too self-consciously poets. They need to look the part, apparently. She is writing a review of a book on Zen and Japanese culture. Zen is similar to Christianity without the church, Christ, law, and dogma. Catholics think of the church as the body of Christ continuing throughout time. It is a "divine institution"; if not, it may just as well be an Elks Club.

Works: None.

July 18, 1959 (p. 341; 4 par.): From ANDALUSIA. It is perhaps natural to want to go to the wilderness; however, one should not desire to begin life again. She has seen it said that Protestants look for goodness and the Catholics truth, but she accepts this as only partly true. It is easier for a Catholic to comprehend the position of the atheist than the Protestant but less difficult to love the Protestant than the atheist. She has completed her novel and sent it to her publisher. It revolves around a baptism and will probably disgust a number of artsy people.

Works: [*The Violent Bear It Away*].

August 19, 1959 (p. 345; 6 par.): From ANDALUSIA. She can try to answer his questions, but she answers from her opinion, which should not

be taken for Catholic doctrine. She attempts to explain what Catholics believe in, that is, what the church teaches about morality and faith. Learning about Catholicism means learning about the sacraments, the central one of which is the Eucharist. All Catholics are capable of sin, even the pope, who also goes to confession like everybody else. The sacraments help us try to keep the two commandments of loving God and one's neighbor as oneself. There might be times when the Catholic goes about his rituals routinely, almost mechanically. However, this is better than having no habits at all, and grace may enter at any time, even those times.

Nuns rarely if ever lie. His friend may be responding to those who are innocent and ignorant of the world. She has been in the church 34 years and known many nuns and never known one to lie deliberately. It takes a special person to be a priest, so the neurotic priests his friends sees are probably more overworked than neurotic. They could have better educations.

The church was not promised to be infallible in matters of politics, so it makes mistakes. The church only seems to oppose governments that pretend to be religions, such as communism. This is the reason it would oppose it, not because it does not like the form of government, per se. The church has associated itself with gangsters and others at times when it has been to its benefit and other times not. Protestants make the frequent charge of saying that the Catholic Church is too authoritative, then they criticize it when it does not show enough authority on issues they think it should. The same thing with its members—Catholics are blamed when they do not think alike politically but believe so much the same spiritually.

Works: None.

November 30, 1959 (p. 360; 6 par.): From ANDALUSIA. She should not have put the word merely in front of spiritual, as though diminishing it. It was messy writing on her part. She means spirit without a material aspect, not spirit as less than. She writes about how FRANÇOIS MAURIAC says that books and knowledge are good and "reflect the Creator" (360). She will stay awake for anything similar to his statement of her hiding in the church; however, she does not see this for herself. She wants her soul to be saved but views this as a long process that includes Purgatory, and for now she is most interested not in becoming a saint but in living in the here and now. She has not yet read *The Phenomenon of Man* by Père TEILHARD DE CHARDIN but knows that it has been criticized by Jesuits, so it cannot be wholeheartedly representative of their thinking. She hopes she will see him in December.

Works: None.

March 16, 1960 (p. 381; 7 par.): From ANDALUSIA. She appreciates his comments on the novel. She can take any negative comments he may have and would like to hear them since she values his thinking. There has been a response to the title that people think it comes from the Old Testament. They are Christ's words, but that does not seem to make a difference once people know. She has finished the book by Jung. She admires him. She recommends two other books—Dominican Victor White's *God and the Unconscious* and *Religion and the Psychology of Jung* by a Belgian Jesuit. She likes how Goldbrunner uses Jung.

   She can agree with Jung's points about penance and taking the sins of the world as one's own because this is the same as what she has been taught by the church. When Jung takes on the church, his arguments stoop too low to be taken seriously and show ignorance about the church. Jung is now old, and this may be his last book. It has a pleading quality to it as though he is asking the world to save itself before it is too late. TEILHARD DE CHARDIN and Jung would have had much to talk about with each other.

Works: *The Violent Bear It Away*.

April 9, 1960 (p. 387; 7 par.): From ANDALUSIA. She does not think he is being unfair to her in his comments about her developmental stages. He misses much in her book because of the difference in how they view the Eucharist. The two

most important symbols in the book are water and bread that is Christ. "This book is a very minor hymn to the Eucharist" (387). Water and fire are symbols of purification; water is given by God; fire we bring on ourselves. The story of the novel is Tarwater's selfishness against the lake as the baptismal font and the bread.

   She defends the church in relation to Jung just as fairly as he criticizes it. This is not the only thing she gets out of Jung, however. His friend is incorrect in the suggestion that she is more interested in method than story. From his comments on TEILHARD DE CHARDIN's *The Phenomenon of Man*, she is not sure they have read the same book. It is not about animals; it is about development. He is a scientist. His love of nature would be better explored in his autobiography, not in this book. She is sending him a book by a Frenchman, C. Tremontant, about Teilhard's thought.

   She was in ATLANTA and met two friends of his but did not get their names. She also went to the Grant Park Zoo with a friend who wanted to see the cyclorama. She saw the apes but was too tired from events to give the zoo much energy. She sends Easter greetings.

Works: [*The Violent Bear It Away*].

January 27, 1963 (p. 506; 7 par.): From ANDALUSIA. He has figured out her intention in writing "The Lame Shall Enter First." His analysis pleases her. She does not agree with some of his criticisms of *The Violent Bear* and speaks about these by page and detail. Old Tarwater sees people condemned by themselves; Tarwater gets away from the Devil by taking on his role as a prophet. In the story, Sheppard purchased the telescope when Rufus came and for his benefit, not his son's.

   As to where to submit the article, she suggests *South Atlantic* since he knows someone on staff there, or *The Georgia Review*, or *The SEWANEE REVIEW*.

   She and Jack Hawkes have different views of and uses for the Devil in their fiction. She has known him a long time, and they have discussed this at length.

She appreciates his writing the article and knowing that someone understands her work. She hopes to see him when he travels their way again.

Works: ["The Lame Shall Enter First"], *The Violent Bear It Away.*

RICHARD STERN (two letters) O'Connor met Stern during her visit to give a reading at the University of Chicago in 1959. In her correspondence with him, she often playfully adopted the persona of a southern hick writing to a northern academic. *Pages* HB: 532, 573.

Letters

July 27, 1963 (p. 532; 2 par.): From ANDALUSIA. He needs to come to Georgia to write and not think about anywhere else. Does he want to be known as a writer who publishes one novel per year? She takes seven years to write one and wants to keep it that way. He is showing up writers like her, and he ought to examine his conscience.

Works: None.

[April 14, 1964] (p. 573; 4 par.): From ANDALUSIA. He is doing better than she in keeping up a schedule of work. She has only written a few letters so far this year. She writes that spring is gone, replaced by summer. The Muscovy duck and swans are around the yard; the PEACOCKS make noise. One day he will come to the South to teach. She may catch up to his production since he is working more slowly. She thinks of him often among the intellectuals of the chilly North.

Works: None.

THOMAS STRITCH (11 letters) Stritch was a friend of O'Connor who taught at Notre Dame. *Pages:* HB: 231, 324, 388, 448, 472, 482, 523, 527, 562, 564, 588.

Letters

August 1, 1957 (p. 231; 1 par.): From ANDALUSIA. Writers are now writing for television and do not pay attention to the existence of the South

and its dialects. She was the least important guest at a recent conference that drew more attention for the agent who sold *Gone With the Wind* to Hollywood and a panel on the "Religious Market" featuring two large South Georgia poets. An old man who was the only male there stopped the show at each meeting and was the only bright spot. He quoted from Dickens and the Bible.

Works: None.

March 28, 1959 (p. 324; 2 par.): From ANDALUSIA. She will save her money and not travel. She has purchased a good chair and is considering an electric typewriter. She bought a five-bedroom house out of her Ford Foundation money some years ago that pays $55.00 a month now. She has completed her new novel. It is called *The Violent Bear It Away* after Matthew 11:12.

Works: The Violent Bear It Away.

April, 1960 (p. 388; 1 par.): From ANDALUSIA. She is glad to hear he likes the book. Even though some do and others do not, it is particularly pleasant for her to know he is among those who do like it. She thinks Christians may know her name as an author now as a result of this book.

Works: [*The Violent Bear It Away*].

September 14, 1961 (p. 448; 2 par.): From ANDALUSIA. He should see her swans. If he arranges a reading at Notre Dame for her, she asks that she not have to fly there from Chicago. Her condition has made her use only the least complicated means of travel. She does not know newer German theologians but only Guardini and Adam. She does enjoy Père TEILHARD DE CHARDIN. She got the title of her next story collection from him, "Everything That Rises Must Converge."

Works: "Everything That Rises Must Converge."

May 7, 1962 (p. 472; 3 par.): From ANDALUSIA. She enjoyed talking with him and the visit to Notre Dame. Her mother wants to know about construction matters there, and she is to find out about it if she goes back in June. Her mother met her with a wheelchair that made her feel like 102 years old.

Works: None.

July 3, 1962 (p. 482; 2 par.):   From ANDALUSIA. She hopes he is enjoying himself. Her honorary degree has so far gotten her nothing locally. Her mother wrapped the hood in newspaper and put it away, where it will probably stay.

Works: None.

June 14, 1963 (p. 523; 4 par.):   From ANDALUSIA. She would like to go to the race at Indianapolis, but the crowds will force her to stay home and watch the race on television. She watches the daily sports reports. She advises him that if he has written three drafts of his profile of the cardinal and is still not happy with it, he has a lack of patience and not energy. She lacks energy but is full of patience with herself. They will be happy to see him come visit whenever he is able.

Works: None.

July 4, 1963 (p. 527; 2 par.):   From ANDALUSIA. She writes to him on the Fourth of July, even though she does not normally celebrate it, in order to take a break from her work, which sometimes makes her tired. Their workman, Shot, said he had a cousin's funeral to go to, but they discovered that he and his friends are barbecuing a goat. Regina gave him a speech about not believing the tale about the cousin in order to get time off. The creep-feeder is not working. Regina tells her that the peachickens have eaten $17.50 worth of calf feed, and now Flannery has to pay for half of the feed. KATHERINE ANNE PORTER sent her a review of the French edition of *A Good Man* that describes her as living on a large estate with many animals.

Works: A Good Man Is Hard to Find.

January 22, 1964 (p. 562; 1 par.):   From ANDALUSIA. She did not buy the record player but bought a pair of swans instead. The nuns gave her their old record player after they received a new one for Christmas. The player makes a

popcorn sound that she is told may be dust, but she does not see any dirt anywhere on it, and it works fine for her.

Works: None.

February 11, 1964 (p. 564; 2 par.):   From ANDALUSIA She did not know that Regina would enjoy the record player as much as she does, or she would have tried to get them one sooner. They received the records he has sent and have been making their way down the stack. She is listening to music now for the first time since she left YADDO. She likes that which goes up and down rather than those that slide around. The swans have also arrived. Father Ginder called her from Pennsylvania and asked her how to get his peafowl out of the trees. She did not know how to help, so he may leave them there and buy more, which proves her mother's point that priests have no concept of money.

Works: None.

June 28, 1964 (p. 588; 2 par.):   From ANDALUSIA. She writes to him on her electric typewriter. She works about two hours a day on doctor's orders. He said she can work but not exert herself, and she is not sure yet what that means. She signed a contract with FS&G for a story collection and hopes to rewrite some of them now that she feels better. She was willing to let the publisher gather the stories to prevent Regina from having to do it, but now she thinks she may do some revision anyway, though it will make the book come out later. She enjoys the records, which she listens to when she is not working. The peafowl seem to sing along with the four-hand Chopin piano piece.

Works: [*Everything That Rises Must Converge*].

CAROLINE GORDON TATE (four letters)   Gordon was a writer and teacher. The Fitzgeralds suggested that O'Connor send her manuscript of *Wise Blood* to Gordon for comments on a revision before sending it to Harcourt, Brace. Gordon's comments hit O'Connor as prescient and worthwhile, and she respected her opinion from then on. She provided an important link for O'Connor with the literary world in the crucial time when she first had to return to MILLEDGEVILLE. *Pages:* HB: 257, 305, 331, 454.

Letters

December 10, 1957 (p. 257; 4 par.): From ANDA-LUSIA. She is working with the Holy Spirit, making him a waterstain. She appreciates Caroline's comments on the story and is using them in her revision. She hopes to have another revision completed for her review after Christmas. She is on a new medicine that has made her dizzy. Dr. Gossett has just returned from a Modern Language Association conference where he heard Willard Thorpe give a paper on Southern Literature and the GROTESQUE. She asks Caroline to pray for her so that she may be able to endure the upcoming trip and invites her to visit the farm and find out for herself why she never wants to leave.

Works: ["An Enduring Chill"].

November 16, 1958 (p. 305; 2 par.): From ANDA-LUSIA. She is glad Caroline said positive things about *Wise Blood*. She assumes Caroline has received a copy of *Critique*. She makes a couple of corrections about details from the novel that Caroline should correct before the introduction to the novel that she is writing. The doctor is allowing O'Connor to walk for short bouts around the room without crutches since, he says, her bones are recalcifying. This is God's work, whether at LOURDES or not.

Works: [*Wise Blood*].

May 10, 1959 (p. 331; 5 par.): From ANDALUSIA. She discusses ROBERT LOWELL's self-hospitalization. Robert Giroux thinks it best that Lowell did it himself. She is eager to see Caroline's book. She is working on the middle of her novel, changing it. She likes Ashley's book about *The Malefactors*. She is glad to hear about M. Coindreau and has some newspaper clippings to give to him.

Works: [*The Violent Bear It Away*].

November 16, 1961 (p. 454; 4 par.): From ANDA-LUSIA. They met Caroline's friend Father Charles at the monastery. She was surprised to see that

Abbot had invited her cousin, Msgr. O'Connor, whom she had not seen in 30 years. Caroline's work for the monks means a lot to them. Father Paul was picking up a kiln; they will be doing pottery. She is nearly done with the story Caroline looked at earlier ["The Lame Shall Enter First"]. Her swans are Polish swans. She encloses pictures of herself, as requested.

Works: ["The Lame Shall Enter First"].

JAMES TATE (one letter) Tate and Mary Barbara, his wife, were MILLEDGEVILLE friends of O'Connor's who attended the Wednesday night group meetings at ANDALUSIA. Tate was in Iceland on military duty at the time of this letter. *Page:* HB: 426.

Letter

January 15, 1961 (p. 426; 5 par.) From MILLED-GEVILLE. FOC sends greetings to Tate in Iceland, telling him that she envisions him wearing his baby-blue parka. The Wednesday group had not been meeting lately because of her condition. She writes about one of their members giving talks at Civil War historical gatherings and how local historian Katherine Scott is not pleased that an Englishman is doing this work when someone from town would do just as well. Maryat Lee was in town over Christmas and wore strange clothes made by a costume designer to parties given by people from the college. FOC was given *Remembrance of Things Past* for Christmas and is making her way through it. She recommends it to Tate. Her mother and she look forward to his return to the States and to his fishing at ANDALUSIA.

Works: None.

FURTHER READING

Andretta, Helen R. "A Thomist's Letters to 'A.'" *Flannery O'Connor Bulletin* 26–27 (1998–2000): 52–72.

Arnold, Marilyn. "Sentimentalism in the Devil's Territory." In *Flannery O'Connor and the Christian Mystery*, edited by John J. Murphy, et al., 243–258. Provo, Utah: Center for the Study of Christian Values in Literature, Brigham Young University, 1997.

Babinec, Lisa S. "Cyclical Patterns of Domination and Manipulation in Flannery O'Connor's Mother-Daughter Relationships." *Flannery O'Connor Bulletin* 19 (1990): 9–29.

Baumgaertner, Jill P. "'The Meaning Is in You': Flannery O'Connor in Her Letters." *Christian Century* 23–30 (December 1987): 1172–1176.

Beasley, David. "Flannery O'Connor Compels Scholars, Fan." *Atlanta Journal and Constitution* (17 June 1984): 2C.

Beaver, Harold. "A Southern Diptych: Faulkner and O'Connor." *The Great American Masquerade*. Totowa, N.J.: Barnes and Noble, 1985. pp. 175–195.

Beeching, Paul Q. "Same Belfry, Different Bats." *National Catholic Reporter* (July 18, 1986): 9.

Behrendt, Stephen C. "Knowledge and Innocence in Flannery O'Connor's 'The River.'" *Studies in American Fiction* 17, no. 2 (1989): 143–155.

Brinkmeyer, Robert H., Jr. "A Closer Walk with Thee: Flannery O'Connor and the Southern Fundamentalists," *Southern Literary Journal* 18, no. 2 (Spring 1986): 3–13.

Ficken, Carl, "Theology in Flannery O'Connor's *The Habit of Being*," *Christianity and Literature* 30, no. 2 (Winter 1981): 51–63.

McGill, Robert, "The Life You Write May Be Your Own: Epistolary Autobiography and the Reluctant Resurrection of Flannery O'Connor," *Southern Literary Journal* 36, no. 2 (Spring 2004): 31–46.

Nichols, Loxley F. "Flannery O'Connor's 'Intellectual Vaudeville': Masks of Mother and Daughter," *Studies in the Literary Imagination* 20, no. 2 (Fall 1987): 15–29.

Westling, Louise. "Flannery O'Connor's Revelations to 'A,'" *Southern Humanities Review* 20, no. 1 (Winter 1986): 15–22.

PART III

Related People,
Places, and Topics

A

Accent The magazine was the first to publish O'Connor's fiction with the short story "The Geranium" in the summer 1946 issue (vol. VI). O'Connor had also sent the journal "The Crop," mailing both stories from Currier Graduate House, State University of Iowa at Iowa City on February 7, 1946. "The Geranium" was accepted in March.

America The Jesuit journal where the essay "The Church and the Fiction Writer" was published on March 30, 1957. Friend and spiritual counselor, Father Robert M. McCown, S. J., recommended O'Connor as a writer to Harold Gardiner, S. J., literary editor. Gardiner invited O'Connor to write a piece for the periodical but then infuriated her by editing one paragraph of it before it was published. O'Connor believed that the changed section altered her meaning for readers. The weekly magazine was founded by American Jesuits in 1909 and is still in circulation. Its offices are located in New York City.

American Scholar, The The periodical published O'Connor's review of *The Phenomenon of Man* by PIERRE TEILHARD DE CHARDIN (Harper, 1959) in the fall 1961 issue (vol. 30, no. 4). It is the only review by her to be published in a secular publication. In the review, she writes that the "work demands the attention of scientist, theologian, and poet" (qtd. in Martin 129). Teilhard's book "is a

scientific expression of what the poet attempts to do: penetrate matter until spirit is revealed in it" (130). *The American Scholar* is a scholarly journal published by the Phi Beta Kappa Society and is still in circulation.

See also: TEILHARD DE CHARDIN, PIERRE.

Andalusia O'Connor lived and worked at the farm called Andalusia four miles northwest of MILLEDGEVILLE, GEORGIA, from 1951 until her death in 1964. When she first arrived back in Milledgeville under the care of her mother for LUPUS, O'Connor lived at her mother's family home on Greene Street. Her uncles Louis and Bernard Cline owned the farm. Once O'Connor's health stabilized, she and her mother moved to the farm in March 1951. Several reasons have been theorized as to why. The most prevalent is that the physical layout of the farmhouse was more conducive to Flannery's condition and limitations at the time. The Cline house on Greene Street had several stairways and a circuitous floor plan, and O'Connor could not climb stairs when she first came home from the hospital. In addition, O'Connor's Aunt Katie was in a wheelchair that necessitated use of the only downstairs bedroom. Also, by moving to the farm, Regina and Flannery could set up a lifestyle that freed them of the influence of Regina's sisters, Mary and Katie, which would allow Flannery the privacy and space in which to work.

The main house at Andalusia, O'Connor's farm in Milledgeville, Georgia, where she lived and worked from 1951 until her death in 1964. The bulk of her writing was completed here, and the farm was often an inspirational, at times even literal, setting in many of her short stories. *(Courtesy of The Flannery O'Connor Andalusia Foundation)*

Though it was not in her family then, the land existing as a farm predates O'Connor's time by several generations into the mid-19th century. At that time, the property now known as Andalusia and several acres surrounding it was owned by Joseph and Mary Pleasant "Polly" Stovall. Though it appears that the Stovalls lived in town, the property seems to have been a 1,500–1,700-acre plantation, complete with slave labor. After Polly Stovall died, the land was sold at public auction in 1855. Nathan Hawkins, a three-term mayor of Milledgeville, purchased it for $6.00/acre. Hawkins also served in the state legislature. In 1860, he was one of the richest men in Baldwin County, one of four landowners who documented more than 100 slaves among his property. The main house was probably constructed in the late 1850s by the Hawkins family.

After Hawkins died in 1870, 1,700 acres was recorded as being sold to Kentuckian, Col. Thomas Johnson of Lexington County. A smaller tract of the land was kept for the use of Anna Hawkins, Nathan's second wife, and this is believed to be roughly the boundaries of the current holding. The next owner of the land was Madison A. McCraw of Milledgeville, who purchased it in 1905.

In 1930, Mrs. Alice E. McCraw died intestate, and Hugh T. Cline was designated to dispense with the property. The 1,700 acres of land was divided into halves; one half was set aside to settle with Judge Allen. The other half was subdivided into three lots of approximately 200–300 acres each. Cline sold one lot to his brother, Dr. Bernard T. Cline in 1931; a McCraw relative sold another lot to Bernard Cline in 1933.

Bernard called his farm Sorrel Farm, named after the light reddish-brown horses he kept there. He hired workers to maintain the farm and acquired some other land to the north of the section he owned. He sent his sister, Regina, to ATLANTA to be trained as a bookkeeper so that she might be able to do the accounting of the farm's business. In 1947, while Flannery was at graduate school at the UNIVERSITY OF IOWA, Dr. Cline died, leaving the land, the house, and surrounding buildings to his other brother, Louis Cline, and their sister, Regina Cline O'Connor.

Louis Cline lived and worked in ATLANTA and tended to the farm's concerns in Milledgeville primarily on the weekends. Through a chance meeting on a bus with descendants of previous owners in 1946, O'Connor learned that during the 19th century, the farm used to go by the name of *Andalusia*. The name, with the spelling *Andalucia*, is a province in southern Spain. O'Connor wrote to her mother, who passed the name by Dr. Cline, who liked it. From that time on, the farm has been called by that name. Regina worked the farm as a dairy farmer, and since her brother stayed in Atlanta, she ran the business with the help of hired workers, such as Jack and Louise Hill and their boarder, Willie "Shot" Manson. The image of the woman farmer in several of O'Connor's stories takes its inspiration from the author's mother.

The 544-acre Andalusia property contains hills, hayfields, pastures, natural and developed ponds for livestock, and woodlands once used for selective timbering. Tobler Creek runs through it. The farm buildings exist on about 21 acres of the property and are made up of the main house, the Hill house, a main barn, shed for equipment, shed for processing milk, smaller barn, Nail House (a garage), water tower, well/storage house, horse stable, pump house, and three houses for tenant farmers. Visitors to the farm are not only O'Connor enthusiasts. The site is of interest to historians, archaeologists, and naturalists who study the wildlife living on the lands.

Andalusia is identified with O'Connor not only because she wrote the bulk of her life's work there but also because the farm serves as the direct or inspirational setting for many of her short stories. Most scholars agree that the longer story, "The Displaced Person," is the one most identifiable with the farm. Several other stories, however, feature a woman and a daughter living on a farm with hired help. While many of these fictional farm women appear to be struggling financially, Regina O'Conner was a successful businesswoman. She may have shared some of the same sentiments about people, life, and the difficulties of maintaining the farm as O'Connor's characters.

Atlanta, Georgia   As the other major city in the state along with SAVANNAH, Atlanta played a part in O'Connor's life, though she was never a fan of the city. In the summer of 1937, when she was 12 years old and living in Savannah, her mother enrolled her in a summer reading course at the Atlanta Public Library. The certificate indicating that she completed the program is part of her papers at the Georgia College and State University. O'Connor biographer, Jean Cash, notes that she and her mother stayed with a relative in the city while the girl completed the program. Notes from Flannery and her mother thanking the relative are archived at the Woodruff Library at Emory University.

The author also lived for a short time in Atlanta as a child in 1938. Early that year, her father, Edward O'Connor, accepted a position in the city with the Federal Housing Administration as a real-estate appraiser. The family lived at 2525 Potomac Street, N. E. O'Connor enrolled at the parochial school of St. Joseph's Church, where she completed the remainder of her seventh-grade year. Neither she nor her mother enjoyed living in Atlanta and had trouble adjusting. By the start of Flannery's fall term, they moved to MILLEDGEVILLE to the Cline ancestral home on Greene Street. Edward stayed

in Atlanta living in the rooming house, Bell House, where Regina's brothers, Dr. Bernard and Louis Cline, lived for a few years. Edward visited his family in Milledgeville on weekends. He left Atlanta and went to Milledgeville when his LUPUS became so severe that he needed to retire from the FHA.

O'Connor's health was treated in Atlanta by internist Dr. Arthur J. Merrill in the fateful year of 1951 when she first came home from living with the Fitzgeralds in Connecticut. Merrill diagnosed lupus to the family physician in Milledgeville and treated O'Connor at Emory University Hospital in Atlanta in February 1951. There she was given blood transfusions and massive ACTH injections. While in the hospital, O'Connor continued to work on the manuscript for *Wise Blood* by hand at the same time that Dr. Merrill was warning Regina that her daughter may die. She left the Emory University Hospital in March 1951 to move with her mother to ANDALUSIA.

In her adult life, O'Connor gave several lectures in Atlanta. On December 1, 1955, she spoke at the annual meeting of the Georgia Writers' Association on "Some Problems of the Southern Writer." On March 16, 1956, she addressed the Georgia Council of Teachers of English there, where her topic was "The Georgia Writer and His Country." On January 11, 1957, she took part in the Emory University Community Education Service adult education program titled "How the Writer Writes." The program featured a different visiting writer each week who spoke to adult students throughout the semester. Her essay "The Nature and Aim of Fiction" likely contains material from her presentation. In a letter to Maryat Lee before her talk, she indicated that she would be telling the students in her conclusion that it is as good to not write as it is to write, implying that admitting when one does not have talent is wise.

awards   O'Connor won several awards during her career as a writer, and a few notable prizes were given to her posthumously. Many of the awards she received during her lifetime involved grant money or fellowships that covered her expenses at the time she was writing. Other prizes were awarded for the writing itself, such as the O. HENRY AWARD for the year's best short story.

Among O'Connor's awards, honors, and other distinctions were: Scholarship in journalism to the State UNIVERSITY OF IOWA (1945); English Department fellowship (1946); Rinehart-Iowa Fiction Award for a first novel competition (1947); an invitation to attend the YADDO artists' colony in Saratoga Springs, New York (1948); a fellowship at Iowa (1948); KENYON REVIEW fellowship (1952); second prize O. Henry Award for "The Life You Save May Be Your Own," (1953); *Kenyon Review* Fellow (1954); first-prize story in the O. Henry Awards for "Greenleaf" (1956); National Institute of Arts and Letters grant (1957); Ford Foundation Grant (1959); honorary Doctor of Letters, Saint Mary's, women's college of Notre Dame (1962);

first prize O. Henry Award for "Everything That Rises Must Converge" (1962); honorary degree from Smith College (1963); and a first prize O. Henry Award for "Revelation," (1964).

Prizes awarded to O'Connor's work since her death include the National Book Award in 1972 for *Flannery O'Connor: The Complete Stories*. This award is rarely given posthumously, but the work was considered so outstanding that it was honored. *The Habit of Being: Letters*, edited by her friend Sally Fitzgerald, received a National Book Critics Circle Special Award for 1979.

O'Connor depended on some of her grant and fellowship money in part to pay for books and medical expenses such as blood transfusions and ACTH.

B

Bishop, Elizabeth (1911–1979) *American poet and short-story writer* Born in Massachusetts, Bishop was schooled at Vassar College and spent much of her adult life traveling and living in South America. Her work often appeared in *The New Yorker*. She was the poetry consultant to the Library of Congress (in the position now called Poet Laureate) from 1949 to 1950. Her *North & South: A Cold Spring* (1955) won the Pulitzer Prize. She taught writing at Harvard from 1970 to 1977. Among her works are: *The Complete Poems* (1969); *Brazil* (1962); and *Questions of Travel* (1965). As a New Englander who frequently wrote about the Tropics, Bishop did not attract the attention of O'Connor until the poet initiated a correspondence with her in 1957.

ROBERT LOWELL once showed O'Connor a photograph of Bishop sitting on a porch in Florida. She tells this to Bishop in her response to Bishop's first letter in which the poet tells O'Connor how much she admires her work. They also know the Fitzgeralds in common, and she tells Bishop that Robert always spoke of her favorably (HB 198). Though she never visited ANDALUSIA at O'Connor's invitations, she did call the writer once from aboard a frighter in SAVANNAH when they docked there unexpectedly on a trip to Brazil (HB 248).

The two exchanged letters several times. In 1958, O'Connor replied to Bishop, thanking her for the copy of *The Diary of Helena Morley* (1957), which O'Connor said she and her mother both enjoyed.

O'Connor adds Bishop to the list of writers whom she would like Robert Giroux to be sure to get review copies of *The Violent Bear It Away* (HB 353). Bishop once sent her an altar (that she mistakenly called a crucifix) in a bottle that she purchased on one of her trips to South America (HB 518–19).

book reviews In addition to writing fiction, essays, lectures, and letters, O'Connor was a frequent and regular book reviewer who wrote approximately 12 reviews per year for nearly a decade. Between 1956 and 1964 when she died, she reviewed 143 titles in 120 distinct reviews. The majority of these articles appeared in *The BULLETIN*, the Catholic diocesan paper of Georgia, but others appeared in *The SOUTHERN CROSS* and *The AMERICAN SCHOLAR*. Among the types of works she reviewed, 50 were religious and homiletic, 21 were biographies and lives of the saints, and 19 were sermons and theology. She reviewed not only religious titles but also 17 works of fiction, eight of literary criticism, six related to psychology, four history, four collections of letters, four periodicals, three intellectual history and criticism titles, and one work of art criticism.

Readers often ask why O'Connor spent so much time reviewing the work of others, especially for smaller circulation periodicals such as Catholic diocesan papers. The papers were not particularly known for journalistic rigor or even for good writing, and they certainly had no other writers of her stature on staff. Carter W. Martin, who edited a collection of her reviews called *The Presence of Grace*, contends that O'Connor took on the task as a kind of charitable mission for her fellow Catholics: "She chose this means, and took it as a charitable duty, to raise the level of Catholic intellectual life by speaking not to theologians, Jesuits, and priests, but to the ordinary layman, to all the Mrs. McIntyres, who (in "The Displaced Person") are embarrassed if Christ becomes part of the conversation" (4).

Among the common themes that recur in the reviews are O'Connor's advocacy of freedom of thought among Catholics (while maintaining a concern for orthodoxy), and a desire to open up the church's policies involving Catholics' explorations of art and the Bible. She treats both Protestant and Catholic works with an equally balanced critical eye.

Reading O'Connor's reviews of titles of the day that were of interest to the church gives important insight into her aesthetics, her views about certain subjects (including the work of her fellow Catholic fiction writers), her theology, and personal spirituality. Scholars are also interested in the reviews because they provide evidence of the volume and wide range of O'Connor's reading and the timing of that reading in relation to her own writing and publications.

Several book reviews that were unpublished in her lifetime exist in O'Connor's papers. The reviews have since been published in the collection *The Presence of Grace*. They include: *How to Read a Novel*, by Caroline Gordon (Viking, 1957); *Religion and the Psychology of Jung*, by Raymond Hostie, translated by G. R. Lamb (Sheed & Ward, 1959); *Joseph, Son of David*, by Sister Emily Joseph, C. S. J. (St. Anthony's Guild Press, 1961); *Reason and Revelation in the Middle Ages*, by Étienne Gilson (Scribners, 1961); *The Christian Opportunity*, by Denis de Rougement (Holt, Rinehart & Winston, 1963); *Hear His Voice Today*, by J. Edgar Bruns, S.T.D. (Kenedy, 1963); *Zen Catholicism*, by Dom Aelred Graham (Harcourt, Brace, 1963); and *Zen Dictionary*, by Ernest Wood (Philosophical Library, 1962).

Bulletin, The   O'Connor reviewed books for this Catholic diocesan paper beginning in early 1956. In a letter to Betty Hester, she wrote that publishing in the paper represented her "first emergence into the Catholic press" (HB 137). *The Bulletin* began as a monthly publication in 1922 when the entire state was in the diocese of SAVANNAH. In 1956, it appeared every other week, a schedule it continued after a separate diocese of Atlanta was formed. Eventually, the two dioceses had new papers called *The Georgia Bulletin* (for the Diocese of Atlanta) and *The SOUTHERN CROSS* (for the Diocese of Savannah).

At first she worked with book review editor, Eileen Hall, but when Hall took a job in Florida in the summer of 1960, the future of the book review section of the paper became uncertain. A layman from Atlanta, Leo J. Zuber, who had been writing reviews for *The Bulletin* since 1949, volunteered to take over as book review editor at the paper. O'Connor doubted the success of the section after Hall's departure, considering the review section under her leadership "the most intelligent thing they had in the paper, which is pedestrian otherwise" (qtd. in Martin 2). Soon, however, she not only kept writing reviews under Zuber's editorship, but she also came to enjoy Zuber and his family as friends, who visited her at ANDALUSIA. As a tribute to O'Connor, Zuber had begun to compile her reviews into a book, but the project remained unfinished at his death in 1980. Carter W. Martin finished editing the book, which appeared as *The Presence of Grace and Other Book Reviews by Flannery O'Connor*, and was published by the University of Georgia Press in 1983.

Reading O'Connor's reviews of books of the day that were of interest to the church gives important insight into her aesthetics, her views about certain subjects (including the work of her fellow Catholic fiction writers), her theology, and personal spirituality. Scholars are also interested in the reviews because they provide evidence of the volume and wide range of O'Connor's reading and the timing of that reading in relation to her own writing and publications.

Books that O'Connor reviewed in *The Bulletin* in 1956 include: February 18?—*All Manner of Men*, edited by Riley Hughes (Kenedy, 1956); March 31—*The Presence of Grace* by J. F. Powers (Doubleday, 1956); and *The Malefactors*, by Caroline Gordon (Harcourt, Brace, 1956); April 28—*The Rosary* of Our Lady by Romano Guardini (Kenedy, 1955); May 26—*Two Portraits of St. Thérèse of Lisieux* by Étienne Robo (Regnery, 1955); June 9—*Humble Powers: Three Novelettes* by Paul Horgan (Image, 1956), June 23—*Letters from Baron Friedrich von Hügel to a Niece*, edited with an introduction by Gwendolen Greene (Regnery, 1955); July 21—*Beyond the Dreams of Avarice*, by Russell Kirk (Regnery, 1956); August 4—*In Soft Garments*, second edition, by Ronald Knox (Sheed & Ward, 1956); September 1—*The Catholic Companion to the Bible* by Ralph L. Woods (Lippincott, 1956); September 29—*The Archbishop and the Lady*, by Michael de la Bedoyere (Pantheon, 1956); and November 24—*Meditations Before Mass*, by Romano Guardini (Newman, 1955).

Reviews in 1957 include: January 5—*The Metamorphic Tradition in Modern Poetry*, by Sister Bernetta Quinn (Rutgers, 1955); January 19—*A Path Through Genesis*, by Bruce Vawter, C. M. (Sheed & Ward, 1956); *The Two-Edged Sword*, by John L. McKenzie, S. J. (Bruce, 1956); March 2—*Writings of Edith Stein*, edited and translated by Hilda Graef (Newman, 1956); April 27—*The Spirit and Forms of Protestantism*, by Rev. Louis Bouyer (Newman, 1956); May 11—*Criticism and Censorship*, by Walter F. Kerr (Bruce, 1956); June 8—*A Popular History of the Reformation*, by Philip Hughes (Hanover, 1957); God the Unknown, by Victor White, O. P. (Harper, 1956); *The Inner Search*, by Hubert Van Zeller, O. S. B. (Sheed & Ward, 1957); and *Occult Phenomena*, by Dr. Alois Wiesinger, O. C. S. O. (Newman, 1957); July 20—*The Holy Fire*, by Robert Payne (Harper, 1957); August 3—*God's Heralds* by J. C. Chaine, translated by Brendan McGrath, O. S. B. (Wagner, 1955); August 31—*Essays and Addresses on the Philosophy of Religion*, volumes 1 and 2, by Friedrich von Hügel (Dutton, 1950); October 12—*The Ordeal of Gilbert Pinfold*, by Evelyn Waugh (Little, Brown, 1957); *Give Me Possession* by Paul Horgan (Farrar, Straus & Cudahy, 1957); October 26—*Letters to Men and Women*, by François de Salignac de La Mothe Fénelon (Newman, 1957); *The Character of Man*, by Emmanuel Mounier (Harper, 1957); *Lines of Life*, by FRANÇOIS MAURIAC (Farrar, Straus & Cudahy, 1957); December 21—*St. John of the Cross*, by Bruno de Jesus Marie, O. C. D. (Sheed

& Ward, 1957); *Doctor Rabelais* by D. B. Wyndham Lewis (Sheed & Ward, 1957);

Titles reviewed in 1958 include: January 4—a series called Canterbury Books (Sheed & Ward) with the titles: *The Roots of the Reformation*, by Karl Adam; *Marriage and the Family*, by Francis J. Sheed; *Confession*, by John C. Heenan; *The Rosary*, by Maisie Ward; and *The Devil*, by Walter Farrell; February 22—*Prayer in Practice*, by Romano Guardini (Pantheon, 1957); *Come South Wind*, edited by M. L. Shrady (Pantheon, 1957); April 5—*The Meeting of Love and Knowledge*, by M. C. D'Arcy, S. J. (Harper, 1957); *The Christ of Faith*, by Karl Adam (Pantheon, 1957); May 3—*The Transgressor*, by Julian Green (Pantheon, 1957); *Painting and Reality* by Étienne Gilson (Pantheon, 1957); July 12—*Patterns in Comparative Religion*, by Mircea Eliade (Sheed & Ward, 1958); October 4—*Further Paradoxes*, by Henri de Lubac, S. J. (Newman, 1957); November 1—*American Classics Reconsidered*, edited by H. C. Gardiner, S. J. (Scribners, 1958); November 15—*Order and History*, Volume 1, Israel and Revelation, by Eric Voegelin (Louisiana State University Press, 1956); and November 29—*Late Dawn*, by Elizabeth Vandon (Sheed & Ward, 1958).

Reviews in 1959 include: January 10—*Freud and Religion*, by Gregory Zilboorg (Newman, 1958); *Temporal and Eternal*, by Charles Péguy (Harper, 1958); January 24—*The Nature of Belief*, by M. C. D'Arcy, S. J. (Herder, 1958); *Order and History*, Volume 2, The World of the Polis, by Eric Voegelin (Louisiana State University Press, 1957); February 7—*Religion and the Free Society*, by Miller, Clancy, Cobsen, Howe, and Kempner. Fund for the Republic; March 7—*Harry Vernon at Prep*, by Franc Smith (Houghton Mifflin, 1959); May 2—*Order and History*, Volume 3, Plato and Aristotle, by Eric Voegelin (Louisiana State University Press, 1958); *Christian Asceticism and Modern Man*, edited by Louis Bouyer (Philosophical Library, 1955); June 27—*Tell Me, Stranger*, by Charles B. Flood (Houghton Mifflin, 1959); July 11—*Light in Silence*, by Claude Koch (Dodd Mead, 1958); July 25—*Nine Sermons of St. Augustine on the Psalms*, translated by Father Edmund Hill (Kenedy, 1959); August 8—*The Image Industries*, by William Lynch, S. J. (Sheed &

Ward, 1959); August 22—*The World to Come,* by R. W. Gleason, S. J. (Sheed & Ward, 1959); *Faith and Understanding in America,* by Gustave Weigel, S. J. (Macmillan, 1959); October 17—*Zen and Japanese Culture,* Bollingen Series 64, second edition, by D. T. Suzuki (Pantheon, 1959); November 14—*Rosmini,* by Claude Leetham (Helicon, 1958); and December 12—*The Devil's Advocate,* by Morris L. West (Morrow, 1959).

O'Connor continued writing regular BOOK REVIEWS for *The Bulletin* into the 1960s. In 1960, her reviews included: February 6—*Jesus Christus,* by Romano Guardini (Regnery, 1959); *Mary, Mother of Faith,* by Josef Weiger (Regnery, 1959); February 20—*The Phenomenon of Man,* by PIERRE TEILHARD DE CHARDIN (Harper, 1959), which O'Connor also reviewed in the fall 1961 issue of *The* AMERICAN SCHOLAR; *Pierre Teilhard de Chardin,* by Claude Tresmontant (Helicon, 1959); April 16—*Sister Clare,* by Loretta Burrough (Hougton Mifflin, 1960); *The Pyx,* by John Buell (Farrar, Straus & Cudahy, 1959); May 14—*God's Frontier,* by J. L. M. Descalzo, S. J. (Knopf, 1959); *The Modernity of St. Augustine,* by Jean Guitton (Helicon, 1959); July 23—*The Christian Message and Myth,* by L. Malevz, S. J. (Newman, 1958); August 20—*Christ and Apollo,* by William F. Lynch, S. J. (Sheed & Ward, 1960); September 3—*The Son of Man,* by François Mauriac (World, 1960); October 1—*The Science of the Cross,* by Edith Stein (Regnery, 1960); *Beat on a Damask Drum,* by T. K. Martin (Dutton, 1960); October 15—*Pierre Teilhard de Chardin,* by Nicolas Corte (Macmillan, 1960); October 29—*Soul and Psyche,* by Victor White, O. P. (Harper, 1960); November 12—*Christian Initiation,* by Louis Bouyer (Macmillan, 1960); and December 24—*Modern Catholic Thinkers,* edited by A. Robert Caponigri (Harper, 1960).

In 1961, the reviews included: February 4—*The Divine Milieu,* by Pierre Teilhard de Chardin (Harper, 1960); March 4—*Catholics in Conversation,* by Donald McDonald (Lippincott, 1960); March 18—*The Life St. Catherine of Siena,* by Raymond of Capua (Kenedy, 1960); April 1—*Cross Currents,* edited by Joseph E. Cunneen (West Nyack, N. Y. Quarterly); May 27—*The Conversion of St. Augustine,* by Romano Guardini (New-

man, 1960); June 10—*The* CRITIC: *A Catholic Review of Books and the Arts* (Thomas More Association); *Stop Pushing,* by Dan Herr (Hanover House, 1961); June 24—*Life's Long Journey,* by Kenneth Walker (Nelson, 1961); July 22—*The Meaning of Grace,* by Charles Journet (Kenedy, 1960); August 5—*Selected Letters of Stephen Vincent Benét,* edited by Charles Fenton (Yale University Press, 1960); September 16—*The Resurrection,* by F. X. Durrwell, C. Ss. R. (Sheed & Ward, 1960); *Themes of the Bible,* by J. Guillet, S. J. (Fides, 1961); September 30—*The Mediaeval Mystics of England,* by Eric Colledge (Scribners, 1961); October 28—*Freedom, Grace, and Destiny,* by Romano Guardini (Pantheon, 1961); November 25—*The Range of Reason,* by JACQUES MARITAIN (Scribners, 1961); December 9—*The Bible and the Ancient Near East,* edited by G. E. Wright (Doubleday, 1961); *The Old Testament and Modern Study,* edited by H. H. Rowley (Oxford Paperbacks, 1961); December 23—*Teilhard de Chardin,* by Oliver Rabut, O. P. (Sheed & Ward, 1961); and *The Novelist and the Passion Story,* by F. W. Dillistone (Sheed & Ward, 1960).

Reviews in 1962 included: January 6—*Conversations with Cassandra,* by Sr. M. Madelva (Macmillan, 1961); February 3—*Talk Sense!* by Edward Gryst, S. J. (Macmillan, 1961); February 17—*Christian Faith and Man's Religion,* by Marc C. Ebersole (Crowell, 1961); *Christianity Divided,* edited by Callahan, Oberman, and O'Hanlon (Sheed & Ward, 1961); February 17—JUBILEE, edited by Edward Rice, (A. M. D. G. Publishing Co.); March 2—*The Georgia Review* (University of Georgia, Quarterly); *Evidence of Satan in the Modern World,* by Leon Christini (Macmillan, 1961); March 17—*The Conscience of Israel,* by Bruce Vawter, C. M. (Sheed & Ward, 1961); March 31—*The Victorian Vision,* by Margaret M. Maison (Sheed & Ward, 1961); May 12—*Toward the Knowledge of God,* by Claude Tresmontant (Helicon, 1961); August 4—*The Council, Reform and Reunion,* by Hans Küng (Sheed & Ward, 1961); *The Integrating Mind,* by William F. Lynch, S. J. (Sheed & Ward, 1962); August 4—*The Cardinal Spellman Story,* by Robert I. Gannon, S. J. (Doubleday, 1962); August 18—*Mystics of Our Times,* by Hilda Graef

(Hanover House, 1962); and November 24—*The Catholic in America,* by Peter J. Rahill (Franciscan Herald Press, 1961).

In 1963, O'Connor's reviews in *The Bulletin* included: July 11—*St. Vincent de Paul,* by M. V. Woodgate (Newman, 1960); *The Holiness of Vincent de Paul,* by Jacques Delarue (Kenedy, 1960); *St. Vincent de Paul,* by von Matt and Cognet (Regnery, 1960); and September 26—*Image of America,* by Norman Foerster (University of Notre Dame, 1962); *The Modern God,* by Gustave Weigel, S. J. (Macmillan, 1963).

See also: The AMERICAN SCHOLAR, BOOK REVIEWS, *The* SOUTHERN CROSS.

C

Capote, Truman (1924–1984) *American author*
A contemporary of O'Connor's, Capote was also
born in the South (New Orleans) a year before her.
He wrote short stories, wrote about his Catholicism, and attended the writer's colony, YADDO, in
the same time frame as O'Connor. He also shared
O'Connor's fascination with violence. He is most
well known for his "nonfiction novel," *In Cold
Blood* (1965) in which he describes in detail the
1959 murder of four members of a Kansas farming
family, the Clutters. His other major works include:
Other Voices, Other Rooms (1948); *The Grass Harp*
(1951); *Beat the Devil* (1954); and *Breakfast at
Tiffany's* (1958). For all their similarities, Truman
Capote and Flannery O'Connor could hardly have
been more different.

Capote became a member of the social elite
in New York City through his work for the *New
Yorker* and other publications. *Breakfast at Tiffany's* was made into a feature film starring Audrey
Hepburn, propelling Capote's fame as a writer into
the national spotlight. Though many considered
him a gifted writer, one who mingled with and
observed the rich and famous from inside their
world yet who remained determined to write about
it from a sharp objective angle on the margins, his
well-publicized eccentric and flamboyant lifestyle
began to compete with his stature a prose stylist.
His expensive parties, bold statements, drug use,
and sexual exploration in the 1950s and 1960s

kept him as a controversial figure on the national
scene.

Capote appeared to stop working on a novel
about the famous people he knew, *Answered Prayers,*
after a few sections of it appeared in ESQUIRE and
turned many of his celebrity friends against him.
The failure to complete the novel undercut, in the
minds of some, the promise he had shown earlier in
his career.

For her part, O'Connor did not mince words in
her opinion of this fellow southern Catholic writer
with whom she might have had much in common.
In 1955, she wrote to Betty Hester, "Mr. Truman
Capote makes me plumb sick" (HB 121).

cartoons Like many writers, O'Connor was also
a gifted visual artist. Her visual art took the form
of drawing and painting. There is a well-known
self-portrait of the writer and a pheasant that is frequently mistaken for a PEACOCK. Her most frequent
drawings, however, were cartoons. The cartoons
were published in student publications long before
her writing became well known.

In fact, O'Connor's first publications of any kind
were her cartoons that appeared in the PEABODY
HIGH SCHOOL's *Peabody Palladium.* In October 1942,
her work began to appear in the GEORGIA STATE
COLLEGE FOR WOMEN newspaper, *The COLONNADE.*
Many featured satires of the WAVES on campus,
marching in unison to class while other students

looked on. In 1944, she was selected to be the art editor of the college yearbook, *The* SPECTRUM. Her artwork is featured throughout, as well as on the inside of the covers of the 1944–45 edition.

O'Connor used linoleum-block prints for many of her cartoons. This involved cutting images into linoleum that was attached to wood. She then covered the image with a single color of paint and used the block to print the image on paper. The cartoons were then printed in black and white.

O'Connor drew one known wall mural during her lifetime. This appeared on the wall of the basement of Parks Hall at GSCW in what was the new campus student center. The cartoons, described by a representative of the school as "Thurber-esque," unfortunately, do not survive. The pictures were there for many years until exploding heat pipes flooded the walls, ruining the mural. The mural was painted over when the basement was renovated.

When she went to the UNIVERSITY OF IOWA, O'Connor's interest in drawing continued. She took two courses in advanced drawing, hoping that she might develop her artwork to the point that it might sell and help support her writing. She submitted cartoons to *The New Yorker* and elsewhere, but none of them were accepted. Soon afterward, she turned her attention more to her writing.

See also: The Colonnade, The SPECTRUM.

Cathedral of St. John the Baptist   Located on Lafayette Square in Savannah, Georgia, the Cathedral of St. John the Baptist is where O'Connor received the sacraments of Baptism, First Penance, First Eucharist, and Confirmation. The cathedral was first dedicated on April 30, 1876. Its architecture is of the French Gothic style with imposing nave and transepts. The main altar and four side altars are white Italian marble. In 1898, the cathedral suffered a major fire and needed to be reconstructed on the inside. It was rededicated in 1900 and has been refurbished several times since then.

The cathedral dominates Lafayette Square, where O'Connor spent her childhood. She could see the spires from her childhood home, and the trip to MASS was a short, easy walk. The bells tolling several times per day still serve as a constant reminder of the passage of time on the square.

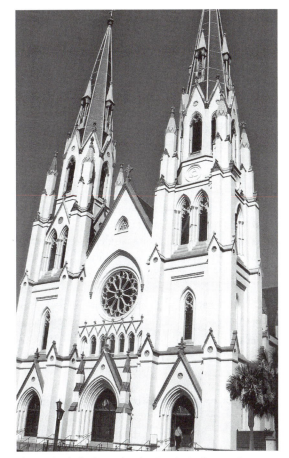

The Cathedral of St. John the Baptist in Savannah, where O'Connor was baptized and formed an early and deep connection to Roman Catholicism. O'Connor's childhood home is only a few steps away, in Lafayette Square. *(Courtesy of Ken Kirk)*

Catholicism   *See* Roman Catholicism.

Colonnade, The   *The Colonnade* was the biweekly student newspaper at GEORGIA STATE COLLEGE FOR WOMEN when O'Connor attended. It remains the name of the official student newspaper today at Georgia College & State University. During her three years at GSCW, O'Connor contributed a linoleum-block cartoon for each issue. She became art editor of the paper in November 1942 and remained in that role until she graduated in June

1945. In the 1942–43 school year alone, she contributed more than 20 cartoons for the publication.

Her first cartoon appeared in the October 9, 1942, issue. Titled "Physical Fitness Day," it features a big, stiff student walking with a cane. The cartoon expressed the students' feelings about the day. Two cartoons in particular are autobiographical in nature. In the January 1943 issue, two students talk longingly about how they missed the dean's list for the fall 1942 term. This happened to O'Connor herself and was the one and only time in her college career that it did. The second autobiographical cartoon appears in the April 3, 1943, issue. A small wallflower wearing glasses stands alone at a dance where she is the only student not dancing. She whispers behind her raised hand that at least she can always keep working toward a Ph.D.

Since GSCW was a women's college, most of O'Connor's cartoons do not feature males. One exception, however, is the cartoon published in the March 7, 1944, issue. In it, two overweight teenage boys walk past the campus and comment that they hope the rules will be relaxed there before they are old enough to date.

O'Connor was probably best known and remembered for her cartoons satirizing the existence of the WAVES on campus. The January 23, 1943, issue, for example, published a cartoon of two students watching WAVES march across the GSCW campus. One student asks the other if she thinks a WAVE would let her try on her military hat. For the February 20, 1943, issue, O'Connor drew two students watching as a WAVE goes through her duffel bag. One wonders to the other if she might be carrying gunpowder. A student holds a bow and arrow aimed at the marching WAVES in the March 27, 1943, issue. In the April 24, 1943, edition, the two students observe the WAVES' hats and coats hung up in neat rows and by number. One mischievously asks the other if they would still make the dean's list if they mixed up the hats on purpose.

The Colonnade remains the official student newspaper at the college. Its stated mission is "to cover events and issues of importance to the campus community and to provide a forum for public debate and discussion." Recent issues of *The Colonnade* appear online at: www.gcsunade.com.

Conrad, Joseph (1857–1924) *British novelist and short-story writer* O'Connor admired Conrad's work greatly and said in 1958 that, along with Henry James, Conrad was her favorite author. She admitted in a 1953 letter to Robie Macauley that she had read "just about everything" Conrad wrote. She said she keeps reading the novels even though she knows nothing about them analytically because she hopes they will affect her writing. Specific titles she mentions reading include: *The Secret Agent* (1907) and *Under Western Eyes* (1911). More than a decade later, she compares her uncle to Captain McWhirr in *Typhoon and Other Stories* (1903) in a letter to Betty Hester and recommends the story to her if she has not read it yet.

Joseph Conrad was born of Polish descent in Ukraine and named Józef Teodor Konrad Korzeniowski. Conrad's father, Apollo, was a Polish insurrectionist working against Russia. Because of his activities, he was exiled to Vologda in northern Russia, where his family joined him. The harsh climate there facilitated Conrad's mother's early death from tuberculosis. His father began to translate English literature as a source of income. At the age of eight, Conrad had his first exposure to the English language and grew up reading Sir Walter Scott, James Fenimore Cooper, Charles Dickens, and William Makepeace Thackeray in both Polish and English.

In 1869, Conrad's father died in Cracow from tuberculosis. His maternal uncle, Tadeusz Bobrowski, was a lawyer who assumed responsibility for Joseph and raised him with care. He gave him advice and financial assistance when he needed it. Bobrowski sent his nephew to Cracow to be educated and then to Switzerland. However, Conrad wished to escape the formal schooling which he found boring. He longed to go to sea to have exotic adventures. Bobrowski gave him a yearly allowance and connected the boy with a French merchant whom he knew who would take him to sea.

Conrad sailed the seas as a passenger, then as an apprentice, and later as a steward. After voyages to the West Indies as a member of the French merchant navy, he was hired onto a British freighter and sailed to Constantinople. On the return from this voyage, Conrad first set foot in England in

June 1878. He knew English then, which served him well, but not quite so well as it would once he began his writing career in that language. For the next 16 years, Conrad worked in the British merchant navy.

In 1889, while staying in London waiting for his next sea appointment, Conrad began to write *Almayer's Folly*. This task was interrupted when he had the chance to live a childhood dream. While a child in Poland, Conrad had once taken a map of Africa and in a game, closed his eyes and put his finger, down on the map. It landed in the dead center of the continent—in the Congo. Conrad said then that he would go there sometime in his life. In 1889, Conrad was able to get an appointment in Brussels for a trip on a Congo River steamboat. This journey into the deepest heart of Africa would change Conrad's life forever.

Conrad wrote about his experiences during four months in the Congo in his masterpiece, "Heart of Darkness." The title refers not only to the center of a continent so unknown to much of the rest of the world but also metaphorically to the darkness that can exist within the hearts of human beings. This darkness could be evil, loneliness, or corruption. Conrad left the Congo a changed man. Not only was his health damaged permanently, but he was also affected psychologically and spiritually. He went to sea a few more times after returning, but by 1894 he left his sea life and took up writing. After several published novels and short stories and an illustrious career, Conrad died in Canterbury, Kent, on August 3, 1924, the year before O'Connor was born.

Conrad's novels not mentioned above include: *An Outcast of the Islands* (1896); *The Nigger of the "Narcissus"* (1897); *Lord Jim* (1900); with E. M. Hueffner (Ford), *The Inheritors* (1901); *Nostromo* (1904); *Chance* (1913); *Victory* (1915); *The Shadow-Line: A Confession* (1917); *The Arrow of Gold* (1919); *The Rescue* (1920); *The Rover* (1923); and with F. M. Ford, *The Nature of a Crime* (1924).

Additional story collections by Conrad include: *Youth: A Narrative, and Two Other Stories*, "Heart of Darkness" and "The End of the Tether" (1902); *A Set of Six* (1908); *Twixt Land and Sea* (1912); *Within the Tides* (1915); and *Tales of Hearsay* (1925). Other works include: *A Personal Record*

(1912); *Notes on My Books* (1921); and *Last Essays* (1926).

Conrad first became popular for his sea stories, but his fiction has lasted in world literature for more serious interior themes of human beings dealing with good and evil. Many of his works speak to the problem of people losing or giving up something they have been faithful to and the exploration of what happens to the ever-present force of evil when this barrier to its expression is destroyed. This more intense and complex aspect of Conrad's work must have intrigued Flannery O'Connor.

O'Connor discusses her meaning of the moral basis of poetry in relation to Conrad's assertion that his aim as an artist was "to render the highest possible justice to the visible universe" (HB 128). O'Connor indicated that, to her, the visible universe reflects that which is invisible. Both O'Connor and Conrad were interested in what lurks beyond what one sees.

O'Connor disliked a biography of Conrad, *Joseph Conrad: A Personal Remembrance*, written by Ford Maddox Ford in 1924. Her comment about the biography had more to do with Ford as a writer than of Conrad's life as an artist.

Corinthian, The   This was the literary magazine at GEORGIA STATE COLLEGE FOR WOMEN when O'Connor attended. It is now a student research journal that publishes journal articles and conference and article abstracts.

As might be expected, O'Connor was a frequent contributor to *The Corinthian*. In her freshman year, she contributed three essays, a free-verse poem, and a brief short story. In the fall 1942 issue, she wrote a satire on the way her fellow students lounge on the grounds of the campus in an essay called "Going to the Dogs." She wrote a timely piece for the winter 1943 issue called "Why Worry the Horse?" This piece speaks facetiously about returning to horses for a mode of transportation in light of the gasoline and parts shortages during World War II. In this issue, she also wrote a book review for a children's book, *The Story of Ferdinand* by Munro Leaf, jokingly recommending it to her college classmates (the book is, incidentally, highly regarded by serious children's literature critics).

The brief short story in the spring 1943 issue, "Elegance Is Its Own Reward," shows the influence of EDGAR ALLAN POE, which O'Connor acknowledged. It also foreshadows the violence that will play such a large role in O'Connor's later work. In the story, a husband kills two wives, decapitating one and wringing the neck of another. Though he claims he did it because the women were both dull, he actually did it because they did not give him the money that was promised in a dowry. He feels as though the decapitation murder lacked finesse and feels guilt over it, so before he wrings the neck of the second wife, he speaks to her in romantic language.

The free-verse poem "Effervescence" starts out parodying a line from JAMES RUSSELL Lowell's "The Vision of Sir Launfal"—"Oh, what is so lovely as a day in June?" The poem is less than effective in its satire of student laziness.

In her second year at GSCW, O'Connor served as literary assistant to *The Corinthian*. She published three stories in the journal that year: "Home of the Brave" and "Doctors of Delinquency" in the fall 1943 issue; and "Biologic Endeavor in the spring 1944 issue. In "Home of the Brave," the longest of the three, O'Connor writes of three gossipy women on the home front during the war. They gather to wrap bandages and talk as they work. Two of them are jealous of each other's sons' positions in the military. One son ends up secretly marrying the other mother's daughter, while the other son contracts mumps on the way to Australia. The story shows the hypocrisy of the "home front" when it describes the women secretly hoarding food that should be rationed.

In "Doctors of Delinquency," O'Connor's targets are the ways that children are taught too leniently about morality and education. The child character Elbert is so misbehaved and uneducated that he kills his brothers and uncle with a time bomb. O'Connor decries other elements of modern-day life such as nutrition and the media. She paints billboards, radio, and movies with a dark brush as working to separate children from nature and reading.

In "Biologic Endeavor," O'Connor continues her attack on modern living by first setting out an anecdote, this time of Great-Uncle Benedict who dies in 1882 at the age of 88. He dies from eating bad meat. Her argument maintains that people's eating habits now are bad compared to his. They eat processed foods and then try to overcome the effects by taking products such as Tums and Ex-Lax.

In her third year at GSCW, O'Connor worked as editor of *The Corinthian*. That year, she also contributed an introductory note for the fall 1944 issue that set the tone for her editorship; an illustrated essay, "Fashion's Perfect Medium;" "PFTT," a poem; and cartoon illustrations for an essay written by Joyce Moncrief called "You Can Have My Share."

The fashion essay attacked her classmates' preoccupation with their looks. Both her essay and her drawings complain about such faux pas as overlong sweaters that nearly alleviate the need for a skirt to go under them; frizzy hair; reversible raincoats; long bead necklaces; and loose shoes.

In the final issue of her senior year, O'Connor drew the cover. This consisted of a cartoon of an overweight cowboy enjoying a drink while relaxing underneath a beach umbrella. She pokes fun at her classmates on the contents page by pointing back to the drawing and describing it as illustrating the lassitude of most GSCW students. In that issue as well, O'Connor contributed an essay, "Education's Only Hope," and a two-quatrain poem, "Higher Education." The poem pokes fun at the gap between professors and the students who do not listen to them.

The essay, "Education's Only Hope," anticipates some of the author's later essays in the way it attacks student apathy and lack of involvement as being the direct result of their "progressive" educations. Speakers on campus, O'Connor claimed, overestimate the students' promise for courageous involvement in society after graduation. Most students on campus are too lazy and weak-minded. They do not participate in student government, which would be a training ground for their future involvement; they do not question the way they are being taught by their professors; and they do not read the newspaper.

O'Connor was known throughout college for her CARTOONS and writing, much of it appearing in

The Corinthian. Her readers on campus had mixed reactions to her work. Some thought the writing was of obvious quality, while others thought her stories ranged from strange to bizarre. Clearly, O'Connor cut some of her publication teeth in her contributions to *The Corinthian* as a writer, illustrator, and editor. Her use of violence in short fiction, satire in essays, and opinionated stance on progressive education are threads that are recognizable to O'Connor's readers today.

Critic, The   Once a Catholic book review magazine, the publication began to publish fiction in the fall 1960 edition. They accepted O'Connor's "The Partridge Festival" for that issue as she describes in a August 10, 1960, letter to Cecil Dawkins (HB 404). O'Connor also writes of meeting Al Miller, the former book-review editor. She does not like the interview of her that appears in one issue that she writes about in 1963, though she says the accompanying picture is not bad (HB 525).

D

Dostoyevsky, Fyodor (alternative spelling used by O'Connor: Feodor Dostoevsky) (1821–1881) *Russian novelist and short-story writer* Dostoyevsky is normally the first in line when O'Connor mentions in her letters that she "read the Russians." By this she means not Tolstoy but Dostoyevsky, Turgenev, Chekhov, and Gogol (HB 98–99). In her advice about fiction writing and antagonists to Betty Hester, she explains that the writer must find herself in the character in order to make the adversary real. She responds, apparently, to a question or comment by Hester that she does not know whether finding oneself in the adversary was Dostoyevsky's problem or not (145).

She once sent to Cecil Dawkins an article by Romano Guardini on the Russian author (243) and recommended Guardini's work also to Dr. T. R. Spivey in 1958. She discusses Dostoyevsky's work in the "The Legend of the Grand Inquisitor" (from *The Brothers Karamazov*) saying that he uses the Inquisition to represent the entire church, meaning that the whole institution is corrupt (304). In 1959, she writes to Maryat Lee that if her relatives start to read Freud or Dostoyevsky in their old age she will "leave home . . ." (331). In 1960, she quips that Ayn Rand, whose work she deplores, makes Mickey Spillane, another popular writer, look like Dostoyevsky (398). Biographer Jean W. Cash notes that Dostoyevsky's *Notes from the Underground* was one of the works discussed at ANDALUSIA during the regular weekly and biweekly meetings O'Connor held there.

Dostoyevsky's works include: *Notes From the Underground* (1864); *Crime and Punishment* (1866); *The Idiot* (1868–69); *The Possessed* (1872); and *The Brothers Karamazov* (1879–80).

E

Esquire O'Connor's story, "Why Do the Heathen Rage?" appeared in the July 1963 issue of *Esquire* magazine. The author found it humorous to discover how many of the locals around MILLEDGEVILLE indicated that this publication meant that she had hit the big time in her career. With a history that continues to this day of articles and features geared toward the stylish and predominantly urban male, *Esquire* was not a magazine to which O'Connor assumed many rural Georgia men subscribed.

The magazine was founded in 1933 by Arnold Gingrich and David Smart. Though it began as a fashion magazine for men, by the 1960s it had a reputation for publishing some of the best fiction writers and essayists in the country, including Tom Wolfe, Langston Hughes, William F. Buckley, F. Scott Fitzgerald, Gore Vidal, and Gordon Lish. The magazine later helped establish careers of writers such as Raymond Carver. The current slogan of the magazine is "Man at His Best."

F

Faulkner, William (1897–1962) *American novelist and short-story writer* Probably the best-known quote from O'Connor about her fellow American

William Faulkner. O'Connor avoided reading much of Faulkner's fiction, lest her "own little boat . . . get swamped." *(Courtesy of the Library of Congress)*

southern fiction writer, William Faulkner, is "I keep clear of Faulkner so my own little boat won't get swamped" (HB 273). Another, lesser-known quote is "Probably the real reason I don't read [Faulkner] is because he makes me feel that with my one-cylinder syntax I should quit writing and raise chickens altogether" (HB 292).

Even in O'Connor's time, Faulkner was regarded as a giant in American and world literature. His long, convoluted sentence style and stream-of-consciousness technique, along with his masterly explorations of the American South, solidified his reputation as an artist of the highest order. He was awarded the Nobel Prize in literature in 1949. That same year, O'Connor turned 24, was finishing her extra year at Iowa, and making her way toward completing her first novel at the YADDO artists' colony near Saratoga Springs, New York.

Like NATHANIEL HAWTHORNE before him, Faulkner added a letter to the original spelling of his name (Falkner), possibly to separate himself from a great-grandfather of whose history he was too well aware. Colonel William Clark Falkner not only fought in the Civil War, but he also built a railroad and wrote a popular romantic novel, *The White Rose of Memphis*. Faulkner's father was the business manager of the University of Mississippi in Oxford, and the young boy grew up with a typical middle-class white southern childhood of the period. He had a gun and a pony and went hunting.

He did not finish high school but was given constant and free-flowing reading material by a family friend, attorney Phil Stone. In July 1918, under visions of martial grandeur and with a downcast heart from a jilted relationship, he enlisted in the British Royal Air Force (RAF) in Canada. He hoped to see military action in Europe. However, the armistice later that same year ended his training. He took a few college courses and then moved to New York for a while, where he worked in a bookstore.

Eventually, he returned to Oxford, where he ran the university post office starting in 1921. His inefficiency and problems with alcohol forced him to resign. Phil Stone helped him publish his first book-length project in 1924 and helped him stay on his feet until his publications began to take hold. He married Estelle Oldham in 1929. Though the marriage did not stay a happy one and Faulkner had numerous affairs over the years, the two did have a daughter, Jill, in 1933.

Except for bouts of working in Hollywood for money when he needed it and occasional writer's residencies at the University of Virginia in Charlottesville, where his daughter lived, Faulkner spent most of the rest of his life at his pre–Civil War home called Rowan Oak in Oxford, Mississippi. Plagued throughout his life by alcoholism, Faulkner died in 1962 from a heart attack brought on from years of hard living and physical unrest.

Faulkner's career spanned roughly 40 years, from the publication of early stories and a verse piece, *The Marble Faun*, in 1924 to his first novel, *Soldier's Pay*, in 1926 through several screenplays in Hollywood, to *The Reivers* in 1962, published one month before he died. By contrast, Flannery O'Connor's entire life of 39 years extended roughly the same length of time as Faulkner's career.

Other than his distinctive prose style, Faulkner is known for his creation of a fictional county in Mississippi that he named Yoknapatawpha County. The county was based chiefly on Oxford, which is the county seat for Layfayette County. This became the fictional landscape and setting for a good many of Faulkner's novels. Novels were set in various communities in the county, and inhabited by characters that overlapped from one work of fiction to another.

Faulkner's major works include *The Sound and the Fury* (1929); *As I Lay Dying* (1930); *Light in August* (1932); *Absalom, Absalom!* (1936); *Go Down Moses* (1942); *Intruder in the Dust* (1948); and *A Fable* (1954). He also wrote what was known as the "Snopes trilogy," *The Hamlet* (1940); *The Town* (1957); and *The Mansion* (1959). Faulkner's short fiction was gathered together in *Collected Stories* (1950). *The Portable Faulkner* (1946), edited by Malcolm Cowley, helped boost Faulkner's American reputation as a writer who was building his own legend of the South.

In 1953, O'Connor wrote to the Fitzgeralds that she liked Faulkner's review of ERNEST HEMINGWAY's *The Old Man and the Sea*. Faulkner says in the review that perhaps Hemingway found God in the writing of his novella (HB 56). She tends to link Faulkner with FRANZ KAFKA and JAMES JOYCE when she speaks of those whose work she had not even heard of, much less read, until she went to Iowa (98).

Another amusing anecdote regarding O'Connor and Faulkner comes in a letter O'Connor wrote to ELIZABETH BISHOP. O'Connor describes meeting a man who was a structural engineer. He told O'Connor he had a friend in Mississippi who was a writer. O'Connor asked the writer's name, and the engineer replied, "His name is Bill Faulkner. I don't know if he's any good or not but he's a mighty nice fellow." O'Connor said she replied that "he was right good . . ." (HB 344).

G

Georgia State College for Women Located in MILLEDGEVILLE, GEORGIA and now called Georgia College and State University (GCSU), O'Connor's undergraduate alma mater was founded in 1889 as the Georgia Normal and Industrial College. It has also been known as the Women's College of Georgia and Georgia College. The school is designated as the public liberal arts university in the state, now offering 40 undergraduate and 18 graduate degrees from the School of Liberal Arts and Sciences, the J. Whitney Bunting School of Business, the School of Health Sciences, and the John H. Lounsbury School of Education. Enrollment is about 5,500 undergraduate and graduate students with a teacher-student ratio of 15:1. In-state tuition is currently less than $2,000 per semester with most of the student body living off campus. School colors are navy blue and hunter green; the school's sports team is the Bobcats, and its Alma Mater is "O Beacon Bright." The college had a lasting effect on O'Connor's life and work and continues to play an important role in her legacy.

The author attended the college in an accelerated three-year program during World War II from 1942 to 1945, when she graduated with a bachelor of arts in social science. O'Connor's activities at college included working on the staffs of the yearbook, The SPECTRUM; the newspaper, The COLONNADE; and in her senior year serving as editor of The CORINTHIAN, the school literary magazine. The student body knew classmate O'Connor especially for her humorous CARTOONS made from linoleum cuts, which appeared in all three of these publications. She also served as a member of the Honor

O'Connor, around the time she was attending Georgia College for Women *(Courtesy of Flannery O'Connor Collection, Georgia College & State University)*

Committee in her sophomore year. The committee is described in the yearbook as a group concerned with encouraging individuals to take responsibility for their own honor and reputations and have concern about the same for their classmates.

One of the distinguishing features of the college in O'Connor's time was the presence of a U.S. Navy WAVES (Women Accepted for Volunteer Emergency Service) encampment on campus. Their marching across the campus to class brought the war home to the all-female student body, many of whom were there learning to become teachers. The encampment also caused overcrowding in the dormitories. As a "town girl," a student from the local community who came to campus each day from home, O'Connor often made the WAVES the subject of her published cartoons. Most of these satirical cuts feature civilian students watching from a distance as WAVES march or perform duties around the campus seemingly oblivious to the other students. The cartoons also include a witty caption.

At Georgia State, O'Connor confirmed her desire to become a writer even if she did not gain the tools she thought necessary to do so. Her English professors immediately recognized her creativity and gift for writing, though some of the older faculty, such as Dr. William Wynn, thought her work could be more graceful and "lady-like" and tried to influence her to change her style. Wynn's opinion had such a strong negative effect on O'Connor that she avoided majoring in English simply because Wynn was the only professor who taught two courses required for the major—Shakespeare and a course in grammar. Professor Hallie Smith, on the other hand, appreciated O'Connor's wit and gave her high marks for her writing, encouraging her to submit pieces to *The Corinthian*. Professor George W. Beiswanger, who taught philosophy, told O'Connor about fellowships in writing available at his alma mater, the UNIVERSITY OF IOWA, and encouraged her to apply there. When she did, he wrote her a letter of recommendation.

Perhaps because the school was so close to home or because she graduated in only three years, O'Connor did not always recall her education at Georgia State favorably when speaking of it years

later. She once indicated that the literature she read there was what was expected to be read by most low-paid Georgia high school English teachers. Either she did not find the curriculum particularly challenging or up to date in terms of contemporary literature or she found it lacking in preparation for what she expected to need as a future writer, or both.

Since O'Connor's alma mater is located near her home at ANDALUSIA and is also the location for the largest collection of the author's papers, the college has become a locus for O'Connor studies since the author's death. The Ina Dillard Russell Library began its collection of O'Connor materials soon after the publication of her first short story, "The Geranium," in 1946. The first donation of manuscripts in 1970 by Regina Cline O'Connor encouraged serious scholars to regard the school as an important repository of O'Connor documents. Additional manuscripts and other materials were added to the collection. It now houses more than 6,000 manuscript pages as well as the author's own personal library of more than 700 books and journals. Critical works, photographs, tape recordings, memorabilia, films, letters, and vertical file materials add depth to the collection. Georgia College and State University is also the home of the *Flannery O'Connor Review*, the premier scholarly journal dedicated to O'Connor studies.

Greene, (Henry) Graham (1904–1991) *British novelist, short-story writer, playwright, and journalist* O'Connor frequently mentioned Greene when she was listing the Catholic novelists she had read. Others included FRANÇOIS MAURIAC, Bernanos, Bloy, and Waugh. In 1955, she sent Betty Hester an issue of *Thought* in which there was an article about Graham Greene. She writes that she has not read Greene recently enough to know how she would feel about his work now, but she remembers his work fondly enough to feel defensive for him when reading the article (HB 119). Later, she wrote to Maryat Lee that this same article, written by Elizabeth Sewell, was the best one she has seen on Greene (201). She mentions that the article describes Greene as having a different sensibility than his convictions. Though his convictions were

Catholic, his sensibilities were Manichean, and, O'Connor says, one writes from one's sensibilities.

In 1957, she wrote to Betty Hester, recalling an article of Greene's in *The Lost Childhood* but not recalling what it said (258). In 1960, she described perhaps the biggest difference between her work and Greene's in a letter to John Hawkes. There, she says that their fiction and probably their theologies are different. An old lady character in Greene's fiction, for example, would have a foul disposition and would break if dropped. In an O'Connor story, if an old lady were dropped, she would bounce back and scream that Jesus loves her. Unlike Greene, whose view starts from somewhere else, O'Connor thinks that the basis for the way she sees is comic (400).

One trait in her own writing that O'Connor identified as either coming from Graham Greene or coming from her own instincts is her tendency to put her most favorite characters under the greatest suffering (HB 120–21). In a letter to Father J. H. McCown in 1956, she commented that she has read the Catholic novelists like Greene but eventually they start to lose return on the effort. A writer then should turn, she says, to the likes of ERNEST HEMINGWAY, who appears to seek a Catholic sensibility in his work, and JAMES JOYCE, who cannot rid himself of it no matter how hard he tries (HB 130).

Greene converted to Catholicism in 1926, principally because of the influence of his future wife, Vivien Dayrell-Browning. The two married in 1927. Greene worked at different times as a copy editor for *The Times*; as a film critic and literary editor at *The Spectator*; and as a freelance journalist for three decades. In his latter work, he traveled, looking for settings for his novels.

Greene's works include: *Babbling April* (1925), a book of verse; *The Man Within* (1929); *Stamboul Train* (1930); *A Gun for Sale* (1936); *Brighton Rock* (1938); *The Confidential Agent* (1939); *The Ministry of Fear* (1943); *The Heart of the Matter* (1948); *The Third Man* (1949); *The End of the Affair* (1951); *A Burnt-Out Case* (1951); *The Quiet American* (1956); *Our Man in Havana* (1958); *The Comedians* (1966); *The Honorary Consul* (1973); *The Human Factor* (1978); *Monsignor Quixote* (1982); and *The Tenth Man* (1985). His plays include: *The Living Room* (1952) and *The Potting Shed* (1957). His

short fiction was collected in *Twenty-One Stories* (1954), and his *Collected Essays* was published in 1969. Greene published two memoirs, *A Sort of Life* (1971) and *Ways of Escape* (1980).

Several of Greene's works were also made into feature films.

grotesque   Originating from the Italian word *grotteschi,* in architecture and decorative sculptural art the term refers to a mixed design of human, plant, and animal forms. *Grotteschi* are the grottoes in Italy where such designs were found when several houses were excavated in about 1500. These excavations included that of the Golden House of Nero, the Domus Aurea.

During the Renaissance, the design was revived by the school of Raphael in Rome. It became popular throughout Italy and Europe in the 16th century and remained so until the 19th century. In the 17th century, the design became popular in decorations such as case furniture in England and America. Used to a great extent in fresco decoration, grotesque design normally did not have symbolic significance. Occasionally, animal heads were intended to hold heraldic or other symbolic importance, but for the most part, grotesques were purely decorative.

In literature, the grotesque refers to a story structure in which some sudden and unexpected element is introduced, and the reaction to that unexpected element becomes part of the story. Often, grotesque plays on elements of the estranged world clashing with those of the everyday in a way that makes resolution difficult or seemingly impossible. The tension between the estranged and the everyday can be terrifying since it often turns what the character (or reader) thought she or he knew upside down, eluding both definition and correction. The elements, seemingly incompataible with one another, remain unresolved.

Among the estranged in O'Connor's world are the "freaks" of the carnival; men in gorilla suits; shrunken mummies; and, interestingly, the disabled, including people with mental challenges, clubbed feet, missing limbs, and other difficulties. Many readers wonder if there are so many characters with disabilities in O'Connor's fiction because of the sense of estrangement she must have felt in dealing with the debilitating effects of LUPUS.

For O'Connor, the grotesque gave her an avenue through which she could have a realistic view of that which lies at a distance. She wrote in "The Grotesque in Southern Fiction" that a writer with a theological world view cannot hold a mirror up to society and think that this mirror will show that society something new about itself. There is an unseen element, a vision, that needs to be brought out. O'Connor uses the grotesque for that intrusion of the unseen world into the seen world. This is why so many of her stories are jarring and uncomfortable, sometimes even unpleasant. The clash of worlds, the incompatible that appears to defy either definition or correction, turns the reader toward a sense of the mysterious and unexplained. This occupation in the sense of mystery is O'Connor's territory.

Why would a young man steal a woman's prosthetic leg? Why would a one-armed man abandon his mentally challenged wife in a diner and drive away? Why does does a man blind himself? These grotesque actions and so many others in O'Connor's fiction force readers to stretch the boundaries of the world in which they normally live to ask questions they would not normally ask.

H

Harper's Bazaar O'Connor wrote letters to her agent, Elizabeth McKee, as early as October 1952, impatiently asking when the story purchased by *Harper's Bazaar*, "A Late Encounter With the Enemy," was going to be published. The story did finally appear in the September 1953 issue. Unlike the early 2000s, during this period in the 20th century, *Harper's* and other magazines published fiction regularly. Of O'Connor's stories, *Harper's* also published "A Temple of the Holy Ghost" in the May 1954 issue; "Good Country People" in the June 1955 issue; and "The Enduring Chill" in July 1958.

The magazine debuted in a weekly newspaper format in the United States in 1867. At that time, it featured fashions from Germany and Paris. Known as the first fashion magazine, the publication was aimed at an audience of middle- and upper-class women. In 1901, the magazine moved to its current monthly format. The current magazine, produced by the Hearst Corporation, strives to be sophisticated in its photography, writing, and design.

Hawthorne, Nathaniel (1804–1864) *American novelist and short-story writer* One of the authors with whom O'Connor is most frequently compared, Hawthorne stands among the most revered of all American writers. His novels *The Scarlet Letter* (1850) and *The House of the Seven Gables* (1851) are American classics. Like O'Connor, Hawthorne

is concerned with the role of Christian religion and spirituality in people's lives as well as the paradigm of good versus evil and a conscious awareness of the presence of the devil. Also like Hawthorne,

Nathaniel Hawthorne. O'Connor said she felt more of a "kinship" with Hawthorne than with any other author. *(Courtesy of Library of Congress)*

whose work is set exclusively in New England, all of O'Connor's stories are set in the South or with characters who endure a deep longing for that region of the country.

If readers see similiarities when encountering the short stories of both writers, O'Connor might say that they are not alone. She once wrote, "Hawthorne interests me considerably. I feel more of a kinship with him than with any other American, though some of what he wrote I can't make myself read through to the end" (HB 457). In the same letter, she wrote that she would admit to writing what Hawthorne called romances. These are not romances in terms of stories centered on love between two people, but rather they are the literary kind of romance that came about particularly in the 19th-century writing of Hawthorne, Herman Melville, and EDGAR ALLAN POE.

Romance, as Hawthorne called his stories, represents a difference from strict realistic fiction. Though the stories are mostly written as though they could actually happen, that is, in a real world and real time and place, they are infused with a dose of imagination that puts them on a slightly different plane. In other words, with the romance, the author is more free to use his or her imagination in composing the story and its events, even if that means that the realism of the story is stretched.

An example is Hawthorne's short story and allegory "Young Goodman Brown." The scene in the middle of the forest stretches the realism of the rest of the story. Readers of O'Connor can recognize these effects in her stories as well, particularly in her frequent use of GROTESQUE characters. In her essay "The Grotesque in Southern Fiction," O'Connor explains that the writer of a romance is interested in mystery over verisimilitude and possibility over probability.

In a 1955 letter to Betty Hester, O'Connor admits to having "learned something" from Hawthorne, among other writers (HB 99). She was also particularly fascinated that the order of the nuns who asked her to help them with the *Memoir of Mary Ann* was founded by Hawthorne's daughter. In 1956, she wrote that this act perhaps was

God's way of "rewarding Hawthorne for hating the Transcendentalists" (145). One of her friends from Nashville told her that the author would leave out the back of a building if Emerson or any of the others came in the front. If he could not avoid meeting them, Hawthorne would ask sarcastically how their oversouls were doing that morning.

Other than the classic novels mentioned above, some of Hawthorne's most notable works include: a collection of stories, *Mosses from an Old Manse* (1846); and the novels *The Marble Faun* (1860), and *The Blithedale Romance* (1852).

Hemingway, Ernest (Miller) (1899–1961) *American novelist and short-story writer* Hemingway was one of the most influential American writers of the 20th century. He is perhaps best known for his spare, minimalist sentence style and his masculine perspective on themes of adventure, love, and various forms of battle and war. He won the Nobel Prize in literature in 1954. O'Connor saw in his work what she thought of as an earnest search for God.

O'Connor comments on Hemingway's *The Old Man and the Sea* (1952) in a 1953 letter to Sally and Robert Fitzgerald. She mentions WILLIAM FAULKNER's review of the book. In it, he reflects that he thinks Hemingway found God as the Creator in the book. O'Connor writes, "What part I like in that was where the fish's eye was like a saint in a procession; it sounded to me like he was discovering something new maybe for him" (HB 56). She also wrote in 1956 to Father J. H. McCown about what she sees as Hemingway's "hunger for a Catholic completeness in life" (130). She does not like what Cozzens says about *The Old Man and the Sea* in an article and calls that writer a hack compared with Hemingway (240).

In her counsel about writing to Betty Hester, she tells her to expect rejection. She holds Hemingway up as an example; it was thought that he received 200 rejection slips before one of his stories was published (242). Novelists use novels, she further counsels Hester, for many different purposes in their lives. Hemingway used the writing of a novel to "test his manhood" (451).

Other than *The Old Man and the Sea* that so impressed O'Connor, key works by Hemingway include: *A Farewell to Arms* (1929); *Death in the Afternoon* (1932); *For Whom the Bell Tolls* (1940); and *A Moveable Feast* (1964).

Holiday   The essay "King of the Birds" first appeared in *Holiday* in the September 1961 issue under the title, "Living With a Peacock." It had one paragraph missing. O'Connor received $750 for the article. She wrote to Betty Hester that this sum doubled her next highest payment. Though at first she hesitated at writing the article when asked to do so, she wrote in a letter that though she dislikes writing articles she likes money and would probably do it. After it was accepted, O'Connor wrote an October 1, 1960, letter to Hester confessing, "Crime pays" (HB 165). In February 1961, she wrote to Cecil Hawkins that she and her mother were expecting the photographer from *Holiday* to come take pictures of the peafowl. She expects that it will go badly—that it will rain, the birds will hide in the woods or sulk, or that a worn-out outbuilding will show up somewhere in every picture. When the article did appear, she wrote to Maryat Lee in August 1961 that the editors changed the title to "something stupid" and that they cut an important paragraph. The picture of the peafowl, however, was "splendid" (HB 447).

J

James, Henry (1843–1916) *American novelist* Henry James was born in the United States (New York City) but became a British citizen. His long and influential career spanned 51 years, during which he wrote 20 novels, 112 stories, 12 plays, several books of travel and literary criticism, and many journalistic pieces. The main theme of his fiction concerned the dramatization of what he saw as the clash between the vitality and innocence of the New World (America) and the decaying morality yet retained wisdom of the Old World (Europe). James's prose influenced many writers when he enjoyed renewed interest in the 1940s and 50s. Not least of those who noticed and studied his work at that time was Flannery O'Connor.

James was named after his father. His older brother, William, was a philosopher. When the James boys were small, they were taken abroad but spent much of their preadolescent years in Manhattan. In their teen years, they returned to Europe where they spent time in Geneva, Paris, and London and picked up languages that few Americans in those days had acquired. Right before the American Civil War, the James family established a home in Newport, Rhode Island, and Henry grew to know New England and Boston well. At 19, he enrolled at Harvard Law School but spent most of his time reading such authors as Charles-Augustin Sainte-Beuve, Honoré de Balzac, and NATHANIEL HAWTHORNE.

James became friends with William Dean Howells, who was editor of *The Atlantic Monthly*. Howells published James's writing often, and together they

Henry James. In her letters, O'Connor admitted to reading almost all of James's fiction "from a sense of High Duty." *(Courtesy of Library of Congress)*

are often singled out as the pair who established realism in American fiction. By the time he was in his 20s, James was publishing regularly, though critics often found fault with his early efforts, saying that they were too much of the mind of the privileged class with not enough emphasis on action.

In 1869, he made his first trip back to Europe as an adult, spending time on a grand tour of England, France, and Italy. The trip was the first of several, and he began to observe the contrast between European and American lifestyles, observations that became the bases for his most enduring work.

O'Connor wrote that she read James in an effort to improve her own writing, though she did not know how it might happen (HB 68). She disagreed with James when he observed that the women of the future would know nothing of mystery or manners. She writes that he should not limit this speculation to one gender only (92). She would like to be able to not admit that she has read and been influenced by James, but it would be a lie to say so (98). She has, she writes in a 1955 letter, read nearly all of his work "from a sense of High Duty and because when I read James I feel something is happening to me, in slow motion but happening nevertheless" (99).

O'Connor referred to James frequently throughout her letters. She said that he could write better about vulgar people than anyone else she knew, and she suspected that it was because he had so little vulgarity in himself and that he must have hated it through and through. She recalled that he once said that the morality of a work of fiction comes from the "felt life" within it. She added quickly that one can get in too deep very quickly, pondering a phrase like that for very long. She understands St. Thomas's explanation more clearly—that one need not be a good person to write good fiction (103). By contrast, she wrote to Denver Lindley in late 1955, that she is glad to hear that a Georgia writer liked her speech but that it was really nothing more than plainly spoken truth from Henry James (123).

In her writing advice to Betty Hester, O'Connor wrote about Caroline Gordon as a follower of James. She, like him, attempts to tell a story through what James called a "central intelligence." O'Connor uses Strether in *The Ambassadors* as an example

(157). O'Connor shared with Hester that she likes Elizabeth Stevenson's book on Henry James (211) and advises Hester that James needs to be judged on *The Portrait of a Lady* (1881), not his more minor works such as *The Spoils of Poynton* (1897) or *The Sacred Fount* (1901) (226).

She did admit to not having read *The Golden Bowl* but remarks that Betty Hester probably did not like James because he was never tempted and that Caroline Gordon likes him too much because of his technical expertise (258). She advises Hester in the writing of her own novel to allow James to influence the structure of her work rather than the style of it (317). In 1959, her conversation with Hester about James continued when she wrote about his masterly writing in concrete detail about vulgar people. Part of his greatness is his ability to recognize the vulgarity in people. She finds *What Maisie Knew?* particularly moving (332–333). She keeps cautioning Hester against measuring the work of the author by her thoughts about the author personally (335).

James was good at diplomacies like thanking an author for a book, even when he did not enjoy it (383). She offers to let Hester borrow James's travel book, *The American Scene,* where a section of SAVANNAH, she notes, has James writing about his unhappiness with the lack of a sense of mystery (462).

Important James works include: *The American* (1877); *Daisy Miller* (1879); *The Bostonians* (1886); *The Turn of the Screw* (1898); and *The Ambassadors* (1903).

Joyce, James (1882–1941) *Irish novelist and short-story writer* Joyce was one of the foremost fiction writers of the 20th century. He is known for his experimentation with the English language and his narrative technique. In *Finnegans Wake* (1939), he virtually makes up his own language. In his masterpiece, *Ulysses* (1922), he employs a technique known as stream of consciousness to express Leopold Bloom's thoughts throughout the novel, which takes place in Dublin, Ireland, in the course of one day.

Joyce was the eldest of 10 children. When he was six years old, his father sent him to Clongowes Wood College, a Jesuit boarding school. Joyce's father had problems with debt and alcohol, so the boy did not return to school in 1891 but instead tried to educate himself at home with his mother going over his work. In 1893, he and his brother were enrolled in Belvedere College, a Jesuit school in Dublin, where their family was not required to pay tuition. Joyce was a superior student and was elected president of the Marian Society (an honorary position) twice. His departure from the school, however, was not a triumphant one because it was determined that he had lost his Catholic faith.

He continued a rebellious streak against the church when he entered University College, Dublin, then another institution where students were taught by Jesuits. There he gravitated toward books not recommended by the Jesuits. He was active in the university's Literary and Historical Society and studied Dano-Norwegian. He studied the language so that he could read the work of Henrik Ibsen in the original language. As a consequence, he wrote a review of Ibsen's new play, *When We Dead Awaken*, published in the London *Fortnightly Review* just after he turned 18 in 1900. In 1901, he published an essay, "The Day of the Rabblement," criticizing the Irish Literary Theater (later named the Dublin Abbey Theater) for pandering too much to popular taste.

Joyce managed to complete his B.A. degree in 1902 but had a difficult time securing and keeping employment. He began to write what he called "epiphanies," story fragments that conveyed moments of sudden revelation for their characters. After a brief time in Paris, he went home to Dublin in 1903 because his mother was dying. There he tried different jobs and taught for a while, living in various locations throughout the city. One notable site is the Martollo tower, now a Joyce museum, and the location of what would be the opening scene of *Ulysses*.

Joyce started to write *Stephen Hero*, based on his life, a book that would later become *A Portrait of the Artist as a Young Man*, when he was approached by George Russell in 1904 to write a series of stories about people from around the city. The purpose of the stories was to entertain readers of a farming periodical called *The Irish Homestead*. Joyce left *Stephen Hero* for the time being and launched into

a series of stories that Russell soon found not useful to him. These were, however, the stories that formed the collection *Dubliners*.

On June 16, 1904, the date that would later be the time for the action of *Ulysses* and which has come since to be known as "Bloomsday," Joyce met Nora Barnacle, an unprentious woman from the west coast of Ireland. Though he did not marry her at the time, he convinced her to leave Ireland with him. Though they did make at least two trips back to the country, the Joyces lived out most of their lives in continental Europe, including times in Trieste, Zurich, and Paris.

The Joyces had two children, George and Lucia. They were always short on cash and stayed afloat primarily through the help of benefactors such as Edith Rockefeller McCormick and Harriet Shaw Weaver, who was editor of the *Egoist* magazine. Weaver became Joyce's publisher when they could find no one to print *Portrait*. The publishing histories of Joyce's works are among the most ironic in world literature. When *Ulysses* also failed to find a publisher, a bookstore owner named Sylvia Beach, who ran "Shakespeare and Company," moved the future classic novel into print on February 2, 1922.

O'Connor read Joyce at the UNIVERSITY OF IOWA, and his influence is clearly evident in her master's thesis. Miss Willerton in "The Crop," for example, the woman who sits at her typewriter and has difficulty writing a story, contains elements of Joyce's Little Chandler in "A Little Cloud" from *Dubliners* (1914). "The Barber" attempts to show the conflicts an individual intellectual encounters with people of his town found in the barber shop. The intellectual clashing with other people in society is a common theme throughout *Dubliners* and *A Portrait of the Artist as a Young Man* (1916).

When she gave writing advice to Ben Griffiths, O'Connor mentions that it is important to get into a story details about the setting unobtrusively. She advises Griffiths to read Joyce's story "The Dead," (from *Dubliners*) and study what he accomplishes with the snow in that story (HB 84). She advises allowing the scenery and the details the character notices about it to reflect his mood or state of mind. This allows the writer to avoid telling these feelings directly to the reader. Readers will respond more readily to emotions characters feel on their own. O'Connor uses the snow in "The Dead" to teach Griffiths one of the principles of fiction writing—"show, don't tell."

She wrote to Father J. H. McCown that Joyce cannot seem to rid himself of his Catholic sensibility, no matter how hard he tries (130). Joyce had such difficulty with the attitudes of his fellow Dubliners that he ended up leaving the city in what he called a self-imposed exile. Even while living far away from them, however, Joyce continued to write about Dubliners for the rest of his life. O'Connor admires an Irish poet who visited ANDALUSIA in 1958 and spoke about how Irish writers like Joyce who leave the church end up cutting themselves off from what they have grown up with, since the Catholic Church is so much a part of everyday life (262).

O'Connor knew the value of Joyce's contribution to literature, even if she did not share his criticisms of the church. She advises Betty Hester in 1957 that if she has not read "The Dead" or *Dubliners* as yet, that she should "study those stories, as you can learn an awful lot from them" (HB 203).

Jubilee In *The Habit of Being,* O'Connor writes frequently about reading *Jubilee,* a Catholic publication distributed in the middle 20th century. In June 1960, she wrote to Betty Hester about the "good" review of *Wise Blood* by Paul Levine that appears in *Jubilee.* Levine sent her "very intelligent" questions in a written interview for the article. In December of that year, she notified Hester that *Jubilee* will publish her "Introduction to the Memoir of Mary Ann." The piece appeared in the May 1961 issue.

The full title of the magazine was *Jubilee—A Magazine of the Church and Her People.* The title comes from the Latin of Psalm 100, *"Jubilate Deo, omnis terra,"* translated "Sing joyfully to God, all the earth." The magazine was in print from 1953 to 1967 and was the first picture magazine about the church in America. One of the missions of the magazine was to help the faithful understand the changes in the church that came about as a result of the Second Vatican Council. Another function was to integrate life in the church with life outside of the church, in politics, culture, and so forth. A fundamental question the magazine tried to address was what it was like to be a Catholic in the 20th century. Editors of *Jubilee* included Edward Rice, Thomas Merton, and Robert Lax.

At its height, the number of subscriptions reached 72,000. Readers tended to be well-read middle- to upper-class professionals, so the magazine was thought to be more sophisticated than some of the more doctrinal-based church publications. Its articles were said to avoid sentimentality and ultraconservatism. One reader commented that it was the only Catholic magazine one could feel comfortable passing on to one's non-Catholic friends.

Kafka, Franz (1883–1924) *German language fiction writer* Anyone who has read Kafka's stories "The Metamorphosis" or "The Hunger Artist" will recognize aspects of the GROTESQUE that O'Connor's work shares with his. O'Connor tried to explain who he was to her mother in 1952 in a story she relates by letter to Sally and Robert Fitzgerald. Regina asks who is Kafka, and O'Connor replies that he is a German Jew, she thinks. She explains, "He wrote a book about a man that turns into a roach" (HB 33). Regina exclaims that she cannot tell people about that. O'Connor tells the Fitzgeralds that her mother is becoming literary.

Though many readers find echoes of Kafka's *The Castle* or *The Trial* in O'Connor's *Wise Blood,* O'Connor dismissed the connection. She never managed to finish either novel. She goes on to say that she would not be able to expound in any way on the author except that perhaps reading a little of his work makes a writer "bolder" (HB 68).

Kafka is known for his explorations of alienation and anxiety. His principal works include *The Trial* (1925) and *The Castle* (1926), both published posthumously, and several stories.

Kenyon Review, The Poet-critic John Crowe Ransom founded this literary journal in 1939. It is based at Kenyon College in Gambier, Ohio. During the 1940s and 1950s, the journal was arguably the most influential and well known of its kind in the country. During the years, *The Kenyon Review* has not only published work by Flannery O'Connor but also by Allen Tate, Robert Penn Warren, William Empson, Mark Van Doren, Kenneth Burke, Delmore Schwartz, Robert Lowell, and Peter Taylor, among many others.

In 1969, financial difficulties halted publication for a decade. In 1979, the magazine revived under the new full-time editorship of Marilyn Hacker. Hacker's influence widened the scope of the journal to include more female and minority authors and their viewpoints. In 1994, seeking more cost-reducing measures, the journal changed editors once again, this time sharing part-time responsibility for editorship with an English professor of Kenyon College.

The Kenyon Review published five O'Connor stories for the first time. These were: "The Life You Save May Be Your Own," in spring 1953; "A Circle in the Fire," in spring 1954; "The Artificial Nigger" in spring 1955; "Greenleaf" in summer 1956; and "The Comforts of Home" in fall 1960.

Equally important to O'Connor's career, she received the $2,000 *Kenyon Review* Fellowship for two years in a row, 1952 and 1953. The fellowship was funded by the Rockefeller family and administered by Ransom. She wrote in her letters that she used the fellowship money to pay medical bills and to buy books. With the second fellowship and her savings, she also invested in rental property—an inexpensive yellow, four-room house "on the way to the waterworks" (HB 223). The investment was a wise choice for her future. The following year she related to Thomas Stritch that she was earning $55 per month in rent from the house.

L

Lourdes (France) O'Connor visited the grotto at Lourdes, France, on her pilgrimage to Europe in 1958. To Catholics, the grotto is a holy shrine based on what is believed to be an apparition of the Blessed Virgin Mary to St. Bernadette in 1848. Many people afflicted with physical illnesses or other concerns make a pilgrimage to Lourdes to immerse in the water of the grotto, praying for a cure or other miracle. O'Connor traveled with her mother as well as her Aunt Kate Semmes, who also paid for their trip.

When she arrived at Lourdes, O'Connor was less than impressed. She found the situation unsanitary with so many people with sores and other ailments entering the water, and she was also not pleased with the commercialization of the site with its souvenir shops, and so forth. She did, however, step into the water of the grotto, where she said she prayed more for her book than for her legs. After she returned home from her trip, the author enjoyed a time of relief from pain as well as renewed energy and interest in activities (such as learning to drive) and continued zest for her work.

Lourdes is located in the heart of the Pyrenees Mountains bordering France and Spain in the southwest region of the country. About 5 million people visit Lourdes each year. On February 11, 1848, young Bernadette Soubirous, along with her sister and a friend, was looking for wood in the area of the grotto. She removed her socks to cross the stream when she heard a noise like wind and turned to see the vision of a lady in the grotto. According to Bernadette, the lady wore a white veil and robe with a blue belt, and she stood barefoot with a yellow rose on each foot. The girl made the sign of the cross and prayed the rosary with the lady. When they finished the rosary, the lady disappeared. Bernadette felt compelled to visit the spot again on February 14, when the lady also appeared and prayed the rosary with her.

On her third visit on February 18, Bernadette said, the lady spoke to her. The lady told her that she would not promise her happiness in this world but in the next. She asked if she would visit the spot for two weeks and requested that a church be built at the spot. Bernadette did as the lady asked, and word of the apparition spread. Visitors in the hundreds and then thousands began to come with her and to pray as she knelt in prayer at the grotto before the vision only she could see. The visions and messages continued for two weeks for a total of 18 apparitions. Despite some challenges even within the Catholic Church about the authenticity of the visions, most believers accepted them as true events, and Bernadette received the support of Catholic clergy in many local and regional circles. The church for which the lady had asked was built.

Young Bernadette Soubirous went on to live a life full of different kinds of challenges. She died on April 16, 1879. Bernadette was beatified in

1925 and was canonized a saint by Pope Pius XI in 1933.

Lowell, Robert (Traill Spence), Jr. (1917–1977)

American poet   Lowell was born in Boston and educated at Harvard and Kenyon College. He married his first wife, writer Jean Stafford, in 1940 and converted to ROMAN CATHOLICISM. During World War II, Lowell was sentenced as a conscientious objector to serve one year and one day in a federal penitentiary. He served five months in a penitentiary in Danbury, Connecticut, and writes about his experience in his poems "In the Cage" and "Memories of West Street and Lepke."

Lowell's collection *Lord Weary's Castle* won the Pulizer Prize in 1947. Two poems from that collection are among his best known, "The Quaker Graveyard in Nantucket" and "Colloquy in Black Rock." Also in 1947, he was appointed poetry consultant to the Library of Congress, a position now called Poet Laureate. His collection *Life Studies* won the National Book Award for poetry in 1959. He won a second Pulitzer Prize for poetry in 1973 for *The Dolphin*. Lowell also wrote essays, plays, and translations.

O'Connor met Lowell at YADDO in 1948, and through him she became acquainted with several other people in the literary world. He was good to her, and she never forgot it. He recommended her for a Guggenheim, which she did not win (HB 7). O'Connor was also a friend of the writer who became Lowell's second wife, Elizabeth Hardwick, who was also at Yaddo. The two took her to a dinner party where she met writer MARY MCCARTHY and made the well-known remark to her about the Eucharist. Lowell also introduced O'Connor to Robert Giroux, who would later become her editor. In a letter to poet ELIZABETH BISHOP, O'Connor mentions Lowell showing her a picture of Bishop sitting on a porch in Florida and always speaking highly of her (HB 198).

O'Connor lived with Hardwick for a short time in New York City after the three left Yaddo in protest over its admissions policies and the practices of its director. During the years, O'Connor stayed in contact with Lowell and Hardwick and followed their careers. In 1952, she asked Giroux to send the couple a copy of *Wise Blood* (HB 34). She was pleased when Lowell wrote to tell her that he liked the gorilla; she wrote back that she hoped he would like the rest of the book as well, since a copy was on its way.

From O'Connor's letters to him and the way she speaks of him to others, O'Connor felt deeply for the poet and his troubled spirit. They had an easy, joking relationship with each other. In several letters, O'Connor teases Hardwick and Lowell to bring their daughter, Harriet, down south where she would get a good education (HB 311). In another, she scolds him for telling stories about her from their Yaddo days.

In 1956, O'Connor wrote to Betty Hester about one of Hester's stories and compared one of her characters to an imaginary friend of "Cal" Lowell's. The friend was named "Arms" and was half-man, half-bear, and worked as a policeman. Lowell called him "Arms of the law," and claimed he said the more outlandish things that Cal was too polite to say (HB 188). This example and others shows the closeness that existed between the two writers, even though they rarely saw each other after the early days at Yaddo.

O'Connor grieved over Lowell's psychological problems, but especially over his leaving the church. When she met him at Yaddo, he had just left his first wife, Jean Stafford, and also the church. She was overjoyed when, over the course of the winter of 1948, she observed him come back into the church. When he left a second time, it appeared to be for good, and it pained her greatly. She thought he had not yet convinced himself that he did not believe, and she prayed that he might find an easy way back. In a 1956 letter to Betty Hester, she wrote, "He is one of the people I love and there is a part of me that won't be at peace until he is at peace in the Church" (HB 152).

Lowell divorced Elizabeth Hardwick in 1972 and married Irish novelist and journalist Lady Caroline Blackwood the same year. Plagued by frequent hospitalizations for mental illness, Lowell died in New York City in 1977.

Other works by Lowell include: *For the Union Dead* (1964); *The Old Glory* (1965, rev. 1968); and *Notebook, 1967–68* (1969).

lupus   The disease that killed O'Connor at the age of 39 and her father when she was 15 is a chronic autoimmune disease of the blood in which the person's immune system attacks the body's own tissues and vital organs. Causes for the disease are still unknown, though genetics are thought to play a role. Symptoms range from mild to severe and may be triggered by a variety of factors, including exposure to sunlight, infections, certain chemicals, and medications. Hormonal links appear to be present but are still not clearly understood. Symptoms of the illness include fatigue; joint pain (sometimes known as lupus arthritis) especially in the smaller joints of the wrists, hands, elbows, knees, and ankles; skin rashes; fever; and a sensitivity to light. Other symptoms may include nervous system problems such as loss of memory and severe headaches; heart problems; anxiety and depression; weight and hair loss; and discolorations of the skin. The kind of treatment for the disease depends on the severity of symptoms, whether the organs are being damaged, and to what extent the symptoms are interfering with the person's daily life. Treatments may involve lifestyle changes and frequent monitoring of the disease by a physician, medications such as nonsteroidal anti-inflammatory drugs, and biological and relaxation therapies. Surgery, such as a kidney transplant, may be performed if the disease becomes severe enough to cause damage to organs.

Many patients with lupus manage their disease through caring for themselves at home with frequent checkups by a physician. Doctors ask their patients to be on the alert for "flares," or episodes of symptoms and to try to create a lifestyle that will help avoid triggers. For example, stress is thought to be a trigger for lupus symptoms. Doctors recommend the patient avoid stress and its accompanying fatigue by keeping to a simple daily schedule, delegating and avoiding obligations to other people as much as possible, exercising regularly such as taking a daily walk, and using calming techniques like yoga or meditation. During remissions, doctors may scale back or change the patient's medication. Danger signals for lupus sufferers that require a doctor's immediate attention include symptoms of heart attack or stroke, sudden numbness or paralysis, blurring or darkening of vision, shortness of breath, fainting, seizure, or any sudden dizziness, severe headache, or clumsiness.

O'Connor's diagnosis of lupus at the age of 25 marked an important turning point in both her life and her career. The first onset of illness while she was home on a visit to her mother in 1950 landed her in the hospital, where she stayed for some time. In order to live with her incurable disease and ease symptom triggers, O'Connor needed to modify her lifestyle in a way that would curtail stress and reduce outside obligations. This meant leaving the kind of literary life she had launched in New York and Connecticut and returning to the small southern town of MILLEDGEVILLE, GEORGIA, to reside permanently under the care of her mother. She was also told to avoid all salt, even that naturally occurring in milk, and was given an experimental drug at the time, ACTH, which required a daily self-inoculation.

Even in her first days in the hospital, O'Connor continued to work on her first novel, *Wise Blood.* During the next 14 years, she continued to write on a limited schedule each day and in fact went on to write her best-known work. During remissions, O'Connor traveled to give talks and lectures at universities and made one trip to Europe, where she sought healing from the waters of the LOURDES grotto in France and had an audience with the pope.

Lupus manifests itself in O'Connor's work, many critics observe, through the physical deformities in some of her characters, such as Joy, the girl with the artificial leg in "Good Country People." Others argue that the disease made O'Connor even more sensitive to loss that caused emotional suffering in her characters. Some claim that her illness fueled the rage and violence in her stories, that writing about such angry and troubled characters was her way of fighting back. Still others argue that living with a debilitating disease affected O'Connor's writing most by influencing her lifestyle, causing her to return home to rural Georgia and write the largest share of her mature work under the constant vigilance and care of her mother.

M

Mademoiselle The magazine published O'Connor's story "The Turkey," in its November 1948 issue (vol. 28) under the title, "The Capture (later revised to "An Afternoon in the Woods")." O'Connor mentioned the forthcoming fall publication in the magazine in her June 19, 1948, letter to Elizabeth McKee when she writes to solicit her services as an agent. When it appeared, the story had been heavily revised by the author from the version in her master's thesis. In 1961, the magazine reprinted the story in a collection *Best Stories from Mademoiselle*, edited by Cyrilly Abels and Margarita G. Smith. After O'Connor's death, *Mademoiselle* published "The Crop" in its April 1971 issue (vol. 72, no. 6), with an explanation of the posthumous publication by Robert Fitzgerald.

Mademoiselle was established in the 1930s as an American fashion magazine aimed toward a female audience. At the same time as it featured articles and advertising on style and trends in fashion, it also published fiction and poetry from enduring authors such as O'Connor and poet Sylvia Plath. Plath, a contemporary of O'Connor's, worked as a student guest editor in New York on the college issue in the summer of 1953, less than five years after O'Connor's story appeared in the magazine. Cyrilly Abels, who helped choose and edit O'Connor's story for the collected best stories of the magazine, was the inspiration for the character Jay Cee in Plath's autobiographical novel, *The Bell Jar*. As Esther Greenwood does for Jay Cee, Plath reported to Abels during her guest editorship in New York. More than 60 years after its first issue, the magazine suspended publication in November 2001, transferring subscribers to its sister publication, *Glamour* magazine.

Maritain, Jacques (1882–1973) Jacques Maritain was a French philosopher and thinker who wrote in the Thomist tradition. He helped bring the teachings of St. Thomas Aquinas to a broader reading public in the 20th century. His works include *Introduction to Philosophy* (1920); *The Degrees of Knowledge* (1932); *Art and Faith* (1948); *The Range of Reason* (1948); *Man and the State* (1951); and *Approches de Dieu* (1953). Maritain's lasting influence can be seen in such legacies and tributes to his work as the University of Notre Dame's Jacques Maritain Center, several journals, and more than 20 national associations organized and named in his honor.

Though Maritain was a philosopher, Flannery O'Connor appreciated his understanding of the nature of art (HB 216) and learned much of her understanding of St. Thomas Aquinas from his work (157). She quoted him in a letter to Elizabeth Hester dated September 24, 1955, that to create a work of art requires the "constant attention of the purified mind" (105). In the context of her letter, she says that the duty of the purified mind is to exclude all from a work of fiction that does not belong. Sally

This is believed to be O'Connor's First Communion photo, taken at age seven. *(Courtesy of Flannery O'Connor Collection, Georgia College & State University)*

Fitzgerald, in her introduction to *The Habit of Being*, claims that O'Connor obtained much of her aesthetics from Maritain, including the idea of cultivating a "habit of art" (xvii). O'Connor claimed that she cut her "aesthetic teeth" on *Art and Scholasticism* (216).

In 1960, O'Connor wrote to Robert Giroux to ask him to be sure to send a copy of *The Violent Bear It Away* to Maritain at Princeton. She had heard from Maurice Coindreau that after he translated *Wise Blood* into French, he gave it to Maritain, who read it and was so impressed that he invited Coindreau to discuss it.

Mass O'Connor was a faithful and practicing Roman Catholic, which meant that she attended Mass at least once a week on Sundays as well as on the Holy Days of Obligation throughout the church year. The Holy Days of the year include: New Year's Day; the Ascension of Christ into heaven after Easter; the Assumption of the Blessed Virgin Mary into heaven; the Immaculate Conception; All Saints Day; and Christmas Day. Catholics also attend Mass on feast days of the saints throughout the year that may be special to them, such as on the feast day (deathday) of their namesake. They may ask that a Mass be said in honor or in memory of a living or deceased loved one, and then they, and usually their family members, will attend that particular Mass.

O'Connor frequently attended weekday Mass, which means that she went to church as part of her school or workday routine in addition to regular Sunday attendance, either early in the morning, around midday, or in the evening. This was one of her practices while in graduate school at the UNIVERSITY OF IOWA. When she lived at the artists' colony YADDO in Saratoga Springs, New York, she attended Mass with the domestic workers of the mansion and grounds since many of the artists were nonbelievers, of other faiths, or were, like poet ROBERT LOWELL, nonpracticing Catholics.

Roman Catholics believe that the Mass is a reenactment of the Last Supper of Jesus Christ, during which bread and wine become not symbols of the body and blood of Christ but of the actual physical presence of the Lord in the form of the body and blood, a mystery Catholics accept called transubstantiation. O'Connor was careful to make this distinction between Catholic and Protestant beliefs (Communion as symbol or as transubstantiation) whenever given the opportunity. The difference was not a subtle one to her; it was crucial.

A typical Roman Catholic Mass in the United States lasts about an hour. Depending on the level of respect shown in the different parts of the Mass, the congregation stands, sits, or kneels. The parts of the Mass include: the Entrance (procession); the Penitential Rite (asking for forgiveness of sins); the Liturgy of the Word (readings and homily); the Offertory Rites (offering of gifts); the Liturgy of the Eucharist (consecration of the bread and wine into the body and blood of Christ); and the Concluding Rites (blessing and recessional). Hymns are frequently sung at different points in the Mass, and the homily is a sermon given by the priest or his representative at the closing of the Liturgy of the Word. Frequently, the homily explains or interprets the readings. Catholic writers such as O'Connor frequently cite growing up in the church listening to the Liturgy of the Word as integral to their appreciation, comfort, and facilitation with language and the importance or sacredness of words.

Catholics believe that the Mass is the church's greatest prayer. Most churches have at least one Mass per day and more than one on Sundays. After the Second Vatican Council, Saturday evening Masses were added for the purpose of giving more options to congregants to meet the Sunday obligation of attending Mass. A Catholic may not receive Communion more than once per day.

Mauriac, François (1885–1970)   Mauriac was a French Catholic novelist whose work O'Connor admitted influenced her own. She writes about reading his work and mentions him frequently until days before her death. Mauriac won the Nobel Prize in literature in 1952. His complete works were published in 12 volumes between 1950 and 1956. In 1957, O'Connor wrote to Elizabeth Hester that she had eight of his novels.

Mauriac was born in Bordeaux, and his father died when he was just 18 months old. The youngest of five, Mauriac lived a rather sheltered childhood, guarded by his mother and then schooled by the Marianites. He studied in Bordeaux and Paris and published poems and other works. He became famous in 1922 after the publication of *Le Baiser aux lepreux* (*A Kiss for the Leper*). Other works include *Le Cahier noir* (*The Black Notebook*), using the pseudonym Forez while living in hiding in World War II, and *Le Desert de l'amour* (*The Desert of Love*) in 1925. Mauriac wrote plays that were produced by the Comédie-Française. He worked as a journalist, serving as contributing editor to the periodical *Figaro*.

O'Connor mentions Mauriac works specifically in *The Habit of Being* including: *God and Mammon* (143); *Lines of Life* (also called *Destinies*) (237); *The Lamb* (241); *The Stumbling Block* (263); *Questions of Precedence* (345); and *Mémoires Intérieurs* (431). A few days before her death in 1964, O'Connor wrote to Janet McKane to thank her for the Mauriac book that she hopes to get to sooner or later when she is feeling better.

O'Connor stated that Mauriac was one of the French Catholic novelists who helped her. She wrote that readers interested in Catholic novelists should begin with him, Bloy, and Bernanos. She noticed at one point that his work does not dramatize evil intruding on the good life in order for a shocking act of grace to occur but instead has the good intrude on the evil. Mauriac claimed that God does not care what the writer writes but uses it (360), so O'Connor added that this means the writer needs to write the best that he or she can for God's purpose and leave the ultimate purpose of the piece to God. O'Connor called Mauriac one of her "admirations" (356). She noted, "Mauriac says *only* fiction does not lie and I believe him" (152).

McCarthy, Mary (Therese) (1912–1989)   *American critic and novelist*   In 1952, O'Connor thanked Robert Giroux for sending her McCarthy's *The Groves of Academe*, a novel that satirizes the academic world during the Joseph McCarthy era (HB 37). In 1953, O'Connor wrote to the Fitzgeralds that Randall Jarrell's *Pictures from an Institution* was perhaps good in terms of Jarrell but was not excellent fiction. She described it as being "of the School of Mary [McCarthy]" (54). O'Connor knew that McCarthy continued to write about the Catholic Church after leaving it at the age of 15. She called her, sarcastically, a "Big Intellectual" (124).

McCarthy was exposed to Catholicism in Minnesota, where she lived for many years after becoming orphaned at the age of six. The strictness of her orthodox relatives turned her away from the church, and she admitted to losing her faith at age 15. She later went to live with her grandparents in Seattle, which she found much more congenial. The years in Minnesota left their mark, however, and McCarthy continued her interest in the church as a writing subject. Most notable, perhaps, is her autobiographical account, *Memories of a Catholic Girlhood* (1957).

She attended private schools and received her B.A. from Vassar College in 1933. McCarthy was employed as a critic for *The New Republic,* the *Nation,* and the *PARTISAN REVIEW.* She served on the editorial staff of the *Partisan Review* from 1937 to 1948, where she contributed articles on art, politics, theater, and travel. Four marriages included one to the critic Edmund Wilson in 1938; Wilson encouraged her to write fiction.

Chief among the topics of McCarthy's work are satire and commentaries on such subjects as the expression of sexuality, the institution of marriage, the role of women in contemporary urban life, and the weaknesses and failures of intellectuals.

Perhaps most important to O'Connor studies is the fact that Mary McCarthy is the writer to whom O'Connor stated her most famous one-line defense of the sacred Eucharist. At a dinner party with McCarthy and others, O'Connor listened as McCarthy spoke about the Sacred Host. She said that as a child, she always thought of the Host as the Holy Ghost, since that was the person of the Trinity (God the Father, the Son, and the Holy Spirit) whom she envisioned as the most "portable." Then she went on to describe the Host as a symbol and implied that as a symbol it worked pretty well. After listening to this talk, O'Connor could no longer contain herself. In a shaky voice, she spoke up and said, "Well, if it's a symbol, to hell with it" (125).

By 1957, O'Connor's comments about McCarthy soften in her letters, though there remains a slight distancing from McCarthy's intellectualism. Perhaps this attitude came about as a result of their mutual friend, Elizabeth Hardwick, ROBERT LOWELL's wife and fellow writer. It could also be that she finally accepted her as a contemporary colleague. McCarthy joined Robert Fitzgerald, O'Connor, and others in the receipt of a $1,000 grant from the National Institute of Arts & Letters in 1957 (218).

O'Connor defended McCarthy's intelligence either directly or indirectly in reference to a review written about a work of Jean Stafford's. In a let-

ter to Betty Hester she wrote that male reviewers take cheap shots at her writing (Stafford's and/or McCarthy's) because she is so much more intelligent than they are (203). She commented on McCarthy's article in the *Partisan* entitled "The Fact in Fiction," which she had heard about but not read herself. O'Connor understands that she states that there are no miracles allowed in fiction, and she wonders if McCarthy considers the Eccentric Tradition in her analysis (413). In 1963, she remarked to Cecil Dawkins that KATHERINE ANNE PORTER sent her a review from France in which *A Good Man* is reviewed alongside McCarthy's *The Group.* She calls this placement with McCarthy in a French review journal "Fancy" (553).

Among several travel works, essays, reviews, and many other pieces, McCarthy's *The Group* (1963) is her best-known novel.

Milledgeville, Georgia   O'Connor lived in Milledgeville beginning in 1938 as a child of 13 until she graduated from college in 1945 at GEORGIA STATE COLLEGE FOR WOMEN. She also lived there again as an adult from 1951 until her death in 1964. In all, the small southern city, or the farm ANDALUSIA four miles outside of it, was home to the author for a total of 20 of her 39 years.

Milledgeville is the former state capital of Georgia. It was founded in 1804 specifically for that purpose and named after Georgia governor John Milledge, whose ancestors dated back to the original colonists. Prior to that time, the area was known as a trading-post region along the Oconee River for Europeans and Creek Native Americans. The town expanded and became richer due to the building boom of the 1820s. In 1839, the state built an executive mansion in the city in which the governor would live, and the railroad to the town was completed in 1852.

During the Civil War, the city hosted several Confederate officers. On November 23, 1864, General Sherman arrived in Milledgeville on his way to SAVANNAH during the famous Sherman March to the Sea. While there, he took up residence in the governor's mansion. Soldiers raised the American flag on the state capitol and held a mock meeting of the legislature where soldiers played representatives. It was from this location that Sherman ordered Special Field Order No. 127, commanding Union soldiers to treat citizens by harsh means if they tried to interfere with their march to the sea. Though he spared the mansion the capitol building, and other nonmilitary sites in the city, Sherman destroyed 50 years of state records.

After Reconstruction, Georgia had two governors, one military and one political. The military branch of government chose to headquarter in ATLANTA because it served as a hub for the railroad network in the state. When the political governor in Milledgeville left the state, it was decided to move the state capital to Atlanta in 1868. After this departure of its main function and founding purpose, Milledgeville lost most of its strength and vitality. Some government offices kept in the town helped it survive.

The Cline ancestral home on Greene Street in Milledgeville was the temporary residence of the governor until the mansion was completed in 1838. It was built in 1837 and is known was known as Government House. Peter James Cline, O'Connor's grandfather, was elected mayor of Milledgeville in 1888. One of his accomplishments in that role was helping the city install a water system in 1891.

N

New World Writing A chapter that would later be revised before inclusion in *Wise Blood* called "Enoch and the Gorilla," appeared in volume 1 of this publication in April 1952. That issue was edited by Arabel Porter. NWW also published an early version of the opening chapter of *The Violent Bear It Away* called "You Can't Be Any Poorer Than Dead," in volume 8, October 1955. Lastly, O'Connor's work was published in the volume 19, 1961 issue edited by Theodore Solotaroff. This was "Everything That Rises Must Converge."

New World Writing was a paperback anthology of fiction, drama, poetry, and essays and was published from 1952 to 1959. The works included were similar to those published by small literary journals. Writers published here in addition to O'Connor include W. H. Auden, Robinson Jeffers, Dylan Thomas, James Baldwin, and Jack Kerouac.

O. Henry Award Named after the writer O. Henry, the awards are arguably the most prestigious recognition given to the best short stories published in English periodicals in the United States or Canada in the previous year. The stories are compiled and republished in a book anthology. O'Connor had stories included five times with two of them as the prize-winning story—in 1955, edited by Paul Engle and Hansford Martin, "A Circle in the Fire"; in 1957, edited by Paul Engle and Constance Urdang, the first-prize story, "Greenleaf"; in 1959, edited by Paul Engle and Constance Urdang, "A View of the Woods"; in 1963, edited by Richard Poirier, "Everything That Rises Must Converge"; and the first-prize story in 1965, edited by Richards Poirier and William Abraham, "Revelation."

The O. Henry Award began in 1918, eight years after the death of O. Henry, when the Twilight Club, founded in 1883 (later called the Society of Arts and Letters) honored the late O. Henry at a dinner at the Hotel McAlpin in New York City. O. Henry was so warmly remembered by those who knew him that a committee met at the Hotel Biltmore that December to set up a memorial to the writer. The committee came up with the idea of reading short stories published each year and handing out AWARDS in O. Henry's name to help draw attention to the short-story form that O. Henry loved as well as to encourage new writers. The O. Henry Award Stories have been published in an annual anthology ever since the first volume appeared in 1919.

P

Partisan Review   While she lived in New York, O'Connor published two early versions of what would become chapters in *Wise Blood* in *Partisan Review*. "The Heart of the Park" was published in February 1949, and "The Peeler" was published in December 1949. The journal also published "A View of the Woods" in the fall 1957 issue.

Partisan Review was founded by William Phillips and Philip Rahv in 1934 as an outgrowth of the John Reed Club. It began as a quarterly arts publication supporting the American Communist Party but evolved into an anti-Communist publication after Stalin. Publication ceased from 1936 to 1937, then resumed until its last issue in 2003. The journal had only 15,000 subscribers at its peak but was particularly influential from the late 1930s to the early 1960s. *Partisan Review* published such renowned writers as Saul Bellow, T. S. Eliot, George Orwell, Isaac Bashevis Singer, and Susan Sontag.

Peabody High School   Located in Milledgeville, Georgia, this was O'Connor's secondary school alma mater, which she attended from 1938 and graduated in 1942. It was one of 10 "experimental" schools in the state of Georgia and was affiliated with the local college, Georgia State College for Women (now Georgia College and State University). O'Connor was not impressed with the school's progressive curriculum, involving student-selected rather than state-mandated subjects and teachers

who circulated among subjects every six weeks. She believed that she did not get the education there that she needed as a future writer. Even so, she did participate in extracurricular activities, such as

O'Connor, most likely a school photo from Peabody High *(Courtesy of Flannery O'Connor Collection, Georgia College & State University)*

serving as art editor for the *Peabody Palladium* as well as submitting CARTOONS, essays, and reviews.

Peabody Model School began in 1891 as a school established for the purpose of providing student-teaching experience for the Georgia Normal and Industrial College in Milledgeville (later named Georgia State College for Women and Georgia College and State University). It also provided the first public education in Baldwin County. A high school was added in 1927, and the high school built and moved into its own facility in the 1930s. By the 1970s, Peabody experienced decreasing enrollment due to the development of the public school system in Baldwin County as well as education students from the college moving their student teaching into those schools. The facility remained part of the college as the Peabody Child and Family Center until it was closed suddenly in 2000 due to budget cuts.

peacocks   O'Connor enjoyed birds, chickens, and exotic fowl all of her life, but she appreciated no single species as much as the peacocks she raised at ANDALUSIA for many years. The most common type of the famous bird with the beautiful plumage is the Indian peafowl; its scientific name is *Pavo cristatus*. *Peacock* is actually the name of the male peafowl; the female is called a peahen; however, over time *peacock* has become into common use as a generic term for the bird. The peacock is a member of the pheasant family; the male is about the size of a turkey. The large fan of plumage on the male is called its train. The long feathers of the train are actually grown from the back of the male, not the tail, though *tail* and *train* are often used interchangeably in speaking about this part of the bird. Males spread their train and parade slowly in front of a female during courtship. The males are characterized by an iridescent blue-green color around

Peacock in full array. O'Connor took great pleasure in the flock of more than 40 peafowl she raised at Andalusia, and often featured peacocks in her writings. In "The Displaced Person," Father Flynn compares a peacock that he sees with flared feathers to Christ's Transfiguration. *(Courtesy Getty Images—John Foxx)*

the neck and breast, with purplish blue feathers in the under parts. The feathers of the magnificent train can reach more than two feet in mature birds. The train feathers are metallic green with a brilliant iridescent spot at the end that is called the eye. Females are smaller, have less bold colors to their feathers, and do not have a train. They make their nest on the ground in a protected spot and lay about 10 brownish eggs. Peafowl have been known to live as long as 35 years.

The Indian peacock does not like changeable climates; it is native to India and Sri Lanka, where it can be found roaming wild or in city parks and on large estates. The bird can be raised tame elsewhere where there is enough land. It feeds on snails, frogs, insects, fruit, grains, juicy grasses, and bulbs. When Regina Cline O'Connor first objected to Flannery wanting to raise them at ANDALUSIA, it was partly because she had heard that peacocks eat flowers. Flannery told her they would eat the feed they gave to the other fowl; however, her mother turned out to be right.

One of the benefits of moving back to the farm at MILLEDGEVILLE for O'Connor was that it allowed her to rekindle her interest and activity in raising exotic birds. In September 1951, she wrote to Robert and Sally Fitzgerald about her flock of 21 brown ducks, five geese, and 15 turkeys. She added pheasants by May 1952, and in late summer of that year she answered an ad and purchased a peacock, a peahen, and four peachickens. She once wrote, "My quest, whatever it was actually for, ended with peacocks. Instinct, not knowledge, led me to them" (*Collected*, 832) (MM4–5; FOC157). Evidence from her letters indicates that the flock grew under her care. In July 1955, she writes of having 16 peachickens. Nine years after the arrival of her first peacocks, she claims she had "forty beaks to feed" (834). She found the birds not only hardy and fairly easy to care for but also prolific—her flock grew relatively quickly until she no longer kept an accurate census.

O'Connor was fascinated with the birds. She writes in letters of sitting on the back steps for long periods studying them. It is no surprise, then, to note that the creatures appear in her fiction and essays. In "The Displaced Person," for example,

Mrs. McIntyre's three remaining peacocks may be understood to represent her declining recognition of God's grace in her life. The peacock's magnificent beauty transcends the physical world to symbolize the spiritual realm. When Father Flynn sees the peacock spread its train and he murmurs, "The Transfiguration," Mrs. McIntyre does not understand the priest's reference to Jesus' transfiguration described in the Bible.

O'Connor's essay "The King of the Birds," which appeared in HOLIDAY magazine in September 1961, best relates the details and her feelings about her history with these birds. She describes when and how her interest began, how she started her flock, how it grew, habits of the peacocks as she observed them, and what it was like to live with so many of the birds on the property. She enjoyed the thought of peacocks so much and wanted to have so many that she could not walk anywhere on the farm without encountering them. Apparently, the author got her wish. In the essay, she describes her peacocks flying to the rooftops, sitting on fenceposts, eating flowers, and screaming their calls all through the day and night. O'Connor's patience and delight in the birds saved them not only from her mother's displeasure but also from similar responses from farm workers, neighbors, and visitors.

After she died and her mother moved into town, the birds apparently left on their own or died off. No known descendants of O'Connor's flock exist at Andalusia. Hopeful speculation by some fans that someone over the years may have adopted a bird or two from O'Connor's flock and is knowingly raising its descendants elsewhere has not been verified. Neither has any local peacock flock been proven or disproved to bear descendants of wanderers from O'Connor's brood.

Peacocks were the subject of a poem O'Connor enclosed in a February 1953 letter to Robert and Sally Fitzgerald. In "The Peacock Roosts," she compares the eyes of the peacock's train to suns. Images of peacock feathers have graced the covers of several books associated with O'Connor, most notably *The Complete Stories*. The long green train feathers with the gold and blue, iridescent eyes are so connected with the author that they are even sold at the Andalusia gift shop. Sales help support the Andalusia Foundation in its efforts to restore and maintain the farm for the use and enjoyment of visitors and scholars.

Percy, Walker (1916–1990)   *American novelist* Percy was a contemporary of O'Connor's. Both were southern writers and Catholic. Percy's concerns were of the changes taking place in the New South as a result of technology and industrialization. His first novel, *The Moviegoer* (1961), won the National Book Award.

Percy was orphaned after his father committed suicide, and his mother died in a car crash. He lived with his brothers at their father's uncle's; he was an unmarried lawyer. Percy received degrees at the University of North Carolina and Columbia and worked as a pathologist at Bellevue Hospital in New York City. While there, he contracted tuberculosis and was forced to recuperate at a facility upstate. During this time, he read widely, converted to ROMAN CATHOLICISM, and decided to turn his career toward writing.

Percy's other works include: *The Last Gentleman* (1966); *Love in the Ruins: The Adventures of a Bad Catholic at a Time Near the End of the World* (1971); *The Message in the Bottle* (1975); *Lancelot* (1977); *The Second Coming* (1980); *The Thanatos Syndrome* (1987).

On March 29, 1962, Flannery O'Connor thought enough of her colleague's fiction that she wrote a letter to him, congratulating him on winning the National Book Award. She writes, "I'm glad we lost the War and you won the National Book Award. I didn't think the judges would have that much sense but they surprised me. Regards" (HB 470).

Poe, Edgar Allen (1809–1849)   *American short-story writer, poet, critic, and editor* Poe is the author of such classic poems as the "The Raven," and the stories "The Fall of the House of Usher," "The Cask of Amontillado," "The Tell-Tale Heart," and "The Black Cat." As one interested in violence, death, the macabre, and the unusual, Poe has much in common with O'Connor. They also share a dark sense of humor. It should be no surprise to O'Connor readers that she claimed Poe as an early influence.

Poe was the son of actors. When his mother died, he was taken in by John Allan, a family friend, and his wife, a childless couple. From 1815 to 1820, he was educated in Scotland and England and continued his education in Richmond, Virginia. In 1826, he attended the University of Virginia for 11 months, but his proclivity for gambling and losing angered John Allan, who withdrew his support, and Poe's enrollment at UVA ceased.

After a try at military service and West Point, Poe's drinking drove him out of the service, and he landed in Baltimore and then Richmond, where he continued to write. In 1835, he worked as an editor and reviewer at the *Southern Literary Messenger*. While in Richmond, he married his 13-year-old cousin, Virginia Clemm. Despite the youth and close relation of his bride, accounts indicate that Poe was a devoted husband.

Edgar Allan Poe, 1848. Poe's *The Humorous Tales of Edgar Allan Poe* were an early influence on O'Connor. *(Courtesy of Edgar Allan Poe Society)*

Poe suffered from abuse of alcohol, though some reports indicate that he was rarely drunk, but when he was, he was often seen in public. Consequently, his reputation for drinking was larger than his actual habit. There is also debate about whether or not Poe was addicted to drugs. Poe's wife died in 1847, and he had several platonic and romantic relationships afterward. He died from excessive drinking combined with a weak heart and is buried in Baltimore.

In 1955, Elizabeth Hester asked her new friend Flannery O'Connor what she read early in life that most influenced her writing. O'Connor responded that as a child she mostly read the Greek and Roman myths from a collection called *The Book of Knowledge*. Then she offered several remarks about what she calls her "Poe period." Her time reading Poe lasted for several years. Chief among her reading and rereading of his work, she says, was a book called *The Humerous* (spelled that way) *Tales of Edgar Allan Poe*.

The Humerous Tales contains 21 stories. Some of their titles have a certain ring of familiarity to O'Connor readers: "The Duc de L'Omlette"; "Lionizing"; "Tale of Jerusalem"; "Bon-Bon"; "The Man That Was Used up"; "King Pest"; "Loss of Breath"; "Four beasts in one — The Homo-Cameleopard"; "The Devil in the Belfry"; "Three Sundays in a Week"; "Never bet the Devil your head"; "Why the little Frenchman wears his hand in a sling"; "The Angel of the Odd"; "The Business Man"; "Literary Life of Thingum Bob, Esq"; "How to write a Blackwood article"; "A Predicament"; "X-ing in a Paragrab"; "Diddling"; "Von Kempelen and his discovery"; and "Mellonta Tauta."

Interestingly, the three stories O'Connor recalls in her brief summaries of them to Betty Hester are not all from this collection. One that is from the book is "The Man That Was Used Up" (about a fine man who gradually removes wooden limbs, a wig, and so forth). The other two are not. Instead, "The Spectacles" (about a man who will not wear glasses and accidentally marries his own great-great-great-grandmother) is from the collection, *The Works of the Late Edgar Allan Poe* (1850). The other story about lunatics taking over the asylum is likely "The System of

Dr. Tarr and Professor Fether" from the same collection.

Influences from the three stories O'Connor recalled are worthy of further investigation. On the surface, similarities between "The Man That Was Used Up" and O'Connor's stories with missing or artificial limbs such as "Good Country People" and "The Life You Save May Be Your Own" seem clear. The misguidedness of faulty vision from "The Spectacles," though humorous in Poe's story, may resonate with the blindness in *Wise Blood*. The controlling behavior of the patients in "The System of Dr. Tarr and Professor Fether" may echo through the doctor's waiting room of "Revelation" and the actions of Singleton in the state asylum in "The Partridge Festival."

Porter, Katherine Anne (1890–1980) *American novelist and short-story writer* Porter joins fellow writers EUDORA WELTY and WILLIAM FAULKNER on O'Connor's list of contemporary writers of whom she had never heard or read until she went to graduate school in Iowa. Of the three, however, Porter is the only one with whom O'Connor might be said to have had a somewhat active acquaintance.

Educated in private and convent schools in the South, Porter later worked as a journalist in Chicago and Denver and then went to Mexico, which provided the setting for several of her stories. Her first published story was "Maria Concepcion," which appeared in 1922. Her first collection was *Flowering Judas* (1930). Porter's short fiction, which consisted of long stories with complex character development normally found only in novels, secured her reputation as a fiction writer. Her style was impeccable as well. O'Connor particularly liked Porter's early work.

Despite her reputation as a fine stylist of short fiction, Porter did not enjoy financial success. She supported herself primarily through writer's residencies at colleges and universities, through fellowships, and through stints doing uncredited screenwriting work in Hollywood. Despite this, her work earned AWARDS and accolades. Porter's *Collected Short Stories* (1965) won both the National Book Award and the Pulizer Prize for fiction. Her story "Holiday," (1962) won an O. HENRY AWARD.

Her one and only novel, *Ship of Fools*, was much anticipated by those who had followed her career.

The publication of the novel in 1962 improved Porter's financial situation. Not only did the book become a best seller, but it was also made into a feature film in 1965. The story involves a group of Germans on an ocean voyage back to Germany from Mexico just before Hitler's rise to power in 1931. The psychological insight and the precision of her ironic style are hallmarks of the novel just as in her shorter fiction.

In 1957, O'Connor wrote to Cecil Dawkins that she had heard what may be an exaggerated version of Porter's writing process, that Porter envisions the whole story before starting to write. O'Connor indicates that at that time she starts with an idea and then follows her nose as she goes along at two pages a day (248). Later that year, also to Dawkins, she wrote of hearing that Porter is very pleasant with both women and men whom she knows have met her. She writes that catty remarks about women writers being rivals are probably found between writers of lesser quality (260). She mentions to Maryat Lee in 1958 that Wesleyan is having Porter visit and can afford "the best people" (266).

O'Connor did not have to live the rest of her life relying only on rumors about her fellow southern Catholic writer, Katherine Anne Porter. The two met in the spring of 1958 when Porter gave a reading in Macon, Georgia, and was then brought by the Gossetts to ANDALUSIA for lunch. O'Connor wrote to Betty Hester about the encounter in a letter about a week later. They spoke about LOURDES, that O'Connor and her mother were planning to go there, and Porter said she had always wanted to go. Porter said that she wished to pray for the completion of her novel (*Ship of Fools*). She had, by that time, been working on it for 27 years. (Later, when O'Connor did step into the waters of the grotto, she reported that she prayed not for the healing of her legs but for the successful completion of her own novel.)

When the conversation at lunch turned to death, as it can do said O'Connor when writers and professors dine, Porter said that she would like to think that all of them would meet again one day in heaven but that she really did not know for

sure. She mentioned that she would be pleased to go where she was expected if she knew for sure where that was. O'Connor relays her impression of Porter's comment: "It was a little coy and a little wistful but there was a terrible need evident underneath it . . ." (HB 275).

O'Connor also described her meeting with Porter to Cecil Dawkins. Porter was about 65, she thought, and was very nice. She loved the PEACOCKS at Andalusia and stepped through the yard in her spike-heeled shoes to see the different varieties of chickens. She heard that the reading went well and shared details of what Porter reportedly wore. Apparently, this included a black halter dress without a back and long black gloves that made it difficult for her to turn the pages of her story. According to O'Connor's sources who attended the reading, she made a wobbly curtsy at the applause after every story (276). Details such as these traded among the younger women writers indicate a mixture of affection and admiration for their elder colleague. O'Connor's letters describing Porter indicate a level of respect that borders on reverence.

In a letter in the same time frame, O'Connor asked Ashley Brown who George Garrett is, since she says that someone in Macon told her that Porter said O'Connor's stories reminded her of Sacheverell Sitwell and Garrett (277). She hopes that they are satisfactory writers since Porter compared her to them. She is also plagued in another letter to Betty Hester concerning Porter's taking 27 years so far to complete her novel. O'Connor says that a novel either "runs" or it does not and that she hopes she escapes the problem of spending so long on a novel that may or may not be working (279–280).

O'Connor maintained her interest in and contact with Porter over the years. She responded to correspondence from the author in early 1960 and thanked her for having her sign a card. O'Connor referred to her own published book and how seeing it in print makes her see all of its imperfections, though she is still glad to have it finished. She also speaks about her Chinese geese and the peacocks (371).

Later that spring, O'Connor wrote to Betty Hester that she is glad to see "Miss Katherine Anne"

having her say about the publishing issue surrounding *Lady Chatterley's Lover* in the February
issue of *Encounter* (390, 394). In 1963, she wrote
to Thomas Stritch that Porter sent her a French
review of *A Good Man,* the translation of which she
doubts since she is described as living among "many
beasts" on a "vast estate" (528).

Porter visited Andalusia again in the fall of 1960
when she read at Wesleyan with Caroline Gordon and then paid a call for dinner. O'Connor was
impressed with the gentle lady once again when
Porter asked after a particular chicken O'Connor
had had on the farm two years earlier. Since it
was nighttime and she could not see the chicken
on this visit, Porter told O'Connor that she was
disappointed because she had hoped to see it again.
O'Connor, clearly astonished that Porter would
remember such a minute detail about her previous
visit, remarked, "I call that social grace . . ." (416).

Flannery quipped about her mother reading
Ship of Fools. Regina says that they are fools all
right; her timing has been off, since she tends
to read scenes that upset her stomach before
they dine. O'Connor defended Porter against her
mother's complaints, saying that Porter does have
the ability to make things seem real, even the
unpleasant facets of life (480–481). As for herself,
she admired the novel, though she says it may be a
fine book but not a great one. She thinks that the
bulldog is like a sculpture, carved perfectly (484).
In 1963, she wrote to the Fitzgeralds that perhaps
Porter will receive the Pulitzer that year. Together
with WALKER PERCY getting the National Book
Award, perhaps the attention of prizes will help

combat the image that Catholics do not contribute to the arts (511).

Though in O'Connor's time Katherine Anne
Porter seemed to be the dean of southern women
writers and her place is certainly secure in the study
of American fiction, O'Connor's work has received
arguably more attention within the academy.

prayer of St. Raphael   Said to be written by Ernest
Hello, the full text of the prayer follows. O'Connor
referenced it in a letter of July 1, 1964, to Janet
McKane, just weeks before her death. She indicated that she said the prayer every day for many
years. She encloses the prayer in a letter to McKane
on July 14, 1964.

"O Raphael, lead us toward those we are waiting for, those who are waiting for us: Raphael,
Angel of happy meeting, lead us by the hand
toward those we are looking for. May all our
movements be guided by your Light and transfigured with your joy.

Angel, guide of Tobias, lay the request we now
address to you at the feet of Him on whose
unveiled Face you are privileged to gaze. Lonely
and tired, crushed by the separations and sor-
rows of life, we feel the need of calling you and
of pleading for the protection of your wings, so
that we may not be as strangers in the province
of joy, all ignorant of the concerns of our country.
Remember the weak, you who are strong, you
whose home lies beyond the region of thunder, in
a land that is always peaceful, always serene and
bright with the resplendent glory of God."

R

Roman Catholicism One of the world's great religions, Roman Catholicism traces its origins to Jesus Christ and the Twelve Apostles. The religion has a worldwide congregation of more than 1 billion believers, the largest population of any single organized religion in the world. Roman Catholicism is one of three major branches of Christianity, along with Eastern Orthodoxy and Protestantism, the latter two breaking off from the former in historical schisms over doctrinal matters. The word *catholic* derives from the Latin *catholicus* and the Greek *katholikos*, and means "universal and including many or most things" such as someone having a catholic taste in food. Flannery O'Connor was a lifelong practicing and devout Roman Catholic who said, "I write the way I do because (not though) I am a Catholic" (HB 90). Consequently, knowledge of basic tenets of the faith and doctrines of the religion are essential to a more complete understanding of the author and her work.

The history of the church begins with Christ and his 12 Apostles, specifically with Peter, whom Catholics regard as the first pope, or head of the church. In the Gospel, Jesus said, "And I tell you, you are Peter [Greek, *petra*], and on this rock I will build my church" (Matthew 16:18). Catholics believe that this is the charter of the church, originating it with Christ and establishing the papacy with Peter as the first leader, given his authoritative and fatherly role from Christ himself. Peter's asso-

ciation with Rome in his life, along with Rome's position as the capital of the Roman Empire led to the ascendancy of the city as the geographic and organizational headquarters of the papacy and the church. Two separations from the church, the East-West schism of 1054 and the Reformation of the 16th century, led to the establishment of the Greek Orthodox Catholic Church and the many Protestant denominations. Simplified considerably, the disagreements of the Eastern church centered on territories of influence between Rome and Constantinople, married versus celibate priesthood, and other matters. Martin Luther and his followers during the Reformation denounced the infallibility of the pope (occupants of the papal office had, over the centuries, sometimes been corrupt) and set the Bible as the authoritative source of their teachings, rather than the church. They also disagreed with Catholic devotional practices involving Mary, the Mother of Jesus, and the saints and, perhaps most important, asserted that the individual's relationship with God did not need intermediaries in the form of priests, bishops, and other members of the church hierarchy.

Though the church has a highly structured and organized bureaucracy of bishops, archbishops, cardinals, priests, religious, and other offices, the average Catholic parishioner in the pew of a small-town church, such as O'Connor throughout her adult life, most frequently encounters the parish priest or perhaps parochial-school staff members such as nuns and other active members of the laity. Most see the bishop of the diocese only on special occasions. Urban parishioners are more likely to interact with higher levels of church hierarchy on a more frequent basis, such as having the bishop of the diocese also serving as the pastor of their parish, which is usually centered at a cathedral. O'Connor's home church as a child in SAVANNAH, GEORGIA, was the CATHEDRAL OF ST. JOHN THE BAPTIST, a beautiful gothic structure that she could see across the street every day and that likely made an enduring impression.

Central to Catholic belief and practice is participation in the celebration of weekly or daily Eucharist, commonly called the MASS. Catholics believe that the Mass is a reenactment of the Last Supper, at which Christ broke bread and blessed it and proclaimed it to be his body, which would suffer for the sins of all. Likewise, he blessed the cup of wine mixed with water and proclaimed it to be his blood. At the Last Supper, the night before he died, referring to the blessing of bread and wine, Jesus said, "Do this in memory of me" (1 Corinthians 11:25). Catholics take this command of Christ literally, that the bread and wine are transfigured through the Mass and the grace of God into the actual body and blood of Christ. This is called transubstantiation. That the elements of bread and wine still have the appearance and taste of bread and wine is regarded as one of the great mysteries of the church.

Flannery O'Connor accepted mystery, that we must believe through faith what we have been told by God but which we do not and cannot understand intellectually. She uses this element of mystery as a moment when God's grace may touch one's life throughout much of her work. She once said about the Eucharistic mystery that the bread and wine are not symbols or metaphors of Christ as Protestants believe. Endorsing the mystery of transubstantiation, she once said to lapsed-Catholic writer MARY MCCARTHY, who had proclaimed at a party that she now thought of the Eucharist as only a symbol although a good one, "Well, if it's a symbol, to hell with it" (HB 125). She went on to write to her friend Betty Hester that the Eucharist

"is the center of existence for me; all the rest of life is expendable" (HB 125).

Catholics also have a basic belief in the seven sacraments: Baptism, Reconciliation, Eucharist, Confirmation, Last Rites, Matrimony, and Holy Orders. Catholics believe that the sacraments are an outward sign of inward grace. Outwardly, the sacraments appear to be church ceremonies or traditions that happen once in life or many times and sometimes not at all depending on one's vocation. Most important for believers, they are moments at which God is present to them in a special way and through which they obtain grace. Baptism, Eucharist, and Confirmation are sacraments of initiation. Baptism brings a newborn child or a person later in life into the church. Eucharist is the daily or weekly celebration of Christ's sacrifice on the cross for the forgiveness of sin. Confirmation represents a maturing in the church and one's faith through free will to join the church community. Reconciliation, also commonly called Confession, is a time when the faithful confess their sins to a priest and pray for forgiveness and a change of heart and a mending of ways. Believers are encouraged to go to confession at least once per year. The sacrament of Holy Orders is given only to men who are ordained as priests; Matrimony is the sacrament of marriage. Last Rites, once known as Extreme Unction, are special prayers and gestures once given only at times when death seemed imminent and in preparation for death. More recently the sacrament is given at times of grave illness as a prayer for healing. O'Connor was baptized at the Cathedral of St. John the Baptist on April 12, 1925, received her first Communion (Eucharist) on May 8, 1932, and was confirmed on May 20, 1934.

There have been three councils in church history, long meetings held to review beliefs and practices of the church and to recommend changes that parishes around the world would all adopt—the Council of Trent (December 13, 1545, to December 4, 1563); Vatican I (1869–1870); and the Second Vatican Council (October 11, 1962, to December 8, 1965). O'Connor lived during the time of the Second Vatican Council and commented on news emitting from it, though she did not live to see all changes resulting from it adopted. Mass said in the vernacular of the local congregation rather than in Latin was one change from Vatican II. The priest facing the congregation rather than saying Mass with his back to the people was another.

O'Connor attended Catholic elementary schools SACRED HEART SCHOOL FOR GIRLS and ST. VINCENT'S, both in Savannah. Several of O'Connor's friends were Catholics, such as Sally and Robert Fitzgerald. She knew many priests and nuns personally, such as Father J. H. McCown and Sister Evangelist and read widely among Catholic theologians such as ST. THOMAS AQUINAS and PIERRE TEILHARD DE CHARDIN. She wrote BOOK REVIEWS for a Catholic diocesan newsletter called the The BULLETIN and her essay "Introduction to A Memoir of Mary Ann" was written for a book composed by Dominican nuns about a young cancer patient.

The church and O'Connor's faith in its teachings and practices deeply influenced her writing and her core being: "I feel if I were not a Catholic I would have no reason to write, no reason to see, no reason ever to feel horrified or even to enjoy anything" (HB 114). "When people have told me that because I am a Catholic I cannot be an artist, I have had to reply, ruefully, that because I am a Catholic I cannot afford to be less than an artist" (MM 146).

S

Sacred Heart School for Girls O'Connor attended this parochial school on Bull Street in SAVANNAH, GEORGIA, starting in 1936 in fifth grade through part of seventh grade, when she left with her mother to join her father in ATLANTA in early 1938. She had been transferred there from ST. VINCENT'S GRAMMAR SCHOOL FOR GIRLS, though the reason for the transfer is unclear. O'Connor may have wanted to join friends there, or her mother may have had a disagreement with the nuns' strict rules at St. Vincent's. Also, Mrs. O'Connor may have considered the families at Sacred Heart a step up in social class. The teachers at the school were all Sisters of St. Joseph of Corondolet. At Sacred Heart O'Connor could no longer walk to school as she had at St. Vincent's. Instead, she rode in Katie Semme's electric car, the only electric car in Savannah.

St. Thomas Aquinas (1225–1274) Widely regarded by the Roman Catholic Church as its most noteworthy Western philosopher and theologian, St. Thomas Aquinas had a profound effect on Flannery O'Connor and her work. She wrote to Elizabeth Hester in 1955 that she read the Dominican monk's *Summa theologiae* for 20 minutes each night before going to sleep. She also comically noted that if her mother came in while she was reading and told her to turn out the light, she would make some kind of philosophical statement such as the light could not, in truth, ever be turned off, so the more accu-

rate request would be to shut one's eyes. O'Connor sums up her feelings for the theologian: "I feel I can personally guarantee that St. Thomas loved God because for the life of me I cannot help loving St. Thomas" (HB 94). Though some of Aquinas's ideas have been challenged in the church, his work is still considered a foundation of Catholic teaching.

Thomas was born in 1225 in Roccasecca, near Aquino, Italy. He died on March 7, 1274, and was canonized on July 18, 1323. His feast day is January 28. Thomas studied at the University of Naples, where he read the science and philosophies of Greeks and Arabs whose works were then being translated. While in Naples, Thomas decided to join the Dominican order of monks. In 1245, Thomas went to Paris and studied at the convent of Saint-Jacques, the center of Dominican scholarship, and the University of Paris.

Thomas attended the school at the same time that Arab-Aristolean ideas were becoming better known to theologians. At this time, scientific rationalism was first confronting believers and theologians, some of whom regarded it with great suspicion. At the same time, European society was evolving from an individualistic agrarian structure to more urban lifestyles emphasizing community with such new features as trade guilds and a marketing economy.

In 1256, Thomas earned his degree in theology and began to teach at the University of Paris. He spent the rest of his life reading, studying, writing, thinking, and teaching, both in France and in Italy. His key writings consist of theological treatises, biblical commentaries, commentaries on Aristotle, philosophical treatises, as well as hymns and liturgical compositions.

In 1274, Thomas was called by Pope Gregory X to the second Council of Lyons. The council was intended to repair a divide between the Greek and Latin churches. On the way, Thomas became ill and stopped at the Cistercian abbey of Fossanova, where he died on March 7.

Key to Thomist thought is the idea that faith and reason need not compete with each other. Like Aristotle, whose writings he studied, Thomas believed in a theory of knowledge in which senses and the natural world play a large part in human understanding. Spiritual truth, according to Thomas, dwells outside human understanding, but it is not in opposition to it. These spiritual truths are made known to human beings through revelation. Faith as a moral choice is another Thomist idea.

Thomist thought underscores several of O'Connor's works, either explicitly or implicitly. One example is "Tantum Ergo," which comes from Aquinas's Eucharistic poem, "Pange Lingua," and which O'Connor features in "A Temple of the Holy Ghost." A more subtle example is the Thomist idea that "prophetic vision is not a matter of seeing clearly, but of seeing what is distant, hidden" (HB 365). In *The Violent Bear It Away*, Tarwater does not see what is hidden, but he accepts prophetic vision through faith.

St. Vincent's Grammar School for Girls   This was the first school O'Connor attended, from first grade in 1931 until fifth grade in 1936, when she transferred to Sacred Heart School for Girls. The school was located across Lafayette Square from her house in Savannah, Georgia. All of the teachers at the school were Sisters of Mercy, many of them young Irish women who crossed the Atlantic Ocean to study in Baltimore, Maryland, who were then assigned to teach in grammar schools around the country. The school building itself was a house built in the 1800s located near the Cathedral of St. John the Baptist. In addition to reading, writing, mathematics, and other subjects, the

nuns also took the students to Mass, which was said in Latin, and prepared them to receive their first Communion. Another hallmark of O'Connor's education at St. Vincent's was the emphasis on the Palmer method of penmanship.

Since O'Connor lived right across the street from the school, she went home for lunch rather than eat with her classmates. Classmates of O'Connor recall her being a quiet girl who set herself apart from others, frequently reading. Sister Consolata remembered O'Connor as an ordinary girl in the class, well-behaved and a good student. She seemed to feel more comfortable speaking with adults than the other children did, a typical trait of an only child. Sister Consolata remembered O'Connor's interest in chickens and how excited she would become when talking about them to her teachers. It is no surprise that her teachers also remembered her interest in reading and writing and showing an aptitude for both.

Savannah, Georgia   O'Connor was born in Savannah in 1925 and lived there until she moved with her mother to join her father, who was working in a new position in Atlanta in March 1938. As a child, she lived at 207 Charlton Street, across Lafayette Square from the Cathedral of St. John the Baptist. The house property adjoined her mother's second cousin's ("Cousin" Katie Semmes) mansion and garden located behind it. Edward Francis O'Connor, Jr., established the Dixie Realty Company (later expanded to include the Dixie Construction Company) in Savannah with money given to him and his wife by this same cousin as a baby gift at Flannery's birth. O'Connor's earliest memories were of Savannah and especially her church life at the cathedral across the street and the two parochial schools that she attended in the city, St. Vincent's Grammar School for Girls at the cathedral and the Sacred Heart School for Girls on Bull Street.

Founded in 1733 by Joseph Edward Oglethorpe, who also founded the state of Georgia, Savannah is known as the state's first city. It is an industrial seaport located where the mouth of the Savannah River empties into the Atlantic Ocean. In the 18th and 19th centuries, principal businesses depending on the city included tobacco and cotton, grown on nearby plantations. It was the seat of the colony and capital of the state until 1786. During the Civil War, the city was blockaded by the Union forces and was the objective of General Sherman's march to the sea. He captured the city, after its citizens held out for some time, on December 21, 1864. The city was organized around a series of public squares, which have now been made into parks with large trees draped in Spanish moss and flowers that add character and natural beauty to the city. This feature, the port, the cathedral, and the stately historical homes in Georgian Colonial and Greek revival styles make Savannah one of the most picturesque cities in the United States.

The city was the birthplace of the Girl Scouts, founded by a local resident, Juliette Gordon Low (O'Connor spent a short time as a Girl Scout when she lived there). In 1994, parts of the film *Forrest*

O'Connor's childhood home on Lafayette Square, Savannah, Georgia, where she lived from birth in 1925 until 1938, when her family moved to Atlanta. It is located at 207 East Charlton Street and has recently been renovated for visitors. *(Courtesy Connie Ann Kirk)*

Gump, starring Tom Hanks, were filmed in Savannah's Chippewa Square.

Sewanee Review, The *The Sewanee Review* proudly never missed publication of a single quarterly issue since its founding in 1892. The journal hails out of the University of the South in Sewanee, Tennessee, and during its illustrious history has published writers such as ROBERT PENN WARREN, Hart Crane, Anne Sexton, Harry Crews, Fred Chappell, Andre Dubus, and Cormac McCarthy. The journal owes much of its longevity and reputation to the fine editorship in the 1940s of Andrew Nelson Lytle (one of O'Connor's instructors at Iowa) and Allen Tate. Lytle published the journal's first short story in December 1943 and a long excerpt from Robert Penn Warren's novel *At Heaven's Gate* in the spring issue. He and Tate also published critical works of well-known writers such as Cleanth Brooks, Randall Jarrell, and ROBERT LOWELL.

O'Connor's familiarity with Andrew Lytle and his admiration for her work made *The Sewanee Review* a welcome home for many of her stories. The journal published "Train," an early version of a chapter from *Wise Blood*, in April 1948. "The River" appeared in the summer 1953 issue, and "The Displaced Person" was published in October 1954. "The Lame Shall Enter First" was published in the summer 1962 issue.

O'Connor wrote to Betty Hester that she knew that she could make $1,500 by sending "Revelation" to ESQUIRE, but she decided to send it to Lytle at *Sewanee*, where it appeared in the spring of 1964. It was the last short story she saw published before her death that summer. Her comment to Hester on the reason for sending it to SR was "I emulate my better characters and feel like Mr. Shiftlet that there should be some folks that some things mean more to them than money" (HB 563).

In 1962, Andrew Lytle dedicated a significant portion of the summer issue to O'Connor and her work. In it, he featured a critical article titled "Flannery O'Connor's Devil" by the novelist and O'Connor correspondent John Hawkes. The article was one of the first major literary analyses of her work.

Southern Cross, The In 1963, the Diocese of SAVANNAH began to publish *The Southern Cross*, a diocesan paper in the line of *The BULLETIN*, after the establishment of the separate Diocese of Atlanta. Prior to that time, there was no Diocese of Atlanta, and Savannah was the sole seat of the Catholic Church in the state. The Atlanta diocese later renamed *The Bulletin* as *The Georgia Bulletin*, and O'Connor reviewed for both papers. *The Southern Cross* is still the official newspaper of the Diocese of Savannah, and *The Georgia Bulletin* remains the official newspaper of the Catholic Archdiocese of Atlanta.

All of O'Connor's reviews in *The Southern Cross* appeared in 1963. They include: March 2—*The Bible: Word of God in Words of Men,* by Jean Levie (Kenedy, 1962); March 9—*Frontiers in American Catholicism,* by Walter J. Ong, S. J. (Macmillan, 1957, 1961); March 16—*New Men for New Times,* by Beatrice Avalos (Sheed & Ward, 1962); *Seeds of Hope in the Modern World,* by Barry Ulanov (Kenedy, 1962); March 23—*The Wide World, My Parish,* by Yves Congar, O. P. (Helicon, 1961); April 27—*Letters from a Traveler,* by PIERRE TEILHARD DE CHARDIN (Harper, 1962); October 24—*Evangelical Theology: An Introduction,* by Karl Barth (Holt, Rinehart & Winston, 1963); October 31—*The Cardinal Stritch Story,* by Maria Buehrle (Bruce, 1959); *Leo XIII: A Light from Heaven,* by Br. William Kiefer, S. M. (Bruce, 1961); November 27—*What Is the Bible?,* by Henri Daniel-Rops (Gyild, 1960); *Faith, Reason and the Gospels,* edited by John J. Heaney, S. J. (Newman, 1962); and *Morte d'Urban,* by J. F. Powers (Doubleday, 1962).

Spectrum, The   This is the yearbook of the GEORGIA STATE COLLEGE FOR WOMEN when O'Connor attended. She was the feature editor of the 1945 edition, and the issue is filled with her CARTOONS, so much so that they give continuity to the publication that was unusual for that time.

Most striking, perhaps, are the endpapers to the yearbook, which are reproductions of a large cartoon showing construction on the front campus amid rain, mud, raincoats, and the usual activity of students running to and fro alongside the unusual sight of the WAVES marching by. Betty Love, a classmate of O'Connor's, once commented that the endpapers captured perfectly the commotion of the campus during the spring of 1945.

Other O'Connor cartoons in the yearbook included "This is Jessieville," a cartoon of Parks Hall, an administrative building, with dogs asleep in front of it. A cartoon showing two women in caps and gowns was recognized as featuring the dean of women and the academic dean. Another cartoon, "Wayfarers," shows four students holding a heavy load of books. Six drawings enlarged from the front of the book recur to head different sections of the yearbook: "Our Naval Escort," "We Learn to Lead," "We Record Our Travels," "Points of Interest," "Having a Wonderful Time," and "Where Our Pennies Go."

Since *The Spectrum* that year was O'Connor's own senior yearbook, she appears in several photographs, including her senior picture, in which she appears without her glasses. She also appears in two photos for *The CORINTHIAN*, one for the Newman Club and one for the International Relations Club. She is missing from the photo, though listed as participating as the feature editor of *The Spectrum* and a member of the Town Girls' Club.

O'Connor, during the time she was part of The Spectrum staff *(Courtesy of Flannery O'Connor Collection, Georgia College & State University)*

T, U

"Tantum Ergo" This hymn, mentioned in the story "A Temple of the Holy Ghost," is the last two stanzas of the "Pange Lingua," a Eucharistic poem written by St. Thomas Aquinas. The hymn/chant is sung during Benediction of the Blessed Sacrament. In Roman Catholicism, Benediction is the ceremony of adoration celebrating the exposure of the Blessed Sacrament in the form of the Sacred Host, usually in an elaborate gold vessel called a monstrance. The monstrance is a portable shrine that often takes on the shape of a large, radiant sun atop a tall stand. The Sacred Host is displayed in a circular glass case in the center of the sun. The monstrance may be carried in procession and then set on the altar for adoration. O'Connor's frequent imagery of the sun as a symbol of divinity may trace some of its origin from the sunlike shape of the monstrance.

In Latin, the two stanzas of "Tantum Ergo" read: "Tantum ergo Sacramentum / Veneremur cernui: / Et antiquum documentum / Novo cedat ritui: / Praestet fides supplementum / Sensuum defectui. // Genitori, Genitoque / Laus et iubilatio, / Salus, honor, virtus quoque / Sit et benedicto: / Procedenti ab utroque / Compar sit laudito. // Amen.

In English, the text reads: "Down in adoration falling / Lo! The sacred Host we hail, / Lo! o'er ancient forms departing / Newer rites of grace prevail: / Faiths for all defects supplying, / Where the feeble senses fail. // To the everlasting Father, / And the Son who reigns on high / with the Holy Spirit proceeding / Forth from each eternally: / Be salvation, honor blessing, / Might and endless majesty. // Amen.

Teilhard de Chardin, Pierre (1881–1955) *French theologian and paleontologist* Pierre Teilhard was a French Jesuit priest who was a theologian and also a paleontologist. O'Connor found her title, *Everything That Rises Must Converge*, from the foreword to one of Teilhard's works, *Building the Earth*, written by Max H. Begouen. She found inspiration in Teilhard's writings, particularly in his famous theory of the Omega point.

Teilhard was born to a gentleman farmer and his wife on May 1, 1881. Teilhard's mother was the great grandniece of Voltaire. His father was interested in geology and encouraged Teilhard's fascination with fossils. Teilhard studied in France, joined the Jesuit priesthood, and also spent time in Cairo, Egypt. During World War I, though he was already a priest and could have served as chaplain, Teilhard chose to serve as a stretcher-bearer instead. His courage on the battlefield earned him membership in the Legion of Honor.

In his work in paleontology, Teilhard traveled to China, Gobi, Sinkiang, Kashmir, Java, and Burma. His contributions to the field include broadening the knowledge of Asia's sedimentary deposits, stratigraphic correlations, and dating fossils of the continent. He was there in 1929 when the skeletal remains of an early human being thought to be

250,000–400,000 years old were discovered in China (the remains were later called the Peking Man).

In theology, Teilhard meditated for long periods and then wrote about his thoughts. Much of what he wrote was controversial among the Jesuit community, so much so that they banned him from publishing his work during his lifetime. Though his faith and loyalty to the church were never questioned, his ideas were thought too challenging to Catholic orthodoxy. Teilhard moved to the United States, where he continued to work in paleontology at the Wenner-Gren Foundation in New York City. From there, he took two archaeological and paleontological trips to South Africa. Teilhard died in New York on April 10, 1955. After Teilhard died and his books began to appear in print at last, a monitum, or simple warning, was issued by the Holy Office in 1962 for the Catholic faithful to read his writings with a critical eye.

Interestingly, one of those critical eyes reading Teilhard at this initial period was Flannery O'Connor. Then reviewing for the Georgia Catholic diocesan periodical, The BULLETIN, O'Connor wrote several reviews of Teilhard's books. These included The Phenomenon of Man (reviewed on February 20, 1960); The Divine Milieu (February 4, 1961); and Letters from a Traveler (April 27, 1963). O'Connor also reviewed books that began to appear about the Jesuit, including Pierre Teilhard de Chardin: His Life and Spirit by Nicolas Corte (October 15, 1960); Teilhard de Chardin: A Critical Study (December 23, 1961); and Claude Tresmontant's Pierre Teilhard de Chardin: His Thought (reviewed in the same issue as The Phenomenon of Man, February 20, 1960).

Interested in both theology and science, Teilhard wrote about human beings evolving both mentally and socially to a spiritual oneness, or Omega point. Teilhard argued that evolution drives toward increasingly more complexity and that human beings are different because they not only know as animals do, but they *know* that they know. He called this "knowledge to the square."

Teilhard also stated that now that human evolution has perfected itself physically, the next great evolution will be the social evolution of the human species. He saw this form of evolution

already well under way in technology, communications, and what would now be called the globalization of the economy.

Jesus' role in this overall plan, according to Teilhard, is not to conquer evil but to culminate the process of evolution through the second coming. At that time, the height of the material and human worlds will unite with the spiritual in Christ. According to Teilhard, evil was simply a byproduct of the evolution process, similar to growing pains, as disorder moves toward an increasingly complex and unified sense of order.

Though she admitted a limited understanding of Teilhard's philosophy, O'Connor wrote that his ideas fueled her creativity, and she argued in favor of them, particularly The Phenomenon of Man. When asked to list outstanding books of the three decades 1931 to 1961 in an article for the fall 1961 issue of AMERICAN SCHOLAR, O'Connor argued for the accomplishments of The Phenomenon of Man. In her article, "Outstanding Books, 1931–1961," she wrote that this book was "a scientific expression of what the poet attempts to do: penetrate matter until spirit is revealed in it" (618). She found Teilhard to be a kindred spirit, saying in a letter that he worked to turn the scientific age toward Christ (HB 388). The very reason his work was good was because it was "dangerous" (571).

University of Iowa, (State)   The college where O'Connor earned her master of fine arts degree in creative writing is now called the University of Iowa and is located in Iowa City. When she attended from 1945 to 1948, the college was known as the State University of Iowa. Presently, there is an Iowa State University in Ames, but this is a different school altogether.

Creative writing education has a long history at Iowa. Beginning in the 1920s, students were allowed to submit creative work for a master's thesis in English. When O'Connor entered the school in the mid-1940s, the creative writing program was administered by Paul Engle. Engle was one of the first students at Iowa to earn an M.A. degree with a creative thesis—a collection of poems called One Slim Feather, which he submitted for his degree in 1932. Engle took over the creative writing workshop at Iowa in 1942 and developed it from a modest program of 12 graduate students to more than 250 by 1965.

Engle was a strong influence in the beginning of O'Connor's time at Iowa. The story of his not understanding her strong southern accent on their first meeting and her writing down for him the declarative sentence "I am a writer" is legendary. Engle later acknowledged that he only needed to read a short passage of O'Connor's writing to recognize that she had "pure talent." The other two years of O'Connor's time at Iowa, however, Engle spent mostly in Florida and elsewhere publicizing the college's creative-writing program. She did not appreciate his comments later on about her novel, *Wise Blood*; she thought that they did not show a comprehension of what she was trying to do. Engle would later comment on what he perceived to be an insufficient acknowledgment of his role in the development of her work as well as the role of the Iowa workshop. O'Connor did, however, dedicate her master's thesis to him.

O'Connor was one of only three women in the program when she enrolled. The other two women were Kay Burford and Mary Mudge Wiatt. The rest of the class was made up predominantly of World War II veterans who exchanged and validated one another's stories about the war. Classmates recalled O'Connor as one of Engle's obvious favorites. She was quiet in class unless she had something to say, and then she articulated her comments brilliantly. Her stories showed her talent, and classmates ended up talking more about their content than the writing itself. Some classmates read her reserve and intelligence as arrogance; others thought perhaps her strong accent made her self-conscious and inhibited her from speaking more freely.

Toward the end of her time at Iowa, O'Connor studied with fellow southern writer Andrew Lytle. Lytle worked with her more closely than any other instructor at the school. They had one-on-one conferences over her work, and Lytle reported that she spoke freely and often in those more private meetings. She was a quick learner and did not make the mistakes he pointed out more than once. With a talent like hers, Lytle claimed that all he could do was point out things to her that he did not think were working. He believed that no one could really teach her, though he seemed to have some quality that she valued in that regard.

Writers such as Robie Macauley who were at Iowa when O'Connor was there claimed that Lytle, even though a southerner, was more of a sophisticated stylist who had reservations about O'Connor's "redneck" characters. True or not, O'Connor wrote of Lytle frequently in her letters after leaving the college.

Other instructors, either on staff or visiting, critiqued O'Connor's early work, including Paul Horgan, ROBERT PENN WARREN, and Allen Tate.

O'Connor earned her M.F.A. in creative writing in June 1947 but stayed in Iowa City for one more year, working on her novel with the support of the Rinehart-Iowa Fellowship. During that year, she came to know writers such as Jean Williams (Wylder), Walter Sullivan, Clyde McLeod (Hoffman), and Robie Macauley.

While in Iowa City, O'Connor lived at 32 East Bloomington Street (no longer standing), which was a house annexed to the Currier Dormitory for Women. She also lived at 115 East Bloomington Street in a boardinghouse that was not far from the Currier Annex.

Among graduate students in creative writing today, the workshop at the University of Iowa enjoys a high reputation for its distinctive and historic program. Flannery O'Connor holds a strong place on the list of great American writers to come out of the workshop. Iowa alumni counted among twenty-first century writers include fiction writers Marilynne Robinson and Michael Cunningham, and the poet Mark Strand.

W

Warren, Robert Penn (1905–1989) *American novelist, poet, critic, and teacher* Warren was a southern writer who was concerned with the dissolution of traditional values at a time when the South was moving away from being a strictly agrarian society. Much of his work concerns the tension brought about by the resulting moral questions. He was the first poet laureate of the United States, an appointment he received in 1986. His novel *All the King's Men* (1946) won the Pulitzer Prize for fiction, and he won the same honor for poetry in 1958 and 1979. With Cleanth Brooks and Charles W. Pipkin, he founded *The Southern Review*, serving as editor from 1935 to 1942. At the time, the journal was one of the most influential literary publications in the country.

Warren was born in Kentucky and educated at Vanderbilt (B.A.), the University of California at Berkeley (M.A.), and Yale. From 1930 to 1950, he taught on the faculties of several colleges and universities, including his alma mater, Vanderbilt, and the University of Minnesota. With Cleanth Brooks, he coauthored two landmark textbooks that helped spread the theory of New Criticism, *Understanding Poetry* (1938) and *Understanding Fiction* (1943). O'Connor recommended the latter to young writer Ben Griffith in 1955. She also shared her own copy "full of juvenile notes" with Betty Hester (HB 197).

As a fellow writer from the South, O'Connor was aware of Warren's presence on the literary landscape. Besides recommending *Understanding Fiction* to younger writers, O'Connor was aware of Warren's association with the Tates, Caroline and Allen, in a group of writers who called themselves the Fugitives. Caroline Gordon Tate was the first reader of O'Connor's novels and offered valuable comments for revision. O'Connor often asked that Warren receive a copy of her book in galleys so that he might review it. In 1960, she wrote to Betty Hester that she did not expect "Red" Warren to like her book (*The Violent Bear It Away*) so was pleased when Caroline sent her his good review (HB 390).

As for Warren's work other than the textbook, O'Connor once wrote that she favored *All the King's Men* to *Band of Angels.* She offered to send her copy of the long dramatic poem, *Brother to Dragons,* to Maryat Lee in 1960. She called her colleague "a lovely man" (HB 396) and once shared an anecdote about their mutual feelings toward public speaking. When asked by a meeting organizer in Pennsylvania what he charged to give a lecture, he replied, "$400 and I'm not worth it" (481).

Among Warren's other works are: *At Heaven's Gate* (1943) and *New and Selected Poems, 1923–1985* (1985).

Welty, Eudora (1909–2001) *American short-story writer and novelist* Welty was a contemporary of O'Connor's and also hailed from the South, the state of Mississippi. Like O'Connor, she spent time working at the artist's colony, YADDO; she never married; and she lived most of her adult life in one place—Jackson, Mississippi. Also similar to O'Connor, Welty's work focuses on small-town southern life. Welty was interested in photography in the way that O'Connor was interested in cartooning, but Welty did have some of her photographs published professionally.

About 16 years her senior, Welty saw her first story in print in 1936 when O'Connor was still a young girl. From then on, Welty published in both smaller periodicals such as *The Southern Review* and major magazines such as *The New Yorker.* In 1941, her collection of stories, *A Curtain of Green*, containing the often anthologized "Why I Live at the P. O." and "The Petrified Man," brought her popularity with an even larger readership.

Welty's works include the short novel *The Robber Bridegroom* (1942); *Delta Wedding* (1946); *The Ponder Heart* (1954); and *Losing Battles* (1970). *The Optimist's Daughter* (1972) won the Pulitzer Prize. Her later collections of short stories include *The Wide Net and Other Stories* (1943); *The Golden Apples* (1949); *The Bride of Innisfallen and Other Stories* (1955); and *The Collected Stories of Eudora Welty* (1980). *The Eye of the Story* (1978) is a collection of essays. An autobiographical work, *One Writer's Beginnings,* was published in 1984.

Though Welty was widely published by then, O'Connor had never heard of her until she went to graduate school at Iowa. She blames the GEORGIA STATE COLLEGE FOR WOMEN for not exposing her earlier to contemporary writers. In a 1963 letter to Betty Hester, O'Connor commented on one of Welty's stories, "Where Is That Voice Coming From?" The story was inspired by the assassination of Medgar Evers and was published in *The New Yorker.* O'Connor did not like the view of the South that she thought the story portrayed. She wrote that it would give the northern liberals more on which to feed in their contempt of the South. She notes by comparison that her story "Everything That Rises Must Converge" puts a plague on both houses, both races. The black woman on the bus does not come off any more favorably than Julian and the lingering 19th-century views of his mother.

According to the memories of some who took part in them, Eudora Welty's stories were discussed among many other works at O'Connor's weekly or biweekly gatherings at ANDALUSIA. She did not, however, offer any comments on the author to Robert Drake in his meeting with her at Andalusia in August 1963. On the other hand, she did write to Louis Dollarhide, mentioning that she was pleased to hear that Welty had another collection of stories coming out. An operation had kept her, O'Connor wrote genially, from doing the same thing.

In 1955, she noted that she had read some of Welty's early work. The following year she wrote that she is "not one of the subtle sensitive writers like Eudora Welty" (HB 141). She appears to mean that genuinely since she then writes about needing to speak about what is obvious and obtuse, as she does in her story "Greenleaf." In a letter to Cecil Dawkins in 1958, she wrote briefly about Welty's use of *churren* for *children* in relation to how the characters in a Dawkins story she has read should speak. She indicates that this is what they say (HB 296).

In 1959, O'Connor filled in for Welty at a writer's residency at the University of Chicago. Welty's brother had become ill, and the school asked O'Connor if she might fill in. She did not entirely enjoy the experience, which consisted of a public reading and two workshop classes. Though she received $700 (enough, she claimed, to live on for a year), she was disappointed in the students at the workshop and the public-reading attendance.

O'Connor and Welty met when they each presented their work at Converse College in April 1962. In a letter O'Connor wrote about it later, she noted that she "really liked Eudora Welty" and appreciated what she called Welty's lack of "presence," or pretense, as a successful author. She said she was "just a real nice woman" (HB 471).

O'Connor related an amusing anecdote about WILLIAM FAULKNER that Welty told her. Welty knew a woman who ran a beauty parlor and also wrote novels. The woman's subject matter was the Northwest Mounted Police. The operator, Welty's story went, sent one of her love scenes to William Faulkner for a critique. When she had not heard back from him by mail, she called him up.

Welty related to O'Connor that the woman asked Faulkner what he thought of her little love scene. Faulkner replied, "Honey, it isn't the way I would do it, but you go right ahead, you go right ahead" (HB 472).

Williams, Tennessee (1911–1983) *American playwright* A contemporary of O'Connor's, Williams was born in Columbus, Mississippi. Like O'Connor, Williams graduated from the UNIVERSITY OF IOWA and wrote much of his work set in the American South with themes focused on life and concerns in that region. Williams is best known for his plays, principally *The Glass Menagerie*, which opened in Chicago in 1944; *A Streetcar Named Desire*, which opened in New York in 1947; and *Cat on a Hot Tin Roof*, which was produced on Broadway in 1955 and released as a film in 1958.

On a visit to New York in 1955 for an appearance on the television program *Galley Proof* and for a *New York Times* interview related to the upcoming television adaptation of her story, "The Life You Save May be Your Own," O'Connor was taken to the stage production of *Cat on a Hot Tin Roof*. It is the only Broadway play she is known to have seen. "I did not like Tennessee Williams' play," she wrote to her agent, Elizabeth McKee on June 29, 1955. "I thought I could do that good myself. However, on reflection I guess it is wise to doubt that" (HB 88). In a letter to Betty Hester later the same year, she pairs Williams with TRUMAN CAPOTE as writers who both make her "plumb sick" (HB 121).

Yaddo The artists' colony in Saratoga Springs, New York, is based at the 1900 Spencer and Katrina Trask mansion and comprises other buildings and approximately 40 acres of grounds. When the Trasks' four children died and they had no remaining heirs, they decided to leave their large estate for the use of creative artists such as writers, painters, and musicians. They wanted to provide a quiet place where creative artists could stay and work away from the distractions of everyday life. In the years since the colony opened to artists, those who have worked at some time at Yaddo have garnered collectively 61 Pulitzer Prizes, 56 National Book Awards, 21 National Book Critics Circle Prizes, and one Nobel Prize, among other prizes and honors. Acceptance for a residency at Yaddo is considered an honor as well as an endorsement of their work by the artists who apply or who are invited to stay by the foundation. Writers and poets who have had residencies at Yaddo include: James Baldwin, Saul Bellow, ELIZABETH BISHOP, Gwendolyn Brooks, TRUMAN CAPOTE, John Cheever, Grace Paley, Sylvia Plath, KATHARINE ANNE PORTER, William Stafford, and many others.

O'Connor was invited by the Yaddo Foundation to a residency while she was still at the UNIVERSITY OF IOWA. She wrote at Yaddo from June 1948 to the end of February 1949, principally working on completing her first novel, *Wise Blood*. She found many of the other writers and artists too secular in their worldviews and "artsy," as she described them, for her taste. She often attended MASS with the domestic staff. While at Yaddo, she became friends with writers Edward Maisel, Elizabeth Fenwick, and Elizabeth Hardwick, and painter Clifford Wright. She also benefited from getting to know ROBERT LOWELL, who read and critiqued her manuscript and later introduced her to editor Robert Giroux.

Along with Lowell, O'Connor was one of a small group of Yaddo residents who began to question admission policies of the director, Elizabeth Ames. It turned out that Ames and the colony itself had been under investigation by the FBI for several years for suspicion of housing Soviet spies, namely, radical journalist and known spy Agnes Smedley. Lowell and his group met with the Yaddo board and demanded Ames's dismissal on the grounds that her activities, including favoring Smedley's residency, were endangering the colony. In the end, the board supported Ames, along with several other Yaddo artists who placed an ad in the newspaper on her behalf. O'Connor left Yaddo with Lowell and Hardwick at the end of February 1949, making her way to New York where she would meet and later take up residence with Robert and Sally Fitzgerald.

PART IV

Appendices

CHRONOLOGY OF LIFE AND WORKS

1925 March 25

Mary Flannery O'Connor is born in Savannah, Georgia, to Edward Francis O'Connor, Jr. and Regina (Cline) O'Connor.

April 12

Baptized at the Roman Catholic Cathedral of St. John the Baptist, Savannah.

1926–27

Maternal second cousin, Mrs. ("Cousin Katie") Raphael Semmes, gives financial gift to the baby's family, which Edward uses to begin the Dixie Realty Company, expanding to the Dixie Construction Company.

1928–30

Summers at 311 W. Greene Street, Milledgeville, Georgia, her mother's birthplace and childhood home.

1931

Enters St. Vincent's Grammar School at St. John the Baptist Cathedral, in first grade. Taught by Sisters of Mercy from Ireland. Enjoys unusual domestic fowl as a child and teaches a "frizzled" chicken to walk backward. Filmed demonstrating the trick by Pathé News newsreel company of New York.

1932 May 8

Receives the sacrament of First Holy Communion at the cathedral.

1934 May 20

Receives the sacrament of Confirmation at the cathedral.

1935

Father encounters more business difficulties as Depression deepens.

1936–37

Transfers to Sacred Heart School, Bull Street, where she is taught by Sisters of St. Joseph of Corodolet.

1938

Moves to 2525 Potomac Street, N.E., Atlanta, when father takes job as zone real-estate appraiser for the Federal Housing Administration (FHA). Finds adjustment difficult; moves with mother to Milledgeville. Enrolls in Peabody High School midterm.

1939–40

Writes and draws cartoons in attic studio for high-school newspaper, *Peabody Palladium*. Father so ill he leaves FHA and retires to Milledgeville.

1941 Feb. 1

Father dies of lupus.

1942

Graduates from Peabody High School. Begins freshman year in summer at Georgia State College for Women, one block from her house.

1943

Contributes to *The Corinthian*, college literary magazine. Meets Marine Sergeant John Sullivan.

1944

Art editor of *The Spectrum*, the college yearbook. Commercial publishers do not take her stories, poems, or cartoons; continues to publish in *The Corinthian*. Corresponds with John Sullivan. Faculty member George Beiswanger encourages her to apply to the State University of Iowa for creative writing.

1945

Receives AB degree. Admitted to Iowa Workshop. Writes mother daily from Iowa City. Makes decision to submit short-story collection for master's thesis.

1946

Begins reading tutorial with Paul Engle, encountering Joyce, Kafka, and others for the first time. "The Geranium" accepted by *Accent*. John Sullivan writes that he is studying for the priesthood; correspondence with him fades. Begins work on first novel.

1947

Wins Rinehart-Iowa Fiction Award, $750 for first novel. Submits thesis, *The Geranium: A Collection of Short Stories*. Receives M.A. in May. *Mademoiselle* accepts "The Turkey"; *Sewanee Review* accepts "The Train."

1948

Works at Yaddo, artist's colony, Saratoga Springs, New York. Solicits Elizabeth McKee as literary agent.

1949

Leaves Yaddo at end of February over politically charged incident. Moves to New York City, then to Ridgefield, Connecticut, with Robert and Sally Fitzgerald.

1950

Has operation at Milledgeville; returns to Ridgefield. Completes early draft of first novel, *Wise Blood*. Becomes ill before Christmas and makes it home to Milledgeville, where she is treated for arthritis with cortisone.

1951

Dr. Merrill of Atlanta diagnoses lupus over the telephone; Flannery is not told. Moves to Andalusia with Regina.

1952

Submits revised and corrected version of *Wise Blood*; novel published in May. Is told about lupus in summer and writes for Fitzgeralds to send books and clothing back to Milledgeville.

1953

Paints self-portrait. Erik Langkjaer, a textbook salesman for Harcourt, Brace, visits Andalusia often and becomes a possible love interest.
Publications: "A Stroke of Good Fortune," *Shenandoah*; "The Life You Save May Be Your Own," in *Kenyon Review*—wins O. Henry Prize; "The River," in *Sewanee Review*. "A Good Man Is Hard to Find" is published in *Modern Writing I*. Spends three weeks in Ridgeville, Connecticut, with the Fitzgeralds. Polish immigrants soon working on the farm; takes draft of "The Displaced Person" to Connecticut and reads it to Fitzgeralds. Begins to plan *A Good Man Is Hard to Find and Other Stories*.

1954

Upset when Erik Langkjaer decides to return to Denmark. Limping begins; using cane by the end of the year.
Publications: "A Temple of the Holy Ghost, *Harper's Bazaar*; "A Circle in the Fire," *Kenyon Review*; "The Displaced Person," *Sewanee Review*. Accepts contract for *Wise Blood* with Neville Spearman Ltd. in England; "A Circle in the Fire" wins second prize O. Henry Awards.

1955

Sends self-portrait for the cover of *A Good Man*, but they decline to use it. After completing "Good Country People" in just four days, she sends it to Giroux to replace "An Afternoon in the Woods" and "An Exile in the East." Hears that Erik Langkjaer is getting married. Travels to New York to appear on *Galley Proof* television show, where she is interviewed about the upcoming dramatization of "The Life You Save May Be Your Own." Does not like Tennessee Williams's *Cat on a Hot Tin Roof*, the only Broadway play she will ever see. *A Good Man Is Hard to Find and Other Stories* is published by Harcourt, Brace in June and sells well. Receives and responds quickly to the first letter from Betty Hester ("A" in *The Habit of Being*), who will become a life-long friend and correspondent. Begins to use crutches for the first time; told she will be on them a year or so because she cannot have an operation with lupus.

Other publications: "Good Country People" in *Harper's Bazaar*, June. *Wise Blood* in England by Neville Spearman Ltd. "You Can't Be Any Poorer Than Dead" (first chapter of new novel), *New World Writing*.

1956

Maurice-Edgar Coindreau translates *Wise Blood* into French. Betty Hester visits Andalusia for the first time after exchanging letters every two weeks with O'Connor. Meets William Sessions and Jesuit James McCown. Andalusia gets first telephone. Receives $800 from television production company for "The Life You Save" and buys Regina O'Connor a refrigerator with it. Meets Maryat Lee, a playwright and sister of the President of Georgia State College for Women.

Publications: "Greenleaf," *Kenyon Review* (wins O. Henry Prize); *A Good Man Is Hard to Find and Other Stories*, New American Library.

1957

Receives and responds to letter from Elizabeth Bishop. Writes essays "The Church and the Fiction Writer" and "The Fiction Writer and His Country." Meets Louise Abbot at the farm. Lectures at Notre Dame in South Bend, Indiana. Meets Thomas Stritch. Cecil Dawkins initiates what will be a long correspondence. Buys house in town for rental income. Thinks about *The Violent Bear It Away* as title for novel she is working on.

Publications: "The Church and the Fiction Writer," *America*; "The Fiction Writer and His Country," *The Living Novel: A Symposium* edited by Granville Hicks.

1958

Works on novel. Does not reapply to Yaddo when approached to do so by Elizabeth Ames. Signs on with Robert Giroux at Farrar, Straus and Cudahy. Makes trip to Europe with Regina, seeing Paris, Lourdes, Rome. Reluctantly enters waters of Lourdes, praying for her book rather than her bones. Passes driving test on second try, though seldom drives. John Hawkes and Theodore Spivey see her at the farm. Mrs. Semmes hears about her not needing crutches before Semmes dies; she inherits Savannah house.

Publications: "The Enduring Chill," *Harper's Bazaar*.

1959

Finishes first draft of *The Violent Bear*. Substitutes for Eudora Welty as short-term visiting instructor for University of Chicago writing program. Receives $700 there for teaching two workshops and low-attended public reading. Meets Cecil Dawkins. Receives $8,000 Ford Foundation grant. Works on revisions and publication concerns for *Violent Bear*. Battles jaw necrosis that makes eating difficult. Adds on to the farmhouse a sitting room, bedroom, and bath out of savings from publications and awards.

1960

Angry that *Time* magazine review of *Violent Bear* mentions her lupus. Robert Lowell, Andrew Lytle, Thomas Stritch, Robert Penn Warren all write to tell her that they like the book. Is approached by Sister Evangelist, Superior of Our Lady of Perpetual Help Cancer Home in Atlanta, who asks for help in writing and editing *A Memoir of Mary Ann*. Coindreau visits Andalusia. Gives lecture, "Some Aspects of the Grotesque in Southern Fiction" at Wesleyan College in Macon. Writes introduction to nuns' book and send manuscript to Giroux without much expectation for publication. Goes to Piedmont Hospital in Atlanta for bone tests. Bones are deteriorating from steroids used to treat lupus. Lower dosages are attempted.

Publications: "The Comforts of Home," *Kenyon Review*; *The Violent Bear It Away*, Farrar, Straus and Cudahy; "The Azalea Festival," *The Critic*; "The King of the Birds," *Holiday*.

1961

Hears from Giroux that Farrar, Straus will publish *Mary Ann*. Sister Evangelist wins pair of peacocks from her in bet about publication. The nuns give her a used television set that she likes more than she expected. Drugs for hip pain last only two weeks at a time. Hip-replacement operation rejected by Dr. Merrill to avoid lupus complications. Speaks to Benedictine nuns at Marillac College in St. Louis.

Publications: "Introduction" to *A Memoir of Mary Ann*, *Jubilee*; "Everything That Rises Must Converge," *New World Writing*; *A Memoir of Mary Ann*, Farrar, Straus.

1962

Dr. Merrill rejects second idea for hip operation. Has flu in the winter. Speaks at four colleges in spring to earn money, one of which is Converse College in Spartanburg, South Carolina. Meets Eudora Welty and Cleanth Brooks in South Carolina, where they all participate on a panel. Granville Hicks visits Andalusia. Receives honorary Doctor of Letters degree from Saint Mary's University, Notre Dame women's college. Follows Second Vatican Council with active interest. Injection helps with hip pain. Makes speeches at four colleges in six days for money, including schools in Texas and Louisiana. Tours New Orleans. Purchases electric typewriter to save her energy but can only do busy work and letter-writing on it, not creative work. "Everything That Rises Must Converge" wins O. Henry Prize.

Publications: "The Lame Shall Enter First," *Sewanee Review*.

1963

Watches and enjoys W. C. Fields films on television. Goes to Boston with Regina to visit aunt and cousins and to Northampton, where she receives an honorary degree from Smith College. Sees Robert Fitzgerald. Sees 14 peacocks out of her flock of 40 all fanning tail feathers in full plume at once. Buys Chevrolet that has power brakes adapted for her use. Weak; diagnosed with anemia and begins to take iron. Hips show improvement. Speaks at Hollins College in Roanoke, Virginia; Notre Dame of Baltimore, Maryland; and Georgetown University in Washington, D. C. Cecil Dawkins given permission to adapt several of O'Connor's stories for the stage. Finishes draft of "Revelation" in eight weeks. Faints before Christmas.

Publications: "Why Do the Heathen Rage?" *Esquire*; *Three By Flannery O'Connor*, New American Library.

1964

Given record player from nuns at cancer home, listens to records brought by Thomas Stritch. Begins to plan new collection of stories with Giroux. Anemia is caused by fibroid tumor; operation is planned despite risk to lupus. Wants surgery at Baldwin County Hospital in Milledgeville so that Regina can also be near Mary Cline, who has had a heart attack. Tumor is removed. Treated with antibiotics for kidney infection. Very upset over Mary Ann's parents threatening a lawsuit, which they drop. Returns to hospital. Gets transfusion and cortisone, but is still very weak. Goes to Piedmont Hospital in Atlanta, all the while working on new collection of stories that will now have reprints rather than revisions of previously published stories. Also working on new story, hiding it under her pillow at the hospital. Sends "Judgment Day" to Catherine Carver for critique. Revises "Parker's Back" until too tired to work anymore. Receives Sacrament of the Sick. Hears that "Revelation" won O. Henry Award. Enters Baldwin County Hospital at end of July and slips into coma on August 2. Dies soon after midnight, August 3, of kidney failure. Low Requiem Mass at the Sacred Heart Church in Milledgeville on August 4. Buried beside father in Memory Hill cemetery.

Publications: "Revelation," *Sewanee Review*—wins first prize, O. Henry Awards.

BIBLIOGRAPHY OF O'CONNOR'S WORKS

Works by Flannery O'Connor

O'Connor, Flannery. *Conversations with Flannery O'Connor*. Edited by Rosemary M. Magee. Literary Conversations. Jackson: University Press of Mississippi, 1987.

———. *Everything That Rises Must Converge*. New York: Farrar, Straus and Giroux, 1965.

———. *Flannery O'Connor: Collected Works*. Edited by Sally Fitzgerald. New York: The Library of America, 1988.

———. *Flannery O'Connor: The Complete Stories*. New York: Farrar, Straus and Giroux, 1971.

———. *Flannery O'Connor: The Habit of Being*. Edited by Sally Fitzgerald. New York: Farrar, Straus and Giroux, 1979.

———. *A Good Man Is Hard to Find and Other Stories*. New York: Harcourt, Brace, 1955.

———. *Mystery and Manners: Occasional Prose*. Edited by Sally Fitgerald and Robert Fitzgerald. New York: Farrar, Straus and Giroux, 1969.

———. *The Violent Bear It Away*. New York: Farrar, Straus and Cudahy, 1960.

———. *Wise Blood*. New York: Harcourt, Brace, 1952.

Collections (Multiauthor) Containing O'Connor's Work

Gordon, Caroline, and Allen Tate, eds. *The House of Fiction: An Anthology of the Short Story, with Commentary*. New York: Scribner, 1960.

Hicks, Granville, ed. *The Living Novel: A Symposium*. New York: Macmillan, 1957.

O'Connor, Flannery. "Wanted: An American Novel," *Life*, September 12, 1955: 48.

O'Connor, Flannery, and Brainard Cheney. *The Correspondence of Flannery O'Connor and the Brainard Cheneys*. Edited and introduced by C. Ralph Stephens. Jackson: University Press of Mississippi, 1986.

Secondary Works

Abbott, Louise H. "Remembering Flannery." *Flannery O'Connor Bulletin* 23 (1994–95): 61–62.

Aiken, David. "Flannery O'Connor's Portrait of the Artist as a Young Failure." *Arizona Quarterly* 32, no. 3 (1976): 245–259.

Alexander, Alice. "The Memory of Milledgeville's Flannery O'Connor is Still Green." *Atlanta Journal* (March 28, 1979), B1, B3.

Allen, Suzanne. "Memoirs of a Southern Catholic Girlhood: Flannery O'Connor's 'A Temple of the Holy Ghost.'" *Renascence: Essays on Value in Literature* 31 (1979): 83–92.

Allen, Walter. "Welty, McCullers, Taylor, Flannery O'Connor." *The Short Story in English*. Oxford: Clarendon, 1981, 310–328.

Allen, William Rodney, "The Cage of Matter: The World as Zoo in Flannery O'Connor's *Wise Blood*." *American Literature: A Journal of Literary History, Criticism, and Bibliography* 58, no. 2 (May 1986): 256–270.

Allen, William Rodney, "Mr. Head and Hawthorne: Allusion and Conversion in Flannery O'Connor's 'The Artificial Nigger.'" *Studies in Short Fiction* 21, no. 1 (Winter 1984): 17–23.

Amason, Craig R. "From Agrarian Homestead to Literary Landscape: A Brief History of Flannery O'Connor's Andalusia." *Flannery O'Connor Review* 2 (2003–04): 4–15.

Andreas, James, "'If It's a Symbol, to Hell With It': The Medieval Gothic Style of Flannery O'Connor in Everything That Rises Must Converge." *Christianity and Literature* 38, no. 2 (Winter 1989): 23–41.

Andretta, Helen R. "A Thomist's Letters to 'A.'" *Flannery O'Connor Bulletin* 26–27 (1998–2000): 52–72.

Angle, Kimberly Grace. "Flannery O'Connor's Literary Art: Spiritual Portraits in Negative Space." *Flannery O'Connor Bulletin* 23 (1994–95): 158–174.

Archer, Emily. "Naming in the Neighborhood of Being: O'Connor and Percy on Language." *Studies in the Literary Imagination* 20, no. 2 (1987): 97–108.

Archer, Emily. "'Stalking Joy': Flannery O'Connor's Accurate Naming." *Religion and Literature* 18, no. 2 (1986): 17–30.

Archer, Jane Elizabeth. "'This is My Place': The Short Films Made from Flannery O'Connor's Short Fiction." *Studies in American Humor* 1, no. 1 (1982): 52–65.

Arnold, Marilyn. "Sentimentalism in the Devil's Territory." In *Flannery O'Connor and the Christian Mystery*, edited by John J. Murphy, et al., 243–258. Provo, Utah: Center for the Study of Christian Values in Literature, Brigham Young University, 1997.

———. "*The Violent Bear It Away*: Flannery O'Connor's Reluctant Compromise with Mercy." *The McNeese Review* 28 (1981–82): 25–33.

———. "*Wise Blood*: Flannery O'Connor's Lonely Gospel of Hope." *Drew Gateway* 46, nos. 1–3 (1975–76): 78–84.

Asals, Frederick. "Differentiation, Violence, and The Displaced Person." *The Flannery O'Connor Bulletin* 13 (1984): 1–14.

———. "The Double in Flannery O'Connor's Stories." *The Flannery O'Connor Bulletin* 9 (1980): 49–86.

———. *Flannery O'Connor: The Imagination of Extremity.* Athens: University of Georgia Press, 1982.

———. "Flannery O'Connor's 'The Lame Shall Enter First.'" *Mississippi Quarterly: The Journal of Southern Culture* 23 (1970): 103–120.

———. "Hawthorne, Mary Ann, and 'The Lame Shall Enter First.'" *The Flannery O'Connor Bulletin* 2 (1973): 3–18.

———. "The Mythic Dimensions of Flannery O'Connor's 'Greenleaf.'" *Studies in Short Fiction* 5 (1968): 137–140.

———. "'Obediah, Obadiah': Guys and Dolls in 'Parker's Back,'" *The Flannery O'Connor Bulletin* 21 (1992): 37–42.

———. "The Road to *Wise Blood*." *Renascence: Essays on Value in Literature* 21 (1969): 181–194.

———. "Some Glimpses of Flannery O'Connor in the Canadian Landscape." *Flannery O'Connor Bulletin* 23 (1994–95): 83–90.

Asals, Frederick, ed. *Flannery O'Connor: "A Good Man Is Hard to Find."* New Brunswick, N.J.: Rutgers University Press, 1993.

Askin, Denise T. "Anagogical Vision and Comedic Form in Flannery O'Connor: The Reasonable Use of Unreasonable." *Renascence: Essays on Values in Literature* 57, no. 1 (Fall 2004): 47–62.

Atkins, Christine. "Educating Hulga: Re-Writing Seduction in 'Good Country People.'" In *'On the Subject of the Feminist Business': Re-Reading Flannery O'Connor*, edited and introduced by Teresa Caruso, 120–128. New York: Peter Lang, 2004.

"Author's Beloved Peacocks Come to Violent End." *Charleston Post and Courier*, November 29, 1991. B10.

Babinec, Lisa S. "Cyclical Patterns of Domination and Manipulation in Flannery O'Connor's Mother-Daughter Relationships." *Flannery O'Connor Bulletin* 19 (1990): 9–29.

Bacon, Jon Lance. "A Fondness for Supermarkets: *Wise Blood* and Consumer Culture." In *New Essays on Wise Blood*, edited by Michael Kreyling, 25–49. New York: Cambridge University Press, 1995.

Baker, J. Robert. "Flannery O'Connor's Four-Fold Method of Allegory." *The Flannery O'Connor Bulletin* 21 (1992): 84–96.

Baldanza, Frank. "O'Connor, Mary Flannery." *The Encyclopedia of Southern History*, edited by David C. Roller and Robert W. Twyman. Baton Rouge: Louisiana State University Press, 1979, 533, 727, 935–936.

Balée, Susan. *Flannery O'Connor: Literary Prophet of the South.* Great Achievers: Lives of the Physically Challenged. New York: Chelsea House, 1995.

Bamberg, Marie Louise. "A Note on the Motif of Midday Crisis in Flannery O'Connor's *The Violent Bear*

It Away." *AN&Q: American Notes & Queries* 23, nos. 1–2 (1984): 19–21.

Bandy, Stephen C. "'One of My Babies': The Misfit and the Grandmother." *Studies in Short Fiction* 33, no. 1 (Winter 1996): 107–117.

Barnes, Linda Adams. "The Freak Endures: The Southern Grotesque from Flannery O'Connor to Bobbie Ann Mason." *Since Flannery O'Connor: Essays on the Contemporary American Short Story,* edited by Loren Logsdon and Charles W. Mayer. Macomb: Western Illinois University Press, 1987, 133–141.

Bart, Robert S. "The Miraculous Moonlight: Flannery O'Connor's 'The Artificial Nigger.'" *St. Johns Review* 37, nos. 2–3 (1986): 37–47.

Bass, Eben. "Flannery O'Connor and Henry James: The Vision of Grace." *Studies in the 20th Century: A Scholarly and Critical Journal* 14 (Fall 1974): 43–67.

Bauer, Margaret D. "The Betrayal of Ruby Hill and Hulga Hopewell: Recognizing Feminist Concerns in 'A Stroke of Good Fortune' and 'Good Country People.'" In *'On the Subject of the Feminist Business': Re-Reading Flannery O'Connor,* edited by Teresa Caruso, 40–63. New York: Peter Lang, 2004.

Baumbach, Jonathan. "The Acid of God's Grace." *The Landscape of Nightmare: Studies in the Contemporary American Novel.* New York: New York University Press, 1965, 87–100.

Baumgaertner, Jill P. "'The Meaning Is in You': Flannery O'Connor in Her Letters." *Christian Century* 23–30 (December 1987): 1,172–1,176.

Baumgaertner, Jill Peláez. *Flannery O'Connor: A Proper Scaring.* Wheaton Literary Ser. Wheaton, Ill.: Harold Shaw, 1988; rev. ed. Chicago: Cornerstone, 1998.

Behrendt, Stephen C. "Knowledge and Innocence in Flannery O'Connor's 'The River.'" *Studies in American Fiction* 17, no. 2 (Autumn 1989): 143–155.

Beiswanger, George. "From the 'Office of Fiction,'" *Flannery O'Connor Bulletin* 25 (1996–97): 175–182.

Bellamy, Michael O. "Everything Off Balance: Protestant Election in Flannery O'Connor's 'A Good Man Is Hard to Find.'" *Flannery O'Connor Bulletin* 8 (1979): 116–124.

Ben-Bassat, Hedda. "Flannery O'Connor's Double Vision." *Literature & Theology* 11, no. 2 (1997): 185–199.

Benoit, Raymond. "The Existential Intuition in of Flannery O'Connor in *The Violent Bear It Away.*" *Notes on Contemporary Literature* 23, no. 4 (September 1993): 2–3.

Beringer, Cindy, "'I Have Not Wallowed': Flannery O'Connor's Working Mothers." In *Southern Mothers: Fact and Fictions in Southern Women's Writing,* edited by Warren Nagueyalti, et al., 124–141. Baton Rouge: Louisiana State University Press, 1999.

Betts, Doris. "Talking to Flannery." *Flannery O'Connor Bulletin* 24 (1995–96): 77–81.

Beutel, Katherine Piller. "Flannery O'Connor's Echoing Voices in *The Violent Bear It Away.*" *Journal of Contemporary Thought* 4 (1994): 23–36.

Bieber, Christina. "Called to the Beautiful: The Incarnational Art of Flannery O'Connor's *The Violent Bear It Away.*" *Xavier Review* 18, no. 1 (1998): 44–62.

Blasingham, Mary V. "Archetypes of the Child and of Childhood in the Fiction of Flannery O'Connor." *Realist of Distances: Flannery O'Connor Revisited,* edited by Karl-Heinz Westarp and Jan Nordby Gretlund. Aarhus (Denmark): Aarhus University Press, 1987, 102–112.

Bleikasten, André. "Writing on the Flesh: Tattoos and Taboos in 'Parker's Back.'" *Southern Literary Journal* 14, no. 2 (Spring 1982): 8–18.

Bloom, Harold, ed. and intro. *Flannery O'Connor: Comprehensive Research and Study Guide.* Bloom's Major Short Story Writers Series. Broomall, Pa.: Chelsea House, 1999.

———. *Flannery O'Connor. Modern Critical Views.* New York: Chelsea House, 1986.

Blythe, Hal. "The Misfit: O'Connor's 'Family' Man as Serial Killer." *Notes on Contemporary Literature* 25, no. 1 (January 1995): 3–5.

Blythe, Hal, and Charlie Sweet. "Darwin in Dixie: O'Connor's Jungle." *Notes on Contemporary Literature* 21, no. 2 (1991): 8–9.

Bolton, Betsy. "Placing Violence, Embodying Grace: Flannery O'Connor's 'Displaced Person.'" *Studies in Short Fiction* 34, no. 1 (Winter 1997): 87–104.

Bonney, William. "The Moral Structure of Flannery O'Connor's 'A Good Man Is Hard to Find.'" *Studies in Short Fiction* 27, no. 3 (Summer 1990): 347–356.

Boren, Mark. "Flannery O'Connor, Laughter, and the Word Made Flesh." *Studies in American Fiction* 26, no. 1 (1998): 115–128.

Borgman, Paul. "Three Wise Men: The Comedy of O'Connor's *Wise Blood.*" *Christianity and Literature* 24, no. 3 (1975): 36–48.

Brinkmeyer, Robert H., Jr. "A Closer Walk with Thee: Flannery O'Connor and Southern Fundamentalists." *Southern Literary Journal* 18, no. 2 (Spring 1986): 3–13.

———. "'Jesus, Stab Me in the Heart!': Wise Blood, Wounding, and Sacramental Aesthetics." In *New Essays* on Wise Blood, edited by Michael Kreyling, 71–89. New York: Cambridge University Press, 1995.

Britt, Brian. "Divine Curses in O'Connor's 'Revelation' and 2 Samuel 16." *Flannery O'Connor Review* 1 (2001–02): 49–55.

Brown, Thomas H. "O'Connor's Use of Eye Imagery in *Wise Blood.*" *South Central Bulletin* 37 (1977): 138–140.

Browning, Preston M., Jr. *Flannery O'Connor.* Carbondale: Southern Illinois University Press, 1974.

———. "'Parker's Back': Flannery O'Connor's Iconography of Salvation by Profanity." *Studies in Short Fiction* 6 (1969): 525–535.

Bryant, Hallman B. "Reading the Map in 'A Good Man Is Hard to Find.'" *Studies in Short Fiction* 18, no. 3 (Summer 1981): 301–307.

Burke, William. "Displaced Communities and Literary Form in Flannery O'Connor's 'The Displaced Person.'" *MFS: Modern Fiction Studies* 32, no. 2 (Summer 1986): 219–227.

Burns, Dan G. "Flannery O'Connor's 'Parker's Back': The Key to the End." *Notes on Contemporary Literature* 17, no. 2 (March 1987): 11–12.

Burns, Stuart L. "The Evolution of *Wise Blood.*" *Modern Fiction Studies* 16 (1970): 147–162.

———. "Flannery O'Connor's Literary Apprenticeship." *Renascence* 22 (1969): 3–16.

———. "Flannery O'Connor's *The Violent Bear It Away*: Apotheosis in Failure." *Sewanee Review* 76 (1968): 319–336.

———. "Structural Patterns in *Wise Blood.*" *Xavier University Studies* 8, no. 2 (1969): 32–43.

Buzan, Mary. "The Difficult Heroism of Francis Marion Tarwater." *The Flannery O'Connor Bulletin* 14 (1985): 33–43.

Byars, John. "Mimicry and Parody in *Wise Blood.*" *College Literature* 11, no. 3 (Fall 1984): 276–279.

Carson, Ricks. "O'Connor's *Wise Blood.*" *Explicator* 49, no. 3 (Spring 1991): 186–187.

Cash, Jean. *Flannery O'Connor: A Life.* Knoxville, University of Tennessee Press, 2002.

Cash, Jean W. "O'Connor on 'Revelation': The Story of a Story." *English Language Notes* 24, no. 3 (March 1987): 61–67.

———. "O'Connor on *The Violent Bear It Away*: An Unpublished Letter." *English Language Notes* 26, no. 4 (June 1989): 67–71.

Cheatham, George. "Jesus, O'Connor's Artificial Nigger." *Studies in Short Fiction* 22, no. 4 (Fall 1985): 475–479.

Chew, Martha. "Flannery O'Connor's Double-Edged Satire: The Idiot Daughter Versus the Lady Ph.D." *The Southern Quarterly: A Journal of the Arts in the South* 19, no. 2 (Winter 1981): 17–25.

Church, Joseph. "An Abuse of the Imagination in Flannery O'Connor's 'A Good Man Is Hard to Find.'" *Notes on Contemporary Literature* 20, no. 3 (May 1990): 8–10.

Ciuba, Gary M. "From Face Value to the Value of Faces: *Wise Blood* and the Limits of Literalism." *Modern Language Studies* 19, no. 3 (Summer 1989): 72–80.

Clark, Michael. "Flannery O'Connor's 'A Good Man Is Hard to Find': The Moment of Grace. *English Language Notes* 29, no. 2 (December 1991): 66–69.

Clasby, Nancy T. "'The Life You Save May Be Your Own': Flannery O'Connor as a Visionary Artist." *Studies in Short Fiction* 28, no. 4 (Fall 1991): 509–520.

Coles, Robert. *Flannery O'Connor's South.* Baton Rouge: Louisiana State University Press, 1980. Athens: University of Georgia Press, 1993.

Cook, Martha E. "Flannery O'Connor's *Wise Blood*: Forms of Entrapment." In *Modern American Fiction: Form and Function*, edited by Thomas Daniel Young, 198–212. Baton Rouge: Louisiana State University Press, 1989.

Corn, Alfred. "An Encounter with O'Connor and 'Parker's Back.'" *The Flannery O'Connor Bulletin* 24 (1995–96): 104–118.

Coulthardt, A. R. "Flannery O'Connor's 'A View of the Woods': A View of the Worst." *Notes on Contemporary Literature* 17, no. 1 (January 1987): 7–9.

———. "Flannery O'Connor's Deadly Conversions." *The Flannery O'Connor Bulletin* 13 (1984): 87–98.

Crawford, Nicholas. "An Africanist Impasse: Race, Return, and Revelation in the Short Fiction of Flannery O'Connor." *South Atlantic Review* 68, no. 2 (Spring 2003): 1–25.

Currie, Sheldon. "Freaks and Folks: Comic Imagery in the Fiction of Flannery O'Connor." *The Antigonish Review* 62–63 (Summer–Fall 1985): 133–142.

———. "A Good Grandmother Is Hard to Find: Story as Exemplum." *The Antigonish Review* 81–82 (Spring–Summer 1990): 143–156.

Darretta, John L. "From 'The Geranium' to 'Judgement Day': Retribution in the Fiction of Flannery O'Connor." In *Since Flannery O'Connor: Essays on the Contemporary American Short Story,* edited by Loren Logsdon and Charles W. Mayer, 21–31. Macomb: Western Illinois University, 1987.

Davis, William V. "'Large and Startling Figures': The Place of 'Parker's Back' in Flannery O'Connor's Canon." *Antigonish Review* 28 (1977): 71–87.

Demory, Pamela H. "Violence and Transcendance in *Pulp Fiction* and Flannery O'Connor." In *The Image of Violence in Literature, the Media, and Society,* edited by Will Wright and Steven Kaplan, 187–194. Pueblo, Colo.: Society for the Interdisciplinary Study of Social Imagery, University of Southern Colorado, 1995.

Denham, Robert D. "The World of Guilt and Sorrow: Flannery's O'Connor's 'Everything That Rises Must Converge.'" *Flannery O'Connor Bulletin* 4 (1975): 42–51.

Desmond, John F. "Flannery O'Connor and the History Behind the History." *Modern Age: A Quarterly Review* 27, nos. 3–4 (Summer–Fall 1983): 290–296.

———. "Flannery O'Connor and the Idolatrous Mind." *Christianity and Literature* 46, no. 1 (Autumn 1996): 25–35.

———. "Flannery O'Connor's Misfit and the Mystery of Evil." *Renascence: Essays on Values in Literature* 56, no. 2 (Winter 2004): 129–137.

———. "The Mystery of the Word and the Act: *The Violent Bear It Away.*" *American Benedictine Review* 24 (1973): 342–347.

———. "The Lessons of History: Flannery O'Connor's Everything That Rises Must Converge." *Flannery O'Connor Bulletin* 1 (1972): 39–45.

———. *Risen Sons: Flannery O'Connor's Vision of History.* Athens: University of Georgia Press, 1987.

———. "The Shifting of Mr. Shiftlet: Flannery O'Connor's 'The Life You Save May Be Your Own.'" *Mississippi Quarterly* 28 (1975): 55–59.

———. "Sign of the Times: Lancelot and the Misfit." *The Flannery O'Connor Bulletin* 18 (1989): 91–98.

Detweiler, Jane A. "Flannery O'Connor's Conversation with Simone Weil: The Violent Bear It Away as a Study of Affliction." *Kentucky Philological Review* 6 (1991): 4–8.

DiRenzo, Anthony. *American Gargoyles: Flannery O'Connor and the Medieval Grotesque.* Carbondale: Southern Illinois University Press, 1995.

Donahoo, Robert. "O'Connor's Ancient Comedy: Form in 'A Good Man Is Hard to Find.'" *Journal of the Short Story in English* 16 (Spring 1991): 29–40.

———. "O'Connor's Catholics: A Historical-Cultural Context." In *Flannery O'Connor and the Christian Mystery,* edited by John V. Murphy, et al., 101–113. Provo, Utah: Center for the Study of Christian Values in Literature, Brigham Young University, 1997.

———. "The Problem with Peelers: *Wise Blood* as Social Criticism." The *Flannery O'Connor Bulletin* 21 (1992): 43–57.

———. "Tarwater's March Toward the Feminine: The Role of Gender in O'Connor's *The Violent Bear It Away.*" *CEA Critic: An Official Journal of the College English Association* 56, no. 1 (Fall 1993): 96–106.

Doxey, William S. "A Dissenting Opinion of Flannery O'Connor's 'A Good Man Is Hard to Find.'" *Studies in Short Fiction* 10 (1973): 199–204.

Drake, Robert. *Flannery O'Connor: A Critical Essay.* Grand Rapids, Mich.: Eerdmans, 1966.

Driggers, Stephen G., and Robert J. Dunn. *The Manuscripts of Flannery O'Connor at Georgia College.* Athens: University of Georgia Press, 1989.

Driskell, Leon. "'Parker's Back' vs. 'The Partridge Festival': Flannery O'Connor's Critical Choice." *Georgia Review* 21 (1967): 476–490.

Driskell, Leon V., and Joan T. Brittain. *The Eternal Crossroads: The Art of Flannery O'Connor.* Lexington: University Press of Kentucky, 1971.

Duckworth, Victoria. "The Redemptive Impulse: *Wise Blood* and *The Color Purple.*" *Flannery O'Connor Bulletin* 15 (1986): 51–56.

Dyer, Joyce C. "'Something' in Flannery O'Connor's *Wise Blood.*" *Notes on Contemporary Literature* 15, no. 5 (November 1985): 5–6.

Dyson, J. Peter. "Cats, Crime, and Punishment: The Mikado's Pitti-Sing in 'A Good Man Is Hard to Find.'" *English Studies in Canada* 14, no. 4 (December 1988): 436–452.

Edmondson, Henry T., III. "Modernity versus Mystery in Flannery O'Connor's Short Story 'A View of the Woods.'" *Interpretation: A Journal of Political Philosophy* 29, no. 2 (Winter 2001–02): 187–204.

———. *Return to Good and Evil: Flannery O'Connor's Response to Nihilism.* Lanham, Md.: Lexington Books, 2002.

———. "'Wingless Chickens': 'Good Country People' and the Seduction of Nihilism." *Flannery O'Connor Review* 2 (2003–04): 63–73.

Edmunds, Susan. "Through a Glass Darkly: Visions of Integrated Community in Flannery O'Connor's *Wise Blood*." *Contemporary Literature* 37, no. 4 (Winter 1996): 559–585.

Egan, Kimberly. "Ruby Turpin in Flannery O'Connor's 'Revelation.'" *Notes on Contemporary Literature* 28, no. 1 (March 1998): 8–9.

Eggenschwiler, David. *The Christian Humanism of Flannery O'Connor.* Detroit, Mich.: Wayne State University Press, 1972.

Elie, Paul. *"The Life You Save May Be Your Own": An American Pilgrimage: Flannery O'Connor, Thomas Merton, Walker Percy, Dorothy Day.* New York: Farrar, Straus and Giroux, 2003.

Ellis, James. "Watermelons and Coca-Cola in 'A Good Man Is Hard to Find': Holy Communion in the South." *Notes on Contemporary Literature* 8, no. 3 (1978): 7–8.

Ellis, Juniper. "O'Connor and Her World: The Visual Art of *Wise Blood*." *Studies in the Humanities* 21, no. 2 (December 1994): 79–95.

Emerick, Ronald. "*Wise Blood*: O'Connor's Romance of Alienation." *Literature and Belief* 12 (1992): 27–38.

Enjolras, Laurence. *Flannery O'Connor's Characters.* Lanham, Md.: University Press of America, 1998.

Evans, Robert C. "Poe, O'Connor, and the Mystery of the Misfit." *Flannery O'Connor Bulletin* 25 (1996–97): 1–12.

Fahey, William A. "Flannery O'Connor's 'Parker's Back.'" *Renascence: Essays on Value in Literature* 20 (1968): 162–164, 166.

Farmer, David R. *Flannery O'Connor: A Descriptive Bibliography.* Garland Reference Library of the Humanities. New York: Garland, 1981.

Farnham, James F. "Further Evidence for the Sources of 'Parker's Back.'" *Flannery O'Connor Bulletin* 12 (1983): 114–116.

Feeley, Kathleen. *Flannery O'Connor: Voice of the Peacock.* New Brunswick, N.J.: Rutgers University Press, 1972. New York: Fordham University Press, 1982.

Feeley, Margaret Peller. "Flannery O'Connor's *Wise Blood*: The Negative Way." *Southern Quarterly: A Journal of the Arts in the South* 17, no. 2 (1979): 104–122.

Feldman, Kathryn. "Back to Back: Flannery O'Connor: Art and Reality." *Nassau Review: The Journal of Nassau Community College Devoted to Arts, Letters, and Sciences* 7, no. 1 (1995): 85–88.

Fenwick, Ruth. "Final Harvest: Flannery O'Connor's 'The Crop.'" *English Journal* 74, no. 2 (February 1985): 45–50.

Ficken, Carl. "Theology in Flannery O'Connor's *The Habit of Being*." *Christianity and Literature* 30, no. 2 (Winter 1981): 51–63.

Fickett, Harold, and Douglas R. Gilbert. *Flannery O'Connor: Images of Grace*, Illus. by Douglas R. Gilbert. Grand Rapids, Mich.: Eeerdmans, 1996.

Fike, Matthew. "The Timothy Allusion in 'A Good Man Is Hard to Find.'" *Renascence: Essays on Values in Literature* 52, no. 4 (Summer 2000): 311–319.

Fiondella, Maris G. "Augustine, the 'Letter,' and the Failure of Love in 'The Artificial Nigger.'" *Studies in Short Fiction* 24, no. 2 (Spring 1987): 119–129.

Fitzgerald, Sally. "Happy Endings." *Image: A Journal of the Arts and Religion* 16 (Summer 1997): 73–80.

———. "The Owl and the Nightingale." *The Flannery O'Connor Bulletin* 13 (1984): 44–58.

Fodor, Sarah. "Proust 'Home of the Brave' and Understanding Fiction: O'Connor's Development as a Writer." *Flannery O'Connor Bulletin* 25 (1996–97): 62–80.

Folks, Jeffrey J. "'The Enduring Chill': Physical Disability in Flannery O'Connor's Everything That Rises Must Converge." *University of Dayton Review* 22, no. 2 (Winter 1993–94): 81–88.

———. "The Mechanical in Everything That Rises Must Converge." *Southern Literary Journal* 18, no. 2 (Spring 1986): 14–26.

Fowler, Doreen. "Deconstructing Racial Difference: O'Connor's 'The Artificial Nigger.'" *The Flannery O'Connor Bulletin* 24 (1995–96): 22–32.

———. "Writing and Re-Writing Race: Flannery O'Connor's 'The Geranium' and 'Judgment Day.'" *Flannery O'Connor Review* 2 (2003–04): 31–39.

Fowler, James. "In the Flesh: The Grace of 'Parker's Back.'" *Publications of the Mississippi Philological Association* (2004): 60–66.

Friedman, Melvin J., and Beverly Lyon Clark, eds. *Critical Essays on Flannery O'Connor.* Critical Essays on American Literature. Boston: G. K. Hall, 1985.

Friedman, Melvin J., and Lewis A. Lawson, eds. *The Added Dimension: The Art and Mind of Flannery O'Connor.* New York: Fordham University Press, 1966.

Frieling, Kenneth. "Flannery O'Connor's Vision: The Violence of Revelation." In *The Fifties: Fiction, Poetry, Drama,* edited by Warren French, 111–120. DeLand, Fla.: Everett/Edwards, 1970.

Gatta, John. "*The Scarlet Letter* as Pre-Text for Flannery O'Connor's 'Good Country People.'" In *Hawthorne and Women: Engendering and Expanding the Hawthorne Tradition,* edited by John L. Idol and Melinda M. Ponder, 271–277. Amherst: University of Massachusetts Press, 1999.

Gentry, Marshall Bruce. "The Eye vs. the Body: Individual and Communal Grotesquerie in *Wise Blood.*" *MFS: Modern Fiction Studies* 28, no. 3 (Autumn 1982): 487–493.

———. *Flannery O'Connor's Religion of the Grotesque.* Jackson: University Press of Mississippi, 1986.

———. "The Hand of the Writer in 'The Comforts of Home.'" *Flannery O'Connor Bulletin* 20 (1991): 61–72.

———. "How Sacred is the Violence in 'A View of the Woods'?" In *'On the Subject of the Feminist Business': Re-Reading Flannery O'Connor,* edited by Teresa Caruso, 64–73. New York: Peter Lang, 2004.

Getz, Lorine M. *Flannery O'Connor: Her Life, Library and Book Reviews.* Studies in Women & Religion 5. New York: Edwin Mellen, 1980.

———. *Nature and Grace in Flannery O'Connor's Fiction.* Studies in Art and Religious Interpretation 2. New York: Mellon, 1982.

Giannone, Richard. "'The Artificial Nigger' and the Redemptive Quality of Suffering." *Flannery O'Connor Bulletin* 12 (1983): 5–16.

———. *Flannery O'Connor and the Mystery of Love.* Urbana: University of Illinois Press, 1989, New York: Fordham University Press, 1999.

———. *Flannery O'Connor: Hermit Novelist.* Urbana and Chicago: University of Illinois Press, 2000.

———. "'Greenleaf': A Story of Lent." *Studies in Short Fiction* 22, no. 4 (Fall 1985): 421–429.

———. "The Lion of Judah in the Thought and Design of *The Violent Bear It Away.*" *Flannery O'Connor Bulletin* 14 (1985): 25–32.

———. "Paul, Francis, and Hazel Motes: Conversion at Taulkinham." *Thought: A Review of Culture and Idea* 59, no. 235 (December 1984): 483–503.

———. "Warfare and Solitude: O'Connor's Prophet and the Word in the Desert." In *Flannery O'Connor and the Christian Mystery,* edited by John J. Murphy, et al., 161–189. Provo, Utah: Center for the Study of Christian Values in Literature, Brigham Young University, 1997.

Gidden, Nancy Ann. "Classical Agents of Christian Grace in Flannery O'Connor's 'Greenleaf.'" *Studies in Short Fiction* 23, no. 2 (Spring 1986): 201–202.

Golden, Robert E., and Mary C. Sullivan. *Flannery O'Connor and Caroline Gordon: A Reference Guide.* Reference Guides in Literature. Boston: G. K. Hall, 1977.

Gordon, Sarah. *Flannery O'Connor: The Obedient Imagination.* Athens: University of Georgia Press, 2000.

———. "The News From Afar: A Note on Structure in O'Connor's Narratives." *Flannery O'Connor Bulletin* 14 (1985): 80–88.

Gordon, Sarah, ed. *Flannery O'Connor: A Celebration of Genius.* Athens, Ga.: Hill Street Press, 2000.

Gray, Jeffrey. "'It's Not Natural': Freud's 'Uncanny' and O'Connor's *Wise Blood.*" *Southern Literary Journal* 29, no. 1 (Fall 1996): 56–68.

Green, James L. "Enoch Emery and His Biblical Namesakes in *Wise Blood.*" *Studies in Short Fiction* 10 (1973): 417–419.

Gregory, Donald. "Enoch Emery: Ironic Doubling in *Wise Blood.*" *Flannery O'Connor Bulletin* 4 (1975): 52–64.

Griffith, Albert J. "Flannery O'Connor's Salvation Road." *Studies in Short Fiction*, 3 (1966): 329–333.

Grimes, Ronald L. "Anagogy and Ritualization: Baptism in Flannery O'Connor's *The Violent Bear It Away*." *Religion and Literature* 21, no. 1 (Spring 1989): 9–26.

Grimshaw, James A., Jr. *The Flannery O'Connor Companion*. Westport, Conn.: Greenwood Press, 1981.

Haddox, Thomas F. "The City Reconsidered: Problems and Possibilities of Urban Community in 'A Stroke of Good Fortune' and 'The Artificial Nigger,'" *Flannery O'Connor Review* 3 (2005): 4–18.

———. "'Something Haphazard and Botched': Flannery O'Connor's Critique of the Visual in 'Parker's Back.'" *Mississippi Quarterly: The Journal of Southern Cultures* 57, no. 3 (Summer 2004): 407–421.

Han, Jae-nam. "O'Connor's Thomism and the 'Death of God' in *Wise Blood*." In *Flannery O'Connor and the Christian Mystery*, edited by John J. Murphy, et al., 115–127. Provo, Utah: Center for the Study of Christian Values in Literature, Brigham Young University, 1997.

Hardy, Donald E. "Free Indirect Discourse, Irony, and Empathy in Flannery O'Connor's 'Revelation.'" *Language and Literature* 16 (1991): 37–53.

———. "Why Is She So Negative? Negation and Knowledge in Flannery O'Connor's 'A Good Man Is Hard to Find.'" *Southwest Journal of Linguistics* 17, no. 2 (December 1998): 61–81.

Harrison, Margaret. "Hazel Motes in Transit: A Comparison of Two Versions of Flannery O'Connor's 'The Train' with Chapter 1 of *Wise Blood*." *Studies in Short Fiction* 8 (1971): 287–293.

Havird, David. "The Saving Rape: Flannery O'Connor and Patriarchal Religion." *Mississippi Quarterly: The Journal of Southern Culture* 47, no. 1 (Winter 1993–94): 15–26.

Hawkes, John. "Flannery O'Connor's Devil." *Sewanee Review* 70, no. 3 (1962).

Hawkins, Peter S. *The Language of Grace: Flannery O'Connor, Walker Percy, and Iris Murdoch*. Cambridge, Mass.: Cowley, 1983.

Haykin, Marti. "A Note on the Prints." *Flannery O'Connor Bulletin* 25 (1996–97): 103–104.

Hegarty, Charles M., S. J. "A Man Though Not Yet a Whole One: Mr. Shiftlet's Genesis." *Flannery O'Connor Bulletin* 1 (1972): 24–38.

Heher, Michael. "Grotesque Grace in the Factious Commonwealth." *Flannery O'Connor Bulletin* 15 (1986): 69–81.

Hendin, Josephine. *The World of Flannery O'Connor*. Bloomington: Indiana University Press, 1970.

Hewitt, Avis. "'Ignoring Unmistakable Likeness': Mark Fortune's Miss-Fortune in 'A View of the Woods.'" In *'On the Subject of the Feminist Business': Re-Reading Flannery O'Connor*, edited by Teresa Caruso, 129–154. New York: Peter Lang, 2004.

Hicks, Granville, ed. *The Living Novel: A Symposium*. New York: Macmillan, 1957.

Horton, James W. "Flannery O'Connor's Hermaphrodite: Notes Toward a Theology of Sex." *Flannery O'Connor Bulletin* 23 (1994–95): 30–41.

Humphries, Jefferson. *The Otherness Within: Gnostic Readings in Marcel Proust, Flannery O'Connor, and François Villon*. Baton Rouge: Louisiana State University Press, 1983.

Hyman, Stanley Edgar. *Flannery O'Connor*. University of Minnesota Pamphlets on American Writers, series 54. Minneapolis: University of Minnesota Press, 1966; reprint in *Seven American Women Writers of the Twentieth Century: An Introduction*, edited by Maureen Howard. Minneapolis: University of Minnesota Press, 1977, 311–355.

Jauss, David. "Flannery O'Connor's Inverted Saint's Legend." *Studies in Short Fiction* 25, no. 1 (Winter 1988): 76–78.

Johansen, Ruthann Knechel. *The Narrative Secret of Flannery O'Connor: The Trickster as Interpreter*. Tuscaloosa: University of Alabama Press, 1994.

Johnson, Gregory R. "Pagan Virtue and Christian Charity: Flannery O'Connor on the Moral Contradictions of Western Culture." In *The Moral of the Story: Literature and Public Ethics*, edited by Henry T. Edmondson III, 237–253. Lanham, Md.: Lexington, 2000.

Johnson, Rob. "'The Topical is Poison': Flannery O'Connor's Vision of Social Reality in 'The Partridge Festival,' and 'Everything That Rises Must Converge.'" *Flannery O'Connor Bulletin* 21 (1992): 1–24.

Jones, Madison. "A Good Man's Predicament." *The Southern Review* 20, no. 4 (Autumn 1984): 836–841.

Jorgenson, Eric. "A Note on the Jonah Motif in 'Parker's Back.'" *Studies in Short Fiction* 21, no. 4 (Fall 1984): 400–402.

Kahane, Claire. "The Maternal Legacy: The Grotesque Tradition in Flannery O'Connor's Female Gothic." In *The Female Gothic*, edited by Julian E. Fleenor, 242–256. Montreal: Eden, 1983.

Keetley, Dawn. "'I forgot what I done': Repressed Anger and Violent Fantasy in 'A Good Man Is Hard to Find.'" In *"On the subject of the feminist business": Re-Reading Flannery O'Connor*, edited by Teresa Caruso, New York: Peter Lang, 2004.

Kehl, D. G. "Flannery O'Connor's Catholicon: The Source and Significance of the Name 'Tarwater.'" *Notes on Contemporary Literature* 15, no. 2 (March 1985): 2–3.

Kessler, Edward. *Flannery O'Connor and the Language of the Apocalypse*. Princeton Essays in Literature. Princeton, N.J.: Princeton University Press, 1986.

Kilcourse, George. "'Parker's Back': 'Not Totally Congenial' Icons of Christ." In *Flannery O'Connor and the Christian Mystery*, edited by John J. Murphy, et al., 35–46. Provo, Utah: Center for the Study of Christian Values in Literature, Brigham Young University, 1997.

Kinnebrew, Mary Jane. "Language From the Heart of Reality: A Study of Flannery O'Connor's Attitudes Toward Non-Standard Dialect and Her Use of It in *Wise Blood, A Good Man Is Hard to Find*, and *The Violent Bear It Away*." *Linguistics in Literature* 1, no. 3 (1976): 39–53.

Kinney, Arthur F. *Flannery O'Connor's Library: Resources of Being*. Athens: University of Georgia Press, 1985.

Kowalewski, Michael. "On Flannery O'Connor." *Raritan: A Quarterly Review* 10, no. 3 (Winter 1991): 85–104.

Kreyling, Michael, ed. *New Essays on* Wise Blood. New York: Cambridge University Press, 1995.

Kropf, C. R. "Theme and Setting in 'A Good Man Is Hard to Find.'" *Renascence: Essays in Values in Literature* 24 (1972): 177–80, 206.

Kwon, Jong Joon. "The Elements of Mystery in *Wise Blood*." *The Journal of English Language and Literature* 37, no. 2 (Summer 1991): 465–490.

Larsen, Val. "A Tale of Tongue and Pen: Orality and Literacy in 'The Barber.'" *Flannery O'Connor Bulletin* 22 (1993–94): 25–44.

Lasseter, Victor. "The Genesis of Flannery O'Connor's 'A Good Man Is Hard to Find.'" *Studies in American Fiction* 10, no. 2 (Autumn 1982): 227–232.

———. "Manor House and Tenement: Failed Communities South and North in Flannery O'Connor's 'The Geranium,'" *Flannery O'Connor Bulletin* 20 (1991): 88–103.

Lawson, Lewis A. "Flannery O'Connor and the Grotesque: *Wise Blood*." *Renascence: Essays on Value in Literature* 18 (1965): 143–147, 156.

LeClair, Thomas. "Flannery O'Connor's *Wise Blood*: The Oedipal Theme." *Mississippi Quarterly: The Journal of Southern Culture* 29 (1976): 197–205.

Lee, C. Jason. "Criticism and the Terror of Nothingness." *Philosophy and Literature* 27, no. 1 (April 2003): 211–222.

Liu, Dilin. "'A Good Man Is Hard to Find': The Difference between the Word and the World." *Short Story* 2, no. 2 (Winter–Spring 1992): 63–75.

Littlefield, Daniel F., Jr. "Flannery O'Connor's *Wise Blood*: 'Unparalleled Prosperity' and Spiritual Chaos." *Mississippi Quarterly: The Journal of Southern Culture* 23 (1970): 121–133.

Logsdon, Loren, and Charles W. Mayer, eds. *Since Flannery O'Connor: Essays on the Contemporary American Short Story*. Essays in Lit. 7. Macomb: Western Illinois University Press, 1987.

Magistrale, Tony. "An Explication of Flannery O'Connor's Short Story 'A View of the Woods.'" *Notes on Contemporary Literature* 17, no. 1 (January 1987): 6–7.

———. "Flannery O'Connor's 'A View of the Woods': An Expectation." *Notes on Contemporary Literature* 34, no. 1 (January 2004): 9–11.

———. "Francis Tarwater's Friendly Friends: The Role of the Stranger in *The Violent Bear It Away*." *Notes on Contemporary Literature* 15, no. 3 (May 1985): 4–5.

———. "O'Connor's 'The Lame Shall Enter First.'" *Explicator* 47, no. 3 (Spring 1989): 58–61.

Maida, Patricia D. "'Convergence' in Flannery O'Connor's 'Everything That Rises Must Converge.'" *Studies in Short Fiction* 7 (1970): 549–555.

Male, Roy R. "The Two Versions of 'The Displaced Person.'" *Studies in Short Fiction* 7 (1970): 450–457.

Malin, Irving. "Singular Visions: The Partridge Festival.'" In *Critical Essays on Flannery O'Connor*, edited by Melvin J. Friedman, et al., 180–186. Boston: Hall, 1985.

Marks, W. S. "Advertisements for Grace: Flannery O'Connor's 'A Good Man Is Hard to Find.'" *Studies in Short Fiction* 4 (1966): 19–27.

Martin, Carter W. *The True Country: Themes in the Fiction of Flannery O'Connor*. Nashville, Tenn.: Vanderbilt University Press, 1994.

Martin, Karl. "The Prophetic Intent of O'Connor's 'The Displaced Person.'" *Flannery O'Connor Bulletin* 23 (1994–95): 137–157.

Martin, Regis. *Grace, Grotesquerie, and God: A Short Study in the Unsentimental Art and Faith of Flannery O'Connor*. Steubenville, Ohio: Franciscan University Press, 1991.

Martin, W. R. "A Note on Ruby and 'Revelation.'" *Flannery O'Connor Bulletin* 16 (1987): 23–25.

May, John R. *The Pruning Word: The Parables of Flannery O'Connor*. Notre Dame, Ind.: University of Notre Dame Press, 1976.

May, John R., S.J. "*The Violent Bear It Away*: The Meaning of the Title." *Flannery O'Connor Bulletin* 2 (1973): 83–86.

Mayer, Charles W. "The Comic Spirit in 'A Stroke of Good Fortune.'" *Studies in Short Fiction* 16, no. 1 (Winter 1979): 70–74.

Mayer, David R. "Apologia for the Imagination: Flannery O'Connor's 'A Temple of the Holy Ghost.'" *Studies in Short Fiction* 11 (1974): 147–152.

———. *Drooping Sun, Coy Moon: Essays on Flannery O'Connor*. Kyoto, Japan: Yamaguchi, 1996.

———. "Outer Marks, Inner Grace: Flannery O'Connor's Tattooed Christ." *Asian Folklore Studies* 42, no. 1 (1983): 117–127.

McCullagh, James C. "Symbolism and the Religious Aesthetic: Flannery O'Connor's *Wise Blood*." *Flannery O'Connor Bulletin* 2 (1973): 43–58.

McDermott, John V. "Dissociation of Words with the Word in *Wise Blood*." *Renascence: Essays on Value in Literature* 30 (1978): 163–166.

———. "O'Connor's 'A Stroke of Good Fortune.'" *Explicator* 38, no. 4 (Summer 1980): 13–14.

———. "O'Connor's 'The Train.'" *Explicator* 60, no. 3 (Spring 2002): 168–169.

———. "The 'Something Awful' of Flannery O'Connor's 'The Turkey.'" *Notes on Contemporary Literature* 31, no. 1 (January 2001): 4–5.

McFarland, Dorothy Tuck. *Flannery O'Connor*. New York: Frederick Ungar, 1976.

McGill, Robert. "The Life You Write May Be Your Own: Epistolary Autobiography and the Reluctant Resurrection of Flannery O'Connor." *Southern Literary Journal* 36, no. 2 (Spring 2004): 31–46.

McGill, Robert James. "O'Connor, Flannery." *The Literary Encyclopedia*. November 8, 2002. The Literary Dictionary Company. Available online. URL: http://www.litencyc.com/php/speople.php?rec=true&UID=3373>. Accessed November 27, 2005.

McKenzie, Barbara. *Flannery O'Connor's Georgia*, foreword by Robert Coles. Athens: University of Georgia Press, 1980.

McMillan, Norman. "Dostoevskian Vision in Flannery O'Connor's 'Revelation.'" *Flannery O'Connor Bulletin* 16 (1987): 16–22.

McMullen, Joanne Halleran. *Writing Against God: Language as Message in the Literature of Flannery O'Connor*. Macon, Ga.: Mercer University Press, 1996.

McNiff, John Likha. "Flannery O'Connor: The Art of Revelation." *Flannery O'Connor Bulletin* 10, no. 2 (1988–89): 24–56.

Michaels, J. Ramsey. "'The Oldest Nun at the Sisters of Mercy': O'Connor's Saints and Martyrs." *Flannery O'Connor Bulletin* 13 (1984): 80–86.

Middleton, David L. "Meaning Through Form: A Study of Metaphorical Structure in Flannery O'Connor's *Wise Blood*." *The Texas Review* 5, nos. 1–2 (Spring–Summer 1984): 47–57.

Millichap, Joseph R. "The Pauline 'Old Man' in Flannery O'Connor's 'The Comforts of Home.'" *Studies in Short Fiction* 11 (1974): 96–99.

Monroe, W. F. "Flannery O'Connor's Sacramental Icon: 'The Artificial Nigger.'" *South Central Review: The Journal of the South Central Modern Language Association* 1, no. 4 (Winter 1984): 64–81.

Monteiro, George. "The Great American Hunt in Flannery O'Connor's 'The Turkey.'" *Explicator* 51, no. 2 (Winter 1993): 118–121.

Montgomery, Marion. "On Flannery O'Connor's 'Everything That Rises Must Converge.'" *Critique: Studies in Modern Fiction* 13, no. 3 (1971): 15–29.

—. *Why Flannery O'Connor Stayed Home.* Prophetic Poet and the Spirit of the Age 1. La Salle, Ill.: Sherwood Sugden, 1981.

—. *Why Hawthorne Was Melancholy.* Prophetic Poet and the Spirit of the Age 3. LaSalle, Ill.: Sherwood Sugden, 1984. [includes discussion of O'Connor]

—. *Why Poe Drank Liquor.* Prophetic Poet and the Spirit of the Age 2. LaSalle, Ill.: Sherwood Sugden, 1983. [includes discussion of O'Connor]

Muller, Gilbert H. *Nightmares and Visions: Flannery O'Connor and the Catholic Grotesque.* Athens: University of Georgia Press, 1972.

—. "*The Violent Bear It Away*: Moral and Dramatic Sense." *Renascence: Essays on Value in Literature* 22 (1969): 17–25.

Napier, James J. "The Cave-Waiting Room in O'Connor's 'Revelation.'" *NMAL: Notes on Modern American Literature* 5, no. 4 (Fall 1981): Item 23.

—. "Flannery O'Connor's Last Three: 'The Sense of an Ending.'" *Southern Literary Journal* 14, no. 2 (Spring 1982): 19–27.

—. "In 'Parker's Back': A Technical Slip by Flannery O'Connor." *Notes on Contemporary Literature* 11, no. 4 (September 1981): 5–6.

Nichols, Loxley F. "Flannery O'Connor's 'Intellectual Vaudeville': Masks of Mother and Daughter." *Studies in the Literary Imagination* 20, no. 2 (Fall 1987): 15–29.

Nielsen, Erik. "The Hidden Structure of *Wise Blood.*" *New Orleans Review* 19, nos. 3–4 (Fall–Winter 1992): 91–97.

Nisly, Paul W. "Wart Hogs From Hell: The Demonic and the Holy in Flannery O'Connor's Fiction." *Ball State University Forum* 22, no. 3 (1981): 45–50.

Oates, Joyce Carol. "The Action of Mercy." *Kenyon Review* 20, no. 1 (Winter 1998): 157–160.

Ochshorn, Kathleen G. "A Cloak of Grace: Contradictions in 'A Good Man Is Hard to Find.'" *Studies in American Fiction* 18, no. 1 (Spring 1990): 113–117.

Okeke-Ezigbo, Emeka. "Three Artificial Blacks: A Reexamination of O'Connor's 'The Artificial Nigger.'" *College Language Association Journal* 27, no. 4 (June 1984): 371–382.

Olschner, Leonard M. "Annotations on History and Society in Flannery O'Connor's 'The Displaced Person.'" *The Flannery O'Connor Bulletin* 16 (1987): 62–78.

Olson, Steven. "Tarwater's Hats." *Studies in the Literary Imagination* 20, no. 2 (Fall 1987): 37–49.

Orvell, Miles. *Invisible Parade: The Fiction of Flannery O'Connor.* Philadelphia: Temple University Press, 1972. Reprint with new preface, *Flannery O'Connor: An Introduction.* Jackson: University Press of Mississippi, 1991.

Owen, Mitchell. "The Function of Signature in 'A Good Man Is Hard to Find.'" *Studies in Short Fiction* 33, no. 1 (Winter 1996): 101–106.

Ower, John. "The Penny and the Nickel in 'Everything That Rises Must Converge.'" *Studies in Short Fiction* 23, no. 1 (Winter 1986): 107–110.

Paulson, Suzanne Morrow. "Apocalypse of Self, Resurrection of the Double: Flannery O'Connor's *The Violent Bear It Away.*" *Literature and Psychology* 30, nos. 3–4 (1980): 100–111.

—. *Flannery O'Connor: A Study of the Short Fiction.* Twayne's Studies in Short Fiction, series 2. Boston: G. K. Hall, 1988.

Pepin, Ronald E. "Latin Names and Images of Ugliness in Flannery O'Connor's 'Revelation.'" *ANQ: A Quarterly Journal of Short Articles, Notes, and Reviews* 6, no. 1 (January 1993): 25–27.

Perisho, Steve. "The Structure of Flannery O'Connor's 'Revelation.'" *Notes on Contemporary Literature* 20, no. 4 (September 1990): 5–7.

Perrealt, Jeanne. "The Body, the Critics, and 'The Artificial Nigger.'" *Mississippi Quarterly: The Journal of Southern Cultures* 56, no. 3 (Summer 2003): 389–410.

Perry, Keith. "Straining the Soup Necessarily Thinner: Flannery O'Connor's 'Greenleaf' and Proverbs 11:28." *English Language Notes* 42, no. 2 (December 2004): 56–59.

Peters, Jason. "O'Connor's *Wise Blood.*" *Explicator* 63, no. 3 (Spring 2005): 179–181.

Petry, Alice Hall. "Julian and O'Connor's 'Everything That Rises Must Converge.'" *Studies in American Fiction* 15, no. 1 (Spring 1987): 101–108.

—. "O'Connor's 'Parker's Back.'" *Explicator* 46, no. 2 (Winter 1988): 38–43.

Pierce, Constance. "The Mechanical World of 'Good Country People.'" *Flannery O'Connor Bulletin* 5 (1976): 30–38.

Powers, Douglas. "Ruller McFarney's Cutting Loose." *Flannery O'Connor Bulletin* 18 (1989): 70–78.

Quinn, John J., ed. *Flannery O'Connor: A Memorial.* Scranton, Pa.: University of Scranton Press, 1995.

Ragan, Brian Abel. *A Wreck on the Road to Damascus: Innocence, Guilt, & Conversion in Flannery O'Connor.* Chicago: Loyola University Press, 1989.

Rath, Sura P. "Ruby Turpin's Redemption: Thomist Resolution in Flannery O'Connor's 'Revelation.'" *Flannery O'Connor Bulletin* 19 (1990): 1–8.

Rath, Sura Prasad. "Comic Polarities in Flannery O'Connor's *Wise Blood.*" *Studies in Short Fiction* 21, no. 3 (Summer 1984): 251–258.

Rath, Sura, and Mary Neff Shaw, eds. *Flannery O'Connor: New Perspectives.* Athens: University of Georgia Press, 1996.

Rechnitz, Robert M. "Passionate Pilgrim: Flannery O'Connor's *Wise Blood.*" *Georgia Review* 19 (1965): 310–316.

Reiter, Robert E., ed. *Flannery O'Connor.* St Louis: B. Herder, 1968.

Renner, Stanley. "Secular Meaning in 'A Good Man Is Hard to Find.'" *College Literature* 9, no. 2 (Spring 1982): 123–132.

Riso, Don, S. J. "Blood and Land in 'A View of the Woods.'" *New Orleans Review* 1 (1979): 255–257.

Robillard, Douglas, Jr. "Flannery O'Connor and the Tragedy of the South." *Flannery O'Connor Review* 1 (2001–02): 94–98.

Roos, John. "The Political in Flannery O'Connor: A Reading of 'A View of the Woods.'" *Studies in Short Fiction* 29, no. 2 (Spring 1992): 161–179.

Rout, Kathleen. "Dream a Little Dream of Me: Mrs. May and the Bull in Flannery O'Connor's 'Greenleaf.'" *Studies in Short Fiction* 16 (1979): 233–235.

Rowley, Rebecca K. "Individuation and Religious Experience: A Jungian Approach to O'Connor's 'Revelation.'" *Southern Literary Journal* 25, no. 2 (Spring 1993): 92–102.

Russell, Shannon. "Space and the Movement Through Space in Everything That Rises Must Converge." *Southern Literary Journal* 22, no. 2 (Spring 1988): 81–98.

Saunders, James Robert. "The Fallacies of Guidance and Light in Flannery O'Connor's 'The Artificial Nigger.'" *Journal of the Short Story in English* 17 (Autumn 1991): 103–113.

Saunders, Kay. *Letters From the Other Side: The Gift of Flannery O'Connor.* Appleton, Wis.: Saunders, 1998.

Schellenberg, Susan. "A Response to 'The Displaced Person.'" *Flannery O'Connor Bulletin* 25 (1996–97): 30–33.

Schroeder, Michael L. "Ruby Turpin, Job, and Mystery: Flannery O'Connor on the Question of Knowing." *Flannery O'Connor Bulletin* 21 (1992): 75–83.

Scouten, Kenneth. "'The Partridge Festival': Manuscript Revisions." *Flannery O'Connor Bulletin* 15 (1986): 35–41.

———. "The Schoolteacher as a Devil in *The Violent Bear It Away.*" *Flannery O'Connor Bulletin* 12 (1983): 35–46.

Seel, Cynthia. *Ritual Performance in the Fiction of Flannery O'Connor.* Studies in American Literature and Culture. Rochester, N.Y.: Camden House, 2000.

Sessions, W. A. "How to Read Flannery O'Connor: Passing By the Dragon." In *Flannery O'Connor and the Christian Mystery,* edited by John J. Murphy, et al., 191–215. Provo, Utah: Center for the Study of Christian Values in Literature, Brigham Young University, 1997.

———. "'Blessed Insurance': An Examination of Flannery O'Connor's 'Greenleaf.'" *Flannery O'Connor Bulletin* 19 (1990): 38–43.

Sexton, Mark S. "Flannery O'Connor's Presentation of Vernacular Religion in 'The River.'" *Flannery O'Connor Bulletin* 18 (1989): 1–12.

Shaw, Mary Neff. "'The Artificial Nigger': A Dialogic Narrative." *Flannery O'Connor Bulletin* 20 (1991): 104–116.

Shaw, Patrick W. "*The Violent Bear It Away* and the Irony of False Seeing." *Texas Review* 3, no. 2 (Fall 1982): 49–59.

Shields, John C. "Flannery O'Connor's 'Greenleaf' and the Myth of Europa and the Bull." *Studies in Short Fiction* 18, no. 4 (Fall 1981): 421–431.

Shloss, Carol. *Flannery O'Connor's Dark Comedies: The Limits of Inference.* Southern Literary Studies. Baton Rouge: Louisiana State University Press, 1980.

Shrine, Mary S. "Narrative Strategy and Communicative Design in Flannery O'Connor's *The Violent Bear It Away*." In *Studies in Interpretation*, edited by Esther M. Doyle, et al., 45–59. Amsterdam: Rodopi, 1977.

Simpson, Melissa. *Flannery O'Connor: A Biography*. Westport, Conn.: Greenwood Press, 2005.

Slattery, Dennis P. "In a Pig's Eye: Retrieving the Animal Imagination in Ruby Turpin's 'Revelation.'" *Flannery O'Connor Bulletin* 25 (1996–97): 138–150.

Slattery, Dennis Patrick. "Faith in Search of an Image: The Iconic Dimension of Flannery O'Connor's 'Parker's Back.'" *South Central Bulletin* 41, no. 4 (Winter 1981): 120–123.

Sloan, Gary. "Mystery, Magic, and Malice: O'Connor and the Misfit." *Journal of the Short Story in English* 30 (Spring 1998): 73–83.

———. "O'Connor's 'A Good Man Is Hard to Find.'" *Explicator* 57, no. 2 (Winter 1999): 118–120.

Sloan, LaRue Love. "The Rhetoric of the Seer: Eye Imagery in Flannery O'Connor's 'Revelation.'" *Studies in Short Fiction* 25, no. 2 (Spring 1988): 135–145.

Smith, Francis J., S. J. "O'Connor's Religious Viewpoint in *The Violent Bear It Away*." *Renascence: Essays on Value in Literature* 22 (1970): 108–122.

Smith, Marcus A. J. "Another Desert: Haze Mote's Missing Years." *Flannery O'Connor Bulletin* 18 (1989): 55–58.

Smith, Peter A. "Flannery O'Connor's Empowered Women." *Southern Literary Journal* 26, no. 2 (Spring 1994): 35–47.

Spivey, Ted R. *Flannery O'Connor: The Woman, the Thinker; the Visionary*. Macon, Ga.: Mercer University Press, 1995.

Srigley, Susan. "O'Connor and the Mystics: St. Catherine of Genoa's Purgatorial Vision in 'Revelation.'" *Flannery O'Connor Review* 2 (2003–04): 40–52.

Steed, J. P. "'Through Our Laughter We Are Involved': Bergsonian Humor in Flannery O'Connor's Fiction." *Midwest Quarterly: A Journal of Contemporary Thought* 46, no. 3 (Spring 2005): 299–313.

Stephens, Martha. *The Question of Flannery O'Connor*. Baton Rouge: Louisiana State University Press, 1973.

Stephenson, Will. "Ruby Turpin: O'Connor's Travesty of the Ideal Woman." *Flannery O'Connor Bulletin* 24 (1995–96): 57–66.

Stewart, Michelle Pagni. "A Good Trickster Is Hard to Find: A Refiguring of Flannery O'Connor." *Short Story* 3. no. 1 (Spring 1995): 77–83.

Stoneback, H. R. "'Sunk in the Cornfield with His Family': Sense of Place in O'Connor's 'The Displaced Person.'" *Mississippi Quarterly: The Journal of Southern Cultures* 36, no. 4 (Fall 1983): 545–555.

Streight, Irwin Howard. "Is There a Text in this Man? A Semiotic Reading of 'Parker's Back.'" *Flannery O'Connor Bulletin* 22 (1993–94): 1–11.

Strickland, Edward. "The Penitential Quest in 'The Artificial Nigger.'" *Studies in Short Fiction* 25, no. 4 (Fall 1988): 453–459.

Swan, Jesse G. "Flannery O'Connor's Silence-Centered World." *Flannery O'Connor Bulletin* 17 (1988): 82–89.

Sweeney, Gerard M. "O'Connor's *Wise Blood*." *Explicator* 56, no. 2 (Winter 1998): 108–109.

Tate, J. O. "The Essential Essex." *Flannery O'Connor Bulletin* 12 (1983): 47–59.

Tedford, Barbara Wilkie. "Flannery O'Connor and The Social Classes." *Southern Literary Journal* 13, no. 2 (Spring 1981): 27–40.

Thiemann, Fred R. "Usurping the Logos: Clichés in Flannery O'Connor's 'Good Country People.'" *Flannery O'Connor Bulletin* 24 (1995–96): 46–56.

Tolomeo, Diane. "Flannery O'Connor's 'Revelation' and the Book of Job." *Renascence: Essays on Value in Literature* 30 (1978): 79–90.

Trowbridge, Clinton W. "The Symbolic Vision of Flannery O'Connor: Patterns of Imagery in *The Violent Bear It Away*." *Sewanee Review* 76: (1968): 298–318.

Walden, Daniel. "Flannery O'Connor's Dragon: Vision in 'A Temple of the Holy Ghost.'" *Studies in American Fiction* 4 (1976): 230–235.

Walker, Alice. "Beyond the Peacock: The Reconstruction of Flannery O'Connor." In *In Search of Our Mother's Gardens*. New York: Harcourt, 1983, 42–59.

Walker, Sue. "The Being of Illness, The Language of Being Ill." *Flannery O'Connor Bulletin* 25 (1996–97): 33–58.

———. "Spelling Out Illness: Lupus as Metaphor in Flannery O'Connor's 'Greenleaf.'" *Chattahoochee Review* 12, no. 1 (Fall 1991): 54–63.

Walters, Dorothy. *Flannery O'Connor.* New York: Twayne, 1973. Macmillan, 1976.

Weisenburger, Steven. "The Devil and John Hawkes." *Review of Contemporary Fiction* 3, no. 3 (Fall 1983): 155–163.

Westarp, Karl-Heinz, and Jan Nordby Gretlund, eds. *Realist of Distances: Flannery O'Connor Revisited.* Aarhus, Denmark: Aarhus University Press, 1987.

Westling, Louise. "Flannery O'Connor's Revelations to 'A.'" *Southern Humanities Review* 20, no. 1 (Winter 1986): 15–22.

———. *Sacred Groves and Ravaged Gardens: The Fiction of Eudora Welty, Carson McCullers, and Flannery O'Connor.* Athens: University of Georgia Press, 1985.

Whitt, Margaret. "Creative Responses to O'Connor's *Wise Blood*: Those Shoes Aren't Like Mine, the Eyes That Matter, and Maude with the Cow Dressed like a Housewife!" *Flannery O'Connor Review* 2 (2003–04): 84–86.

———. "Letters to Corinth: Echoes From Greece to Georgia in O'Connor's 'Judgement Day.'" In *Flannery O'Connor and the Christian Mystery,* edited by John J. Murphy, et al., 61–74. Provo, Utah: Center for the Study of Christian Values in Literature, Brigham Young University, 1997.

Whitt, Margaret Earley. *Understanding Flannery O'Connor: New Perspectives.* Understanding Contemporary American Fiction. Columbia: University of South Carolina Press, 1995.

Wilson, Carol Y. "Family as Affliction, Family as Promise in *The Violent Bear It Away.*" *Studies in the Literary Imagination* 20, no. 2 (Fall 1987): 77–86.

Witt, Jonathan. "*Wise Blood* and the Irony of Redemption." *Flannery O'Connor Bulletin* 22 (1993–94): 12–24.

Wood, Ralph C. "Flannery O'Connor, Martin Heidegger, and Modern Nihilism: A Reading of Good Country People." *Flannery O'Connor Bulletin* 21 (1992): 100–118.

Wray, Virginia. "Narration in 'A Good Man Is Hard to Find.'" *Publications of the Arkansas Philological Association* 14, no. 1 (Spring 1988): 25–38.

Wyatt, Bryan N. "The Domestic Dynamics of Flannery O'Connor: Everything That Rises Must Converge." *Twentieth Century Literature: A Scholarly and Critical Journal* 38, no. 1 (Spring 1992): 66–88.

Yaeger, Patricia Smith. "The Woman without Any Bones: Anti-Angel Aggression in *Wise Blood.*" In *New Essays on* Wise Blood, edited by Michael Kreyling, 91–116. New York: Cambridge University Press, 1995.

Young, Thomas Daniel. "Flannery O'Connor's View of the South: God's Earth and His Universe." *Studies in the Literary Imagination* 20, no. 2 (Fall 1987): 5–14.

Yumiko, Hashizume. "Urban Experience in Flannery O'Connor's 'The Artificial Nigger.'" *Sophia English Studies* 11 (1986): 41–58.

Zoller, Peter T. "The Irony of Preserving the Self: Flannery O'Connor's 'A Stroke of Good Fortune.'" *Kansas Quarterly* 9, no. 2 (1997): 61–66.

Zornado, Joseph. "A Becoming Habit: Flannery O'Connor's Fiction of Unknowing." *Religion and Literature* 29, no. 2 (Summer 1997): 27–59.

INDEX

Note: Page numbers in **boldface** indicate main entires. Page numbers in *italic* indicate photographs.

A

"A." *See* Hester, Betty
Abbot, Louise 11, 185
  letters to 185–186
Abbott, Shirley 186
  letters to 186
Abels, Cyrilly 348
Accent (magazine) 7, 298, **313**
ACTH 12, 206, 207, 347
adolescent(s). *See also* child(ren)
  in "The Lame Shall Enter First" 89, 90, 91–92
  in "A Temple of the Holy Ghost" 117–118, 119
  in *The Violent Bear It Away* (*See* Tarwater, Francis Marion)
  in *Wise Blood* (*See* Enoch Emery; Hazel Motes)
adult-child relationships 141–142
adult education program 269, 315
African Americans. *See* black(s); race relations
"Afternoon in the Woods, An" (short story) **21–24**
  commentary 22–23, 140

early versions 7, 21, 22, 23
letters 24, 115
Manley (character) 21–23, **23–24**
publication 22, 348
synopsis 21–22
agent(s). *See also* McKee, Elizabeth
FOC on 194, 269, 273
Algren, Nelson 226–227, 272
Ali, Muhammad. *See* Clay, Cassius
America (magazine) 15, 35, **313**
  in letters 209, 210, 213, 237, 239
American Association of University Women (AAUW), lecture for 13, 191, 224–225, 226, 232, 233, 234, 286
American novels 64, 65, 66
American Scholar (magazine) **313**, 317, 370
Ames, Elizabeth 8, 163, 200, 375
Amis, Kingsley 195, 217
Ananias 165
ancestors (of FOC) 3
Andalusia (farm) **313–315**
  bequest of 7, 314
  and "The Displaced Person" 12, 49, 55, 315
  history of 314
  house 314
  life at 9–13, 14

move to 8, 9, 313, 315
peacocks at 9–10, 88–89, 356, 357
stories reflecting life at 12, 37, 315
today 17, 357–358
visitors 10–11, 12
writing career at 10, 13, 14–15
angel(s) 232
  Gabriel 153–154
animals, in *Wise Blood* 172
Answered Prayers (Capote) 322
Arendt, Hannah 201, 264–265
Aristotle 366
art
  by Catholics 34, 212, 361, 364
  Maritain (Jacques) on 287, 348, 349
  obscenity and sentimentality in 34, 221, 287
  Pasternak (Boris) on 304
  in "The River" 109, 110
art (by FOC) 322–323. *See also* cartoons
  at Andalusia 207, 282
  at GCSW 5, 322–323, 323–324, 332, 333
  in school years 4, 322
  self-portrait 207, 216, 220, 230, 292, 299, 322
  wall mural 323

Art and Scholasticism (Maritain) 193, 206 , 239 , 349
art editorial work 323–324
"Artificial Nigger, The" (short story) **24–28**
  characters 27
  commentary 25–27
  letters 27–28
    as favorite story 25, 187, 228, 269
    interpretation 26, 220, 221, 228, 243, 258
    origin and title 25, 287
    publication 15, 215, 241
    public readings 196, 245
    writing 235
  Mr. Head (character) 24–27, **27**, 220, 221, 243, 258
  Nelson (character) 24–27, **27**, 220, 228, 258
  publication 25, 215, 241, 343
  synopsis 24–25
artist(s). *See also* writer(s)
  Catholics as 34, 212, 361, 364
  failed, in stories 44–45, 58, 59, 101, 102
  inspired by FOC 17
  and truth 66, 247
artists' colony. *See* Yaddo
Asa (biblical figure) 177